How to Do Everything with Your PC

How to Do *Everything* with Your

PC

Robert Cowart

Osborne/**McGraw-Hill**

Berkeley   New York   St. Louis   San Francisco
Auckland   Bogotá   Hamburg   London
Madrid   Mexico City   Milan   Montreal   New Delhi
Panama City   Paris   São Paulo
Singapore   SydneyTokyo   Toronto

Osborne/**McGraw-Hill**
2600 Tenth Street
Berkeley, California 94710
U.S.A.

For information on translations or book distributors outside the U.S.A., or to arrange bulk purchase discounts for sales promotions, premiums, or fund-raisers, please contact Osborne/**McGraw-Hill** at the above address.

How to Do Everything with Your PC

234567890 CUS CUS 01987654321

ISBN 0-07-212776-7

Publisher	Brandon A. Nordin
Vice President &	
Associate Publisher	Scott Rogers
Editorial Director	Roger Stewart
Project Editor	Pamela Woolf
Acquisitions Coordinator	Cindy Wathen
Technical Editor	Bill Bruns
Copy Editor	Marilyn Smith
Proofreader	John Gildersleeve
Indexer	Jack Lewis
Computer Designers	Lauren McCarthy, E. A. Pauw
Illustrators	Bob Hansen, Michael Mueller, Lyssa Wald, Beth E.Young
Series Design	Mickey Galicia
Cover Design	Dodie Shoemaker
Cover Illustration	Joe and Kathy Heiner

This book was composed with Corel VENTURA™ Publisher.

Dedication

I've decided to dedicate this book to you, the reader. And why not? After all, whether you are a spring chicken, middle-aged, or a senior, you've taken a step of courage to expand your horizons and embark on a new and exciting adventure, to tackle a complex technology. Many people simply resign, accepting that computers are something they'd rather not struggle to understand. But computers are here to stay, and you've chosen to get on board. So my accolades are to you. And hey, you've purchased my book, and for that I'm grateful.

You're about to embark on an exciting new adventure into the world of computing. All I ask of you is that you use your computer for constructive purposes. It's a powerful machine that can be used for making the word a better place. So please make a small contribution to society with your PC from time to time. You can do that by more fully engaging in your world, our global community—a community that computers are bringing closer and closer with each passing season. Do your bit by sending letters to your government representatives, forming online communities, facilitating international or intercultural understanding through letter writing or building Web sites, or simply educating yourself and your family by creatively browsing the Web. Then I'll feel I've made my little contribution to bettering the world, too!

Bob Cowart
Berkeley, CA, USA

About the Author

Robert Cowart (a.k.a. Bob) is a Windows and PC expert who makes his living as a freelance author. Writing for about 18 years now, he's authored more than 35 books about computing, and over 100 articles for major computer magazines. Some of his Windows books have been major bestsellers in the ranks of computer books.

Holding a degree in psychology from Temple University (Philadelphia, PA), and a digital-electronics degree from Merritt College (Oakland, CA), Bob entered the computer industry in 1981 at Northstar Computers, one of the first PC manufacturers. Combining his people skills with his technology background, Bob provided technical support for usually-desperate computer dealers for about a year. Wanting to work his own hours (this was California, after all) he became a freelance computer programmer and systems integrator a year or so later. He has been an avid promoter of personal computers and technology ever since.

When he's not holed up in his office writing computer books, Bob is involved in the music world, hosting a classical chamber music concert series in his home. He's also a pianist and a teacher of the Transcendental Meditation technique. His latest venture is an online training company using streaming video, producing what he believes will be the next wave in technology education at www.brainsville.com. Brainsville.com is collaborating with Osborne/McGraw-Hill to produce a new series of books with interactive video on CD-ROM called *Virtual Classroom*.

Contents at a Glance

Contents

PART IV   **Upgrading, Maintaining, and Troubleshooting Your PC**

CHAPTER 16   **Adding Peripherals** **459**

Acknowledgments

Thanks to everyone at Osborne—it's been a real joy to put this book together and do a brain dump of the general knowledge I've accumulated about PCs over 20 years. Normally I have to write about one specific topic. This book has been really fun. Thanks especially to Roger Stewart, editorial director at Osborne, who offered me the opportunity to participate in this exciting book series designed for new computer users. Along with Cindy Wathen who managed project traffic flow, you two made the way smooth for this book to hit the store shelves in a timely manner.

Many thanks to the various assistant authors and editors who contributed their expertise efforts: Elaine Kreston, Brian Knittel, Rowena White, Don Rittner, Bill Karow, Peter Kuhns, C. Michael Woodward, Laurie Ulrich, and Dave Johnson. Kudos to Pamela Woolf for project editing and Marilyn Smith for copyediting, and to the illustrators and production team who helped make this book look so nice. No book gets to market successfully without the endless phone calls, street pounding, and deal making of the sales, marketing, and public-relations folks. Seldom thanked and often invisible to authors, these folks bring the book to you the reader. Thanks you guys!

Great appreciation goes to my business partner, Daniel Newman, for his patience during my hiatus from my other endeavors at the office.

Finally, as always, thanks to Chris Van Buren of Waterside Productions, the agent who represents me and oversees my contractual and promotional matters.

Introduction

Welcome to *How to Do Everything with Your PC,* the book especially written for folks who are new to computers, yet who don't think of themselves as "dummies." In writing books and teaching people to use PCs for close to 20 years now, I have discovered that there are tens of thousands of intelligent people who are excited about learning to use a computer, but who are still intimidated by them. If you're one of these people, this book is for you. Learning to use a PC is a complicated matter, but I believe this book can really help anyone get up and running quickly and with a minimum of wincing. I can't guarantee there won't be any head-scratching, but that's just the nature of computers. (Heck, I do it every day, myself!)

By contrast, if you're already adept with computers and are tired of your answering machine filling up with technical support pleas from your friends, well, this book is for you, too! Buy a carton of them and give them to your friends so you can grab a beer and watch *The Simpsons* when you get home from work instead of returning all those phone calls.

In planning these 600 or so pages, I first brainstormed what the most important skills for using a PC with today's current technology would be—from unboxing, plugging in, and turning on your new PC all the way through upgrading and maintaining a typical PC, you'll find clear, concise explanations of each topic, in plain English, not a lot of computer jargon. When I explain how you perform the related tasks, I use simple step-by-step procedures, and I explain not only how you perform a particular task, but why. With computers changing too quickly, it's valuable for you to understand a concept so you can apply it in the future as the technology evolves. When there are additional sources of information available, I always try point you to them (such as Web site locations).

Even if you are totally new to PCs, don't worry. The first chapter of this book doesn't even assume you own a computer yet. I'll tell you how to shop for one and explain what all those numbers in computer ads mean. From there, the rest of Part I covers how to turn on the computer and get it running, how you interact with it, and how to use Windows (the software that makes the computer tick).

Part II gets you started doing actual work with your PC (what, you only wanted to play games?). We start with simple tasks such as using a word processor to write letters and producing various business documents (such as spreadsheets and databases). Then you learn how to get connected to the Internet, send e-mail, cruise the World Wide Web, and start interacting with the hundreds of online communities that are out there on the Internet waiting to greet you.

If you really *did* want to play games, we've got you covered in Part III, with a whole chapter devoted to all the latest gaming techniques and gear, including interactive Internet gaming. Then we move on to such cool topics as making your own Web site, working with those new-fangled digital cameras, creating your own movies on your PC, managing your checkbook and investments, playing and collecting music on your PC, and connecting with handheld computers (like the Palm Pilot).

Part IV covers the popular upgrades you might consider making to your PC, from adding internal "cards," upgrading the computer's memory, to plugging in a scanner, printer, external and internal hard disks, and so forth. Then we get into maintaining your PC, keeping your data safe, and preventing loss of your precious documents. In the last chapter, I'll show you how to solve the common problems that always seem to come up with computers and how to keep Windows and your PC running in peak condition.

At the back of the book, you'll find a glossary. Even though I always explain terms as they come up in the book, it's convenient to have a handy reference for computer jargon all in one place.

This book is written in an easy-to-read style so you can sit down and read it page by page, or you can use the book as a reference to learn how to do specific tasks. To make this book easy and quick, you'll find the following features:

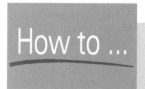

Check out these boxes for fast and easy information about certain tasks.

These boxes give you extra information about a variety of topics. Check these out as you read each chapter.

 *These icons point out some quick, helpful information.*

 *These icons give you additional information you might find helpful.*

 Some configurations can cause problems, and these icons point out danger areas.

Also, be sure to check out the Table of Contents and the index to quickly find information you need. So, are you ready? Then let's go, and by the way, you can talk to me at bob@cowart.com or visit me on the Internet at http://www.cowart.com.

Enjoy your PC—and enjoy this book!

Chapter 1

Everything You Wanted to Know About Your PC (but Were Afraid to Ask)

How to...

■ Identify the parts of your PC

■ Recognize different kinds of software

■ Make sense of the jargon in computer ads

■ Set up your PC

Welcome to the world of personal computers, also known as PCs. Whether you already own a PC or are thinking of acquiring one, this book will help you understand what your PC can do and possibly bail you out if you run into snags. Getting to know your PC and exploring the things you can do with it is an experience you will share with millions of other people all over the world. It may even bring you in contact with some of those people.

If you don't already own a PC but are thinking about buying one, you have probably already been confronted by advertisements boasting a puzzling array of specifications involving gigabytes, megahertz, and baud rates. What's the best deal? Which of those options matter for what you plan to do with your PC? Will it run the next version of SimCity or Dreamweaver?

You may have already bought your first PC and felt hopelessly lost as you opened the box and set the components on your desk. How do you get from hooking up the cables to the monitor and the printer to actually building your own Web site, which is what you really want to do? Maybe you don't care to own a PC at all but just started a new job where you're expected to be as proficient as everyone else in the office at using your PC—but, of course, there is no training program. If you match any of these profiles, this book is for you. It will act as a roadmap to guide you safely and soundly through some of the more interesting and useful areas of PC Land. (If Nick at Nite can have "TV Land," we should be able to have "PC Land"!) Soon, you'll even be doing the cool things you heard about from friends or read about in magazines.

What Is a PC?

The PC is more than a tool, although it is surely the most versatile tool ever invented. It is more than a toy, although it opens a door into a world of 3D games and graphics that could never have been conceived of before its invention. It is more than a communications device, although with the advent of the Internet the PC allows us to connect with one another more than ever before. The combination of the PC and the Internet may, in fact, rank as the one of the most significant inventions of the twentieth century.

What is the PC then? An accurate description would be to call it a "general-purpose computing device," but that's too dull. Perhaps a better way to say it is that the PC is the "anything machine." At the heart of your PC is a chip called a *microprocessor* that allows it to perform millions of calculations, or computations, in the blink of an eye. What sets the PC apart from other machines is the fact that the microprocessor isn't designed to do any particular task; rather, it is designed to do anything it is told.

The way we tell a microprocessor what to do is by writing sets of instructions, called *programming code*. Consisting of just two numbers—one and zero—these binary instructions are the only thing your computer really understands. Still, it's enough to allow you to process the words that may become the next Great American Novel, to generate and display realistic graphics that may form a game or become part of a Hollywood movie, or to connect you to Web sites and fellow computer users all over the world.

Before we begin our tour of the PC or boot up the operating system and start using some applications (don't worry if this jargon is meaningless to you right now—it will become clear), let's take a short look back at where the PC came from. Learning a little history is useful for getting an overview of PC technology and a sense of where it is heading.

A Brief History of the PC

The PCs that you can buy for $1,000 or so today have mind-boggling capabilities compared to their ancestors of just 5 or 6 years ago. Back in 1965, Gordon Moore predicted that microprocessors would double in complexity every two years, but recently the computer industry seems to be outdoing even the predictions of "Moore's Law." The speed, storage capacity, and other capabilities of the newest PCs far surpass anything that would have been imagined a few years ago.

The Mainframe Era

Until about 20 years ago, computers were energy-hogging, room-sized gadgets that only true geeks—guys with flat-top haircuts and glasses with thick, black frames—knew how to work. These huge machines were mostly kept busy running banks or doing other kinds of behind-the-scenes corporate business administration. On TV and in Hollywood movies, these monster computers were often portrayed as threats to humanity, tyrannically controlling the population of entire planets. (Well, until someone like Captain Kirk came along and delivered a logical full nelson that caused its circuits to burn out.)

In those days, office workers, corporate managers, and even scientists didn't have easy access to computing power. Typically, to do anything on a computer, the average person had to make a request to the MIS department techno-jocks, who functioned almost as a priesthood surrounding and protecting the machine. These requests usually entailed having a "batch job" run on the corporate mainframe computer when time was available. The whole process was similar to ordering a car at the local dealership. If you were lucky, you might see the results in a week or two; and, if the gods were willing, you would actually get what you ordered.

You Say You Want a Revolution...

In the late 1970s, a small Silicon Valley-based company named Intel—co-founded by Gordon Moore, whom we mentioned earlier—manufactured a little gadget called a *microprocessor*. Although it was only about the size of a large postage stamp, this chip could perform many of the same computations that previously required humongous machines sporting tens of thousands of separate (also known as *discrete*) transistors. These new circuits, by contrast, were integrated into a single chip and thus were called *integrated circuits*.

At first, nobody really knew what exactly average folks would do with a computer in their home or on their office desk, or how they would learn to use it, but that didn't matter to the microcomputer revolutionaries. To the hobbyist engineers behind the early PCs, it was exciting enough that the machines could work at all, that so much computing power could be packed into anything smaller than a Buick, and that it didn't need its own air-conditioner to keep it cool.

The first Intel microprocessor was called the 4004 and was only capable of 4-bit computations, not powerful enough for building a general-purpose computer, but good enough for industrial control—running stuff like traffic lights and washing machines. After the 4004 came the 8008 and eventually the 8080—direct predecessor to the chips used in your computer today. Motorola, which was already a big company in comparison to Intel at the time, was working on similar developments. (The eventual triumph of the Intel processor makes this one of those David and Goliath stories.) Around the same time that Intel produced the 8080 chip (see Figure 1-1), MOS Technologies came out with the 6502, which was fairly similar.

> **NOTE** *The terms* integrated circuit, chip, *and* microchip *all mean the same thing. The terms* CPU (central processing unit) *and* microprocessor *are also synonymous.*

Once Intel announced its 8-bit 8080 and MOS Technologies released the 6502, the microcomputer revolution was in full force. Steve Jobs and Steve Wozniak launched a company called Apple Computer from a garage in Silicon Valley, basing the Apple I on the 6502 from MOS Technologies. "Woz," as the co-founder of Apple is affectionately known, is said to have chosen the 6502 because it was cheaper than the competition. Meanwhile, several other upstart companies, such as MITS, Altair, and Imsai, built their machines around Intel's 8080 or an almost identical chip called the Zilog Z-80. The early visionaries behind all of these startup companies saw enormous potential in the powerful, little CPU (central processing unit) chips, believing that they would usher in a new age of high technology, bringing the power of those behemoth computers to the average citizen.

Eventually, these microcomputers diverged along the two lines that we know best today. The Intel machines became Windows-based PCs, while the Apple/Motorola computers became the Apple family of Macintosh, iMac, and iBook computers. Each type of personal computer—PC

FIGURE 1-1 An early microprocessor—the Intel 8080

and the Mac—has its strengths and weaknesses, its admirers and detractors. In this book, we are concerned only with the Intel-based family of PCs that run the Windows operating system. Intel-based computers will also run the increasingly popular Linux operating system, but the PC with Windows is by far the most popular and common type of personal computer in use today.

Did you know?

The History of the PC

The history of the computer may be said to have begun with the invention of the abacus, as long ago as 500 B.C.E., in ancient China. The modern timeline for the invention of the computer begins with Charles Babbage.

1832	Charles Babbage's never truly completed "Difference Engine No. 1" was the first successful automatic calculator and is regarded as a milestone in the early history of computing.
1876	Lord Kelvin (William Thompson) demonstrated that machines can be programmed to solve problems.
1888	William Burroughs invented an adding machine.
1943	Alan Turing and his associates developed the first all-electronic calculator, called Colossus.
1945	John Eckert and John Mauchley invented ENIAC, the first stored-program computer, which used over 18,000 vacuum tubes (see Figure 1-2).
1951	Eckert and Mauchley built UNIVAC, the first commercially available electronic computer.
1975	The Altair 8800 computer kit appeared on the cover of *Popular Electronics*. This first PC was based on the Intel 8080 chip, and Bill Gates and Paul Allen licensed BASIC as its programming language.
1977	The Apple II ready-made personal computer was released to instant commercial success.
1981	Adam Osborne completed the first "portable" computer. It weighed just 24 pounds and featured a 5-inch display, 64 kilobytes of memory, a modem, and two 5 ¼-inch floppy disk drives. IBM launched its PC that year and introduced DOS (Disk Operating System).

FIGURE 1-2   The ENIAC, the world's first full-scale digital electronic computer that used stored programs

A Typical PC System

When you buy a PC today, you get more than just the computer box containing the microprocessor. Several components are now considered "standard" parts of a typical PC system. Additionally, you can acquire a wide range of PC add-ons to customize your PC system.

Standard Parts of a PC

You may own a desktop PC or a laptop PC. Either type of PC setup will likely consist of similar parts, which are described in the following sections.

The Computer Box (CPU)

The box that houses the "guts" of your computer is sometimes called the CPU, just like the microprocessor that is the heart of the system. It's where the software is installed, all of the actual computing is done, and all of the peripherals (the hardware devices attached to the PC, such as the monitor, keyboard, and printer) typically connect. The box is also where you install special-function add-ons (such as network and modem cards) and where the RAM, hard disk drive, and floppy disk drives are usually located.

The Monitor (Screen)

If the eyes are the window to the human soul, the monitor (screen) is the eye into the computer's brain. It's where you view what you're doing with the computer and see the benefits of your work or play. Monitors come in a variety of sizes, shapes, and resolutions. The monitor plugs directly into the CPU's *video display card*, which is hidden inside the box. Laptops have screens built in, and most laptops can also be connected to an external monitor so they can use a bigger screen.

> **NOTE** *Prior to the invention of the computer monitor, users interacted with a computer by reading paper printouts, which were generated by giant printer-like gizmos called Teletypes. The early monitors were dubbed "glass Teletypes."*

The Keyboard

Virtually all computers come with a keyboard, even if it's a cheap one. Most keyboards look about the same, and connect directly into the computer, via a little, round hole on the back of the CPU called a PS/2 port. (A computer port is a connector on the computer box.) These days, you can buy all kinds of ergonomic replacement keyboards that are better for your hands and wrists, as well as keyboards that are specialized for different languages.

Mouse

People used to rely solely on a keyboard for interacting with a PC. Then, with the advent of graphical operating systems like Windows, the mouse became an extremely important tool. You use the mouse to make selections, move objects and windows around on the screen, activate links on Web pages, edit text, draw pictures, and many other tasks. In addition to the common variety that most people recognize, mice come in many flavors, from the little "eraser-head" pointer on laptops to the trackpad, which is sensitive to your finger as you slide it over the surface.

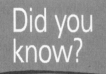

About Alto

The mouse, screen icons, toolbars, and menus were all parts of Xerox's Alto computer (see Figure 1-3) in the early 1980s. This was well before the invention of the Mac (or even its predecessor, the Lisa). After seeing the Alto, Steve Jobs and Steve Wozniak quickly went to work building their new computer, borrowing basic concepts they saw at Xerox's PARC (Palo Alto Research Center) in California. It's ironic that years later, Apple sued Microsoft for supposedly copying the Mac interface for use in Windows.

FIGURE 1-3   The Alto computer from Xerox PARC was the inspiration for the Apple computer and, indirectly, for the Windows operating system

The reality is that a guy named Doug Engelbart, who was working at Stanford Research Institute in California, came up with the concepts that led to "windowing" on the computer screen. Doug also developed such concepts as online publishing, video-conferencing, e-mail, and software that allows several people in different locations to work on one document at the same time. It was Doug who invented the mouse, which he called the "X-Y position indicator." He got only one check, in the amount of $10,000, for his invention until 1997, when he was given $500,000 as winner of the third annual Lemelson-MIT Prize for American Innovation.

Floppy Disk Drive

The floppy disk drive is for transferring relatively small files to and from your computer via an inexpensive diskette. People typically use floppy disks for trading files with friends and colleagues or for making backup copies of files. (Other media are preferable for large-scale backups of your data.) Floppy disks aren't actually floppy anymore, but they used to be—and so they still keep the name. Floppies are now housed in hard, plastic 3 ½-inch shells.

Hard Disk Drive

The hard disk drive, shown in Figure 1-4, is where your programs and documents are stored long-term—like a big memory bank. Hard disk drives are almost always hidden away inside the computer box because you don't need to physically access them, so you may never actually see your hard drive. When you turn off the computer, assuming you saved your work, your data stays on the hard disk for use the next time that you turn on the computer.

FIGURE 1-4   A typical hard disk drive is hidden inside your computer; you can see the numerous exposed hard-disk platters

Hard disk drives have steadily gotten smaller in size and larger in capacity in recent years, owing to miniaturization techniques developed for laptops. Hard disks come in vastly different storage capacities, but suffice it to say you can store a heck of a lot of stuff on today's typical drives. Unless you are doing a lot of work with digital photography, video, or audio CDs, or you are cataloging the entire Library of Congress, you probably won't need to worry about running out of space on your hard disk.

CD-ROM Drive

Programs you buy at the store used to fit on a handful of floppy disks, but not anymore. Today's programs include more and more features, so programs are now shipped on CD-ROMs (which stands for compact disc read-only memory). A CD-ROM disk can hold 451 times as much stuff as a floppy disk—up to 650 megabytes of information.

Every new PC (with the exception of a few very small laptops) comes with a CD-ROM drive. As a bonus, your CD-ROM drive also plays music CDs—so you can pop in Brahms or Britney Spears and whistle while you work.

The ROM part of CD-ROM means that you can't replace the contents of the CD with your own data. However, there are special CDs, called CD-R or CD-RW, that allow you to create your own CDs, including audio CDs that play on any audio CD player.

Printer

Technically, the printer is not part of the computer—it's a peripheral. But, if you want to put your work or information you've pulled from the Internet onto paper, you need a printer. It should be considered standard equipment with any computer system. The printer typically hooks up to the *parallel port* (sometimes called the *printer port*) on the back of the computer box. However, more and more printers can connect to a new style of socket called a *USB* (*Universal Serial Bus*) *port*, which operates faster than the parallel port.

USB ports are hot swappable, *meaning you can plug and unplug peripherals to the port while the computer is on, and it will detect the devices. You can also connect several devices at once to a single USB port through a USB hub. For example, you could have a printer, scanner, Zip drive, mouse, and modem all connected to the same USB port simultaneously. USB cables and connectors are less bulky than older parallel port cables and connectors.*

PC Add-ons

In addition to the standard components described in the previous sections, many PC setups also include add-ons to increase your computer's versatility. Common PC add-ons are described in the following sections.

Modem

A modem (which is short for modulator/demodulator) may be a card inside the computer, a plug-in card for a laptop, or a little box that attaches to the computer externally. It lets your computer "talk" to other computers. Typically, modems are used for connecting to the Internet or to an information service such as America Online (AOL) or Microsoft Network (MSN). Many people today are connecting to the Internet via DSL (Digital Subscriber Line) or cable modems, which are specialized modems that transfer data between computers at a higher rate of speed than standard phone-line modems.

Backup Storage System

If you're not worried about your computer gobbling up your Ph.D. thesis, well, you should be! Ignore Murphy's Law at your peril. *Backing up* your data simply means saving an extra copy of your work in case your hard disk drive fails or you accidentally delete a file you meant to keep. It happens. You'll want to develop your own backup strategy and decide how often you need to save extra copies of everything. (See Chapter 17 for suggestions on backup and security.)

A wide variety of backup systems are available. The most popular is called a Zip drive, as shown in Figure 1-5. Backup devices can be internal or external to the CPU box.

Scanner

If you're a photographer or a graphic artist, a scanner is a must. It's the easiest way, short of snapping pictures with a digital camera, to get photos (or other graphics) into your computer. Once you've transferred your images into the computer, you can manipulate them, remove redeye (or zits), resize, retouch, print, or e-mail them.

FIGURE 1-5   This Zip drive can protect you from losing your valuable data

Scanners come in a wide variety of shapes, sizes, and specialties. Some excel at document and text scanning, while others are better for photos. Scanners are always external to the CPU. A typical scanner is shown in Figure 1-6.

FIGURE 1-6   If you want to manipulate photos and other types of artwork, having a scanner is essential

DVD-ROM Drive

DVDs are the big brothers to CDs. They look about the same as music CDs or CD-ROM discs and can even be inserted into a CD-ROM drive, but that's where the similarities end. DVDs can store about 26 times more data than a CD-ROM can. DVD-ROM discs typically have movies on them, but they aren't limited to that. In fact, DVD stands for digital versatile disk (not digital video disk as some people think). More expensive computers have CD-ROM drives that can double as DVD players. Drives that allow you to write data to a DVD are now just beginning to appear.

Game Controllers

One of the most often cited reasons that people give for buying home computers is to play games. For many types of computer games, a game controller of one kind or another can enhance the experience. The mouse and the keyboard are all you need for most types of puzzle, adventure, and role-playing games. But race car, combat, and aircraft simulations often demand that you have a joystick, as shown in Figure 1-7.

Other types of controllers may range from a game pad that simulates the type of controller found on a video game machine to expensive steering wheels or moving chairs that simulate the inside of a cockpit. A popular feature in current joysticks is "force feedback," which makes the joystick jump about and vibrate in your hand to give the sensation that you've been hit or that the vehicle is out of control.

Game controllers typically attach to a special game port on the back of the computer.

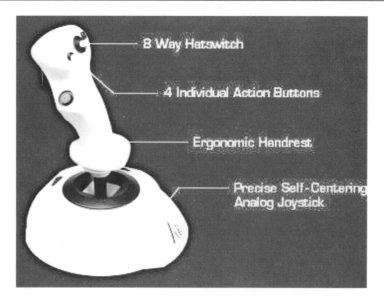

FIGURE 1-7   If you are into high-speed action games, a joystick will be an essential addition to your PC system

TIP *A good game computer will also have a sound card inside, and many of today's popular games require a 3D graphics accelerator video card. A standard modem is fine for simple online games such as bridge or Scrabble®, but for tournament-style multiplayer games such as Quake or Unreal, you'll want a high-speed Internet connection.*

PC Software

There's a classic joke among computer people about the two engineers who point the finger at each other when trying to solve a computer glitch. The software engineer claims it's a hardware problem, and the hardware engineer claims it's a software problem. In the end, the problem is never resolved.

Okay, so what is hardware and what is software? Put simply, *hardware* is the physical components that your computer is made of—nuts and bolts and chips and circuit boards. The term also includes the monitor, mouse, and keyboard, as well as add-ons like the printer, modem, and scanner. For the most part, what we have talked about so far in this chapter is hardware.

Software consists of the instructions that make the computer work. These may be stored in magnetic or optical form, but ultimately they become electrons flying around inside your microprocessor. Without software, the computer would be a hunk of metal, plastic, and silicon (the glass-like compound chips are made of) taking up real estate on your desktop. It would be as useless as a stereo without CDs or a VCR without any tapes to play.

NOTE *Don't worry if all this talk about software and hardware seems a bit esoteric at first. You'll understand it much better, almost intuitively, as you start to play with your computer. And that's just exactly what you should call it—play. People get too serious about these darned things, as though technology controls their lives. It should be the other way around!*

There are several basic types of software, which are described briefly in the following sections.

The Operating System

The operating system (OS for short) is essential software for every computer. After the BIOS (basic input/output system) kick-starts the computer, the operating system wakes it up, sort of like the Prince delivering that initial smooch to Snow White.

NOTE *The BIOS is embedded in the hardware (in the BIOS chip), so it's often called firmware. It's not exactly software or hardware; it's something in between.*

After the BIOS wakes up the computer (called *booting up*), the operating system then provides the means by which all other software programs work. For example, when you want to print a document, the operating system makes it happen. When you type on the keyboard, the operating system takes the keystrokes and displays the characters on the screen. When you open or save a file on the hard disk, the operating system handles the chore. All those little icons on the screen, the pointer, the menus, and the windows are the work of the operating system.

In 99 percent of the PCs in general use today, the operating system is some version of Microsoft Windows. The Windows operating system usually comes preinstalled on your computer.

Application Software

Application software, application programs, programs, and apps are all names for the same thing. (I prefer the word *program* myself, because it reminds me of being at a concert or a play, rather than in front of my computer.) Simply put, an *application* is software you buy at the local computer store or download from the Web that allows you to accomplish whatever tasks you have in mind.

Store-bought application programs usually come on a CD-ROM these days. You stick the CD into your CD-ROM drive and run a setup program that installs the application onto your computer's hard disk. (Most setup programs run automatically when you insert the CD.) After that, you can run your new program whenever you want by clicking an icon on the screen.

Popular application programs include Microsoft Word, TurboTax, PhotoShop, Netscape Navigator, and so on. You also get a bunch of application programs free with Windows, including Outlook Express, WordPad, Notepad, Calculator, Media Player, and more. So even if you didn't purchase or download programs for your new computer, you'll have a few already installed. Often, you will find programs that are designed to work well together bundled together in what is called a software *suite*. The most popular example is Microsoft Office, although there are many others, such as Microsoft Works, Corel WordPerfect Office 2000, and Lotus SmartSuite.

NOTE   *The truth is many people don't need everything that is included in a typical software suite bundle. It's a little like those late-night infomercials about the amazing Ginsu Knives—"Order now and you'll also get...". Then you're stuck with 14 Chia Pets.*

Utility Software

Utilities can be thought of as a subset of application software, but they are usually treated as a category of their own. As opposed to application programs that allow you to perform your work, such as to create spreadsheets or balance your checkbook, utility programs are used to maintain your computer in one way or other. For example, there are utilities for making more space on your hard disk, scanning for viruses, making your desktop look cool, adding nifty screen savers, managing your fonts, partitioning your hard disk, and so on.

Shopping for a PC (What Do All Those Numbers Mean?)

Although you can still put together your own computer, as most hobbyists did in the early days of the microcomputer revolution, I advise against it. Putting together a PC from scratch is not really worth the hassle. Any PC manufacturer worth its salt these days has engineers and testers whose job is to iron out software and hardware incompatibilities so that you don't have to lose sleep over them.

When you buy your computer, get it from a reputable dealer—preferably someone who will provide some sort of service plan and guarantee it to work with the operating system you have in mind. Make sure those guarantees are in writing. Get as many of the essentials and the options you desire in the box as you can, including video, audio, modem, and network cards; CD-ROM, hard disk, Zip, and floppy disk drives; and USB, serial, and parallel ports. (You can still add extras later, if you want.) The basic system, with keyboard, monitor, mouse, and drives, should all boot up and work just fine the first time you turn it on. If it doesn't, take it back.

Did you know?

About All Those 1s and 0s

Computers operate using a numbering system that is different from the base-ten system most people are used to. We use ten as the basis for our number system because we started counting—way back in the days of Neanderthals—on our fingers. (Heck, I still do that now.) Base ten is also called *decimal*.

Computers use a different numbering system called *binary*, which has only two numbers—zero and one. (You see, they're dumber than you thought!) Computations in your PC are all based on little electronic switches, like light switches. Each switch (called a *bit*) can be either on or off. That's it. As you would imagine, not much computing can be done with one little bit, but the computer can process zillions of them, organized in groups of eight, in very little time. This grouping of eight was chosen because that's the number of little switches it takes to encode (using combinations of on and off) all of the stuff we use computers for, including the letters of the alphabet and the numbers in our human numbering system. Each of the eight bits together is called a *byte*. Byte actually stands for *binary term*.

Large numbers of byte are indicated in terms that make them easier to talk about. Computer specifications use the letters K, M, and G. K stands for thousand and indicates a kilobyte (really 1,024 bytes without rounding off). M is for million and indicates a megabyte (1,048,576 bytes). G means gigabyte (1,073,741,824 bytes). A floppy disk that can hold 1.44 megabytes, for example, is capable of storing approximately 1.4 million characters (letters and numbers), or about 3,000 pages of text.

Quiz: How many pages of text could be stored on a 20G drive?

Answer: 42,666,666 pages!

Break Down the Terminology

If you are currently shopping for a new computer, what do you look for? The typical PC advertisement in your local paper may boast of such features as a 700MHz Pentium III processor with 128M RAM (expandable to 384M), with a 128 L2 cache and 20G HD, 1.44M floppy drive, 56K internal modem, 32x CD-ROM, and 17-inch monitor. *What do all these numbers mean?* How do you know if this is the computer you need or if another computer in the same ad that offers a similar array of confusing and impenetrable options is a better choice?

Let's take the options and features mentioned in this hypothetical advertisement one at a time and decipher their meaning. The heart of the PC is the microprocessor, or CPU. The speed of the microprocessor determines the overall capabilities and limitations of the computer, so this is the number that is usually the most ballyhooed in the advertisements. We'll begin there.

700MHz Pentium III Processor

This tells you the speed and the type of the CPU, the brain in the computer. The MHz designation means *megahertz* or, literally, millions of hertzes (Hz). No, we're not talking about rental cars. Heinrich Rudolf Hertz (1857–94) was a German physicist who studied how things vibrate, especially things that vibrate really, really fast. So they named the unit of frequency—the hertz— after him. Wiggle your finger back and forth once every second. You could now say your finger wiggles at 1Hz. Now wiggle your finger 700 million times in one second. Ouch, now that hurts!

In a CPU, a clock controls how fast the microprocessor can do computations. The number in the CPU specification tells you how fast the CPU's clock is ticking, and thus, how fast computations are going to be performed.

New processors are coming out every week, with names like Athlon, Duron, and Crusoe, and some have even broken the 1,000MHz speed barrier (1GHz). Do you need to buy the computer with the fastest processor available? It depends on what you plan to do with your computer, but the answer is probably not. I'm doing just fine writing this book with my trusty 333MHz Celeron laptop—word processing doesn't require that much processing speed. I have another computer that's based on a 400MHz AMD K6-2 chip, and I use it to do video editing, work with PhotoShop, and play my MP3 music files. You need the latest possible CPU running at the fastest possible speed only if you're going to be doing a lot of CPU-intensive work, such as serious graphics processing or video editing. By purchasing "behind the technology wave" (meaning one generation older products), you'll usually save a lot of dough and be perfectly happy.

TIP   *If you want to run a particular program, check with its maker to find out what speed and brand of CPU the manufacturer recommends using. There might be requirements for the CPU.*

Did you know?

What You Need

The motherboard (the main circuit board in the computer that holds the CPU and RAM) should be Plug-and-Play compatible (check that it has an actual Plug-and-Play BIOS). It should also support the ACPI (Advanced Configuration and Power Interface) power management scheme (not just APM, or Advanced Power Management) and have a reasonably quick processor (at least 300 to 500MHz range). A Pentium Celeron, Pentium, Pentium Pro, Pentium II, Pentium III, AMD K6-2, or K6-3 is fine. It should have a 100MHz internal bus, support for AGP graphics, a flashable BIOS for later upgrading, and should actually have been designed around the processor you have in mind. Sometimes system builders plug in a CPU that will work, but you don't reap all the advantages that the motherboard could provide if the correct CPU were installed.

Don't overpay on the latest, fastest processor. It's not worth being on the bleeding edge. Keep in mind that the CPU must work in concert with the rest of the system. Many people think that a system with a super-fast CPU chip guarantees a fast computer, but this isn't true. Efficiency of the CPU is interdependent with several variables such as the support chipset, the hard disk, and the internal system bus speed. In fact, contrary to popular belief, the efficiency of the computer is more affected by the chipset than by any other factor. If you want to get techy when shopping, read the computer magazines, either in print or on the Web, and look for speed comparisons of various brand-name computers. These real-world tests are more reliable than simply comparing CPU speeds of the computers you're thinking about purchasing.

128M RAM Expandable to 384M

This notation translates to "128 megabytes of random access memory installed that can be raised to a maximum of 384 megabytes if you want to purchase more in the future." *RAM* (*random access memory*) refers to the chips in your computer that store your applications and documents in "live" mode while you are actually working on them. Turn off the computer, and RAM loses its memory—that's why you need to save your documents before exiting the program. For this reason, RAM is also called *volatile memory*.

Don't confuse RAM with memory stored in the hard disk (the "HD" amount). Think of RAM as being like the operating room in a hospital. The bigger the operating room (the greater the RAM), the more doctors and support staff you can have in there at once; otherwise, you would have to ask one specialist to leave so that another one could enter.

Even a computer with a middle-of-the-road CPU and a lot of RAM can outperform a faster CPU with less memory, so it makes sense to put your hard-earned greenbacks into extra RAM. Many systems come stocked with only 64M of RAM, which is the minimum you need to run today's operating systems and applications. Pay a bit extra to get at least 128M of RAM. You can also purchase RAM upgrades and add RAM to your computer. If you're upgrading the RAM on a computer you already have, make sure that you get exactly the kind your computer needs.

 *The price of RAM chips is very volatile, so I can't tell you how much to pay. Suffice it to say, however, that retailers will often charge twice what you can get them for at a discount shop or over the Internet. Some big-name computer manufacturers will charge three times more than bargain-basement prices.*

128K L2 Cache

Another kind of RAM that can speed up your computer is called *Level 2 (L2) cache*. This is different from system RAM. A hotly discussed topic in the computer magazines, cache RAM is very fast RAM used by the CPU to temporarily store data as it is sent to and from system RAM, speeding up memory fetches. RAM caching has been shown to increase system speed considerably.

Today's CPUs have an L2 cache built into them. The Intel Pentium II has 512K. The Intel Celeron and AMD K6-2 have 128K. The Pentium III has 256K, as do the AMD Athlon and K6-III. If your computer is very old, it might not have a built-in cache or even an option to add one.

When shopping for a notebook or desktop computer, go for at least a 128KB L2 cache, and preferably a 256KB or 512KB one.

20G HD

This translates to "20 gigabyte hard disk." As explained earlier in this chapter, the hard disk is the internal device that stores your operating system and applications, as well as the documents you create. You don't see it, but you can hear it whirring inside the computer box at super-high speed (typically 5,400 times per minute or higher). By almost anyone's standards, the sizes of today's hard disks are astronomical. Only a year ago, we were just breaking the 1-gigabyte limit; now hard disk sizes seem to grow by at least a factor of 10 each year.

In reality, most folks could get by with a 2G drive. However, most of us are lazy about keeping our hard disks tidy, and we accumulate programs we never use—digital photographs that take up lots of space, MP3 music files, and so on. So spring for a system with as much space as you can afford. But don't sweat it if you can't afford the latest zillion-gigabyte drive!

1.44M Floppy Drive

Almost all floppy drives store 1.44M of data, so this is the standard you will find on most systems. You can get 2M floppy drives these days, as well.

56K Internal Modem

This means that the computer has a modem built into it—an *internal* modem. Most computers come with an internal modem these days. The speed of 56K is as fast as dial-up modems (those that use standard phone lines to access the Internet) get right now. If you are shopping for a new computer, a 56K modem is the minimum you should buy.

If you're planning on getting a high-speed connection to the Internet via DSL or cable, an internal modem will only be of use to you in a pinch—that is, when your DSL or cable service goes offline for some reason.

32x CD-ROM

This tells you that there is a CD-ROM drive included in the computer and that the speed of the drive is 32 times the base rate. The faster the drive, the faster you'll be able to load in software from a CD-ROM. Drives are measured as a factor of speed faster than the original CD-ROM drives, which established a baseline of 1x speed. As of this writing, the fastest CD-ROM drives are running at 72x. If you only install new software once in a while and you don't use CD-ROMs to play games, don't worry about the speed too much. For serious gamers, though, CD-ROM speed can be crucial.

17-Inch Monitor

Since you have to look at the screen virtually all the time you're using the computer, you'd better get something you like. I could write an entire book about monitors, but you only need to know the basics when you're selecting one for your computer.

Monitor Basics   There are three main areas that you should be concerned with when shopping for a monitor:

- **Size**   In size, screens typically range from 10–21 inches, measured diagonally. Dealers may throw in a 15-inch screen with a desktop system, but 17-inch monitors are in more common use. The bulk of laptops come with 12-inch screens but go as high as 15-inch screens.

- **Resolution**   The *resolution* determines how detailed the picture is. As the resolution increases, you can see more of your work on the screen at one time. Resolution is measured in *pixels*, which are the dots on the screen. The lowest standard is called VGA and is 640 pixels across, 480 up and down (designated as 640 x 480). The next step up is called SVGA and is 800 x 600. Then there's XGA, which is 1,024 x 768. If you have a 17-inch monitor, you'll want to be running in at least 800 x 600 resolution, more likely in 1,024 x 768.

- **Color depth**   You also should consider color *depth*, which refers to how many colors your screen can display. You'll want a system that can display at least 64,000 colors for most work. Make sure the screen and card can run at 72Hz refresh rate at the color depth and resolution you desire, too, so you won't see flicker on your screen. Flicker will tire your eyes and can lead to headaches.

The screen is connected by a wire to the video card *inside the computer, so think of these two as Siamese twins. They must work together. Make sure the screen and card both support the number of colors you want at the resolution you want.*

LCD Screens   Are you considering getting one of those thin, flat-screen (LCD) monitors for your desktop? I highly recommend it. I have a 15-inch one on my desktop PC, and it's terrific. Regular TV-like screens (called CRT for cathode-ray tube) jobs are bulky and produce a fuzzier image. Nothing comes close to an LCD's clarity. They makes no noise, use very little electricity, and take up very little space. You can even hang them on the wall like a picture. The ones that come with their own digital video display cards will offer the clearest display. The catch is that you will pay about two to three times more for an LCD display than for a conventional CRT.

Laptops in today's market come with two different flavors of LCD screens, called *TFT* (*thin film transistor*) and *dual scan*. TFT, also known as *active matrix,* is the better-looking of the two, but dual scan can decrease the price of the laptop by a couple hundred bucks. Dual scan is okay, but the image can look dimmer, and can "smear" when you move objects around on the screen quickly. So, for example, the pointer can be hard to find when you're moving the mouse quickly. Or, if you're watching a video, the picture can get blurry. All the desktop-style LCD screens are the TFT kind.

Laptop and other flat-panel screens look very good at only one resolution—their so-called native resolution. Other resolutions may be displayable, but they'll tend to look blocky. Some LCDs look better than others do in non-native resolutions due to built-in *anti-aliasing*. Incidentally, unlike standard CRT monitors, LCD monitors look best at low refresh rates (the rate at which the screen display is recharged). If you do buy an LCD monitor, be sure to set up the refresh rate to 60Hz. It will probably look clearer that way. Unlike with CRT displays, you don't need to worry about flicker on an LCD, so high refresh rates are not an issue. Any advertising about high refresh capabilities of an LCD monitor is bogus and misleading.

Other PC Purchase Considerations

We've covered the terminology in our hypothetical PC ad, and now you have some idea of what the most important numbers in those ads are all about. There are a few more items that you will want to be aware of when making a decision about purchasing a new PC.

Internal Ethernet Connector

Ethernet basically translates to a LAN (local area network). If you plan on connecting two or more computers together so they can share files or peripherals (like a printer), this is something to look for. You can add one in later if you need to, but it's nice to get it thrown in, if possible.

Ports

Ports are the connectors on the back of the computer (not a place where you tie up boats). The ports on your computer determine what kinds of doodads and peripherals you can plug in. Here are the types of ports a computer might have:

■ Serial ports have typically been for stuff like external modems and Palm or Pocket PC cradles.

■ PS/2 ports are for keyboards and mice.

■ Video ports are for plugging in an external monitor.

■ USB and IEEE 1394 (sometimes called *Firewire*) ports are the new kids on the block. These ports were added in hopes of virtually eliminating all the others and improving on them (see the "What's a Legacy-Free Computer?" section later in this chapter).

■ Audio ports are for recording and listening to music and other sounds like voice.

■ Infrared (IR), or IrDA, ports (typical on most laptops) aren't something too many people use, but they can be handy. If you have two laptops each with IR ports, they can communicate with one another through the air, with no wires. Some printers also have IR ports, so you can print to such a printer just by aiming the IR port of your computer at it and issuing the Print command.

As far as I'm concerned, the more ports you have, the better. However, there is a trend afoot to eliminate the old-fashioned serial and parallel ports in favor of the more versatile USB and 1394 ports.

Available Slots

When scoping out a computer, keep in mind that you might want to expand it later with plug-in boards, which are the kind that go inside the computer. (This applies only to desktop units, because laptops have no extra space inside.) The need for extra slots is less important now that more and more hardware is built onto the main boards (VSLI, or very large scale integration, chips make this possible). Often network support, audio, and even video are built into the motherboard, for example. (The computer's *motherboard* is the circuit board that contains the CPU, chips, and other integrated components.) Still, any new computer you buy should have at least a few empty expansion slots.

There are three kinds of slots these days: ISA (Industry Standard Architecture), PCI (Peripheral Connection Interface), and AGP (Accelerated Graphics Port). As of this writing, most computers had a few empty PCI slots, but typically only one empty ISA slot. That's because the ISA standard is a moldy-oldy, and on its way out. Most PCs have an AGP slot for plugging in a fast video card. AGP is based on the PCI bus, but fine-tuned for the needs of high-performance 3D graphics. Since I like to be ready for anything, I recently opted for a machine with five PCI slots, one AGP slot, and one ISA slot. That should be more than enough for most folks' needs. Figure 1-8 shows the typical slots you will find inside a PC today.

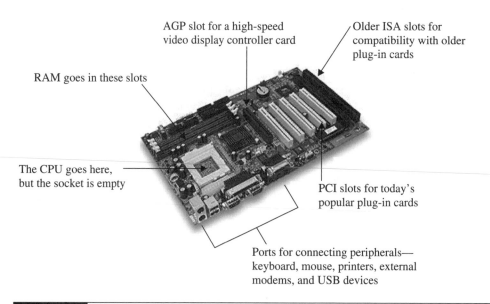

AGP slot for a high-speed
video display controller card

Older ISA slots for
compatibility with older
plug-in cards

RAM goes in these slots

The CPU goes here,
but the socket is empty

PCI slots for today's
popular plug-in cards

Ports for connecting peripherals—
keyboard, mouse, printers, external
modems, and USB devices

FIGURE 1-8 A typical PC's PCI, ISA, and AGP slots

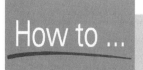 **Stop the Noise**

Are you annoyed by the noise your computer makes? Why should that fan and hard disk
have to make so much noise?

Ambient noise generated by the cooling fans and the hard disk drive has been a critical
hurdle plaguing the PCs capability to fully penetrate the home and become an appliance.
Hard drive noise adds to the noise of the PC power supply fan, and as hard drives become
faster with the 7,200 RPM and 10,000 RPM spindle speeds, the noise level increases. TVs,
phones, and VCRs produce less then 26 decibels of noise, while PCs produce between 36
and 48 decibels when operating. A PC is considerably louder than the typical living room.
The problem worsens as you add more PCs to an office, especially a home office, which is
otherwise quiet. It's one reason many folks opt for laptops.

There is a solution to the noise problem. Several companies now offer noise suppression
kits. When you're upgrading or buying a new PC, you might think about the noise factor.
Check www.silentsystems.com for more on the issue.

Laptop Versus Desktop PC: Which Is Better?

Now that you know what some of the numbers mean, one of the biggest buying decisions you'll need to make is whether to get a desktop computer or the more portable laptop or notebook variety. It's a tough decision for many, though to me it's a no-brainer. I've been a portable-computer fan since the Radio Shack Model 100 hit the streets back in 1983.

Laptops

For many, the convenience and ease of using a laptop computer far exceeds the need for the expansion options a desktop computer offers. It's a lot easier to set up, too; just plug it in and go. You don't need to mess with all those cables or live with what looks like a spaghetti factory after an explosion.

You may be concerned about the size of the screen or the keyboard, but those really are not a problem. A full-sized laptop can have a 15-inch screen, which has an equivalent viewing area of a 17-inch desktop computer monitor. It can also have a full-sized keyboard as far as key size and stroke travel (how far the key goes down when you press it), although it will not have the dedicated number pad over on the right side (accountants and bookkeepers seem to like those). And you can always plug in an external monitor or keyboard if you need larger models. Laptops are quieter and produce less radiation (if you are worried about that sort of thing) than desktop computers, and they save energy.

My personal laptop favorites at this point are the Sony VAIO N505VE sub-notebook and the Dell 7000 full-sized laptop. The Sony weighs in at under three pounds, yet packs a wallop. In fact, this whole book was written on it. It's significantly smaller than a standard sheet of paper and is less than an inch thick. It has a 6.4G drive, 128M of RAM, and a 333MHz Celeron CPU. The screen, though only 10.4 inches, displays 1,024 x 768 (this is called XGA resolution). The Dell has a beautiful 15-inch screen and plays movies on its DVD drive (which look amazing on the bright LCD screen—I'm the envy of the dude in the next seat on the plane). It runs five hours with the extra battery, has a 300MHz Pentium II, 8G hard disk, and 256K of RAM. Admittedly, it weighs in at about 10 pounds with extra batteries and power supply, so when I'm traveling, I'm starting to prefer the Sony, unless I want to see a DVD movie on the plane.

Laptops come with different types of batteries. When shopping, check out the battery performance and rundown times. The computer magazines often compare battery performance of competing brands. You'll want to get a model that will run at least a couple of hours on a battery. Also, look for a machine sporting the latest in battery technology, such as lithium-ion. NiMH (nickle-metal-hydride) rechargable batteries are second best. You should avoid NiCd (nickle-cadmium) batteries because they have shorter lifespans and need to be fully discharged before recharging them, or they cease to recharge fully.

Desktops

If you're going to do work that requires serious expansion, you need specialized video cards or sound cards, or your computer will perform as a network server for a bunch of workstations in an office, then get a desktop machine. Also, if you want the fastest machine possible, remember that laptops always trail behind the desktop units in speed. But by and large, all the power of a desktop computer can be packed into a good laptop, and laptops offer a lot more convenience.

Taking your desktop computer into a conference room (or on your vacation so you can check e-mail despite protests from your spouse) isn't something you want to try.

What's a Legacy-Free Computer?

You might have seen some computers advertised as being "legacy free." Depending on your background, I guess dumping your legacy could have a positive ring to it. In computers, it means a whole different thing. Anything with the word *legacy* in it refers to the bad old days.

The introduction of legacy-free PCs has been a design goal for both Intel and Microsoft for some years now. The theory is that since PCs (this is where the Mac evangelists get excited) were designed and redesigned over and over by individual companies, industry consortiums, and to a great extent by Microsoft, there's a bunch of stuff in them that's pretty useless and confuses the operating systems, notably Windows.

NOTE   *If you've heard a lot about Windows being "crash" prone, well, it's true. In defense of Windows, imagine writing software that needs to run properly (or even half-way reliably) on a zillion different kinds of PCs with a gabillion different combinations of hardware cards and peripherals plugged in. Apple has almost totalitarian control over the Mac and the Mac operating system, so designing it has been a much easier task for the Apple system developers.*

Legacy-free computers are designed to get rid of unnecessary elements in hopes of making things run smoother. They are stripped-down and simpler PCs, primarily with fewer ports. The old serial (COM1 and COM2) and parallel (LPT) ports are hitting the road, leaving only USB and Firewire ports. One way to view them is as a Wintel (combination of Intel CPU and Microsoft Windows) version of the Apple iMac. They have no internal expansion slots accessible to the user. All peripherals will be attached outside. And they're cheap. For example, the Compaq iPaq is only about $400. If you're looking for a no-frills PC for a budget price, a legacy-free PC is the way to go. The newest version of Windows, Windows ME, was designed with legacy-free PCs in mind.

Setting up Your Computer

If you just purchased a new computer, you might be faced with a task that will seem daunting the first time you try it. After you've removed all of the components from their boxes, you find yourself surrounded by disconnected, lifeless, useless chunks of metal, glass, and plastic. How do you bring it all to life and put it to work for you?

Here's some basic advice:

- Don't be in a rush. Expect to spend about 30 minutes to an hour setting everything up.

- You might need a small screwdriver, typically a flat-head type, for screwing in some connectors at the ends of cables.

- You'll need a good place to put your computer, preferably with plenty of room to work.

1

■ Look for a conveniently located AC wall outlet, or find an extension cord or power strip that reaches the outlet.

■ A surge protector is okay, but not required. If you live in an area that has crazy, unreliable electricity, get a good protector capable of protecting against spikes (big increases in line voltage that happen very quickly, such as from lightning strikes).

If you're worried about which cables attach to which connectors on the back of the computers, look over the diagram in Figure 1-9, which shows the various connectors.

Setting up Your Laptop

If you're setting up a laptop, you have only two or three plugs to worry about. Wire it up as you see in Figure 1-10.

Here are the steps for setting up your laptop computer:

1. Remove the wrapping and save it by putting it all into the box. You'll want to save that box in case you need to return the computer for repair or you need to move it to a new location.

2. Find a good spot for the computer. Keep in mind that reflection of lights or windows off of the screen can reduce visibility, strain your eyes, and send you running for a couple of aspirin. Staring past the screen and out a window can also make viewing difficult (because it closes down your iris and consequently makes the screen look dimmer). Look for a spot that avoids these, if possible. Of course, some ambient room light is a good idea, just not too much.

3. Plug the AC power adapter to the wall outlet. Plug the other end into the appropriate receptacle on the computer. If you have a surge suppressor, use it. If not, don't worry about it. If the plug has three connectors (has a ground plug), don't cheat. Laptops typically don't have ground plugs, but if yours does, it's there for a reason. Use a grounded outlet.

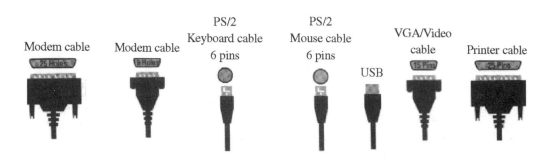

Modem cable   Modem cable   PS/2 Keyboard cable 6 pins   PS/2 Mouse cable 6 pins   USB   VGA/Video cable   Printer cable

FIGURE 1-9   The various cables and their sockets on the computer

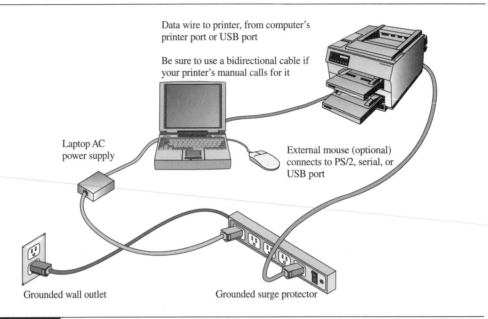

Data wire to printer, from computer's
printer port or USB port

Be sure to use a bidirectional cable if
your printer's manual calls for it

Laptop AC
power supply

External mouse (optional)
connects to PS/2, serial, or
USB port

Grounded wall outlet   Grounded surge protector

FIGURE 1-10   The basic hookup for your laptop

4. Find a safe, secure place for your printer, one where you can get the paper in and out
without a hassle. Plug its AC cord into the wall outlet. Then find the printer cable.
With the computer turned off, firmly attach the cable between the computer and printer.
Most printers plug into the printer port (sometimes called LPT port) on the back of the
computer. It's the long, smooth one with 25 little holes in it. If you have a newer model
printer, it might be of the USB variety and will plug into the USB port. USB ports are
tiny little rectangular holes about an inch long that could be on the side rather than the
back of the laptop. Look around, and also check the laptop's manual for the location.

NOTE   *Some printers don't come with a cable, because the manufacturer doesn't know what kind
of computer you're going to hook up to. You might have to purchase a printer cable.*

You're finished. If you are using a laptop, you can skip the rest of this chapter and turn to
Chapter 2 to start using your computer.

Setting Up Your Desktop PC

Setting up a desktop system takes a little more work than a laptop, but you'll survive. The basic
wiring diagram is shown in Figure 1-11.

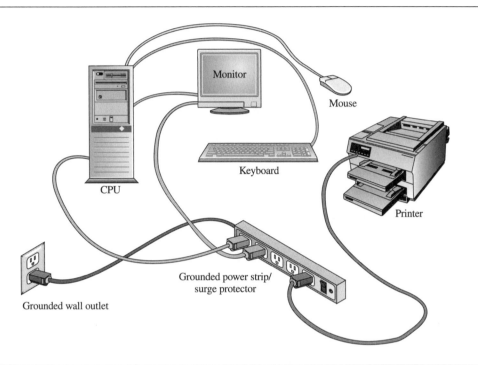

FIGURE 1-11   The basic hookup for your desktop PC

Here are the steps for setting up your desktop computer:

1. Pick a good place for the computer, keyboard, monitor, printer, and other system components. There are two schools of thought about where to put the CPU. Some like it on the desk next to the monitor; others prefer to put it on the floor.

NOTE   *I prefer to keep my desktop PC on the floor, because I don't have to listen to the whir of the internal fan as much. The downside is that it's a hassle to snake the cords down there, and I end up on my knees in the dust bunnies with a flashlight more often than I'd like. If you have a little iPaq or other minimalist computer, putting it right on top of your desk could be fine.*

2. After you choose where to put the CPU, push some papers off your desk, and carefully place the monitor where you want it. The monitor should sit right in front of you, not off to the side, even though that looks cool at banks and stuff. You'll end up needing a chiropractor if you position it that way! Also, see step 2 in the previous section, because the information about positioning a laptop relative to the lighting in the room applies to your monitor.

Some extra-tidy people think they'll keep their lovely new monitor dust-free by leaving the plastic bag over the top. Don't do it! Monitors (especially the CRT variety) need to breathe since they get hot inside. Remove all of the packaging.

3. Find a safe, secure place for your printer, one where you can get the paper in and out without a hassle.

4. Now you need to plug everything in. With all units turned off, you can do this in any order—you won't hurt anything. Because each unit has an AC plug, you'll need three plugs if you bought a printer. So, you're going to probably need a power strip. Don't use one of those little power cubes, since they don't have a ground wire on them. Find the AC cords for each unit and plug into a decent, grounded power strip. (You can forget the ground if none of your plugs have a third connector on them, but at least the one for the CPU probably will.)

5. Connect the printer to the computer, per step 4 in the laptop section above.

6. The monitor will have a special cable with it, either attached or separate. Monitor cables have a connector that looks almost identical to the COM1 (serial port) connector, but have a lot more pins inside. Don't try to push this cable into the wrong connector. You can damage the pins. The video connector has 15 pins; a COM1 connector has only 9 pins.

7. Keyboard placement issues can fill a book, if you're into ergonomics. You want a good place for your keyboard, where you're not in some unnatural position, leaning over, reaching, turning your body to one side. Your hands should be just about parallel to your arms when typing, not raised more than 30 degrees. Your elbows should not be bent more than 90 degrees. Sit up tall, and remember to breathe. Don't smoke, cut down on meat… (whoops, there I go again). Okay, now you need to plug in the keyboard. Snake the wire over or down the CPU.

In the rare situation where the cable isn't long enough, and you have the CPU right where you really want it, jog down to your local computer store and ask for a keyboard extension cable.

And that's it for your desktop PC setup. You're ready to get started with it.

Let's Get Going!

Whew! As the Grateful Dead said, "What a long, strange trip it's been!" We've taken a very brief look at the history of the PC. (You'll find more historical tidbits scattered throughout the book in the "Did You Know?" boxes.) We've taken a look at the basic components of a PC, and we've deciphered those mysterious numbers you see in the PC ads in the newspaper. Finally, we got around to discussing the things you need to do when you are setting up your PC for the first time.

Now, we're ready for some real action! In the next chapter, we will explore the basics of the Windows operating system. Once you know your way around home base, we'll take a look at some popular applications and how they can make your life a whole lot easier.

Chapter 2

Starting Your PC and Using Windows

How to...

- Start your computer
- Use your mouse
- Understand the desktop and parts of the Windows screen
- Use menus
- Use dialog boxes
- Get help when you need it
- Shut down your computer

Did you follow along through the last chapter successfully? Did you get everything hooked up without anyone getting electrocuted? If so, congratulations; you're making headway becoming a PC user. Now it's time to power up your computer system and take it out for a spin.

In this chapter, you'll learn how to start up your computer, the basics of the Windows operating system, and how to shut down your computer. This chapter covers the essential Windows concepts and skills that you'll need to have, no matter what your line of work or what you intend to do with your computer. A solid grasp of these concepts will also help you understand and make the best use of the rest of this book.

Booting Up Your PC

You'll hear computer-savvy people sometimes talk about "booting up" or "booting" their computer. (Do they know where to kick it for those times when it crashes and loses the national budget?) Actually, the term refers to the concept of *bootstrapping*, which comes from the phrase "pulling yourself up by the bootstraps," something that's technically impossible to do (if you've ever tried).

As you might imagine, booting up is actually a fairly tricky process, because the computer starts up from a pretty brain-dead state, and then loads in the operating system (which is Windows in most modern PCs), so that it then becomes ready to run applications and allow you to do useful work. Booting up is a multistage process that starts with the CPU turning on and being forced (through hard wiring) to follow the instructions stored in the BIOS firmware. For your computer, it's a little like waking up in the morning—at first you're groggy, but with any luck, your body remembers how to turn on the Mr. Coffee. The BIOS tells the CPU how to load in the operating system software from the hard disk. Then the operating system takes over, ready and able to do your bidding.

NOTE *The BIOS, pronounced "BYE-ose" (like the beginning of the word biosphere), is an acronym for basic input/output system. The BIOS is the "hardwired" processes your computer always follows when it starts up.*

The Natural Order of Things (What to Turn On and When)

Since your system probably contains a bunch of different pieces of hardware (CPU, printer, scanner, monitor, and so on), you might be wondering which you should turn on first, or if it matters. If you plugged everything into a power strip, it's simple—you can just turn on the power strip's switch, and that will power up everything at once (assuming that all of the individual devices have their power switches turned on.) If you don't have a power strip, it's still pretty simple. Basically, here's the procedure:

1. Remove any floppy disks from the computer's floppy disk drives. Your BIOS always checks the floppy drive first to see if you are trying to boot the computer from there. A "non-system disk" in the drive will cause the startup sequence to pause, and you will be prompted to remove the disk and then press any key to continue.

NOTE *In some cases, the operating system can also boot from a CD-ROM, so don't leave any bootable CD-ROMs in your CD-ROM drive.*

2. Turn on the monitor next, so you can see what's happening when you turn on the CPU. The screen messages will report some things that could be useful to know.

3. Turn on any external drives or storage devices, such as Zip, Jaz, LS-120, or external CD-ROMs before starting the PC. As a rule, turning on external drives before turning on the computer is a good idea, because the computer is more likely to recognize them correctly. However, if your external drives are connected by USB (Universal Serial Bus), it doesn't matter whether you turn them on before or after the computer is switched on. (See Chapter 1 for more information about USB.)

4. Turn on the computer. There should be a button on it that is larger than other buttons and probably has the label "Power," although it might just have an international symbol on it (such as I/0). (For a laptop, if you are unsure of the location of the switch, which is usually pretty small, check the manual.)

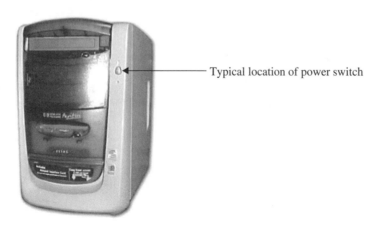

Typical location of power switch

Does pushing the power button to start the computer give you the willies? The original IBM PCs and AT machines had a big red switch, far back around the side of the machine. You really had to reach around the side and flick that switch, and it sounded like a small jackhammer when it flipped. Then things would start to whir. But today's PCs are much kinder and gentler. There is nothing to worry about.

Now you've got your computer up and running. You can typically turn on (or off) your other system components—scanners, speakers, printers, and so on—at any time, even when the computer is running, and it won't damage or confuse your computer. Obviously, whatever of these is turned off won't work then. So, for example, if you turn off the speakers, you won't hear your computer's sounds.

 *Because a laptop's monitor is integrated into the CPU, you don't have a choice of when to turn on the screen. It turns on when you turn on the laptop.*

The Startup Interval (Be Patient)

After you've turned on your computer, you next step is to wait patiently. As Windows loads, you'll usually see some action on the screen. As long as you see some movement—even if it is just shifting color patterns on a bar at the bottom of the opening screen—it means your computer is still alive and responding. Windows is a very big program, and it typically takes quite a while to load from your hard disk into RAM (random access memory).

Your computer will begin booting up by making some funky sounds and going through a little dance that includes a self test, possibly an on-screen display of what brand of PC it is, and then some gobbledygook about the internal settings (the amount of RAM and such). These messages may fly by so quickly that you can't read them, but that's okay, since you usually don't need to know what they say.

Next, the floppy and CD-ROM drives make some clicking or ratcheting sounds. This is all part of the normal startup sequence as your computer wakes up. Even though we think of computers as the ultimate digital appliances, they still have many moving parts that can make a bit of noise.

If your computer truly freezes at any point during the boot sequence (remember to be patient as Windows loads), you may have a serious problem. This is the time to read the on-screen messages, if any, and follow their instructions. (For example, if you see a message about "non-system disk," you might have a floppy disk in the floppy drive. Remove it and press the ENTER key to resume the boot process.) If the computer is still frozen, check the troubleshooting tips in Chapter 19 of this book for some advice.

Once Windows starts, you might be prompted to enter your name and possibly a password, as shown here.

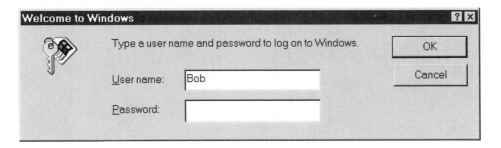

If you have Windows 95, 98, or Me (Millennium Edition), you can actually just press the ESC key (located in the upper-left corner of the keyboard) or click the OK button when prompted for your name and password to skip this dialog box. In fact, you can use Windows without having a password. If this is the first time Windows is being booted up on the computer, simply clicking OK in the login dialog box tells Windows that you won't be using a password. However, if your PC is connected to a LAN (local area network), correctly entering a password can be important because it give you access to shared networked resources, such as remote printers. If you don't know your user name and password, ask your network administrator.

Windows Basics

This book assumes you are running Windows 95, 98, or Me (the latest version). If you are using a very old computer that has Windows 3.1 on it, you will need to consult a book specifically on Windows 3.1. (You really need to get an upgrade, though!) By the same token, if you are working with Windows NT or Windows 2000, you should consult a book that is specifically about those operating systems.

To see which version of Windows you have, watch your screen while your computer is booting up, and you'll see an announcement of which version you have. If the announcement flies by too fast to read, you can check to see which version of Windows you have by clicking the Start button at the bottom of your Windows screen, then clicking once again on the word Help in the pop-up menu. The Windows Help screen that appears next should tell you the version of Windows that you have, or you may need to drill down further by selecting the Introducing Windows topic. (See the "Help!" section later in this chapter for more information about using the Windows Help facility.)

What Do I Do If My Computer Is Stuck?

If you need to quit Windows at any time while you're reading this chapter, just jump to the end of this chapter and read the "Exiting Windows" section for instructions. Also, if at any time you don't understand how to use a Windows command or perform some procedure, you can use the built-in Help facility available within any Windows application. Just press the F1 key on your keyboard. You can read more about the Windows Help facility in the "Help!" section later in this chapter.

The Progression of Windows

Windows has evolved over the past 15 years from Windows 1.0 to the current Windows Me and Windows 2000. The evolution of Windows has diverged along two paths. One path has been oriented toward home users, stand-alone computers, and computers for small businesses and small workgroups. This path includes the following versions:

- Windows 286
- Windows 386
- Windows 3.0
- Windows 3.1
- Windows 3.11 (Windows for Workgroups)
- Windows 95
- Windows 98
- Windows 98 Second Edition
- Windows Millennium Edition (Windows Me)

The other path is geared toward corporate networks and power users. It includes these versions of Windows:

- Windows NT 3.1
- Windows NT 3.51
- Windows NT 4
- Windows 2000

Yet another version of Windows is Windows CE. Some say the CE stands for Compact Edition, but Microsoft will tell you that it doesn't stand for anything in particular. It is the version of Windows that is used to power the popular handheld computers and has a lot in common with the version you use on your desktop or notebook computer.

If you have recently purchased a home computer, it probably has a version of Windows 98 or its successor, Windows Me, on it. If you work in a corporate environment, your computer may possibly have Windows NT or 2000 on it, although Windows 95 and 98 are popular even in big businesses.

2

If you get truly stuck and don't know how to escape from some procedure you're in the middle of, the last resort is to reboot your computer and start up Windows again. You may lose part of any documents you're working on, so this isn't a great idea, but it won't actually hurt your computer. There are several ways to reboot your computer, presented here in the order in which you should try them:

- Click the Start button (located in the lower-left corner of your screen) and choose Shut Down, and then choose Shut Down from the list of options that appears. This is the best method and the way you should always exit Windows.

- Try pressing the CTRL, ALT, and DEL keys simultaneously (in other words, press CTRL and hold, press ALT and hold both, then tap DEL). In the box that appears, click the Shut Down button (no, pressing the ENTER key won't work).

NOTE   *Windows allows you to use keystroke combinations—keyboard keys that you press simultaneously—for many operations. These combinations are denoted by listing the keys separated by hyphens, as in* CTRL-ALT-DEL.

- If your computer is really stuck, you might need to press CTRL-ALT-DEL again (that is, twice in a row). This will likely restart Windows.

- The most drastic but surefire way to reboot the computer is by pressing the computer's reset switch or turning your computer off, waiting a few seconds, and then turning it on again. This will almost invariably get you out of what you were doing, and make the computer ready to use again. Most, but not all, PCs have reset switches, which are located right on the front. Some newer computers require you to press and hold their power switch for four seconds before it will shut off.

Why Is It Called Windows?

Windows' name reflects the fact that it each program or document appears in its own separate frame, or *window*, on the screen. Figure 2-1 shows several such windows.

Many windows can be on the screen at the same time, and you can switch between them at will. Thus, you can be working on several projects at once, just as you can have several folders for various projects open on your office desk. Using the Windows *Clipboard*, you can easily share information between documents in different windows using Cut, Copy, and Paste commands. For example, you could copy digital photographs you've transferred to you computer, as well as some numbers from a spreadsheet, and paste them into the document containing your company's annual report to make it look professional. (See Chapter 4 for more information about using the Cut, Copy, and Paste commands.)

The most obviously useful thing about Windows is that it provides a standard GUI (graphical user interface) that many different programs can use. What is a *user interface* and why is it important to have a standard? To understand this, let's use cars as an example.

FIGURE 2-1   A window is a frame that contains a document or a program on the screen

When you get into any car, even a model you have never driven before, you pretty much already know how to use it because the "interface" is similar from car model to car model and from year to year. The steering wheel is on the correct side (at least for your country), the gas and brake pedals are always in the same location, gear shifts and headlights work the same way, and so on.

The GUI (pronounced "gooey") is a fancy name for the collection of graphical doodads that appear on your computer screen once Windows is up and running. You point at these doodads and click on them with your mouse buttons to get your work done. More accurate names for these GUI doodads are *icons*, *menus*, *buttons*, the *pointer*, and so on.

NOTE   *Before the Windows GUI came along, PC programs lacked a common set of commands. Even in Windows, of course, there are necessarily some differences between programs, but in the pre-Windows days, you had to learn a whole new set of controls and keyboard commands for each program. It was a big hassle.*

About the Mouse

The Windows GUI is designed for use with a mouse. As mentioned in Chapter 1, there are many different types of pointing devices, such as track pads, trackballs (the "upside down mouse"), and pointing sticks that live in the middle of the keyboard. Each has its own peculiarities, but most will have a motion sensor of some type and two switches (*buttons*) you can click.

NOTE   *Don't feel bad if you're not sure how to use a mouse. Consider the case of my mom, who just recently started using a computer. She picked up the mouse and pointed it at the screen like a TV remote control.*

When you move the mouse, the pointer moves around on the screen—move your hand or finger to the left, and the mouse moves to the left; move right, up, or down, and the pointer follows. It can take a little time to get the hang of moving and controlling the pointer, but try not to get too frustrated. Like driving a car or riding a bike, using a mouse becomes automatic after a bit of practice.

When manuals, books, or people talk tell you how to do stuff with your mouse, they'll say to "click," "right-click," or "double-click." Here's what you should do:

- To *click,* position the mouse pointer on the item in question and then click the *left* button once (or, if you've custom configured your pointing device, whichever button you've assigned as the *primary* button).

- To *right-click*, position the mouse pointer on the item and click the *right* button once (or whichever button is configured as the secondary button).

- To *double-click,* click on an item twice in quick succession. You should keep the mouse still and not take too long between clicks.

NOTE   *You don't need to press the mouse buttons hard to make them click. A tap will do the job.*

Speaking of taps, many laptop computers have track pads. With this kind of mouse, simply tapping the pad has the same effect as clicking the left button. Tapping twice in succession results in a double-click. Refer to the manual or an online help file to learn more about how your track pad works.

Parts of the Windows Screen

Now let's take a quick look at the basic parts of the Windows landscape: the desktop, icons, taskbar, and so on. Figure 2-2 shows some of the parts of the Windows screen. Once you understand these essential building blocks, you'll be comfortable working with Windows.

The Windows screen contains the following main elements:

- **Desktop**   The *desktop* is your jumping off point for doing your work in Windows. It's called the desktop because it's analogous to the way you would use the surface of a desk.

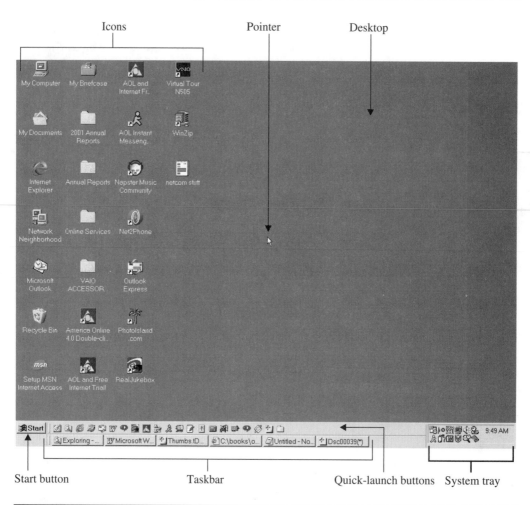

FIGURE 2-2   The Windows desktop

As you work in Windows, you move items around on the desktop, retrieve items, put
away items, and perform your other day-to-day tasks. You do all this using graphical
representations of your work projects. You can store your favorite items on the desktop
to make it easy to find them. Each time you run Windows, those items will be right there
where you left them.

■   **Icons**   An *icon* is a graphical symbol that represents programs, documents, or folders
in your computer. To get your work (and play) done, click on these little graphics to run

the programs or open your documents. Icons have names under them to remind you what they are. Some icons look like little file folders, and they actually represent Windows folders. *Folders* keep related documents or programs together. You can even create folders within folders, a useful feature for organizing your work from the top down.

■ **Start button**   Click the Start button (a *button* is a little square or rectangular icon) to begin most anything in Windows. You can open documents, run programs, or make settings in your computer from here. The *Start menu,* shown below, appears when you click on the Start button. (Your choices may be different than what you see here.)

■ **Taskbar**   The taskbar displays one button for each window you have open at any given time. Clicking any button in the taskbar makes its associated window pop to the front of other windows that might be obscuring it.

■ **Quick-launch buttons**   At the far-left end of the taskbar are the quick-launch buttons. These make it easy to open your most-used programs or documents. Instead of clicking the Start menu and searching for the program you want, you can just add *shortcuts* to programs and documents here, so they're only one click away. (Adding shortcuts is discussed in Chapter 3.)

■ **System tray**   At the far-right end of the taskbar lies the system tray. The icons here pertain to the operating system. For example, you'll see the system time (your computer has a clock in it), a little speaker icon for adjusting the loudness of your speakers, and other goodies. Some programs will add icons to the system tray when you install them.

- **My Computer**   Double-clicking on the My Computer icon opens up a window containing a bunch of icons. Through these icons, you can delve into your computer's contents. For example, you can examine all of the contents of your hard disk and access your dial-up networking function to connect to the Internet.

- **My Documents**   When you create documents while using your computer, you usually will save them inside the computer, so that you can work with them again later. For example, you might want to print them, make changes to them, and so forth. When you save your documents, they are typically stored in the My Documents folder (makes sense, right?), although you can choose to store them in other folders or subfolders if you want. Double-click this folder icon to access your saved documents.

> **TIP**   *Instead of double-clicking icons to open them or run them, you can make Windows act the same way a Web page does. On a Web page, one click on a hot link will activate it. All you have to do to make the Windows desktop act like a Web page is to enable Web view. You can activate Web view from almost any window (such as the My Documents window) by opening the View menu and choosing Folder Options.*

Anatomy of a Window

You can change the size of windows, move them around, and close them (remove them from the screen). All windows work the same way, so once you understand the basic anatomy of one window, all the other windows will make sense to you. Figure 2-3 shows the elements common to all windows. (Some programs have extra stuff like fancy toolbars built into their windows, but you'll learn about those things as you experiment with the particular program.)

In a program window, you will see the following elements:

- **Title bar**   The name of the program, and sometimes the document, appears at the top of its respective window, in what's called the *title bar*. The title bar also indicates which window is *active*. Although you can have a lot of windows on the screen at once, there can be only one active window. The active window is the one you're currently working in. When a window is made active, it jumps to the front of other windows that might be obscuring it, and its title bar changes color. You make a window active by clicking anywhere within its border.

- **Minimize button**   The Minimize button is the first of the three small buttons at the right end of the title bar. When you click on this button to minimize a window, the window zips down to become a button on the taskbar. The window's name is shown beside the icon so you know what it is. To get it back from the minimized state, just click on it.

- **Maximize/Restore button**   The Maximize button is the second of the three little buttons at the right end of the title bar. Clicking the Maximize button makes the window *maximized*, so that it takes up the whole desktop. When you maximize a window, the Maximize button changes to the Restore button. Clicking the Restore button makes the window its restored size, which is neither full-screen nor minimized—it's whatever size it was when it was last between its minimized and maximized states.

2

■ **Close button**   The little button on the far-right side of the title bar is the Close button. Click this button to remove the window from your screen.

■ **Scrollbars**   When there is more information in a document than will fit into a window, there will be *scrollbars* along the edge of the window. Vertical scrollbars along the right side of your window let you scroll up and down through the document. Horizontal scrollbars along the bottom of your window let you scroll left and right. Scrolling lets you look at a large amount of data through what amounts to a small window—your screen. Click the little arrows at the ends of a scrollbar, or drag the little box in the middle of the scrollbar (the *elevator*), to scroll through the document.

TIP   *If you have a "wheel" mouse, such as the Microsoft Intellimouse, you can scroll the window by turning the little roller on the mouse using your index finger.*

Menu bar   Just below the title bar lies the *menu bar.* Notice that the menu bar contains a number of words. If you click on one of the words in the menu bar (called a menu *name*), a menu opens up, displaying a series of options that you can choose from by clicking on them. (Pizza typically won't be a menu, though). Menus are discussed in more detail in the "An Introduction to Menus" section, coming up soon.

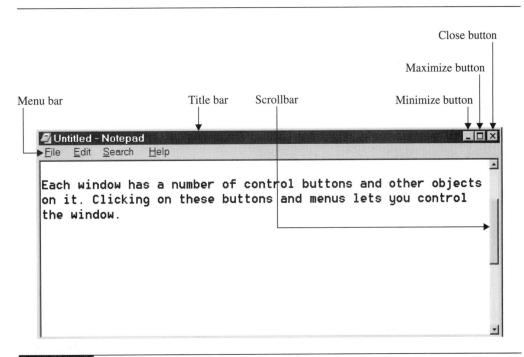

FIGURE 2-3   Common parts of a window

Some windows are divided into panes that have different contents. For example, Outlook Express has one pane that shows a list of e-mails and another that shows the contents of an e-mail after you click it. (See Chapter 7 for coverage of Outlook Express.).

Window Resizing and Repositioning

There are essentially three sizes that a window can have:

- *Normal*, where the window is open on the desktop and you can make it any size you want
- *Minimized*, where the window becomes an icon on the taskbar (as explained earlier)
- *Maximized*, where the window takes up the whole desktop

Sometimes, you'll want to adjust the size of a window manually to a very specific size. You might want to arrange two windows side by side, for example, so you can see them both at once. To resize a window, carefully position the cursor on any edge or corner of the window that you want to resize. When you are in the right position, the cursor shape changes to a two-headed arrow. Now *drag* it (keep the left mouse button depressed and continue to move the mouse). When you are happy with the size, release the mouse button.

When a window is smaller than the full screen, you can reposition (without resizing) it. Just click on the window's title bar, hold down the mouse button, and drag it around. Then release the mouse button when the window is where you want it. Note that for this to work, the window can't be maximized, since that wouldn't leave any screen room for moving it.

An Introduction to Menus

Virtually all programs you run will have menus. Each menu has *commands* on it. Most programs have a File menu, like the one shown below, used for saving your work on the hard disk and later reopening it. Also, most have a Help menu for obtaining help with the program.

You can open a menu by clicking on its name in the menu bar. Alternatively, you can use the keyboard to open menus. Just press the ALT key (typically located next to the spacebar), then look up at the menu bar. There will be an underlined letter in each menu's name. Press that letter, and the respective menu will open.

Once a menu is open, you can select any of the commands in the menu that aren't dimmed. Just click the menu choice or press the underlined letter in the command's name. You can close a menu without making any choices by pressing the ESC key. Some menu commands have special indicators:

- A grayed (dimmed) command name means that this choice is not currently available to you. Grayed commands usually do not apply to the current state of your work in the program. For example, the Paste command will be dimmed until you have cut or copied something to the Clipboard.

- An ellipsis (…) next to a command mean that you will be asked for additional information before Windows or the Windows application executes the command.

- A checkmark (✓) or dot (.) beside a command means that the command is a toggle that is activated (turned on). A *toggle* is a command that is alternately turned off and on each time you select it.

- A triangle (>) to the right of a menu command means that the command has additional subchoices for you to make. This is called a *cascading menu* (because the next menu starts to the right of the previous one and runs down from there, a bit like a waterfall of menus).

- A key combination next to a command indicates the shortcut keys for that command, which you can press to issue the command without opening the menu and selecting it. For example, on most Edit menus, you'll see CTRL-C next to the Copy command. This means that instead of opening the Edit menu and selecting the Copy command, you can press and hold down the CTRL key (located near the spacebar on your keyboard), and then press the C key to copy the selected item.

An Introduction to Dialog Boxes

Windows uses *dialog boxes* when it needs to collect information from you, such as where you want to store a document that you are saving. It's called a dialog box because it's a way the computer can have a little conversation with you. Some dialog boxes ask a simple Yes/No question, some require you to check off options or make choices from a list, and some need you to type in information. After you enter the requested information, you click the OK button in the dialog box, and Windows closes the dialog box and continues on its merry way. Figure 2-4 shows a typical dialog box.

Some dialog boxes, such as the one in Figure 2-4, have *tab pages*, which keep a dialog box to a reasonable size while still letting you adjust a gazillion settings from it. To get to the page of settings you want, just click on the tab with the correct name.

Many dialog boxes have a little question mark in the upper-right corner. This is the What's This? button. Click it, and then click any part of the dialog box you don't understand. You'll see a description of that part of the dialog box. (This is called *context-sensitive* help, because it pertains to what you're trying to do when you ask for help information.) The X button next to the question mark is the Close button, which works just like the Close button in a window: It removes the dialog box from your screen.

Close button

Tab pages   The What's This? button

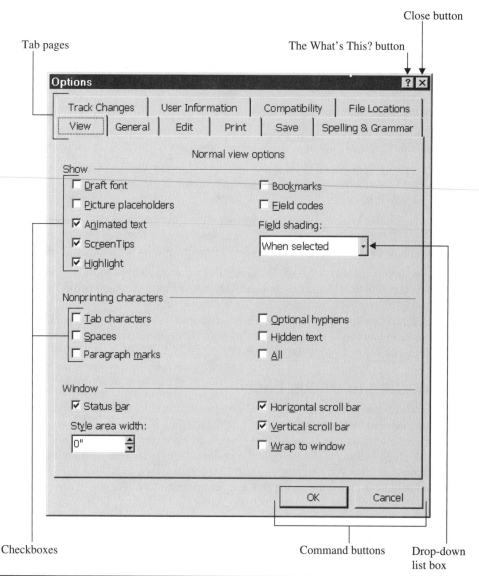

Checkboxes   Command buttons   Drop-down
                                                           list box

FIGURE 2-4   A dialog box that presents an array of options

You interact with dialog boxes by clicking on the section you want to change or fill in. Dialog boxes may contain the following parts:

- **Text boxes**   Just click in the box and start typing. Use the Backspace key to erase characters.

- **Check boxes**   These are toggle settings (as explained earlier) that you activate or deactivate by clicking on the box. When the box is empty, the option is off; when you see a check mark in the box, the option is on. Multiple check box options can be selected at the same time. For example, in Figure 2-3, the Window section at the bottom of the dialog box has four check boxes; three are on (checked), and one is off (empty).

- **Option buttons**   Sometimes called radio buttons, these are round buttons that contain a dot when they are selected (turned on). Unlike check boxes, only one option button can be selected at a time.

          ● Never dial a connection
          ○ Dial whenever a network connection is not present
          ○ Always dial my default connection

- **Command buttons**   These buttons carry out specific actions. For example, most dialog boxes include OK and Cancel buttons, and some also have Apply buttons. Once you've filled in a dialog box to your liking, click on the OK button. The dialog box will close, and your settings will go into effect. If you change your mind and don't want the new settings in the dialog box executed, click the Cancel button instead. This closes the dialog box and ignores any changes you made within it. Clicking the Apply button applies any changes you've already made and keeps the dialog box open for you to make additional changes.

- **List boxes**   These boxes present a list of choices. Just click on the selection you want. Some list boxes are too small to show all of the possible selections. In this case, there will be a scrollbar on the right side of the list box. When a list box is active, you can jump quickly to an area of the list by pressing the first letter in the selection you want to make. For example, in the Font list box shown here, you could type the letter *T* to see the fonts that begin with *T*.

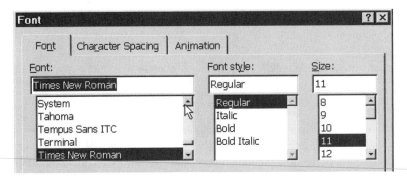

■ **Drop-down list boxes**   Drop-down list boxes are used when a dialog box is too crowded to accommodate regular list boxes. Click on the arrow next to the box to open a list of choices. This list works just like a normal list box, and has scrollbars if there are a lot of options.

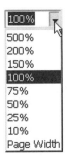

Though most dialog boxes ask you for your input, others are more like monologue boxes (computers make terrible conversationalists); they just announce something. These dialog boxes sometimes have a big letter *I* (for Information) to let you know that they are providing information. Others, like the one shown below, have an exclamation mark (!), indicating that they are alerting you to a situation. More often than not, these boxes only ask you to read them, and then click OK.

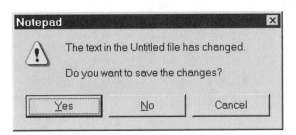

Help!

Sometimes, even if you're a computer jock, there will be times when you don't remember or understand how to use a command or perform an operation (er, how do mailing labels work again?). The good news is that you don't always need to drag out a book to get some quick help.

Both Windows and Windows programs have helpful advice built right in. Sometimes it helps, and sometimes it's about as useful as a bicycle is to a fish. The trick is to know the difference, and to know how to use the Help system to search for what you want. Once you learn how to use the Windows Help system, you'll be able to find answers to many of your questions.

NOTE *Does Help replace books? Nope. Books have certain advantages that can't be easily rivaled by computers. For starters, books let you know intuitively how many pages of material there are on a given topic—you can thumb through them easily. They don't require batteries, and they don't break if you drop them. Using them doesn't really take much expertise (except the ability to read), so you don't have to know how to use the computer before you can figure out how to use the computer! It's easy to tote a book with you to read on the bus or a plane (even during landing and takeoff—the FAA doesn't make you turn off your book).*

There are two broad categories of Help information: You can get help about using Windows itself and help about using one of your application programs. You can always get help about Windows whenever you're running Windows—which is to say whenever your computer is turned on. To get help with a specific program, that program has to be running. Then you just press the F1 key or open the program's Help menu and choose the Help command.

The Windows Help system uses a sensible layout that lets you look things up by topic (sort of like an index in a book) or by browsing a table of contents (also like a book). You can also type in a word that represents the topic you want to find (called a *keyword*).

NOTE *Help screens have evolved over the years and vary in the way they work. Some older programs you run might have Help screens that look a little different than the ones shown here. Even if they don't look exactly the same as the examples in this chapter, Help screens all work pretty much the same way. You may need to poke around a bit in an older Help screen, but it's usually self-explanatory.*

Using the New Help Center

Here's how to get help with Windows topics (help with how to use Windows itself, not with specific Windows programs you might be running). If your computer is on, you might want to follow these steps to experiment a bit.

1. Click the Start button at the bottom of your screen, and then click on Help. A window like the one shown in Figure 2-5 appears. This is the new Help Center for Windows Millennium Edition.

2. Click on one of the topics that interests you.

FIGURE 2-5 The opening Windows Help window

3. You can also click in the Search area at the top of the window, enter a search item (such as "printing") and click Go. That will bring up a list of printing topics. Just click on any underlined topic and in a few seconds you can read about that topic.

4. Note links near the upper edge of the window: Home, Index, Assisted Support, and Tours and Tutorials. Explore these by clicking on them. With some patience and a little fishing around, you'll learn a few things.

Using Help in Typical Applications

The help you'll see in most applications (and in Windows 98, if you are using that) will not look like the Windows Help screen illustrated in Figure 2-5. Instead, it will look more like Figure 2-6.

1. While in your program, press F1, or choose Help from the Help menu of the app.

2. A small window appears. The three tabs at the top of the pane (window portion) on the left represent the three ways you can work with help: Use Search to find help relating to a word you type in, Contents to view the table of contents, or Index to see an alphabetical list of topics.

3. Click the Contents tab. The Help window shows a list of Help topics. Each of the little books on the left means the topic is like a chapter. You can "open" the chapter to see subtopics by clicking it.

4. When you see a little icon that looks like a page of text with a question mark (?) in it, you can click on it to read what it has to say. Usually, another window will open, with information about the topic you selected.

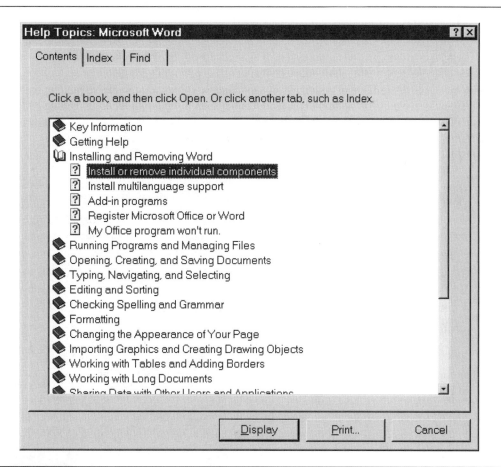

FIGURE 2-6   Using the Help facility's Contents tab to find Help information

5. When the secondary window opens, the Contents window might disappear. To get it back again, click the Help Topics (sometimes called Contents) button:

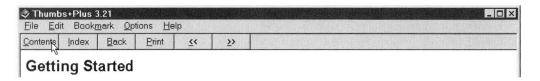

 You can enlarge the Help window to see more information at once. Just click on the Maximize button or manually resize it, as described in the "Window Resizing and Repositioning" section earlier in the chapter. You can also enlarge or shrink each pane by moving the pointer to the bar that divides them until it changes to a double-headed arrow and then dragging it left or right.

Using the Index Tab

The Index tab is the second line of attack if you can't find that elusive topic you're hunting for help with. Actually, when you're doing real work (rather than just passing the time reading Help information about Windows or some program), you'll use the Help index. Just as with a book, the index can help you quickly locate just the piece of trivia you need.

Follow these steps to use the index:

1. Click the Index tab of the Help window. You might see a message that says "Preparing the index for the first time" and a little pen writing on it. This might take a few seconds.

2. Now the left pane displays a listing of topics. Notice that there is a scrollbar to the right of the list. You can scroll the list down to search for your topic, but the quicker way to find a topic is to simply start typing it in.

3. For this example, let's suppose I was having trouble printing from Microsoft Word. After clicking on the Index tab, I typed **print** in the text box above the list box, as shown in Figure 2-7. Notice that the list jumps immediately to topics pertaining to printing.

4. Scroll down until the topic you want is in sight, and then double-click on it. With some luck, you'll now see some useful information pop up in a secondary window. In some cases, before actually getting the Help information, you'll be presented with a list of subtopics to choose from. Double-click on the one you want, or highlight it and click on Display.

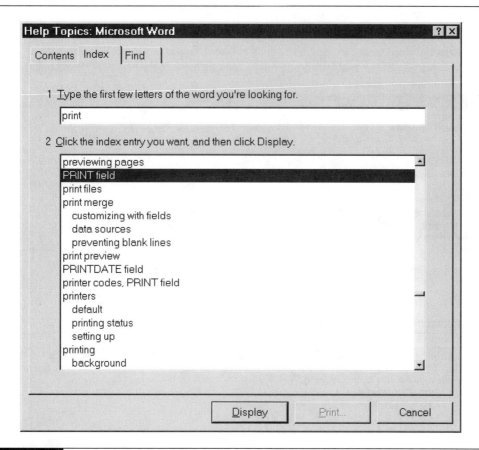

Help Topics: Microsoft Word

Contents   Index | Find |

1 Type the first few letters of the word you're looking for.

print

2 Click the index entry you want, and then click Display.

previewing pages
PRINT field
print files
print merge
    customizing with fields
    data sources
    preventing blank lines
print preview
PRINTDATE field
printer codes, PRINT field
printers
    default
    printing status
    setting up
printing
    background

Display   Print...   Cancel

FIGURE 2-7   Using the Help facility's Index tab to find Help information

Using the Search Tab

The third tab of the basic Windows Help window is labeled Search. This is the "needle in a haystack" option for combing through the Help file for exactly the word you want. I generally resort to this approach if I can't find the information by using the Index tab.

Here's how to do a search:

1.   Click the Search tab. If this is the first time you're running a search, you may be prompted to answer a few questions about creating the search database. It only takes a few seconds. Just follow the on-screen instructions. If you're short on disk space, use the Custom option. Otherwise click on Express, Next, and then Finish.

2. Enter the word you're looking for in the text box at the top of the tab You may type in multiple words. For example, here I'll look for envelopes in the Microsoft Word help file:

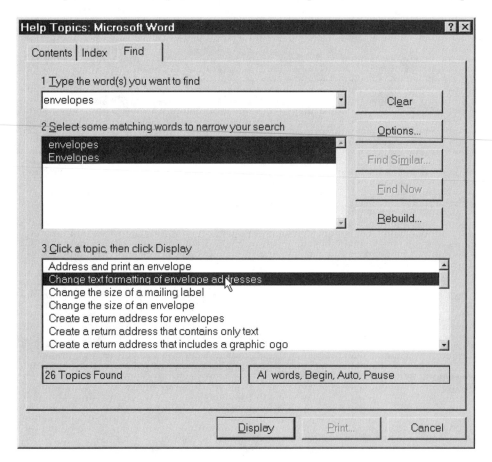

3. If no topics are found, you'll be alerted. If multiple topics are found, you'll need to choose one and click Display (or double-click on a topic). In this illustration, I'm about to click on one.

4. The resulting topic is shown in a secondary window. Typically, each occurrence of your search word is highlighted to help you see where in the text your searched-for word is. If this bugs you, you can click on the Options button in the Help window's toolbar and choose Search Highlight Off.

TIP

The Help window's toolbar also has Back and Forward buttons. If you are tooling around reading Help topics, you often want to retrace your steps to review information. This is a snap with the Back and Forward buttons. Click Back to back up one step in your previous journey, and Forward to go to the next step after the one you're viewing.

Keeping a Specific Help Screen Handy

Some Help windows often seem to disappear when you go back to the task that the Help information is about. This is worse than trying to remember a phone number you just got from the phone company's information and then dialing it from a phone booth.

In reality, the Help window hasn't disappeared; your application window has covered it up. Some Help windows can be told to "stay on top" of other windows. Check their menus for a setting called Stay on Top. Even if a program doesn't have this feature, there are a couple of ways to keep a window full of specific Help information in view or at least easily available:

■ You can shrink the Help window down to a size where you can still read it but it doesn't take up the whole screen. Make it a small, wide band at the bottom or side of the screen, for example, and resize your other windows to accommodate it.

■ You can minimize it, which puts a button for it on the taskbar. When you need to read the Help information again, just click on the Help button's icon to bring the window back up on your screen. This is particularly helpful for quickly recalling lists of key commands or other information that might be difficult to remember.

TIP

In some cases, Help just won't tell you what you're interested in the first time around. Here's a general game plan to try when you can't seem to ferret anything useful out of Help. First, try spending some time wandering through the Help screens. There is a lot of information in the Help files supplied with Windows and the Windows accessories. You can also try entering related terms in the Search (sometimes called Find) tab page.

Exiting Windows

Exiting Windows properly is very important. You can lose your work or otherwise foul up Windows internal settings if you don't shut down Windows before turning off your computer. If you accidentally fail to do so, the computer probably won't die or anything, but at the least, the hard disk will be checked for errors the next time you turn it on, which is annoying and takes several minutes. Even if you are running a program (such as a word-processing program or Web browser), and you close that application, you must still use the Windows Shut Down or Standby command before turning off your computer.

NOTE

Windows Me is better than Windows 95 or 98 is about repairing itself if an important system file is compromised by improper shutdowns. Even so, it's easy to shut down properly, and it should just become a matter of habit for you.

Shutting Down the Computer

Here are the steps for correctly shutting down your PC:

1. Close any programs that you have running. If you forget to do this, Windows will try to close them for you, but it won't always save your work first. Typically, you'll be prompted to save your work, but you might not see the prompt. It's more reliable to manually close any open programs. (Switch to the application's window by clicking on its button in the taskbar, click on File in its menu bar, and choose Exit from that menu.)

2. Click on the Start button and choose Shut Down. You'll see the dialog box shown in Figure 2-8.

3. Click the Shut Down option button.

4. Windows will ask you to confirm that you want to shut down the computer. Click Yes.

5. Wait until Windows completely shuts down and tells you it's okay to turn off your computer. This can take up to about 15 seconds. On many computers, that message will appear only briefly, and the computer will shut down by itself. If the computer doesn't turn off automatically, just wait until the screen says "It's now safe to turn off your computer," and then switch it off manually using the computer's power switch.

6. Turn off any peripherals, such as your printer and monitor.

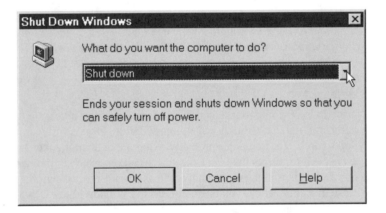

FIGURE 2-8 Shutting down Windows

Using the Standby Feature

Most modern PCs have a feature called APM (Advanced Power Management) or ACPI (Advanced Configuration and Power Interface) that Windows uses to economize on the electricity consumed by your computer. The computer and Windows work together to save you time, as well as save the environment. These computers have a low-power *standby* state that can kick in when the computer hasn't been used for a while or when you shut down using the Standby option. Standby keeps just enough power in the computer so that it doesn't lose track of what you were working on. It's sort of like when the judge calls a 15-minute recess during a trial, after which everything starts back up again just as it was.

If you're using the standby feature, you don't need to exit all your applications before turning off your computer. And when you're ready to work again, you don't need to twiddle your thumbs as Windows boots, then run the programs you were running, find the document(s) you were working on, and find your place in those documents. You can just press a key or button (depending on your computer), and in a few seconds (typically about ten), you are up and running right where you left off.

Note that there is a limit to the amount of time a laptop computer can stay in a suspended state, because there is some drain on the battery even in the standby mode. If the battery runs out while the computer is in standby, the computer will need to be rebooted from scratch when you turn it on, and your work may be lost. If you're going to put a battery-powered PC on standby, check the battery level, and educate yourself about how long the computer can stay in the standby state on a fully-charged battery.

TIP
To be safe, you may be able to use hibernate function, if your laptop supports it (check the manual). There is no time limit with hibernate, since batteries are not used, although it takes a little longer to revive the machine (like about 15 to 45 seconds). The effect is the same as the standby state—you can start working from where you left off. My newest laptop computer (which happens to be a Sony VAIO), has a terrific feature: It will automatically go from standby into hibernate mode if the standby batteries get too low in charge. When you're shopping for a laptop computer, intelligent power management features such as this are worth looking into.

If your desktop computer has the standby feature, you'll have a Standby option in your Shutdown dialog box when you go to exit Windows (as in Figure 2-8, shown earlier). Just use the drop-down list to choose it. Some machines even have a special key on the keyboard for shutting down or standing by (for example, some Compaq machines have a button with a little moon on it). If you're going to use the standby feature, you should save your work first, just to be safe (see Chapter 3 for more information about saving files).

In a few seconds after you choose the Standby option, the computer will go into standby mode. There may be some indication that it's still semi-alive, such as a little light somewhere that blinks. (The indication will vary, depending on your computer). If it's a laptop computer, you can now close the cover and pack it up if you need to take to the streets. When you put a computer into standby, you don't need to turn off the power switch. The computer should go into standby mode on its own.

Chapter 3

Running Programs and Managing Your Files

How to...

- Run programs
- Create and save documents
- Organize your files and folders
- Copy files and folders
- Delete and recover files
- Find files quickly

Now that you know the basics of how to turn on your computer and how the Windows operating system works, you're obviously going to want to start doing stuff with it. Whether you're working or playing, you'll need to know how to run programs, create new documents, save files, and organize your work. This chapter tells you how.

Running Your Programs

Many of the things you'll want to do while using Windows can be achieved a number of different ways, and that applies to the task of running your programs. For example, last time I counted, there were at least ten ways you could run a program. Here, we'll explore the simplest techniques. As you gain experience with Windows, you can try other methods and decide which ones you feel most comfortable using.

Running Programs from the Start Button

One simple way to run your programs is by using the Start button. As you learned in Chapter 2, the Start button resides in the lower-left corner of your screen, on the taskbar. It's called the Start button for a good reason—it's where you can start your programs, make settings, or open documents. Clicking the Start button opens the Start menu.

As supplied from the dealer, your computer includes a number of programs already, all of which can be run from the Start menu. In addition, when you buy a new program and install it, that program's name is almost always added to the Start menu. To start a program, click the Start button, find your way to the program's name in the Start menu, and click it. Finding the program name in the Start menu may be the only tricky part. Sometimes a program will be "nested" several layers deep in the menus, so you might need to click through several levels of menus to find it. (These kinds of menus are called *cascading menus*, as you might recall from Chapter 2.)

As an example of running a program from the Start menu, let's start up Notepad, which is a simple word-processing program that comes with Windows. The Notepad program is grouped with the Accessory programs. Follow these steps to run Notepad:

1. Click the Start button to open the Start menu.

2. Slide the pointer up until it rests on the word *Programs*. Just let the pointer sit there for a second, and the Programs menu will pop out to the right. This menu shows a list of

programs that are installed on your computer. Any selection that has an arrow pointer to the right of the name is not actually a program but a program *group*. Resting the pointer on one of these names opens another menu listing the items in the group.

3. Slide the pointer up or over to highlight *Accessories*. Now a list of accessory programs appears.

4. Slide the pointer down to *Notepad*, as shown below, and click. (If one of the lists disappears because you are not super-coordinated with the mouse, don't worry. Just click the Start button again to start over.)

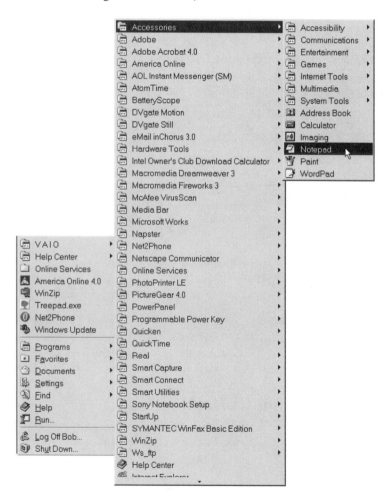

NOTE   *Your Start menu and its cascading menus will look different from the ones shown here, because this is the list of programs on my computer, not yours.*

Assuming you aimed correctly and clicked on *Notepad*, the Notepad program should be running. You should see a blank Notepad window, prepared to accept your keystrokes. Since we're not going to use the Notepad program, just close it by clicking its Close button (the X in the upper-right corner of the Notepad window) or by opening the Notepad window's File menu and choosing Exit.

In the preceding example, you needed to open the Accessories group to find Notepad. If you open the Accessories group again, you'll notice that there are several groups of programs within Accessories, such as Communications, Entertainment, Games, Internet Tools, Multimedia, System Tools, and so on. Clicking on each of these opens another cascading menu that lists the programs in that group. For practice, try running some of the programs in the Accessories group. For example, open the Games group and run Solitaire. When you're finished with a program, just close its window.

If there are too many programs in the menu for the list to completely fit on the screen, you'll see arrows at the top or bottom of the list, as shown below. Click the arrow to scroll the list, and release the mouse button when you see the program you want. Then click it.

Click here to scroll the list

If you accidentally open a list that you don't want to see, you can close it by pressing the ESC key. Each press of ESC closes one level of any open list. To close all the open Start menu lists, click anywhere else on the screen, such as on the desktop or another window.

Here's a little trick for running a program when you can't find it listed in the Start menu or on your desktop: Locate a document that was created with the application in question and double-click it. This will run the application and load the document into it. Usually, you can then close that document, and the program will still be running.

Running a Program from Its Desktop Icon

Many programs, when newly installed, will create a *shortcut icon* on your computer desktop. For example, here's an icon that was added to the desktop by the Real Jukebox program I installed recently:

3

When I double-click this icon, Real Jukebox runs, so I can listen to some tunes. Some folks prefer this desktop-icon approach to navigating through the Start menu. The only problem is that you need to get to the desktop (clear off any obstructing windows) before you can see the icons to click on them.

However, there are easy ways to quickly get to your desktop. You can temporarily clear off the desktop and minimize all of your open windows with a single click. Click the icon to the right of the Start button that looks like a pencil pointing to a piece of paper.

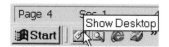

Another way to show the desktop is by pressing the WINDOWS key (the one with the Windows symbol on it, usually located near the spacebar on your keyboard) and the D key simultaneously. Press WINDOWS-D once to minimize any open windows. Press WINDOWS-D again, and they will reappear.

As you'll learn later, you can put shortcut icons in various places, such as on the quick-launch bar, desktop, and Start menu.

Running a Program from Its Quick-Launch Icon

On a newly installed Windows system, there are several quick-launch icons (at the left end of the taskbar), such as those for running Internet Explorer and Outlook Express. Many programs, when you install them, will add icons here.

The quick-launch icons are smaller than the ones on the desktop, but they aren't any less powerful. Since you don't need to clear the desktop to reach the quick-launch icons, they're more convenient than the desktop shortcuts. And they don't even require double-clicking—a single click will do.

Since the little quick-launch icons don't have any text on them, you might forget what each does. You can just rest the pointer on any quick-launch icon to see a pop-up text description before clicking it. Here's an example:

Notice the word Launch in the quick-launch icon's pop-up description. This isn't a reference to boating, but rather to running a program. Launching is the same as running a program.

Switching Between Program Windows

Windows is a *multitasking* operating system. This means that instead of running just one program at a time, it can actually run many—all at once. So you could, for example, be checking your e-mail while at the same time working on a business report, and even calculating a complicated business spreadsheet in the background. A bit like a juggler keeping many balls in the air, Windows can efficiently divide up your CPU's ability to do work, doling out what's called "CPU time" between simultaneously running tasks, in a round-robin fashion. It *appears* as though the computer is doing multiple things at once, when really it is very quickly switching between tasks.

Many PC users think they need to shut down one program, folder, or document before working on another one. But since Windows can multitask, that's really not necessary, nor efficient. How many programs can you run at once? That depends on the speed of your computer and the amount of RAM in it. But most of today's PCs can easily run at least two or three. As I look right now, I see that I have 14 programs running on my laptop computer, which has 128M of RAM. Of course, most of those are not doing any heavy-duty calculations; they're just waiting for me to get back to them to type something in or give a command.

Using the Taskbar

As you learned in Chapter 2, each time you open a new program or open a folder, a new window appears on the screen. So, if you're running a bunch of programs, your screen can become cluttered by all those windows. If you click on a window that's behind another window, it "jumps" to the front of the lot. So if you accidentally click on the wrong one, you can suddenly feel a bit lost, like dropping the book you were reading and needing to find the right page again.

This is where the taskbar comes to the rescue. Each window on the screen also has a corresponding button on the taskbar. Simply clicking one of those buttons brings back the program or folder's window. Clicking the button again causes the window to minimize down to the taskbar again.

For the first several programs you run, the buttons are long enough to read the names of the programs or folder, as shown here.

As you run more programs, the taskbar buttons automatically get narrower, so the names on them are truncated, as in the example here.

If you rest the pointer over a taskbar button, its full name will pop up, as you see here. This helps you know what each button is for.

Switching with ALT-TAB

If you don't like the taskbar approach, there is another way to switch between windows. Press the ALT key and hold it down. Now, press the TAB key (you know, that key just above the CAPS LOCK key and to the left of the Q). You'll see a box in the center of your screen showing you an icon of each program or folder that's running, like this:

Each time you press the TAB key (while holding down the ALT key), it will advance the outline box one notch to the right. The outline box indicates which program you'll be switched to when you release the ALT key. Notice that the name of the program or folder is displayed at the bottom of the box. This is especially useful when you're choosing folders, because all folders look the same. Release the ALT key, and the corresponding window will jump up on the screen. While cycling through running programs with this technique, you can back up one program (move the box to the left), by pressing ALT-SHIFT-TAB.

Adding a New Program to Your Computer

Suppose you see an exciting new program that slices, dices, and calculates your taxes for you. How do you install it on your computer? Well, first you want to check a few things:

- What are the system requirements for the program? Does your computer have enough RAM, enough hard disk space, or a fast enough CPU to run it? Are there other hardware requirements?

- What is the price of the program? If it's an expensive commercial product, try shopping around on the Internet for it, or ask for a competitive price from a local dealer. On the other hand, perhaps it's shareware or freeware. *Shareware* is a marketing scheme that lets you try out a program first. If you like it, then you pay for it. *Freeware* is totally free software, without any strings attached.

After you have the computer program in hand, you need to *install* it on your computer before you can run it. How you do this differs a bit from one program to another. Programs typically come with installation instructions. Look on the box, on the CD, in the manual, or on the Web page that you downloaded the program from. You'll likely find instructions there. Many CDs containing software will run their installation programs automatically when you insert the CD into your CD-ROM drive.

If none of these techniques works, look for a file called Readme.txt or Readme on the floppy disk, in the download folder, or on the CD that the software came on. Double-clicking on such a file usually opens a text file in a Notepad window, and this file may tell you how to install the software.

Although by clicking on Start, Settings, Control Panel, and then double-clicking on Add Remove Programs, you will run a wizard (a program that walks you through a procedure) for installing programs, nobody does it this way. This approach is only used for removing programs you have installed on your computer and no longer use. That's something you do when you're in the mood for spring cleaning or are running out of hard disk space.

Creating, Saving, and Opening Files

So far, we've only talked about how to run programs. As you probably know, your programs are primarily used for creating documents and other kinds of files. All the documents you create and save (and even the programs you run) are stored on the hard disk as files. A file can take up very little of your hard disk's space or quite a lot of it. Files are measured in kilobytes (K) and megabytes (M), just like RAM is (as discussed in Chapter 1).

For your work, you will most likely want to create new documents (files), save them to disk, and later open them.

Creating New Documents

There are several ways to create new documents. Most people do it from within a program. You decide which program you want to create the document with, and then you find and run that program (as described earlier in this chapter). Using that program, you create a new document, usually by using the New command on the File menu. But there's another way that can be useful, too.

You can create a new document without running any program at all, by simply right-clicking in a folder or on the desktop and using a few menus. To use this method, follow these steps:

1. Open the destination folder where you want the new document stored. It can be a folder or the desktop (the desktop is really just a folder). For example, double-click the My Documents icon on your desktop to open the My Documents folder. (See the "Managing Your Files and Folders" section later in this chapter for information about viewing all the folders on your computer.)

2. Right-click in the folder, and then slide the pointer over *New*. A menu of document type choices pops up. Click on the type of document you want to create. Figure 3-1 shows an example of creating a new Microsoft Word document from the desktop.

Saving Files

You learned about dialog boxes in Chapter 2. There's a special kind of dialog box called a *file dialog box* or simply *file box*. You're most likely to see this type of dialog box when you want to save a document you've been working on, or when you want to open it again later. When you open the File menus in most programs, there will be Open, Save, and Save As commands on it.

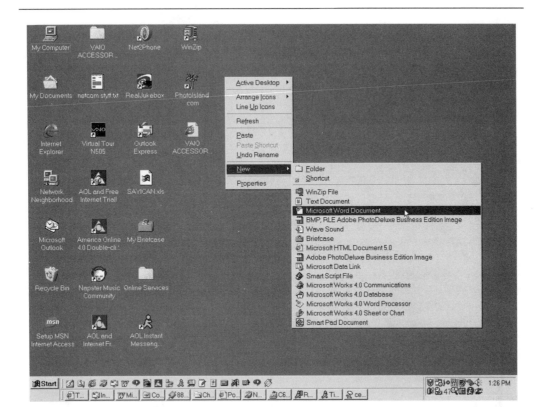

FIGURE 3-1 To create a new document, you can right-click in a folder or on the desktop and choose New, followed by the document type

Choosing any of these commands will display a file dialog box on your screen, similar to the one shown in Figure 3-2.

TIP *File dialog boxes can be confusing. If you're new to Windows, mark this section with a paper clip and refer back to it when you need to save or open a file for the first time. File dialog boxes vary somewhat from program to program, even though they perform the same job.*

After you've created a new document, you will usually want to save it on your hard disk, so that you can work with it again later. These are the general steps for saving a document for the first time:

1. In the program you've created the document in, choose the Save command from the File menu. (The Save As command works the same as the Save command if this is the first time you're saving a file.) The Save As dialog box appears (see Figure 3-2).

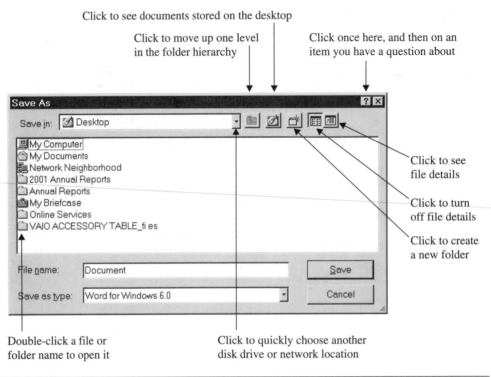

Click to see documents stored on the desktop

Click to move up one level
in the folder hierarchy

Click once here, and then on an
item you have a question about

Click to see
file details

Click to turn
off file details

Click to create
a new folder

Double-click a file or
folder name to open it

Click to quickly choose another
disk drive or network location

FIGURE 3-2   A file dialog box

2. Notice the Save As section at the top of the box. This tells you which folder's contents
    are being displayed in the dialog box. You can click on this drop-down list to choose
    another drive or folder you want to look in. It's easiest to store your documents in the
    folder called My Documents, and most programs use this as a default location, so this
    will often come up automatically.

3. If you're a neatnik, you can organize your files in subfolders, each with a specific name
    related to its category. (For example, you might want to keep all your personal letters in
    a folder called Personal Letters and all your business letters in a folder named Business
    Letters.) To do this, click the Create New Folder button in the dialog box's toolbar. A
    new folder, called New Folder, is automatically created. Its name is highlighted, waiting
    for you to type in your desired folder name. Type in the name and press the ENTER key
    to rename the new folder. Now double-click it to switch to it.

4. Once you're looking at the contents of the correct folder, position the pointer in the File
    Name text box in the dialog box, click, and type in the name. The names for files and
    folders can be really long (up to 250 letters, numbers, and spaces), such as "All the

3

letters I wrote since 1995 including those I sent to Mom," but there are some rules to know about when choosing names. If you are saving a file, you cannot use the following punctuation marks in a name: ? * < > / \ | . If you try to use a character that isn't allowed, a dialog box will alert you.

5.   Optionally, in the Save as Type section of the dialog box, you can change the file type. Under certain circumstances, you may want to change this setting. For example, suppose you were writing a business letter in Microsoft Word, but your colleague has WordPerfect (a different word-processing program). You could opt to change the Save as Type setting to WordPerfect, so that your colleague could open the file in his program.

Opening Files

Opening a file stored on your hard disk works much the same way as saving it. When you use the Open command on your program's File menu, you'll see a dialog box similar to the one shown in Figure 3-2, except that it's named Open. You could type in the name of the file you're looking for, but it's easier to just navigate to the file.

In the Open dialog box, scroll to the file you're looking for, and then double-click it. If the file is in a different folder, first double-click the folder to open it; and then double-click the file. If you don't see the folder you're aiming for, you might need to move down or back up the tree of folders a level or two. You back up a level by clicking the Up One Level button. You move down a level by double-clicking a folder and looking for its subfolders.

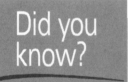
Did you know?

What's This I Hear About the Last Three Letters of a File's Name?

All files on PCs (and thus in Windows) are given a file name *extension*. An extension is a three-letter suffix tacked onto a file's name. For example, Microsoft Word files have the extension *.doc,* so a file named annual report is actually called *annual report.doc* when the file is saved on the hard disk.

The extension is used by Windows to figure out which program to use for editing or modifying the file when you click on it. Generally speaking, you don't have to worry about the extension. This is because Windows keeps a list of known file extensions in its internal settings, called the Registry. In fact, extensions that Windows knows are normally hidden from your view. They are assigned automatically when you create new files of known types. But for document file types that are not in the Registry list, the extension will be displayed.

The idea of the extension goes back to the days before Windows and before the GUI, when DOS (short for Disk Operating System) was the operating system used on PCs. Back then, and even up until Windows 95 came out, file names could not exceed eight characters in length, followed by the three-character extension.

Instead of scrolling around to find a file or folder, you can jump to it. Just click once on a folder or file in the box (any one will do), and then type the first letter of the item you're looking for. That will jump the highlight to the first item that starts with the letter, and probably bring your target into view. Pressing successive keys will move through each item that starts with that letter.

Managing Your Files and Folders

After you've been using your computer for a while, you're likely to end up with a lot of documents scattered around your hard disk, or worse yet, a lot of documents lumped together in the same directory with no sense of organization. In interviewing users and teaching people about Windows over the years, I've found that most people haven't the foggiest idea where their work files are. They know they're on the hard disk, but that's about it. To avoid this problem, you should do a little housecleaning on a regular basis.

To get organized, you can move files around, make copies of files (perhaps on floppy disks for backup purposes), and delete files that are no longer needed. You'll probably also want to create new folders and rearrange those, too. The following sections discuss how these chores are accomplished.

Viewing Your Computer's Contents

There's an easy way to see all of the stuff that's in your computer. The door to your computer's contents is the icon in the upper-left corner of your desktop called My Computer.

Double-click the icon, and you'll enter the folder system for your computer. Figure 3-3 shows the result on my system.

You will undoubtedly have a C drive in your folder. This is your primary hard disk. Double-click on it to open it, and you'll see a lot of folders and some other files in there. Figure 3-4 shows what's stored on my C drive.

Notice that the folders look like a manila folder. Folders always look like this in Windows, and clicking on them opens a window revealing their contents. For example, by double-clicking the My Documents folder, you can reveal its contents, as shown in Figure 3-5.

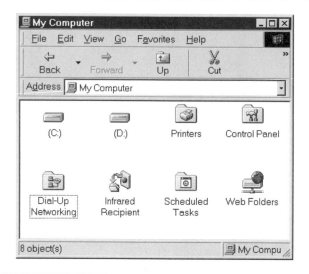

FIGURE 3-3   My Computer is a folder that provides an entryway into your computer's holdings

By clicking on the View menu or the View button in the toolbar, you can change the view of the listing. Normally, as in Figure 3-5, it is Large Icon view. To see more information, such as date the items were created, choose the Details view. Figure 3-6 shows an example of a folder contents in Details view.

Making New Folders

As explained in the "Creating New Documents" section earlier in this chapter, when you're saving a new document from an application, you'll see the file dialog box. At that point, you have the option of creating a new folder to save your new document. However, you can create folders and rearrange your files quite easily at any time you like, not just when you're saving a file. In fact, you can create new folders and new documents right from the desktop or inside any folder.

NOTE   *The desktop is actually a specialized folder and has many of the qualities of any regular folder. You can right-click on the desktop and choose New, Folder. Lots of folks make folders right on the desktop for storing their work documents and other folders. This makes it very easy to get to them. It's faster than opening My Computer, because that takes an additional step after getting to the desktop by clearing off open windows.*

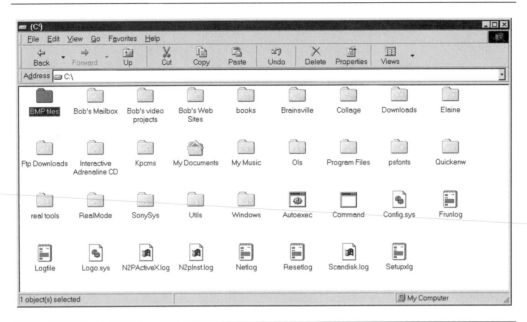

FIGURE 3-4 Opening drive C reveals the files and folders stored there

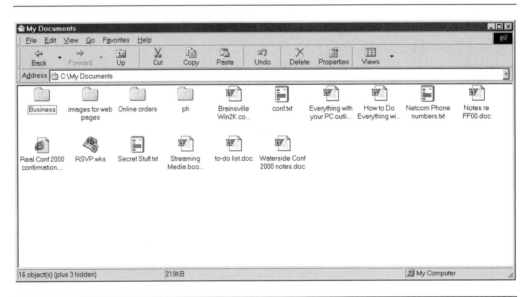

FIGURE 3-5 Opening My Documents reveals its contents

3

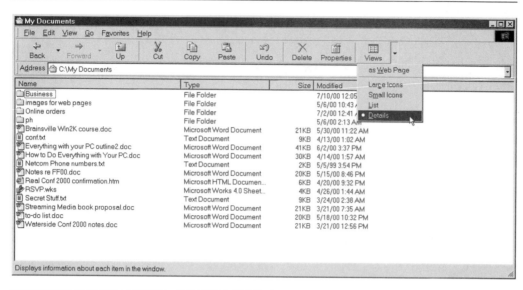

FIGURE 3-6   Changing the view of the contents of any folder to Details reveals additional information about its contents

To create a new folder, follow these steps:

1. Right-click inside the folder you want to create the new folder inside of. Choose New from the menu that pops up.

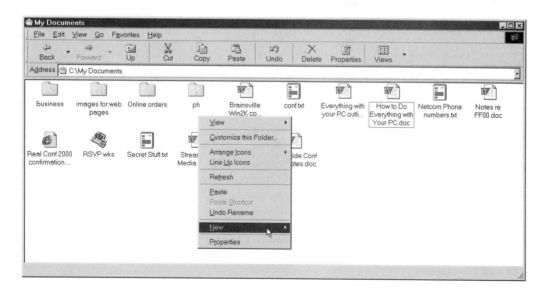

2. In a second, a cascading menu will pop up. Slide the pointer over to Folder and click on it. Now a new folder appears, called New Folder. Its name is highlighted and ready for editing. Whatever you type will replace the current name.

3. Finalize the name by pressing the ENTER key. Now you should have a new folder.

4. You can now open the folder by double-clicking on it.

If you forgot to name the folder, it is automatically given the name New Folder. You can always change the name later. Just click once on the name of the folder (not the folder itself). It will become highlighted, with the I-beam cursor sitting in the name, blinking slowly. Type in a new name and press ENTER.

Moving Items Between Folders

Even if you've been careful in your creation of folders and documents, you'll probably eventually want to move them around between folders. You can easily move items between folders. You can even move folders between folders (for when you're nesting folders several levels deep).

To move items between folders, follow these steps:

1. Open the destination folder. (Actually, you don't have to open the destination folder, but what you're about to do is more graphically understandable if you do.)

2. Size and position the destination folder's window so you will be able to see the folder(s) you put in it.

3. Open the destination folder's window and position that so you can see both windows.

4. Drag folders from the desktop inside the perimeter of the destination folder's window. Be careful not to drop items on top of one another. Doing that can put the dropped item *inside* the item under it. Figure 3-7 illustrates the process.

To drag an item, click once on the item you want to move and hold down the mouse button. Now, keeping the mouse button depressed, move the mouse. When the item you're dragging is over the destination area, release the mouse button.

You can drag and drop most objects in Windows using this same scheme. In general, if you want something placed somewhere else, you can drag it from the source to the destination.

As noted in step 4, when dragging and dropping, you should aim carefully before you release the mouse button. If you drop an object too close to another object, it can be placed inside that object. For example, when you're moving folders around, or even repositioning them on the desktop, watch that a neighboring folder doesn't become highlighted. If something other than the object you're moving becomes highlighted, that means it has become the target for the object. If you release the mouse button at that time, your object will go inside the target. If you accidentally do this, you can correct your mistake in several ways:

■ Just open the target and drag the object out again.

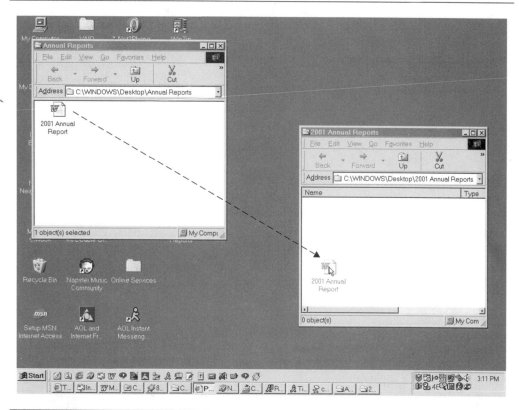

FIGURE 3-7   Rearranging your work is as simple as organizing your desk drawer; just drag and drop items from one folder to another

- ▪ If the incorrect destination was a folder, open any folder and choose Undo Move from the Edit menu.

- ▪ Right-click on the desktop and choose Undo Move from the pop-up menu.

- ▪ If you press ESC before you drop an object, the dragging process is canceled, and the item bounces back to its previous location.

Copying Files and Folders on Your Hard Disk

Copying a file or folder means making a replica of the item in the new destination, as opposed to moving a file or folder, which means relocating the original. Sometimes you'll want to make a copy rather than moving the original. A good example is when you want to make a backup copy of an important document or a folder full of documents.

The procedure for copying a file or folder is pretty much the same as moving it. When you drag an item from one folder to another, Windows does its best to determine whether you intend to move it or copy it. The general rule about moving versus copying is simple. When you move something by dragging, the mouse pointer keeps the shape of the moved object, as shown here.

But when you copy, the cursor takes on a + sign, as in this example:

You can easily switch between moving and copying by pressing the CTRL key during the dragging process. The + sign will show up in the icon so you know you're making a copy.

There's also an easy way to ensure what's going to happen when you drag and drop an item. What you do is something called the *right-click-drag*. (Sounds like a tap-dance move, doesn't it?) You place the pointer on the object you want to move or copy, and then press the right mouse button (or left button if you're left-handed and have reversed the buttons) and drag the item to the destination. When you drop the object, you'll be asked what you want to do with it, like this:

Copying Files and Folders to and from Floppy Disks

Regardless of whether you're sending a file to a colleague around the world, "sneaker-netting" some work down the hall, or simply making a backup of some important files, copying to and from floppy disks is one of those basic computer housekeeping chores.

First, you'll need to insert the floppy disk into your computer's floppy disk drive. On desktop PCs, you'll typically find the floppy disk drive on the front. On laptops, it's somewhere around the bottom edge of the machine, often in the front. On some very thin laptops, the floppy drive is external and plugs into the USB or printer port.

Regardless of the location of the floppy disk drive and type of computer you have, you work with your floppy disks in the same way.

3

Working in the Floppy Disk Drive Window

An easy way to work with floppy disks is from the floppy disk drive's window. To open this window, open My Computer, and then double-click the floppy disk icon.

3½ Floppy (A:)

A window will open, much like the window for your hard disk or a folder. Now you can create, copy, move, or delete files and folders just as with your hard disk. Just drag and drop items into the window. When you drag a file into the floppy disk's window, Windows assumes that you want to make a copy of it, and so the icons you drag will have the + sign on them as you drag them into the destination window.

Sometimes, when you're trying to work with a floppy disk, you'll see an error message alerting you that the disk has not yet been formatted, that the disk can't be read, or something else, such as the disk is *write-protected*, as in the message shown here.

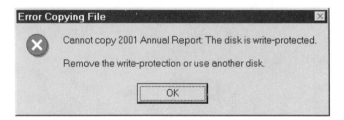

On 3 1/2-inch diskettes, there's a little tab on the back of the disk that must be in the closed position before the diskette can have new files stored on it. If it's in the open position, then it's write-protected. You can physically move the tab into the closed position so that you can put files on the disk.

Before copying files to a floppy disk, you'll want to make sure that there is room on the diskette. Normal diskettes only store 1.44M of data, which isn't much. You can easily overrun that. So, sometimes you'll need to erase something from the diskette before you can add something new.

To see how much room is left on any disk drive, including a floppy, right-click on the drive in My Computer, and choose Properties. You'll see a display of the disk's free and used space. Figure 3-8 shows an example of a floppy disk's Properties dialog box.

On a PC, when you eject one floppy disk and insert another, the computer doesn't know about it automatically (as it does on the Mac). So, after you swap floppy disks, the contents of any open floppy disk windows will remain the same, even though the disk might contain a completely different set of files. You'll need to update the display by pressing the F5 key or by choosing the Refresh command from the View menu of the window displaying the floppy's content.

Copying Files to a Floppy with Send To

Rather than going through the floppy disk window, there's a shortcut that you can use to copy files to your floppy disk. Here's how to use the shortcut:

1. In your floppy disk drive, insert a floppy disk that has enough free space on it to hold the items you intend to copy.

2. Right-click the source file or folder icon and select Send To from the menu that appears.

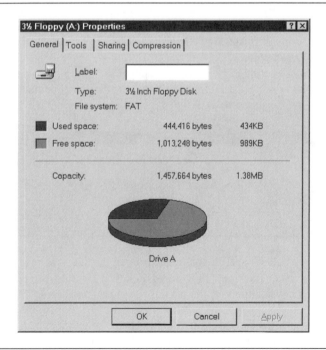

FIGURE 3-8   Viewing a floppy disk's properties

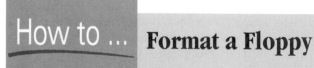

Format a Floppy

Floppy disks need to be *formatted* to work. Formatting is like weeding and tilling a field before planting the crops. If the disk isn't formatted—because you just bought it (or it was used in another kind of computer or device, such as a Mac), you can't write anything on it. Most diskettes come "pre-formatted" from the store. Their box will usually say so. But if your diskette is not formatted for some reason, then here's how you do it:

1.   Open My Computer, right-click the floppy drive's icon, and choose Format. You'll see this box:

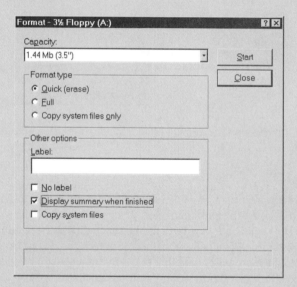

2.   Choose between the Quick and Full format types. (The Copy System Files Only, type is used to make a bootable floppy, which lets you start up your computer from a floppy disk.)

- ■ Use Full if the disk is new or if you want to erase everything from the drive in such a way that nobody can ever see what was on it previously. This will take a couple of minutes.

- ■ Use Quick if you want to quickly free up space on the disk. The entire disk's contents will be freed up, but there will still be remains that some sneaky people could discover if they really cared to. (It would take some work, though).

3.   Click Start. The formatting will begin. When it's finished, you'll be notified. Then you can copy files to the diskette.

3. A second menu will appear. Depending on your computer's setup, you'll have different choices in the Send To list, but you'll have at least one floppy-disk option, as shown here.

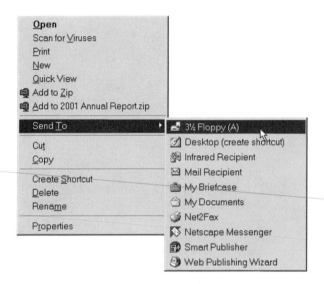

4. Click on the desired drive. The items will be copied to the drive you specify.

Creating Shortcuts

A *shortcut* is sort of like a pointer to the item. It's not the item itself. Create a shortcut to an item when you don't want to take up the extra hard disk space required to make a copy of an item. Shortcuts are efficient and small, and they don't use up much disk space. Double-clicking on a shortcut has the same result as clicking on the original. So, for example, rather than dragging a document file (and certainly a program) out of its home folder just to put it on the desktop for convenience, you'll should make a shortcut out of it. You can also drop shortcuts on the quick-launch bar or Start menu so that even if the desktop is covered with windows, you can get to you favorite programs, documents, and folders, quickly. Then with a single-click of the mouse—no matter what you're doing with your other programs—you can quickly see the programs, folders, and documents you use most. Regardless of destination for your shortcut, the technique is the same:

1. Locate the item you want to create a shortcut for—almost any icon will work. For example, while working on this book, I often need to get to the same folder time and time again because it holds all the chapters of the book. So, I added a shortcut to the folder on my quick-launch bar, on my desktop, and on my Start menu.

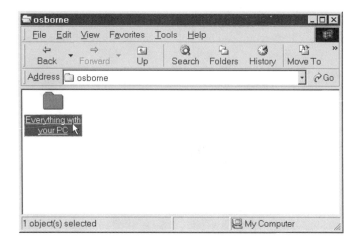

2. Drag the item to the location(s) where you want the shortcut using a right-click drag (hold down the right mouse button and drag the item to the destination). Start by dragging to the desktop.

3. When you release the mouse, you get a pop-up menu. Choose Create Shortcut(s) Here.

Windows creates a shortcut to the folder. You can double-click it at any time to open the folder. It's a great time saver.

You can use the same technique to drop an item on your Start button. This creates a shortcut on the first menu you see when you click the Start button.

Likewise, you can drop an item on the quick-launch bar. Notice that I have lots of items on mine. Before dropping the item (releasing the mouse button) you can move it left or right to choose where the new shortcut will end up.

If your computer gets cluttered with shortcuts, you can easily remove them. The need for this is common because programs often dump shortcuts on your desktop without asking permission. Follow these steps to get rid of some of the clutter:

1. Right-click the shortcut icon. (In the case of the Start menu, this requires opening the Start menu, and then right-clicking the item.)

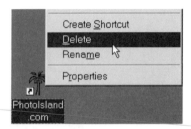

2. Choose Delete from the resulting menu, as you see here.

 *Be careful when deleting shortcuts. Make sure you are actually deleting the shortcut and not the item it points to, such as a program file or a folder containing important files. The icon should have the little arrow on it, denoting that it's a shortcut.*

Remember that shortcuts are *not* the original file. So, for example, copying a document's shortcut to a floppy disk doesn't copy the document itself. If you copy only the shortcut of your annual report to a floppy disk and then give it to a colleague, she won't be able to open it on her computer. If you are in doubt about what is getting copied, look at the icon resulting from the procedure. If it has a little arrow in it (as in the icon on the right), it's a shortcut. If it doesn't have an arrow (as in the icon on the left), it's the actual file.

2001 Annual   2001 Annual
Report   Report

Deleting Files and Folders

Getting rid of the old stuff in your computer is really important. If you don't do it on a regular basis, you can become like everyone else—strapped for disk space. Deleting documents and folders is pretty straightforward.

You might have noticed the Recycle Bin icon on your desktop. This is essentially a trashcan—the place you chuck stuff that you don't want. Anything you put in the Recycle Bin stays there until you empty the trash, so you can get it back if you need to, as explained in the next section.

To delete a file, follow these steps:

1. Select the file wherever it is, such as in a folder or on the desktop. (Selecting is done by clicking once on the item, unless you are using Web View, in which case you just point to the file.)

2. Drag the item on top of the Recycle Bin, press the DEL key on your keyboard, or right-click the item and choose Delete from the menu. Now you're asked to confirm the deletion.

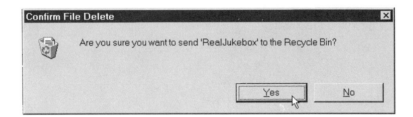

3. Click Yes, and the item goes into the Recycle Bin.

You can delete a folder the same way you delete a file. There's only one difference— deleting a folder deletes all of its contents. When you drag a file over to the Recycle Bin (or delete it using one of the other methods), you'll see a confirmation message warning you that all the contents—any shortcuts, files, and folders (including files in those folders!)—will be deleted. Take care when deleting folders, because they may contain many juicy items you want to keep.

 *You should look inside a folder before you delete it. Open the folder and choose the Details or List command from the View menu to examine what's in the folder, check the dates the files were created, and so forth. Check the contents of any folders within the folder by opening them; you might be surprised by what you find.*

Oh No! (When You've Deleted Something You Wanted)

Have you ever had the experience of accidentally locking your keys in the car?! Who could forget that beautifully indescribable moment when you realize that somehow you've done something that confirms you're one pork pie short of a picnic. Well, guess what? You get to have that lovely feeling with your computer, too. To be specific, you can self-flagellate when you've accidentally deleted some important file like your Ph.D. thesis. The good news with your car is that you can call AAA to break into it and get your keys out. Likewise, there's hope for recovering your erased file(s), if you act quickly enough. Here's how:

1. Get to the desktop so you can see the Recycle Bin.

2. Double-click the Recycle Bin icon to open the bin. A window opens, showing all the files and folders that have been deleted since the last time the Recycle Bin was emptied.

3. Right-click the item you want to restore and choose Restore, as shown in Figure 3-9. If you choose a folder, all the contents of the folder will be restored along with the folder.

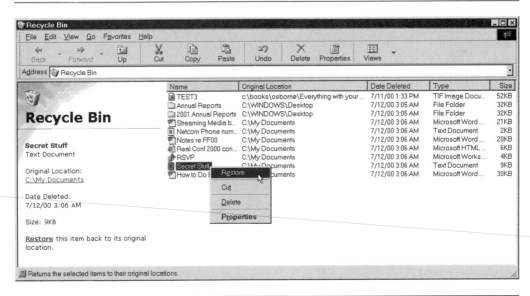

FIGURE 3-9   In the Recycle Bin, right-click an item and choose Restore; it will be returned to its previous location

You should occasionally empty the Recycle Bin so that the items are not consuming hard disk space unnecessarily. The Recycle Bin continues to fill up with items you delete. If it gets too full, you'll be alerted, but this can take quite a long time. To empty it, click Empty Recycle Bin or right-click the Recycle Bin icon on the desktop and choose Empty Recycle Bin.

   The Recycle Bin will hang onto your deleted items only until you empty the bin. Once you empty the bin, everything in it is gone.

Where Is That File I Made?

One of the most useful commands in Windows is the one that searches through your whole computer looking for a file. Instead of spending tens of minutes looking around through all of your folders just trying to find that one document you need again, use the built-in Find command. Here's how:

1.   Click the Start button and select Find. You'll see the dialog box shown in Figure 3-10.

2.   Enter the name of the file or folder you're looking for in the Named text box. You can enter just a portion if you want. In the example in Figure 3-10, I entered *annual* to look for the Annual Report folder.

3.   In the Look in drop-down list, choose where you want to look. Typically, it will be on the C drive. Choosing My Computer (as in Figure 3-10) looks on all the drives in your computer, including any floppy disks or CD-ROMs that are in the computer's disk drives.

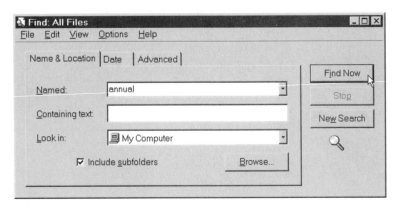

FIGURE 3-10   The Find dialog box lets you search for files or folders

4. Click Find Now. The search will begin. The results will be displayed in a list at the bottom of the dialog box, as shown in Figure 3-11. From that list, you can double-click a document to open it, right-click it to see a menu of choices, or drag it from the dialog box into a folder.

The Find dialog box provides many other features for refining your search. You can actually look for a file by entering some of the text you know it contains in the Containing Text box. The Date and Advanced tabs offer other options for searching for specific files.

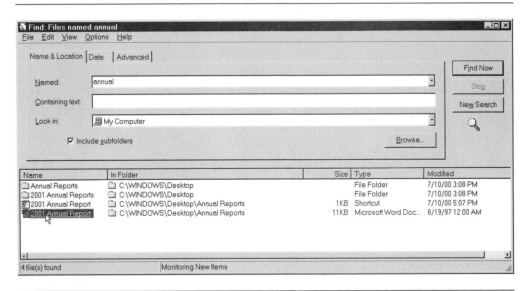

FIGURE 3-11   Results of a search are listed at the bottom of the Find dialog box

Part II

Putting Your PC to Work

Chapter 4

Using Common Applications

How to...

- Create text documents with a word processor
- Print documents
- Use a spreadsheet
- Create a database

Despite all the neat things you can do with a PC, the truth of the matter is that most folks purchase a computer expecting to run only a few specific programs. They will use it for only a few select tasks, such as writing their great American novel or managing the finances of a small company. In this chapter, we're going to talk about three of the all-time most popular types of programs—word-processors, spreadsheets, and databases.

Individual Programs Versus Suites

You may have heard the term *office suites*, or *integrated* applications. Since the three primary programs—spreadsheets, word processing, and databases—work so well together and are so essential to the operations of the average business, there have been attempts to either package the three separate programs and sell them together, or to write a single program that offers similar functionality.

When you're shopping for these traditional office productivity applications, you'll certainly run into Microsoft Office, which is one of the most successful of the suites. Office is a collection of different programs designed to work well together. By contrast, Microsoft Works is a single program that has all of the basic abilities of a suite. Programs like Works are more tightly integrated but have fewer of the frills than the office suite products, and typically cost one-fifth the price of the more expensive office suites. What few people know is that they will suffice quite well for most home and home-office computer users' needs.

Another approach to assembling your essential office tool pack is to pick individual programs best suited to each task (or at least the ones you like the most)—sort of a mix-and-match approach. For example, you might want to use WordPerfect for your word processing and Microsoft Excel for spreadsheets. This approach works, but an integrated program like Works or a suite of tools such as Office (all from the same software company) will be simpler to work with, especially if you want the programs to interact in an intelligent way. For example, you might want to "cut and paste" bits of information between your database, spreadsheet, and word-processing documents and have the data look good and be formatted nicely without a lot of hassle. That kind of task is more likely to work seamlessly in products from the same company.

Word Processing: A Better Way to Write

Word processors let you write, perfect, and then print all manner of documents, such as business letters, form letters, lists, company reports, contracts, invoices, magazines, and even books.

Some word processors even let you write in different languages. The big advantage of a word processor over a typewriter is that you can throw away your eraser and forget about "white-out" forever. If you make a mistake using a word processor, you just press the BACKSPACE key and fix it.

As you probably know, using a word processor amounts to typing on your computer's screen instead of on a piece of paper. As you type on the computer's keyboard, the letters are displayed on the screen, and they are simultaneously stored in the computer's memory.

It is by virtue of the fact that your words are in the computer's memory (sometimes called RAM, for random access memory) that you can move the words around right on the screen and make revisions until you are satisfied with the way your document looks. The computer, responding to your commands, shifts the words around within RAM. When you are happy with the revisions, you can save the file so you can retrieve it later. Optionally, you can instruct the computer to print your document on paper, using your printer.

Common Word Processor Features

Word processors can come with a variety of features, including the following:

- **Built-in spelling and grammar checking**   Spelling and grammar checkers can proofread your entire document after you've finished writing. When they find a mistake, they let you correct the error. Some spelling and grammar checkers actually work as you type, causing the computer to make a beeping sound or underline a word or phrase; then, if you like, they can make suggestions for correcting the spelling or grammar.

NOTE   *Of course, a spelling checker won't catch a word spelled correctly but used improperly, and a grammar checker may misunderstand syntax. You'll still need to read over your documents.*

- **Word count**   Some word processors have a tool that will automatically count the number of words or pages you've written. This feature is particularly useful if you get paid by the word (as many professional writers do) or you're a student writing a term paper with a length requirement.

- **Search and replace**   This capability will hunt down occurrences of a particular word in your document and alter it automatically, while readjusting the surrounding text to fit the line. The search-and-replace feature is useful if you find you have made a misspelling repeatedly, or if you want to abbreviate a long word to speed your typing and let the computer replace it later with the full word.

- **Auto-text**   Some word processors will correct common mistakes (such as *teh* instead of *the*) as you type, or you can set up special shortcut words that the word processor will expand automatically for you as you type. For example, I can type in **os,** and my word processor will type *operating system* for me. This can save not only time, but cut down on repetitive stress disorders that can result from extensive typing.

■ **Thesaurus**   Some word processors include a built-in thesaurus that can be very handy when you find yourself stuck for a word. Use a simple command, and synonyms for a word appear. Press another key, and the word drops into your document automatically.

■ **Multi-column and table support**   If you want to create three-fold brochures or newsletter-style documents, you'll want a word processor that lets you snake your text around on multiple columns within a single printed page. Likewise, if you need to organize tables of text and/or numbers, you'll want a word processor that lets you easily create and edit tables without undue effort. (Trying to align columns of numbers using the spacebar or the TAB key as you would on a typewriter is ancient history, and really doesn't work on a computer.) Figure 4-1 shows an example of a word-processing document that includes both a table and columns.

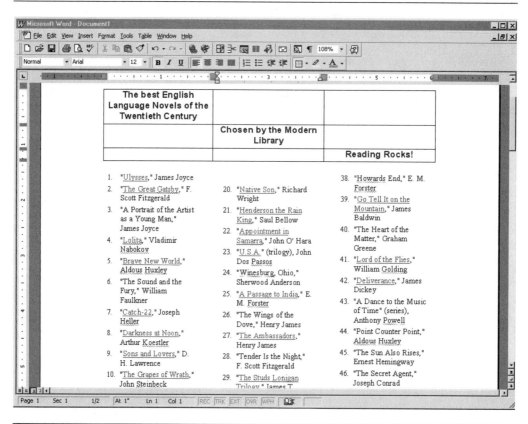

FIGURE 4-1   Fancier word-processing programs have powerful layout capabilities for tables and columns of text

■ **Special insertions**   Many word processors let you insert symbols (such as ornamental or mathematical characters), pictures, charts, and even sounds right into the document. (Inserted sounds will play when you're viewing the document on the computer.)

■ **Integration with other programs**   With some word processors that are designed to work with other programs (generally those that are part of a suite), you can insert elements from those other programs directly into your word-processing program, and even have changes made to those elements in the other program reflected in your document. For example, you could insert a section of spreadsheet data from a spreadsheet document. When the data in the spreadsheet is altered, the word processor document's data is automatically updated. Thus, you could create a company report that uses essentially the same text each month, but the chart of company performance would be updated automatically each month, before you print.

4

■ **Multiple file formats**   Most word processors have the capability to save your documents in a number of different file formats. This allows you to exchange your files with people who use a different brand of word processor.

■ **Printing options**   Any decent word processor allows you to manipulate exactly how your text will appear on the printed page. You typically can use a wide variety of fonts (typestyles) in your documents, limited only by the fonts you have installed in the Windows operating system. Fonts are widely available at minimal cost, or even free (easily downloadable from the Internet.) You should also be able to adjust such details as margins, tabs, headings and footings (text that appears at the top and bottom of each printed page), and page numbering. Better word processors will show you a preview of what your printout will look like, so you can avoid wasting paper and ink.

■ **View modes**   Some word-processing programs have multiple viewing modes that show your document in various ways. For example, Microsoft Word has normal, online, outline, page layout, and master document modes. The modes make it easier to organize, preview, and edit documents.

The type of word processor you should use depends on the features you need for your word-processing tasks. You don't have to run out and purchase Microsoft Word (or Microsoft Office) for hundreds of dollars unless you need some advanced features. For example, Microsoft Works, which is bundled with many PCs these days, has many of the features that most home users and small-business folks need, including spelling checking, a thesaurus, envelope and form-letter printing, and much more. For basic word processing, you can use the WordPad program, which comes with every copy of Windows.

Basic Word Processing

All word processing in Windows programs use a basic set of text-editing functions, and then expand on them. In this chapter, we'll experiment with the Windows WordPad program. WordPad is a no-frills word processor, but it lets you use different typestyles, set headers and footers, and search and replace. It doesn't have spelling checking, a thesaurus, or other fancy formatting, such as multiple-columns and tables.

NOTE   *Notepad, a word processor even more basic than WordPad, also comes free with Windows. Notepad has very minimal formatting features. It's good for the very simplest of text editing. Programmers use it for things like editing Web pages and writing computer programs. You can run it by clicking the Start button and selecting Programs, then Accessories, then Notepad.*

Entering Text

Let's open WordPad and start processing some words:

1. To start a new WordPad document, click the Start button, select Programs, Accessories, and then WordPad. The WordPad window will appear with a new, empty document window open for you. If the WordPad window isn't already maximized, maximize it so it fills the whole screen. Your screen should now look like the one shown in Figure 4-2.

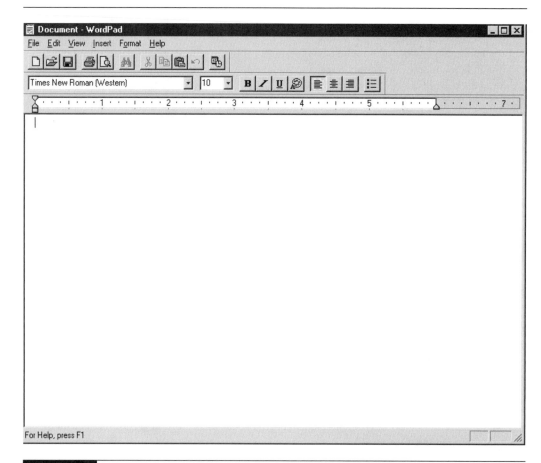

FIGURE 4-2   The initial WordPad screen with no text in the document

2. Notice the blinking vertical bar, called the *insertion point* or *cursor* (no, a cursor isn't a person who swears a lot). Type some characters and notice what happens. Text appears, and the cursor moves to the right.

3. Type in a few sentences. Notice that you don't need to press the ENTER key when you reach the end of a line to move down to the next line. The text automatically wraps around to the next line when it reaches the right margin.

As you type, the cursor moves along with you, always at the end of the line where you're typing. To fix an error just after you typed it, you simply press the BACKSPACE key (look in the upper-right corner of the keyboard). Each press of BACKSPACE wipes out another letter to the left of the blinking cursor, even snaking back up to the previous line if you press enough times. Holding down the BACKSPACE key will cause it to *repeat* and gobble up your letters really quickly. To delete characters to the right of the cursor, press the DEL key.

TIP *If you delete anything accidentally and are suddenly surprised by its disappearance, you can retrieve it by choosing Undo from the Edit menu, clicking the Undo button on the toolbar, or pressing* CTRL-Z.

Fixing errors with the BACKSPACE or DEL key as you type is one way to correct text, but you'll often want to edit a piece after it's written. Obviously, you don't want to retype what you have written just to fix a misspelling in the middle of a document. Instead, you can move to the error and fix it.

The first step in working with word-processed text, then, is learning how to move the cursor around to get to the place where you want to make a change. From there, you can insert text, remove words, fix misspellings, or select blocks of text for cutting, copying, and pasting elsewhere.

Moving the Cursor

The easiest way to move the cursor is just to point and click. When the mouse pointer is over the document window, it looks like a large letter *I* or a steel beam (this shape is often called the *I-beam pointer*). Move the I-beam pointer so that the vertical line is over the place in the text where you want to begin editing or typing. When you click, the blinking insertion point will jump from wherever it was to this new position.

NOTE *After positioning the cursor with the mouse, don't forget to click; otherwise, you'll end up making changes in the wrong place.*

You can also use the arrow keys to move the cursor. This is often quicker than using the mouse when you need to move the cursor by only a few characters or lines. Practice these techniques to get used to moving the cursor using both the mouse and the keyboard:

1. Click somewhere in your practice text to see the insertion point move immediately. Try aiming to get the position exactly where you want it.

2. Press the → (right arrow) key and hold it down for a few seconds. Notice that the cursor moves one character to the right, pauses briefly, and then moves rapidly to the right. When it gets to the end of the first line, it wraps around to the start of the second line, continuing to the right from that point.

3. Press the ← (left arrow) key and hold it down. The cursor moves steadily to the left until it reaches the beginning of the line, then jumps to the end of the previous line. When the cursor gets to the beginning of the document, your computer starts to beep, because the cursor cannot go any farther.

4. Press the ↓ (down arrow) key to move the cursor down a line. If you hold down the key, the cursor will keep moving down until it reaches the last line in the text. (If a document has more text than will fit in the window, the text will scroll up a line at a time until the end of the document is reached.)

5. To move up one line at a time, press the ↑ (up arrow) key. Again, the text will scroll until the cursor reaches the very first line in the document.

6. Press CTRL-→. Each press of the arrow key moves the cursor ahead one word. CTRL-← moves it a word at a time in the other direction.

7. Press CTRL-HOME. The cursor jumps to the very beginning of the document. To jump to the end of the text, press CTRL-END.

Because writing relies heavily on the keyboard, WordPad provides several keyboard combinations that can be used to move the insertion point. Most of these are used by other word-processing programs, as well. Table 4-1 lists all the keystrokes for moving the cursor around in WordPad.

Keystroke	Moves the Insertion Point...
–	Up one line
↓	Down one line
←	Left one character
→	Right one character
CTRL-←	Left one word
CTRL-→	Right one word
CTRL-HOME	Beginning of document
CTRL-END	End of document
CTRL-PGUP	Top left of current window
CTRL-PGDN	Bottom right of current window

TABLE 4-1 Keys for Moving the Insertion Point in WordPad

Selecting Text

Much of editing with a word processor centers on manipulating a *selected* portion of text. A *selection* is one or more consecutive text characters (letters, numbers, punctuation, and so on). For example, you might want to select a bunch of text and then change its font or italicize it, move it to a new location, or delete it altogether. Figure 4-3 shows a block of text selected in a WordPad document. Notice that a selection is always *highlighted*.

There are two main ways to select a text block: with the mouse (by dragging the I-beam pointer over the area you want to select) or with the keyboard. To use the keyboard, you hold down the SHIFT key while moving the cursor with the arrow keys. To *deselect* (remove the highlighting), just click elsewhere within the text.

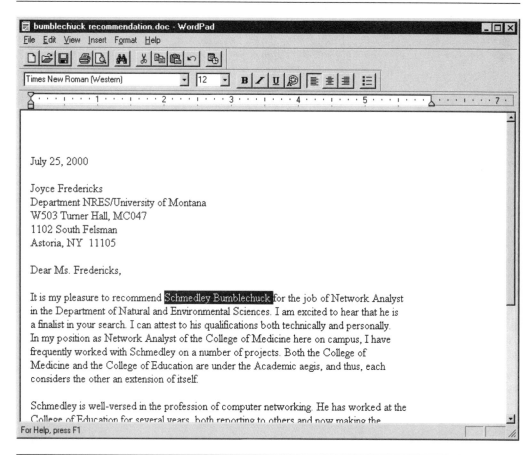

FIGURE 4-3   When you select a portion of text, it becomes highlighted; your actions will now affect only the highlighted text

Once you've selected a block, be careful about the keys you press. If you type A, for example, the text of the whole block (the selection) will be replaced by the letter A. If this happens accidentally, choose the Undo command from the Edit menu, press CTRL-Z, or click on the Undo button on the toolbar before doing anything else, and your text will be returned to its previous state.

Selection is particularly intuitive and simple with the mouse. Try this:

1. Deselect any selections you may have made already by clicking anywhere in the text.

2. Move the I-beam pointer to the beginning of a word somewhere.

3. Hold down the left mouse button and move the pointer down several lines. As you move the mouse, the selection extends. When you release the mouse button, the selection is completed.

4. Click anywhere in the document to deselect the selection.

5. Move the I-beam pointer to any point within a word a double-click, The whole word is selected. If you want to replace one word with another word, double-click the word and start typing the new word.

6. Click anywhere in the document to deselect the word.

The anchor point *is the point you first clicked. Dragging downward extends the selection downward from the anchor point. If you were to keep the mouse button down and drag above the anchor point, the selection would extend from the anchor point upward.*

Most word processors offer many ways to select text. For example, to select the whole document to make a change that affects all of the text (such as changing the font size), choose Select All from the Edit menu or press CTRL-A. Some programs—such as Word, WordPad, and Works—let you easily select complete lines of text from the left edge of the window. Move the pointer over to the left edge of the document's window, and the pointer will switch direction, now pointing right instead of left. Then click the mouse button and drag up or down along the margin to select complete lines of text quickly.

Using Word-Processor Toolbars

Most word processors have a number of bars at the top of their window with buttons on them. These are called *toolbars*. If you don't see the toolbar in WordPad or in another word processor, someone has probably turned it off. Typically you can display it by choosing Toolbar from the View menu. Here is the toolbar in WordPad:

Clicking on the toolbar buttons gives you one-step access to some of the most common word-processing commands. Many toolbar buttons will be the same from program to program. For example, the formatting buttons for Bold, Italic, and Underlining are very common. Just select some text, and then click on one of these buttons to see the effect. Also notice the options on the toolbar for setting the font, size, color, alignment (left, right, or center), and bullets. Many programs also have a Find button—the one showing a pair of binoculars—that lets you search for specific passages of text and an Undo button (the one with the arched arrow pointing to the left) that lets you get rid of your last editing action.

TIP *There are also keyboard shortcuts for many of the toolbar buttons. For example, the character formatting shortcuts are CTRL-B for Bold, CTRL-I for Italic, and CTRL-U for Underlining.*

In most Windows programs, you don't need to memorize what each button does. Just position the mouse pointer over the button and wait for a couple seconds. A small text box with a one- or two-word description of the button's function will pop up.

Using Cut, Copy, and Paste

As mentioned briefly in Chapter 2, Windows has commands called Cut, Copy, and Paste. Cut removes the text from the original location, Copy leaves the text intact and makes a copy of it, and Paste puts the copied or cut text in the location you specify. These commands are real time-savers when you want to move large portions of text, such as paragraphs, within a document. Rather than retyping the paragraph in the new location, you can pick it up from one place and move it to another.

Cut, Copy, and Paste are achieved via something internal to Windows called the *Clipboard*. The Clipboard is a temporary holding area for the material you cut or copy, until you paste it. You can cut, copy, and paste not only within a document, but between different documents and even between programs. For example, you could copy a picture from your image-editing program (such as an Adobe Photoshop window), and then switch to your word-processing window and paste the picture into a document, such as a letter to a friend. Once you've used the Cut or Copy commands, you can paste as many times as you want, because the text stays on the Clipboard until you replace it with new information by using the Cut or Copy commands.

To use these commands, first select the text you want to cut or copy. Then choose Cut or Copy from the Edit menu (or press CTRL-X to cut or CTRL-C to copy). Move the insertion point to the place where you want to insert the text. Then choose Paste from the Edit menu (or press CTRL-V).

Using Symbols

If you need to insert characters that aren't available on your keyboard, such as a ™ or ©
symbol, you can use the Character Map accessory. (If your system doesn't have the Character
Map accessory, you can install it from the Windows CD-ROM). Follow
these steps to use Character Map:

1. Click the Start button and select Programs, then Accessories, then System Tools,
   then Character Map. The Character Map window opens, as shown here.

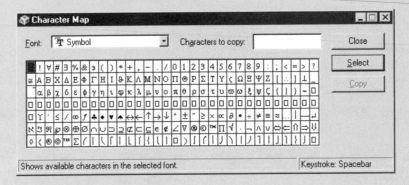

2. From the Font drop-down list, choose the font you want to use (typically Wingdings,
   Symbol, or Dingbats).

3. In the character grid, double-click the symbol you want to insert.

4. Switch back to your word-processing program.

5. Choose Paste from the Edit menu (or press CTRL-V). The symbol will be inserted
   into your document.

6. Close the Character Map window.

Some word-processing programs have Symbol as an item on their Insert menus. This lets
you insert a symbol (using the same basic technique as in the steps here) directly from the
word processor, without starting from the Character Map program.

TIP   *Most word-processing toolbars have toolbar buttons for Cut, Copy, and Paste.*

In WordPad and many other word-processing programs, clicking the right mouse button over the document pops up a small menu offering immediate access to some common editing commands, as shown below.

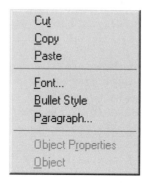

You can use these commands to quickly cut, copy, and paste text, as follows:

1. Select the section of text you want to cut or copy.

2. Click the *right* mouse button anywhere over the selected block. The pop-up menu appears.

3. Choose Cut or Copy from the pop-up menu, depending on what your goal is.

4. Position the pointer where you want the text to go and click, again with the *right* button.

5. From the pop-up menu, choose Paste.

Sometimes, after moving paragraphs around, you'll need to do a little adjusting, such as inserting or deleting a line or some spaces. You can always insert a line by pressing the ENTER key. If you have extra blank lines after a move, you can delete them by putting the insertion point on the first space of a blank line (the far-left margin) and pressing the BACKSPACE key.

Saving Your Work

Another important feature of word processors (and this is true of most other computer programs as well) is that your work is not lost when you turn off the computer. You can save your documents for later printing or revisions by storing them on floppy disks or a hard disk. Word-processing programs, with the help of your computer's operating system, store your work on your disk as files. Each file is stored separately, and it can later be reloaded into the computer's RAM, revised (edited), and printed. It can even be joined with other files to create new documents. This way, you can cut and paste various versions of, say, a contract for different clients without needing to retype each component part of the contract again and again. This will increase your productivity and decrease your typos at the same time.

To avoid losing your work while you are creating a document—because the power to your computer suddenly went down, your program had an error and shut itself down, or some other reason—you should save your work often. You can always save your document, and then continue working. I usually save my writing every ten minutes or so.

You can save your documents with either their Save or Save As command on the File menu, or you can use the keyboard shortcut CTRL-S. The first time you save a document, you're asked for a name to give your document; in this situation, the Save and Save As commands work the same. After the initial save, programs typically assume you want to use the current name unless you indicate otherwise by using the Save As command. For details on saving files, refer to Chapter 3.

 If you try to save a document using the same name as a file that already exists in the same folder, the program will ask you to verify that you want to replace the already existing file. If you say yes, the other file will be gone!

How About Printing?

Before printing a document, you should always save it. For some reason (Murphy's Law, probably), things can go wrong during printing; if the computer "hangs," you might just lose your document.

Another step you should take before printing your document is to preview it. Instead of wasting paper on a document with an obvious layout mistake, use the program's Print Preview command (if the program has one) to inspect your work before you print. Preview displays your document on the screen just as it will look when printed, as in the example shown in Figure 4-4. Typically, you can look at entire pages to check the overall layout or zoom in on a particular portion to check details.

After you've saved your precious prose, do the following to preview it, and then print it on paper to share with the masses (or for reassurance that it won't be lost to the world of electronic goblins):

1. Choose Page Setup from the File menu and choose the correct type of paper and orientation you intend to use. The most important setting here is Orientation, which is either Landscape or Portrait. Portrait is the normal setting that you use for documents like business letters, term papers, and your Ph.D. thesis. For wide documents, use Landscape. (If these names confuse you, think of a landscape painting versus a portrait painting such as the Mona Lisa.)

2. Optionally, set up page numbering and headings/footings to print at the top and bottom of each page. Check the Help file of your word-processing program to determine how to add page numbers, headings, and footings. (See Chapter 2 for details on using Help files.)

3. To see a preview, choose Print Preview from the File menu, or click the Print Preview button on the toolbar. Check over the preview version, and then click the Close button in the preview window's toolbar.

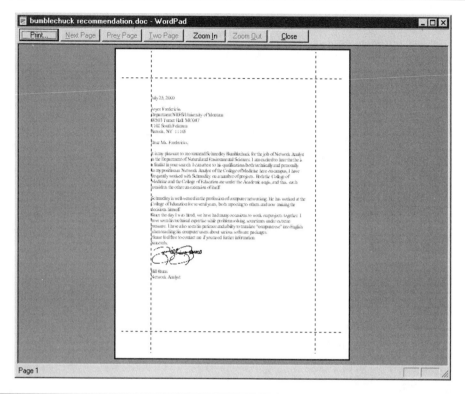

4

FIGURE 4-4   Checking a document with Print Preview before printing it can save you paper
and hassle

4. Make any adjustments you think are necessary for the document to look correct when
    printed, such as changing margin sizes, font size, and so on.

5. Turn on the printer and make sure it has paper in it.

6. Select Print from the File menu. The Print dialog box will appear, as shown in Figure 4-5.

NOTE   *Depending on your type of printer, you'll have other option tabs in your Print dialog
box, for things such as choosing different qualities of paper, printing in color versus
black and white, testing the printer, and so on. Explore the other tabs at your leisure
so you know what your adjustment options are.*

7. If the printer you plan to use isn't already chosen in the Name box, choose it from the
    drop-down list of your installed printers. Click Find a Printer if you want to print to a
    network printer (one shared by another person on your local area network).

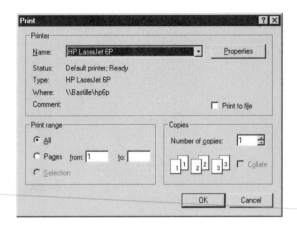

FIGURE 4-5 The Print dialog box in WordPad

NOTE *In order to use a printer, it needs its driver to be installed. The printer driver is usually installed when the original printer setup is done, so you probably don't need to worry about it.*

8. If you want to print all the pages, click on All in the Print Range section of the dialog box. If you want to print specific pages only, click on Pages and type in the range of page numbers you want to print in the From and To boxes. If you want to print only text that you selected, click on Selection.

9. In the Number of Copies box, specify the number of copies of each page to be printed.

10. Check the Collate check box if you want each complete copy to be printed one at a time, in page order (more convenient but slower). Leave it unchecked if all copies of each page should be printed before moving onto the next page (quicker but requires you to hand-collate). This option applies only if you're printing more than one copy of the document.

11. Click OK to close the Print dialog box and start printing your document.

12. When the document is finished printing, close the file. Also close the program you're using if you are through with it and won't be editing any more documents.

As I mentioned at the beginning of this section, printing is one of those areas where things may not go as smoothly as they're supposed to. If you are having trouble printing, refer to Chapter 20 for some troubleshooting tips.

Spreadsheets 101

If you have ever seen an accountant poring over a wide notebook of green-ruled paper that has a lot of columns and rows, you know what a spreadsheet is. Many businesses use these tables for keeping records of transactions, budgets, receivables, payables, general ledgers, and the like. Just as word processors are the electronic counterpart to the typewriter, computerized spreadsheets are the electronic version of an accountant's or manager's multicolumn accounting paper. Of course, the computation capabilities of the computer add some interesting twists.

Most spreadsheets are used to store numbers, and those numbers are usually part of some overall mathematical formula. Take a column of expenses, for example. Chances are the column is to be added, with a total appearing at the bottom. To arrive at the total, an accountant would normally sit down with a calculator and manually punch in the numbers. But since a computer likes nothing better than to sit around adding, subtracting, and multiplying numbers, why not have the computerized spreadsheet do all of the calculations? This is precisely what a microcomputer spreadsheet program does.

Spreadsheet programs vary widely in the number and types of functions they offer. Some are designed for business and financial analysis. Others excel at scientific and engineering problem solving. Some really expensive programs (often costing tens of thousands of dollars) let you hook your PC up to a mainframe computer to perform statistical analysis of very large databases.

Parts of a Spreadsheet

A spreadsheet appears on the computer as a table of columns and rows, as shown in Figure 4-6. Each intersection of a column and a row creates a box called a *cell*. Cells are referenced by their location on the spreadsheet, such as A1 (column A, row 1) or G3 (column G, row 3). Each cell can hold text, a number, or a formula.

NOTE

Spreadsheets vary in the number of cells allowable. By and large, the spreadsheet size is dictated by the amount of RAM in your computer, because most programs require that your entire spreadsheet reside in RAM while you work with it. Windows, due to its virtual memory management capabilities, breaks this barrier and lets you have larger spreadsheets.

A *formula* is used to calculate the cell's numeric value, usually with reference to other cells in the spreadsheet. For example, by entering the formula shown into cell A6 in Figure 4-6, you tell the spreadsheet to calculate the total of cells A1 through A5 and place the result into cell A6. Notice that formulas always reference other cells by their location. Also, spreadsheet programs generally don't display the formula in the cell, but rather the result of the numerical calculation performed by the formula. Some programs will let you see both the formula and value simultaneously. This useful feature serves as a reminder of the relationships between cells.

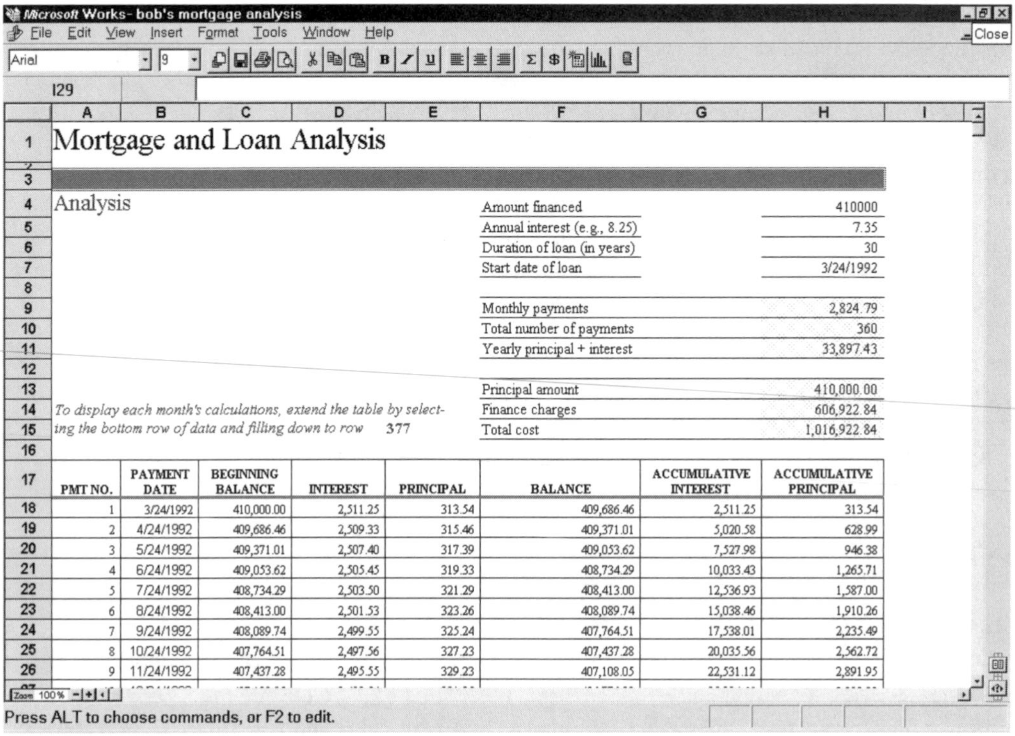
Microsoft Works - bob's mortgage analysis
File Edit View Insert Format Tools Window Help
Close
Mortgage and Loan Analysis
Analysis
Amount financed 410000
Annual interest (e.g., 8.25) 7.35
Duration of loan (in years) 30
Start date of loan 3/24/1992
Monthly payments 2,824.79
Total number of payments 360
Yearly principal + interest 33,897.43
Principal amount 410,000.00
Finance charges 606,922.84
Total cost 1,016,922.84
To display each month's calculations, extend the table by selecting the bottom row of data and filling down to row 377
PMT NO. PAYMENT DATE BEGINNING BALANCE INTEREST PRINCIPAL BALANCE ACCUMULATIVE INTEREST ACCUMULATIVE PRINCIPAL
1 3/24/1992 410,000.00 2,511.25 313.54 409,686.46 2,511.25 313.54
2 4/24/1992 409,686.46 2,509.33 315.46 409,371.01 5,020.58 628.99
3 5/24/1992 409,371.01 2,507.40 317.39 409,053.62 7,527.98 946.38
4 6/24/1992 409,053.62 2,505.45 319.33 408,734.29 10,033.43 1,265.71
5 7/24/1992 408,734.29 2,503.50 321.29 408,413.00 12,536.93 1,587.00
6 8/24/1992 408,413.00 2,501.53 323.26 408,089.74 15,038.46 1,910.26
7 9/24/1992 408,089.74 2,499.55 325.24 407,764.51 17,538.01 2,235.49
8 10/24/1992 407,764.51 2,497.56 327.23 407,437.28 20,035.56 2,562.72
9 11/24/1992 407,437.28 2,495.55 329.23 407,108.05 22,531.12 2,891.95
Press ALT to choose commands, or F2 to edit.

FIGURE 4-6 A Microsoft Works spreadsheet

Built-in Spreadsheet Functions

Beyond simple mathematical computations, the real power of the newer electronic spreadsheets derives from their many advanced built-in functions. These functions allow the numbers in the spreadsheet to be used in analytical, trigonometric, and statistical modeling computations. Some perform date calculations as well.

With these additional capabilities, spreadsheets can be used as "what-if" tools for sophisticated and rapid business analysis. As an example, if you change the data in any of the cells A1 through 5 in Figure 4-6, the total in cell A6 will automatically change to reflect the alterations. With a complex spreadsheet containing many cells and formulas, say, a proposed annual budget for a business, you could quickly experiment with the bottom-line effect of altering key variables. This can be an invaluable aid in the corporate or even small-business decision-making process.

The latest versions of top-notch spreadsheet programs such as Quattro Pro, Excel, and 1-2-3 take what-if analysis a step further. They allow you to set the desired bottom line and let the program alter the key variables, such as budget allocations, that would provide the desired result. This is called *backsolving*.

Some better programs also provide three-dimensional modeling, whereby multiple spreadsheets (two-dimensional—columns and rows) are combined into a single three-dimensional matrix. This allows cells in one spreadsheet to reference cells in another.

Using a Spreadsheet

If you have Microsoft Works, you have a spreadsheet in your PC already. The spreadsheet that is part of the Works program includes a full range of editing commands, similar to those in a word processor. You can add or delete columns or rows, or change their sizes or positions within the spreadsheet's matrix. You can sort the spreadsheet according to data in specific rows, and scroll through large spreadsheets (because all the data may not fit on the screen at one time) while "freezing" the column and row names so as not to lose your reference points. You can also alternate between seeing the numeric values or the formula contents of cells. Works spreadsheets are compatible with other programs, such as Excel, so if you have spreadsheets created in those programs, you'll probably be able to load them into Works.

Like most spreadsheets, Works will let you decide how you want the numbers in each cell to be displayed. For example, you may want dollar amounts to display the $ symbol, or you may want figures to show a certain number of decimal places. Cells can also contain text information (called labels) rather than just numbers. Usually, such labels would be the names of columns or rows. Without labels, it is easy to forget what each cell's contents represent.

As an aid while working on larger spreadsheets, you can split the screen to display up to four sections of the same worksheet simultaneously. Another command lets you decide whether to have the spreadsheet automatically recalculate its formulas every time you alter a cell's value or wait until you have made all of your changes first.

You can print a wide variety of reports from your spreadsheets that can include all or just a portion of the matrix. The printed version can incorporate titles or descriptive phrases and can use various font styles and sizes.

If you want a graphic version of the spreadsheet data, you can use a single command to instantly make it a chart. With Works, as with other spreadsheets, you can choose from a wide variety of chart formats. Colored bar, line, pie, and scatter charts can be viewed on the screen and printed, complete with borders, legends, and labels.

If you have Microsoft Works, you can try out its spreadsheet. Here's a simple example:

1. Click the Start button, select Programs, and then Microsoft Works. Works will start and display the Works Task Launcher dialog box.

2. Click the Works Tools tab, and then click the Spreadsheet button. The spreadsheet window will appear, with cell A1 outlined, meaning that it is the active cell.

NOTE   *If this is the first time you've launched this Works tool, you will see a First-time Help dialog box offering to show demos for creating a new spreadsheet. Click OK to close this dialog box.*

3. Enter a number, such as **15**, in cell A1.

4. Press the ↓ (down arrow) key to move down to cell A2 (you can also click a cell to move to it), and then enter a number in that cell.

5. Enter numbers in cells A3, A4, and A5.

6. In cell A6, type **=sum(A1:A5)**. The equal sign tells Works that you are entering a formula. The formula tells Works to compute the sum of cells A1 through A5.

7. Press ENTER. The sum of cells A1 through A5 will appear in cell A6. You can see the formula that the cell contains in the entry bar above the spreadsheet grid.

8. Select cells A1 through A5. The easiest way to select cells is to click in the first one you want to select and drag to the last cell in the selection. The selected area is called a *range*.

9. Select New Chart from the Tools menu. You will see a dialog box in which you can make basic and advanced settings for a chart. A preview of the default chart type, a bar chart, will appear in the dialog box.

10. Click OK. You now have a new window that displays the bar chart of your selected data.

11. Close the chart window, then the spreadsheet window, then the Task Launcher dialog box, and finally Works.

You can edit, save, and print spreadsheet and chart files in the same way that you save and print word-processed documents.

Databases 101

A database is really nothing more than a list of items you want to remember. In fact, most of us use databases every day, but we just don't call them by that name. Encyclopedias, phone books, and shopping lists are examples of databases. Just as with electronic spreadsheets and word processors, the difference between a computer database and one on paper is convenience. With a computer, you can rearrange the items in the list by sorting them or you can quickly search through the list to find specific items.

Computer databases are typically used in business environments for customer lists, inventory management, transaction tracking, and so forth. But you can also use a database for household chores such as organizing your phone numbers or holiday card mailing lists.

Parts of a Database

Information in a database is stored in columns and rows, in a layout similar to that of a spreadsheet. This is sometimes called a *table*. The columns in the table are called *fields*, and the rows are called *records*. You might think of each field as a category, and each record as a separate entry in the list. For example, Figure 4-7 shows a simple contacts database. In this example, the three fields are Name, Address, and Phone. Each entry (or person) in the contacts list constitutes one record.

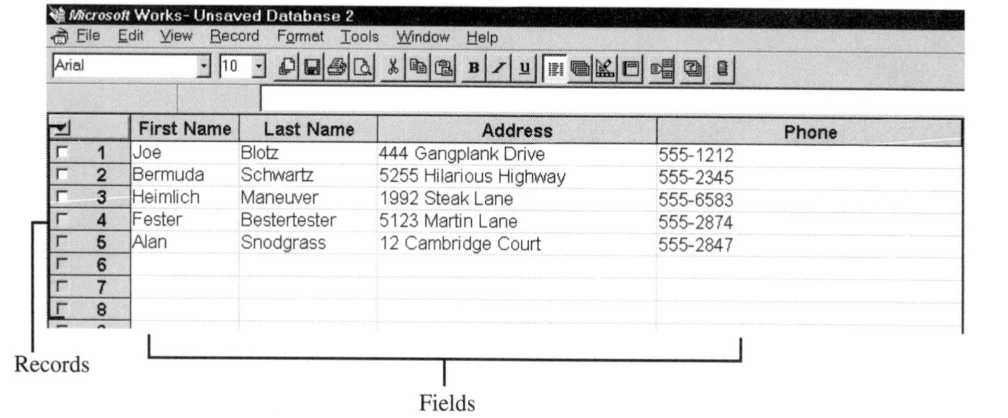

Microsoft Works– Unsaved Database 2

File Edit View Record Format Tools Window Help

Arial   10

		First Name	Last Name	Address	Phone
	1	Joe	Blotz	444 Gangplank Drive	555-1212
	2	Bermuda	Schwartz	5255 Hilarious Highway	555-2345
	3	Heimlich	Maneuver	1992 Steak Lane	555-6583
	4	Fester	Bestertester	5123 Martin Lane	555-2874
	5	Alan	Snodgrass	12 Cambridge Court	555-2847
	6				
	7				
	8				

Records

Fields

FIGURE 4-7   A simple database

As opposed to the cells in spreadsheets, database fields are designed to let you easily find a particular piece of information quickly. If you need to look up a particular phone number or see a list of everyone who lives in a certain city, a computerized database can quickly provide you with the correct information. A database's fields are simply pigeonholes for storing information. Think of a database as analogous to a filing cabinet.

Database programs vary in their capacities for holding data. Some can handle enormous quantities of information; others have strict limitations. Also, the maximum size of each record and the size of each field might be constrained by certain limitations. Some more sophisticated programs will allow you to link or join separate databases temporarily or permanently, to achieve the effect of a larger one, or to pull out only selected subsets of data from one database to create an entirely new one.

Some database programs include what is called a *programming language*. With a programming language, you can design database systems to perform very specific tasks, such as recording sales as they are transacted in a store or tracking inventory as it arrives and is scanned by a bar-code reader. Popular programmable databases include dBASE, Paradox, Microsoft Access, Oracle, and Microrim's R:base.

Using a Database

Along with its word processor and spreadsheet functions, Microsoft Works (which may have come preinstalled on your computer) also includes a database. The Works database can perform quite a number of useful functions, with its built-in wizards and templates. You can easily coordinate the printing of form letters using names and address information you keep in a mailing list database, for example.

Like any database program worth its salt, Works will allow you to print your data on paper in a variety of formats, selectively showing only desired records and fields and even performing calculations such as totals and subtotals in the process of creating the report. You can also create forms to display and print data in. Forms are great when you want to print, say, envelope mailing labels from your database of old school chums, table place-cards for your wedding reception, or recipes on index cards for easy access in the kitchen.

If you have Works, you can follow these steps to experiment with its database:

1. Click the Start button and select Programs, Microsoft Works. Works will start and display the Works Task Launcher dialog box.

2. Click the Works Tools tab, and then click the Database button. The Create Database dialog box will appear.

If this is the first time you've launched this Works tool, you will see a First-time Help dialog box, offering to show demos for creating a new database. Click OK to close this dialog box.

3. Enter **Name** in the Field Name text box. Notice the Format options. You can click the option button for each format to see the Appearance options available for each format. For this example, leave the default General format and click Add.

4. For the second field, enter **Phone** in the Field Name text box and click Add. Then click Done. The database window will appear with the Name and Phone fields.

5. Enter a name in the first record. Then press TAB to move to the Phone field, and enter a phone number.

6. Press TAB to move to the Name field for the second database record, enter a name, press TAB, and enter a phone number.

7. Continue to enter a few more names and phone numbers. If you make a mistake while typing, use the BACKSPACE key to erase characters. If you notice a mistake after you've moved to another cell, double-click the cell with the error. You can now use regular editing techniques to make corrections. Press ENTER when you're finished.

8. You probably need to widen columns so that the whole entry fits in the field. Place your cursor in the field names row, on the right edge of the field you want to widen. The cursor changes to a double-sided arrow, with the label ADJUST. Drag the column to the desired width and release the mouse button.

9. Choose Sort Records from the Record menu. The Sort Records dialog box will appear. The Name column and Ascending sort are selected by default as the sort criteria. Click OK. Your database records will now be rearranged to appear in alphabetical order.

10. Close the database window, then the Task Launcher dialog box, and finally Works.

This gives you some insight into what you can do with a database. For databases that contain many records, the sorting and searching capabilities are invaluable tools.

Works, like many databases, lets you view your data in a number of different ways. Figure 4-7 shows a typical "list view" where data is arranged in columns and rows. But databases really come in handy when you can dress them up and display data in "form view" such as you see in Figure 4-8. Works has quite a number of canned forms, like this one for a sports roster. You can, of course, whip up a custom form to display any of your data, using a "forms design" mode. Many database programs offer something like this to make data entry of information easier on the eyes, or for your hired help to more easily understand what each column or row of data contains.

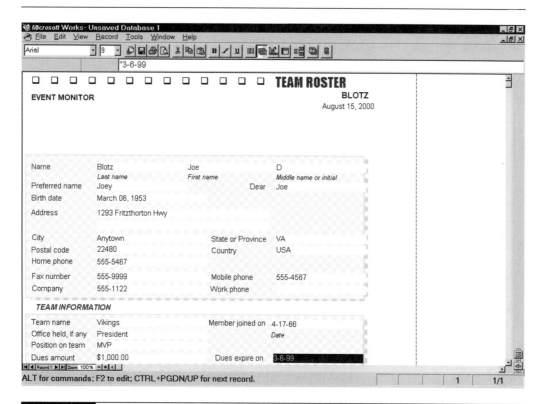

FIGURE 4-8   A simple database in form view

Chapter 5

Managing Your Money

How to...

- Manage your checking, credit, asset, and debit accounts
- Receive and pay bills over the Internet
- Create monthly budgets and plan your retirement
- Generate reports and keep tax records
- Trade stocks and track your portfolio online

One of the most practical uses for your personal computer is organizing and managing finances. Whether you want to balance your checkbook each month or wrestle the accounting and payroll demands of a growing company, you will be amazed at how much time (and money!) you can save when you let the computer do the bean counting for you.

When money management programs first hit the streets more than a decade ago, they were little more than a series of spreadsheets with built-in calculations. Today's applications go far beyond simple addition and subtraction. You can use them to do just about anything even remotely related to money, from keeping track of all of your financial accounts, to planning a budget, to shopping for a cheaper insurance policy, to applying for a loan. What's more, if you are connected to the Internet, you have direct, round-the-clock access to some of the most respected online resources for financial news, events, and advice.

Choosing the Right Financial Software

Despite manufacturers' claims, "one size fits all" is rarely the case. There are just too many different body sizes and shapes to make that claim a practical reality. The same is true of money management software: What is perfect for one person, or even most people, won't work at all for others.

If you don't have many special considerations and just want to keep track of your monthly bills and expenses, you may want to stick with one of the more basic programs, such as Quicken Basic. On the other hand, if you run a business and need to manage payables, receivables, payroll, and employee details, consider a more feature-rich package, such as QuickBooks Pro.

New versions of money management products are released annually in the fall. Be sure to buy the most current version of the product available, but don't feel like you must buy the newest version every single year. Most of them include an easy way for you to update the software to reflect the latest changes in financial, tax, and banking laws—usually by downloading product upgrades. The software itself will continue to function indefinitely, but you should consider upgrading to a newer version at least every few years to take advantage of new features and improvements.

The most popular financial applications are versions of four products:

- Microsoft Money (www.microsoft.com/money)
- Intuit Quicken (www.intuit.com/quicken)

- Intuit QuickBooks (www.intuit.com/quickbooks)
- Peachtree (www.peachtree.com)

The following sections provide an overview of these applications, grouped by the type of money management they can handle. To learn more about the various products and which one might be the best choice for your situation, visit the manufacturers' Web sites.

If you are planning to use your financial software in conjunction with some financial institution's services, check with that institution's representatives to see if they have a preference or recommendation before you decide which application to buy. Although most programs can convert from competitor's formats, some software might not be supported.

5

Personal and Family Finances

The most popular programs for personal finances are the Intuit Quicken packages and Microsoft Money. Quicken is available in a variety of flavors depending on the complexity of your needs. Here are descriptions of the two biggest Quicken sellers and the Microsoft Money package:

- **Quicken Basic**   As the name suggests, Quicken Basic is the no-frills, low-overhead edition of Quicken. Simple features let you manage your bank accounts and track where your money goes. If you don't need to keep track of your investments and other more complex financial accounts, Quicken Basic will suit you just fine. Quicken Basic sometimes comes free with some new computers.

- **Quicken Deluxe**   Quicken Deluxe includes all of the features of Quicken Basic, plus a number of tools to track investments online, plan for your future, and reduce your tax burden. Quicken Deluxe is currently the number one best-selling personal finance software on the planet.

- **Microsoft Money**   Although it was very clunky and ill-designed when initially introduced, Microsoft Money has shown massive improvements since its early releases. Today's Money is a slick tool that gives Quicken a real run for the money, so to speak, and it's a viable alternative. The reviewers at *PC Magazine* liked Money 2000 so much they gave it their "Best of 1999" award and commented, "If you're shopping for personal finance software for the first time, consider Money 2000 first." Money does nearly everything Quicken does (and some things it doesn't), but it takes a different visual approach. A basic version of Microsoft Money is often included free with some computers.

NOTE

Quicken Deluxe is the leader in the money management software category, capturing more than 80 percent of the market. For the examples in this chapter, we'll look at the capabilities of Quicken Deluxe 2000. Keep in mind that the competitors' products have similar features.

Small Business Finances

If you have a home business or are managing a small business, you can step up to the versions of Quicken and Money designed for your needs:

- **Quicken Home and Business**   Quicken Home and Business offers all of the features of Quicken Basic and Quicken Deluxe. It also lets you create invoices, track accounts payable, and simplify your business tax payment process. It's ideal for the home office or small business, especially if your business and personal finances tend to intermingle.

- **Money 2000 Business & Personal Edition**   Microsoft promotes this deluxe version of Money as ideal for sole proprietorships because it so seamlessly integrates all of your finances in one place. A contact management tool is one helpful feature of the Microsoft suite.

Business Accounting

When you cross the line from sketchy startup records to heavy-duty accounting needs, make sure your financial support grows with you. You may be interested in the following products:

- **QuickBooks**   QuickBooks (from Intuit, the makers of Quicken) offers a wide range of business and commerce tools, including payroll features, detailed reporting capabilities, and many helpful financial hints and suggestions.

- **QuickBooks Pro**   If plain old QuickBooks isn't quite enough firepower, the Pro version supports progressive invoicing and job costing, and is fully integrated with Microsoft Office 2000. It also supports multiple users.

- **Peachtree Complete**   Peachtree Software, Inc., is not as well known as Microsoft or Intuit, but its financial software products have a strong and loyal following. Because Peachtree has been focusing on business users all along, it's no surprise that some people think Peachtree leaves all the competitors in the dust. (Every underdog has a group of diehard loyalists behind it, right?)

 Like Intuit and Microsoft, Peachtree also offers some lower-end solutions for the home/small business if the full-blown version is more than you want to tackle.

Minimizing Money Madness

Some people were born with a genetic trait that makes them meticulous about keeping track of their records. They balance their checkbooks to the last penny every month by hand; they save every receipt they get and write down every single purchase they make; and they always know exactly which bills are due when and for how much. Does that sound like you? I didn't think so!

Although I wondered where they found the time, I used to admire those people for being so organized. Now I just smile, because I found the secret to painless and successful money management—let Quicken do it for you! The process of getting myself organized enough to even think about setting up things in Quicken was the hardest part, but I only had to do that once. Since then, Quicken has really helped to minimize the amount of time I spend dealing with money matters—and that is exactly the way I like it.

Here are some of the best things about using Quicken as your check register:

- You don't need to do the math.
- You can assign categories for expense tracking and tax information.
- Quicken carries all your information over to other areas and features (like budget planning), so you only need to enter it once.
- If you enter upcoming bills and payables into Quicken, it will remind you a few days before a bill is due and even write the check for you (optional).

In this section, you'll get a taste of the ways in which you can use Quicken or another money management program to help you stay on top of things in a fraction of the time it used to.

Recording Banking Activity

Once you've gone through the initial software setup steps, the most tedious process is entering all of the transactions you make into the computer. Some people prefer to do this every day or every few days; others find it easier to do at a single sitting when their monthly statements arrive. Either way, it's a very important step because it ensures that your records and balances are accurate.

You can enter your transactions manually, which makes sense if there aren't too many of them. Another, quicker approach is to download all of your account activities directly from your participating bank or credit card company's Web site into Quicken. No more missing checks or forgotten ATM withdrawals!

If you sometimes download your transactions and sometimes enter them manually, be careful that you don't end up entering the same transaction twice. Duplicate entries can throw off your balance one way or the other. And according to Murphy's Law, the error will never be in your favor.

Entering Transactions Manually

Quicken Deluxe includes a shortcut tool called QuickEntry that you can use to record your account activity just as you would in a paper check register. Rather than deal with the whole program when all you want to do is enter the damage from this afternoon's shopping spree, use QuickEntry. Figure 5-1 shows an example of using QuickEntry to enter some transactions in Quicken Deluxe.

Downloading Your Statements

If you only have one or two dozen transactions each month, entering them manually is no big deal. On the other hand, if you write a lot of checks or make numerous credit card purchases, you'll find that entering each one by hand is time-consuming. Thanks to the explosion of Internet banking, there's a faster way.

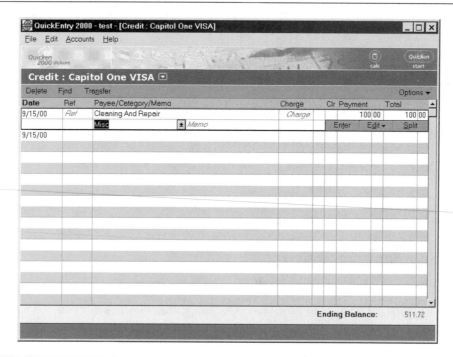

FIGURE 5-1 QuickEntry makes it easy to record your transactions in Quicken

NOTE *Before you can download your financial statements, you'll need some way to connect to the Internet and an Internet service provider. You might also need to get special software from your financial institution, if they require it. See Chapter 6 for details on getting connected to the Internet.*

All you need to do is log in to its Web site and download your account history to your hard drive (usually in the Quicken-compatible standard QIF format). Figure 5-2 shows an example of downloading an account history file from a credit card company's Web site.

After you've downloaded the file and saved it to your hard disk, your next step is to open Quicken and import the file. The QIF Import dialog box, shown next, makes this a simple process.

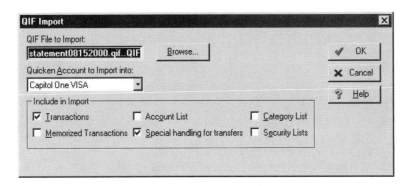

5

Finally, after the transactions are imported, all you need to do is compare it to your notes and receipts. Figure 5-3 shows an example of imported transactions in a Quicken register.

About the only downside to the download method (at least in my experience) is that you often can only draw from the most recent two- to four-month period of history. Some sites may make older records available, but don't count on it.

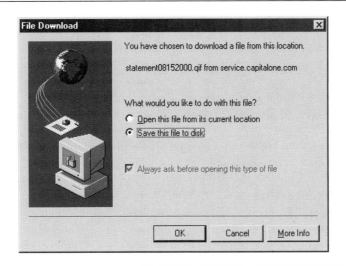

FIGURE 5-2   Downloading an account file from a financial institution's Web site

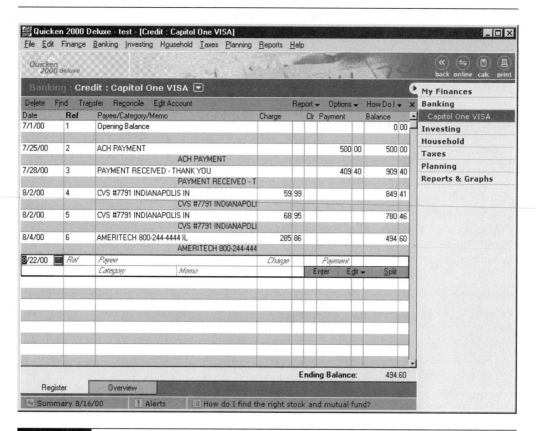

FIGURE 5-3   Transactions you've imported are listed in the appropriate Quicken register

Reconciling Your Accounts

One of the main points of keeping your transactions in a money management program is to make sure your checkbook is balanced. Here's how easy is it to balance (or *reconcile*) your accounts at the end of the month in Quicken:

1. Open the account register for the account you want to balance.

2. Enter or import all the transactions for the month. Figure 5-4 shows an example of check register entries in Quicken.

3. Click on Reconcile in the register's toolbar. The Reconcile Bank Statement dialog box will appear, as shown next.

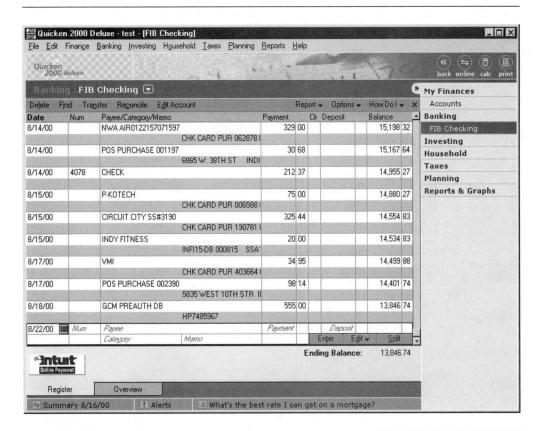

FIGURE 5-4   A Quicken checking account register

4. Enter the opening and closing balances, along with any finance charges or interest earned, and then click OK. The Reconcile Bank account window will open.

5. Click on each verified transaction so that a check mark appears next to it, as shown in Figure 5-5. If you entered the transactions manually, verify your entries against your statement. If you downloaded the statement, verify its entries against your notes and receipts.

6. Use the New, Edit, and Delete buttons on the Reconcile Bank Statement window's toolbar to make adjustments to the balance sheet as needed. When everything is balanced, the difference will be 0.

7. Click the Finished button in the lower-right corner of the window.

That's it. Your account is reconciled, and you don't need to think about it again until next month.

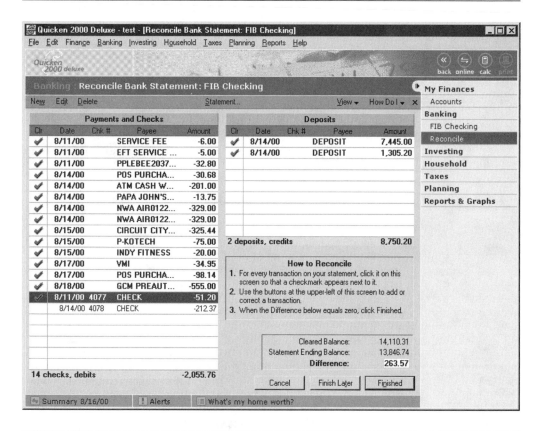

FIGURE 5-5   Reconciling a bank statement

Tracking Investments and Pensions

In addition to simple checking and credit card activity, Quicken can help you keep track of your entire investment portfolio, including IRA, 401(k), and brokerage accounts. Set up a Quicken account for each investment using the Account Setup Wizard, as shown in Figure 5-6. Then you can sit back and watch your nest egg grow.

By tracking all your family's investment accounts in the same place, you get a much more accurate view of your current financial health, as well as how well you are doing toward your future and retirement goals. Figure 5-7 shows the many ways that Quicken shows information about your investments.

If you choose to take advantage of the program's online and Web-based features, you'll become an even wiser investor. See the "Using Online and Web-based Financial Services" section later in this chapter for more information about using online features and money-related Web sites.

Tracking Assets and Liabilities

Managing your cash-based accounts with the computer is easy, but what about keeping track of all your other valuables? You may have a home, a car, a boat, a coin collection, or a vintage Gibson electric guitar. You'll want to keep track of how much these items are worth, as well as how much you owe for them (if anything). Rather than relying on stacks of paper records or a nice, neat (but very expensive) printout from your accountant every year around tax time, you can use Quicken to manage your assets. Figure 5-8 shows an example of using a household asset account to keep track of the value of a guitar.

FIGURE 5-6   Setting up an investment account

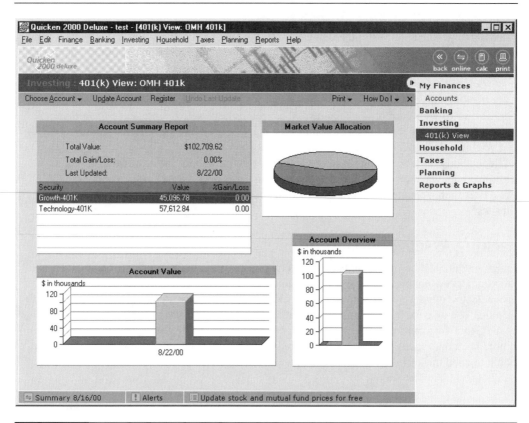

FIGURE 5-7   Viewing information about a 401(k) account

> **TIP**   *You can even use Quicken to track activities related to collecting and hobbies. Use the account register, for example, to record your coin collection inventory and each piece's value. Then update the total worth as you buy and sell individual pieces in the collection. Whether your hobby grows into a commercial venture or your collection is just for your family's enjoyment, you'll really appreciate having this kind of information.*

Similarly, you can set up accounts to track your loans and other liabilities. Quicken makes it easy to create accounts for amortized or other types of loans. Then you can keep track of what you've paid and what you still owe. Quicken also provides a Loan Planner feature to help you figure out what your payments would be on loans you are considering.

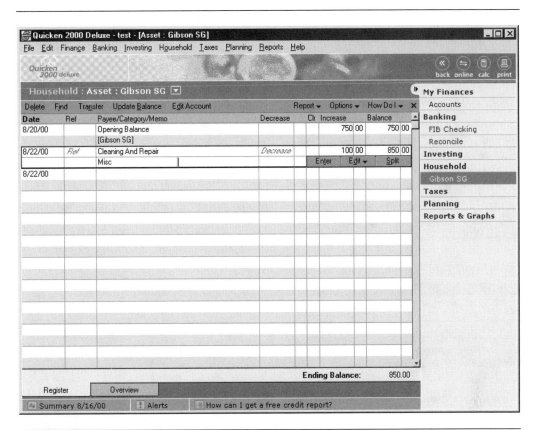

FIGURE 5-8   Using Quicken to keep track of an asset

Viewing Reports and Graphs

Perhaps the best part about money management programs is not the day-to-day work they save you, but the cumulative data your efforts produce over time. Quicken lets you view, analyze, and sort your information into more kinds of reports and graphs than you'll probably ever use.

After you have several months of data in Quicken, it's very easy to take a look back and see how things are going. In fact, sometimes even just a few months' records can say a lot. Quicken's robust reporting and graphing features let you examine all types of information about you and your money. Here are just a few examples of how you might use Quicken reports:

- Supply prospective creditors, such as mortgage brokers, with the all the information they need to approve your application

■ Generate a report on how much you own and how much you owe

■ Help you recognize and correct bad spending habits

Figure 5-9 shows the Quicken reports available for seeing how you are spending your money.

Budgeting and Forecasting

Suppose that after using Quicken's reports to analyze your expenses for the last six months, you think that perhaps you are spending too much money on dining out. You wonder how much you could you save if you cut those expenses in half over the next six months. How long would it take to build up enough for a short vacation? Can you tighten your belt in others areas, too, and hop on that plane even sooner?

Quicken can help you set up a monthly budget and make adjustments to your spending or plan for a future goal such as a vacation, your child's college tuition, or the down payment on a new car. Working from a budget each month takes some getting used to, but if you can tough it

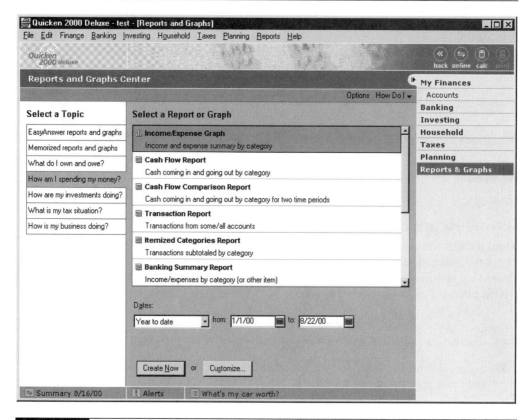

FIGURE 5-9 Quicken provides many reports and graphs on various money-related topics

out for the first few months of growing pains, you'll see how worthwhile your patience can be—especially if you have some big-ticket items or events down the road that you want to make sure you can afford.

In a series of simple steps, Quicken's Planning Center walks you through some questions and assumptions about yourself and your situation, as shown in Figure 5-10.

You can create a budget with Quicken in one of two ways. Quicken can create a budget for you, based on your income and expense history. After it sets up the budget, you can make adjustments as necessary. If you open Quicken's Budget window and don't already have a budget set up, Quicken will assume that you want it to create one, as shown here.

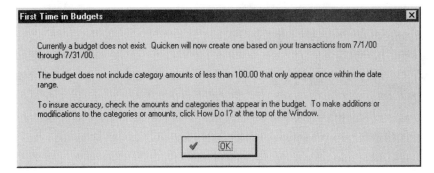

The other way to create a budget is to start from scratch. This is the long way, but often worth the exercise. Using this approach forces you to think long and hard about what you are spending and how much you really need every month for that category.

Taking Care of Taxes

If you're interested in preparing your own tax returns, you might want to use a specialized tax program, such as TurboTax. However, Quicken has an entire Taxes Center and Taxes menu to help you gather tax-related information, as shown in Figure 5-11.

You can plan and estimate your taxes, find tax deductions, and prepare reports for your tax accountant. You can even download a demo of TurboTax and try it out.

Using Online and Web-based Financial Services

As with nearly every other industry, the Internet is having a huge impact on the way banks work and how we do business in the twenty-first century. Five years ago, it was hard to find a bank that had a Web site, let alone one that supported online banking. Today, you can do most of your regular financial activities via the World Wide Web.

To use online and Web-based financial services, you'll need to have your Internet connection and service set up. These topics are covered in detail in Chapter 6.

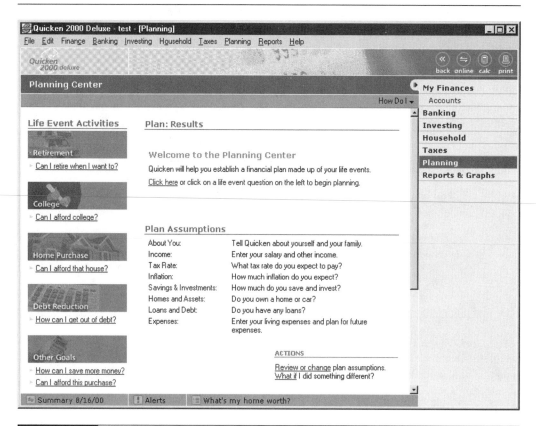

FIGURE 5-10   The Planning Center in Quicken is the key to slaying the finance dragon

Money management software packages work with the Internet to make your life easier. Here are some of the things you can do online:

- Pay bills directly from your checking account
- Get statements and invoices from creditors
- Use e-mail to contact customer service about your account
- Get up-to-the-minute financial news and information on the Web
- Buy, sell, and monitor stocks
- Manage your entire investment portfolio
- Join online interest groups
- Read advice and tips from industry experts

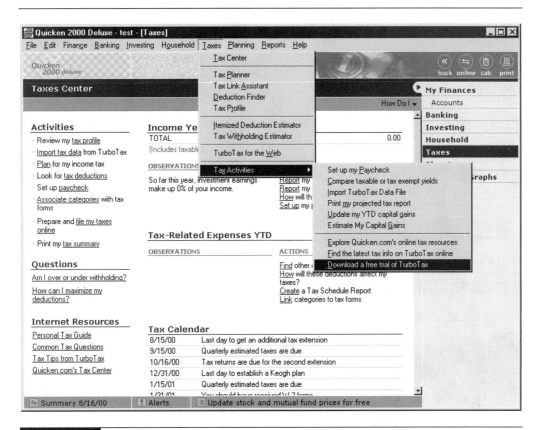

FIGURE 5-11   Quicken includes many features for organizing your tax information

See Chapter 7 for details on using e-mail. For information about online interest groups, see Chapter 8.

In this section, we'll take a look at a few of these features in more detail. After you've become familiar with the World Wide Web, you're sure to discover many other online resources on your own.

Receiving and Paying Bills Online

As explained earlier in this chapter, you can download your bank and credit card statements and import them directly into your financial management program. In some cases, you can even receive your bills online (or via e-mail) and pay them, too. Paying your bills online has many benefits—no paper, stamps, or checks involved, and they're accurate and on time. How much easier can it get?

If all of your banks and credit card companies offer online billing and payment, you can take one of two different approaches to managing your accounts online:

- Visit each creditor's Web site each month. Check your statement online and, while you're there, authorize a payment from your checking account (or whatever account you want to use), and then record that transaction in your Quicken with QuickEntry. If you don't have a lot of different accounts or you're not concerned about the details of your credit card spending and only want to track the balance and payments, this might be the way to go. Figure 5-12 shows an example of visiting a credit card company's Web site.

- Download your statements into Quicken or enter the transactions manually and use Quicken's Online Payment feature to authorize and record the transaction simultaneously. When you're serious about saving money, sticking to budgets, and improving your worth, consider this method. It can take a bit longer to ensure you've entered every transaction for every account, but you'll get the best cumulative results this way. Figure 5-13 shows an example of downloading account records from a bank's Web site.

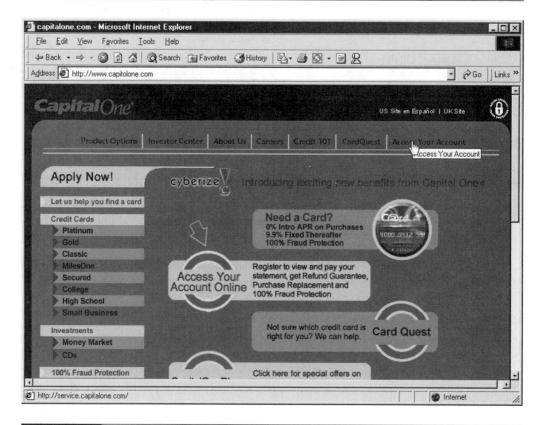

FIGURE 5-12   You can visit your financial institution's Web site, access your account, and pay your bills from there

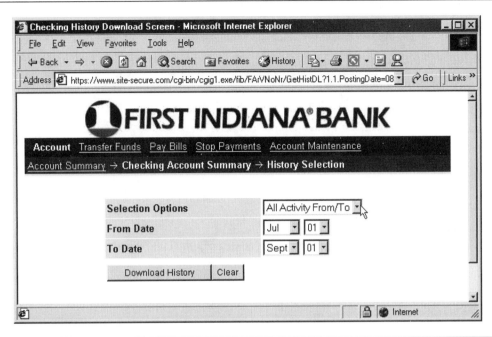

FIGURE 5-13   You can download your records from your financial institution's Web site

TIP *If your bank does not directly support payments via your money management program, you might consider using a service such as CheckFree. This type of checking service writes, posts, and mails checks for you, deducting the payments right out of your checking account and your Quicken account register. You can send an online payment to anyone you would send a regular handwritten check to—schedule a regular monthly payment to your landlord for the rent or send a one-time $25 check to your nephew for his birthday (unfortunately, they won't send a birthday card long with it).*

Online Investing and Stock Trading

Some of the best advice my father ever gave me (or at least advice that I actually listened to) was this: Start investing when you're young. I had a corporate job then, so investing via paycheck deductions was simple. They kept part of my check, added to it, and socked it away in an interest-bearing account for me. I, as dad so wisely advised, left it alone. In time, the money grew. That really was very easy, but what I didn't know back then was that I had choices over the years about the distributions of my investments. If I had a more direct involvement and understanding of my investment options early on, that total corporate nest egg might have accounted for a larger part of my net worth when I retire. Your money management software and Internet resources can provide a great deal of information about the investment options available to you.

 *If you're new to investing, you can gain some understanding of how to make the best of your returns and track the potential growth by running Quicken's Investment Basics. This is an animated training clip that walks you through the important concepts and procedures.*

A variety of investment securities are available, and most successful investors have very diverse portfolios, because different types of securities offer different types of benefits. No matter what combination of assets you have—brokerage accounts, IRAs and Keoghs, 401(k) plans, dividend reinvestment plans, or other investments—they are your future. You can use your money management software as your portfolio's "command center," tracking all of your investments and account activity.

By consolidating all your accounts in a personal portfolio, you can manage your investments in a variety of ways:

- Easily determine summary totals
- Know the value of your securities on any given day
- Track a variety of activities and generate dozens of situational reports, charts, and graphs

Having immediate access to your portfolio and being able to create consolidated summaries in quick, easy steps saves an incredible amount of time. And, of course, you can do all this without having to do any of the math!

Setting Up Investment Accounts

After you gather your latest statements from each of your brokers and investment firms, Quicken makes it easy to set up the individual accounts in the portfolio. Figure 5-14 shows the Quicken Investing Center window and the dialog box for setting up a new investment account.

Entries from your account records contribute to your historic data, which produces more accurate reports, gives you a better assessment of your current financial situation, and helps you make more realistic plans. As explained in the next section, you can simplify input by downloading your personal account activity into your Quicken investment account, where it instantly becomes part of your portfolio.

If you need help setting up your investment account, a click of the mouse in the Investing Center window will give you the information you need. For example, you can learn about *asset allocations*, or how to calculate what your asset allocations should be to meet your investing needs, as shown in Figure 5-15.

Getting Online Investment and Stock Information

After you've established your individual accounts, you can get market value updates, account transactions, and balances as often as you like. All you need to do is tell Quicken what you want to know, and then connect to the Internet to get the most recent information. You can also get real-time stock quotes, the latest news tips, reminders about maturity dates, and more.

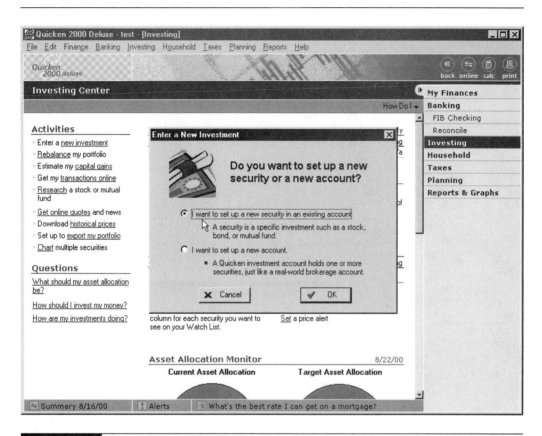

FIGURE 5-14   Setting up a new investment account

Be sure that your broker or investment firm supports your money management software. Some will be in an exclusive arrangement with Quicken, others with Money, and still others will support any type of money management package.

Quicken offers a nice feature that combines your Internet access with your favorite stock quotes. Set up the quotes you want to track and recall the updated information at any time. You also can watch your stock tickers in Quicken.com, as described in the next section.

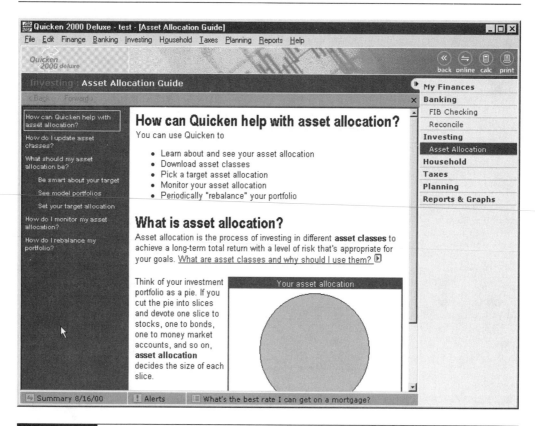

Getting information about asset allocation

Accessing Online News, Advice from the Experts, and Helpful Resources

Your money management software's associated Web site is your online portal to your personal account information and links to a wealth of resource information. You can use most of the resources for free, although some related services or subscriptions might require an additional fee. Figure 5-16 shows MSN's MoneyCentral Web site, designed for Microsoft Money users.

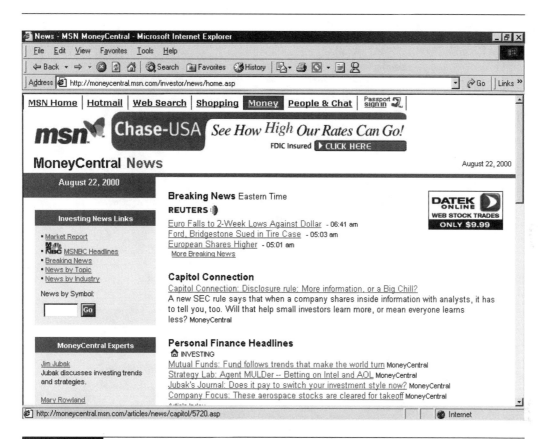

5

FIGURE 5-16   MSN's MoneyCentral Web site is the online investment and financial management center for Microsoft Money users

Quicken.com is the mission control center for online investing and financial management for Quicken users. Here are just some of the resources you'll find at Quicken.com:

- If you're shopping for a mortgage or home equity loan, click the Mortgages tab to get started.

■ To see information about the stock tickers you specified, as well as historical stock information and news article links, go to the Quicken.com Stocks page.

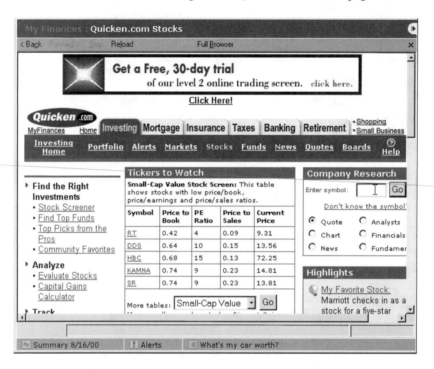

■ Do you need a bank account that you can access 24 hours a day from anywhere in the world? Click on the Banking tab and find the one that's right for you.

■ On the Investing page, you'll find current headlines from the most respected financial news sources, such as CBS.MarketWatch.com and Dow Jones.

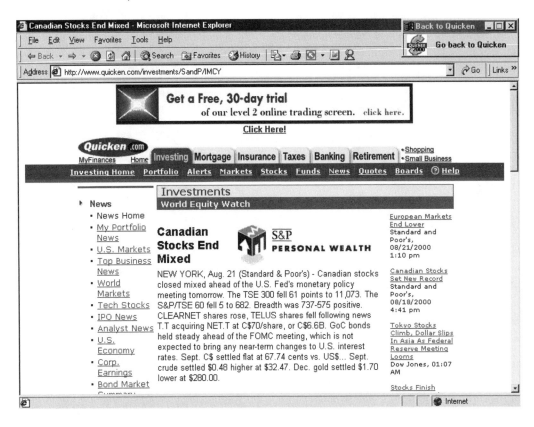

■ Are you on the prowl for better insurance rates? See what Quicken recommends on the Insurance page.

■ Do you want to get some expert advice on planning for your retirement? You'll find answers to your questions and much more on the Retirement page.

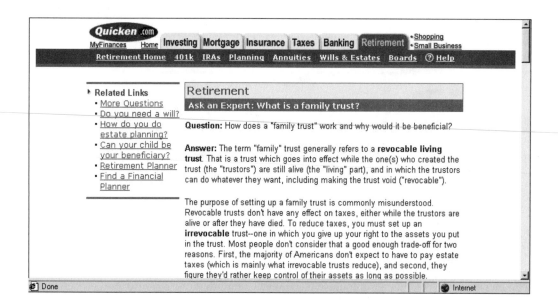

■ Are you a small business owner (or thinking about becoming one)? Check out the Small Business page.

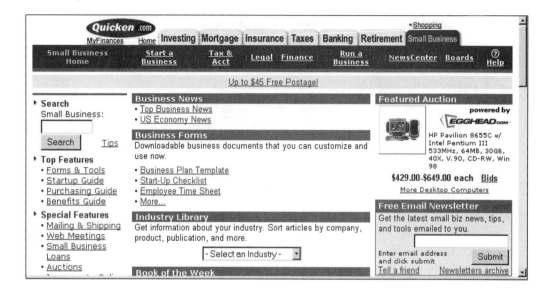

■ Do you need a quick definition of a term? Use the Quicken.com Glossary (www.quicken.com/glossary) to find terminology and concepts defined in plain English.

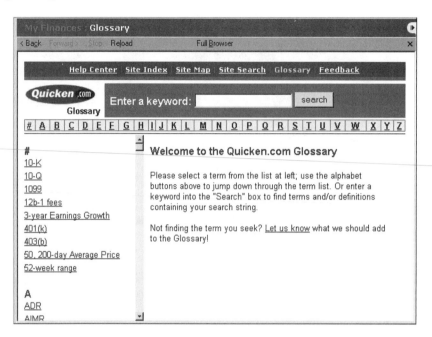

TIP *Your Quicken accounts are available even when you can't access your personal Quicken software. If you synchronize your accounts with your Quicken.com online account before you leave town, you can pay bills and monitor your bank accounts while you travel. When you get home, just log onto Quicken.com and walk through the steps to download the WebEntry activities that occurred while you were gone.*

Once you've made the decision on which financial management program to use, take the time to really explore everything it has to offer. The software developers work hard to make their tools the best they can be, and you really can't go wrong with any of them. If you take full advantage of the features and resources, you'll not only be healthier, wealthier, and wiser, but you'll have a lot more time for what you really want to do: surf the Web!

Chapter 6

Becoming an Internet Expert

How to...

- Pick an Internet service provider
- Choose an Internet connection method
- Use a Web browser
- Navigate to Web sites
- Shop on the Web

One of the biggest advantages of owning a computer is having access to the Internet. By now, you've probably heard enough ranting in the mainstream media about how the Internet is great, evil, useless, or any number of descriptions. They're all true. But the Internet also is an amazing resource that, filtered through your judgment, can be tremendously useful in a vast number of ways. Before you can discover this for yourself, you need a means of connecting to it.

In this chapter, you'll learn about the services and connections you need to hook up to the Internet. Then you'll be introduced to the Web browsers and navigation tools that allow you to get around on the Internet. Finally, you'll get some information on shopping on the Web.

Choosing an ISP

There are two factors that control your Internet surfing speed: your connection from your computer to your ISP (Internet service provider) and the connection across the Internet from your ISP to the site you're seeking. Depending on the time of day, Internet routing problems, and the responsiveness of the site you're trying to reach, even the fastest connection can feel sluggish at times. Regardless of that warning, it makes sense to get the fastest and most cost-effective connection to the Internet that you can.

Unless you're a wealthy hobbyist who wants to have a massive pipeline to the Internet regardless of the expense (and if this is you, I can tell you'll need extensive personal assistance at my quite reasonable hourly rates), you'll be relying on an ISP to provide your connection to the Internet. A few years ago, ISPs were often local operations, but as the market has grown, many local ISPs have been bought and conglomerated into bigger regional or even national operations. Now you have the choice of using a regional or national ISP, a national online service (like AOL), or your phone or cable company. Each has its advantages and disadvantages.

What you will find is remarkable parity between pricing schemes. The widespread availability of ISPs has squeezed pricing pretty hard, which is good for you. For a dial-up connection, you shouldn't need to pay more than $20–$25 per month for unlimited use.

National ISPs

National ISPs are great if you travel frequently. You should be able to find a local access number in most major cities, allowing you to dial in and check your e-mail without incurring toll charges. For a business traveler, this is a big plus.

What is the downside? Well, if you run into a problem, it may not be easy to get personal service from a huge outfit. It's not like a local ISP where you can just march to the office and ask for help. Check for toll-free support numbers, and if you're skeptical, call with a support question even before you sign up. If you are stuck on hold a long time, consider it a warning.

Local ISPs

Local ISPs can be great. From a good outfit, you can get personal service, any services you need on an a la carte basis, and local dial-in numbers. If you run into strange configuration problems or need some special services, the attention of a local provider can be invaluable. In some towns, a local ISP may be your only way to get a local Internet access number. It's also nice to help out the local economy.

Unfortunately, some local ISPs do not provide good service. You may run into an insufficient number of modems and improperly configured servers. You may experience all kinds of odd problems, including mysterious hangups, dropped connections, and lousy performance.

Customer service is a good indication of the service you'll get from an ISP. Stop by a local ISP, or call and ask for help. If the customer service personnel can't find time for you before you sign up, the odds aren't good they'll turn it around once you give them money.

> **TIP** *Ask your friends who already have Internet access who they use. Are they happy? Did they try another ISP first?*

Online Services

Online services are another way to get onto the Internet. AOL (America Online) and CompuServe both offer added-value content in addition to serving as your ISP. Some folks live for their IMs (instant messages) on AOL, and both AOL and CompuServe have built a community beyond just the Internet. Prodigy and MSN (Microsoft Network) have both morphed into primarily Internet providers and have reduced their emphasis on added-value content.

Despite some well-publicized problems in making sufficient phone lines available for demand, AOL has done a good job of providing connections. And both AOL and CompuServe, having been in existence as stand-alone dial-up services, have tons of local access numbers. However, you should still verify that you are using a local number before you run up a huge bill!

> **NOTE** *In Chapter 7, you can read my discussion about why I think AOL is a pain to use. Check it out before signing up for AOL.*

Choosing a Connection Type

Along with deciding on an ISP, you also need to figure out how you will actually connect to the Internet. The most common method is through a dial-up phone line via your modem, because it's generally the cheapest method. ISDN (Integrated Services Digital Network) might be another alternative available to you. Another option is a cable modem, handily provided by your cable TV provider. DSL (Digital Subscriber Line) connections are dropping in price rapidly. Satellite connections are also available.

Dial-Up Connections

Nearly every computer ships with a modem, and even the fastest modem isn't all that expensive if yours is slow or nonexistent. There has been a long history of modem speed improvement, ranging from 300bps (bits per second) in the distant past up to the current 57,600bps (more commonly written as 56Kbps). Realistically, you may run into 28.8Kbps or 33.6Kbps modems, but those are at the lowest end of acceptable connection speed. If you don't have a 56Kbps modem and you'll be using a dial-up connection, this is a good spot for an upgrade. (See Chapter 17 for more information about adding a new modem to your computer.)

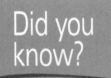

The Truth About Modem Speed

Modems are advertised at 56Kbps, but you'll never see that speed. Connections are currently limited to no more than 53Kbps because of an arcane FCC regulation, but even that is over a perfect, noise-free connection under ideal circumstances. Depending on the distance between you and your ISP, the quality of the phone lines between you, and even the weather, you will see lower speeds. In reality, anything approaching 50Kbps is quite good.

In order to make a near-56Kbps connection, several conditions need to be in place:

- One end of the connection needs to be digital (the end at your ISP).

- One end of the connection must be analog (typically, the line connecting your modem to the phone company's equipment).

- Both ends must have 56Kbps capability.

ISDN Connections

ISDN is a digital connection, eliminating the analog-to-digital conversion challenges that normally limit modem speeds. There are two types of ISDN circuits: the BRI (Basic Rate Interface) and PRI (Primary Rate Interface). The PRI circuit is substantially faster (running at up to 2000Kbps), more expensive, and better suited for commercial use.

BRI consists of two B channels, each capable of 64Kbps, and one D channel carrying 16Kbps. Each B channel can carry a voice call independently, and most ISDN modems have plugs for a phone handset to attach to them. The service is capable of running at 128Kbps (the sum of the two B channels), then dropping to half that speed if an incoming call is received on one of the channels. This doesn't mean you can get rid of your POTS (plain old telephone service) number once you get ISDN service, however. A power outage renders your ISDN service worthless, while your good old phone line remains operable.

In many parts of the country, ISDN is an idea whose time has come and gone. ISDN connections require phone company intervention. Ideally, it should be a simple process for the phone company to install the modem, configure the lines at the phone company's end, and test the connection. However, my experience in attempting to install ISDN through the phone company indicates that simple installations are a rarity. Pricing for this service is often reasonably high, although it varies from area to area. Additionally, ISDN service requires that you be within three miles of the phone company's switching station. If you're not, stop. You can't have ISDN. These constraints, coupled with the availability of more attractive alternatives, are beginning to sound the death knell for ISDN.

Cable Modem Connections

If you're in an area served by Time-Warner Cable, you can't avoid ads for their Roadrunner service. Cable modems are a big improvement over standard modems in speed and ease of installation, and unlike the treatment ISDN got from most local phone companies, cable companies have cleverly marketed their Internet service. Cable connection speed is rated at a 10Mbps maximum, but is typically closer to 1.5Mbps.

Cable modem service varies by provider. Locally, it involves your cable company installing an Ethernet card and connecting the card to an outlet the cable company provides. Actual cable modems are used in other areas; they are connected to the cable service and then to the PC. Depending on the cabling in your area, cable modems are either two-way or receive-only, with a modem connection for return service. The two-way kind is preferable, since it doesn't cause a bottleneck for your outgoing traffic, and it doesn't require the expense of a second phone line. But you don't get to pick—you'll be told what's available. You can either live with it or move to a new neighborhood.

There are downsides to cable service. First, you need to ensure that file and printer sharing is turned off on your machine. By installing a cable modem, you've joined a network along with all of your neighbors who share the circuit. If your neighbors don't disable file and print sharing, do the honorable thing—send a warning about it to their printers!

Because you're sharing a network circuit, you're also limited in speed by how many others are using that circuit at the same time. Depending on the number of users and how much bandwidth they are using, you may be slowed at times to nearly dial-up speeds. But the speed improvement you'll experience on average makes cable modem Internet access a great value.

DSL Connections

DSL is becoming a popular means of accessing the Internet. You'll often see it as *x*DSL, since there are several variants, including ADSL, HDSL, SDSL, VADSL, and VDSL, among others. ADSL (Asymmetric DSL) is the most relevant for our purposes, since it's offered at the lowest cost.

DSL requires that you be within a certain distance of the phone company, and it isn't available everywhere yet. But if DSL is available in your area and the pricing is reasonable, it may be your very best approach. DSL service ranges from about 1500Mbps to 9000Mbps, a substantial improvement in access speed. What makes it particularly attractive is that you don't share the circuit—it's all yours. DSL uses your existing copper wiring, and even when you're downloading files at huge speeds, you can make and receive voice calls (because the Internet traffic is carried inside a high-frequency carrier signal that doesn't interfere with the range used by voice data).

Satellite Connections

Satellite service is available, often in connection with TV mini-dishes. It is one-directional, so you'll need a second phone line to send information to the Internet. Satellite connection performance is good, and if you don't have access to cable modems or DSL connections, it may be your only high-speed choice.

What's It Going to Cost Me?

Table 6-1 shows the various connection types, their speeds, their relative speed (with 1X as the base, or slowest speed), and an approximation of your monthly costs. Keep in mind that these charges vary widely depending on your location, so it pays to check for yourself.

Table 6-1 does not include the hardware and installation costs for higher-speed connections. See Chapter 17 for information about costs for hardware for Internet connections.

Connection Type	Speed / Relative Speed	Monthly Cost
Dial-up over POTS line	33.6–50Kbps / 1X	$20 plus phone line
ISDN	56–128Kbps / 2–4X	$30–$60 plus connect time (usually a few cents per minute depending on time of day)
Cable	1.5–10Mbps / 40–100X	$40–$60 plus return phone line if needed
Satellite	400Kbps or higher / 10–500X	$20–$40 plus ISP charges and return phone line if needed
xDSL (ADSL, HDSL, SDSL, VADSL, and VDSL)	9Mbps maximum (ADSL)–more than 50Mbps (VDSL) / 50–1500X	$60 (128Kbps service)–$1,000 (very high-speed service)

TABLE 6-1   Internet Connection Alternatives

6

NOTE   *There are two kinds of connection problems when accessing the Internet: one you can fix and one you just get to complain about. The connection from your PC to the ISP may be faulty. That you can fix, even if it involves a support call to the ISP. The other kind of problem is when the Internet itself is totally bogged down, and no amount of magical incantations directed at your PC can fix that.*

Windows includes easy setup for new accounts on AOL, MSN, AT&T World Net, CompuServe, Prodigy, and other services, right out of the box. Refer to Chapter 15 to learn how to set up your Internet connection.

Getting to Know Your Browser

The two primary browsers are Microsoft Internet Explorer, which according to Microsoft is an integral part of Windows, and Netscape Communicator. (Netscape's browser was formerly called Netscape Navigator.) While the buttons aren't called the same things, both browsers offer most of the same features. Each browser has its own charms and quirks, but both are really amazing considering how primitive they were just a few short years ago.

Internet Explorer

Internet Explorer (IE), shown in Figure 6-1, is the browser provided with Windows. You can open it from the quick-launch bar, its desktop icon, or by selecting Start, Programs, Internet Explorer.

IE's appearance can be customized, so it may not always look like the example shown in Figure 6-1. You can choose to start on the MSN home page (by default), a different page, or a blank page. (See Chapter 18 for details on changing your home page).

The IE screen contains the following main elements:

■ **Toolbar** The toolbar buttons will get you places pretty quickly. To get back to the site you were at just before you arrived at your current site, click the Back button. Once you've gone backward using the Back button, you can also click on the Forward button to return to the site you visited last. Clicking on the Home button will take you back to the MSN page, or whatever page you've selected as your home page. Clicking the Refresh button reloads the page you're on, which can be useful if the site changes regularly; for example, from a news site, you may want to occasionally click Refresh to update the news coverage.

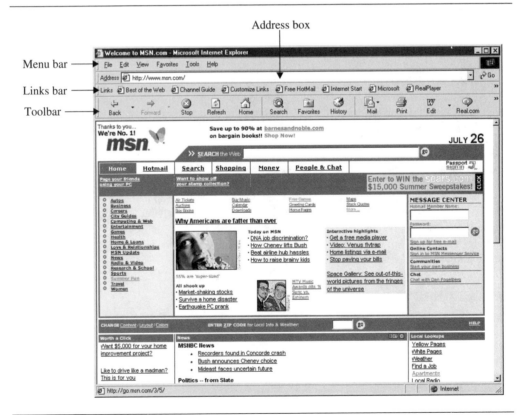

FIGURE 6-1 Internet Explorer with its default home page, MSN

NOTE

If the Back button on the toolbar is grayed out, the link you just selected actually opened another browser window, so you're already at the first Web site in that browser window, and you can't go backward any farther. You can open multiple browser windows at the same time.

TIP

Clicking the Back button is something you'll do a zillion times a day if you surf the Web a lot. A shortcut for this that doesn't require the mouse is to press Alt+Left Arrow.

- **Menu bar**   The menu bar contains all of the menus for IE. All the "under-the-hood" stuff happens here, such as adjusting the browser's settings or saving a Web page to a file. The menus contain commands for opening, closing, and saving files (File menu); copying and pasting selections (Edit menu), controlling the elements displayed in the IE window (View menu); managing bookmarks (Favorites menu); managing IE settings (Tools menu); and getting help (the Help menu).

- **Links bar**   The Links bar can be configured to your liking. By default, it has a handful of default icons provided by Microsoft, but you can add any Internet shortcuts there that you like. You can drag any shortcut from your Favorites menu to the Links bar, and back again. For example, if you have a site that you visit frequently, but you don't want to make it your home page, you might want to put its shortcut on the Links bar.

- **Address box**   When you know the address of the site that you want to visit, you can simply type it in the Address box, and then click the Go button to its right or press ENTER. IE will take you to that address (known as a URL, as you'll learn later in the chapter). Clicking the arrow on the right side of the Address box opens a drop-down list of previous addresses accessed through the Address box. You can select an address from this list to go to that Web site.

Netscape Communicator

Netscape Communicator, shown in Figure 6-2, is the only major competitor to IE. Netscape Communicator (I'll call it Netscape from now on) operates in a manner similar to IE. It has a menu bar, a toolbar, and a Netsite box (which has the same purpose as the IE Address box). The Bookmarks bar is similar to IE's Links menu.

One nice touch in Netscape is the quick-launch bar at the bottom-left corner of the browser window, shown here. These buttons allow instant access to a lot of the extra features built into Netscape, including the mail inbox, newsgroup access, address book, and Composer (a Web page design program).

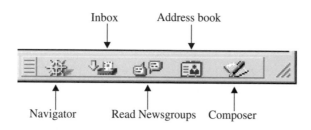

Netsite box

Bookmarks

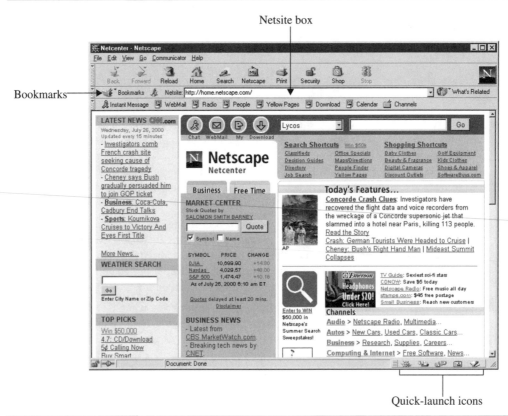

Quick-launch icons

FIGURE 6-2   Netscape Communicator opened to its default home page

Finding Your Way Around the Internet

Finding your way around the Internet can be a daunting task. Without some map or idea where you want to end up, it's like wandering into a strange city wearing a blindfold. However, if you have an address in mind or some way of finding the information you're seeking, you'll be able to get where you want to go. Web addresses are known as URLs. Search engines can help you find the information you're looking for. Also, Web pages contain hyperlinks, which you can click on to jump to another page with more information about the linked item.

URLs

URLs (Uniform Resource Locators) are the format for Web addresses. They follow the format of *<protocol>*://*<domain name>*/*<path>*. If a path isn't given, the URL opens to the default home page (usually called index.html) for that site. HTTP (Hypertext Transfer Protocol) is the protocol for all WWW (World Wide Web) documents.

You might find URLs for interesting Web sites in various places—books, newspapers, magazines, radio, TV, even billboards! That's the ubiquitous "dot com" you're hearing everywhere. To visit that Web site, type the URL in your browser's address area (the Address box in IE or the Netsite box in Netscape). It's not necessary to type the http:// part of the address; unless informed otherwise, the browser will provide it. You can see examples of the URLs in Figures 6-1 and 6-2 (shown earlier in the chapter). MSN's home page URL (http://www.msn.com) appears in Figure 6-1, and Netscape's home page URL (http://home.netscape.com) appears in Figure 6-2.

Hyperlinks

6

Navigating around the World Wide Web using hyperlinks is pretty intuitive. When you click on a hyperlink—which can be a text link or an image link—you jump to the target of that hyperlink, which is usually another Web page.

In IE, you can move your mouse cursor until it turns from an arrow to a hand. When you see the hand, this means that you're over a hyperlink. Click to jump to the information associated with that link (the speed of your "jump" depends on the speed of your Internet connection).

Search Engines

The best friend you can have on the Internet is a good search engine. To use a search engine, you go to its Web site, type the words you want to find in its Search box, and click the Search button. The search engine will look for your search entry in its database, and then display a list of URLs that match. Each URL contains a hyperlink to the found information. Just click on a hyperlink to see where it leads. When you're finished at the linked site, click on the browser's Back button to go back to the search engine's site. You can explore each of the items in the search engine's results list this way.

There are many search engines, and their number seems to grow daily. Popular search engines include Search.com, Lycos, and Excite, just to name a few. My personal top choices are AltaVista (http://www.altavista.com), shown in Figure 6-3, and Google (http://www.google.com), shown in Figure 6-4. Inevitably, search results can turn up some entries that will make you wonder what that site could possibly have to do with your request, but Google and AltaVista do as good a job as anyone in finding useful sites.

Another good search engine is Hotbot (http://www.hotbot.com). The nice thing about it is that you can easily specify how you want the search engine to combine your criteria during the search. On some search engines, you have to use quotes and other punctuation marks when searching based on a phrase, formal name, and so on. Hotbot lets you choose this stuff from a simple drop-down list such options as "all the words," "exact phrase," or "the person."

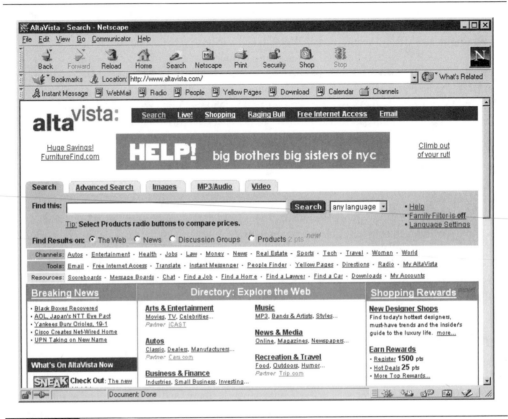

FIGURE 6-3   The AltaVista search site

Bookmarks

The more time you spend rummaging around on the Internet, the more sites you'll find that you may want to visit again. You can *bookmark* these sites (make a shortcut to them) in your browser. Internet Explorer calls these shortcuts *favorites*, and Netscape calls them *bookmarks*. In IE, you can add a bookmark to the site you're currently visiting by selecting the Add to Favorites command from the Favorites menu on the menu bar. In Netscape, you can add a bookmark by choosing File, Add Bookmark.

Once you bookmark a Web site, how do you use the bookmark to get back to your favorite location? In Internet Explorer, you open the Favorites menu, find the bookmark, and click it. In Netscape, click Bookmarks on the toolbar. To make your bookmarks more quickly available, if you're using Internet Explorer, just click Favorites in the toolbar, or click View, Explorer Bar, Favorites. A panel will open up over on the left margin of your browser, listing all your favorites. Just click on a favorite to go to the Web. If you have organized your favorites into different folders, clicking on a folder will open it so you can see the favorites stored within.

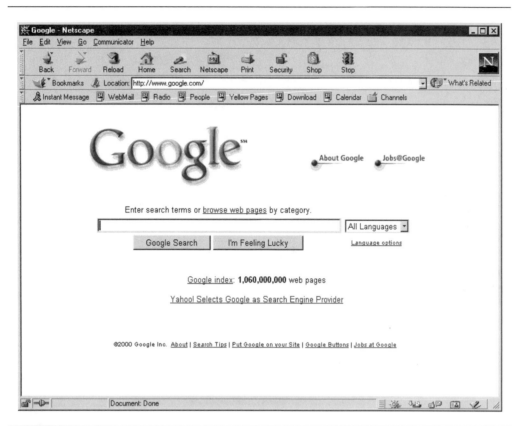

FIGURE 6-4   The Google search site

If you take advantage of bookmarks, which are a very handy way to navigate to your favorite Web sites, you will soon accumulate a pile of shortcuts. Without some form of organization, these shortcuts can become a nuisance to sift through.

Both IE and Netscape allow you to organize your bookmarks in folders. I categorize my shortcuts into broad categories, sticking to 20 or fewer, so that they'll all appear without scrolling the list. Each category can be broken into as many subcategories as needed.

To organize your favorite shortcuts in IE, select the Organize Favorites option from the Favorites menu on the menu bar. You'll see the Organize Favorites dialog box, as shown in Figure 6-5, which allows you to organize your links to your heart's content.

Netscape takes a slightly different approach. It stores your Bookmarks file as an HTML file. To add a bookmark in Netscape, click on the Bookmarks bar, and then select Edit Bookmarks. This opens your Bookmarks file, as shown in Figure 6-6. In this window, you can arrange your bookmarks into folders by clicking to expand folders, creating new folders, and dragging your bookmarks between folders.

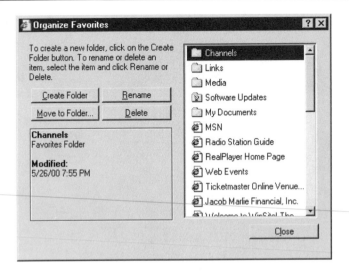

FIGURE 6-5 The Organize Favorites dialog box in IE

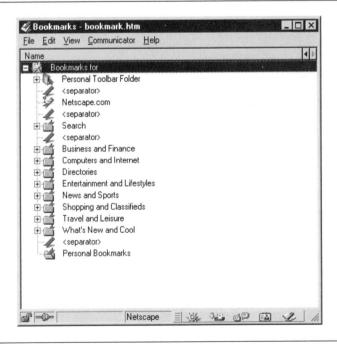

FIGURE 6-6 Netscape Communicator's Bookmarks file

Shopping on the Web

Contrary to what you may have read in the mainstream media, online purchasing is as risk-free as using you credit card anywhere else. Until banks offer the same level of protection to debit card holders that they offer to credit card holders, I recommend you use a credit card rather than a debit card for all online purchases. (Debit cards are those check cards that directly hit your checking account, but have Visa or Mastercard logos and are accepted everywhere that credit cards are.) By using a credit card, you can contest a debit before being forced to pay for it. Contact the bank issuing the credit card and begin a discussion regarding the false charge.

Encryption

Encryption is built into both IE and Netscape to offer online security. The highest security available for exports within U.S. and Canada is 128-bit encryption. Outside those borders, 40-bit security is the highest security available.

6

Rather than delve into the technical details of encryption, the best advice is to be sure you have a browser with 128-bit encryption enabled. Brute force computer attacks can break 40-bit encryption, but 128-bit offers sufficient extra security that it's worth seeking.

Cookies

Cookies are a necessary evil. When you shop online, you often store items for later purchase. Instead of storing this information on the site's server, the site instead places a small file in your computer—a *cookie* file—to store your selections. Next time you go to that site, you're saved the inconvenience of re-entering your shopping list.

There are two kinds of cookies: session and persistent cookies. Session cookies go away when you shut down your browser. Persistent cookies linger for some defined period of time. Persistent cookies can be used to identify you each time you show up at a site, so you don't need to log on or enter your address information each time. But persistent cookies do present a potential risk, because they can be also be used by evil-doers.

Because Web pages are often a collection of parts grabbed from across the Web, a machine that feeds your computer any part of a Web page can leave a cookie behind and fetch it later. This comes in handy for Web advertising firms, who can then tell that you viewed two separate ads on two distinct pages, but both ads were provided by the same ad company. They can track your interests and what you've clicked on. Using this type of information, such companies can start gathering a database of your preferences, without your knowledge. It's difficult, but not impossible, for them to tie these interests back to you directly.

What's the solution? You can disable cookie support in your browser, although this makes e-commerce sites a bit of a nuisance. To disable cookies in IE, select the Internet Options option from the Tools menu on the menu bar. Then click the Security tab shown in Figure 6-7. Set the security to High to disable cookies.

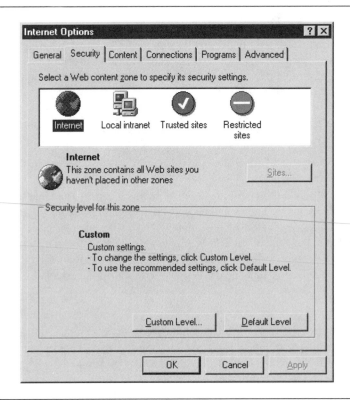

FIGURE 6-7   IE's Security tab page

To manage cookies in Netscape, select the Preferences option from the Edit menu on the menu bar, and then click on Advanced to see the options shown in Figure 6-8. You can disable or partially enable cookie support here. (Notice that Netscape provides more options for fine-tuning cookie settings than IE does.)

Another security option is to use cookie management software, which is a rapidly growing field. For example, Webwasher (www.webwasher.com) blocks advertising banners and their cookies without blocking other cookies, which is a good approach.

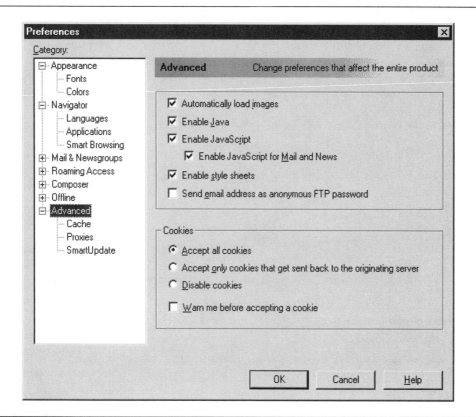

FIGURE 6-8   Netscape's cookie configuration

Controlling Objectionable Content

As you probably know, the World Wide Web holds the most diverse range of information and content of any library in the world. Unfortunately, that includes a vast array of material that you might deem objectionable. Especially if you're a parent, you'll be well advised to consider implementing some controls so that your kids cannot access sites on the Web that deal with adult information that is explicitly violent, sexual, or otherwise bad news. There is no perfect way of protecting yourself from it short of never going online. However, IE incorporates a feature called the Content Advisor, a tool to help you screen out much of the things you or the other people using your computer would rather not see.

The Content Advisor evaluates Web content using a rating system developed by RSACi (Recreational Software Advisory Council on the Internet). (You can use other rating systems, but this is the default.) You have to enable to Content Advisor manually, but once set up the Advisor can be password-protected so that only you can adjust the settings. To enable the Content Advisor, open the Internet Options dialog and perform the following steps:

1. In any IE Window click Tools, Internet Options.

2. Click the Content tab to bring it to the front, and then click Enable to open the Content Advisor dialog.

3. The Content Advisor dialog contains four tabs, as shown in Figure 6.9. On the Ratings tab you can move the slider back and forth to set a rating level in each of the four categories presented.

4. Click the Approved Sites tab to bring it to the front. List specific Web sites here to control access to them. Click Always to make it easily acceptable or Never to restrict access.

5. On the General tab, choose whether un-rated sites can be viewed. Keep in mind that many objectionable sites will not be rated. You can also set a password to let people in to un-rated or restricted sites on a case-by-case basis, or add another rating system here.

6. Click the Advanced tab. If you plan to use a ratings bureau or PICSRules file you obtain from the Internet, your ISP, or another source, add it here. Click OK when you are finished.

CAUTION

Rating of Web pages is voluntary. Web site owners are supposed to set the ratings for their sites in the "meta tags" of the sites, based on their own evaluation of their site's content. However, they don't always do this, and besides, their evaluation of what is objectionable may not align with yours. The RSACi periodically audits rated sites, and Web developers generally try to rate their sites as accurately as possible. However, if you really want to play it safe, you can disallow viewing of any unrated sites. The only down side to this is that you could inadvertently prevent your kids from viewing pages with innocuous or educational content that aren't rated.

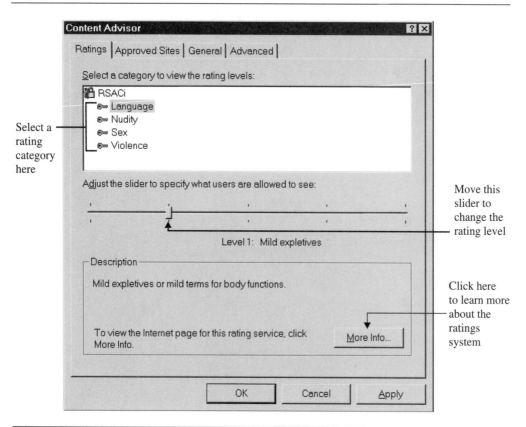

Select a rating category here

Move this slider to change the rating level

Click here to learn more about the ratings system

FIGURE 6-9   Move the slider back and forth to change the rating level

Chapter 7

Communicating with E-mail

How to...

■ Choose an e-mail program

■ Set up an e-mail account

■ Send and receive e-mail

■ Manage your e-mail address list

■ Use stationery and personal signatures in your messages

■ Organize your mail

■ Use AOL and Web-based accounts

■ Avoid e-mail viruses and spam

These days, it's likely to have happened to all of us. Our street address and telephone numbers aren't enough. Without an e-mail address, there are some people who can't seem to find a way to contact us, as if they think we have stepped off of the planet. And of course, no business, regardless of size or specialty, can seem to manage through a day's work without being e-mail enabled. Do you have friends who haven't returned a letter since the @ replaced the stamp and envelope (not to mention the trip to the post office)? Do they ask you how you can possibly survive without e-mail? If you're beginning to wonder the same thing, this chapter is for you.

Here are just some of the many benefits of e-mail:

■ You can keep in touch with family and friends all over the world, and feel confident that they've received your message almost instantly.

■ You can contact people at any time of day or night without worrying about waking them or interrupting a meal.

■ Whether your contacts are traveling or at home, you can use the same e-mail address to get in touch with them.

■ You can make scheduling meetings simple by contacting all attendees simultaneously.

■ You can maintain communications at a speed similar to a phone call for a fraction of the cost, or even for free, if you e-mail from a public computer.

■ It really is easier to click on the Reply button than to use an envelope and a stamp!

In this chapter, you'll learn all about using e-mail, starting with picking an e-mail program and ending with managing all of the mail you'll get once you have an e-mail address.

Selecting an E-mail Program

The first step in setting up your computer for use with e-mail is to choose the program you will use to read, write, and send messages. Even if you've already chosen an e-mail program, skim through this list to see if another one better suits your needs:

■ **Outlook Express**   This excellent e-mail program is bundled with Internet Explorer as a freebie with Windows. It is a fairly simple program that can handle both e-mail and newsgroups. You can create multiple accounts for other members of your family or colleagues in your office. It can also easily display formatted messages that have different kinds of fonts, colors, and so on (sometimes called HTML-formatted). Not all e-mail programs can do this.

> NOTE
>
> *Although it would seem that Outlook Express is a small sampler version of Microsoft Outlook (part of the Microsoft Office suite of applications), they are actually quite different programs. Outlook is a larger program, requiring more disk space, and has more features such as a personal calendar, journal, and fax capability.*

■ **Netscape Messenger**   A part of the Netscape Communicator package, Netscape Messenger is similar to Outlook Express in its handling of e-mail and newsgroups. It does not, however, have the ability to handle multiple e-mail accounts or identities, which is essential for many families and businesses.

■ **Eudora Pro**   This good-quality program from Qualcomm manages e-mail well and includes additional features such as voice messaging, McAfee Virus Scan protection against viruses sent through e-mail attachments, and a built-in compression agent that shortens download time when using a dial-up connection. It does not have a newsgroup reader.

■ **America Online**   The ubiquitous AOL is an ISP (Internet service provider) that also functions as an e-mail program, Web browser, and online community rolled into one. AOL is incredibly successful, yet it has some major shortcomings. For example, reading HTML-formatted mail or opening attachments is a pain in AOL. It is filled with features that can help you navigate the Web, but many find the multitude of features to be confusing and distracting.

> TIP
>
> *There are many other e-mail programs from which to choose. You can find a listing at http://dir.yahoo.com/Computers_and_Internet/Software/Internet/Email/.*

Obviously, you have numerous choices for your e-mail solution. This chapter focuses on Outlook Express, which comes with your computer, and also provides information about AOL and Web-based e-mail accounts.

Getting Started with Outlook Express

Outlook Express (OE for short) is easily accessible from your Windows desktop. To open the program, double-click on its desktop icon, click on the Outlook button on the quick-launch bar, or choose Start, then Programs, then Outlook Express. The first thing you'll want to do is maximize the window. The opening view of OE, shown in Figure 7-1, gives you an overview of OE's capabilities, but you may not find it useful on a daily basis. (See the "Reading Your E-mail" section later in this chapter for some suggestions on customizing your display.)

Setting up an E-mail Account

You need to have an e-mail account in order to send or receive e-mail. When you get an account with an ISP (see Chapter 6), you will receive the following information, which you'll need to have available when setting up your e-mail account in OE. (Don't worry about what it all means; just copy down the information carefully and keep it handy.)

- Your e-mail account and password
- The type of server to be used for incoming mail
- The names of the servers for incoming mail and outgoing mail
- The local phone number for access to your server

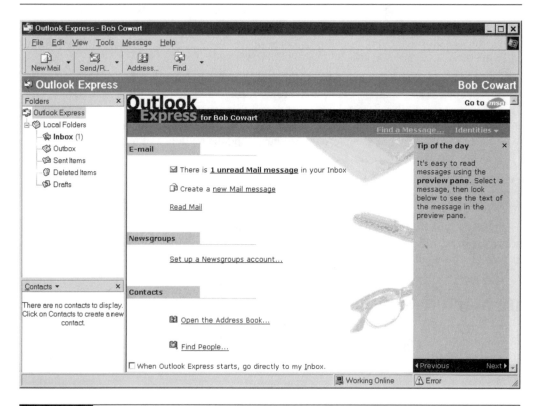

FIGURE 7-1   The opening view of Outlook Express

If you didn't get an e-mail account when you signed up with an ISP, or if you're using some offbeat means of getting onto the Internet (such as via a no-frills free service), you'll need to create a new one. First we'll cover using the e-mail address you got from an ISP, and then we'll go through the steps for creating a free Web-based e-mail account.

Using Your Existing Address

To set up OE with your existing ISP e-mail account information, follow these steps:

1. Start OE, and then click on Tools in the menu bar and select Accounts.

2. Click Mail tab, Add, Mail to start the Internet Connection Wizard, as shown in Figure 7-2.

3. Enter your name as you would like it to appear on the e-mail you send, and then click Next.

4. If you already have an e-mail address, click that option and enter your address in the E-mail Address text box, as shown in Figure 7-3. Then click Next.

7

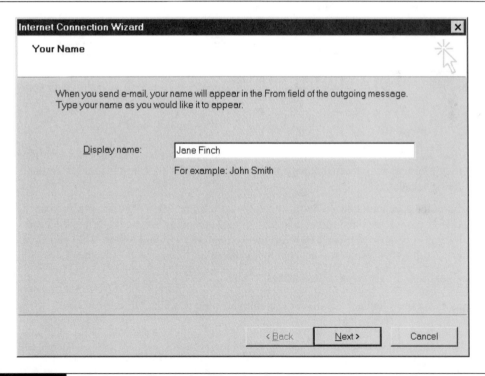

FIGURE 7-2   The Internet Connection Wizard makes it easy to set up an e-mail account

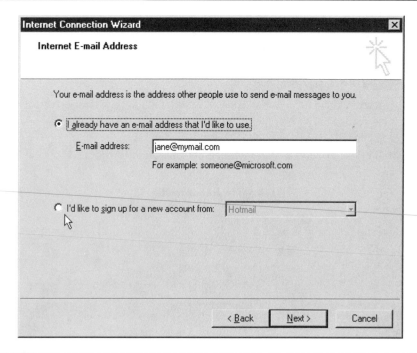

FIGURE 7-3 Entering your e-mail address in OE

5. You will be asked for the server names provided by your ISP. (This is where you'll need that information you jotted down earlier.) Enter the information in the text boxes, and then click Next.

6. Enter the account name and password that you selected when signing up with your ISP. If you are the only one with access to your computer, or you don't feel the need to protect your e-mail, you can select the Remember Password option. This saves your password so that you don't need to enter it every time you start the program.

7. Click Next, Finish to save the settings.

Repeat these steps for each additional account you want to add to OE.

Using a New Hotmail Address

If you don't have an e-mail address already, you can sign up for a new one. To sign up for a new Hotmail account, follow steps 1–3 in the previous section. Then select the option for signing up for a new account (see the lower section in Figure 7-3). When you click Next, Finish, you will be connected to MSN to sign up for a free Hotmail account.

If you would prefer to have an address with a different provider, go to their Web site and follow the directions there to sign up for new service. Then open OE and set up an account for this address by following the instructions for using an existing address. (See the "Using Web-based E-mail" section later in this chapter for more information about Web-based e-mail accounts.)

> **TIP**   *There are literally thousands of places to get a free e-mail address; www.hotmail.com and www.yahoo.com are two of the most popular. You can find a listing of providers at www.emailaddresses.com/guide_types.htm.*

Writing and Sending Your First E-mail Message

Now that you have set up an e-mail program and have an address of your own, you're ready to surprise your friends by sending your first e-mail message. Let's start with something simple. You can get an idea of what it all looks like in Figure 7-4.

Follow these steps to create a new e-mail message:

1. Open OE and choose New Message from the Message menu, click on the New Message button on the toolbar, or press CTRL-N. You will see a New Message window, with your own address already in the From box.

2. Move the cursor to the To box and enter the e-mail address of the person to whom you wish to write. Note that some e-mail addresses are case-sensitive. If you are not sure, use all lowercase letters.

3. Enter a subject in the Subject box. The subject is the first thing that recipients will see when they receive your mail, and it is also a handy way to keep track of incoming and outgoing messages, so it is a good idea to put a relevant subject here. Later on, when you want to look up this message, it will be easier to find it if the subject is "Movie tonight?" than if it simply says "Hi."

4. Move the cursor to the large box at the bottom of the window and write your message. It is as simple as if you were typing on a blank piece of paper in a typewriter. Here, though, you have the bonus of text-editing options similar to those in word processing, (such as a spelling checker) and a variety of fonts.

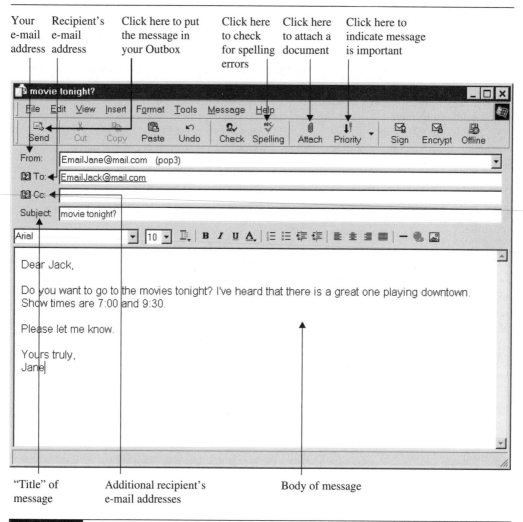

Your   Recipient's   Click here to put   Click here   Click here   Click here to
e-mail   e-mail   the message in   to check   to attach a   indicate message
address   address   your Outbox   for spelling document   is important
                                                errors

"Title" of   Additional recipient's   Body of message
message   e-mail addresses

FIGURE 7-4   Elements of an e-mail message

5. After you've composed your message, click on the Spelling button in the toolbar to use the spell check function. The spelling checker will start from the beginning of the message and look for typos. If a spelling error is found by the program, it'll ask you what to do, like this:

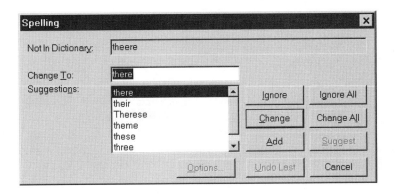

6. If the spelling checker finds any errors in your message, you can highlight the correct spelling and click Change, or if you want the word to remain as is (if it is a person's name or intentionally misspelled for some reason), click Ignore. The spelling checker will then move to the next error and ask you what to do. When the spelling check is complete, you will be notified in a separate window.

NOTE

The spelling checker cannot find every error, so look over the message yourself. For example, it won't let you know if you should have typed "its" instead of "it's," since they're both correct spellings individually.

7. When you are ready to send your message, choose Send Message from the File menu or click Send on the toolbar. When you choose to send an e-mail message, it goes into the Outbox folder, waiting to be sent. If you are currently connected to the Internet, the mail should be sent out almost immediately. If you are not online, it will stay in the Outbox until you are online.

That's it! Your first e-mail should be on its way, and if the recipient is online, it's possible that he or she is already reading it. That sure beats the postal service on delivery time.

TIP

If you want, you can opt to have your outgoing messages stack up in your Outbox, even while you're online, until you tell OE explicitly to send all your mail. This gives you a second chance to edit your messages. To do this, open the Tools menu, click Options, click the Send tab and turn off Send Messages Immediately. Then click OK. Now, when you want to send ad receive email, make sure you're online, and then click the Send/Receive All button on the toolbar. This sends out all messages that have accumulated in your Outbox. (As a keyboard shortcut, you can instead press CTRL-M or F5 to send and receive all of your mail.).

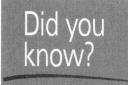

E-mail Etiquette

Some social critics have suggested that even though the Internet may be improving the typing and language skills of a populace that is becoming frighteningly illiterate, its contribution to polite and considerate interpersonal communications may be questionable. It only takes a few additional moments to look over your message to make sure that it is courteously worded before sending it, so please do. When composing your e-mail messages, the usual customs of etiquette (sometimes called *Netiquette*) apply:

- Include a greeting and a closing to your message.
- Use complete sentences.
- Use capital letters sparingly. Writing in all uppercase letters makes it seem like YOU ARE YELLING!
- Use both uppercase and lowercase letters and punctuation where appropriate, because they make the message easier to read.
- Include the original message in your e-mail, if you are responding to another person's message. (This is covered later in this chapter.)
- Before sending your message, use the built-in tools such as the spelling checker to ensure you haven't made any major spelling blunders.

All of these steps together will make your recipient feel that your message is worthy of attention and a response.

Sending Messages to Multiple Recipients

Now that you're getting the hang of sending messages without the need for envelopes and stamps, you might want to know about another feature that can save even more time. You can just as easily send a single message to multiple recipients. This is useful for sending party invitations to a slew of friends, announcing committee meetings, updating all your grandchildren on the latest activities down at the farm, and so on.

When you are sending out an invitation to your family members or a group of friends or colleagues that are already in contact with one another (or who will need to be), enter the e-mail addresses in the To field or the Cc field (see Figure 7-4, shown earlier). This will allow recipients to see the addresses of everyone to whom the message was sent. Put primary recipients in the To field, and those who should see a copy of the letter in the Cc field. (The Cc stands for courtesy copy, similar in function to carbon copy, a relic from the old days of writing multiple letters by inserting sheets of carbon paper between pieces of paper.)

If you are sending a message to a group of folks who don't know each other, it's considerate to enter their e-mail addresses in the Bcc field. (The Bcc stands for blind courtesy copy.) This feature hides the addresses entered here. If your distribution list is large, you certainly should use this feature; otherwise, your recipients will need to scroll through a long list of names and addresses before they can even begin to read your message.

To display the Bcc field, choose the All Headers option from the View menu. Your e-mail messages will now be displayed like this:

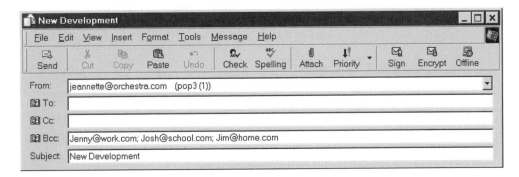

All recipients can still see addresses in the To and Cc fields, so enter the addresses carefully. This protects the privacy of others and can cut down on your recipients' spam (bulk e-mail). Just as you wouldn't carelessly give out a person's phone number or street address, you should be prudent when giving out e-mail addresses.

If you've set up names and e-mail addresses in your Address Book, you can click the To, Cc, or Bcc button in your outgoing e-mail message to bring up the Address Book in a separate window, as shown in Figure 7-5. Scroll through the names, and double-click those who should receive the message. Adding addresses to your Address Book is covered later in this chapter, in the "Managing Your Address Book" section.

Reading Your E-mail

By now, you should have some messages in your Inbox. To read your mail, click the Inbox folder in the Folder bar. No one wants to see an empty mailbox, so the folks at Microsoft made certain that you would have at least one e-mail message by including a welcome letter, which will appear in your Inbox the first time you open OE, as shown in Figure 7-6. If you've subscribed to any free services or made any purchases on the Internet, you are likely to be a very popular person indeed.

You will notice that the right side of the window is divided. A list of incoming mail appears in the top-right pane, showing the sender and the subject of each message, as well as the date and time it was sent. A preview of the selected message appears in the lower-right pane.

The simplest way to view your e-mail is by using the preview pane. Highlight one of the messages with a single-click to read it in the preview pane. Then you can quickly scroll through your messages by using the down or up arrows to highlight different ones.

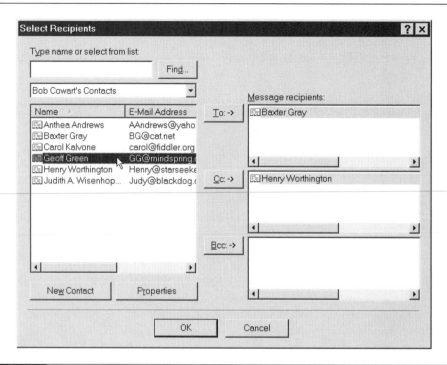

FIGURE 7-5   You can select your e-mail recipients from the Address Book

Alternatively, you can double-click a message in the upper pane, and it will appear in a separate window. After you read the message, close its window to help keep OE clutter-free. Otherwise, before you know it, you could have 10 windows open.

Since we all want to check our incoming mail frequently, the Inbox is likely to be the first thing you want to see when you open OE. You can change the opening view by choosing Options from the Tools menu and clicking the General tab. Select the When Starting, Go Directly to My 'Inbox' Folder check box, and then click OK.

Customizing the Inbox Display

There are several things you can do to customize the look of the Inbox. Figure 7-7 shows the Inbox with all elements displayed. As you can see, displaying every option can look a bit messy. Compare the window shown in Figure 7-7 with the simplified version shown in Figure 7-6.

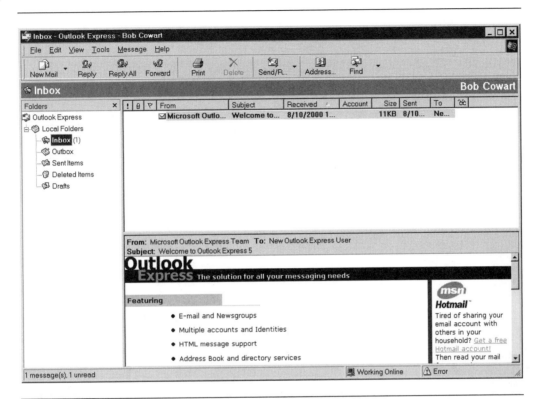

FIGURE 7-6   The OE Inbox shows your incoming messages

By hiding the panes you don't think you'll be using often, you will have a cleaner look and more room for the information that is important to you.

The Folders bar can be a helpful tool in organizing your mail and moving around OE (see the "Organizing Your E-mail with Folders" section later in this chapter). Click on the divider between the panes to make the Folders bar as narrow as possible while still displaying the folder names clearly. This way, you'll have more room to view your mail. The Outlook bar, an ineffective duplication of the Folders bar, is best kept hidden. The Contacts bar, which displays the first few entries in your Address Book, is not very helpful once you have more than about ten people listed. You can easily view your entire Address Book in a separate window when you're writing a new message (see Figure 7-5, shown earlier). See the "Managing Your Address Book" section later in this chapter for details on using the Address Book.

Folders bar   Incoming mail list

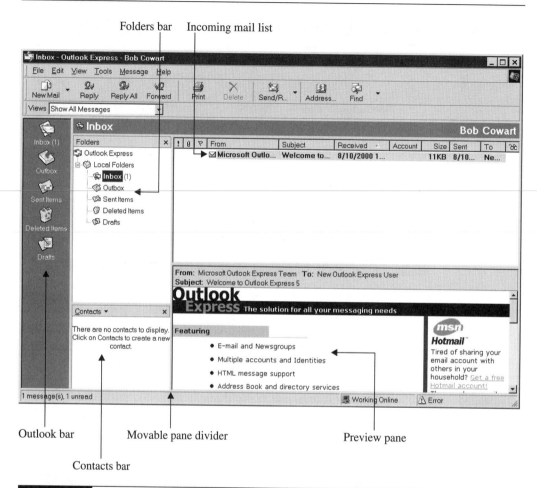

Outlook bar   Movable pane divider   Preview pane

Contacts bar

| FIGURE 7-7 | The Inbox window with all of its elements visible |

Choose Layout from the View menu to change the layout. The Window Layout Properties dialog box appears, as shown in Figure 7-8. In this dialog box, you can select or deselect the elements you would like to see or hide. Try a few different settings. If you decide you prefer a different look, just choose Layout from the View menu again and change the settings.

You can also change the sizes of the panes by moving the dividers separating the panes. To do this, click one of these bars and drag it until the pane is of desired size.

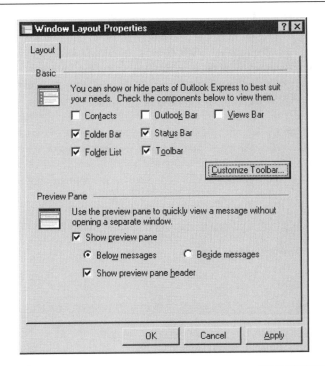

7

FIGURE 7-8 The Window Layout Properties dialog box allows you to design the look of your Inbox

Reading Your Mail at Another Time

When you want to quickly check your e-mail, but don't have the time to read every message, you'll want to know about a couple of features that will make it easier for you later: marking messages as unread and flagging messages.

Unread messages are listed in bold. If you've opened a message to skim it, but want to remember to read it fully later, you can mark it as "unread." Highlight the message by clicking it, and then choose Mark As Unread from the Edit menu. When you have a bit more time, you will be able to easily see those messages that were pushed aside.

If you have a message that requires more attention, you can flag it—literally. When you flag a message, a little red flag appears to the left of the message, making it easy to find. To flag a message, click in the Flag column to the left of the message in the list. If this column is not showing, choose Columns from the View menu and mark the box next to Flag. (This is also the place where you can choose the order and width of the columns.) You can also sort your messages to display the flagged ones first. Just click on the Flag button (to the right of the From header) in the row of column headers. (Sorting your messages is covered in more detail in the "Finding a Needle in the Haystack" section later in this chapter.)

Responding to E-mail

You can reply to a message directly from the preview pane view. Highlight the message and click on the Reply icon in the taskbar, press CTRL-R, or choose Reply to Sender from the Message menu. A separate window will open, displaying a new mail message with the From, To, and Subject fields already filled out. Type in your reply, and then click Send. The new window will disappear, and the message will go to your Outbox.

When a message is sent to a group of people, it is helpful in some cases to reply to everyone who received it, not just the sender. If someone is setting up a meeting, for example, it would be more helpful to respond to everyone with "Tuesday and Wednesday work for me, but I won't be available Friday," or "I'll bring a copy of the video – who has a projector?" To respond to the sender as well as all of the other recipients, click the Reply All button or choose Reply to All from the Message menu.

Be careful when using the Reply All command or button. If the message was originally sent out to, say, 50 people using the Cc feature, and you choose Reply to All, all 50 people will get your response.

Forwarding a Message

Did someone just send you a hot new tip, a picture of your grandson, or a joke that you think is actually worth sharing? You can forward a message to others by clicking the Forward button, pressing CTRL-F, or choosing Forward from the Message menu.

A word of caution: Think carefully before forwarding a message to a bunch of people (or to one person, for that matter). First, make sure that the original sender wouldn't mind if the message were circulated. Then, consider whether the forwarded message would be worth others' time. Just like the boy who cried "wolf," your recipients are likely to begin skipping over the messages you send if you're constantly forwarding those jokes and "did you knows" that are floating around the Internet. You'll also be guilty of tying up the Internet unnecessarily if you forward messages with the slightest whim.

Including Originals in Reply

It is usually a big help to include the sender's original message in your reply. With so many e-mail messages floating around these days, it can be difficult to keep track of the correspondence on a specific subject. By including the original message, the sender has a quick refresher on the subject at hand. To set up OE to do this for you, choose Options from the Tools menu, click the Send tab, and mark the box next to Include Message in Reply.

Keeping a Record of Messages You've Sent

Every time you send a message successfully, a copy of it is made and put into your Sent Items folder. You can turn off this feature, but I suggest you leave it on. It's a great way to keep track of what and when you've written. Often, especially in business correspondence, you'll want to

Did you know?

Chain Mail Can Litter the Information Superhighway

You may read alarming "news" in the form of chain letters that arrive in your e-mail box. Some letters look suspicious from the start, but others can fool even the most wary. When you see something like this in your Inbox, "Please sign and forward this petition to as many people as you can, before Congress permits the flying mongoose to have exclusive rights to our waterways, which will damage the ecosystem forever…," look into it before jumping to the conclusion that it is a true and a worthy cause.

The Internet can only transmit so much information at once. Just as too many cars on the highway can cause a traffic jam, e-mail can proliferate and get out of hand. One silly urban legend can end up spreading around the world and replicating at an exponential rate. So be considerate of others by helping to not bog down the Internet with unnecessary or redundant information.

Before forwarding any chain mail, investigate it further. You can check the validity of claims by going to one of these Web sites: http://ciac.llnl.gov/ciac/ CIACChainLetters.html#pbsnpr, http://urbanlegends.about.com/science/urbanlegends/ library/blhoax.htm, or www0.delphi.com/navnet/legends/legends.html.

review what you've written to a colleague. This is particularly useful if the other person fails to include the original e-mail message in his or her response to you. By simply opening your Sent Items folder, you can locate the original. (See the "Finding a Needle in the Haystack" later in this chapter for tips on how to quickly locate specific e-mail messages.)

Adding and Choosing Identities

OE allows you to create different "identities" for different users. This is a feature that families and small offices sharing a single computer may find useful. It's also convenient if you have a houseguest who would like access to e-mail. You can quickly set up a new identity for your guest without that person's mail interfering with yours. This can cut down on a lot of clutter for everyone, since each person's e-mail, Address Book, and preferences are kept separate.

To create a new identity, choose Identities from the File menu, and then select Add New Identity. Type the name you would like to use for this identity in the text box at the top of the window. If you would like to keep your information private, select the Require a Password check box. Click OK, and the identity will be added. A window will pop up asking you if you would like to switch to that identity. Note that OE must close to switch identities (it will reopen with the new identity).

When OE reopens with a new identity, it will look like it did when you first set it up. If you've already been using OE (under a different identity), you might panic. The Address Book and e-mail folders will be empty (except for the single e-mail that Microsoft includes with the program), and you'll need to reformat the look of OE to suit your needs. You can import your data by choosing Import from the File menu. You'll be guided through the steps of importing your messages, Address Book, and other data.

You can switch between identities by choosing Switch Identity from the File menu and selecting the identity (created earlier) to which you want to change. To modify or delete an identity, choose Identities from the File menu, and then select Manage Identities.

Using Digital Signatures

Because of the popularity and convenience of e-mail communications, and the unfortunate ease with which people can falsify their identity in e-mail, consumers began to ask for a way to ensure proof of the sender's identity. Programmers have developed a system that uses digital signatures, which are special documents that enable you to prove your identity in electronic transactions.

Before sending or receiving a message that is digitally signed or encrypted, you must get a digital ID. To do this in OE, choose Options from the Tools menu and click the Security tab. In this window, you can select the options to encrypt or digitally sign all of your outgoing e-mail. Click on Get Digital ID. You will be sent to a Web page that will instruct you how to obtain a digital ID.

After you have a digital ID, when you want to encrypt or digitally sign a message, choose Digitally Sign or Encrypt from the Tools menu when you are creating the new message.

Managing Your Address Book

It may only take a few messages for you to realize that e-mail addresses can be long and complex. A simple misspelling or unwanted capital letter is all it takes for your sent message to be bounced back to you. Fortunately, e-mail programs have an Address Book feature, which allows you to store names and e-mail addresses for easy access while composing messages.

Entering Information in the Address Book

When you're getting started, you'll probably need to add some names to the Address Book in the traditional way, as you do in your trusty leather binder, by entering the names and addresses by hand. There are also faster ways to add addresses.

Entering Addresses Manually

When someone has given you an e-mail address at a party or on a business card, you can open the Address Book and enter the address. In OE, choose Address Book from the Tools menu, or click Addresses on the toolbar. When the Address Book window opens, choose New Contact from the File menu, as shown in Figure 7-9 (you can also press CTRL-N to add a new contact).

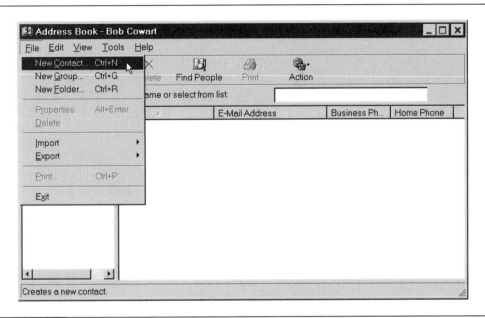

FIGURE 7-9   You can add new contacts through the Address Book window

You can enter as much or as little information as you want about each person. At a minimum, enter the person's name and the correct e-mail address, as shown in Figure 7-10. You may find it helpful to enter a nickname or some additional information about the person. After you've entered the information, click on Add. You can even use the OE Address Book as your primary address book. Just click the tabs along the top to access the other pages for adding more information.

Adding Names from Incoming Mail

When you begin to receive mail from others, you can add those names to your Address Book quickly and easily. Right-click the sender's name in the Inbox and select Add Sender to Address Book from the pop-up menu. This will open an Address Book window with the selected e-mail address already entered. You can click the text boxes or tabs to add additional notes about the person.

NOTE   *Sometimes, the sender is added directly to the Address Book without opening the Address Book window. To edit the entry, open the Address Book and double-click that contact's e-mail address.*

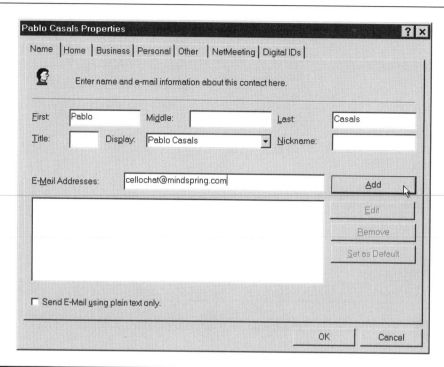

FIGURE 7-10   Entering information in an Address Book Properties dialog box for a contact

Adding Names Automatically

Another way to build up your Address Book is to allow OE to do it for you. Choose Options
from the Tools menu and click the Send tab to display the Send page of the Options dialog box,
as shown in Figure 7-11. Select the Automatically Put People I Reply to in My Address Book
check box and click OK. This can be a helpful feature, since the assumption is that if someone
is important enough to receive a reply, they're important enough to be in your Address Book.

Cleaning up Your Address Book

Since you want your Address Book to be helpful instead of mind-boggling, try to sort through
the contact information regularly and add identifying information. I've found that after about a
month of the automatic-add feature, I have a dozen or so entries that I can't identify. You may
find that you communicate with people with addresses such as coolcat3924809@mail.com. It
is a good idea to check to see that your Address Book contains your contacts' names as well
as their e-mail addresses. (If your contacts didn't disclose their names when they set up their
Internet accounts, OE cannot automatically include their names in the Address Book.)

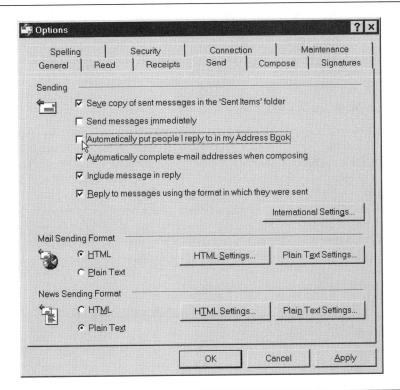

FIGURE 7-11   Choosing to have OE add names to your Address Book automatically

Not every contact deserves a place in your Address Book. For example, if you're communicating with a consumer representative from the Web site where you just bought your niece's birthday present, it's unlikely that you'll want to write to that person regularly. You can delete an entry by opening the Address Book, highlighting it in the list, and clicking on Delete.

Creating Groups

Do you write to a group of people regularly? Would you like to click on a single button to announce the Girl Scout camping trip? If so, you can create a group in your Address Book.

To create a group, open the Address Book and choose New Group from the File menu. Enter a name for the group. Then click Select Members and enter names from your Address Book. When you are finished, click OK.

After you create a group, it will appear as a new entry in your Address Book. Simply enter the name of the group in the To field (or use Bcc if appropriate), and your message will be on its way to every member of the group.

Creating Unique (HTML) E-mail

Just like a word-processing program, OE allows you to use a variety of styles, sizes, and colors of text. You can even have a background (called stationery) or a virtual letterhead (called a signature).

To HTML or Not to HTML

HTML is an acronym for Hypertext Markup Language, and it's the programming language that is used to create Web pages. HTML is what allows you to create a fancy message, filled with colors, a variety of fonts, pictures, and even the electronic equivalent of stationery. The good news is that you don't have to be a programmer to use HTML in your e-mail. Then why not use this all the time?

The problem is that there are a lot of folks out there whose e-mail programs translate all of these fancy options to gobbledy-gook and make your message difficult or impossible to read. Figures 7-12 and 7-13 show the difference. For the folks who don't get HTML mail, you'll want to use plain text. Choose Plain Text from the Format menu before you send your message.

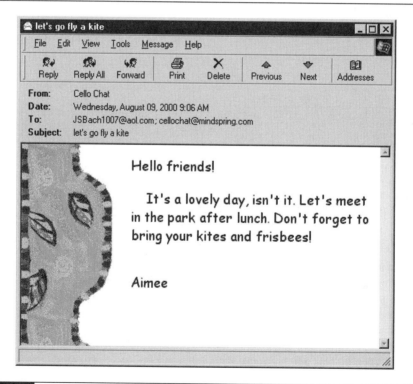

FIGURE 7-12   HTML mail as it was meant to be

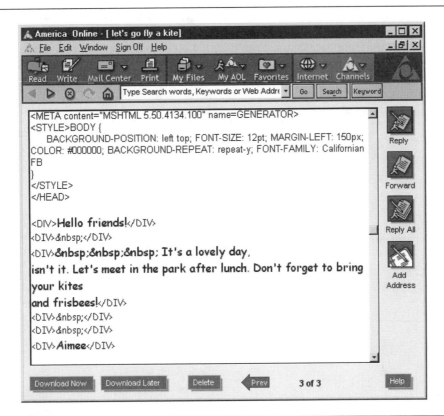

FIGURE 7-13   HTML mail seen on a program or through a server that can't view it properly

> **TIP**   *You may not know if a certain recipient can read HTML mail or not. If it is an important message, it's best to send it in Plain Text or ask first.*

To have OE remind you of the recipients who should get plain text messages, you can mark this preference in their Address Book entry. Open the Address Book, double-click the contact you want to mark, and click the Name tab. At the bottom of the dialog box, select the Send E-Mail Using Plain Text Only check box (see Figure 7-10, shown earlier). When you try to send a message to this person using HTML, a pop-up window will appear warning you to send it as plain text.

Using Stationery

If you are beginning to feel nostalgic for the days when you would walk down to the dime store and pick out a new box of stationery to impress and delight your pen pals, you'll appreciate the Stationery feature of OE. Just as you can choose from a variety of stationery at the store, you can select colorful backgrounds for your e-mail. An advantage here is that you can choose a different design for each new message without having to use up an entire box of stationery.

To send a message using the electronic equivalent of stationery, open a New Message window and be certain that you are creating the message in HTML. The Rich Text (HTML) option should be selected on the Format menu. Then choose Apply Stationery from the Format menu. A list of pre-designed stationery options will appear, as shown below. Click one of them to apply it to your current message.

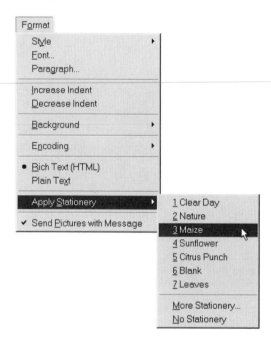

Did you notice the More Stationery option listed on the Apply Stationery submenu? If you want to create your own stationery, choose this option and click Create New. This will take you to the Stationery Setup Wizard, shown in Figure 7-14, where you can add pictures, patterns, colors, and fonts.

Select the picture and color for your stationery background. Click the Next button to move to the page for specifying the margins of your stationery, as shown in Figure 7-15. If you've added a border, make sure to increase the margin so that your text will not overlap with the image.

The final step is to give your new stationery a name. Make it descriptive so that you can find it easily (the name My Stationery is not going to help much, once you've created more than one design).

Personalizing Your Messages with Signatures

An e-mail signature is a useful feature with a function similar to letterhead. With the simple click of a mouse, you can add personalization at the beginning, middle, or end of an e-mail message (although it is customary, in e-mail, to add your signature at the end). You can choose to list your

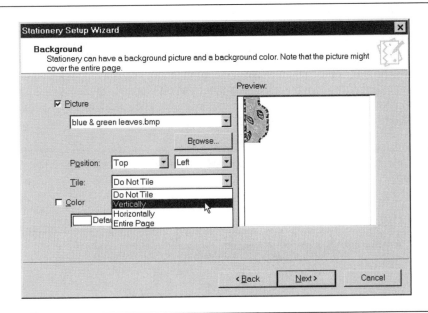

FIGURE 7-14   The Stationery Setup Wizard allows you to create your own stationery

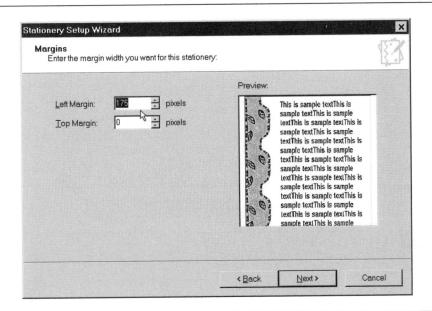

FIGURE 7-15   Setting stationery margins

name, phone numbers, addresses, profession, a mini-resume, and even a favorite quote. You can create multiple signatures here for different purposes. You may want to have one for business use and a different one for personal use.

To set up a signature, choose Options from the Tools menu and click on the Signatures tab to open the Signatures page of the Options dialog box, as shown in Figure 7-16. Click New to add a signature. Name the signature in the upper text box. Add the elements of the signature in the lower text box. To add a signature to every outgoing message, select the Add Signatures to All Outgoing Messages check box. Finally, click Apply.

If you would rather have more control over when your signature is added to a message, leave the Add Signatures to All Outgoing Messages box unchecked. When you are ready to insert a signature into an e-mail, choose Signature from the Insert menu and select one of the signatures you have created.

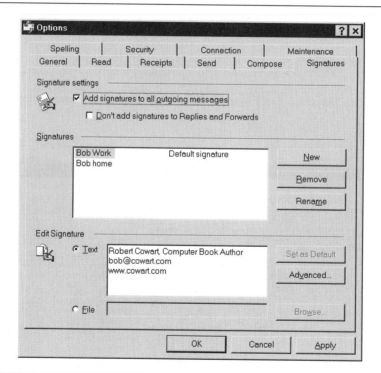

FIGURE 7-16 Creating a signature for your e-mail

Sending and Receiving Attachments

Besides providing a convenient way to write messages, e-mail offers the powerful capability to transfer files. Many types of document and image files can be attached to an e-mail message, just as you would include a current project outline on a separate piece of paper when sending a letter in an envelope.

Sending Attachments

To attach a document to an e-mail message, click the Paperclip button (Attach) in your message. OE displays the Insert Attachment dialog box, which is a standard file-browser dialog box, as shown in Figure 7-17. Select the file(s) you want to send and click the Attach button in the dialog box.

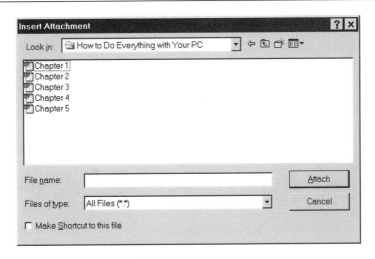

FIGURE 7-17   Attaching a document to an e-mail message

The file name will appear in the Attach text box of your e-mail message, as shown here. You can repeat the procedure to attach multiple files to the message.

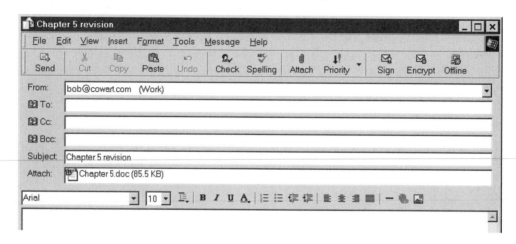

It is a good idea to let the recipient know that you are attaching a document to the e-mail message. Otherwise, the recipient may suspect that the attachment is unknown to you, making it a likely candidate for a virus (e-mail viruses are discussed later in this chapter, in the "Protecting Against Viruses and Unwanted Mail" section). It is also thoughtful to say in the Subject line or body of the message what type of file is attached, such as "Excel 2000 file attached," so the recipient will know the best way to open it.

When you're sending e-mail attachments, you should try to keep the size of an individual e-mail message as small as possible. It can be cumbersome to have your Inbox filled with large files, and annoying when your work is put on hold by an incoming e-mail. (Computers will slow down considerably while receiving a large file.) Your goal is to create interesting and eye-catching e-mail, without creating problems for the recipient.

 If you're sending your entire photo collection of your latest family trip, make sure your recipient has a fast Internet connection, or prepare to lose a friend.

The maximum size allowed for attachments depends on the rules of the server machines involved in the transaction (your ISP and the one that your recipients use). Typically, however, it's about 5MB. Most documents will fall well under this, but video files and high-resolution digital photographs may push the limit. Check the size of the attachment before sending by looking in the Attach text box (next to the name of the file that you've attached).

To give you an idea of how long it takes to download files, if you're sending a 100K file, it will take about 28 seconds to download with a connection speed of 28.8Kbps, or about 14 seconds with a connection speed of 56.6Kbps. Now consider what happens when you send a 5M file. With a 28.8Kbps connection, this takes a bit more than 24 minutes; with a 56.6Kbps connection, the download time is a bit more than 12 minutes.

NOTE   *Dial-up connections with modems typically are about 28.8Kbps or 56.6Kpbs. DSL (digital subscriber) and cable connections provide much faster connections.*

How to ...   **Send a Web Page**

7

Suppose that you're surfing the Web and find something that Uncle Charlie might find interesting. You could write him an e-mail and laboriously type in the www.blahblahblah stuff and risk misspelling it, which is a pain. But here's a trick to make it easy to share Web pages with people. You can e-mail the page directly from your browser, using e-mail. Here's how:

1. Go to the Web page that you want to tell someone about.

2. Click the Mail icon when you are viewing the page, and select Send Page.

3. A New Message window will open. Enter an address as you would for any e-mail message. You can even add text by typing in the body of the message, as you would ordinarily do when composing an e-mail message. The Web page will drop down as you add text to the top of the message.

4. When you're ready, send the e-mail message to the lucky recipient.

Receiving Attachments

If someone has sent you an e-mail containing an attachment, the paperclip symbol will be in the upper-right corner of the preview pane for that message, and just to the left of the sender's name in the Inbox list. You have two choices: you can open an attachment or save it to disk.

To open an attachment (one that you do not want to edit), click the Paperclip button in the preview pane. Highlight the attachment you wish to view and click it. A dialog box will appear, asking you what to do with the file, as shown here.

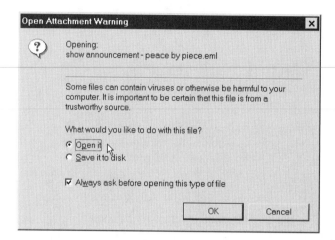

If you are confident with the sender of the attachment (see "Protecting Against Viruses and Unwanted Mail" later in this chapter), click Open It. A new window containing the attachment will open. When you have finished reading the attachment, close the window. Remember not to edit an attachment opened this way.

In Outlook Express, image attachments, such as .gif and .jpg files, will display in the e-mail body itself; you don't have to manually open such attachments to view them. Just scroll down the e-mail preview window and you should see images.

If you will be editing and returning the document, save it to the hard disk first, under a new name. Choose Save It to Disk when you're asked what to do with the file. OE will display the Save Attachment As dialog box, allowing you to browse through your computer to choose a place to store the document, as shown in Figure 7-18. When you've found the folder you want to save it in, click the attachment's name in the File Name text box. So that you don't confuse it with the original attachment, rename the file by entering a new name in the text box. Otherwise it's stored under some very cryptic name in a weird "temp" directory somewhere. Now you can view the document at any time by opening Windows Explorer and opening the folder and file that you've set up.

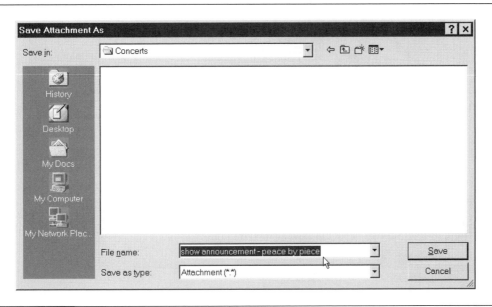

FIGURE 7-18   Saving an attachment to disk

Managing Your E-mail

I like to keep copies of most of the e-mail that I send and receive, and just when I think I might never need a message again, an occasion arises when it's helpful to refer to it. If you also save your messages, you'll soon find that you need a system for organizing all of them, finding specific ones, and clearing away the ones you really don't need. You'll also want to back up your mail and Address Book.

Organizing Your E-mail into Folders

OE allows you to arrange your message into different folders. This makes keeping track of an ongoing conversation easy. It also helps to keep your Inbox manageable.

When you highlight the heading Local Folders in the Folders bar, you will see a list of the folders that already exist, such as Inbox, Outbox, Sent Items, and Drafts. To create a new folder, right-click on Local Folders and choose New Folder to bring up the Create Folder dialog box, as shown in Figure 7-19. Make sure that Local Folders is highlighted in the folder list in this dialog box. By adding all your new folders to the main list, they will be easy to see in the Folder bar. (Later on, you can get fancy by adding folders inside of other folders you've created.) Enter a name for the new folder in the Folder Name text box at the top of the dialog box, and then click OK. The new folder will now be listed, alphabetically, in your Folders bar.

To rename a folder, simply right-click on the folder, choose Rename, and enter the new name in the text box. To delete folders from the Folders bar, first be certain that you do not need

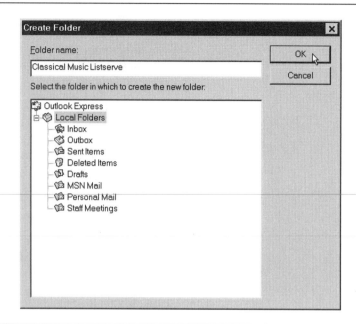

FIGURE 7-19   Creating a new OE folder

any of the messages that are stored in the selected folder. Then right-click its name in the Folders bar and choose Delete. (If you've made a mistake, you can retrieve it from your Deleted Items folder before it's emptied.)

Moving Messages Between Folders

Your new folders can function as working folders, storage folders, or both. After you have responded to a message that you want to save, move it from your Inbox to the storage folder.

You may anticipate receiving messages about a project that you would like to keep separate from other mail. You can move this mail to a folder before you even read it. OE will remind you that a folder contains unread mail by displaying the folder name in bold.

When you want to keep close tabs on a current project, begin the folder's name with an A, such as A house search instead of just house search. This will place the folder at the top of your list for easy access. Once the project is completed, you can rename the folder, deleting the "A", and the folder will drop down to its place in the list alphabetically.

To move a message from your Inbox to a different folder, highlight the message in the right pane and drag it to the desired folder in the left pane. To drag multiple messages, click the first message, hold down the SHIFT key, and pull your mouse to the last message you want to move. Click again in the list (which will now be highlighted) and drag the messages to the desired folder.

Automatically Directing Incoming Mail to Folders

If dragging messages into folders becomes too tedious, you can have OE sort your mail for you. You can keep messages about specific topics out of the Inbox altogether by having OE search for certain messages and put them directly into a folder you specify. (This is particularly useful if you've joined a group that regularly exchanges messages.)

You set up this automatic sorting by establishing *message rules* for your mail. As an example, suppose that you want to move relevant messages into a folder labeled Staff Meetings. Here are the steps:

1. Click the Tools menu and select Message Rules, Mail. The New Mail Rule dialog box will open, as shown in Figure 7-20. In this dialog box, you can set up the conditions under which a message should be acted upon, as well as the action that should be taken. This can involve one or more actions, including moving, copying, deleting (careful!), forwarding e-mail messages, and more.

2. In the top section, labeled 1. Select the Conditions for Your Rule, select the Where the Subject Line Contains Specific Words check box. Your new condition will appear in the 3. Rule Description section of the dialog box.

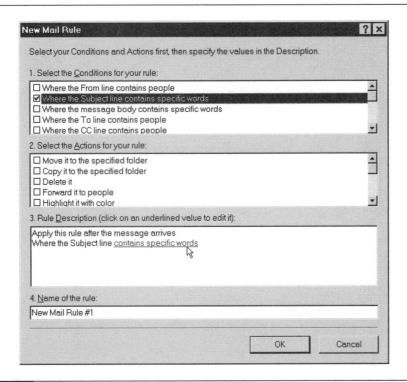

FIGURE 7-20   Creating a new mail rule

7

3. Click the underlined portion of the description (which is in blue). A new dialog box will open, as shown below. Enter words here that are sure to be in the subject line of incoming mail you want to redirect. For example, if your office circulates e-mail announcing staff meetings with subject lines like "Staff Meeting Friday," and "Staff Meeting postponed," it is safe to say that **Staff Meeting** would be an appropriate entry here. After you've entered the words, click Add, and then OK. You will be returned to the previous window.

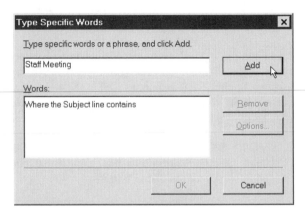

4. In the 2. Select the Actions for Your Rule section, select the Move It to the Specified Folder check box. In the Rule Description section, this instruction appears with *specified* underlined and in blue.

5. Click the underlined word. A dialog box with a list of folders appears, as shown here. Highlight your chosen destination folder, and then click OK. You will be returned to the previous window.

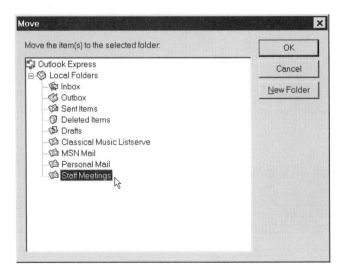

6. Enter a name for this rule in the Name of the Rule section of the dialog box.

7. To complete the task, click OK twice. Now OE is set up to look for and move any message with "Staff Meeting" in its subject.

Once you've created a rule or two, don't forget to look beyond the Inbox for new mail. A folder name in bold indicates that the folder contains unread e-mail, as shown here.

> *A rule applies only to new mail. It doesn't sort mail that you've already received. You'll need to do this yourself. (See the previous section for instructions on moving messages between folders.)*

NOTE

Finding an Elusive Piece of E-mail

Often, we remember who sent the message we're looking for, so it's as simple as looking through messages from that person to find the information we need. It is possible to sort by sender, subject, date, or a variety or other characteristics by simply clicking on the appropriate heading at the top of the mail pane, as shown here. To sort by sender, for example, click the From button.

Sorting your messages can help you find the one you're looking for in many cases, but what if all you remember is a specific reference within the message (who was it that said something about the redwood forest?). OE's Find function lets you search for a word or phrase in a message or subject. Choose Find from the Edit menu, and then choose Message. You'll see the Find Message dialog box, as shown in Figure 7-21. Fill in the applicable fields to supply information about the message you are trying to locate, and then click Find Now.

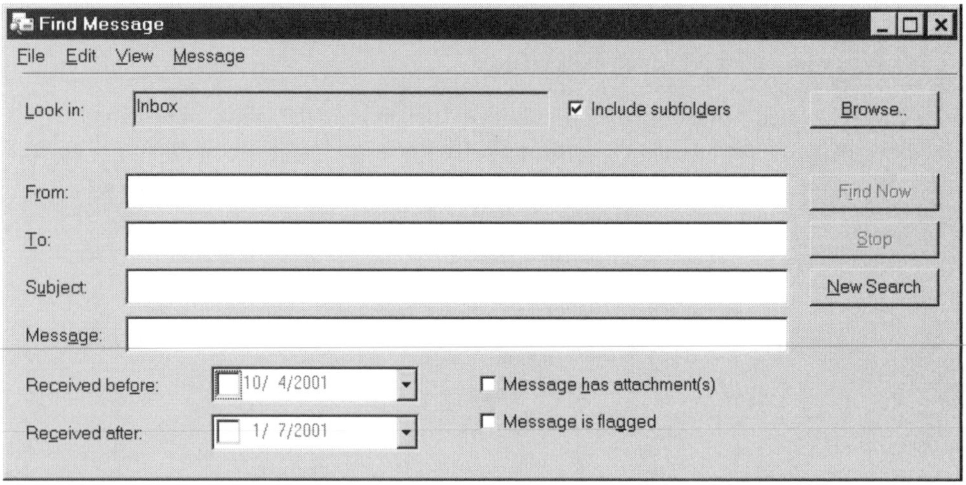

FIGURE 7-21   Finding a message

Cleaning up Your Folders

From time to time, it is a good idea to sort your mail by size (by clicking on the Size column header in the mail pane), and look for especially large files that should be deleted. Each folder must be sorted individually. One common culprit is the Sent Items folder. If you have sent pictures or a Web page to someone, and those messages remain in your Sent box, they will use up a large amount of memory.

Also remember to empty your Deleted Items folder regularly. This is another common place where hard disk space is used unnecessarily. Right-click the Deleted Items folder and choose Empty 'Deleted Items' Folder. If you don't want to be regularly bothered with this chore, you can open the Tools menu, choose Options and click the Maintenance tab. On the Maintenance page, shown in Figure 7-22, make sure that the Empty message from the 'Deleted items' Folder on the Exit check box is not selected. This option sets the program to empty the folder automatically whenever you exit Outlook Express.

Backing up Your Mail

Backing up your mail and address list is very important. If you don't know why, you are either a very lucky person or you have owned a computer for only a few days. Things happen—a few keys get pressed accidentally, the power goes out, or your computer crashes. For those and countless other reasons, it can save you time and headaches to back up your files regularly.

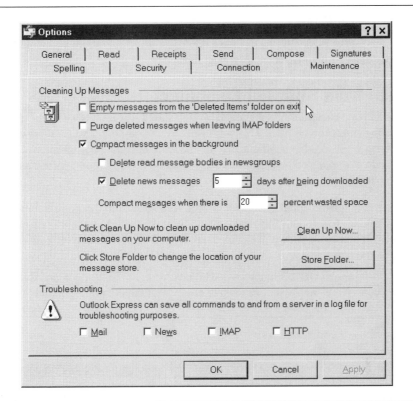

FIGURE 7-22   The Maintenance page of the Options dialog box includes options for automatically cleaning up your messages

Follow these steps to back up your saved e-mail messages:

1. In OE, compact your folders by clicking the File menu and choosing Folder, Compact All Folders.

2. Open Windows Explorer and find the folder file containing your email. (Your email files are typically stored in the vicinity of the folder \Windows\Application Data\Identities....) If you have multiple mail identities, there will be several directories. You might have to do a little sleuthing to determine which one you want. OE mail folders have a .dbx extension. So, if you want to backup "Business Deals 2002," you're looking for a file called "Business Deals 2002.dbx." A quick way to find it is by searching for it with the Start button's Search command.

3. Copy the files to a backup folder, network drive, or floppy disk. (Usually, a floppy disk is not a practical choice, since many message files are too large to back up onto a floppy disk.)

You can back up your Address Book by exporting it to a file. Open your Address Book in OE and choose Export from the File menu, Address Book. A standard file-save dialog box will appear, as shown in Figure 7-23. Choose or create the folder and drive where you would like a backup copy to be stored. It will be saved as a .wab file.

Using E-mail from Different Computers

If you use more than one computer, it's a good idea to choose a single one to be your main computer for storing and sorting e-mail. This way, you have a consistent thread of messages on a single machine, while still having the luxury of checking in from other machines.

You need to adjust settings on both your remote e-mail computer (or computers) and your main e-mail computer, as follows:

■ In OE, on each remote email computer, choose Accounts from the Tools menu and double-click on an account. Click the Advanced tab and select Leave a Copy of Messages on Server, as shown in Figure 7-24. Repeat this procedure for each account, and on each remote computer.

■ On your main e-mail computer, choose Accounts from the Tools menu and double-click on an account. Click the Advanced tab and ensure that the option to bring in your mail and remove it from the server is enabled. Repeat this procedure for each account.

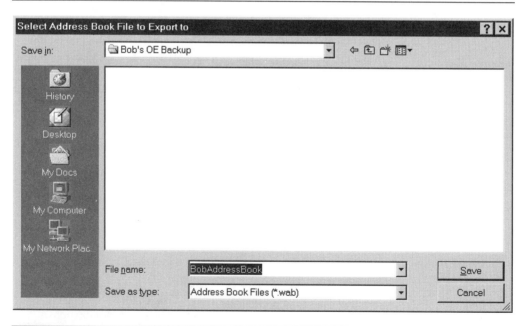

FIGURE 7-23   Exporting your Address Book

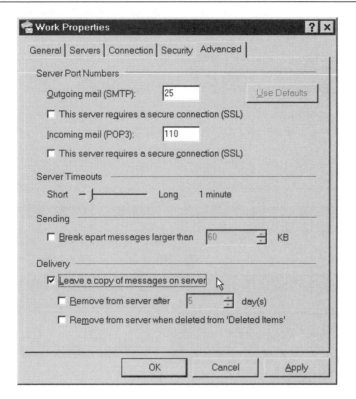

FIGURE 7-24   Setting up a remote (secondary) e-mail computer

Using America Online

Now that you've read about all the great things you can do using e-mail programs like Outlook Express, you may wonder why so many people still choose AOL. One reason is that people are tempted to load the software on their machine that they receive, unsolicited, in the mail. They get it going, enjoy the free minutes, and by the time the trial period is up, they don't want to bother contacting another ISP and changing their address.

Since AOL is such a large company, it has another advantage. There is likely to be a local access number in nearly every place you're traveling, with a good dial-up connection speed. This can be a real convenience when you're moving around with your laptop and you want to plug it into a phone line and get some work done… at a hotel, a friend's home, or even an airport.

If possible, I recommend that you avoid AOL and take advantage of the multitude of e-mail and Web browser programs available. However, perhaps you're stuck with AOL, because your office chose to use it, you live in an area that does not yet have many ISP options, or your parents picked it for the home account and you can't get them to change their minds. (Let your folks read this book, and try again.) For whatever reason, if you're still set on going with AOL, I'll give you a few pointers.

Figures 7-25 and 7-26 show two views of AOL. As you can see, the multiple windows, icons, and general arrangement make it difficult to find the information you need.

TIP   *If you're overwhelmed with the number of windows open in AOL and want to focus on a single window you've selected, choose Close All Except Front from the Window menu.*

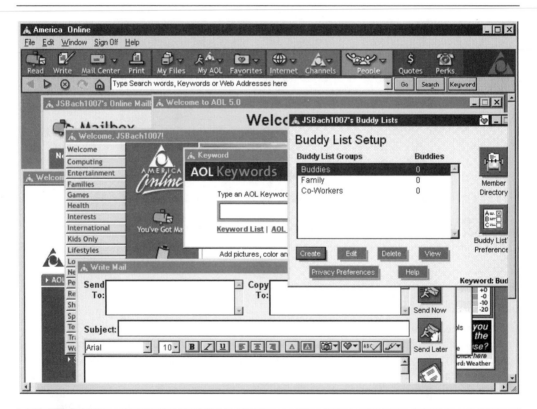

FIGURE 7-25   A typical view of AOL after you've opened a few things; it's a confusing jumble of windows that are difficult to switch between

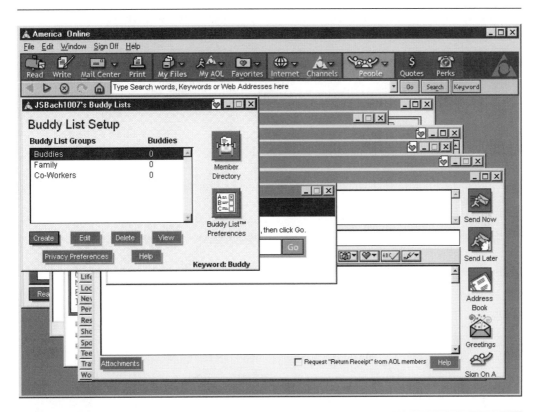

FIGURE 7-26   A slightly cleaner view of AOL, after choosing Window, Cascade; it's not much better

Opening Attachments in AOL

Opening attachments is difficult and cumbersome, for the AOL customer as well as the person on the other end who receives the mail sent through AOL. When you receive an e-mail message with a disk icon attached, this indicates that there is a file attached to the message. You will need to download the file while you are online. Pay attention to where you tell your computer to save this file, because you will need to remember this in order to read the attachment. The most likely place it will go is in a Download folder in AOL. Open Windows Explorer and look for these folders. Once you've downloaded a few attachments, though, it can be difficult to locate a specific one (especially since a single attachment is often broken up into several files).

To make it easier to find these files later, you can create a new folder when AOL brings you to the Download Manager.

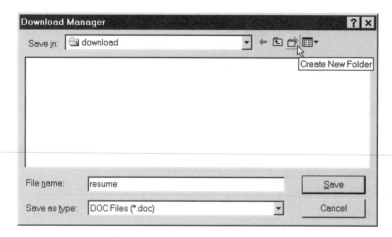

Here are the steps for creating a new folder in AOL:

1. Give the folder a name that clearly identifies the attachment you are downloading, such as Resume. If you don't know what the attachment is, give it a temporary name, such as the sender's name and the date it was sent. Then view the attachment and rename it.

2. Double-click the new folder to open it, and then click Save.

3. Now you can find this attachment more easily. Open Windows Explorer and go to the AOL\downloads\resume folder. Choose AOL, Downloads, Resume.

4. You will find the elements of the attachment in that folder. Click one of the more significant-looking files and hope for the best. It's likely that you won't need to view every file in the folder.

TIP   *When you're forwarding an e-mail using AOL, you can make it easier for the recipient by opening the message and copying and pasting it into a new message. This way, the forwarded message will appear in the simple form of a regular e-mail message instead of as an attachment.*

Using a Different E-mail Program with AOL

One software development company, eNetBot, has a program that allows you to bring your AOL mail into an e-mail program of your choice. (It works with Outlook Express, Netscape, Eudora, and others.) Download the software at www.enetbot.com, and install the program to begin receiving your AOL mail in OE. (It will only import mail still on the AOL server, so the mail you've already downloaded can not be transferred using eNetBot.)

You'll need to have eNetBot and OE (or another e-mail program of your choice) running simultaneously in order for this to work. The eNetBot window, shown in Figure 7-27, can be a

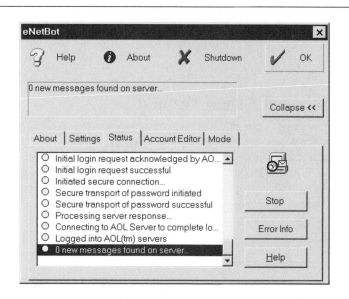

FIGURE 7-27   The eNetBot window

little annoying, since it remains in the front even if you click on another window. To hide the eNetBot window, click OK in the upper-right corner of the window. You'll see the icon in your system tray when the program is running.

The bad news is that you'll still have difficulty opening attachments or viewing Web pages that others have sent to you. Web pages are sent through eNetBot and AOL in a WinZip file that contains all of the separate components of the Web page. It's similar to receiving eggs, butter, and flour when you were expecting a cake.

Using Web-based E-mail

If you don't have a laptop or Palm-type device with you, how can you check your e-mail when you're on the road? What if your PC dies—how do you get your e-mail then? Yahoo! *et al* have a solution for you. They want you to see their banner ads, but the price is a small one to pay. Here's how it works: All you need is an Internet connection and a browser. (A computer helps, too.) You can find these almost anywhere these days—at a friend's house, in a public library, or in the increasing number of establishments known as cyber-cafes.

Cyber-cafes worldwide are making Web-based e-mail accessible even in remote corners of the globe. I have a friend who returned from a recent trekking trip in Nepal, even a bit disappointed with how easy it was to get his e-mail during his trip. That didn't stop him, though.

Creating a Web-based E-mail Account

There are many places where it is possible to get a free e-mail account. Web sites like www.hotmail.com and www.yahoo.com make signing up quick and easy. Just go to the Web site (for example, enter www.yahoo.com), look for an e-mail link (Check Email, or something of the sort), and click it. Figure 7-28 shows the Yahoo! Mail page. You will be guided through the process of creating a new account. After choosing an e-mail address and password and answering a few questions, your account will be set up and ready to use.

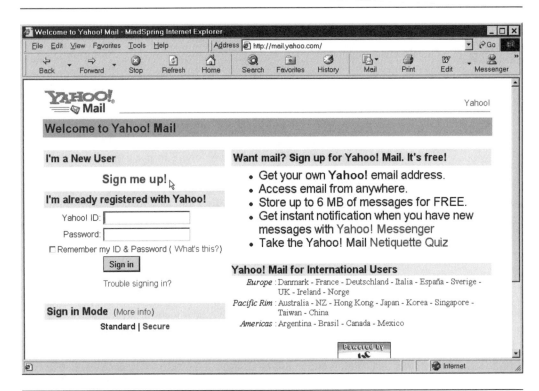

FIGURE 7-28   Signing up for, and signing in to, Yahoo! Mail

When you set up a Web-based account, consider creating an anonymous e-mail identity. You might find that there are times that you want to send e-mail while maintaining your privacy. If your standard e-mail account is RebeccaBrown@home.com, you may find it useful to create a different address such as Bluebird@hotmail.com.

This type of account can also reduce the amount of spam (unsolicited e-mail) entering your Inbox. When you fill in Web forms or order stuff over the Internet, you are often asked for your e-mail address. If you use your anonymous e-mail identity on such forms, the spam resulting from this transaction will be kept separate. Since you can sort and delete messages directly at the site of your Web-based account, you can sign up for online promotions without fear of a crowded Inbox or follow-up phone calls. See the "Protecting Against Viruses and Unwanted Mail" section later in this chapter for more on spam.

> **TIP**
>
> *If you have a Hotmail account and want to keep it separate from the mail you bring into OE, MSN can notify you of new Hotmail while you are online. In OE, choose Options from the Tools menu and click on the General tab. Select the Automatically Log on to MSN Messenger Service check box. (Or, you can log on to the MSN Messenger Service manually, whether or not OE is open.) An icon will appear in the system tray, and a small window will pop up in the lower-right corner when you are online and you receive new Hotmail. Click the window to go to the Hotmail Web site and read your mail online.*

Checking Your Home E-mail from a Remote Computer

Now that you have a Web-based e-mail account established, did you know that you can use it to gain access to your normal, home e-mail account? This is a real godsend when you're expecting an important message and you don't have the time to run home to check your email there.

Here's the general game plan:

1. Open a Web browser window, go to the service's Web page (for example, enter www.yahoo.com), and click the e-mail link there. For example, with Yahoo!, click Check Email.

2. Log into your Web-based account. Enter your user name and password, and click the Sign In button.

3. Now look for Options (or another place to change your preferences), and then look for something like Check Other (POP) Mail or Check Other Mail. Select this option, and you will be guided through the process of entering information so that you can check mail from your other accounts. For example, when you click Check Other (POP) Mail in Yahoo!, you will go to another page where you should click Add Mail Server.

4. A new window will open, as shown next, where you'll need that information from your ISP that you entered when you set up your main e-mail account. (See the "Setting

up an E-mail Account in Outlook Express" section earlier in the chapter.) Enter the information, and then click OK.

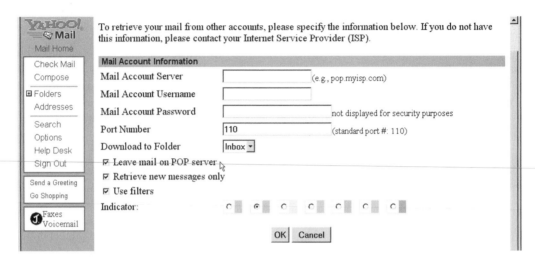

 Make sure the Leave Mail on POP Server check box is selected if you want to pull all of your mail into your computer when you return home. Otherwise, your mail will be in multiple locations and difficult to organize.

Saving Information Online

You can also use your Web-based account as a virtual filing cabinet. Let's say you're on vacation when you meet a person who could be a valuable business associate. You've left your resume and business plan in your office (you're supposed to be taking a break from work, after all), so you don't have them handy. However, if before your went on your trip you sent an e-mail, with the documents attached, to your Web-based e-mail account, you can go to any computer and open the files. Then you have the options of printing your documents or forwarding the e-mail with the attachments to your new contact.

There is a catch to saving messages in your Web-based accounts. There is a maximum storage allowance online, which varies depending on the server. Emptying your Deleted Items folder can make more space available. In fact, many servers empty your Deleted Items folder on a regular basis, so don't count on being able to rescue items from there. In addition, you must sign on from time to time (at least once each 60 days for Hotmail) in order to keep your account active.

Protecting Against Viruses and Unwanted Mail

Sadly, there are malicious software programmers that are bent on wanting to hurt your computer or mess up your data. They create software programs that will erase your hard drive, delete files, or replicate themselves so they slow down the operation of your computer. There is a whole family of these harmful programs, and they go by the names Trojan horse, worm, or virus. Regardless of what they're called, catching one can give you hours of trouble. There are hundreds of these nasties on the PC platform, but there are antidotes. There are shareware and commercial virus killers that will do the job of keeping your PC virus and trouble free.

The people that send you junk mail aren't usually malicious, but they certainly are irritating. Although spam is now pretty much a fact of Internet life, there are a couple of things you can do to avoid it.

Using Anti-Virus Software

Viruses fall into several categories and attack differently, but the end result is usually the same: You have lost valuable hours of time or precious data. Some viruses attack the boot program that is stored on every bootable floppy disk or hard disk; others directly attack and modify the program files, like those with the extension .exe or .com. The latest form, called macro viruses, use the built-in programming capability in Microsoft Word and Excel and run when you download them unsuspectingly. There are even viruses that send messages to mobile cell phones.

One of the most common ways to catch viruses is by downloading them from the Internet, but even the commercial online services such as AOL and CompuServe have been infected (although they maintain that their software is checked for viruses before they are made available for downloading).

Commercial anti-virus software, such as Norton AntiVirus or McAfee VirusScan, can do the job of tracking down and killing computer viruses nicely. As new bugs enter the community, these commercial companies (and shareware developers) send out patches or updates to their software to kill them.

Norton AntiVirus (www.symantec.com/product/enterprise-av.html) has a feature called LiveUpdate that will automatically launch AOL (if you're using that service) and download updates. It will also inform you automatically when new virus threats are reported or cures are created. It scans your e-mail looking for viruses in attachments, like the dreaded I LOVE YOU virus, which hit many computers not too long ago.

 Be sure to keep your anti-virus files up to date. Anti-virus software that is even a month out of date can allow yesterday's new virus to endanger your data.

McAfee's VirusScan (www.mcafee.com/anti-virus/) is programmed to look automatically for undiscovered viruses or even as yet undetected new ones. It also checks e-mail. A quarantine feature isolates suspected files and provides a safe area on your hard drive to store important files.

Before opening any attachment, be certain it is from a trusted source. Be especially suspicious of any file with an .exe extension. Unless you know who sent it, and you send them an e-mail first, asking if they meant to send it, don't open an .exe file. Some viruses attach themselves to e-mail messages without the sender knowing about it. Make sure the sender is someone you know, and that he or she has run the program safely. Then, even if it is from a trusted source, use a program such as McAfee's VirusScan or Symantec's Norton AntiVirus to scan the attachment before you open it.

> *There are many resources that provide more information about viruses. Visit F-Secure's Web site at www.datafellows.fi and the Anti-Virus Resource site at http://www.hitchhikers.net/av.shtml. There is an excellent Web site maintained by the U.S. Department of Energy's Computer Incident Advisory Capability (CIAC) group (http://ciac.llnl.gov/ciac/CIACHoaxes.html). The site lists and explains Internet hoaxes and teaches you how to identify a new hoax or real warning, and what to do if you think a message is a hoax.*

If possible, you should avoid downloading programs from the Internet directly to your hard drive if they are from unknown or untrusted sources. Instead, download to a Zip disk, floppy, or another backup device. Then run your anti-virus program to check it for viruses before you run the download program. Only then copy the file to hard disk.

Disabling Macros in Word Files

Microsoft Office products (Word, Excel, Access, and Outlook) have a built-in programming language called VBA (Visual Basic for Applications). Documents for these programs can run scripts called VBA scripts (or *macros*) for automating some of their functions. It's possible for an unscrupulous programmer to write a script in VBA that can mess up your computer. Therefore, when you receive and open a Word, Excel, or Access file that has macros in it, you should be careful. Opening the document file could automatically run the macro and erase files on your computer. You can protect yourself by turning off the ability for Word or other Office tools to run macros.

To watch for macros in Word documents, in Microsoft Word, choose Options from the Tools menu and click on the General tab. Make sure that the Macro Virus Protection option is selected, as shown in Figure 7-29, and then click OK. Now when you open a document with macros, a warning dialog will appear. You'll be given the option to run macros or not.

Freeing Yourself from Junk Mail (Spam)

Unfortunately, it didn't take long for people to figure out how to send junk mail to e-mail boxes. Just as we were beginning to appreciate the time-saving attributes of e-mail, our Inboxes began to be filled with unwanted e-mail for us to sort through.

Fairly early on, this type of mail began to be referred to as spam, probably through association with the luncheon meat of the same name. In the context of e-mail, spam refers to a single message sent to a large number of recipients through e-mail, similar to the junk mail you receive from the post office, but easier, cheaper, and faster to distribute. (The folks at SPAM don't seem to mind the negative association, and have even set up a Web site.)

The good news is that it is a lot easier to rid yourself of spam (and not as big a drain on the environment) than it is to avoid the junk mail that is delivered in your snail-mail box.

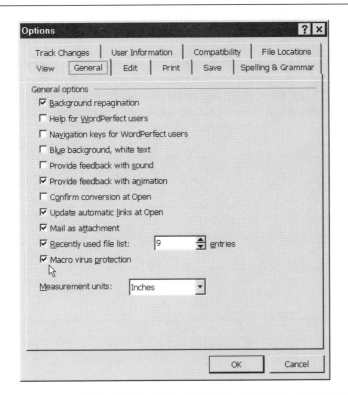

FIGURE 7-29   Enabling macro virus protection in Microsoft Word

Also, your server is on your side, and very likely uses software that attempts to identify and remove spam before it gets to you. The best way to handle it is to highlight the offending message and click Delete.

 Senders of junk e-mail often include a note at the bottom of their message instructing you to reply to the message to be taken off of the list. Don't fall for this trick! All you're really doing is showing that your address is a live one, guaranteeing you'll get even more spam. Delete any message you do not want to have.

While there are often tempting offers on how to make a million dollars overnight or to receive a college diploma in just 30 days, use the same judgment you would use with information from any other anonymous source. Just because a message arrived in your very own Inbox, in your very own computer, does not mean that the offer is legitimate.

 *For tips on getting rid of spam, go to www.ecofuture.org/ecofuture/jnkmail.html.*

If there is a particular e-mail address from which you are sure you don't want to receive mail, OE can block this sender. Unfortunately, this technique does not help much in preventing bulk e-mail, since senders of spam know about this feature and change their addresses frequently. To deflect unwanted mail from a specific e-mail address, choose Message Rules from the Tools menu, select Block Senders, and enter the e-mail address.

Chapter 8

Online Communities

How to...

- Chat online with Instant Messenger services
- Join chat rooms
- Become a member of a newsgroup
- Get mail from a mailing list server
- Explore Web rings and other online communities

Now that you've learned how to use e-mail, you may be eager for even more ways of connecting with others through the Internet. The vastness of the Internet and the Web makes it easier, cheaper, and faster than ever before to communicate with people worldwide. There's sure to be a group somewhere covering any subject you can think of, accessible at any time of day or night.

You may want instant communications, via online conversation. If so, online chatting is for you. Instant Messenger services and online chat rooms bring the speed of communication to real time. Is there a particular subject you can't get enough of? Then look into newsgroups and mailing list servers. Newsgroups and mailing list servers (sometimes referred to as listservs) allow people to share information and discuss specific topics in an organized way with a far-reaching impact.

It's good to know that a sense of community is coming back to our fast-paced society, even if it is in cyberspace. People that used to have more of a true neighborhood presence, such as politicians, are once again within reach, as they seem to be easier to contact online. Some online connections develop into offline relationships as well. There are an increasing number of community-oriented sites that have begun to organize meetings, gatherings, and parties where people can once again connect face to face.

In this chapter, you'll learn how to find communities of interest to you and how to interact with them. We'll start with ways to have online conversations with people you already know, and then move onto other ways of communicating in cyberspace.

Chatting with Friends Through Instant Messenger Services

It's likely that you have friends, family, or colleagues who are already online and chatting. If so, a good place to start is with the IM (Instant Messenger) service that they use. When you are online and logged into a particular IM service, you can see who else is logged into the same service. With a simple click of the mouse, you can communicate with a friend in real time.

AOL (America Online) introduced an IM service, called the Buddy List, back in 1990. Chatty teenagers knew a good thing when they saw it, and they were hooked right away. It took longer for the rest of us to catch on. About six years later, ICQ introduced a messenger service that anyone could join for free. (Even though AOL later acquired ICQ, the two systems remain incompatible.) Other companies, including Yahoo and MSN, introduced their own IM services. It is now estimated that 3 million new users sign up with an IM service every month.

You can choose from among dozens of IM services downloadable for free, and you can join as many as you wish. Although some IM services are beginning to join together to allow users of different systems to communicate with each other, for the most part, IMs are closed systems that require you and the person you wish to chat with to sign into the same service.

Using AOL Instant Messenger

After reading the last chapter, you may think I'm not a fan of AOL. Well, you're right—that's true when we're talking about e-mail services. However, AOL has a fabulous and easy-to-use chat program called AIM (AOL Instant Messenger). You can get AIM for free by downloading it from the Internet. (If you are an AOL member, it is included as part of your AOL service.)

You may choose to use AIM simply because it's the most widely used IM program. With the number of users estimated to be over 100 million (and as many as 170 million), you are likely to find someone you know who is an AIM user.

AIM allows you to share pictures, files, and sounds (including the ability to communicate by voice with a buddy). It also has a news- and stock-ticker available. There are other IM programs with more features, but AIM offers the essentials in a simple format. Figure 8-1 shows an example of an AIM Buddy List window.

8

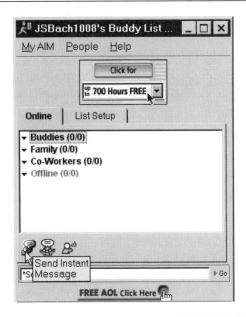

FIGURE 8-1   AIM's Buddy List

The version of AIM that loyal, paying AOL customers receive as part of their AOL service is more cumbersome than the service AOL offers over the Internet for free. For example, an Internet AIM user might have four or more AIM chats going on simultaneously while also working on a Word document, surfing the Web, and checking e-mail. However, the AOL user might not be able to "multitask" as easily, because the AOL AIM service can disrupt other activities. When chatting with people using the AOL service instead of the Internet service, be patient with their replies, which will likely take more time than yours. In other words, don't bug them.

Downloading AIM from the Internet

Here's how you can sign up for AIM and start chatting:

1. Connect to the Internet and go to www.aol.com/aim/home.html.

2. Choose a screen name and password, and enter them along with an e-mail address.

3. Download, install, and run the program.

4. A New User Wizard will give you an overview of the program and guide you through creating a Buddy List and setting preferences. You can look through this now or read it later.

5. If you want to get started right away, click Cancel. The Buddy List window will appear.

6. In the Instant Message window, type the screen name of the person you want to talk with in the upper text box, and type your message in the lower text box, as shown here.

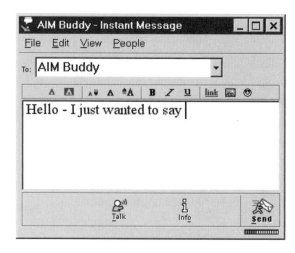

7. Click the Send button in the lower-right corner of the window or press ENTER to send your message (press SHIFT-ENTER for a carriage return). Now your message will be delivered instantly, and you've started a conversation!

You can leave AIM running whenever you are signed on to the Internet, and once you have created a Buddy List, you'll be able to see your buddies sign on and off. By leaving AIM running, you'll allow others who know your screen name to send messages to you as well, whether or not they're on your Buddy List.

Receiving AIM Messages

When you receive a new AIM message, the IM window pops up, front and center. It will actually "steal" text away from whatever document you were working on. If you don't catch it in time, you will send that text off to your buddy the next time you press ENTER. (You can avoid this by setting preferences in AIM indicating how you want to allow others to contact you.)

Avoiding Receiving Viruses Through AIM

Before accepting files from others over IM, you should install antivirus software. (See Chapter 7 for details on antivirus programs.) AIM has a nice feature that will automatically run your installed checker against any file you accept. To activate this feature, from the Buddy List window, choose My AIM, Edit Options, Edit Preferences. Click the Virus Checker tab to see the screen shown in Figure 8-2. Check the top two check boxes and specify the location of your anti-virus software. Then click OK.

Using AIM as an AOL Member

If you are an AOL member, AIM will look and act a bit different from the AIM that Internet users use. For example, when you sign on to AOL, AIM will run automatically (unless you choose the option to turn it off). You'll see the Buddy List window right away, which will show an invitation to set up a Buddy List if you haven't already done so, as shown in Figure 8-3. After you've set up your list, sending and receiving messages works basically the same as in the Internet version. On AIM's AOL version, press CTRL-ENTER to send a message. Press ENTER for a carriage return.

If you are busy with e-mail or the Web and feel pestered by well-meaning friends who want to chat, remember that they are having an easier time of it on their end. (As mentioned earlier, Internet users can easily multitask without their computers slowing down.) You can send a quick message letting them know that you're busy and would prefer to chat later.

If you would like to keep the chat feature open, but don't want to be so obvious, you can "hide" so that you don't appear on the Buddy Lists of other AIM users. Here's how to keep your name off other AIM users' Buddy Lists when your Buddy List is open:

1. Click My AOL in the AOL window's toolbar.

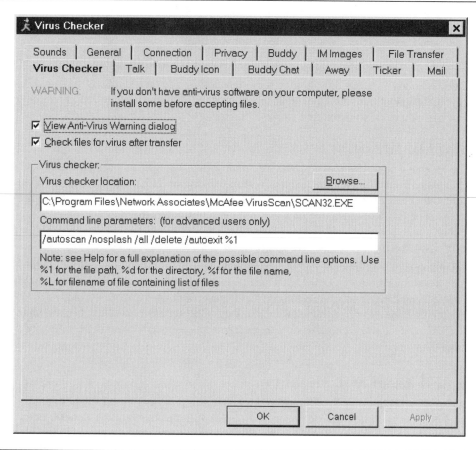

FIGURE 8-2   AIM's virus-checking options

2. Click Preferences, Privacy. You will see the Privacy Preferences window, as shown in Figure 8-4.

3. In the Choose Your Privacy Preferences section, select the Block All AOL Members and AOL Instant Messenger Users option.

4. In the Apply Preferences to the Folllowing Features section, select the Buddy List option.

5. Click Save to save your settings.

FIGURE 8-3   An invitation to set up your buddies from the AOL window

Using Other IM Services

There are so many IM programs, it would be impossible to mention them all here. You can try some out and get a sense of the different flavors that are available. The number of contacts that you have on any given service will probably determine the one you use most often. The following IM services have many of the same features, like chat, group chat, the ability to create an online photo album, and much more.

TIP   *If you decide to sign up with several IM services, try to simplify your life by choosing a single chat name and password. If this is not possible, keep a file on your computer where you store all of this information. As the number of your user names and passwords increases, it can become frustrating to try to remember the right one at the right time.*

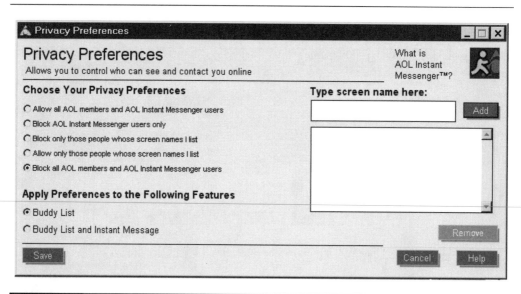

FIGURE 8-4   Setting privacy options in AOL

ICQ

ICQ is a popular IM program with over 74 million users worldwide. Its name is cleverly derived from the words "I Seek You." ICQ has many more features than AIM, which is either appealing or confusing, depending on your needs. It's a bit less user-friendly than AIM, since instead of choosing a screen name, you are identified by a string of numbers that ICQ selects. (You can add more information about yourself, such as a nickname and e-mail and physical addresses.) Figure 8-5 shows an example of an ICQ window. The upside of ICQ's identification system is that their search engine is one of the better ones for finding fellow IM-ers. You can enter as much or as little as you know about a person to find out if they have an ICQ address.

Like many IM programs, ICQ allows you to chat, send messages and files, and exchange Web page addresses. In addition, you can play games and even create your own home page. ICQ displays what you write as you write it, creating a more immediate connection by mimicking an actual face-to-face conversation. The person you're chatting with can respond as you write, without waiting for you to compose your thought and click Send. Although your conversations can have a more direct flow this way, the downside is that you don't have the luxury of making quick revisions before sending messages.

MSN Messenger

When you log into MSN Messenger, not only do you see which MSN buddies are online at the same time, you can also easily monitor your Hotmail. The MSN Messenger window displays

FIGURE 8-5   ICQ's IM service

how many unread messages are in your Hotmail mailbox, as shown in the example in Figure 8-6. If you stay logged into the service, a pop-up window will automatically appear in the lower-right corner of your screen when you get new Hotmail. You can also initiate a NetMeeting directly from the MSN Messenger window (choose Tools, Send an Invitation).

NetMeeting

NetMeeting is a bit different because it is a more office-oriented instant communication system than the others. It allows interaction through video, audio, a whiteboard, and file sharing, as well as written chatting. As you draw on the whiteboard or write in the chat window, your work is instantly displayed without the need to click on a button or press a key to send it. See Figure 8-7 to get an idea of what a NetMeeting can look like, complete with active whiteboard, chatting, audio and video.

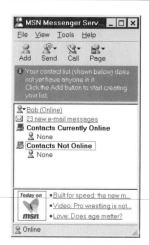

FIGURE 8-6   MSN Messenger

FIGURE 8-7   A NetMeeting in progress

It's possible to collaborate on a particular document, such as a Word file, or a technical drawing, even if the other person doesn't have the program you're using to create a document. You can even share your entire computer with another person in your individual NetMeeting. You can literally hand over the controls and watch as another person across the office or on the other side of the world accesses your computer. For lots of information about using NetMeeting, see www.meetingbywire.com.

Here you see a listing of people on one of the many NetMeeting "ILS" servers. Note that you can see who has a video camera and who has a microphone. Once you are set up, you can easily click on one of the people in the list to "call" them. If you both have a camera and microphone, you can see and hear each other while chatting.

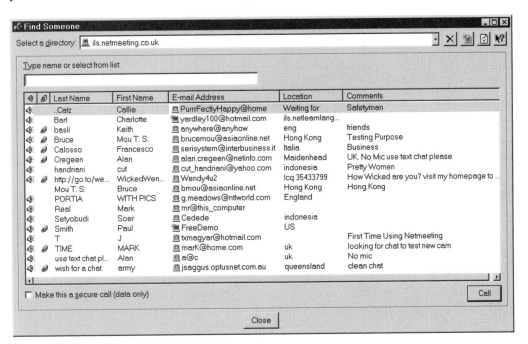

Yahoo! Messenger

Yahoo! Messenger, Yahoo's IM program, is similar to other IM services. As you might suspect, it will notify you if you receive new Yahoo! mail. It also allows you to enter other e-mail addresses so that you will be notified when you get new mail from those servers. You may appreciate clicking through the tabs on the Yahoo! Messenger window to read news, check stocks, get sports scores, and see your online Yahoo! calendar. Clicking on the Chat button will allow you to enter one of many chat rooms or create your own. Figure 8-8 shows an example of a Yahoo! Messenger window.

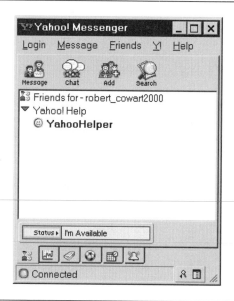

FIGURE 8-8   Yahoo! Messenger

Meeting New People Online in Chat Rooms

In the unlikely event that your friends or colleagues have not yet subscribed to any IM services, or you've logged on and no one else is "home," you can chat with the millions of people who are online in chat rooms or forums, at any time of day or night. You can search for online chat rooms in a variety of places and then join in when you find one that sounds interesting.

NOTE

What's the difference between a chat room and a forum? Chat rooms allow for instant communication between people, in real time. The speed of a conversation in a chat room can escalate at an astonishing rate, especially if the subject matter is stimulating and if there are many active participants. A forum is an online discussion group, where you can post a question or comment and check back later to see the response. Similar to a newsgroup, it's a bit like a slow-motion chat room. When participating in forums, it helps to quote the small section to which you are actually referring so that the conversation is easier to follow.

Searching for Chat Rooms

The Internet is heavily populated with chat rooms. You'll find them at www.yahoo.com, www.MSN.com, and your ISP's home page. Here is another good place to look for chat rooms: http://host99.com/freechat.htm.

There really are so many out there, it's best to allow yourself to wander a bit. Go to one of your favorite sites, and it's likely that you will find a chat room or forum set up there. Some sites have regular chat rooms as well as special-event chats, where a notable person is interviewed by whoever signs on during the scheduled chat. The following sections present a few more ideas to get you going.

Magazine, Newspaper, and TV Show Chats

Did you know that you may already be a part of a community that has a chat room? Your favorite magazine is likely to have a Web site that offers online chat rooms and/or forums. To chat about current events, go to the Web site of a local, national, or international newspaper. Here are a couple of places to look for a favorite (or find a new one):

- www.magazinesatoz.com
- www.newsrack.com

Local and international TV programs are another likely source of chat rooms. You'll find the popular cable TV news network has chat rooms at www.cnn.com/chat. Oprah Winfrey has created a vast and international community through her TV show, magazine, and book club. They all come together in her Web site, www.oprah.com. If you're a fan, or even mildly interested, it's likely that you'll find people with whom you will enjoy chatting there.

Comic Chat

Here's a fun way to chat: go to www.kns.net/comichat/room.htm. At this address, you can download software that enables you to become a character in a comic strip. Instead of mere words at your disposal, you can choose a character and use expressions and gestures to convey meaning.

Napster

You may have heard of Napster. It's one place where people share their music online. It is more than that—it is a community of music lovers. Let's say you're downloading a tune from someone signed into Napster, or you see someone downloading one of your music files. You can click on their name and begin an instant conversation with them. There's a pretty good chance you'll have something in common, since you share musical tastes! Napster also hosts chat rooms on various music topics. (See Chapter 11 for details on downloading music files.)

CompuServe Forums

One of the first online services, CompuServe, is still alive and well. It continues to support a large number of forums, but now it also includes chat and IM services. Take a look at www.compuserve.com.

8

Did you know?

Why Napster Is So Interesting

As we all know, college kids love to share music with one another. A college student nicknamed "Napster" wrote a program (called Napster) to make it easy for students to share MP3 files over the Internet. You just tell a master database what files you have on your computer that you would like to share, leave your connection to the Internet on all the time (as they typically are on college campuses), and give people a way to search the database for the songs they want. That way, people could easily find and download their favorite music.

The success of his program encouraged Napster to incorporate. The Napster site soon caught on like wildfire. People were happy to be able to find anything from the Four Seasons to Metallica and download it automatically, even if they weren't there to monitor the computer. You just put your desired songs into the download queue and go get lunch.

It wasn't long before the recording industry got up in arms, of course. Now the courts, Congress, and the record industry are in the process of trying to sort out how to control Internet dissemination of artists' music.

Joining a Chat Room

Going into chat rooms is quite simple. Here are the general steps:

1. Connect to the Internet and go to one of the numerous Web sites with chatting features. You can go to one mentioned in the previous sections or look for chat rooms using any search engine.

2. Sign on by entering a nickname and password. If you haven't signed onto the particular site before, it's likely you'll need to sign up by choosing a user name and password, and possibly entering some additional information. Sometimes, you can just lurk and then make up a user name on the spot.

3. Browse through the available topics. When you see a topic of interest, click on it.

4. Watch the conversation unfold, and when you're ready, join in!

5. If you don't like what you see, go back to step 3 and choose another room, or go to a different Web site.

Most chat rooms will display the number of people currently in a room. You may find a chat room with more than 100 people overwhelming, or you may find it stimulating. If the chat room you've signed onto seems too large or too small, move to another one. Some rooms even have a maximum number of people who are allowed in (just like elevators, but this rule is enforced). If the room is full, you can be locked out.

Some chat rooms have monitors to keep the conversation civilized, which means you can get kicked out for bad behavior and using inappropriate language. If the room you are in doesn't seem to have a monitor, and you would like to stay if it weren't for a particular person or two, you can look for an option commonly called Ignore. You will be able to remain active in the chat room, but you won't see (or be bothered by) what that particular person is saying.

You'll find that many chat rooms operate as in real life (it *is* real, after all). If a person begins to harass someone, others in the chat room are likely to stick up for the underdog and defend him or her.

Chatting with IRC

IRC (Internet Relay Chat) used to be the only way of communicating in real time on the Internet. Although it still exists, the Web's easy-to-use and easy-to-access chat rooms have become a more popular alternative. To use the Web, all you need to do is open a browser window and search for a group or topic that interests you.

On the other hand, to use IRC, you must run a program (an IRC client) to connect to a server on one of the IRC networks (or nets). The IRC system is made up of many different and separate networks of IRC servers, which are machines that allow users to connect to IRC. The server relays information to and from other servers on the same network. When you're connected to a server on a network, you can join one of the "channels" and communicate with other users there. As in Web chat rooms, you can choose to have conversations that are displayed to the entire group or to a single user.

The scope of IRC is larger than chat sites on the Web and more formally organized. There can be more than 12,000 channels on a network, each with a unique topic. Often, there are more than 32,000 people at once. Now *that* is a large house! For more information about using IRC, go to www.irchelp.org.

Dealing with the Dangers of Strangers

We've probably all heard the horror stories about the dangers of meeting strangers online. How much should we worry, and how can we protect ourselves?

The biggest rule to live by as you explore the many online communities is to treat the people who you meet online the same way that you would treat people you meet on the street. This goes both ways: You should treat others with courtesy and respect, but also be wary when meeting strangers. Remember that there is a person behind every user name. Just as in the real world (again, remember that it *is* the real world), there are wonderful people and, unfortunately, there are those who have bad intentions. The greatest danger of meeting people on the Internet is that it's a lot easier to hide one's true identity.

The Bad News

The problem is that the bad news can be really bad. There is the story of the 13-year-old girl, who, thinking she was chatting with someone close to her own age, developed a close friendship with a person she met in an online chat room. After Katie was drawn in emotionally, this man—still essentially a stranger—began to suggest that they meet in person. When they did, it was in a room of the hotel where her swim team was staying. She was shocked to find that the person she had thought was her best friend had a different name and identity. He was a 41-year-old pedophile who had committed multiple crimes.

What fooled her? He seemed sensitive and intelligent. She said her guard was down since she was communicating from the privacy of her own home. It seemed harmless, and she had a lot to talk about. Their meeting was planned at the last moment, only a few days before the event, and she was too distracted to give it much thought. When they did meet, she was confused since she cared about him and feared him at the same time.

This story has a positive ending, since Katie had told a friend where she was going. Her mother was able to gather security guards and come to her rescue. In addition, Katie (Katherine Tarbox) took her case to court. It was one of the first successful prosecutions of a pedophile under the 1996 Communications Decency Act. Katie went further, since she had a desire to

Protect Yourself and Your Children Online

Here are some guidelines for avoiding danger:

- Get to know and understand the Internet (your children do!).

- Don't give out personal information online—such as your home address or any information that would enable someone to find your home address—unless you are sure your privacy is honored. (Don't allow your children to give out any personal information at all.)

- If you decide you would like to meet a person you've developed an online relationship with, choose a public place to meet and bring a friend.

- Talk to your children about where they can and cannot go on the Web.

- Use blocking and/or screening software. (For more about protecting your children from content on Web pages, see Chapter 6.)

- Establish rules for what your children should and shouldn't say and do in chat rooms or on IM services. Know who their "buddies" are.

- Use your common sense, and treat the Internet as you would any other city your children visit, with neighborhoods you would like them to stay out of and those in which you're happy to have them spend time.

- For more guidance, visit www.cyberangels.org.

share her story and help prevent the same thing from happening to others. She wrote a book, *katie.com*, and has established a Web site, www.katiet.com.

The Good News

It's not all bad—even Katie says so, as she encourages others to enjoy the Internet. (Some caution is in order, however, and parents should keep an eye on what their children are doing online.)

Both scholars and average citizens have been lamenting the loss of community as people become more independent, travel farther, and lose touch with family and friends. The Internet now allows people to connect in a new way. Someone living in a remote area has instant access to people all over the world. Those who are confined to bed or a wheelchair can now find a person to chat with at any time of day or night. And the families that are separated by thousands of miles now have an easy, immediate, and inexpensive (even free) way to keep in touch.

Joining Newsgroups

8

A newsgroup is a group of people who create a collection of articles about a specific subject. Newsgroups are a great way to learn and share information about practically anything. You'll find experts and enthusiasts, as well as the curious.

Newsgroups are similar to e-mail exchanges, in that you can respond to what someone else has written (in newsgroup terms, what they have *posted*) or you can send a question or comment of your own. You can direct your posting to the whole group or to an individual. Since postings are threaded, it is easy to follow a specific discussion.

Internet newsgroups are uncensored. You can find just about any view on any subject at any time. No person or committee or government has authority over newsgroups as a whole. If you find groups, articles, or people offensive, don't go there. You'll see later in this chapter how you can filter out these articles. In any case, be prepared to come across some shocking stuff out there.

Accessing Newsgroups

To read newsgroups, you need a news server and a newsreader. Your ISP will provide you with the name of its news server. Get your pencil ready, since it will likely be something like news.*yourISP*.com. While you're at it, ask your ISP if you need a user name and password to log on to the news server, and keep this information handy.

Next, you'll need a newsreader. OE (Outlook Express) News is a good newsreader, and it is included free with Windows. If you think you'll be working with newsgroups a lot, you might consider another newsreader such as Free Agent, which has several more features, but Outlook Express is quite acceptable. Free Agent is available as freeware, downloadable at www.forteinc.com/agent/freagent.htm.

Since OE News is already on most computers, we will focus on the OE format for reading newsgroups. You can customize the layout of OE in the same way you did for e-mail (see Chapter 7 for details on using OE).

Setting up a News Account

To set up your OE news account, follow these steps:

1. Start OE and choose Tools, Accounts.

2. Click the News tab and choose Add, News. The Internet Connection Wizard will start.

3. Enter the name you would like to have displayed when you communicate with the newsgroup, and then click Next.

4. Enter the e-mail address you wish to use for newsgroups, and then click Next.

5. Now you'll be asked to enter the information you were given by your ISP. Enter the name of the news server. If your ISP requires you to use an account name and password to access newsgroups, check the My News Server Requires Me to Log On check box. Then click Next.

6. Enter any necessary information, and then click Finish.

Now you're ready to browse through and participate in newsgroups.

NOTE   *If you don't want your name and/or e-mail address displayed when you visit newsgroups, you can enter aliases in the appropriate dialog boxes of the Internet Connection Wizard. You can enter anything you like, but realize that others can do the same. Some ISPs have policies against this, so check to be sure that entering a false name does not violate these policies. A good alternative is to create an anonymous e-mail address with a Web-based e-mail account. (See Chapter 7 to learn how to do this.)*

Finding Newsgroups

After you've set up your news account, you can see what's available by downloading a list from your ISP's news server. Connect to your ISP and open OE News by choosing Newsgroups from the Tools menu, pressing CTRL-W, or clicking your news server in the Folders bar. You'll see the dialog box shown below. Click Yes to download a list of newsgroups available on your server.

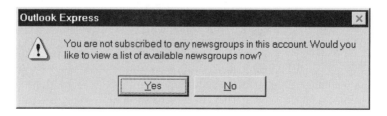

The speed of your connection will determine how long the downloading process takes. It could take some time. As the process is underway, you will be entertained with a counter that shows the number of newsgroup titles being downloaded.

NOTE *To save time and disk space, only the names of the newsgroups are downloaded to your computer. Update this list from time to time by clicking on Reset List.*

After the download is complete, you'll see a long list. How do you begin to make sense of it and find something you're truly interested in? You can scroll down the list a bit, to see what's there. This may be fun once or twice, but soon becomes a frustrating and time-consuming practice. You may notice that the list is organized alphabetically by category, so one way to begin is to go to the category of interest. Here is a partial list of what these categories are

- alt = alternative
- biz = business
- comp = computer
- misc = miscellaneous
- news = news
- rec = recreational
- sci = science
- soc = social issues
- talk = talk

A more efficient way to find what you're looking for is by performing a search. Once all the groups' names are downloaded, you can then type in a search word, as you see in Figure 8-9. This will comb through the list of thousands of newsgroups to find one you may be interested in. Click the Go to button to check out the newsgroup, or click the Subscribe button to subscribe to it.

Unfortunately, after you go to a newsgroup you found, OE News doesn't retain the list that your search found in the Newsgroups dialog box. To select another newsgroup that was in the "found" group, you must repeat your search.

There's another way to search through the thousands of newsgroups available. You can open a web browser and go to www.deja.com/usenet. Deja.com allows you to search among even more newsgroups in a more user-friendly format. It is not as critical here to know the name of the newsgroup, since Deja.com will search the articles as well as the names of the groups to help you find what you're looking for. You can post a message or subscribe to a newsgroup directly from the Web site.

NOTE *Deja.com was founded as Deja News in 1995. Four years later, the company was renamed Deja.com and introduced Deja Ratings, a service that collects opinions directly from consumers on thousands of products and services and posts them for all to read. It is a good place to explore before making a big purchase.*

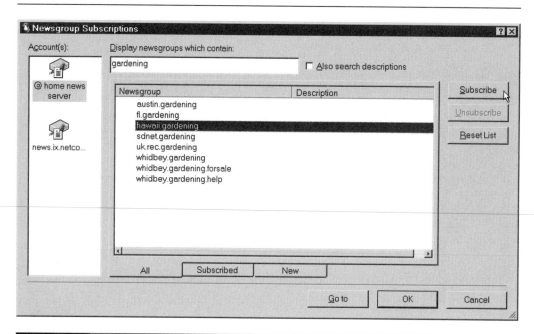

FIGURE 8-9 A list of newsgroups found using the search word "gardening"

Liszt (www.liszt.com/news) is another place to find several types of Internet discussion groups, including mailing lists, newsgroups, and IRC chat channels.

 Web-based newsgroups are available at www.easyusenet.com, which eliminates the need for a news server and newsreader. They're not for everyone, though, because newsgroup readers allow you to synch your messages and store them locally for reading later.

Newsgroup Reading, Responding, and Posting

After you've found a newsgroup that you would like to read, click on its name, and then click Go To. From there, you can read an article by clicking on its header, as shown in Figure 8-10. A *header* is the information displayed in the message window. This may include information such as the name of the sender, the subject, the newsgroups to which it is posted, and the time and date the message was sent or received.

 If you double-click the header, the article will open in a separate window. It's usually more practical to avoid this. Before you realize it, you could have dozens of open windows cluttering your screen.

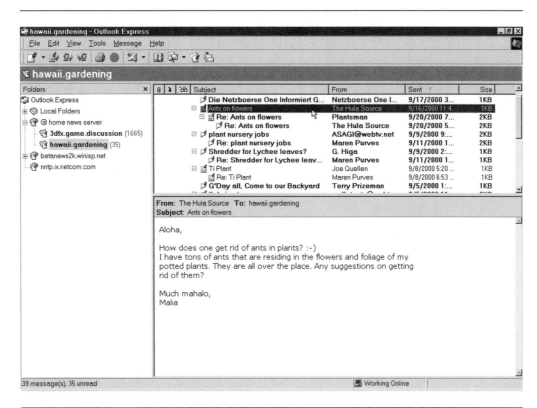

FIGURE 8-10   Reading a newsgroup article

When you view a newsgroup, you will see some messages that are preceded by a plus sign (+). This indicates that the message is part of a thread. A *thread* is a single conversation, including the original message and any posted replies. To view the other messages in the thread, click on the plus sign. Another related message appears. If it is part of a further, ongoing thread, it will also be preceded by a plus sign. When you open a thread to display the further messages, it becomes a minus sign (–). Just click the minus sign to collapse the thread again.

You can scan a newsgroup's messages quickly, reply only to a given message, and if your subject line is the same as the original you're responding to, yours will be threaded under the original one. (If you change the title when you reply to a message, you will start a new thread.)

While you're reading a newsgroup, you have a choice of replying to an individual author of a message or to the entire group. If you think your response will be of interest to the entire group, post your reply. However, if it is directed specifically at one person, keep things simple by responding only to that person.

Guidelines for Posting to Newsgroups

Although newsgroups are not controlled by any single entity, there are some rules for participating in the community, akin to a "gentlemen's agreement." Following these guidelines helps show respect for others and reduce clutter on newsgroups:

- Remember that real people contribute to newsgroups. Treat others with the same respect you would have when joining any group, online or off.
- Check out a group ("lurk") before you post to get a sense of the group and see if it's one you would like to join.
- Realize that system administrators are not responsible for their users' behavior.
- Never assume a person's postings represent his or her organization's view.
- Be considerate in your comments about others (millions may read what you post).
- Be brief.
- Use titles with accurate descriptions.
- Include a summary in your follow up.
- Post a message only once.
- Think about your audience.
- Don't assume that you can hide in anonymity; post ideas and comments that you would be proud to share in person.
- Be careful in your use of humor and especially sarcasm. It is easy to misread a joke without an accompanying facial expression.
- To follow up with a specific person, e-mail that individual directly.
- Cite appropriate references.
- Don't infringe on copyrights and licenses.
- Keep signatures short and simple.
- Avoid posting the same message to multiple newsgroups.

TIP   *You may see requests from time to time that responses be directed toward the individual and not the group. Respect the group's wishes (and each person's valuable time) by honoring these requests.*

To reply to an individual, click on the Reply button. To reply to the whole group, click on the Reply Group button (the name of the group will appear in the To field). Then type your message in the message window and click Send. To reply both to the author and to the newsgroup, choose Message, Reply to All. You can also use the Message menu to forward articles. To post a new message to a group, click the New Post button.

Subscribing and Unsubscribing to Newsgroups

When you read a newsgroup, it appears as a subfolder in your News folder. These folders are deleted from the Folders bar when you exit Outlook Express, unless you *subscribe* to a given newsgroup.

Once subscribed to a newsgroup, that newsgroup subfolder is retained in the Folders bar when you exit OE News. The next time you access your news server, you can simply click this folder to open the newsgroup. (Any messages you've downloaded can also be read offline.) There are two ways to subscribe to a newsgroup:

- In the Newsgroup Subscriptions window, select a group and click on Subscribe.
- With the newsgroup open, right-click on the newsgroup's listing in the Folders bar and choose Subscribe.

You can unsubscribe while viewing a newsgroup by right-clicking on the newsgroup's listing in the Folders bar and choosing Unsubscribe. Alternatively, click on the News Groups button, click the Subscribed tab, select the name of the newsgroup, and click Unsubscribe.

Setting Newsgroup Synchronization

You can download messages from a newsgroup so you can read them when away from the Internet. This makes especially good sense if you have to limit your connection time to the Internet, or are travelling with a portable computer. You do this using the *synchronization* settings in OE.

1. To reach the settings, click the news server's name in the Folders bar. All the groups you've subscribed to will be listed now, showing synchronization settings for each one. You'll also see the number of messages currently in the group, and how many you still have not yet read.

2. Select the newsgroup you want to synchronize, and review its settings. Normally only new messages will be synched, but you can alter this via the Settings button. The idea is to keep the list of messages in your computer updated to your liking. The choices are:

- Don't synchronize: No synching is done. You just click on the newsgroup when you are online and OE downloads one message at a time, as you click on the headers.
- All messages: This downloads all the message headers and bodies, but it could take quite a long time to download!

8

■ New messages only: This is a sensible solution for many folks.

■ New headers only: This is the quickest setting (after "Don't synchronize"), but you won't be able to read the messages while offline.

3. Click in the little box to place a check mark next to the group you're making the settings for.

4. Connect to the Internet, and then click the Synchronize Account button. You can disconnect after the messages are downloaded.

Filtering Newsgroups and Messages

Remember that most newsgroups are not censored in any way. However, you can be your own censor by choosing which newsgroups and messages appear on the message list and are downloaded to your computer. This is called *filtering*. People decide to filter groups and messages to avoid saving and scrolling through messages on topics that don't interest them, and to screen out old messages.

To filter newsgroups and messages, use the Message Rules feature (just as when you organize e-mail, as explained in Chapter 7). For example, if you want to delete any messages that contain objectionable words in the subject line, follow these steps:

1. Select Message Rules from the Tools menu and click News. The New News Rule dialog box will open.

2. In section 1, click the box next to a rule you want to use. Choose Where the Subject Line Contains Specific Words.

3. In section 2, click the box next to the action you want taken: Delete It.

4. In section 3, click the blue links as needed to provide more specific information. Click the Contains Specific Words link, and then enter the words you find objectionable.

5. Click OK when you are finished.

To display only certain messages, click on the View menu, choose Current View, and select an option from the drop-down menu.

Subscribing to Mailing List Servers (Listservs)

A mailing list server is a server that manages mailing lists for groups of users. In other words, it facilitates an Internet e-mail discussion group. When e-mail is addressed using one of these servers, it is automatically sent to everyone on the list. The result is not unlike a newsgroup or forum, but since the messages are sent as e-mail, they are available only to those on the list.

NOTE

LISTSERV is a brand name for a specific mailing list server. Similar to asking for a Kleenex when you want a tissue, or looking for a snack in the Frigidaire ("Fridge") instead of the refrigerator, the term listserv is used far more frequently than mailing list server. I use the term listserv generically in this chapter.

Unlike the easy-to-follow threads on newsgroups, individual e-mails in a listserv require some repetition of messages. But nothing can compete with e-mail as a medium, since it comes to you, not the other way around. (Increasingly, messages are available through Web searches, but to see the whole picture, you must be on the list.) As you might suspect, a common mailing list server is LISTSERV. Another popular mailing list server, Majordomo, is available as freeware.

Joining a Mailing List Service

You may be thinking, "Another mailing list? My mailbox at home is flooded with catalogs I don't want. Why would I want to *join* one?" A better way to characterize a mailing list server may be to think of it as a discussion tool or online newsletter. Here are some of the common uses of listservs:

- Announcements of meetings and events to members of a group or club
- The efficient exchange of ideas among members of a group
- An economical way to keep a group with members in many different countries informed
- Communication between politicians and their constituents, manufacturers and their international sales forces, and the like
- Notification of product updates by software companies to their registered users
- Broadcasting of last-minute travel deals by airlines to subscribers
- Communication between educational institutions and/or their professors and/or their students

Joining a mailing list service is quite simple: You just submit your e-mail address. One place to see the services that are available is www.egroups.com. Search for a subject of interest, and write to the address given to subscribe to the mailing list.

TIP

When you join a listserv, you'll start receiving all of the service's e-mail messages. A good way to stay organized is to take action before the messages begin to flood in. Create a new folder and use rules in OE to keep messages for each listserv in its own folder. (See Chapter 7 for details on using OE rules to automatically direct incoming mail to a specific folder.) Also, you may want to delete anything more than a month old once in a while. (Many listservs have an archive online.)

Subscribing in Digest Form

Most listservs have digest form available, which can be a real help if you're overwhelmed with e-mail. The digest mode assembles a day's worth of listserv e-mail into a newspaper of sorts. It's a good idea to subscribe to most lists in digest form, unless you're an extremely active member or you can't wait until the end of the day to get the postings. By using the digest form, you'll get a single e-mail message instead of receiving tens or hundreds of messages a day.

A downside to the digest is that there are no links to the stories, so you'll need to scroll down and look, which can be tedious. Some may find it easier to search through the messages in non-digest form, especially if they've been directed to their own folder in OE.

Replying to a specific message is a little trickier in digest mode, because you need to copy and paste the header into the subject line of your response. In non-digest mode, you just select Reply, and the header is automatically included in the e-mail you send.

Using the Commands of the Mailing List Server

When you sign up with a mailing list server, you'll be sent an e-mail message explaining the rules and commands of the server. To communicate with the listserv, you'll need to use the commands it understands. Here are some common reasons to use commands:

- To unsubscribe to the listserv (if you no longer want to receive its messages)
- To switch between digest and non-digest mode
- To suspend your subscription while you are out of town (especially if you don't need to know what's going on while you're gone)

NOTE   *Some servers have a maximum size after which all your mail will start to bounce, so check that out before an extended absence.*

Store the list of commands you receive in a safe place for later use. You send these commands to the mailing list server in a simple e-mail message, the same way that you subscribed to the listserv.

Becoming a Part of Other Online Communities

Although chat rooms, newsgroups, and listservs are the most common, there are all types and forms of online communities out there. The following are a few of the other communities that exist on the Internet and the Web.

Web Rings

A Web ring is a different way of surfing the Web. A ring contains home pages with a common theme. It is created on a ring server and maintained by a ringmaster. Web ring users follow links on ring members' home pages to go to the next member's page in the ring. Anyone who fulfills the established criteria for membership of a particular ring is free to join.

Rings are frequently broken or dysfunctional if the navigation HTML fragment is incorrect. Some rings now have a server-side navigation bar feature, which can prevent a ring from breaking and make it easier to look around.

To search for a Web ring, connect to the Internet and point your browser to this address: www.webring.org/#search.

Online Learning

A growing segment of the online community concerns itself solely with the issue of online learning, called distance learning. Through an Internet connection, distance learning can present educational material on everything from computer science to literature. More and more universities, community colleges, technical schools, private-sector institutions, and Web-based startups are charging into the distance-learning market each week.

Imagine taking your entire college course load in the comfort of your home. Using Web pages, teachers can post virtual classroom materials and lectures. Using bulletin board systems, you can interact with your fellow virtual students, as well as with your instructors. Even testing could be administered over the Internet (although it's impossible at this point to monitor whether you cheat on test questions, since nobody can see you while you answer your questions).

Regardless of the potential social consequences of distance learning (such as fewer and fewer people with reasonably refined group etiquette), online learning represents a quickly growing community. Web sites such as blackboard.com and Learn2.com are growing by leaps and bounds, claiming to have thousands of courselets (mini-courses on everything from sock washing to how to build your own Martian lander).

NOTE
As a partner in an Internet startup, I'm also pushing the wave of online learning. If you're interested in using streaming video to learn by watching and doing instead of reading, check out www.brainsville.com.

Customer Service Communities

It used to be that the only way to get technical support or help with a product was to call the company's 800 number and stay on hold for far too long until a customer service representative would be available to talk to you. Technical support and customer service via online instant chat is a great alternative.

User communities are now part of product support on many manufacturers' Web sites. Companies from ISPs (such as www.mindspring.com) to clothing retailers (like www.landsend.com) have this feature on their Web sites. If there is a wait, you can leave the chat window open until a representative becomes available, while you continue to work on other things on your computer. Often, sites allow you to see several people chatting with representatives at the same time; you may learn something by following a different conversation. Some retailers have even come up with the innovative idea of allowing you to chat with fellow shoppers while you shop at their site.

There are other ways of connecting with people interested in the same product or service. Most Web sites have, at a minimum, a link allowing you to e-mail a question. Others are more advanced. For example, Adaptec, the manufacturer of CD-recording software, has a Web site (www.cdrcentral.com) with a User Community link. You can sign up for the related listserv right at the site, and communicate daily with others who use Adaptec products to create CDs.

Online Dating Services

Another growing type of virtual community lets you look for a partner and date online. In addition to provisions for e-mailing potential mates, many of these sites have chat rooms. It's more difficult to create a false identity (in the long term, at least) than it is in other chat rooms, since each member must divulge information in order to register with the service. You may appreciate that authenticity. (Most services keep your information private; you decide when to let others learn more about you. Still, someone in a position of authority knows.)

There are a lot of different services out there. www.match.com is a widely used one, and others are easy to locate with the help of a search engine. Many allow you to experience a free trial period before they require a monthly fee. Typically, you're asked to answer some questions that relate to your interests, values, and personality when you register with a service. You may be encouraged to write a bit about where you're coming from and what you're seeking in a relationship, and to post a photo or two. You begin by communicating with other members using an alias name, and you decide when (and if) to reveal more about yourself.

Your ISP's Community Links

Most ISPs have their own Web sites, which can direct you to chat rooms, other Web sites, and the like. You may enjoy some of these, and discover that others are yet another form of advertising. Take a look around and see if there's something that interests you. One of AOL's top marketing strategies seems to be the promotion of the communities it has created. You can access them by clicking on one of the buttons at the top of the AOL window (in particular, People or Channels) or by using AOL's keyword feature.

Part III

Cool Things to Do with Your PC

Chapter 9

Creating Your Own Web Site

How to...

- Select the right tool for building your Web site
- Design a Web site that meets your needs
- Register a domain name for your site
- Choose a host or online community to store your site
- Get your new site up and running on the Web

Like most things that start out for a simple or relatively pure purpose, the Internet's growth to include the World Wide Web (now just called "the Web") has turned the Internet into a commercial environment. Rather than existing for its original purpose, which was to share scientific findings and the ideas and thoughts of academics, the Web now allows millions of people to sell their products and services, and to pursue their personal interests—anything from travel to investing, from shopping to religion, and a dizzying array of recreational activities in between. If you want to buy it, read about it, find out what others think of it, or sell it in mass quantities from your own garage, the Web is the place to be.

Rather than being a person who merely visits other people's Web sites, you can have your own site—a place to share your self, your family, your business, and your passions with the rest of the Web-surfing world. You may wonder if it's really possible for someone with little or no related experience to possibly set up a Web site. The truth is that it's really rather easy. Anyone with a computer and some basic word-processing software can do it. And if you have a few extra software tools, which may already be on your PC, you can create a really snazzy Web site that you'll be proud of and have fun creating and maintaining for years to come.

Why Have a Web Site?

The reasons to have a Web site are as varied as the people who have them. Individuals, families, companies, churches, charities, social organizations, interest groups, and clubs all have something to share, and have chosen to share it through their Web sites.

As an individual, you might choose to have a Web site to advertise yourself as a potential employee or consultant. You may be looking for a date or want to connect with people with similar interests. A family's Web site can contain all of the information you would find in a holiday newsletter—how the kids are doing in school, where they went for summer vacation, and pictures of the new boat. Figure 9-1 shows an example of a family Web page.

A business Web site can serve as an advertisement, containing the same information as a printed ad in the newspaper or business directory—products or services offered, hours of operation, a phone number, and an address. Add pages to the site that contain product pictures

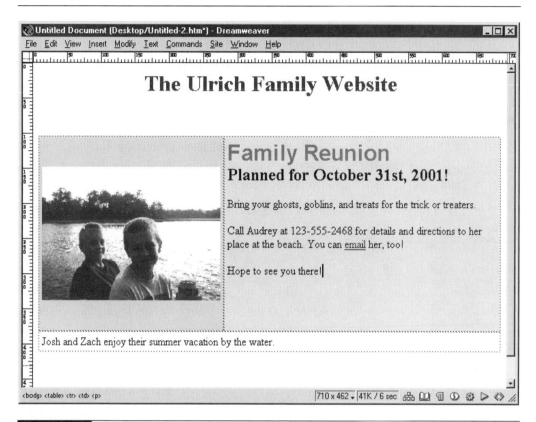

The Ulrich Family Website

Family Reunion
Planned for October 31st, 2001!

Bring your ghosts, goblins, and treats for the trick or treaters.

Call Audrey at 123-555-2468 for details and directions to her place at the beach. You can email her, too!

Hope to see you there!

Josh and Zach enjoy their summer vacation by the water.

FIGURE 9-1   Keep your relatives and friends informed about your family via the Web

and descriptions, customer testimonials, and perhaps even a way to order the products online, and you've found a way to market *and* sell to millions of potential customers all over the world. As shown in Figure 9-2, a business Web site can be very simple.

Charitable, religious, and social organizations have Web sites to promote their causes and beliefs, and to increase their memberships. If you typically run various fund-raising events for your cause, a Web site will not only advertise the events, but can solicit donations and inspire volunteers from a much wider audience. People who were unaware of your cause or your calling will find out about it without leaving their homes. This can be a real boon to many organizations

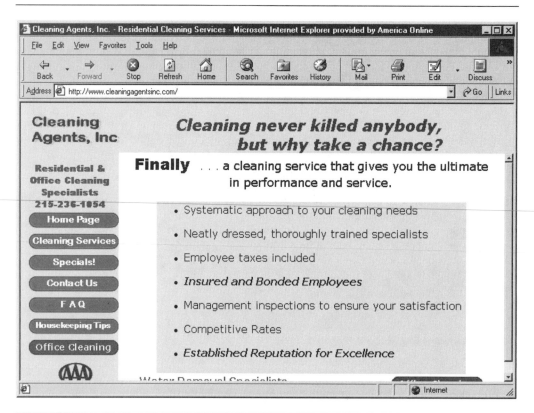

FIGURE 9-2   Take your business online with a Web page

who lack funding and participants simply because it's expensive to get the word out. Figure 9-3 shows an example of an organization's Web page.

Setting up and maintaining a Web site is easy, and can be a lot of fun. You don't have to be a graphic artist or have any knowledge of art or advertising. Of course, the more attractive your site is, the better an impression you'll make on your site's visitors. The more compelling the site's content, the more people you'll turn into customers, friends, or donors.

For people who don't feel confident that they can design an attractive and compelling Web site, there's software that takes the guesswork out of selecting fonts and colors for the site, and makes Web page layout quick and easy. For those who feel they have the requisite design skills, there are tools that allow them to design the site's pages from scratch.

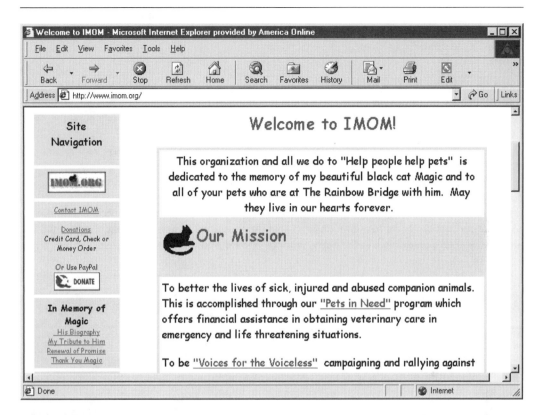

FIGURE 9-3 Gather momentum for your cause with an informative and inspiring Web site

Choosing a Web Design Tool

How you choose to build your Web site is an important decision, but not one that should necessarily delay your starting the process of actually building the site. You already have the basic tool for Web design installed on your computer. Notepad, which comes with Windows, can be used to create Web pages by typing HTML (Hypertext Markup Language) code into a simple text file. That file can then be saved as an HTML file, which makes it readable by Web browsing software. The code you type into Notepad becomes a Web page when viewed online.

Now, don't panic. You don't need to learn HTML to create a Web site. There are a host of tools available, in every price range, that allow you to build Web pages without knowing anything about HTML. You can spend hundreds or nothing on these packages, depending on what you need them to do. You can buy software with a lot of bells and whistles and an equally impressive learning curve, or you can find a package that gives you just the basics and takes just a few minutes to master.

Using a Web Page Template

If your PC came with Microsoft Office 2000, you may already have Publisher or FrontPage, which are two programs that provide Web page templates. A Web page template is a preset layout that dictates fonts, colors, background images, and graphical elements such as buttons, background colors or images, and the appearance of horizontal rules. When you use a template, you can simply type your content and insert your graphics into preset positions.

Microsoft Publisher offers an array of Web page templates to choose from, as shown in Figure 9-4. Fonts, colors, background, and all other graphical elements are chosen for you, so all you need to do is type and choose graphic images to insert. This can be great for people with no time and/or no confidence in their own design capabilities, but the downside is that it's difficult to add any of your own touches to the pages without throwing off the existing layout.

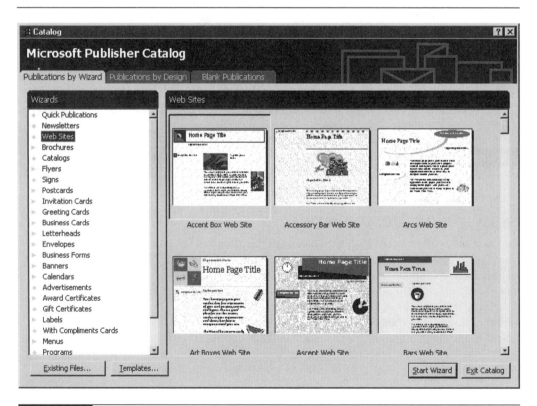

FIGURE 9-4   Use Publisher's preset layouts to create your Web pages quickly and easily

Like Publisher, FrontPage offers preset templates for your Web pages. Unlike Publisher, FrontPage requires you to set up the page layout yourself. You need to choose where text and graphics will be placed, opting to use tables (invisible grids into which text and graphics are placed to give you control over their location on the page), and applying basic text formats to the text you type. This gives you more control over the page's design, but it takes more time than it does to use Publisher. Figure 9-5 shows the FrontPage Themes dialog box, where you choose the colors, backgrounds, fonts, and the overall look for your Web pages.

CAUTION   *A lot of people have come to recognize the Publisher and FrontPage layouts. When they visit a site created in Publisher or FrontPage, they know that's the tool that was used. What conclusions they draw or what impressions are made by this is anyone's guess, but in the case of business Web sites, it's not likely to be a positive one.*

9

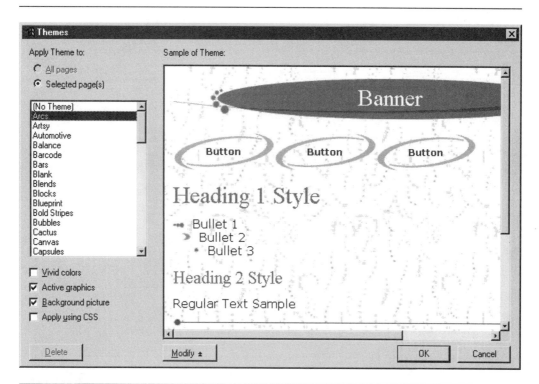

FIGURE 9-5   Choose a FrontPage Theme, and your Web pages are automatically filled with colors, fonts, and graphic elements that look good together

Using a Word Processor

If you have a word-processing program, chances are that it gives you the ability to create a Web page consisting of text and graphics, and to save it as HTML. By saving it as HTML, your text, colors, fonts, and choice of a background color or image are automatically converted to HTML code. What you developed as a document can be viewed as a Web page online. The only skills you need are the ability to type and format text, and to use the Insert menu to add graphics to a document.

Microsoft Word, a program that is part of the Microsoft Office suite, is one word processor that allows you to save documents in HTML format. However, although it's a great word processor, Word is rather limited when it comes to Web page design. You'll find that the pages you create in Word don't always look the same online as they did on your screen when you designed them. Figure 9-6 shows a page under development in Word.

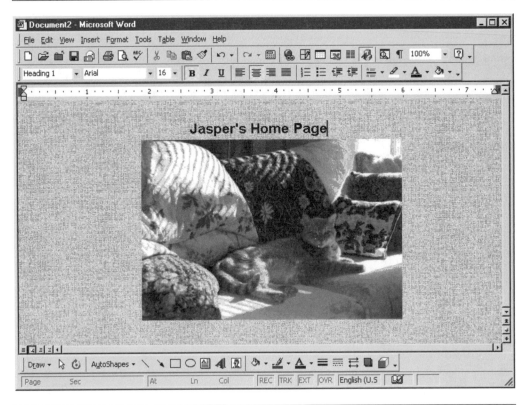

FIGURE 9-6 Word allows you to create Web pages, but doesn't provide the best tools or environment to do so

Another drawback is that if you create a Web page in Word, you may find it hard to edit it later in another Web design program. This is because Word tacks on so much Word-specific code to the HTML that it becomes cumbersome to work on the pages in any other environment. If you never plan to work outside of Word, this may not be a problem. But as most people's interest in the Web and confidence working with software increase, so do their goals for their Web sites. You'll probably be drawn to more complex tools as time goes by, and the pages you made in Word may need to be redone.

NOTE *The extra stuff that Word tacks onto the HTML code consists mainly of information about the graphic backgrounds and themes that Word allows you to apply to your Web page.*

If you have a word processor other than Word, check to see if you can save your files as HTML. Choose File, Save As, and in the Save As Type drop list, see if HTML (or .HTM) is one of the choices. If it is, the software is capable of converting your text and graphics to HTML code. There may even be a Save As HTML command on the File menu, which indicates the ability to save your document as a Web page.

Using Web Design Software

For those of you who are willing to purchase software for Web site design, there is a variety of Web design applications available. These applications provide a WYSIWYG (What You See Is What You Get) environment for designing Web pages and simple mouse and menu operations. They offer many tools and a lot of control over the design process, but these features come at a price. Not only do you need to pay to purchase the program, but you also need to invest your time in figuring out how the software works.

NOTE *WYSIWYG (pronounced wiz-e-wig) stands for What You See Is What You Get. It refers to a graphical or picture-oriented design environment. The software shows your letter, flyer, Web page, worksheet, or other file on your screen as it will appear when printed, or in the case of Web pages, viewed online.*

Macromedia's Dreamweaver and Adobe's GoLive are examples of WYSIWYG Web design applications that allow you to build a Web page graphically, inserting text and graphics and selecting colors, fonts, and layout options as you go. Dreamweaver, from Macromedia Software, costs approximately $200, and you can purchase it directly from Macromedia at www.macromedia.com or from any online software retailer, such as www.zdnet.com or www.amazon.com. GoLive, from Adobe Systems, can be found for about $250, and you can buy it from them at www.adobe.com/store/products/golive.html.

As shown in Figure 9-7, Dreamweaver offers on-screen palettes through which you can format page elements, selecting where to place them, their size, and their color. This level of control allows you to create a completely unique Web page, but it takes time to learn the software well enough to really work with it.

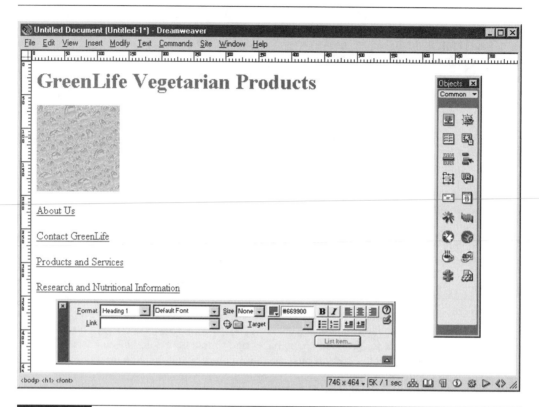

FIGURE 9-7   Dreamweaver allows you to format and customize every element of your page

TIP

Don't let the learning curve scare you. There are many books available about both Dreamweaver and GoLive, and the Help files available through the software are very effective and comprehensive. You can search for books online at www.amazon.com or www.bn.com (Barnes & Noble) or check the Osborne/ McGraw-Hill site (www.osborne.com) for their list of Dreamweaver and GoLive books, and other books on Web design and the Internet.

Using HTML

HTML is a simple mark-up language. *Mark-up languages* differ from programming languages in that they are used to mark up text that will be interpreted by an application, rather than being used to create applications themselves. In the case of HTML, the text is interpreted by and displayed within a browser, such as Internet Explorer or Netscape, and the result is a Web page.

HTML consists of various tags (commands) and their attributes (settings or formats) that determine the placement, color, and alignment of text and graphics. Figure 9-8 shows the HTML code required to create the Web page shown in Figure 9-9.

As noted earlier, you can use a simple text editor such as Notepad to create HTML files. Notepad creates .txt (text) files by default, but you can choose to save files with an .htm extension.

Proponents of Web design through HTML claim it gives you total control over the Web page, and that's true. When you use HTML, you're not limited by any functions of the software, as you might be in Dreamweaver and will be in FrontPage. On the other hand, HTML takes some time to learn. It's a very detailed and specific process, requiring that rules of syntax and structure be followed to the letter. For someone new to Web design, using HTML is probably not the best way to go about creating a first Web site.

Although you might not want to use HTML to create your Web pages, learning enough about HTML to be able to read it and know what specific tags are doing is valuable. This information

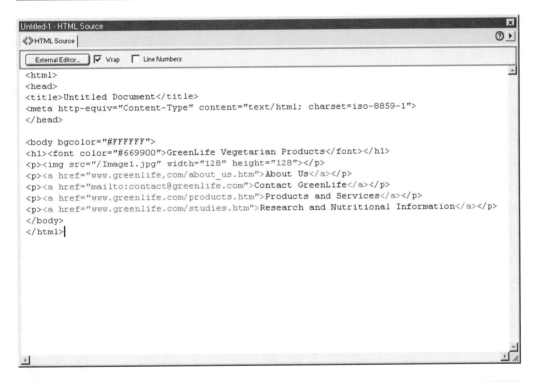

```
Untitled-1 - HTML Source

<> HTML Source

[ External Editor... ]   ☑ Wrap   ☐ Line Numbers

<html>
<head>
<title>Untitled Document</title>
<meta http-equiv="Content-Type" content="text/html; charset=iso-8859-1">
</head>

<body bgcolor="#FFFFFF">
<h1><font color="#669900">GreenLife Vegetarian Products</font></h1>
<p><img src="/Image1.jpg" width="128" height="128"></p>
<p><a href="www.greenlife,com/about_us.htm">About Us</a></p>
<p><a href="mailto:contact@greenlife.com">Contact GreenLife</a></p>
<p><a href="www.greenlife.com/products.htm">Products and Services</a></p>
<p><a href="www.greenlife.com/studies.htm">Research and Nutritional Information</a></p>
</body>
</html>
```

FIGURE 9-8   A series of tags and attributes tell the browser what to display and where to find images on the Web server

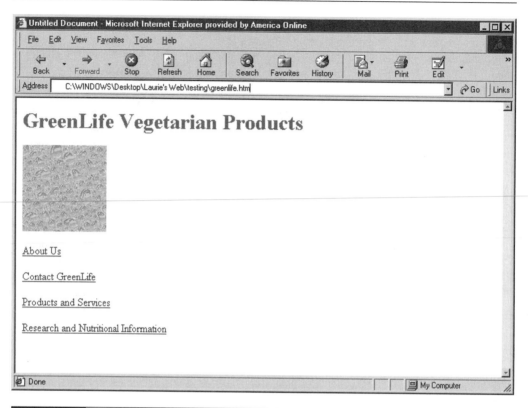

FIGURE 9-9   If your HTML code is perfect, the page will display properly

will help you troubleshoot the HTML code you generate by creating Web pages in FrontPage, Dreamweaver, or some other WYSIWYG environment. A good way to get started is to choose Source from the View menu in Internet Explorer, or Page Source from the View menu in Netscape, to see the HTML code behind the Web page you're viewing through the browser. Much of it will be jibberish to you when you start, but over time, and perhaps with a book on HTML to guide you, things will start to make sense—check out Osborne/McGraw-Hill's *HTML: The Complete Reference* by Thomas A. Powell. You can find the book at Osborne's Web site (www.osborne.om) or any book retailer.

Designing Your Web Pages

Once you've chosen the tool you'll be using to create your Web page, you can dive in. Begin by planning your site, including the pages it will include. Then add your text, graphics, and links. With the tools provided in your software, these tasks are fairly easy to accomplish.

Planning Your Site

The terms *Web site* and *home page* are often, though erroneously, used interchangeably. A Web site contains a home page, but it can and should contain other pages as well. The home page is the starting page—the page that a visitor sees first after typing a Web address (also known as a URL, which stands for Uniform Resource Locator) into a Web browser's address bar.

The role of the home page is to tell the visitor who you are, what information or ideas your site exists to share, what products and services may be for sale, and how to reach you, at least via e-mail. Your site can consist solely of that home page, functioning as a sort of electronic phone book ad, or consist of several pages, all connected to each other via hyperlinks. For example, the home page shown earlier in Figure 9-9 includes a series of text links that tell you what you'll find within the site's pages.

The approach you take to designing the pages for your site depends on the software you're using and your preferences. You can take a site approach, or you can simply design separate pages and set up links between them later.

In the site approach, you set up the site's page hierarchy. The hierarchy defines the order and connections between pages—this page comes up first, then links to this page, which links to that page. Figure 9-10 shows an example of a FrontPage site plan, which appears as a flow chart of pages and their hierarchy within the site.

Creating separate, unrelated pages may be an easier approach for new users, and many seasoned Web designers prefer this approach as well. If you're working in Notepad or Word, you'll be going page by page, without a site plan. FrontPage and Dreamweaver allow you to use either approach: You can set up a site plan before you begin designing pages, or you can create separate pages without a plan.

Adding and Formatting Text

Text is the backbone of many Web pages. Although some pages have little or no text, most have a great deal of it. Text can appear in a variety of fonts and sizes, aligned to the left, center, or right side of the page. You can apply styles to the text, which will produce multiple formats all at once. For example, in Dreamweaver, Heading 1 style text is quite large and is usually applied to the title of a page, shown here.

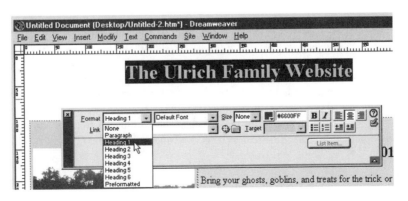

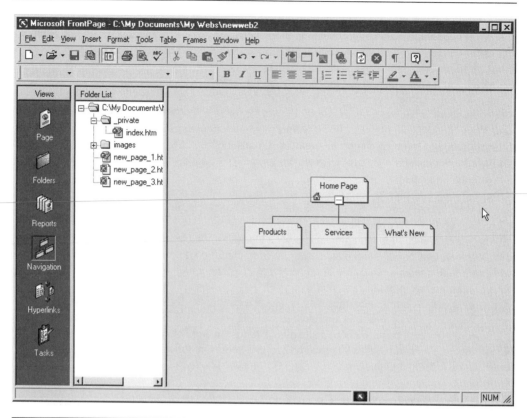

FIGURE 9-10 If you're working in FrontPage, you can create an organization chart of your pages and determine how they'll relate to each other

Entering Text

Getting your text onto the page is easy; you can just type it. You don't need to worry about formatting and placement when you first enter the text. After the text is typed, you can worry about its size, font, and color. It's much more efficient to type without stopping to apply formats as you go, because you'll type faster and make fewer mistakes. Save the aesthetics for later! Figure 9-11 shows an example of entering text in FrontPage.

If the text exists elsewhere, such as in another document, you can use the Clipboard to copy it from the existing location and paste it into your page. The commands to copy and paste are universal. In any application, select the text to be copied and choose Copy from the Edit menu or

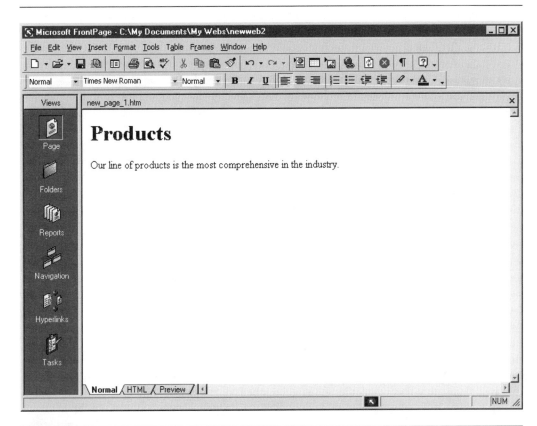

FIGURE 9-11   By default, text you type onto a Web page (in a WYSIWYG environment like FrontPage or Dreamweaver) is left-aligned, 12 points in size, and in the Times New Roman font

press CTRL-C. Then go to the target document (your Web page) and choose Paste from the Edit menu or press CTRL-V.

Formatting Text

How you format your text depends on the program you're using. If you're creating HTML code, you'll use an alignment tag, such as <div align="center"> before the text to be aligned, and a closing tag (</div>) after the aligned text. In programs like Dreamweaver and FrontPage, you can simply select the text with your mouse and apply a format by clicking on a button. For example, in Dreamweaver, you can center text by clicking on the center alignment button on the Dreamweaver Properties palette, as shown here.

Center alignment button

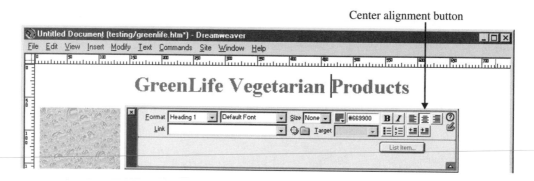

Like alignment settings, it's best to apply fonts, sizes, and colors after you've typed the text, rather than as you type it. You may have made color and font choices before you started typing, but it's easier to apply them to existing text. In many programs, you can just select the text and click on buttons or menu selections to change the text's font, size, and color.

Fonts and font sizes are a bit more limited in Web page design than they are in word processing. While you can apply any one from a pool of hundreds of fonts when you're typing a letter or report, you should stick to a small group of fonts when formatting Web page text. These include Times New Roman, Arial (or Helvetica), Courier, and Verdana, as shown below (offered on Dreamweaver's Properties palette). Other fonts may not be supported by your browser or the browsers of your site visitors, and, therefore, will not be properly displayed.

If you want to use other fonts, it's best to create a graphic in Adobe PhotoShop or an illustration program such as Illustrator or CorelDraw. After you've created the image (which may consist solely of text), insert that into the Web page. Figure 9-12 shows a Web page with text that is really a graphic image.

Adding Graphics

Web pages that only contain text are very dull to look at, and unless the text contains exciting information, text-heavy pages won't garner a lot of repeat visitors. And you want people to come back often—to buy things from your company, contract for your services, or donate their money and/or time to your cause.

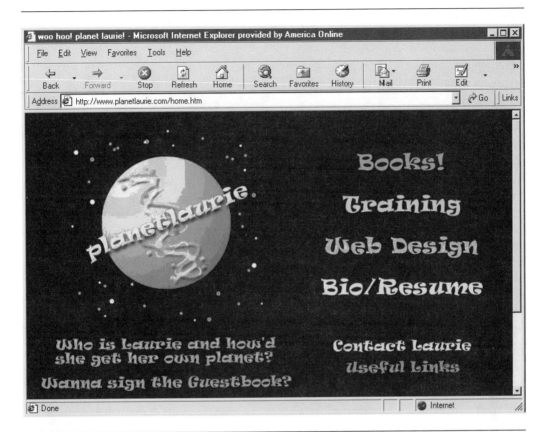

FIGURE 9-12   If you need to use a fancy font, create a graphic of the word or words, and insert it like a picture onto your Web page; site visitors won't be able to tell the difference

Graphics make Web pages more visually interesting. Graphics can be drawings, clip art, photographs, or graphic designs (such as logos) designed in applications such as Adobe PhotoShop, Illustrator, or CorelDraw. By adding pictures of you, your family, your products, your events, or other related images, you involve more of the visitor's brain in the process of viewing your site, increasing their comprehension of your pages.

CAUTION   *When using photos, clip art, or line drawings on your Web page, be sure not to use copyrighted material. You can't simply copy any photo or image from another Web site or from printed originals and reuse them on your site. There are many free images available online and on CD-ROMs that you can buy at most office-supply stores, and you can create your own images as well. Borrowing someone else's artwork or ideas is not only illegal, it reflects poorly on you as a person, and on your organization.*

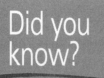

Web Page Design Tips and Tricks

Your Web site says a lot about you. Whether yours is an informal and friendly family Web site or a no-nonsense, conservative business site, you want to make sure that the colors, fonts, and graphic images you use don't contradict the impression you want to make on your site's visitors. Here are some tips for good design and effective color and font choices:

Don't use more than two fonts on any one page. Fonts come in three major types: serif, sans serif, and artistic. You shouldn't combine two from any type, but it's okay to have one serif and one sans serif, or one artistic and one sans serif. Be careful not to use ornate or complex fonts for small text, because it might be illegible on some users' monitors.

Be aware that just because you have some fancy font in your computer, it doesn't mean you can use it successfully in a Web page design. Unless the people viewing your Web site have that font in their computer, they won't be able to see your fancy font. When choosing a font for your text, it's better to stick with the basics—Arial, Verdana, Times New Roman, and Times. Pretty much everyone has these fonts. If you really want to use an offbeat font, search the Web and read up on the topic of embedded fonts for Web pages.

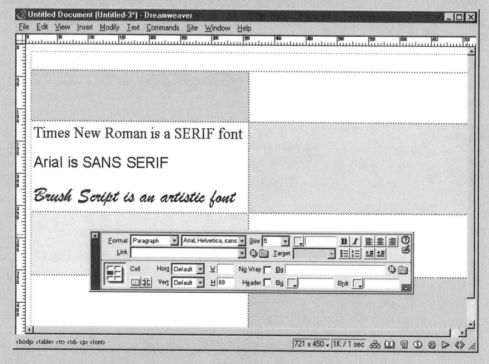

Another point to consider pertains to using graphics.

Do use color, but use it carefully and consistently. Use light and festive colors if you want an upbeat, informal feeling. Use darker, more muted tones if you're trying to convey a serious image.

Don't use a busy background image for your pages. The background image can compete visually with your text and graphics, and it will add significantly to the time it takes your page to load.

Avoid using clip art and cartoon-like images on business Web sites, because they can convey an amateurish feeling. Instead, use photos or simple monotone line art to give your site an elegant, tasteful look.

Keep your layout consistent on each page. If your links and navigation buttons are along the left side of the page on your home page, keep them there on the other pages in your site. Don't make people look around for things on every new page. The more consistent your layout, the easier it will be for people to move around in and experience all the content in your Web site.

Inserting Graphics

To insert a graphic, use the appropriate command in your program. For example, in Dreamweaver, choose the Image command from the Insert menu. In FrontPage, choose the Picture command from the Insert menu, and then select From File. If you're working in HTML, you'll insert an <IMG SRC= *directory path/file name*> tag to tell the browser which graphic to display and where the file is stored.

Choosing a Graphic File Format

Just as the number of fonts that Web browsers can display is rather limited, so is the list of graphic file types that browsers support. At this time, three formats are acceptable: GIF, JPG, and PNG. The most common formats are GIF and JPG. The PNG format has recently been accepted by the W3C (the World Wide Web Consortium) and is growing in popularity among Web designers. New versions of the major browsers (Internet Explorer and Netscape) support it, so it's safe to create graphics in this format.

Other graphic file formats—such as TIF, BMP, and EPS—contain information about the graphic that the browser software can't interpret or turn into a displayed image. Furthermore, these file types generate large files, and large files are to be avoided on the Web. If it takes a long time for your image to display, the visitor will move on out of boredom.

To choose which of the three approved file formats to use for your graphics, consider the graphic content.

- The GIF format is best for line art and simple images such as logos.

- The JPG is the best format for photos or detailed drawings.

- The PNG format is fine for either line art or photos.

There are programs specifically for optimally compressing graphics so they load into Web pages as fast as possible. Check out Fireworks from Macromedia, for example.

If your image is large (in terms of the file size), you can choose to make the image *interlaced* or *progressive,* two terms that mean the same thing. Images that are interlaced or progressive will compose slowly, starting out choppy and blurry, and becoming smooth and clear as the page is fully loaded in your browser. Figure 9-13 shows an interlaced photo composing on the screen.

How big is too big? Try to keep your images below 20K, bearing in mind a simple rule of thumb: For every kilobyte of file size, allow a second of download time. That means a 60K file could take a full minute to appear on the page, which is likely to be too long for most Web users. If the image is essential to the visitor's experience on the page, he or she might not wait around for the page to compose, choosing to go to a site where all the important stuff comes up right away.

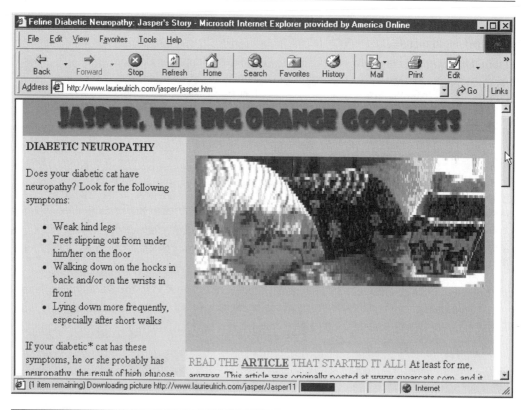

FIGURE 9-13   An interlaced image starts out blurry as it is downloaded to the page

Remember that most Web site visitors use modems, rather than T1 lines or networks connecting them directly to the Internet. Design your page around these users' needs, and keep your pages simple and quick-loading.

Laying Out Your Page with Tables

Whether you're using Dreamweaver, FrontPage, or Word, you're limited in terms of where text and graphics can be placed on the page. As shown in Figure 9-14, if you attempt to insert a graphic next to text, the results will not be what you're looking for, because the two objects

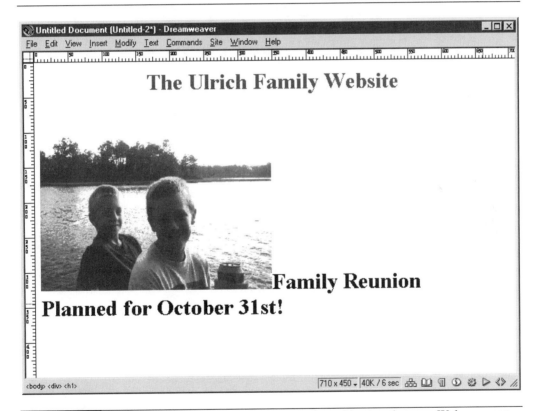

FIGURE 9-14 Finding creative ways to place text and graphics together on a Web page can be challenging

won't align vertically. You can't easily align items, such as centered text next to a picture, so it's difficult to create an interesting or orderly layout for your page.

The solution to producing an orderly layout is to use tables. You can create tables in any Web design application, as well as directly through HTML code. Tables are simply a collection of columns and rows, the width and height of which you can adjust to create a customized grid to house your text and graphics. Figure 9-15 shows the same Web content as in Figure 9-14, but this time, the content is arranged in a table.

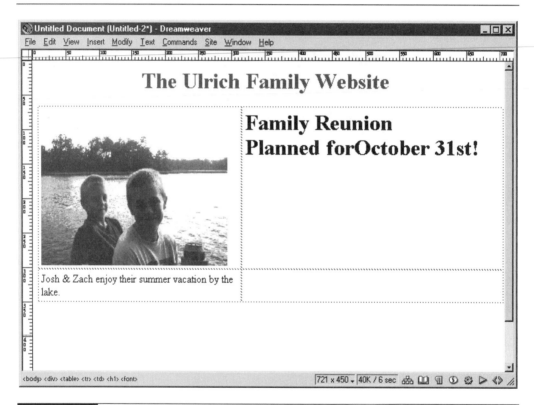

FIGURE 9-15   A table gives you more control over the placement of text and graphics on your Web page

Inserting Tables

In Dreamweaver, you can add a table to your Web page by choosing Table from the Insert menu. If you're working in FrontPage or Word, the command to insert a table is Insert (or Insert Table), which is on the Table menu. These commands bring up the program's Insert Table dialog box, as shown here (in Dreamweaver).

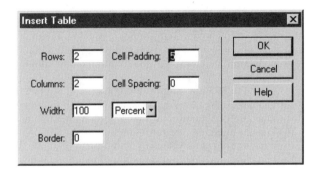

In this dialog box, you specify the number of columns and rows for your table, as well as the following settings:

- **Cell Spacing**   A *cell* is an individual compartment in your table, like a box. The cell spacing establishes the distance between the edges of the cells. Cell spacing is measured in pixels and is set to zero by default. If you don't want your table cell edges to touch, change the Cell Spacing setting to the amount of spacing you want between them.

- **Cell Padding**   The cell padding determines the space between the content of the cell and the cell's edges (like the margins on a document page). Like cell spacing, cell padding is measured in pixels and set to zero by default. To keep your text well away from the edge of your table cells, change the Cell Padding setting to 5 pixels.

- **Width**   The Width setting determines the amount of the Web page that the table should occupy. You can choose to express this in exact measurements (pixels) or as a percentage of the whole page.

- **Border**   The Border setting specifies the thickness of the lines around the table and its cells, measured in pixels. Unless you want a visible frame around each of your cells or your entire table, set your table border to zero.

9

Once your table is created, you can customize it further by dragging column and row borders to adjust the dimensions of columns, rows, and individual cells. You can also merge cells to create one large cell out of two or more smaller cells, or split cells to break up one cell into several cells. The commands work similarly in different software applications. For example, in FrontPage, all table adjustments can be made through the Table menu, as shown here.

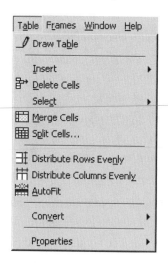

Inserting Text and Graphics into Tables

To place text in a table cell, click in the cell and begin typing. The text will wrap within the cell when it hits the right margin of the cell. You can apply left, center, and right alignment within the cell, using the Properties palette in Dreamweaver or the toolbar in FrontPage.

To place a graphic in a table cell, click in the cell that should contain the graphic, and then choose the program's command for inserting a graphic (Image on the Insert menu in Dreamweaver, or Picture, From File from the Insert menu in FrontPage or Word). After you've inserted the graphic, you can resize the image by dragging its corner handles (to maintain current horizontal and vertical proportions) and align it just as you would align text.

Even though you can size a picture this way, it' considered the cheater' approach. The image can end up looking blurry because the Web browser itself is doing the resizing of the picture. You'll get better-looking results by resizing your image using a good image editing program such as Photoshop, Paintshop Pro, or Fireworks.

Figure 9-16 shows a graphic in a cell alongside a cell containing text. When viewed through a browser, the gridlines will disappear (if a table border of zero is set), and the table outline will be invisible.

You can adjust the color of individual table cells, or leave them unfilled so that your page background color or image shows through. To color an individual table cell, click inside it and

Family Reunion
Planned for October 31st!

Bring your ghosts and goblins, and a treat for us all to share.
We'll be carving pumpkins (and having a contest for the
scariest) at 5 p.m., followed by dinner at 7 and a dance around
the bonfire to frighten off the evil spirits.

Hope to see you there! Call Audrey at 222-555-2468 to get
directions to her house at the beach, or send her an email.

FIGURE 9-16   Tables allow you to neatly align graphics and text

9

choose a color from the palette or toolbar. In Figure 9-17, a table with different colored cells not
only provides a grid into which text and graphics can be placed, but also creates an interesting
visual effect that keeps the viewer's eye moving around on the page.

*Web colors are expressed as a combination of letters and/or numbers. For example,
light blue is CCCCFF, and bright red is FF3300. You don't need to know these
numbers unless you're working in HTML or you're attempting to match a color at your
site with a color found at another Web site or created for use on the Web through a
product such as Adobe PhotoShop.*

Making Links to Pages and Web Sites

Links (also called *hyperlinks*) are what give a Web page depth. Without them, you couldn't go
from page to page by clicking on text or graphics. Instead, you would need to enter new Web
page addresses in the browser's address bar each time you wanted to go somewhere new.

Beyond giving pages functional depth, links enable you to connect your home page to the
rest of your site's pages, as well as to Web sites external to your own. You can create links that
connect your pages to Web sites that offer related information or to sites you simply feel are
interesting and should be shared. If, for example, your business belongs to a professional

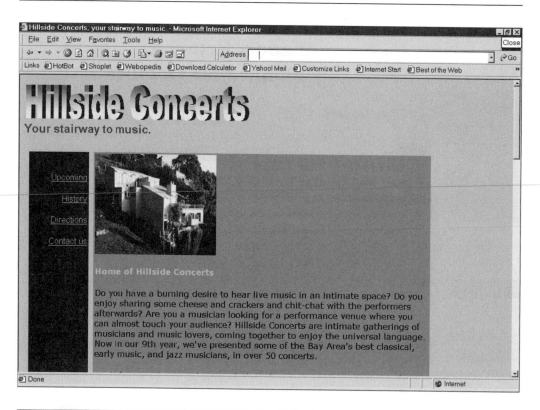

FIGURE 9-17   Adding color to cells can make the layout more interesting

organization, a link to that organization's site would be a great idea. A family Web site might contain links to the Web sites other family members have created or to a genealogy site that people can use to find lost relatives.

Creating links is easy, no matter which tool you're using to develop your pages:

In Dreamweaver, select the text or graphic that should serve as the link, and then choose Make Link from the Modify menu. You can also type the link directly into the Properties palette, as shown here.

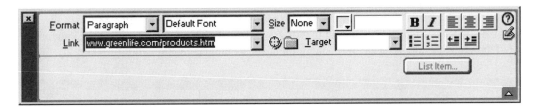

In FrontPage or Word, select the text or graphic that you want to be a link, and then choose Hyperlink from the Insert menu. In the dialog box that appears, enter the address of the target page, as shown here.

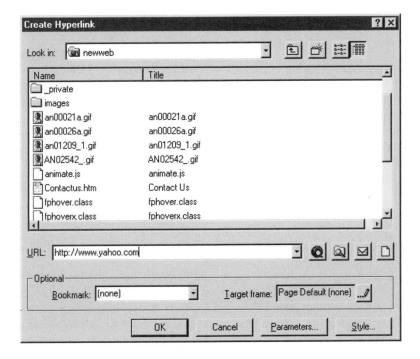

9

If you're writing HTML code, you'll need to create an <A HREF= *Web page address*> tag within the attributes for a given string of text or graphic, as shown below. The tag should include the full path to and address of the Web site or the name of the page within your own site.

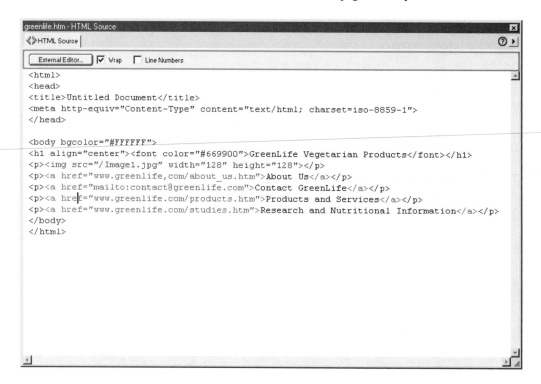

Once the link is created, test it by previewing your page in a browser. Simply save the file and then open it (by choosing the Open command on the File menu) in your Web browser (for example, Internet Explorer or Netscape). When you point to the text or graphic, your mouse pointer should change to a pointing finger, and you should see the Web address to which the link points displayed in the lower-left corner of the browser window. Click the link to go to the designated site or page.

 *In Dreamweaver, you can enter text that will appear in a screen tip when viewers move their mouse over your link. Type the text, such as "Click here to see our Products Page," in the ALT text box in the Properties palette.*

Naming Your Domain

Your domain is your Web site name. It must be unique (two people can't have the same domain name), and it can't have any symbols other than dashes or underscores in it. You'll want a domain name that's the same as your name (for a personal or family Web site), your company's name (for a business site), or your organization's name.

Domain names are registered with the InterNIC, the administrative body that maintains many standards for the Internet. Registration entails selecting an available domain name, providing contact information for you or your organization, and paying a fee to own the domain name. The fee is generally $70 for two years, and you're billed bi-annually. Recently, some domain registry services have started offering one-year registrations for $35.

Researching Available Names

Due to the popularity of having one's own Web site, many names have already been taken. Your own name, such as www.johnsmith.com, might already be taken. Another company or organization may have already registered the domain name you wanted. You may be forced to come up with an alternative, so be prepared by creating a list of names you would be willing to use, rather than assuming the one and only name you like will be available.

> **TIP**
>
> *If your family name is already taken, try Mailbank, a company that owns thousands of family names. You can "rent" your family name with your first names attached (such as john.smith.com) and set up parallel email accounts, such as john@smith.com. This saves your having to come up with an alternative domain name if your family name is taken or the expense of a domain name and ISP/host even if your name is available. Check out Mailbank at www.mailbank.com.*

Before you can register your domain name, you need to be sure the name is available. You can research the available names through any domain registry site, such as those listed here:

- www.networksolutions.com
- www.register.com
- www.domainbank.com
- www.getdomain.com
- www.domainregistry.com

From the registry site, type the domain name you want. The site will then search the database of domain names and let you know if your name is taken. As shown in Figure 9-18, the domain name search process is simple and gives you a quick answer.

You might discover that the .com version of the name you want is taken, but the .net or .org version is available. If you're a nonprofit organization (such as a church, a charity, or a fund-raising organization), you'll be happy to get the .org version. If you're a business, however, you might want to come up with another name, rather than go with the .net version of the name. This is because many people will assume yours is the .com version, and they will end up at someone else's site—not what you want to happen, especially if the owner of the .com version is a competitor!

9

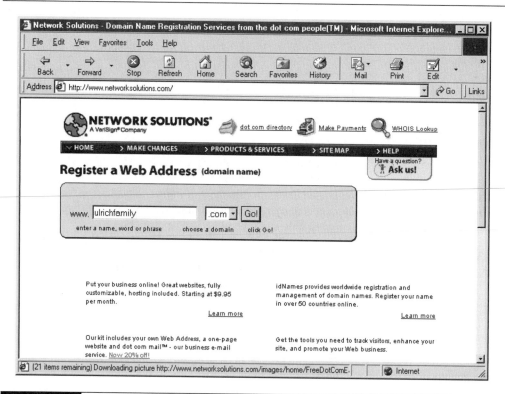

FIGURE 9-18   Type the name you want and click Go (or Search, depending on the site); the status of the name you're researching will appear in just a few seconds

If the domain name you wanted is taken, you can find out who has registered it by executing a "Whois" search. Most domain-registry sites offer this service, through a "Whois" button or a link that indicates that you can find out who has the name you wanted to register. Click the link and view the name and address of the person or organization who owns the domain. You can contact them to see if they are willing to give up the site, or to sell the name to you, but don't count on their being willing to do so.

Registering Your Domain Name

Through the site you used to research the name's availability, you can also register it. The process will involve your filling out an online form, such as the one shown in Figure 9-19. The form asks for your name, address, e-mail address, phone number, and credit card number.

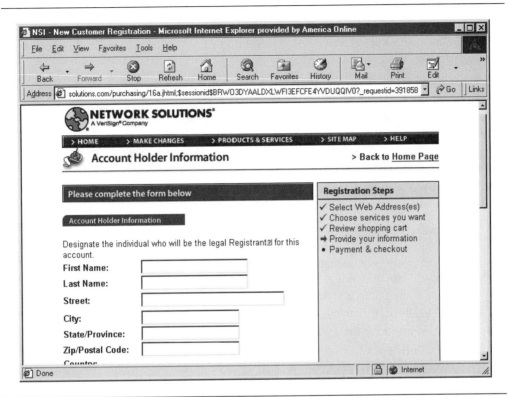

FIGURE 9-19   Identify yourself and provide payment information to register your domain name

You may see the option to "park" your domain (usually for free) with the domain registry company you're using to research and buy your domain name. If you don't have a Web host, you need to park the name until you have a host. If you have a host, you should register the name through the hosting service. After you've found an available domain name, simply exit the registry site and go register your site through your hosting company or ISP's Web site. By registering through the host, your Web space will be allocated under the domain you've chosen at the same time the domain is registered with the InterNIC, saving you time and administrative effort. Finding a host is discussed in the next section.

Finding a Host for Your Web Site

A *host* stores your Web site on its Web server. If you don't have a host to store your Web site, it's easy enough to find one. You can ask friends and colleagues who they use to host their sites, you can find out if your ISP offers hosting services, or you can do a search on the Web.

 *A Web server is a computer that stores Web sites and provides access to them via the Internet. The server is contacted when you type the Web address (URL) into your browser, and the pages stored on the server under your domain name are displayed on the screen.*

To do a Web search, simply type "Web hosting" into the Search box at your favorite search site (such as Yahoo!, AltaVista, HotBot, or Google) and explore the sites that meet your search criteria. That way, you can check out the various hosting company Web sites and choose the one that has the most services and support for the best price.

Choosing a Hosting Service

Before you hand over your hard-earned credit to a hosting company, it's a good idea to understand your hosting options. There are several types of hosting services available:

- **Web hosting companies**   Hosting companies offer Web space for your domain name, e-mail addresses using your domain (such as jsmith@domain.com), and an FTP (File Transfer Protocol) site through which you can upload your Web pages to their server. Many hosting companies will bill your credit card monthly (generally about $20 per month) or allow you to pay yearly, which normally offers some savings over the monthly payment option.

- **ISPs**   You may have some free Web space coming to you through your ISP. Most ISPs offer at least 2MB of space to their subscribers, at no extra charge. The downside is that you probably won't be able to get a simple *yourname*.com domain name this way. Instead, you'll end up with something like www.*ispname*.com/*yourname*/*yourname*.htm. This is probably not a good way to go for businesses or nonprofit organizations, because people wouldn't be able to find your site as easily. However, this approach can be great for families who only want their own family and friends to access the site.

- **Online communities**   Services such as AOL (America Online) also give their members Web space. For example, through AOL, you can set up your Web page (using their design software within the AOL environment) and post it immediately to the AOL server. Again, as in the case of the free space offered by a regular ISP, the Web address is more cumbersome, such as www.aol.com/members/*yourname*.htm.

When evaluating your Web hosting options, look for the service that will meet your most important needs. If you're a business or organization that needs to be easily found by potential clients, working with an ISP or online community may not be the best idea, despite the low or no-cost Web space. If you're going to set up a personal or family Web site and want a little anonymity, working through your ISP or online community might be just the ticket.

Checking Host Features

No matter which service you choose, check out the service before setting up your site. You should investigate the following aspects of the hosting service you are considering:

- ■ **Service and support**   Does the service offer an 800 number to call if you have problems with your Web site? Is customer support available 7 days a week, 24 hours a day? Do you need to wait a long time to get a response from either the customer service or technical support people?

- ■ **Site features**   Does your Web site come with a counter (to keep track of how many visitors you've had), a guest book (to store data about people who visit your site), and an FTP address to use in uploading your site content? Also, some hosting companies can provide log reports for you (for free, or for a small fee) that show you who visited your site, when, and how many times. Ask about this when investigating potential hosts, especially if yours is a business site that relies on frequent and repeat visits.

- ■ **Reputation**   Ask around to see if anyone you know has had experience with the hosting service. Ask the hosting company for a list of references. Of course, they'll only give you the names of people who love them, but if you visit those sites and see that all is running well, at least you know they're doing a good job for someone.

- ■ **Downtime**   All hosts (and ISPs) require some downtime to do system upgrades, fix technical problems, and so on. This shouldn't result in your site being down while these functions are being performed. Ask the customer service people how they handle this and if your site will ever be down due to their technical maintenance schedule. The answer should be "No."

9

Posting Your Page to the Web

Once you've designed your Web site pages, registered your domain name, and found a host, you're ready to post your site to the Web. Posting your site involves uploading the pages and graphic files to your host or ISP's Web server. To do this, you will use an FTP program that allows you to connect via modem to the Web server. (FTP stands for *File Transfer Protocol*, the means by which files are transmitted across from your computer to the Web server.)

FTP software is available for free (through generous trial versions and freeware) online. You can do a search for "FTP software" from a search site, or you can go to any of the following software sites and do a search there for free FTP programs:

- ■ www.hotfiles.com
- ■ www.tucows.com
- ■ www.gnu.org
- ■ www.add-soft.com

You can follow the site's instructions for downloading the FTP software, and then use the setup.exe file that is copied to your computer to install the software for use on your PC. Once the software is installed, simply double-click the program icon and set up your connection to the host's or ISP's FTP site.

Some better Web-design programs have FTP services built into them and will upload your files directly to your Web server without using an external program. Search your Web-page editor for the term "FTP" and you might discover this feature.

Connecting to an FTP Site

Most FTP software works the same way. When you start the program, a two-sided screen appears, one side representing your local computer, and the other side representing the remote FTP site to which you're connecting, as shown in Figure 9-20.

After entering the FTP site address, your user name, and your login password, you click on the Connect button to connect to the FTP site. Most FTP sites are password-protected for security. Your host company or ISP will give you a user name and password when you arrange to use Web space on their server. After you're connected to the remote site, its listing should appear on your FTP program's screen (see Figure 9-20).

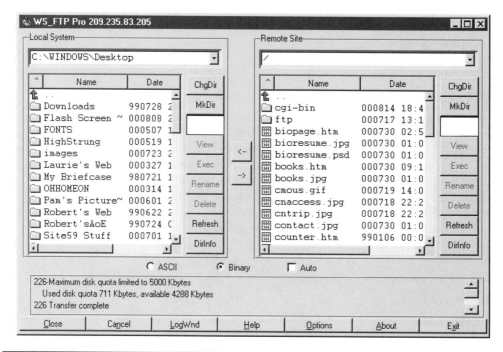

FIGURE 9-20   FTP programs contain lists of the folders and files on your local system and your remote site's system

Uploading Your Pages to the Web

Once your FTP connection is established, select the files on your local computer to copy (upload) to the remote FTP site, and click on the button to copy your files to that site. (In the example shown in Figure 9-20, click on the right-pointing arrow button.) The files will be copied, at a speed dictated by your modem connection, to the FTP site. The FTP software window will provide an ongoing display of the uploading process.

It's important to create the same folder structure on the FTP site as you were working with on your local PC. This is the structure that you used when inserting graphics and establishing links to pages within your site. With the same structure, your references to graphic files and Web pages that you included in your pages will display and function properly. If you don't mimic the local PC's folder structure on the FTP site, your graphics won't appear on the page, displaying instead as missing picture icons, as in the example shown in Figure 9-21.

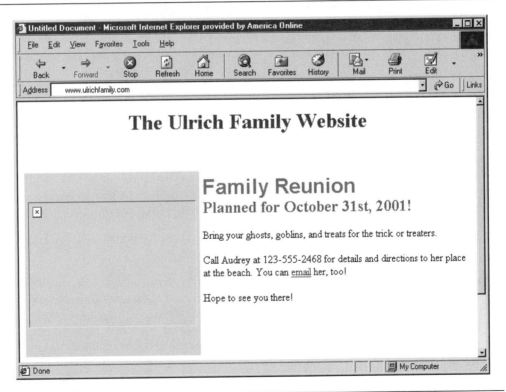

FIGURE 9-21   If the graphics aren't stored in the path that your Web pages' HTML code indicates, the browser won't be capable of displaying your graphic images

If, for example, you saved your graphics in a folder called Pictures, you should create a Pictures folder on the FTP site as well, and copy the graphic files to that folder. Generally, Web pages are stored in the root (main) directory, and graphics are either in their own folder or stored along with the Web pages at the root. To create a folder on the FTP site, click on the File menu and choose New Folder. Name the new folder to match the name of the folder on your local PC, such as Pictures to match your own Pictures folder, as shown here.

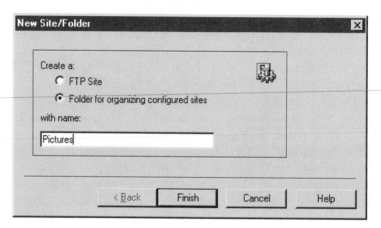

Make sure the folder name is exactly the same as the folder on your local computer. If your local folders have spaces or symbols in their names, rename them on your PC first, so that there are no spaces or symbols used. Most browsers don't support the use of spaces or symbols in file or folder names.

If you're using FrontPage, you can use the Publish command on the File menu. This feature automates the process of posting your pages and related material (graphics, documents, multimedia files) to your host's server.

A common mistake to make when creating Web pages is erroneous links to pictures on your pages. It's easy to accidentally add pictures that have "absolute" file names on them, pointing to a folder on your hard disk. Once you publish this page on the Web, other viewers will see blank images, but if you check the page on your computer, it will look fine. This can be frustrating when friends and colleagues report that your page images aren't working, yet it seems to be fine on your computer. So, you should always do some testing of your Web site on multiple computers, especially on ones other than the one you designed the site on. This will help you iron out errors in your page design. While you're at it, you should look at your site using different browsers, specifically netscape navigator, IE, and the AOL browser. You'd be surprised how differently a page can look on different browsers. You might have to fine-tune your site—pay attention to tables in particular—to work across the various browsers properly.

Chapter 10

Digital Photography

How to...

- ■ Choose a digital camera
- ■ Bring your digital photos into your PC
- ■ Store and organize your digital photos
- ■ Alter your photos using graphic applications
- ■ Share your pictures with others
- ■ Turn digital pictures into prints

You may have seen one or your computer-savvy friends at a recent wedding or other event snapping one of those fancy, new digital cameras. You know, the ones where you instantly see the picture, a bit like a Polaroid, but without the paper? Well, they're all the rage now, but when digital cameras first hit the market, they were well-beyond the average budget, well more than $1,000. The essential imaging portion of a digital camera, (called CCDs for *charge-coupled devices*) were prohibitively expensive to manufacture, thus putting the cameras out of range of the average consumer. As CCD manufacturing costs have come down, camera prices have plummeted. Today, there are scads of very-affordable digital cameras to fuel your photographic imagination and creative instincts. With digital cameras, pictures can be captured, viewed, and in some cases, even printed directly from the camera! This chapter introduces you to the creative world of digital photography. You will learn what digital photography is all about, how to get started, and how to share your photos with others.

Getting a Digital Camera

Before digital cameras, an image or photo needed to be scanned to produce a digital file the computer understands. Scanners have been around for years now, but digital cameras are relatively new, appearing in the mainstream only about four years ago.

Digital cameras have plunged into the computer world like a hot knife through butter, ranking with the Palm Pilot as one of the most popular electronic gadgets of the last few years, despite their relatively high cost. Especially if you intend to share your image-capturing talent over the Internet, a digital camera is a wise and economical choice. The images they produce are perfect for placing on a Web site or sending via e-mail. The better of the digital cameras can produce a quite credible 8 x 10 print, if you have a decent printer at your disposal, too.

Digital Cameras Versus Film Cameras

Relative to a traditional film camera, digitals are now on the order of four times as expensive. Two years ago it was more like eight to one. Although pricey up front, the cost savings in film and processing make digital cameras well worth considering. How many times have you taken pictures that come out black or blurry? Unfortunately, with film cameras, you don't have the opportunity to see the results immediately. Digital cameras enable you to see the picture in less than 10 seconds. If it didn't come out the way you had envisioned, simply delete your last shot and take the picture over again. Also, you can bring your digital photos into an image-capturing program and make all sorts of corrections and add a vast array of special effects—significantly more than are available in a well-equipped darkroom.

Don't get me wrong—film cameras have their advantages. The pictures they produce typically outclass those of a digital camera, even if you use the most expensive digital camera on the market today. If you are a professional photographer or taking photos that will be reproduced in printed material such as magazines or advertisements, you will probably want to stick with film cameras, at least for the time being. You can always use a scanner to get printed photos into your computer if you need to, and treat them just like the shots taken with your digital camera. But standard film might not have the upper-hand on quality for long. I've just seen an eight-foot-square photograph print taken with the latest-generation digital camera that was awesome.

Digital cameras were designed to *interface* (communicate) with computers. Since computers only understand bits (1s and 0s), digital cameras capture images using that technology, breaking images down into binary bits, essentially painting by number.

By contrast, film cameras are analog in nature. Analog film creates essentially an infinite number of shades and colors instead of on or off, black or white, one or zero. The volume control on your radio is a prime example of how analog can be better than digital. If you turn the volume down, and it is digital, you may notice that the change between one volume number and another may be too great. With analog, you can adjust this value to your particular preference. In short, the volume can be fine-tuned.

Currently, the CCDs in digital cameras are not sensitive enough to capture and interpret the many minute differentiations that the human eye can, instead breaking down visual characteristics such that each shade variant is given a numeric value. This value is not the exact shade; it is a value that is the closest match, meaning the shade may be altered slightly, rounded off to the closest value. Also, CCDs don't have the same *dynamic range* as film. This can cause digital pictures to suffer from overexposure in strong light or underexposure in low light. The upshot is that digital cameras, although capable of creating strikingly beautiful images under the right conditions, can take some coaxing and fiddling to do so. Figure 10-1 shows a few of today's digital cameras. Notice the wide variety of shapes and sizes.

What to Look for in a Digital Camera

Digital cameras have come a long way since their introduction into the market. Some of the more expensive cameras produce nearly film-quality images. Other, more affordable, cameras produce photos that look lifelike when viewed on your computer screen, but don't print quite as well as an image from film.

When you shop for a camera, you want to consider how you intend to use it. Are you going to take pictures that will only be viewed on a monitor, or will you want to produce prints at some time? If so, how large and of what quality will those prints need to be? Here are some of the other questions you need to ask before purchasing a digital camera:

■ *Does it have a preview screen where you can view the picture before and after it is taken?* You'll typically want a bright LCD display of two inches or more. In bright sunlight you probably won't be able to see the LCD, so you'll want to have a *optical viewfinder* to aim through, too.

FIGURE 10-1 Digital cameras come in a variety of shapes and sizes partly because there is no film inside that would require specific lens-film positioning

- *How many pictures does it store?* This usually depends on the size of the removable memory card thrown in with the camera, though cheaper cameras sometimes have only internal RAM that can't be expanded. Most cameras have a variety of capture modes that will vary the number of shots you can store, too, so read the specs on the camera carefully. Note that most cameras let you swap out the RAM cards while in the field, so you can, theoretically, shoot indefinitely. However, in reality the cost of the RAM cards prohibits this. As a rule of thumb, using a 2.1 mega-pixel camera, an 8MB card enables you to store approximately 28 pictures.

- *What kind of storage media does it use?* Smart Media, Compact Flash, Sony Memory Stick, or a removable disk? There's a running battle between all these media formats. I prefer the Compact Flash (CF) format. CF cards have a lower per-megabyte cost than the SmartMedia and Memory Stick and are available in higher capacities. CF cards are smaller in size than disks, too, helping to keep cameras more diminutive.

- *What interface does it use to communicate with your system (USB, serial, IR, or another port)?* And thus, how long does it take to transfer a full set of images into your computer?

- *What type of energy source does it require or support (batteries or AC)?* If the camera comes with rechargeable nickel metal hydride (NiMH) or lithium-ion (Li) batteries all the better.

- *How many pictures can the camera take on a single charge of the batteries?* Note that if a camera normally runs on alkaline AA or AAA batteries, a set of NiMH batteries and charger will typically net you more than 10 times the number of shots.

- *If the batteries are rechargeable, does the recharger come with the camera or is it purchased separately?*

- *Does the camera have zoom or panoramic capabilities?* Some cameras have a "digital zoom" but zooming in digitally will produce a fuzzy image. You'll want an optical zoom, preferably 3x or more.

- *What image resolutions does the camera produce?* Along with the lens system, this is the major determinant of image quality and is directly related to the number of *pixels* the camera produces. Pixels are the tiny dots that comprise the picture. When you see ads touting a camera as a 1-megapixel, 2.1-megapixel, 3.2-megapixel, etc., this is what they are referring to. The more pixels a camera's CCD sensor has, the larger and more detailed the images produced. Because you can always reduce a picture's size for, say, putting it on a Web site, large pictures are not a liability except in that they consume RAM in the camera and on your computer's hard disk. But the reverse is not true—that is, you can't create a high-quality enlargement from a small image. So, unless you are going to be taking pictures *only* for use with emails and the Web, you'll want to get a camera with the greatest number of pixels your budget can afford.

- *Does the camera have a decent lens?* Remember, you get what you pay for. A zillion–pixel camera with a bad lens is a waste of money. The good lens makers have been in the camera business for a long time. Look for names like Nikon, Canon, Olympus, Agfa, Kodak, and Fuji. The likes of Sony and Casio can be acceptable, but they are relative newcomers to photography, capitalizing on their knowledge of electronics, not glass optics.

- *Does the camera accept accessory lenses such as wide angle, fisheye, or telephoto?* Many digitals don't. If it does, what is the cost of such attachment lenses?

- *Can the camera capture black and white as well as color?* This can be useful for taking pictures of text documents such as book pages. Software in your computer can change pictures to black and white, so this is not a big deal. However, if the camera can capture in black and white, you can store more images in the camera before having to transfer them into your computer.

- *Does it come with supporting software that helps you manage your photos, create photo albums, print pictures in different sizes, and so on?*

- *How many seconds does the camera require to snap and store a picture, ready to take the next shot?* Some cameras are just too slow, and this will annoy you when you hope to capture the action.

- *Can you override the automatic settings to adjust the f-stop, shutter speed, focus, and so on, or is the camera fully automatic?* If you like to fiddle with your pictures, you'll want both.

- *Can the camera photograph tiny objects using a "macro" mode?*

- *Does it feel good to carry around and shoot with?* This is a big decision point for many camera buffs. Be realistic. Regardless of all the bells and whistles the camera has, you won't be taking many pictures if it weighs five pounds and doesn't fit in your pocket.

10

Digital Camera Information

If you want to know more about various digital cameras on the market today, theseWeb sites offer some good information regarding the features of various cameras: www.dcresource.com or www.steves-digicams.com.

If you want to see some of the author's photographs, including macros and panorama pictures, check www.cowart.com/nikon.

Getting Your Photos into Your PC

There are two basic ways to get an image onto your system. You can download the image from a digital camera, or your scan a printed image. Getting a picture into digital form is known as *acquisition*. Once a photo has been acquired in digital form, it can be altered with image-editing software, sent with e-mail, or added to a Web page.

Downloading Images from a Digital Camera

Getting your photos from your digital camera to your computer is easy. Most digital cameras come with very intuitive software and a cable that attaches to a port on your system. Basically, all you need to do is install the software onto your system, attach the cable to the appropriate port, and voilà, you're ready to copy your images onto your hard drive. If you have a USB port on your computer and on the camera, you're in luck. This is probably the easiest approach.

Windows Me has an applet in the Windows Control Panel called Scanners and Cameras, for easily acquiring images from these devices. Open the Control Panel, run the applet, and follow the instructions to install your camera or scanner. It's best to connect and power up the camera or scanner first so your PC will auto-detect it. After you have successfully installed your device, follow these steps to get your pictures out of it:

1. Click Start, Programs, Accessories, and then click Scanner and Camera Wizard.

2. Click the device you want to get pictures from, and then click OK.

3. Follow the onscreen instructions.

 The Scanner and Camera Wizard only appear on the Start menu after you install a scanner or digital camera.

Some camera brands or models don't have drivers that work through the Scanners and Cameras interface. In that case, you have a couple of alternatives: One is to check to see if there is download software supplied with the camera.

For example, Epson offers a useful application that enables you to copy the images from an Epson digital camera to your system. Just start up this program and choose the View Pictures in the Camera option form the Image Export window, as shown in Figure 10-2. Once you have your pictures in your system, this frees up the RAM in your camera so you can go shoot some more pictures. You can also use the Epson program to organize your photos into albums or adjust the color and lighting to make your photos easier to see.

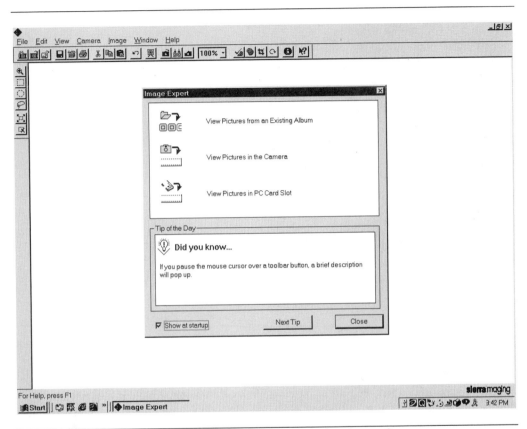

FIGURE 10-2   Using the Epson camera software to acquire pictures from your camera

Depending on the camera model you choose, you might want to use an alternative means of downloading images, especially if your camera and computer don't both have USB ports. As mentioned earlier, most cameras offer removable media, such as Compact Flash, SmartMedia, or a floppy disk (in the case of the Sony Mavica cameras). Being able to remove the media means you can transfer the images into your computer more quickly than over a cable attached to the camera. For example, with the Sony Mavica cameras, all you have to do is remove the disk from your camera and insert it into your system's floppy disk drive to read in the pictures.

With Compact Flash and SmartMedia you'll use a different approach. A small device called a *card reader* attaches to your USB, parallel, or other port on the computer. Figure 10-3 shows several types of card readers available on the market.

Remove the Compact Flash or SmartMedia card from your camera, plug it into the card reader, and the images are sucked into your computer for storage on the hard disk. Avoid card readers that use the serial port on your computer because they are too slow. The solution I use

Internal card reader

PCMCIA CF card adapter

Parallel port card reader

Multiple-format USB card reader

FIGURE 10-3 Various card readers

is even more portable. I have a PCMCIA Compact Flash card adapter. It's the size of a standard PCMCIA card for laptops that my Compact Flash card plugs into. Then I insert the PCMCIA card into the side of the computer, and Windows recognizes it as an external disk drive. I can easily copy the files from it to the hard disk, just as if it were a floppy disk, Zip disk, etc.

Scanning Prints

Scanning enables you to turn your prints into digital images your system can comprehend. Flat-bed scanners for home or office use are affordable and easy to find at your local computer store. You just put your printed photo on the scanner bed, push a button, or choose a command on the computer screen, and the scanner's software converts the picture into a digital photo you can store in your computer. Some scanners include a slide attachment so you can scan slides as well as prints.

An alternative to flatbed scanners that will produce superior images is known as the *film scanner* or *slide scanner*. These specialized scanners are available for prices ranging from a few hundred dollars to more than $1,000. You simply feed in your slides, prints, or negatives, and high-quality images appear on your computer screen. HP makes some very good and affordable ones.

If you have taken pictures with a film camera, another option is to have the exposures saved to a CD-ROM. Most Kodak film-processing shops offer photo CDs at very reasonable prices. Going this route offers a very good way of acquiring excellent-quality digital images, because the image negatives are scanned with a high-resolution drum scanner. A drum scanner works similarly to a regular flat-bed scanner, except the image is placed on a large revolving drum. This process produces better results than flat-bed scanning.

Storing Your Photos

After you've brought your photos into your PCs, you'll need to figure out the best way to store them, sort them, and archive them. You'll also want to know just how they are stored—their file format.

Photo Storage Space

One thing you need to consider when storing photos is space. Digital photos take up a considerable amount of space. Provided you have ample storage available on your hard drive, you can store your images there; however, if your hard disk ever fails (crashes), you have lost your precious pictures.

It is highly recommended that you store your images on removable media such as Zip disks or CD-ROMs. This will save room on your hard drive and will make your photos portable. They can be viewed from other computers or taken to a film-processing shop where they can be printed for you. (See Chapters 16 and 17 for more information about Zip disks, CD-ROMs, and other removable storage.)

Photo Organization

Digital photos have a habit of accumulating rather quickly, even more than regular photos, since you don't have to pay for film or processing. Before you know it, you have folders upon folders of images that have since lost their meaning and magic.

Here are a couple of simple tips that will help keep your precious photos from falling into a mass of confusion:

- Download your photos into a folder that describes the content, with a name such as Summer Vacation – Aug_00.

- View the photos in your photo album. Delete the photos you don't like, and rename the photos you do like. Most photos are named with a number when they are downloaded. Select a file name that best describes the photo, such as August_00_Erika at Lake Annette -.

- If you want to more fully organize, figure out what's the most important criteria for finding photos. I like to organize mine into categories such as "Friends," "Trips," "Natute" and so forth. I have about 20 categories that seem to cover all the bases, including "Misc" for those that don't fit cleanly into one of the categories.

- Unless you need them on your computer's hard disk, erase the hard disk files as soon as you archive the images on external media. That will free up often-scant hard disk space. Until archived, store them under a folder called something like "To be archived," as a memory jogger so you know what's been archived.

10

■ Some cameras number each "roll" of pictures using the same numbering scheme. My old Nikon 900s, for example, labels each first new picture "DSC00001.jpg". Without some care on my part, I'll end up with a bunch of pictures with the same file name, or files that overwrite one another.

Photo File Formats

Digital images are stored in a file format that computers can read. This file format is usually JPEG (Joint Photographic Expert Group) because they take up the least amount of hard disk space. With some cameras, photos can also be saved uncompressed as TIFF (Tagged Image File Format), or as GIF (Graphic Interchange Format) files.

The format is noted in the file name extension on the photo file. For instance, a digital picture of your puppy could be named puppy.jpg. From this file name, you know that it was saved in a JPEG format. (No, you cannot simply change the format extension to change the file format, you have to use an image-editing program to do that.)

JPEG is the desired format for all but the highest-quality photographs. GIF is the desired format for line art and computer-generated graphics. Web browsers can read both formats. The reason that one format is desired over another is due to compression and display issues. JPEG simply does a better job of compressing and displaying photos than GIF. On the flip side, GIF is better at compressing and displaying graphics. TIF formats are the least compressed, so the picture will remain as sharp as possible. However, the TIF format creates large files.

Exercising Your Artistic License

Okay, so now that you have your photos in your computer, what do you do with them? Well, that's the fun part. You can do anything you want. There are many graphic applications that enable you to play with photos. You can make fixes to improve the quality of the photo, apply special effects, add and remove selected photo parts, and much more.

A few popular image-editing programs are PaintShop Pro, Adobe PhotoShop, and PrintShop. All three include many features for working and playing with photos. If you do this sort of thing professionally, or want to someday, PhotoShop is the Rolls Royce of photo-editing programs and is highly recommended. It offers all the features of other graphic applications, plus a few more bells and whistles that generate awesome special effects. It has a steeper learning curve and is a bit more expensive, but it's well worth the time and expense.

The digital image in Figure 10-4 was captured with a digital camera, and then brought into Photoshop. Using various filters, the image was modified to create the effects you see.

Every photographer has experienced red-eye in photos—you know, that funny little red dot on the eye that makes the photo's subject look rather demonic. This red dot occurs when light (usually from the camera's flash) reflects off the eye's retina. In digital format, this problem can be corrected with a click of your mouse button. This stage of digital photography is known as image correction.

Another common chore is *cropping*. That's when you cut out the section of the picture you want to keep and chuck the rest. Even elementary photo editing programs have cropping tools in them. You just select the portion of the picture you want to keep, and choose Crop. Then save the file. I often save cropped or otherwise edited pictures to a new file name, incidentally, so I always have the original to go back to.

FIGURE 10-4   Here's a picture of a boat at my uncle's place in Virginia, modified with
sketch filters supplied with Photoshop

10

Making Panorama Pictures

Ever stood on a mountain top or gaping at a cityscape and taken a series of pictures while
rotating around a pivot point? The limitation of that little picture you see through the viewfinder
is so frustrating that you instinctually want to capture the *big* picture to later show your friends.
Well, creating *panoramas* is one of the coolest things about digital photography! And unlike
with regular prints, you don't have to get out the scissors and tape to make a wide picture
comprised of several shots. The computer is smart enough to create the panorama for you.

There are any number of panorama-picture programs available for your PC. A little
searching on the Net will land you on sites you can download them from. I got mine with my
Nikon digital camera. It's called QuickStitch (because the process of joining the photos is called
stitching) from Enroute. It's pretty awesome. I can stitch together as many as six pictures across
and six pictures vertically, into one huge photograph. You can read more about panoramas at my
Web site: www.cowart.com/nikon. Click Panoramas to see some pictures and read some general
tips. Figure 10-5 shows QuickStitch in action, joining 15 photos into one larger one. The result
of the stitching operation can be seen in Figure 10-6.

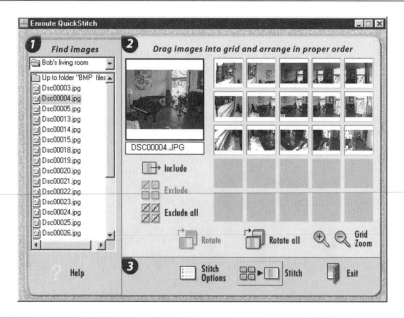

FIGURE 10-5   You can use a panorama program, like Quickstitch shown here, to join a number of smaller images into one larger one

FIGURE 10-6   There are a few jagged edges and an odd perspective, but this is an extreme example of stitching

Some cameras make it easier to take *panos* (as they're called in the trade), but you don't need a special digital camera to do it. You can even use images you scanned in from a regular film camera. But no matter what kind of camera you use, the trick is to set the exposure, white balance, and focus manually so it doesn't change perceptibly from one shot to the next. Otherwise there will be color, focus, and brightness variation within the pano. The other trick is to shoot carefully. You'll want to overlap each shot by about 50 percent. This helps the computer figure out how to stitch the pictures together and does it more gradually, so the final image looks smoother.

TIP *Ever seen those images on the Web where you can look around 360 degrees, and even zoom in and zoom out of an image? This is called VRML (Virtual Reality Modeling Language) imaging. VRML is another kind of image stitching, usually requiring special lenses, such as fisheye, and some specialized viewing software, typically a downloadable plug-in for the person viewing the Web page to install. Ipix is one company that makes software for this kind of application, though they charge a healthy sum for each image you create. There are alternative freebie programs to do the same thing, however. Search the Web for "VRML imaging" to find out more.*

When processing your images, keep the intended purpose of the image in mind. Here are some image-processing considerations:

■ **Image resolution**   If you are processing an image for the Web or an online document, you will want to reduce the image resolution to 72dpi (dots per inch)—the dot pitch of a normal monitor display. Anything higher than that will just take longer than necessary to display and will not serve much purpose. On the other hand, if you would like that image to look good when printed, you want to keep the resolution fairly high. This value varies depending on the output device, but 150dpi is a good average. It is not recommended that you increase the resolution of an image. If the image was captured at 150dpi, do not increase it to 300dpi, or it will look terrible. You can, however, decrease it to 72dpi without loosing clarity, assuming you view the image on a monitor.

■ **Image size**   If an image is viewed on the screen, you can produce a very small size and still have it look great. Size is measured in pixels (dots) or inches. You can reduce the size of an image without risking quality. When you increase the size of an image, all you are doing is spreading the existing dots further apart. The result is a very grainy looking image. If you're going to use an image on a Web page, actually resize the image using an image editor to the exact size of the displayed image. Although Web-design programs let you resize an image right on your Web page, don't do it. It will either tend to look fuzzy or will load slower than it should. Check out programs such as Fireworks to optimize images for Web presentation.

TIP *When taking pictures or scanning images, do so at a high resolution and format. This gives you the freedom to reduce the resolution and size on an as-needed basis.*

■ **Colors**   When processing an image, the color palette you use can play an important role. If the image is going to be shared on the Web, you want to make certain to use a Web-compatible palette, or the image you view on your screen may not look as good on another system across the Internet.

10

 *The Web site http://www.nyip.com has many articles about digital photography. Check this site out. It is a wonderful source of information. Two other sites worth checking are www.shortcourses.com and www.kenmilburn.com.*

Sharing Your Pictures

One of the fun concepts behind digital cameras is the ability to share your photos with family and friends over the Internet or via e-mail.

When you send a picture via e-mail, you do so as an attachment. Simply write your e-mail message and send the image file as an attachment. The recipient on the other end only needs to double-click on the image file to view the picture. If they have Outlook Express or other email program that reads HTML formatted mail, they needn't even do that. The picture will show up automatically, righ inside the email message.

The most important thing when sending photos via e-mail is to make them small, so they don't take too long for you to send and for your recipient to download. Many programs can resize your photos for you. IrfanView, ThumbsPlus, Kai Photo Soap, Lview, and PaintShop Pro are shareware programs that you can use to resize pictures. Higher-resolution pictures will require more time to send (and receive) via e-mail. Aim for image sizes in the 640 x 480 range for typical emailed pictures.

A great way to share your photos with friends and family is to put them on a photo album Web site. You can use special software such as ActiveShare (www.activeshare.com) to create albums and send the photos to Web sites such as eCircles (www.eCircles.com). Your friends and family can visit the site and view your photos.

You can also place your images on Web pages. Photos that are used on the Web should be in either JPEG or GIF format. See Chapter 9 for details on adding photos and other graphics to Web pages. There are many programs—even some Shareware and freeware ones—for creating Web-based photo albums. Some of them are pretty sophisticated, too, with neat transitions, musical accompaniment, and so forth. Try going to www.download.com and searching for "photo album" software. Some will be for publishing your photo albums on the Web.

Printing Your Photos

Digital images are fun, but they are little difficult to put in your wallet. What if you have this awesome photo that you want to frame or carry with you? You have two choices: you can send it to a photo finisher that can produce prints from digital photos, or you can find yourself a good photo-quality printer and print the photos yourself.

Photo Finishers

Some Web sites offer a service that enables you to upload your images and have them processed through a photo-finishing lab. Photo-finishing labs offer various services, ranging from photo touch-up, to prints. Digital photos are processed using digital projection as opposed to using traditional film negatives.

Web sites that offer photo-processing services include: Mystic Color Lab (www.mysticcolorlab.com) and Kodak (www.photonet.com). Ofoto (www.ofoto.com) offers digital touch-up services. If you do a search on "Digital Photo Processing," you can find other labs that offer these services.

Photo Printers

There are three common types of printers that can produce good-quality prints: inkjet, dye-sublimation, and thermal dye. Let's take a look at how each of these types works and which type you might want to use for your prints.

Ink-Jet Printers

Color ink-jet printers generate good-quality color and black-and-white prints. The image is created by spraying jets of ink onto the page. This type of printer is the most economical for the quality it produces.

The most popular ink-jet printers on the market today are those from Epson such as the Stylus series. Hewlett-Packard models, however, are not far behind. The model numbers change weekly, so I won't quote those here. In general, these printers can produce output as high as 1,440dpi. At that resolution, your eye is challenged to even detect the individual dots that make up an image.These printers cost as little as $100 to nearly $1,000.

For the best quality, you need to buy good photo-quality paper specifically designed for ink-jet printers, preferably for *your* brand and model. For archival purposes (prints that won't fade when exposed to sunlight or UV rays from halogen lamps), look into a printer that can work with the new archival inks. Some of the Epsons will do this. Archival inks cost more, but the results are fabulous. For more about printers, see the printers discussion in Chapter 16.

Dye-Sublimation Printers

Dye-sublimation printers, also known as thermal-wax printers, actually roll a wax-coated ribbon against the paper. Heat is applied to bind the wax to the paper. The paper that is used with this process is quite pricey, but the quality is evident. Prints from a dye-sub printer look pretty amazing, with one exception: If you look at them from an angle, you can see *banding*, a fine line between each pass of the print head across the paper. Ink-jet printers don't exhibit this anomaly because they interweave the passes of the print head into a continuous image.

Fargo makes a dye-sublimation printer called FotoFUN. This printer was designed for amateurs, so it is easy to use. The downside is that it produces prints no larger than 4 x 6 inches. This printer costs under $500.

The Olympus P-330 Digital Home Photo Printer is a bit cheaper, at less than $400, and it does not require a computer system. That's right—it can connect directly to an Olympus digital camera. If you don't own an Olympus digital camera, you can connect this printer to your system via the parallel port. It produces 4 x 5.5-inch prints. It also produces up to 30 thumbnail images on a single page for easy proofing.

10

Alps makes some dye-sub printers that are inexpensive and awesome. They'll print up to 8 ½-inch x 11-inch (or thereabouts) and cost only a few hundred dollars. They print very slowly, so don't expect to run a print service using one.

Thermal-Dye Printers

Thermal-dye printers work just like thermal-wax (dye-sublimation) printers, except they use dye instead of wax. They use a glossy, photographic type of paper. This special paper is coated with polyester and can be quite expensive. The quality of thermal-dye printer output is comparable to that of thermal-wax printers. These printers cost around $500. Panasonic's TruPhoto Digital Photo Printer sells for just under $500.

General Printing Suggestions

In general, I suggest going with ink-jet printers for your photos. For one thing, they offer the most versatility—you can print up anything from business letters to photos on them. They are relatively inexpensive to operate, can use a wide range of papers from textured to glossy. Consumables (ink and paper) are fairly inexpensive on them. Finally, they are very reliable and tend to have very good printer drivers with software tools for such things as cleaning the heads, checking the amount of ink in the reservoirs, and so on.

Do consider what size of prints you want to produce too. If you want to print no more than 8 x 10s you can do that on one of the inexpensive ink-jets that take 8 ½-inch by 11-inch paper. If you want to print 11-inch x 14-inch prints, though, check out the larger format ink-jet that takes 11-inch x 17-inch paper. Epson makes several of these.

When you're ready to print, if you're not into serious photographic gymnastics and ready to purchase Photoshop for around $700, do the following to get good, economical printouts:

- *Look around for a reasonably-good printing program, one that uses your fancy photo paper intelligently.* Check out Ulead photo impact, Kai Photo Soap, and Epson Photo Factory (supplied with most Epson printers). There actually *are* programs that will turn and juggle the images so you can cram the maximum number of photos onto a piece of expensive glossy photo paper. This saves your hard-earned money and cuts down on wasted paper.

- *Plan to print on photo-quality glossy paper.* It's expensive (can be as much as $1 per page), but the results are far better than when using normal ink-jet paper. Make sure to adjust your Print settings to indicate the correct kind of paper you've loaded, before you print, though. Printers actually use differing amounts of ink, depending on the kind of paper.

- *If you get into subtle color adjustments in your photo editing program, you'll want to learn how to calibrate your printer and monitor so what you see onscreen is what you get in your printouts.* Color calibration is a somewhat complex topic. Look in the Help file supplied with your editing program and in the Windows Help system for details on color profiles.

Chapter 11

Playing and Recording Music

How to...

- Play CDs
- Play MP3s
- Find music on the Web
- Turn CDs into MP3s
- Put music into your portable player
- Record your own CDs

If music is something you love as much as I do, you'll wonder how you lived without a PC up until now. In the last few years, the technological advances that combine computers and music have been so swift, that it's next to impossible to keep up. You may remember when new music formats came along at the lazy rate of once a decade at most. Recall that the move from vinyl records to CDs took about 20 years. But in the past ten years, we've been handed the MiniDisk (MD), DAT, and now the MP3 formats.

In addition to playing MP3s, your PC can also play standard audio CDs. Some computers will even let you record audio CDs that can play on any standard CD player, like the one in your car, your boombox, or your stereo system.

In this chapter, you'll discover how well music and your PC go together. Before we get to the details of playing and recording music, let's consider what you'll need for your computer sound system.

Setting Up Your Computer Sound System

So, what do you need to play music on your computer? The good news is that most computers are ready to rock and roll, literally. Even a Brand-X computer comes with a sound card (the internal electronics that convert sound files into signals that speakers can then play) and at least a pair of cheesy speakers.

Choosing Your Sound System Approach

Contrary to what some folks will tell you, a computer-based system can sound as delicious as the stereo in your living room. You just need to get some good speakers and hook it all up correctly. There are two approaches that you can take:

- Buy a good set of amplified speakers designed for use with a PC.
- Wire your computer to your existing stereo system.

Let's see what you need for each approach.

Using Amplified Computer Speakers

Speakers for computers need to be amplified one way or another, since the sound card in your computer doesn't have enough power to drive (power) a pair of speakers. This is why computer speakers typically have a power switch and volume control. It's also why they need to be plugged into an AC outlet to provide power to the internal amplifier in the speakers.

To receive the sound signal they'll amplify, most computer speakers connect right into the sound-output jack of your computer. Newer ones connect via the USB port on your computer. The USB ones lead to cleaner sound, but they're more expensive, since essentially, the sound card is in the speakers rather than in the computer.

Few computers come with decent speakers, and there must be a fortune to be made in convincing unsuspecting buyers that a couple of little $5 plastic jobs really have super-turbo bass and awesome 3D sound, or can produce 850 watts. Don't you believe it. For a decent sound from a set of computer speakers, expect to pay $100 or so.

If you plan to use amplified speakers for your computer sound system, purchase a brand-name (Cambridge Soundworks, or Altec Lansing, for example), three-piece speaker system designed for computers. With this arrangement, you'll have one speaker for each of the two stereo channels (left and right), and a *subwoofer* for the middle. The subwoofer goes under your desk or table, and the little "satellite" speakers go up on shelves or on your desktop. The lowest frequencies (bass notes) produced by the subwoofer are nondirectional, so your ear can't tell where those notes are coming from. The higher-pitched sounds—voice, guitars, violins, and such—come out of the little satellite speakers. With this arrangment, you get good sound without having giant speakers sucking up all your desk space. Figure 11-1 shows an example of a three-piece subwoofer/satellite speaker system.

11

The subwoofer is not magnetically shielded and should not be placed close to a monitor. Placing the subwoofer on the floor close to a wall or corner of a room provides maximum bass efficiency.

FIGURE 11-1   The better computer speakers on the market have three pieces; the subwoofer plays the low notes, while the smaller satellite speakers play the higher ones

Look for speakers that can produce in the range of 15–40 watts RMS (Root Mean Squared) power. PMPO (Peak Music Power Output) is usually the inflated number and does not mean much. Also, listen to the speakers before you take them home, or at least make sure that you can return them if the sound isn't satisfying.

Using Your Existing Home Sound System

If you already have a good stereo or a mini-component system, you might want to wire your computer right to that. You just take the output from computer's sound card and plug it into the auxiliary input jack (or other high-level input such as tuner, tape monitor, or CD player) on your stereo's amplifier. Figure 11-2 illustrates the connections.

The advantage of this type of arrangement is that you have the additional amplification and tone controls (and presumably good speakers) of your existing stereo, with no additional expenditure except the cable to attach the parts. You'll need a cable called a *stereo mini male jack to dual RCA male jacks*, which you can pick up for a few dollars from any Radio Shack store or similar vendor. The only potential problem is that your stereo system will be too far away from your computer (such as down the hall and in the next room) to easily run the cable. Then you're better off going with plan A, which is the separate amplified computer speaker system.

Using Headphones for Privacy

For laptop traveling, or playing music at the office without bugging the people in the next cubicle, reach for your headphones. Your computer has a jack for headphones, typically marked with a little headphones icon. (It's actually the same one you use to plug in your speakers or feed your stereo.) On some machines, you will have to look very closely at the little jacks on the back (or edge, in the case of a laptop) to determine which one is the headphone jack.

Just as with speakers, spending a little more on a good pair of headphones can make a substantial difference in sound quality. I have found that the "around-the-ear" style of headphones blocks out external noise better than the "on-the-ear" type. If you've got about $100 to spend, you might try the new "noise-canceling" headphones available from places like the Sharper Image.

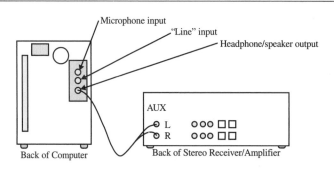

FIGURE 11-2   You can use your existing stereo to play sounds from your PC; look carefully at the jacks on the back of the computer for the output one. Sometimes the markings or symbols are hard to read

Here's an important warning: After you plug in the headphones, don't put them on until you have started playing some music and know for sure that the volume control isn't set to some deafening level. To adjust the volume control for every source on your computer, click on the little speaker in the system tray to pop up a volume-control slider, like the one shown here. Drag the slider up and down until the sound level is reasonable. Then put on the headphones when you're sure you're not going to be blasted.

Playing CDs

Even though computer software is usually what's on CDs that you feed into your computer, your CD-ROM drive can also play music CDs. Whenever you insert a CD into your computer, Windows examines it and decides whether it's a data CD or an audio CD. Then your computer responds accordingly.

As your computer comes from the factory, an inserted music CD should start the Windows Media Player program, which comes with Windows. If it doesn't, click Start, Programs, Accessories, Entertainment, Windows Media Player. Then click CD Audio or the left side of the player. Figure 11-3 shows the Media Player when used for playing CDs.

NOTE   *The Windows Media Player discussed in this chapter and shown in the figures is the one that comes with Windows Me. Windows 95 and 98 come with a more limited Media Player program, as well as a separate CD Player program. If you have an older version of Windows Media Player, you can download a newer one from the Microsoft web site.*

Media Player is a clever little program. It can play a wide variety of file formats, both video and audio, and is really extensive in its capabilities. A bit like a chameleon, it can change its color, size, and texture. For example, click the button in the lower-right corner to switch to compact mode, and the player gets tinier, as shown here.

11

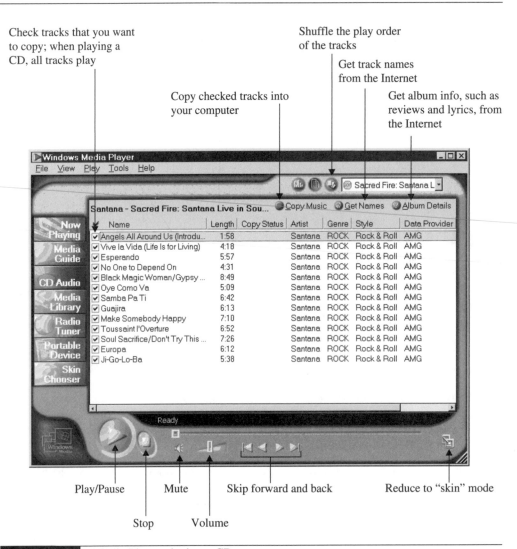

Check tracks that you want
to copy; when playing a
CD, all tracks play

Shuffle the play order
of the tracks

Get track names
from the Internet

Copy checked tracks into
your computer

Get album info, such as
reviews and lyrics, from
the Internet

Play/Pause   Mute   Skip forward and back   Reduce to "skin" mode

Stop   Volume

FIGURE 11-3   Media Player playing a CD

Getting CD Information

One great thing about Media Player is that, if you're connected to the Internet, it can look up the names and other information about all of the songs on your CD automatically, when you insert the CD. It does this by connecting with music databases (such as one called CDDB) over the

Internet. If the CD you inserted is a rare one, or if you're not connected to the Internet, you only see the track number of each cut. You can enter the track and CD title information yourself. Then, it will be stored in the computer so that the next time you insert the CD, the track names come up on the screen, letting you play tracks by name. You can even send this information over the Internet to the CDDB online database so that others can access it if they insert the same CD you have.

Once you've inserted a CD, follow these steps to get information about it:

1. Make sure you're connected to the Internet.

2. Click the CD Audio button on the left side of the player.

3. Click the Get Names button, and then follow the instructions on your screen. The song names and album information will be brought into the Windows Media Player listing.

4. If the CD is not found, you'll see a listing of track numbers without names. You can click on any track number, artist name, or genre, and the name will become highlighted and available for editing, as shown below. Type in the new name and press ENTER.

Media Player also lets you store the CD's music itself on your computer. The music file will be compressed for computer storage.

    As usual, Microsoft is doing things its own way, and doesn't even make clear how it's doing the compression or what kind of files it's creating. If you want to store CD music on your computer's hard disk, I recommend using a more standard MP3 program such as MusicMatch or Real Jukebox, which are discussed later in this chapter.

Shedding Your Skins

You can really change the look of the player by applying a new *skin*, which is like a different shell for the player's image. Skins are a little gimmick you'll see in a number of programs discussed in this chapter. Real Jukebox, MusicMatch, and WinAmp have skins, too, for example.

TIP   *The cool thing about skins for some of these music programs is that regular folks can make up new ones and submit them. Then they become available to everyone over the Internet. The same is true of visualizations, which are discussed in the next section.*

To try out a new skin in Media Player, follow these steps:

1. Click Skin Chooser on the bottom-left side of the Media Player window. A list of available skins comes up.

2. Click on each skin to see a preview in the right pane.

3. Click Apply Skin to see the new skin.

Figure 11-4 shows the Media Player skin called Headspace, along with skins from some other popular media players.

NOTE *Skins only run in the Windows Media Player compact mode. When you switch back to full-size mode, the skin goes away and the full-size mode reappears.*

Visualizing Your Music

Visualizations are the modern-age equivalent of the light shows common in the 1970s. Since your PC has amazing amounts of computing power typically going untapped, the music-player programmers have thought of really neat ways to entertain you while music is playing. Visualizations consist of patterns and moving images that synchronize with the music and dance

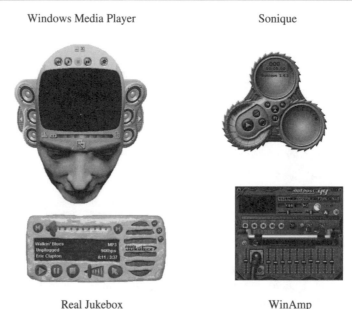

Windows Media Player

Sonique

Real Jukebox

WinAmp

FIGURE 11-4   Many media players on the market have a skin mode that lets you radically change the look of the player

about on your screen in some very mesmerizing ways. (No recreational pharmaceuticals are needed!) Windows Media Player, WinAmp (www.winamp.com), Real Jukebox (www.real.com), Sonique (http://sonique.lycos.com/), and MusicMatch (www.musicmatch.com) players all have visualization modes.

To check out Windows Media Player's visualizations, do the following:

1. Switch to full mode (not compact or skin mode).

2. Select the Visualizations option from the View menu, and then choose any one of the many visualizations available from the cascading menus, as shown in Figure 11-5.

3. Start playing a music cut, either by inserting a CD or clicking on Media Library and choosing an MP3 or other sound file stored on your computer (you can also use radio with visualization).

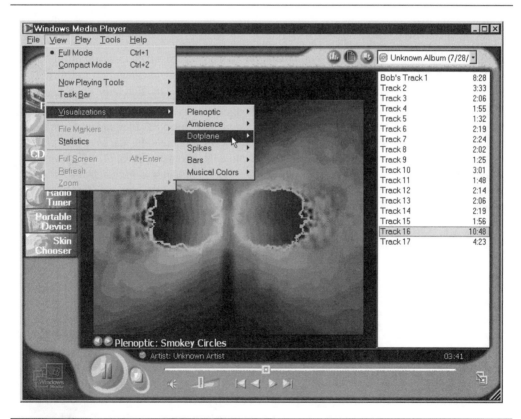

FIGURE 11-5   Choosing a visualization in Windows Media Player

4. Click Now Playing, and the left side of the Windows Media Player window will display the visualization. The buttons at the bottom of the visualization window let you quickly change which visualization is running.

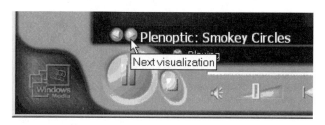

You can spend a full evening playing with the visualization settings and downloading new visualizations for each brand of player. Look for buttons and menu options on your player for experimenting with visualizations. For example, in Windows Media Player, choose Options from the Tools menu, and then choose Visualizations to find some settings that affect the update speed and display size of the visualizations.

Playing MP3s

Several years ago, I bought a Sony MiniDisk recorder and started copying my CDs and vinyl over to that format. But my project was interrupted midstream by the appearance of a new format called MP3. Once I realized I could put *all* my music into my computer on MP3 files and organize them any way I wanted, I was hooked. So what's so great about MP3? Here's the skinny.

An MP3 is a type of compressed audio file that can contain music, spoken text, or any other sounds. These files can be stored and played back on your computer and its attached speakers (or headphones). MP3 files are small compared to their CD-based counterparts. You can store a typical 5-minute song in about 3M of space, whereas it might consume about 50M on a CD. This means that you can store a lot of music on a typical computer's hard disk. It also means music can now be easily sent across the Internet as e-mail attachments, sold from a Web page, or shared between users all over the world via an Internet distribution scheme.

MP3 is an abbreviation for MPEG, audio layer 3. MPEG stands for Moving Picture Experts Group, a bunch of people who work on figuring out how to invent gear for making and playing movies. Since movies have sound in them, the MPEG people developed layer 3 as a way to work with sound only.

Here are some reasons why you might want to use the MP3 format to store music on your computer so it's always there, ready to play back:

■ You tote a laptop and don't want to carry a bunch of CDs just to have music with you.

■ You use a desktop computer, but don't want to rifle through a stack of CDs and insert them just to hear some music.

■ You've found some music on the Internet that you like, and you want to download it and store it on your hard disk for playing whenever you want.

You can download MP3 files (MP3s for short) over the Internet, or you can make your own MP3s from music sources you have at home, such as CDs, cassettes, and vinyl records. You can achieve all this using a growing list of freely downloadable computer programs, the most popular of which are dubbed "jukebox" programs. That's because they turn your computer into the modern-day equivalent of those old jukeboxes you can see in resuscitated diners from the 1950s.

Using an MP3 Player

Basically, all of the MP3 player programs do the same things:

- Organize your MP3 files into a library (actually just a database) so you can see what you have. You can sort your files by artist, album name, and song name. The resorting doesn't actually rearrange the song files themselves, just the database. It's like rearranging the card catalog in a library while leaving the books where they are. This certainly beats reorganizing all your CDs, tapes, and records on your bookshelves.

- Create "play lists" of songs you like to hear together, sort of like those compilation dance tapes you used to make for parties. You can create play lists of dinner music, dance music, opera duets, string quartets, vintage R&B, and so on.

- Search for songs in a variety of ways; for example, you can find all piano sonatas or all Elton John songs. When all the matching songs are found, you can easily play them one after another.

- Use other little tricks such as "shuffling" your songs into different order, playing through your entire collection and so on, much like those CD players that hold 100 or more CDs.

11

Did you know?   How Does MP3 Shrink Sound Files?

MP3s are cool because they take up less storage space on your hard disk (or other storage device such as a floppy or hand-held playback unit) than do the tracks of a CD. How do they do that, you ask? Layer 3 uses something called perceptual audio coding and psychoacoustic compression, a technique that eliminates parts of the music that your ear can't hear, such as redundant sounds or sounds that will be "masked" (hidden) by other sounds in a recording. The result is that MP3s shrink the original sound file from a CD by a factor of about 12, without sacrificing the sound quality appreciably.

MP3 actually uses a technique similar to that used by the MiniDisk (MD) systems developed by Sony. The Sony compression system is called ATRAC, but it works essentially the same way as MP3. The only real difference between MP3 and MD is that there are a lot of portable MiniDisk units available, capable of recording and playing back up to 80 minutes of music and storing it on little removable disks. MP3 players are more limited in function, and they typically use only solid-state media (such as Sony's Memory Stick or compact flash cards), not disks.

In addition to these basic MP3-playing features, some of the popular programs will put icing on the cake, adding other features such as the following:

■ Turning your CDs into MP3 (or other proprietary formats) files for storage on your hard disk. This is sometimes called *ripping* a CD.

■ Playing a wider variety of file formats such as video clips, streaming video, and audio from the Internet, WAV files, Quicktime files, and so on.

■ Recording your MP3 files onto blank, recordable CDs you buy at the store. These can then be played on any audio CD player. This is sometimes called *burning* a CD.

When you run Windows Media Player or install an MP3 player such as Real Jukebox for the first time, these programs will typically ask if they can snoop around your computer looking for music files. Here's an example from Real Jukebox:

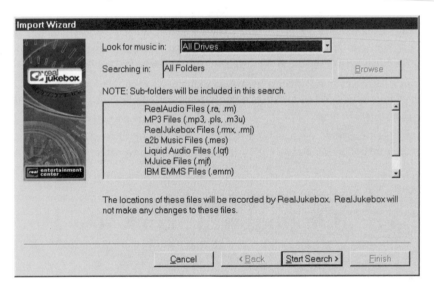

As you can see, it's going to search all of the folders on the hard disk for different kinds of sound files, including MP3. You might as well let your program do a search, unless you have all your music files stored in one location and want to direct the program there. That will be faster, and you'll exclude any files you are not interested in. On the other hand, if you let the program poke around your computer's hard disk(s), it may unearth more selections than you thought you had.

Once the original sleuthing process is done, you should have the beginnings of a music library. Even if you haven't consciously downloaded or recorded MP3 files to your system, you will have some sound files on your hard disk, since there are some included with Windows (but they're not very interesting).

Regardless of the program you're using, you should be able to view your personal library of songs in various ways, such as by artist, album name, track name, and so on. In Real Jukebox, for example, there's a button on the toolbar for listing all your files by artist, subsorted by album. Figure 11-6 shows Real Jukebox's full display.

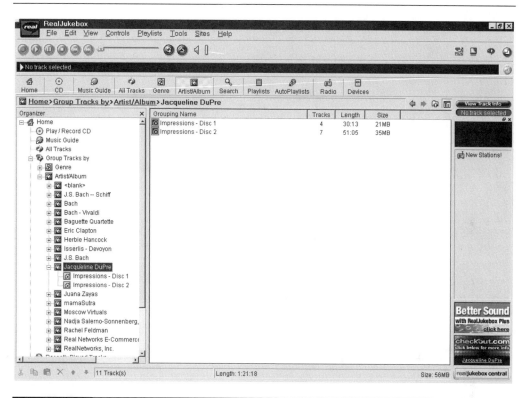

FIGURE 11-6   Real Jukebox has a flexible library display, much like Windows Explorer's interface; you click a + sign on the left to see a sublisting of albums for an artist

Figure 11-7 shows the listing in Windows Media Player. Notice that Real Jukebox makes it clear that I have two Jacqueline DuPre CDs, whereas the tracks from both CDs are lumped together in the Windows Media Player display.

Notice in Figure 11-7 that Windows Media Player will organize your video clips. Expect a repeating game of feature competition between the makers of these programs on capabilities such as these.

Downloading MP3s from the Internet

Downloading MP3 files from the Internet may be the easiest way to get them. They are everywhere and very easy to acquire. The courts have started to crack down on illegal dissemination of music over the Internet, but there are still many sites and services that legally distribute non-copyrighted music. In an hour's time with a fast Internet connection, you can download a healthy music collection. Some services will even send you a new, free, song every day through your e-mail (check out www.mp3.com). Then all you do is save the MP3 attachment to your hard disk and import it into your music library.

Did you know?

Can I Have Multiple MP3 Players Installed?

Importing your MP3, WAV, RM, or other kinds of multimedia files into a media player usually doesn't move or modify the files themselves. All it does is let the player create its own database of your files and their locations. The database is then maintained by the player, so you can easily find, play, and record media files. Therefore, you can install as many media players as you like. I have MusicMatch, Real Jukebox, WinAmp, and Windows Media Player on my laptop, and I switch back and forth between them for testing purposes. One reason to keep more than one program around is for their visualizations.

Generally, I suggest choosing one MP3 player program and doing all your work (and play) with it, since there can be small conflicts between the ways programs organize MP3 files on the hard disk, and preferences in the various programs can conflict with one another. Also, you don't need to manually update several libraries each time you download an MP3 from the Internet.

The one thing to watch out for is the tug-of-war that media players have with one another over their associations with specific file types. Most of these programs want to be the default program that will play, say, MP3, Real Audio, or Windows Media files. So, when you install the program, part of the setup process usually involves answering some questions about this. Unless you're ready to commit to a specific player, don't let it register all those file types. Just deselect the file types you don't want handled by that program.

To find MP3s on the Web, try these approaches:

- Check the player for a button or menu that brings up a list of MP3 sources.
- Surf to www.riffage.com, www.emusic.com, or www.ritmoteca.com.
- Use a search engine and look for "MP3." You'll find many pages with free MP3 files on them.

TIP   *There's a multitude of file-sharing programs available on the Web. Current examples include Napster, Gnutella, Scour Exchange, Freenet, MP3 Friend, Planet.MP3Find, MP3Leech 98, MP3 Album Finder, MP3 Voyeur, and more.*

That should get you started. You can easily burn up an afternoon or evening downloading new music into your library. Many sites will let you hear a piece before your download it. You may need to hear it in low-fidelity, but the MP3 file you download will probably sound much better.

When you download a file, you need to save it on your disk somewhere. I suggest you put your MP3 files in the My Music folder. Most MP3 players will look there first when adding files to their libraries.

FIGURE 11-7   Windows Media Player's library display includes playback of video files

Also, before downloading music, you should check the file size. The Web page probably tells you the size, as in the example shown below. If the size is really large and you have a slow connection to the Internet, it may be a long, painful wait.

As a final note on downloading music, you probably know that there's concern over the publishing of copyrighted music on the Internet. You also are probably aware that we're likely to see a lot more copying and easy availability of music, video, games, books, magazines, and so forth over the Internet. It's going to be difficult to control the pricing and collection of fees for these. You may want to follow the press or read up on the Internet about your rights and responsibilities when making and sharing your MP3s with others, or when downloading MP3s from illegal Web sites or when using programs like Napster or Gnutella.

You can send an MP3 file to a friend by including it as an e-mail attachment. Just make sure that your MP3 file isn't larger than the maximum allowed by your or the recipient's e-mail server (typically 5M). See Chapter 7 for more information about e-mail attachments.

Turning Your CDs into MP3s

Transferring your CD collection into your computer makes it possible to find the music you're looking for instantly and play it in a second. How you actually record your CDs varies from program to program, but the better ones such as MusicMatch or Real Jukebox make it pretty easy. Typically, they will respond when you insert a CD by listing the CD's contents. Then you click the Record button and sit back. (Some MP3 programs only play back and don't record at all; if you can't find the record controls, that might be why.)

Configuring CD Recording

Before you start recording, you should make sure that the program is configured correctly for your system (if the program's setup routine didn't already walk you through this configuration). Typically, these settings are made from the program's recording preferences dialog box. Poke around and look for it. Figure 11-8 shows the CD Audio settings in the Windows Media Player's Options dialog box.

If the program has a wizard for testing the record setup, use it. Tell the program which CD-ROM drive you want to use.

Configure the following settings:

- **Digital or analog** Stipulate whether to use digital or analog recording. Most CD-ROM drives can read the music on the CD in digital format, which will produce better sound and a faster ripping (copying) speed.

- **Sampling rate** Choose the sampling rate you want to use for your recording. The sampling rate determines the quality of the recording. Typical sampling rates are 96K, 128K, and 160K. The higher the rate, the better the sound. Higher rates create sound files that are larger, and thus take up more of your hard disk. Many folks are happy with a 96K rate, which will consume 42M per CD, versus 56M for a rate of 128K, or 69M for a rate of 160K. A rate of 128K is quite good; 96K sounds a little worse than a CD, but is still good. I would not go below that except for spoken-word recordings such as books. Some programs give you 128K sampling with their free product. Some charge you extra for it.

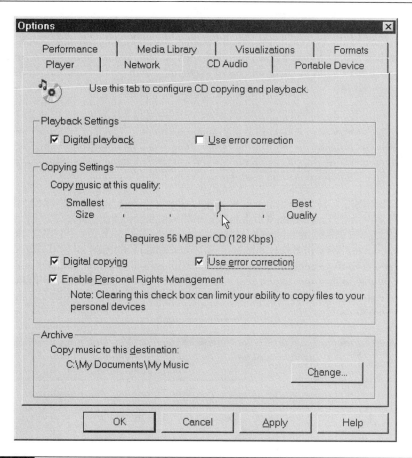

FIGURE 11-8   The CD copying and playing configuration settings in Media Player

Some MP3 programs, such as Real Jukebox and MusicMatch, come in both a free version and an upgrade version. Like some other demo versions of programs, these MP3 player/recorder programs are almost fully functional, missing just a few features. (If you really like the program, you can upgrade for about $30, which typically garners you a "lifetime" of free upgrades.) The feature most often left out of the free versions is the ability to record an MP3 with CD-quality sound. The quality is determined mostly by sampling rate.

■ **Error correction**   Check the error correction setting. I suggest turning on error correction for copying CDs, if your program offers that option. Error correction can prevent clicks and pops from cropping up in the recordings. It will slow down the ripping process, however.

■ **File licenses** Because of the record industry's concern over infringement of copyrighted music, there is an option to personally stamp every piece you copy from a CD. In Windows Media Player, this is called Personal Rights Management. In Real Jukebox, it's called Secure Music Files. When you turn on this feature, songs you record from CDs will have a unique license created for them, which deters people from stealing or copying the file.

If you use Windows Media Player to transfer a file that has a license from your computer to a portable device, a copy of this license is also transferred to your portable device so you can play the file on it. If you clear this check box and disable Personal Rights Management, you might not be able to play some music files on a Secure Digital Music Initiative (SDMI)-compliant portable device.

■ **File storage** Choose where you want your music files to be stored. The folder structure for storing MP3s on the hard disk is adjustable on some of the better MP3 programs. This lets you choose how much information will be included in each MP3 file you rip, and how the files will be organized in different folders. Putting all of the files into one folder can confuse not only you, but the MP3 program's library. The best approach is usually the default one, which creates a structure like the one shown in Figure 11-9 (as seen from Windows Explorer).

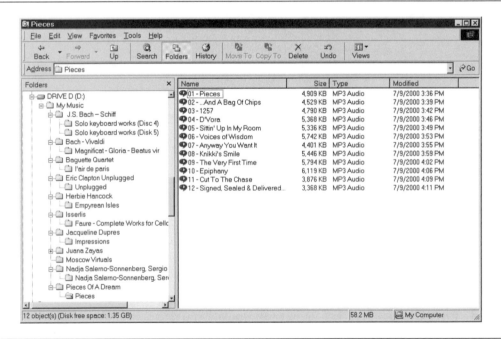

FIGURE 11-9   The best organization plan for your MP3s is with one folder for each artist, and one folder for each CD, tape, or album below that; file names used in this arrangement can be short, including only the track name and number

Ripping the CD

After you've configured the settings for copying CDs, follow these steps to copy a CD into your computer:

1. Insert the CD you want to record. If the track names don't come up, click on the button for getting the names from the Internet. Figure 11-10 shows an example in the Windows Media Player after inserting a Santana CD. With my Internet connection active, the names came up automatically.

2. Make sure that you have enough free space on your hard disk to hold the tracks you aim to record. Real Jukebox and MusicMatch will show you the amount of space needed and the amount free on your target hard disk, as in the example shown here.

| 13 Track(s) Checked | Required: 52MB | | Available (C:) 696MB | realjukebox central |

3. Click Record (or Copy in the case of Windows Media Player) to start recording. Now all you need to do is wait. Your progress while recording each track will be reported. Try not to tax your machine with other tasks while recording, because it can cause static in the recordings, especially if you did not turn on error correction. The recording process will slow down other things you might be doing on your computer, too, because it takes a lot of attention from the CPU.

11

FIGURE 11-10   A CD listing in Media Player

When the process is finished, you'll be alerted, and the files should be added to your hard disk. The new names should appear in your MP3 program's music library window.

Ripping Vinyl Albums and Cassettes

You thought those old vinyl albums were already rather ripped up, didn't you? Well, now you can really rip them, and once they're in your PC, you can play them forever, without inflicting further damage to those delicate grooves. (Of course, you'll need to find a turntable to spin them on, at least one more time.) The same is true for your old cassettes—you still have a cassette deck up in the attic don't you? Dare I even mention your 8-tracks or, worse yet, moldy-old 45s and 78s?

A few MP3 programs will let you record from *analog* inputs in addition to the usual digital CDs. That means that you can record MP3s from just about any music source, even a tape of your garage band or directly from a microphone. Once you've digitized your old tunes, you might even get into cleaning up the sound using some after-market noise reduction software (such as Cooledit, which is discussed in the "Cutting CDs from Your Own Recordings" section later in this chapter).

When you rip CDs, the data typically comes off the CD in digital form, and the track information (length of each track and, optionally, track and album name) are sucked into your computer pretty effortlessly. But things get trickier when you use analog sources, requiring a little more legwork on your part. You will need to do the following:

- The better programs will let you choose the line-in or mic (microphone) input as your recording source. Key in the album name and artist.
- If you don't mind the tracks being labeled Track 1, Track 2, and so on, you can skip typing in the individual track information.
- Set the record level manually.

Setting up for Analog Recording

The first thing you need to do is wire up your analog device to the proper input on your computer. Typically, the source will be the tape output of your stereo, and it will connect to your computer's line input. You'll need to connect the turntable to a preamp, integrated amp, or receiver first, and then connect the tape output to the computer's line input. Figure 11-11 shows a typical wiring diagram for cassette or vinyl recordings.

After you've connected your analog device to your computer, make sure that the input-selection switches on the stereo are set correctly so that your desired signal is actually emanating from the tape-output connector. Note that on virtually all stereos, the tone and volume controls don't affect the tape-output volume. You can usually turn down the volume on the stereo, and it won't affect the recording volume.

NOTE *If you're going to record from a microphone, you can plug that directly into the mic input on the back of the computer.*

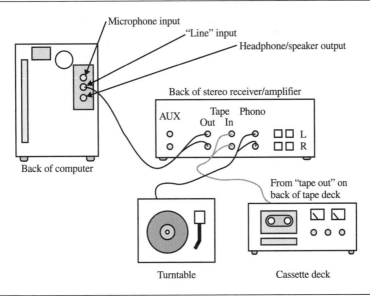

Microphone input
"Line" input
Headphone/speaker output
Back of stereo receiver/amplifier
AUX
Tape Phono
Out In
L
R
Back of computer
From "tape out" on
back of tape deck
Turntable
Cassette deck

FIGURE 11-11   Wiring your turntable or cassette player to your computer

Analog Recording with Real Jukebox

Here are the steps for making an analog recording in Real Jukebox:

1. Choose the Record from Analog Source option from the Tools menu. You will see the Record from Analog Source dialog box, as shown in Figure 11-12.

2. Choose the recording input.

3. Click Adjust Recording Levels. This brings up the Windows sound mixer. You can adjust the sound level for the input you're planning on using. If the sound source you've chosen isn't displayed, click Options, click Properties, put a check mark in the box for the missing volume control, and then click OK. Select only the desired input source (turn off other input sources via the check boxes at the bottom of the Volume Control dialog box).

4. Name the track (for example, enter the name of the album). With this program, you can only record one track at a time.

5. Get the album, tape, or other source ready to play. Then click the Record button. When the track is finished playing, click the Stop button.

11

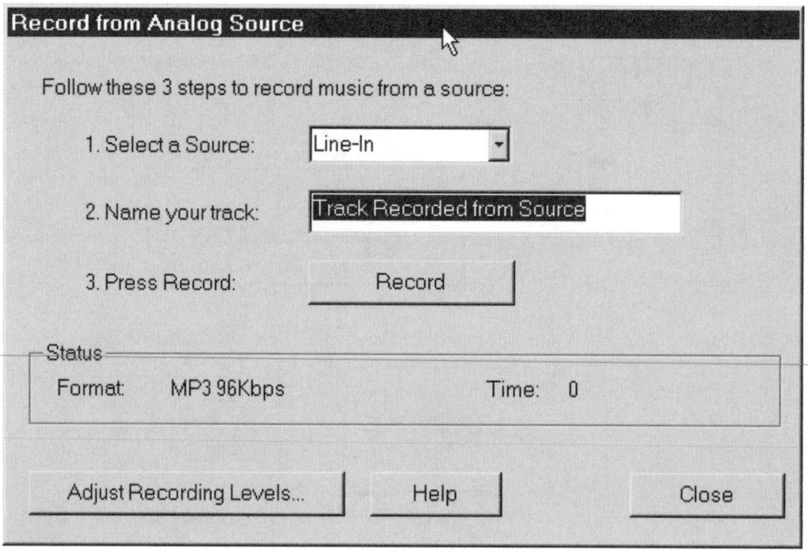

```
┌─────────────────────────────────────────────────────────────────┐
│ Record from Analog Source                              ↖          │
│                                                                   │
│   Follow these 3 steps to record music from a source:            │
│                                                                   │
│      1. Select a Source:     ┌─────────────────────┐▼            │
│                              │ Line-In             │             │
│                              └─────────────────────┘             │
│                                                                   │
│      2. Name your track:     ┌──────────────────────────┐        │
│                              │Track Recorded from Source│        │
│                              └──────────────────────────┘        │
│                                                                   │
│      3. Press Record:        ┌──────────────────┐               │
│                              │      Record      │               │
│                              └──────────────────┘               │
│   ┌─Status──────────────────────────────────────────────────┐   │
│   │  Format:   MP3 96Kbps              Time:   0            │   │
│   └──────────────────────────────────────────────────────────┘   │
│                                                                   │
│   ┌──────────────────────┐  ┌──────────┐   ┌──────────┐          │
│   │ Adjust Recording Levels...│  │   Help   │   │  Close   │      │
│   └──────────────────────┘  └──────────┘   └──────────┘          │
└─────────────────────────────────────────────────────────────────┘
```

FIGURE 11-12   The Record from Analog Source dialog box in Real Jukebox

> **TIP**
>
> *If you want to record the second track on the album, just use the same name. A second file will be created in your music folder (typically My Music, unless you've changed it), with the same name as the first one, followed by a 2 in parentheses, such as James Taylor's Greatest Hits (2). Each time you record another track, the number in parentheses will automatically be incremented for you. Windows does this with any file-name conflict, but in this case, it's really useful, because the automatic numbering corresponds with the track number.*

6. Listen to your first track after you record it. You might find that the recording level is too high or too low. There is no automatic setting to make sure that the levels are good. If the level is too high, you'll get digital distortion in your MP3 file. If the level is too low, you'll need to crank up the volume to hear the playback, and there will be hiss or hum in the playback.

Analog Recording with MusicMatch

Here are the steps for making an analog recording in MusicMatch:

1. Select Options, Recorder, Source, and then choose the input your intend to use.

2. In the player window, click the Rec button to open the recorder window.

3. In the Track 1 spot, the recorder window should say *Edit track name here before beginning.* Click the track name, type in the name, and press ENTER.

4. Click Stop to end the recording. The file will be added to your hard disk and play list.

Downloading MP3s into Your Portable Player

A portable MP3 player is actually just a little computer, with a small CPU, a bunch of RAM to hold the MP3 files, and the digital-to-analog circuitry to turn all those digital numbers back into music that you can hear on a pair of headphones. Since they have no moving parts, there is almost nothing to break or go wrong; portable MP3 players are totally resistant to shock (which makes them good for taking with you when you're jogging). Figure 11-13 shows some examples of portable MP3 players.

When you shop for a portable MP3 player, along with its physical size, check how much music it will hold. You also might want to know what kind of memory it uses. If you have a digital camera, you'll want to get an MP3 player that uses the same kind of memory cards as your camera, so you can get double-duty from the cards. The standard is compact flash cards, but Sony's Memory Stick is another type of memory card you might find in your digital camera and portable MP3 player.

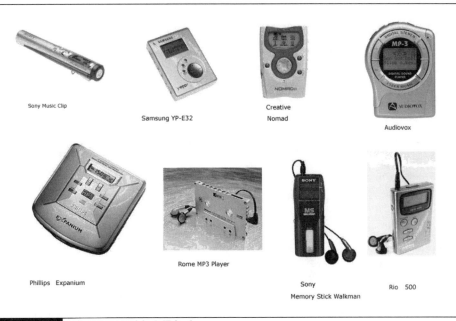

Sony Music Clip

Samsung YP-E32

Creative
Nomad

Audiovox

Phillips Expanium

Rome MP3 Player

Sony
Memory Stick Walkman

Rio 500

FIGURE 11-13   Some portable MP3 players

11

A portable MP3 player can hold only an hour or so of music, unless you get one that can accept high-capacity memory cards. Compact flash cards are available in sizes up to 256M, which can hold about 51 songs, but this type of memory will cost you a few hundred dollars.

There are a couple of ways to get music into your portable player:

- If you have a player that uses removable memory, plug the memory into a card reader or other attachment on your computer (some Sonys have a slot for their Memory Stick, for example), and use the Windows Explorer to drag and drop the MP3 files. This is a little cumbersome, but it works.

- Use the computer port that the player's manual describes as best, such as the infrared, serial, USB, serial (COM), parallel, or firewire port (most will suggest USB). Then use an MP3 management program that supports portable players, such as Windows Media Player, Real Jukebox, or MusicMatch. Figure 11-14 shows Real Jukebox's screen for starting the transfers.

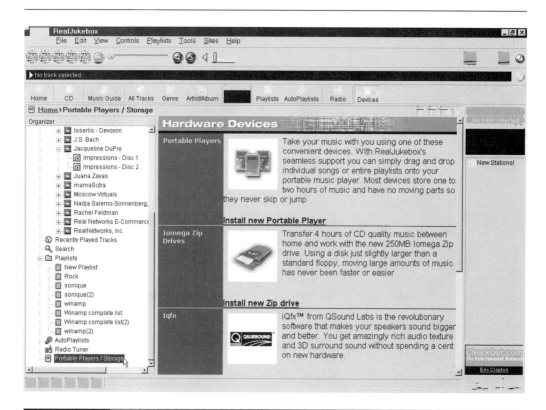

FIGURE 11-14   Beginning the transfer of MP3 files to a portable player with Real Jukebox

Putting Music on Your Web Pages

Many musicians want to post their music on Web pages (creating your own Web site is covered in Chapter 9). If you would like to do this, you'll want to consider a couple of questions first:

■   Do you want viewers to just be able to download your music files so they can play them later? (The wait for the listener could be from a few minutes to much more, depending on the amount of music and the format.)

■   Would you rather the music started playing immediately? (One advantage is that the site visitor cannot easily grab the music file and share it with others.)

After you decide on your approach, you can download or acquire the proper tools to do the work for you.

Allowing Music Downloads

If you want the viewer to be able to click on a file and download it, you can set this up in your Web-page editing software. Add a hyperlink to your page, referring to the location of the MP3 file. Then save the file and post it on your Web server. Make sure to post the MP3 file, too, in the correct folder, so that the link is accurate.

Starting Music Immediately

If you want the music to start immediately, you need to *stream* it. Streaming means that as soon as the first section of the music data reaches the receiving computer, it will start to play. Streaming is a bit like playing music on radio or television. A small amount of the music will be *buffered* first, but then it will start to play.

To add a stream to your Web page, first decide whether you want your viewers to use Windows Media Player or Real Player to hear the music. One way or another, they'll need a player to hear the music. Windows Media Player is shipped with Windows Me, but Real Player is more popular (at least as I write this). Your decision may be based on which formats your Web server people support. Make a phone call or search their Help pages to figure it out. Their server software must match the format of the files you hope to stream.

Once that's decided, you'll need a tool to *encode* (essentially compress for streaming purposes) your music. Free tools exist for both Windows Media Player (Windows Media Tools from Microsoft) and Real Player (Real Producer, from Real Networks) streaming, and you can download them over the Web. Install the encoding software tool of your choice, read how to use it, and encode your music into the target format. Read the tool's Help file to determine how to put the link on your pages and how to find a specialized "streaming server" to host your now-encoded music files.

11

Making Your Own CDs

CD burning—putting your own music on CDs—is something that you can now do fairly easily and cheaply on your own computer. CD recorders (called CD-R or CD-RW drives) have become cheap and commonplace in the last couple of years, to the point where you can get them for a couple hundred dollars nowadays. In fact, many new computers even come with CD-R or CD-RW drives.

CD-RWs can be written on many times, erased, and rewritten. They work just like floppy disks in that way, only they store a whopping 650M of data (about the same as 450 floppies). CD-Rs cannot be rewritten, although with the correct drive, you can write on a CD-R several times until the full capacity of the disk is exhausted. (This is called multi-session CD-R.) The attraction to CD-R disks is that they are really cheap. I have purchased them for as little as 20 cents apiece (after rebates) when I purchase a pack of 50, but typically they're about $1 each. At these prices, even if you mess up recording a CD-R, it's a pretty inexpensive drink coaster for your coffee table! There are also more expensive CD-R disks specifically designed for digital audio (like those for home stereo CD-burners).

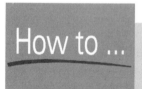

Before recording to a more expensive digital audio CD-R, you might want to try a cheaper CD-R disk, to see if a CD you make plays in your audio CD player. I haven't had any trouble using the TDK brand ones that I buy for less than a buck apiece.

How to ... Create an Instant Radio Station!

There are some free services that will stream your music (or voice) recordings, free of charge. This is great if you don't need your sounds to be part of a fancy Web site. It's a bit like sending a tape to a radio station for the disk jockey to play on the air later. In fact, it's more like creating your own on-demand radio station. Unlike a radio station, people can access your posted music any time they want, not just at the predetermined broadcast time.

Here's how it works: You simply send in your MP3 files (as many as you want, basically), and the service will create your personal radio station with your sound files on it. Then you can send your friends there, or link to it from your Web page, and people can simply click to hear the files stream from that site.

So what's the catch? When people go to your radio station site, they have to look at ads. And unfortunately, you don't get to share in the revenues from those ads. Check the rules at www.live365.com.

You might wonder how the computer can make a CD out of MP3 files so that it's playable on a standard audio CD player. Audio CDs normally have WAV files on them. When you copy a CD into MP3 format, the data gets compressed, and the resulting MP3 files are about one-tenth the size of the original. When you cut a CD from a play list of MP3s, the process is reversed. Your PC can't recreate the data that was removed in creating the MP3 file, because that was thrown out during the original compression, but it can convert your MP3s into WAV files that will play back on a normal CD player. When you tell MusicMatch or another MP3 program to cut an audio CD-R from MP3 files, this is just what it does. The MP3s are converted to WAV file format, then recorded onto the surface of the CD-R.

Creating a CD of Your Favorite Tunes

Some MP3 programs such as MusicMatch let you create a CD of your favorite tunes. CDs you cut can be played on most any audio CD player. The basic game plan for cutting a CD-R with your favorite tunes on it is simple:

1. Typically, you need to create a play list of songs you want on the CD. How you do this differs between the programs, but usually it's by dragging items into the play list portion of the window. If you have saved a play list you want to put on CD, you can open it.

2. Insert a blank, recordable CD in your CD-R or CD-RW drive.

3. Invoke the command for burning a CD. In MusicMatch, the command is Create CD from Playlist, on the File menu, which brings up the dialog box shown in Figure 11-15. Click Help to get information about each of the settings. Typically. you'll want to select Audio for the CD Format option, and you can probably leave the other settings alone. Then click on Create CD.

The MusicMatch program also creates CD inserts for the jewel case (the clear plastic case that holds the CD).

> **TIP**
>
> *You can also copy MP3 files on a CD, but you won't be able to play it on a normal audio CD player like the one in your car (although there are several MP3/CD players under development). Even so, you will be able to play the CD in any computer. So if you want to back up your MP3s, take music on the road with you, or share music with friends who have computers, putting MP3 files on the CD is the way to go. Just choose the Data setting rather than Audio setting when burning the CD from your MP3 program.*

Cutting CDs from Your Own Recordings

What if you want to make professional-sounding CDs of your own recordings, say your kid's piano recital or your garage band? Can you do it with your PC? Sure, but there are a few tricks involved.

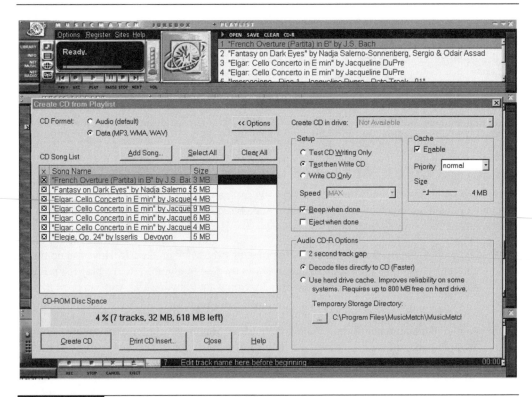

FIGURE 11-15　Cutting a CD with MusicMatch

First, you need a good recording to work with. There's going to be some degradation in the process of making the recording, so the cleaner the sound you start with, the better the final product will be.

You can invest in fancy sound cards, DATs, and professional software, but there's a cheaper way to produce a credible-sounding CD. This approach uses the basic 16-bit sound card that comes with the computer and a sound recorder such as Sony MiniDisk. Here's what you'll need:

- A stereo or mono recording device of some sort (even a Walkman Pro cassette recorder will do)
- A good-quality microphone

> **TIP**　*Spend a couple hundred dollars on a good microphone. It's probably the best place to put your money. I use an AKG uni-point stereo condenser microphone.*

- A computer with a line-in jack on the sound card

- ■ Optionally, a stereo digital reverb unit to add some "room" sound—reverb, like in a concert hall

- ■ Cooledit, a shareware program available over the Internet. Available at http://www.cooledit.com

- ■ A CD-R or CD-RW drive installed and working properly in your computer

- ■ A CD-R or CD-RW program, such as Adaptec Easy-CD or Easy-CD Pro, MusicMatch, or Real Jukebox (Real Jukebox requires you to get a plug-in from Adaptec)

After you have all of the tools, here's how you can make the recording:

1. Record the music you want to put on the CD, using your microphone.

2. After you have your material recorded, connect your MD, DAT, or other recorder's line output to the PC sound card's line-in jack. Optionally, run it through your digital reverb unit to add some nice reverb, but not too much! It's easy to overdo reverb.

3. Download, install, and run Cooledit.

4. Start a new recording in CoolEdit, but don't click on the Record button just yet. Turn on the VU monitors, and check the input levels and set them as necessary using the Windows sound-level mixer dialog box and/or your sound recorder (if it has an output adjustment).

5. Begin your recording. You can record each track individually, or run all of them together and later cut and paste individual sections into tracks and save them as separate WAV files to put on the CD. Figure 11-16 shows an example of a WAV file being recorded and edited.

6. Optionally, edit the individual WAV files using the amplitude envelope adjustment in CoolEdit to fade in at the beginning of the track and fade out at the end of the track. There are presets called Fade In and Fade Out in the program, just for this purpose. This makes the transitions between tracks sound smoother because the background noise doesn't suddenly disappear. CoolEdit also has a noise-reduction option that you can use to get rid of pesky tape noise and noise introduced by the cheesy electronics you might have used to create your recordings.

7. Now you are ready to cut the CD. Insert a blank CD in your recorder. Then run a CD-writer such as Adaptec Easy CD or Easy CD Pro, or for a cheaper solution use MusicMatch, since it will write WAV files to a CD-R. Line up the WAV files in the order you want to record them, insert the blank CD, and start cutting.

8. Make up a nice cover for your CD (using the Adaptec program, PhotoShop, MusicMatch, or another program).

11

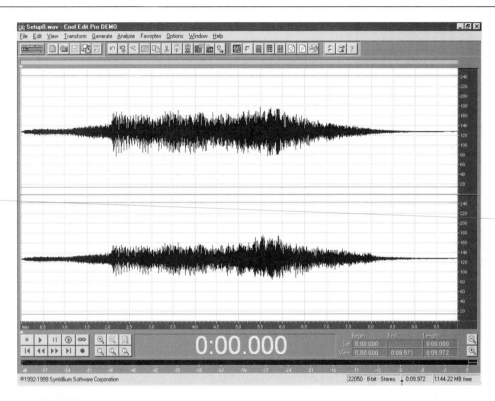

FIGURE 11-16 CoolEdit in action, recording a track

> **TIP**
>
> *If you use Adaptec's program, there is a trick to putting a photo on your CD cover. You need to open the .jpg or other photo file in a program such as PhotoShop, then select the portion of the photo you want to use. Then switch to Adaptec CD Pro and paste the image from the Clipboard. (You can't open a photo image from the Adaptec program.)*

9. Use a program such as CD Stomper Pro (check http://www.octave.com/accessories/cdlabels.html) to create your CD's label.

10. Print the label and place it on the CD. Print the cover art on glossy paper (an inexpensive ink-jet printer works fine). Cut, fold, and insert the cover art/liner notes into the CD jewel case. Figure 11-17 shows an example of a completed CD label and cover in the jewel case.

FIGURE 11-17	A finished CD cover and label

For your initial recording, you can use something like the little MiniDisk recorder from Sony (they cost a couple hundred dollars). The next step up is a DAT recorder (even a DAT Walkman from Sony will do a credible job). If you want the clearest possible starting point, forget the external recorders altogether and record directly into the PC with a high-quality semi-pro recording sound board. A good example is the GadgetLabs Wave (8 lines in, 24 out), which you can get more information about at www.gadgetlabs.com. You'll also want a very fancy program such as SoundForge, or for multi-tracking, Cubase.

11

Chapter 12

Making Movies with Your PC

How to...

- Choose video-editing hardware
- Select video-editing software
- Plan a movie-making approach
- Create movies with Window Movie Maker
- Explore Web movie streaming

Did you know that you can use your PC to produce sophisticated, ready-for-prime-time movies? This fact may seem incredible to anyone familiar with movie editing, but it's true. Just a few short years ago, the possibility of portable, affordable movie editing on a PC was a pipe dream. Now average computer users can not only make movies inexpensively, but they can also view other novice's movies over the Internet.

You can step up to the director's chair next to the likes of George Lucas, Stanley Kubrick, or Steven Spielberg for a few thousand bucks (and that includes the PC). Using a readily available video camera, a PC, some inexpensive software, and possibly an add-in video-capture card, you can set up a small video-editing and production system, right in your own home. Whether you plan to produce semi-professional programs for broadcast or consolidate all of those home videos you have scattered around the house, affordable PC-based video editing has come of age.

"So, how is this possible?" you ask. "Don't you need major Hollywood talent and bucks to write, shoot, edit, and produce a real movie? Don't you at least need an expensive Avid system with a giant stack of hard disks running on a Macintosh?" Well, yes. Don't expect to produce Star Wars 4 on an $800 PC, because films like that are shot on expensive 70mm film (and cost millions of dollars) for good reasons. But remember, many TV shows, documentaries, and independent movies are shot and edited entirely on video, without a frame of old-fashioned film involved in the process. Many are made on shoestring budgets, too.

Once you create a movie on your PC. you can do some very cool stuff with it:

- Play it on your computer
- Play it on your TV
- Send mini-movies to a friend or relative via e-mail
- Stream it over the Web (sort of like TV broadcasting) for anyone with a computer and decent Internet hookup to see
- Have your local public-access cable station broadcast it in your city or town.

This chapter will get you started on your way to producing movies on your PC, starting with a bit of explanation of how it all works.

How Does Video Editing Work?

How does video editing on your PC work? Here's an analogy: Consider how you use a word-processing program to move your words around on the screen to create your magnum opus. First, you type in all the words; then you "process" them by cutting, copying, pasting, and applying formats. Video editors work in much the same way. Instead of the keyboard, your input device is your camcorder or VCR. Your PC captures your moving pictures and sound from the camcorder or VCR. After your video images (called *clips*) are in your computer, you can massage and rearrange sections of them, add special effects, transitions between clips, narration, and sound effects to produce a final document (your movie).

> **NOTE** *You must, of course, start with some good footage. The saying, "garbage in, garbage out" is as true with video as with anything else. Although a computer video-editing system can perform certain miracles, there's a limit to how much you can improve bad footage, even with effects. Special effects, transitions, and titles are the artistic icing on the cake, not compensation for bad planning or shoddy camera technique.*

The big difference between word processing and video editing is that video happens in real time. When you start playing back your movie, events need to be synchronized, and they must occur according to a designated timeline. To make your movie, regardless of the program you use, you'll be working with a timeline tool, such as the one shown below (from Ulead Media Studio Pro). Your job as movie editor is to arrange the order of sound and video on the timeline.

12

Choosing Video-Editing Hardware

Before you can start playing with video in your computer, you need to shoot the video with a camera. This can be video you made with a conventional Hi-8 or VHS camcorder, or with a digital video camcorder. Next, you record the video on the computer's hard disk. This is called *capturing* the video. Then the process of editing begins, with you at the helm.

What Is Nonlinear Editing?

The truly exciting thing about video editing on a computer is that it's *nonlinear*. Here's a little perspective on what the term means. About 10 years ago, a friend of mine was working with a team at George Lucas' Skywalker Ranch, designing something they called the Edit Droid—one of the first nonlinear editors. It was about twice the size of R2-D2 (of *Star Wars* fame) and very expensive. Edit Droid was sort of a precursor to today's desktop video-editing stations.

Linear editing is the traditional form of film editing (major movies are shot on big film, not video) used in the past. Since you had only one master print of the film you were shooting, you had to carefully cut it up and physically splice it together to create the master print of the film. This is called linear editing, because you do it literally in a line, from beginning to end.

Then came devices like the Edit Droid. By copying all the filmed scenes onto video tapes, then controlling a bank of playback VCRs with a computer, a film director could easily try out several different variations of the movie, with scenes in different orders, using different camera angles, and so forth. Once a final edit was approved, the actual film footage would be cut up and spliced together. This was early nonlinear editing.

But even the Edit Droid was primitive compared to today's nonlinear, PC-based systems. The droid was slow since all the source footage was still on VCR tape; it had to be copied piece by piece from one VCR to another for each trial rendering of a movie. There was a lot of tape shuttling (fast forward/rewind action) to get to the right spot on the tapes. With a computer-based nonlinear system, you can record all of the videos on the computer's hard disks. This makes all that video footage instantly available, malleable, and combinable in any number of ways. By just dragging and dropping little thumbnail pictures of each scene, you can electronically splice together a rough version of a film in very short order, and then play it back instantly on your computer screen. It's truly a film editor's dream.

NOTE

Conventional camcorders produce NTSC (National Television Standards Committee)-compressed analog video, which is standard for playing on TVs and VCRs in the United States. Before NTSC video can be processed in your computer it has to be converted into a digital format (digitized). This is done using a combination of a hardware capture card and specialized compression software. Typically, NTSC video gets digitized into something called MPEG, (Moving Picture Experts Group, pronounced m-peg). There are other popular video digitizing standards such as Video for Windows, QuickTime, and Indeo, but MPEG is the most popular. Using MPEG or one of the other compression formats lets you store much more video on your hard disk. Compression works by recording only the differences between each frame of the movie, rather than a complete picture of each frame. The newer digital video camcorders (called miniDVs) produce video in compressed digital format already, which means it doesn't have to be compressed by your computer or a fancy video capture card. It's ready for computer video-editing right out of the camera. Only a simple Firewire cable between the camcorder and computer is needed to copy the movie clips from the DV tape into the computer.

Video-Capture and Audio-Capture Cards

To capture video, you'll need a video-capture card or port. For the audio portion, you'll need an audio-capture card, too. Video-capture cards come in a wide range of prices and capabilities—some as high as a $1,000 or more and others for as little as a tenth of that.

Most video-capture cards have audio-capture capabilities built into them, so you can kill two birds with one stone. It's best to use a card that has both audio and video; otherwise, synchronizing the sound and picture can be a problem. Popular cards are made by Pinnacle, ATI, Miro, and Hercules. An inexpensive one (about $200) is the ATI All-In-Wonder, which in addition to audio and video capture, lets you watch regular TV on your computer. It runs about $200. Here's a Pinnacle DV board:

12

The kind of capture device you'll need depends to a great degree on the video source(s) you want to feed into your computer. The more expensive cards will capture analog (NTSC) output from nondigital camcorders (Hi-8 and VHS), from VCRs, and TV, as well as digital images from the new digital video cameras. Pinnacle has some good solutions, such as the DV500, but they do not come cheaply.

Regardless of the capture device you get, research it thoroughly so you know that all of your equipment will work together. Capture cards specifications will often state a minimum CPU speed, amount of RAM, and hard disk space needed. For example, the Pinnacle DV500 has the following system requirements:

- Windows 98, Me, NT 4.0, or 2000
- Pentium II CPU running at 400MHz or faster
- 32-bit PCI 2.1-compliant slot
- 128M RAM
- 4G AV-certified hard drive running through a SCSI-2 or faster controller
- 16-bit video card with DirectDraw support

TIP

For some good comparisons of video capture cards, check this Web site: http://www.videoguys.com/roundup.htm.

Hard-Disk Requirements

Hard disk space is a major issue when editing video. In general, if you're interested in doing more than 5-minute shorts, you're going to be investing in a big hard disk upgrade. With 80G drives just beginning to appear in the $300 range, this should not be a problem. If you have a smallish (2G to 10G) hard disk, you can still make a long movie, but you'll need to do it in sections, dubbing out each section to tape in order, essentially building the movie from beginning to end. The larger the hard disk, the more of the movie you can have in the computer at one time, and thus the more nonlinearly you can edit it before committing the final cut to tape (or to another medium, such as CD-ROM).

TIP

To capture five minutes of digital video, 1G of hard disk space is required. For 30 minutes of digital video, you'll need 6.5G of space. Disk space used for analog sources varies greatly, depending on frame size, frames per second, number of colors, and type of compression. Refer to the manual that accompanies your software, or contact a vendor to determine the amount of disk space you'll need. You'll need more space on your drive than just enough to store the source files you are capturing. Once you have captured the video to disk, you'll be creating a final "output" file, which will include all the source footage, and more, such as special effects. Thus, you need between two and three times more space than you were thinking, just so you can cut, copy, paste, and render the final movie.

Another consideration for video editing is the speed of your hard disk. Fast hard drives are required for serious video editing. The fastest drives are SCSI-type (which are expensive), although the newer EIDE Ultra-DMA drives (which are less expensive than SCSI) have become competitive in their performance. Some drives are designed for video and are labeled *AV-certified,* which means they don't stop occasionally to recalibrate themselves. Your drive should have at least a 10ms *average access time,* and be capable of 3 megabyte-per-second (MB/sec) transfer rate for 30 frame-per-second analog video capture.

If your computer can handle an IDE Ultra DMA/66 7200 RPM drive, it is a good lower-cost alternative to a SCSI drive. You'll need to dig into your computer's manual or contact the manufacturer of the motherboard to see if your PC can use this type of drive.

Video Cameras

If you can get hold of a digital video (DV) camcorder, it's definitely the way to go for making movies. Get one with a Firewire jack on it, and buy a capture card with a Firewire jack on it. Some PCs, such as the Sony VAIO, have a built-in Firewire jack, in which case, you're home free on the capture-card requirement.

There are four compelling reasons to buy a DV (officially, miniDV) camcorder:

- ■ **Size**   Camcorder models in miniDV format are incredibly small. Many of them fit in a loose-fitting pants pocket.

- ■ **Quality**   MiniDV currently offers the best picture quality of any consumer grade camcorder tape format. They capture more lines of resolution than do VHS or SVHS.

- ■ **Endurance**   The tapes themselves are no sturdier than 8mm, but when you gaze into the crystal ball to see which of the current camcorder formats are likely to be around a decade or two from now... well, you get the idea.

- ■ **Availability**   Every major camcorder manufacturer has adopted the miniDV format. Accordingly, you'll find miniDV camcorders from such arch-rivals as Sony and JVC, as well as from Panasonic, Canon, Sharp, and even RCA. Here's a picture of a small JVC miniDV camcorder:

12

The downside of DV is that it takes up more space on your hard disk than does NTSC-compressed (MPEG-2) analog video from Hi-8, VHS, or S-VHS sources. However, the quality of the final image will be clearer, without dropped frames, jitter, and color abnormalities often seen in analog video.

Microphones

Even the best video can suffer as a result of poor sound recording. You'll want to purchase a good microphone if you intend to put together professional-quality videos. If you're just playing with your home videos, don't sweat it. Your camcorder has a microphone in it that will pick up conversation and ambient sounds well enough, assuming you're not too far away from those sounds.

A good external microphone can be incredibly expensive, but it may also be one of your most essential pieces of equipment. A decent handheld microphone is the Shure BG 5.0, which is available for about $150. Here are some specialized types you might consider:

- A stereo microphone is useful for indoor recordings, such as classical music concerts. An example is the AKG model AT822, which costs about $300.

- A wireless microphone is nice to have if you intend on recording interviews, especially while walking around in an outdoor setting. A Shure wireless microphone (model VLP 93 VHS) costs about $400.

- A shotgun microphone is designed for very directional use (when you need to filter out other sounds in the room or outside). The drawback is that most shotguns make people sound as though they're talking out of a metal garbage can. The Audio Technica AT835B has great sonic response for its price (about $250). A better one (for real professional work) is the Sennheiser ME66 (around $550).

TIP *A shotgun microphone can be mounted on a larger camera with a "shockmount," such as a Beyerdynamic EA86 (about $35). It slides into the accessory shoe of a camera and suspends the microphone in a matrix of short rubber bands, isolating it from camera-handling noises.*

Choosing Video-Editing Software

Specialized software allows you to capture and edit video on your PC. You can choose from the most basic video-editing programs to full-featured ones.

Video-Editing Functions

Video-editing programs perform some or all of the following functions:

- Importing the video images from a source, typically a camcorder or VCR (sometimes called *acquiring* video)

- Breaking up your video into clips so you can rearrange them to your liking

- Adjusting the length of each clip to get rid of extraneous sections at the beginning or end of a clip that you don't want (called *trimming*)

- Adding text (*titles*) to your scenes, typically to introduce a new scene or as credits at the end

- Adding fancy *transitions* between clips such as fades and wipes, spin in, spin out, 3D flying cubes, and so on (there are literally hundreds of these kinds of effects)

- Adding an audio overlay to your production, such as narration or music (high-end video programs provide several audio tracks for compiling and mixing together complex sound tracks with voice-overs, background music, sound effects, and so on)

- Optional *filtering* to clean up sound or video, or apply special effects such as cropping, converting color to black and white or sepia tone, adding echo and reverb to sound, and so on

- Creating a final output file that can be played on your TV or computer (called *rendering*)

- Copying your output file to the destination device, such as DV camcorder or VHS tape

As you might imagine, software that does *all* the above can be fairly expensive, especially if it does everything very well.

Video-Editing Programs

The most popular video PC-based video editor is called Adobe Premiere, and it's expensive. Its list price is close to $800, but you might be able to find it for about $500 (if you shop really hard). A competing product with a very good feature set (in fact, I prefer it) is Ulead Media Studio Pro, selling for roughly the same price.

Fortunately, a new breed of entry-level video software is showing up for hobbyists. You can find no-frills video editors for less than $100 these days. Even though they lack the bells and whistles of their heavy-duty counterparts, they'll still suffice for many smaller jobs. Ulead offers a basic product called Video Studio for under $100.

There are also shareware or freeware programs for video editing available on the Internet. For example, QuickEditor (available for download from http://wild.ch/quickeditor/index.html) costs $35 and does basic editing of QuickTime files. If you do a search on the Web for "video editing software" you will find more than you gambled for.

Additionally, video-editing programs are being included as freebies with computers, just as word-processing and sound-editing programs have been. Windows Me includes such an editor, called Window Movie Maker. Sony VAIO computers come with a program called DV Gate.

Video-editing programs vary in the type of video format they can store on your hard disk, and they can use as clips in your movies. Aside from MPEG, one of the most popular file format for video is called AVI (Audio Video Interleave), followed by MOV files (QuickTime for Windows). To complicate matters, Windows Movie Maker creates output files in the new Microsoft Windows Media format, not AVI or QuickTime. The AVI and MOV formats are highly Windows compatible, so either of these should work fine for most PC video projects.

AVI is the file format Microsoft developed for its Video for Windows standard. Within AVI, there are many options, such as how large the window for the video is in pixels. For example, a common size is 320 pixels wide by 240 pixels high, also called simply 320 x 240. This will create

12

a smallish window on your screen. The larger the window, the larger the video files on the hard disk need to be, and the more processing power you need to capture and play back the video smoothly.

The quality of the finished picture is also limited by the video source. Standard camcorders and VHS decks record in what is called NTSC-format, designed for TV viewing, not the higher resolution of today's PC screens. There is really only a 640 x 480 window's worth of data to display, unless you have some tricky hardware that does *line doubling* or other tricks to improve the image resolution. Hi-8 and Super VHS (S-VHS) sources are a step higher in resolution. Some capture cards have an S-video input for capture, so use it if your video deck or camera has an S output. miniDV has a higher resolution than any of the aforementioned. Video from a DV camera that is captured over Firewire is going to look better than video from an analog source.

The other important option when capturing and editing video on a PC is the number of frames per second (fps) you want to work with. NTSC draws new, complete images on your TV screen 30 times per second, thus fooling the eye into thinking that smooth motion is occurring. (Movies you see at your local theater run at 24fps.) Many of today's PCs are not quite up to the task of recording and playing 30fps on a full screen, so you'll typically need to reduce your frames per second or your display's color depth if you want to display a larger image.

If all of this seems like more than you want to deal with, don't worry. The less-expensive programs don't hassle you with all of these considerations—they just make the choices for you. Only if you use Adobe Premiere or another fancy video editor will you need to have some understanding of frame size, compression algorithms, pixel interpolation, and file formats. And if you're interested, you can easily find this information: Check your program's Help files, subscribe to a video magazine, and/or search the Web.

Choosing a Movie-Making Approach

There are several basic approaches to capturing and editing video (and optionally putting the video back on tape so you can sell your movie down at Blockbuster). The one you choose will depend on your needs and your equipment.

I call the approaches manual, semi-automatic, and automatic. The automatic method is the best, but it requires the latest hardware, including a DV camcorder, Firewire port on your computer, and appropriate software. The other, slower, approaches work with non-DV/non-Firewire camcorders, such as Hi-8 and VHS, or a DV camcorder that doesn't have a Firewire connection. Let's take a look at the basic steps that each approach entails.

The Manual Approach

The manual approach to video editing includes the following steps:

1. Capture video by manually controlling the playback of the camcorder and your video-capture program. Push Start on the camcorder, and then click on Start in the capture software. It's sort of like recording a CD onto a tape recorder.

TIP *Though this depends somewhat on the speed of your computer, it's a good idea to close other programs you might have open, and turn off your screen saver while capturing video. This can result in a smoother-looking video because it helps prevent dropped frames.*

2. Stop the computer and camcorder at the end of the clip, and save the clip as a file (typically an AVI file).

3. Repeat steps 1 and 2 for each clip you want to use in your movie.

4. Once the clips are stored as files, use a video-editing program to arrange your clips in the order you desire, add transitions between clips, add credits, special effects, and so on. This is typically done on a horizontal timeline (as shown earlier in this chapter, in the "How Does Video Editing Work?" section), where you can drag and drop clips, audio tracks, and transitions. You can adjust the timing until you are satisfied.

5. Preview the movie in a small window on your computer screen. Previews are typically displayed in a lower quality than you'll get in your final output.

6. Render the movie. During rendering, the software pieces the clips together in order, applies any effects and scene transitions you might have specified, and merges in any additional audio tracks. It then creates a new output file on the hard disk with your final movie on it. The original source files are left in place, and the new output file is created. You may have options to create output files of different resolutions, window sizes, and so forth, depending on the purpose of your output file (such as streaming it on the Web, sending it via e-mail, or just showing it on your computer).

7. If you want to play the movie on a TV set, output the movie to a VCR to record it.

The Semi-Automatic Approach

Here are the main steps in the semi-automatic approach:

1. Begin the capture of video manually, as in the manual method, but in one long take. Using this approach, you let the tape run through all of the scenes that you would otherwise need to capture and save separately.

2. Stop the computer and camcorder when all the scenes are through playing. The computer program is then smart enough to automatically break up the scenes into separate clips. (It does this by looking for two adjacent frames that are very different from one another, assuming this is a clip boundary.)

3. Arrange your clips and render your video, as described in steps 4–6 in the previous section.

12

The Automatic Approach

For the fully automatic method, you must use a DV camcorder, Firewire cable, and compatible software, such as Adobe Premiere. Depending on your DV setup and software tools, the procedure may differ a bit, but here are the general steps for using the automatic approach:

1. Instruct your video-editing program to scan the entire tape (or portion thereof) and make an index of all the shots on it. It creates a thumbnail picture from the first frame in each shot.

2. Instruct the program to "batch capture" the actual video of clips you want and store the video on your hard disk It does this automatically, controlling the camcorder's mechanism itself (you don't need to press the buttons on the camcorder).

3. Arrange your thumbnails on the timeline, in the order you want them in your movie. Add transitions, effects, and so on, using the appropriate tools.

4. Instruct the program to render the movie to an output file.

5. Optionally, tell the software to output your completed movie onto a blank tape you insert in the camcorder, so you can watch it on TV or broadcast it. It writes the video data back out to the DV camcorder over the Firewire cable.

Using Windows Movie Maker

If you have Windows Me, you already have a simple video-editing program, called Windows Movie Maker. Movie Maker requires the following minimum system configuration:

- Microsoft Windows Me operating system
- 300MHz Pentium II or equivalent
- 64M of RAM
- 2G of free hard disk space
- An audio-capture device
- A video-capture device
- An Internet connection and an e-mail program (if you want to send a movie to a Web server or attach a movie to an e-mail message)

As you can see, the requirements are not too heavy, so most late-model PCs are likely to work with this program.

Movie Maker is intended for the amateur home-video experimenter. The output files are in Microsoft Windows Media format (not AVI format), which limits the image size to 320 x 240. You can view your movies on the computer screen, e-mail them, or play them on a Web page.

To open Movie Maker, click Start, select Programs, and then choose Accessories. You should see Windows Movie Maker listed on the menu. Figure 12-1 shows an example of the Movie Maker window with some clips loaded.

The workspace has two modes: storyboard and timeline. In storyboard mode, you see your clips lined up side by side, as in Figure 12-1. In timeline mode, you can adjust the length of each clip by trimming it from either end, or you can split a track in two.

NOTE *Before you do any work in Windows Movie Maker, it's a good idea to read through its Help files.*

The clips you've recorded in Movie Maker appear in the Collections area of the Movie Maker window, listed under My Collections. My Collections is a lot like Windows Explorer. It's basically a system for organizing all of your video clips. With Movie Maker, you keep all your clips in one place in the My Collections folder system. Then you can drag them around, between folders (to reorganize them) or to the timeline to organize a movie. Once you have a movie set up, you can save the arrangement, so you can open it again later and work with it. This is called a *project*. You save a project with the Save Project command on the File menu.

To introduce you to video editing with Movie Maker, we'll go over the steps for creating a short movie using Movie Maker. Then you'll learn how to e-mail your movie and post it on the Web.

FIGURE 12-1 The Windows Movie Maker window with some clips loaded

Recording Your Movie

After you've shot your video and you've got your capture card connected and working, follow these steps to bring your clips into Movie Maker:

1. Plug your camcorder or VCR into the video-input port and turn on the camera. Queue up the tape to the starting location of your shots.

2. Click Start, Programs, Accessories, and then choose Windows Movie Maker to start Movie Maker.

3. Start the capture process by clicking the Record button in the toolbar or choosing Record from the File menu. This brings up the Record dialog box, as shown in Figure 12-2.

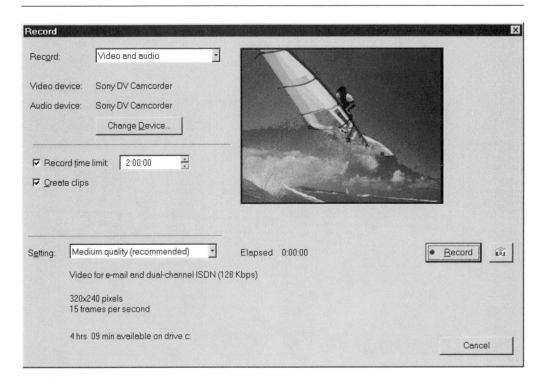

FIGURE 12-2   Adjusting the recording settings before starting the capture process

12

NOTE   *If you see a message warning you that your system may not "provide acceptable performance," try it anyway. It may work.*

4. If the wrong video or audio device appears to be selected, click on the Change Device button and choose the correct one. You may also want to click the Change Device button to use sound from a source other than the camera, such as the line-in jack or a CD in your CD player.

5. Select the Create Clips check box if you want Movie Maker to break the video capture into separate clips for you after it records the incoming video.

6. Check the quality setting in the Setting box on the bottom-left side of the dialog box. This setting controls the number of frames per second and the image size in the final movie. You can pick a quality setting from the Setting drop-down list. The choices are Low Quality (160 x 120 at 15fps), Medium Quality, the default, (320 x 240 pixels at 15fps) and High Quality (320 x 240 at 30fps).

7. Click the Record button. Now start your camcorder playing. The incoming video images will appear in the Record dialog box, and the word *Recording* will flash in the dialog box.

8. Click Stop when the tape reaches the end of the section you want to capture. You will be presented with a file dialog box. Enter a file name and click OK. Movie Maker will automatically give your file a WMV extension. If you told Movie Maker to create clips for you, you'll see the Creating Clips dialog box, as shown here.

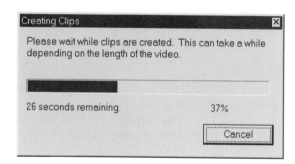

You should now see your clips in the Collections area of the Movie Maker window.

Putting Clips into the Storyboard

Once you have some clips your Collections area, the next step is to drag them onto the storyboard in the order you want them to appear in the movie. Then you can play your movie. Follow these steps:

1. Select the desired folder under My Collections to see the clips stored in it.

2. Identify and drag a clip from the Collections area down to the storyboard.

If you want to see information about each clip, or get more clips on the screen at once, choose Details or List from the View menu.

3. Repeat step 2 for each clip you want in the movie. You can rearrange them by dragging them left and right on the storyboard. Delete a clip from the storyboard by right-clicking it and choosing Cut or Delete.

4. Play your movie! Click the Play menu and select Play Entire Storyboard/Timeline. Your movie clips will play in the order you arranged them. Press period (.) to cancel the playback if you want. Choose Full Screen from the Play menu to make the movie as large as possible.

5. Assuming you like what you see (or it's close enough), you should save the project. Click on the File menu, choose Save Project, and name your project (that is, your movie).

After you've saved your movie, you can easily reopen at any time in Movie Maker by selecting Open Project from the File menu. All the clips and the storyboard will come up in the Movie Maker window.

Adjusting the Timeline

Now that you have the clips in the right order and have saved your movie, you can either call it quits or you can tweak your movie. Often, you'll want to make some adjustments. You might think that some clips are just too long; other clips may have portions in the middle that you don't want to include in the movie. Movie Maker offers solutions to both problems.

NOTE

You can't lengthen a clip in Movie Maker. However, some more advanced video-editing programs will let you do this by stretching the video and creating new frames for it.

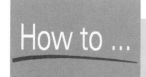

Create Effects with Repeated and Overlapped Clips

You can drag a clip to the Movie Maker storyboard or timeline more than once. For example, suppose that you wanted a few seconds of black screen with just some music, to separate your final movie into segments. You could create a clip that has nothing but black in the video, but has music or some other transitional audio on it, and plug it into the storyboard at appropriate times. You only need to shoot and capture the clip once, but you can enter it into the storyboard as many times as you want.

Here's another idea: Suppose that you want to do a special effect of, say, your pet bird doing some silly motion repeatedly. Create a small clip of the motion, then capture it as a clip and pull it into the storyboard as many times as you want.

You can also make audio and video clips fade into one another and overlap (called a *cross-fade*). If you don't specify a transition type, it will be a straight cut. To create a cross-fade, drag the second of two clips to the left, on top of the clip to its left, as shown here. The amount of overlap determines the amount of time that the cross-fading will occur. Check the Help file for more information about fading and other effects.

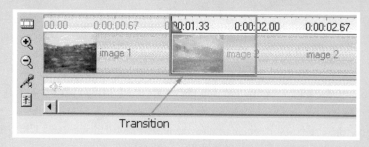

Transition

Trimming a Clip

Trimming clips is one of those recurring jobs in putting together a movie. Luckily, it's easy to do. Here's how:

1. Change the view from storyboard to timeline by clicking on the Timeline icon at the far-left side of the storyboard or by choosing Timeline from the View menu. Notice that now there is a time "ruler" above the storyboard, and each clip's length in time is indicated. You can zoom the view using the + and – buttons to the left of the timeline if you need to get a more detailed look.

2. Click the thumbnail of the clip that you want to trim, and *trim points* will appear above the clip. You can drag these trim points to shorten the clip from either end, as shown here. As you do so, look at the monitor window. It will indicate the exact timeline location and clip duration as you make the adjustment. Or, to increase the precision of the timeline, choose View, Zoom In or Zoom Out. You can "scrub" though the clip, and the monitor will show you just where you are moving the trim point.

3. When you release the mouse button, the clip is trimmed. Movie Maker will tighten up the timeline, pulling adjacent clips up, to fill in the gap.

4. To test the trim job you did, you can play the adjusted clip all by itself. Click the Play button, located just under the monitor window, as shown here.

Splitting a Clip

The automatic clip-splitting option you use during video capture doesn't always work as you planned. As a result, you might have some shots that are joined together in a single clip, so you will need to split them into separate clips. If you're into creating experimental movies, you also might want to cut clips up into fragments so you can rearrange them in weird ways.

Movie Maker makes it quite easy to split up clips. Basically, you set a split point in the clip and click the Split button. It's that easy. Here are the steps:

1. In the Collections, timeline, or storyboard area, click on the clip you want to split. The clip is loaded into the monitor window, with the first frame of the clip displayed.

2. Using the slider below the picture in the monitor area, scrub through the clip to the spot where you want to divide the clip. You can fine-tune the split point by clicking the Previous Frame and Next Frame buttons under the slider.

3. Click the Split Clip button, as shown below. Movie Maker cuts off the clip at the split and creates a new clip out of it. It will be given a name similar to the source clip, such as Clip 10 (1), Clip 10 (2), and so on.

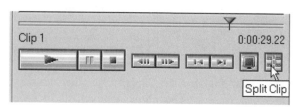

12

You can repeat these steps to split up even a very long clip into smaller segments that you can work with.

You can combine clips by selecting two or more and choosing Combine from the Clip menu.

Adding a Narration

You can add sound to your movie, either on top of the sound in the video files or in place of it. Here's how:

1. Open the project and place clips on the timeline.

2. Click the File menu and select Record Narration. You'll see the dialog box shown here.

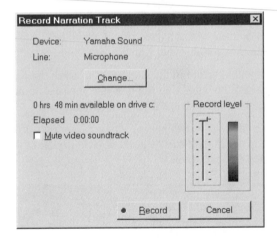

3. Check that the Line selection is accurate. This specifies the audio-input source, which typically is a microphone. If the Line setting is incorrect, click Change and pick the one you want. If you want the soundtrack on the video to be silenced, leaving only your narration, click on the Mute Video Soundtrack check box to select it.

If you're using a laptop computer, I suggest that you plug a good microphone into the mic input on the laptop. Internal microphones in laptops pick up too much of the computer's internal sounds (hard disk spinning, for example), ruining the recording.

4. Click the Record button. The movie will rewind to the beginning, and you can watch the whole thing in the monitor window as you recite your narration. Adjust the sound level if you need to, using the slider. The meter should register somewhere in the middle.

5. Click Stop when you're finished recording the narration.

6. You will be prompted to give your narration file a name. It will be saved as a WAV file and automatically added to the Collections area of the Movie Maker window.

7. Drag the audio clip down to the auto line (just below the timeline), and position it. Typically, you'll position it at the beginning of the movie, as shown below. Audio clips work just like video ones do, in terms of placement. You can drag them left and right on the timeline.

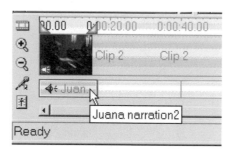

E-mailing a Movie

Sending a movie to someone as an e-mail attachment is fairly easy. However, in order to play your movie, your recipient will need to have a media player that will play a WMV (Windows Media Video) file if you created a movie or WMA (Windows Media Audio) if your clip only had audio and no video. A recent version of Windows Media Player can play MVW files. Real Player (from Real Networks) and some other media players try to keep up with the latest Microsoft video formats for playback, so other players might work as well.

Also, remember that movies can be very large files. Someone with a slow Internet connection may be very displeased if you send them a megabyte-sized file!

Here are the steps for e-mailing a movie to a friend or colleague:

1. Open a saved movie in Movie Maker.

2. Click the Send button on the toolbar and choose E-mail. You'll see the Send Movie Via e-mail dialog box, as shown in Figure 12-3.

3. In the dialog box, choose the desired quality (resolution and pixel size) of the rendered movie. In the Display Information section of the dialog box, you can enter in the movie's title, author, rating (use your discrimination), and a description of the movie. This information goes into the file and will be visible to viewers of your movie, so word it carefully. After you've filled in the dialog box, click OK.

12

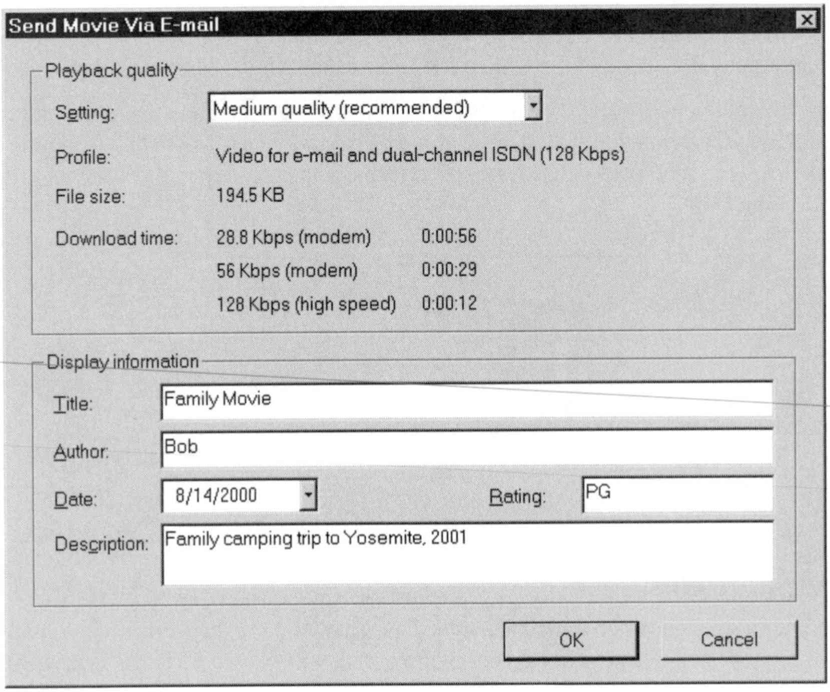

FIGURE 12-3   Sending a movie via e-mail

TIP   *You may want to scale down your movie from a higher quality for e-mailing it over slow connections.*

4. Movie Maker prompts you to enter a name for the file. It will use this file name to store the file on disk before sending it. The name can't include spaces or punctuation marks. Use a short name, like Mymovie. Click OK; then wait while the movie is rendered and saved to a disk file.

5. Movie Maker will ask you which e-mail program to use for sending. Choose the e-mail program you intend to use (for example, Outlook Express).

6. An e-mail message is generated with an explanation for your recipient of how to view the movie, with the movie attached. Just enter your recipient's e-mail address and a subject line. Then you can send the message with the attached movie in the same way that you send other e-mail.

Posting a Movie on the Web

If you want to avoid the hassle of e-mail and post the movie where anyone with a Web browser and a media player can run it, you can post it to a Web server. (For more information about Web servers and Web hosting services, as well as creating your own Web site, see Chapter 9.)

Here are the steps for posting your movie on a Web server:

1. Connect to the Internet.

2. Open a saved movie in Movie Maker.

3. Click on the Send button on the toolbar and choose Web Server. You'll see a dialog box similar to the one shown in Figure 12-3. Choose the quality and enter the title, author, date, rating, and description (as explained in step 3 of the previous section). Then click OK.

4. In the next dialog box that appears, enter a name for the file. Use no more than eight characters, lowercase, without spaces (some Web servers don't like long names or those other characters). Then click OK.

5. You'll see the Send To Web dialog box, as shown in Figure 12-4. This dialog box asks for your Web-hosting information. (POPcast is pretty cool, giving you a lot of space for your movies and features such as movie albums and video "channels" you can broadcast your video shows from.) Fill in the host name, your user name, and your password, and then click OK.

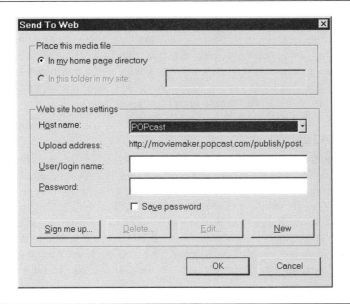

12

FIGURE 12-4   Sending a movie to a Web server

If you don't have a place to present your movies to Web viewers, you can create a new account with one of the growing list of free services that will host for you. Click Sign Me Up in the Send To Web dialog box, and follow the directions on the pages that appear (you need to be connected to the Internet to do this). After signing up (which takes only a minute), you'll have a user ID and password. Enter it in the dialog box, and click OK.

Your movie will be uploaded to the Web site. Make note of the URL (Web address). Now you can e-mail the Web address to people so that they can go see your movie!

Graduating to the Big Time

If you got this far, you're well on your way to movie-making on your PC! It's very addictive, especially if you have struggled with linear video editing before. The power the PC brings to the task is exhilarating.

Using Advanced Video-Editing Software

As you've seen, Movie Maker is a pretty spiffy tool considering it's free, and it's very efficient for what it does. Basically, it replaces what only a month ago I was doing with three separate programs: a capture program that came with my video card, an $800 editor, and Real Producer (a program that prepares video for Web-based streaming).

However, once you master a simple program such as Movie Maker, you'll probably want to move up to a more sophisticated program. Take a look at Figures 12-5 and 12-6 to see what Adobe Premiere and Ulead Media Studio Pro have to offer.

Notice that both of these programs offer multiple video and audio tracks on the timeline. You can easily drag and drop content into a project from Windows Explorer or any folder window. The feature set of these programs is very rich, especially with all the transitions and special effects, filters, and output options they offer. Expect to spend at least a week or two working with either of these video-editing programs to begin mastering it.

Streaming Movies

Due in part to the availability of affordable video editing, there is a trend afoot for small, independent or aspiring film makers and video producers to stream their creations (typically short movies) over the many new streaming movie channels on the Web. This provides them with audiences they normally would never reach, and bypasses the whole Hollywood studio tradition where only a few well-endowed projects with little or no artistic merit get produced.

If you have a high-speed Internet connection (DSL or cable), you'll be able to tune in and watch innovative video with merit ranging from pure junk to the exceptional, any time of day or night. And if you like to roll your own, imagine having an instant global audience for your new short.

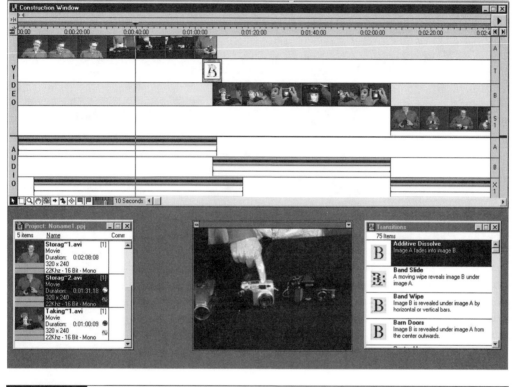

FIGURE 12-5   Adobe Premiere with a project file open

If you want to get serious about publishing on the Web, you'll need to learn about streaming technology. Sign up for Streamedia.com's newsletter (www.streamingmedia.com) and put your thinking cap on (as my kindergarten teacher used to tell us).

> **TIP**
>
> *Trey Parker and Matt Stone sent their short film,* The Spirit of Christmas, *a construction-paper animated short, to a studio executive as a holiday card. It wasn't long before the card was forwarded to anyone who was anyone in Hollywood. Before they knew what hit them, Comedy Central called and gave them a deal to make the now incredibly popular South Park series. If you're interested, you can search for "soxmas.mov" to locate and download the movie.*

12

FIGURE 12-6 Ulead Media Studio Pro 5 with a project file open

Check out the following movie streaming sites:

- IFILM (www.ifilm.com)
- Reelmind (www.reelmind.com)
- AtomFilms (www.atomfilms.com)
- EVEO (www.eveo.com)
- ZeroOneFilms (www.zeroonefilms.com)
- 405 The Movie (www.405TheMovie.com)

If you suspect that there's really a movie writer/director/producer lying dormant somewhere deep inside you, and you're serious about sharing your movie productions, you can try submitting them to channels specializing in streaming movies.

Chapter 13 Playing Games

How to...

- ■ Play games included with Windows
- ■ Find the best third-party games for Windows
- ■ Join multiplayer Internet games
- ■ Host your own multiplayer game
- ■ Use MSN's Zone.com software
- ■ Install game-related hardware

Unlike the television console machines, PC games have always been more serious, more involved, and more complex. Arcade-type games, which focus on instant fun and excessive graphics, continue to dominate on such platforms as Dreamcast and Playstation. PC games, however, continue the tradition of realism, and the detailed experience required by their audience—adults 21–34 years of age.

With more games available for the Windows platform than most consoles, the PC and Microsoft Windows has become the dominant gaming platform. This dominance did not come without serious work though. Microsoft, after a decade of neglecting the gaming market, finally started incorporating game features into Windows 98 and Windows Me. With the inclusion of DirectX version 5 (in Windows 98) and version 7 (in Windows Me), Microsoft has enabled game developers to build advanced, 3D games that run within the Windows operating system. Windows also provides the traditional board and card games. This chapter covers games that you can play alone or with others on the Internet.

Playing the Games Included with Windows

Depending on which version of Windows you have on your PC, you have up to six single-player games already installed on your system:

- ■ Freecell, a solitaire variant
- ■ Minesweeper, a strategy game
- ■ Pinball, a computer version of a pinball machine
- ■ Spider Solitaire, a solitaire variant
- ■ Classic Solitaire, the original, most famous computer game on the planet
- ■ Classic Hearts, a version of the Hearts card game, where your opponents' hands are played by the computer

Windows Me also includes five Internet multiplayer games, which are available through the MSN Gaming Zone (www.zone.com): Internet Backgammon, Internet Checkers, Internet Hearts, Internet Reversi, and Internet Spades.

Launching a Windows Game

To access the games included with Windows, simply click on Start, then Programs, then Games. The Games menu shows all the games installed with Windows, as in the example from Windows Me shown here.

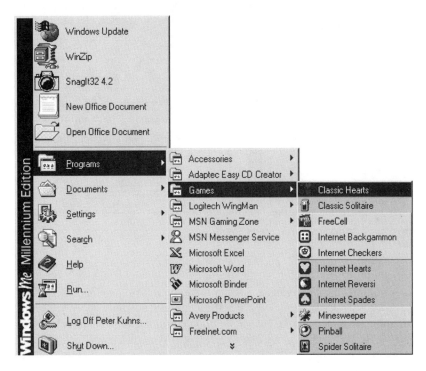

Select a game to launch it. Each game includes a simple interface that resembles the real game. For card games, the computer will deal the cards and mimic as many players as necessary. In Classic Hearts, for example, a game requires four players. The computer creates three of these players for you. Figure 13-1 shows an example of playing Hearts.

Notice that the game window shown in Figure 13-1 includes Game and Help menus on its menu bar. The Game menu includes options you can set for the specific game you are playing,

13

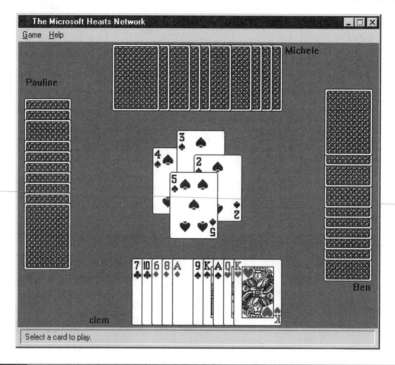

The Microsoft Hearts Network

Michele

Pauline

Ben

clem

Select a card to play.

FIGURE 13-1   Playing Classic Hearts

such as a selection of card deck designs for a solitaire game. The Help menu includes the Help Topics option, which provides information about the game. For example, when you select Help Topics from the Help menu in the Hearts window, you can choose to see rules, scoring, and tips for playing Hearts, as shown in Figure 13-2. Every Windows game includes a useful Help file for new players. Simply select Help Topics from the Help menu or press the F1 key at any time within the game to access the game's Help information.

NOTE   *If you press F1 from the desktop or access Help by choosing it from the Start menu, you will not be able to access instructions on how to play each game. Instead, you'll see general information about accessing the Windows games.*

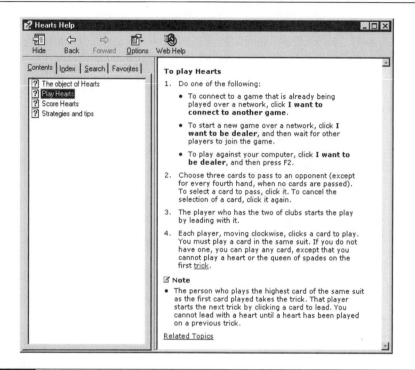

FIGURE 13-2   Microsoft Help for Hearts

Getting Online Quickly with Windows Me Games

Windows Me comes with free Internet games: Backgammon, Checkers, Hearts, Reversi, and Spades. These games are multiplayer only; if you select one of these games from the Games menu, plan on playing with someone else. The Zone.com game Wizard included with Windows Me has reduced multiplayer gaming to a few clicks. Now you can get online and play someone else in seconds after booting your PC.

> **TIP** *You can also access the Internet games included with Windows Me by visiting the www.zone.com Web site. You will need to download the Zone.com software to play. See the "Playing Internet Multiplayer Games" section later in this chapter for details.*

13

To play a Windows Me Internet game, first connect to the Internet, and then select the game you want to play from the Games menu (for example, click Start, Programs, Games, and then Internet Backgammon). The Internet Gaming Wizard window will appear. Click Next, and the wizard will connect to Zone.com and look for an opponent for you to play against, as in the example here.

Next, you will see the window for the game you chose to play. For example, Figure 13-3 shows the Internet Backgammon board. As you can see, you can turn the Chat option on or off. If both you and your opponent have Chat turned on, you can exchange messages using common remarks (in these games, your conversation is limited).

 *Single-player card and board games included in Windows can be paused. If you need to switch out of a game quickly, just minimize the window by clicking the Minimize button. If you're playing someone online, however, you risk forfeiting the game if your opponent loses patience!*

Choosing New Windows Games

More types of games are available for Windows than any other platform. The vast number of choices can make determining which games to buy overwhelming. A good way to begin your selection process is to decide which game genres appeal to you. The main game genres available for the PC and Windows include role-playing, first-person action, simulator, real-time strategy, sports, and puzzles. Let's take a look at each of these genres and some of the most popular games in each one.

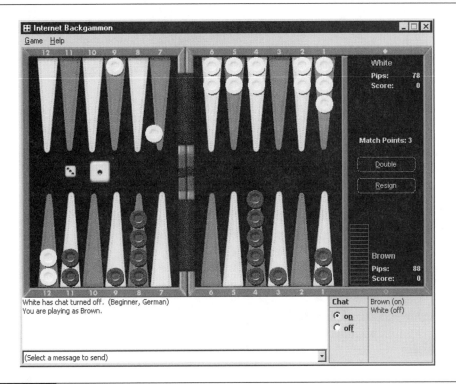

FIGURE 13-3   Multiplayer backgammon using Zone.com's game servers

NOTE

Games continue to evolve and improve. The games mentioned in this chapter may not even be available by the time you read this. Chances are good that at least a half dozen new games in every genre will be available. If you cannot find the games mentioned in this chapter, you may want to check the message boards to find new games that are similar. See Chapter 8 for information about online message boards.

13

Role-Playing Games

Role-playing games (often referred to as RPGs) are based on turns and are much more interactive than any other genre. You create a character and live through the character in a virtual world, such as the one from Everquest shown in Figure 13-4.

This type of game has benefited from the Internet more than any other genre. Massive multiplayer worlds are now first person, 3D environments with cities, forests, oceans, and mountain ranges. Thousands of people can interact in real time, 24 hours a day.

FIGURE 13-4   Everquest is a multiplayer role-playing universe

When you play an RPG, you can meet people through your character, form relationships, create communities, and learn through others. You will meet enemies who you must fight. Other, more peaceful characters in this world may only want to barter, buy, and sell goods using money earned or "borrowed" from enemies. The success and longevity of your character are based on the items you have, your experience, and the amount of points you gain or inflict on enemies.

A few landmark games in the role-playing universe include Everquest, Call of Asheron, Ultima Online, and Icewind Dale.

First-Person Action Games

First-person action games are real-time, detailed (usually violent) games that are viewed from a first-person perspective. These games enable users to wander around everywhere in a "level" and interact (usually blow up!) anything the gamer encounters. The first-person action games have slowly evolved into more complex games that cross several genres. The newest, most exciting variant is team-based play. Groups of people embark on "missions" that must be completed cooperatively.

First-person action games usually require speed, cunning, and a lot of firepower. These games are not for the faint of heart, especially in multiplayer mode.

CAUTION   *First-person action games rely heavily on CPU power and graphics-processing power. If you are using an older PC with a weak video card, you will not be able to enjoy these games, because the frame rate (speed at which the PC processes your moves), will be too slow. As a result, the game will be jerky and will not show the textures of the 3D objects in the game.*

The following are some of the more popular first-person action games:

- **Quake III Arena**   The successor to Quake and Quake II, this purely multiplayer Internet game has the most advanced graphics in the gaming universe. This game is extremely demanding on hardware because of enormous levels (rooms) with thousands of polygons and textures and special lighting. Figure 13-5 shows an example of a scene in Quake III Arena.

- **Unreal**   Released in 1998, this game is still considered a leader in graphics, story, and gameplay. Variations of this game, such as Unreal Tournament, are popular Internet multiplayer games. Unreal is known for its beautiful lighting.

FIGURE 13-5   Quake III Arena is a multiplayer, 3D, intensive, first-person shooter game

13

- **Half-Life** Considered "old" by gaming standards, this game continues to be a top seller for single players and Internet gamers. Half-life is known for its AI (Artificial Intelligence) for the computer-controlled characters in the game.

- **John Clancy's Rainbow Six: Covert Ops** In this game, you command an elite corps of soldiers on various covert missions. Clancy's games are known for extreme realism, including the often slow work of getting from point A to point B.

- **Duke Nukem 3D** This is the original bad-attitude game, which was released in early 1996. You play a tough-talking Rambo in a dirty world full of babes and monsters. A sequel to this immensely popular game has been in the works for several years.

- **Descent** Released originally in early 1994, Descent was the first six-degrees-of-freedom action game available. In this game, you pilot a space ship through endless corridors in search of hostages and enemies.

- **Doom** Doom became a run-away hit among computer gamers because of its great monsters, endless levels, and empowering weaponry (the rocket launcher!). This game, along with Descent and Duke Nukem, are seriously outdated, but they deserve mention because of their importance in the development of first-person game universes.

Simulators

Simulators are complex, intricate, faithful reproductions of actual planes, tanks, ships, and cars. More simulators exist for aircraft than any other vehicle or machine. This genre, which has always been the redheaded stepchild of the game world, also happens to be the best-fit genre for PC gamers. Simulators often require dozens of keyboard keys, special controllers, and peripherals. In addition, they are often not much "fun." As such, a special breed of gamer admires these games.

Good simulators for the PC do not appear with any regularity and come out much less frequently than games in other genres. The reason is that these games are very complex and now take up to four years to develop.

The most popular simulators as of this writing include the following:

- **Falcon IV** Released in late 1998, this is still the ultimate combat flight simulator. Hurry before it disappears off store shelves.

- **SimCity** In this game, you create and manage a city. Design the city properly, and it will grow, providing a healthy world for its inhabitants. Add too much industry or forget housing, and you'll have a rust-belt ghost town. This game can also be considered real-time strategy (see the next section) because of the way that it's played and its graphics.

- **The Sims** This is a new genre that simulates people. The creators of SimCity have created a new, unusual game that has a large following.

■ **MechWarrior III**   In this game, you command giant robots in battle. This first-person action game is so complex it must be defined as a simulator. MechWarrior IV is on the horizon, and it promises to be even more complex and graphically demanding.

■ **The Jane's Combat Series**   These games include numerous flight simulators created under the Jane's Defense weekly title. They are published by Electronic Arts.

■ **Microsoft Flight Simulator**   This simulator, which allows you to fly small airplanes and corporate jets, has a huge following and is very realistic.

■ **X-Plane**   Do you want to learn *all* the controls of a 747 or the space shuttle? If you honestly answer yes, this is the simulator you need for your PC.

■ **Roller-Coaster Tycoon**   In this game, you create a theme park and manage it for growth. It allows you to create your own roller coasters and ride them in first person.

■ **Civilization**   This is a massive, complex strategy game that simulates the creation of empires and dynasties of human history.

Real-Time Strategy Games

In real-time strategy games, you play a commander who moves troops or groups of warriors (people in peaceful games) around using the mouse. These games are usually shown in three-quarters perspective—you view the game from above (a bird's eye view) and control the action below.

This type of game is relatively new. Two companies have dominated real-time strategy for the past five years: Westwood Studios and Blizzard. Both companies have consistently created the top-selling real-time strategy games, including Warcraft, Warcraft II, Command & Conquer, Starcraft, Diablo, and the new Diablo II.

Famous games in this genre include the following:

■ **Diablo II**   A real-time, role-playing game that includes the sword and sorcery of role-playing games in a fast, mouse-controlled environment. Your character must explore, fight, and survive as waves of zombies and evil magicians appear out of the darkness. This game has a huge online following. Most multiplayer games are team-based, with two or more characters taking on legions of computer-controlled bad guys. Figure 13-6 shows an example of a Diablo II scene.

■ **Command & Conquer**   This game involves futuristic warfare on other planets. It is a run-away best-seller that has set the standard for real-time strategy games.

■ **Myth**   The real-time strategy game that ushered in real-time, open-battlefield play.

13

FIGURE 13-6   Diablo II has set the standard for twenty-first century real-time strategy games

- ■ **Starcraft**   In this game, you command troops on other planets. The goal is to build up colonies and then protect them.

- ■ **Age of Empires**   In this game, you build up humankind over centuries from a pack of hunter-gatherer Neanderthals to a massive Roman Empire. This is the game that put Microsoft on the map in the gaming business.

- ■ **Railroad Tycoon**   This game simulates the rail-baron world of the late nineteenth century. You create railroads and then maneuver to build a railroad empire.

Sports Games

Every year, sports games for the PC and consoles get more detailed, realistic, and engrossing. Most of the sports games developed for the PC also are available as console games. The big difference between these two platforms is the multiplayer aspect. The PC sports games allow you to play others over the Internet. As of this writing, consoles were not able to do this.

Sports games are released every year because player lineups change every year. Sports games such as NHL 2000 include all of the professional players in the league for the year 2000. The next release, NHL 2001, will include a new lineup and probably some new features. If you are sports fanatic, watch for upcoming releases of your favorite sports titles so that you have the entire year to play.

Sports games have benefited from the 3D capabilities more than any other genre because of the realism now available during game play. One excellent example is the sport of NASCAR. The release of NASCAR in 1995/1996 was a huge success because of the first-person perspective and realism. Today, every type of sport is available in first person. Most of the new games in this genre include multiplayer options. In addition, playing against other players is now free on almost all the gaming services.

The predominant PC sports publisher is also the king of the console sports games—Electronic Arts (EA). Their major rival is Microsoft, who has purchased a number of smaller publishers with excellent sports titles. Popular games in the sports genre include NHL 2000 Hockey, NFL 2000, Baseball 2001, Links Golf, and NASCAR Road Racing.

Puzzle Games

Puzzle games are brainteasers that either include gorgeous graphics or simple 2D puzzles. Games in this genre span all types of technology and frustration levels. For a while, puzzle games were trying to match the success of Myst, the best-selling game of all time. Puzzle games changed dramatically after people grew tired of the insanely frustrating puzzles included in that landmark best-seller.

A puzzle-type game usually has a character in an unusual world that includes many puzzles that must be solved to advance to the next level in the game. These types of games take many forms, including first person, third person (your watch the character as he or she moves), and even God.

The most famous puzzle games include the following:

■ **Myst**   The best-selling game to date. This brainteaser set a new standard for PC games when it was released in the mid-1990s. The player explores a strange island (in first person) and encounters puzzles along the way.

13

- **Riven**   This sequel to Myst did not become a run-away best seller, but it's an amazingly beautiful game with even more difficult puzzles.

- **Lemmings**   In this game, you must help dozens of lemmings survive by solving puzzles that prevent the lemmings from killing themselves. The first version of Lemmings was originally developed for the Commodore Amiga platform in the early 1990s. The premise remains just as popular today. Figure 13-7 shows a scene from a Lemmings game.

- **Tetris**   In this game, your job is to keep the falling blocks from piling up. Tetris is a simple 2D game that consumed millions of man-hours in the early 1990s. Freeware versions of this game are available on the Web at sites such as www.tucows.com.

FIGURE 13-7   In Lemmings Revolution, you save as many lemmings as possible from killing themselves

Playing Internet Multiplayer Games

The current rage in the PC gaming world is Internet gaming. Players can now team up and combat opposing forces in the sky, on the ground, and in space. In addition, players can tough it out in multiplayer every-man-for-himself games such as Quake III Arena and Half-Life.

Of course, to be able to play Internet multiplayer games, you need to be able to connect to the Internet. See Chapter 6 for details about ISPs (Internet service providers) and Internet connection requirements.

Also, Internet gaming is more fun when you can hear the game, hear the players, and enjoy game soundtracks. This is all possible through your computer's sound card (standard on most new PCs). Most sound cards include a microphone port for in-game conversation. If you have a microphone (one may have come with your PC), you can plug it in and talk over the Internet in a number of games.

Here, you'll learn how to access online games, join multiplayer games, and host games. You'll also learn how to set up for voice chatting with other players during the game. Keep in mind that each game's multiplayer user interface and feature set are different; in addition, every multiplayer Web site is different. We will go through the steps using one or two games as examples, just to give you the general idea.

Accessing an Online Game

Getting onto the Internet through the phone lines involves pretty much the same steps for everyone. Once you're online, however, there are variations in how you access a multiplayer game. Microsoft has provided a new standard for accessing online games using its Internet Gaming Wizard. However, this wizard works only with the card and board games included with Windows Me (see "Getting Online Quickly with Windows Me Games" earlier in this chapter). If you bought a new multiplayer game in the store, or you have heard about a multiplayer game you can play from the Internet, you will need to know how to get online with this third-party game.

The best place to start looking for gamers already playing your favorite game is to visit popular gaming sites such as these:

- **MSN Gaming Zone (www.zone.com)**   This site includes many free games, free access to popular third-party multiplayer games, and access to a few massive multiplayer games for a monthly fee.

- **Gamestorm (www.gamestorm.com)**   At this site, a monthly fee allows you to play the huge multiplayer games Air Warrior, Battletech, and Jack Nicklaus Tour. These games are available only on gamestorm.com. The software for the games is free.

- **Heat.net (www.heat.net)**   This is a large multiplayer site like MSN's Zone.com. It provides access to dozens of multiplayer games. After you register, you need to

13

download the heat.net software. Afterward, you can use heat.net to form game rooms and even voice chat with other players.

■ **Game Spy (www.gamespy.com)** Download the Game Spy software, and it will tell you what games are currently being played over the Internet. This software helps you find the fastest connection to a multiplayer game of your choosing. With a fast connection, you are more likely to survive.

■ **Yahoo! games (games.yahoo.com)** Yahoo includes a number of free card games, board games, and some arcade classics that run as Java applets. All these games are free!

Game Web sites include software that interfaces with your operating system or the game you want to play. Some sites, such as Planet Quake, cater to one game only. Some games cater to only one Web site. Diablo II and Starcraft, for example, work only with Blizzard Entertainment's www.battle.net Web site.

Because of the differences among multiplayer games, the best way to get online quickly with your favorite game is to join a site that can interface with almost all games. The MSN Gaming Zone site allows beginners to get online quickly and start playing. The following sections describe how to sign up with Zone.com and use Zone.com software. After a few minutes of registration and software download, you'll be online and playing!

Joining a Web-based Game Service

If you know exactly what game it is you want to play online, make sure you already own the game and have it installed on your PC. To play on the MSN Gaming Zone site, you need to have the game installed and its CD in your PC's CD-ROM drive.

If you're not sure what game you would like to play, you should still follow the steps in this section. Sign up with Zone.com and play a few card games while you explore all of the different multiplayer games available.

NOTE *Most of the games included at the Zone.com site are free to play. You need to purchase the game and also have Internet access, but beyond that, multiplayer gaming is free. Zone.com's card games and board games do not require registration.*

To access an online game, follow these steps:

1. Log onto the Internet and visit the site www.zone.com.

2. When you arrive at the Zone.com site, you will need to sign up and download some software. Click New to the Zone? Free Signup. The Signup page will appear, as shown in Figure 13-8.

3. You will need to create a Zone.com user name and password. After you specify a zone name and password, click Continue.

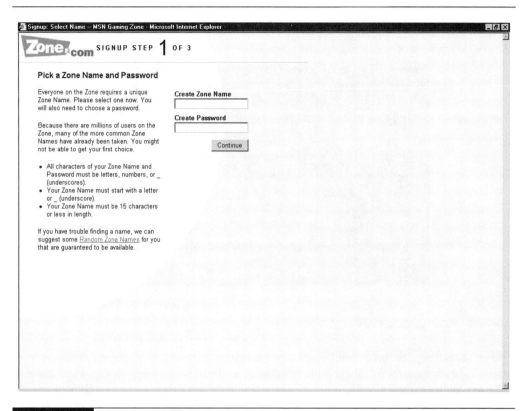

Zone.com SIGNUP STEP **1** OF 3

Pick a Zone Name and Password

Everyone on the Zone requires a unique Zone Name. Please select one now. You will also need to choose a password.

Because there are millions of users on the Zone, many of the more common Zone Names have already been taken. You might not be able to get your first choice.

- All characters of your Zone Name and Password must be letters, numbers, or _ (underscores).
- Your Zone Name must start with a letter or _ (underscore).
- Your Zone Name must be 15 characters or less in length.

If you have trouble finding a name, we can suggest some Random Zone Names for you that are guaranteed to be available.

Create Zone Name

Create Password

Continue

FIGURE 13-8   Zone.com's Signup page

13

TIP   *If you have a Hotmail account or an MSN Messenger user name and password, you may want to use the same ones with Zone.com. Try to use the same user ID and password for all of MSN's features, just to keep things simple.*

4. Zone.com must send you a confirmation e-mail. Specify an e-mail address you can access during registration. Enter your e-mail address, and then click Continue. Zone.com will send you a confirmation e-mail message.

5. Zone.com must download a small executable file that works in conjunction with the Web site. At the next page, click Download to begin the download process. When you see the spade appear on your screen, click the text *Click here when you see the Spade.*

6. The registration process is finished. Click Logon and Take Me to the Games to bring up the Sign In dialog box. Enter your new Zone.com user name and password, as shown in the example here, and then click OK.

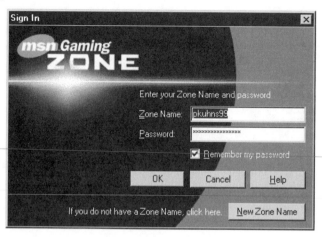

The Zone.com site will appear again. You are ready to play a game! Follow the steps in the next section to start playing one of the MSN Gaming Zone multiplayer games.

Launching a Multiplayer Game

After you register with MSN Gaming Zone and download the Zone.com software, you use the same procedure to join any multiplayer game. As an example, the following steps walk you through the process of logging on to Zone.com and joining a multiplayer version of the simulator MechWarrior III:

1. Make sure that the game you want to play is installed on your PC and the CD-ROM for the game is in your PC's CD-ROM drive. If the CD has an auto-play feature (it opens a window when the CD-ROM drive is closed), close the window. The game should *not* be running when you access Zone.com.

2. In your browser, click the Action link under Game Index on the main Zone.com page. Scroll down until you see the game you want to play (in this case, MechWarrior III).

NOTE *Not all multiplayer games are available at Zone.com. Some games run off of Blizzard's battle.net; others have their own servers that gamers such as you configure. If you don't see the game you want to play in Zone.com's list of games, start your game and access its multiplayer features. It may find a server for you.*

3. Select the game in the list. Zone.com will begin downloading some software to your PC, and then the MechWarrior III page appears, as shown in Figure 13-9. This page lists the various rooms in which you can play.

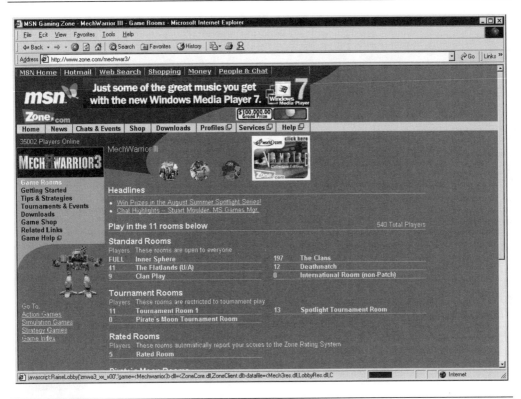

FIGURE 13-9   The MechWarrior III page on Zone.com

13

4. For this example, click on The Flatlands (U/A). A new window appears with row upon row of circles, as shown in Figure 13-10. Each circle represents a separate multiplayer game. A game can be in one of three modes: waiting for players, game in progress, or host. You cannot join a gain that is already in progess. If you click on a circle that says Host, you can set up a game that others will join, as explained in the next section.

NOTE   *If you see a little, yellow lock symbol above the circle, the game is private. These games require a password the gamemaster gave each player. If you don't have the password, you can't join.*

5. Find a circle that says Join and click on it. Make sure it's not a private game. The fastest way to find a game waiting for players (you) is to click the Quickjoin button at the top of the screen. Zone.com will find the first open game and put you in it.

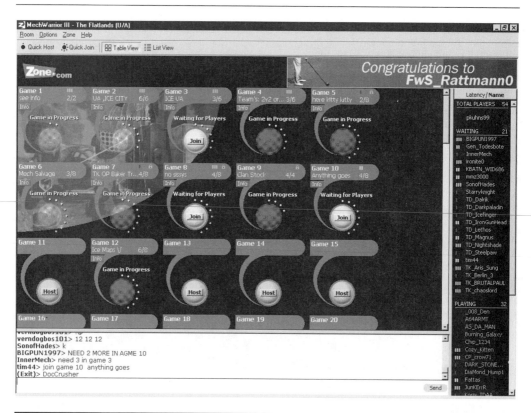

6. A chat window will open, as shown in Figure 13-11. Here, you will become visible to the gamemaster and other players waiting to play. You can talk to everyone and coordinate the game prior to launch.

7. Introduce yourself, and then wait for the gamemaster to launch the game. When the game is launched, a dialog box will appear that says "Launching Game." It can take several minutes for the Zone.com software to find your game and launch it.

8. Your game will start and display a multiplayer window where everyone can continue chatting and discussing the game. Each game window is different, but they all have the same features. When everyone is ready, the gamemaster will launch the game. Go play!

These steps apply to every game available through MSN Gaming Zone, no matter what genre.

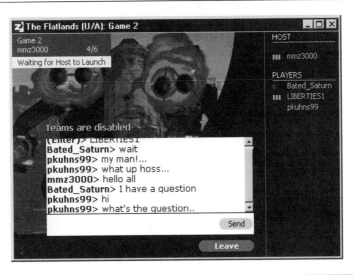

FIGURE 13-11   A chat window where players can meet prior to launching the game

Troubleshooting Zone.com

When you're attempting to play a game at Zone.com, you may experience some problems. The most common problems are that the game cannot be detected, started, or started when a multiplayer game is launched.

If you select a game from the Zone.com list of games and an error message like the one shown below appears when the game's home page displays, the Zone.com software cannot find your game. Make sure your game is installed (this means buying the game and installing it through your PC's CD-ROM).

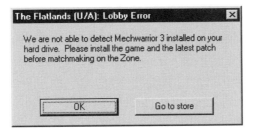

When you are in a room and the gamemaster launches the game so that everyone can play, a dialog box will appear stating that starting a game can take up to 3 minutes. If the dialog box shown below appears a minute or two later, the Zone.com software cannot start your game. If your PC has two or more CD-ROM drives and also several partitioned hard drives, the best way to ensure that the Zone.com software notices the game is to install the game in its default directory, usually on the C:\ drive. Another problem may be that the Zone.com software cannot find or initiate your PC's CD-ROM drive quickly enough. You may need to upgrade your CD-ROM drive to a newer, faster model if this error message continues to appear.

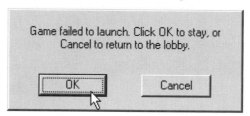

If your Web browser is not configured to accept JavaScript and ActiveX objects, you may not be able to launch the game's opening chat window (refer to Figure 13-10). Follow these steps to ensure your browser security is configured properly (these steps assume you are using Internet Explorer 5.5, which came with Windows Me):

1. Start Internet Explorer and select Internet Options from the Tools menu. The Internet Options dialog box will appear. Click the Security tab to display the Security page, as shown in Figure 13-12.

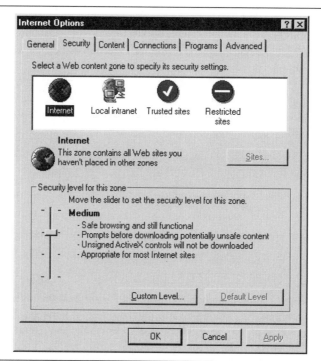

FIGURE 13-12 Security options for your browser

2. Click on the Default Level button. The security settings should say Medium. If this button is disabled (grayed out), click the Custom Level button. The Security Settings dialog box will appear.

3. Scroll down until you see the Active Scripting entry. Make sure that it is set to Enable or Prompt, as shown in Figure 13-13. The Zone.com software requires Active Scripting to operate. When this is set correctly, click OK.

4. You now need to delete cached Internet files. In the Internet Options dialog box, click the General tab. On the General page, click the Delete Files button, as shown in Figure 13-14, and click OK when prompted.

5. Next, you need to reconfigure your browser so that it always checks for more recent files. Click the Settings button on the General page (it's right next to the Delete Files button) to open the Settings dialog box. Click the Every Time You Start Internet Explorer radio button, and then click OK. Click OK again to close the dialog box.

6. Exit Internet Explorer, and then restart it.

You may also need to uninstall, then reinstall the Zone.com software after performing these steps. To uninstall the Zone.com software, choose Settings from the Start menu, and then click Control Panel. In the Control Panel window, click Add/Remove Programs. Find the MSN Gaming Zone entry in the Add/Remove Program list, click the Add/Remove button, and follow the instructions.

13

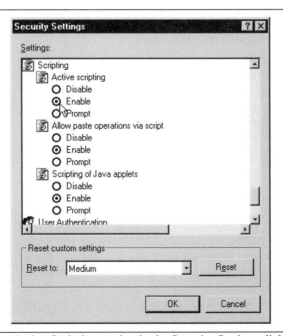

FIGURE 13-13   The Active Scripting setting in the Security Settings dialog box

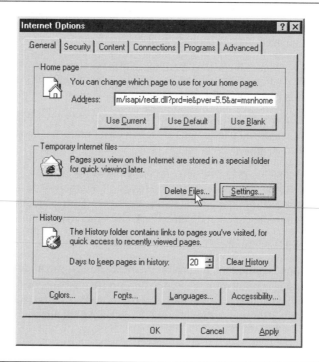

FIGURE 13-14 Deleting temporary Internet files

To reinstall the Zone.com software, exit and then restart Internet Explorer. Navigate to www.zone.com, and select your favorite game. The Zone.com software will begin to install (use your existing Zone.com ID and password). After the Zone.com software is installed, exit Internet Explorer, and then restart it. Return to the Zone.com site. You should be able to play your multiplayer game after performing these steps.

Hosting an Online Game

The MSN Gaming Zone games and most new games allow a player to host a game over the Internet that others can join and play. Hosting a game through MSN's Zone.com is easy. With other games, you may need to set up your own server.

Hosting a Zone.com Game

If you are member of Zone.com, own the game that you would like to host, and are logged onto the Internet, hosting a game involves only a few steps:

1. Navigate to www.zone.com. Log in with your Zone.com user name and password.

2. Start your game and configure it the way you want for multiplayer gaming. Every game has a different interface. You will need to set up the host game the way you want. Exit the game, and then return to the Zone.com site.

3. In the Zone.com home page, click the game you would like to host. If it's not listed on the home page, click a genre underneath the Index button on the left side of the page. For example, MechWarrior III is under Simulation.

4. When the game page appears, click the game room in which you would like to host your game (see Figure 13-9, shown earlier) Try to click on a room where a lot of players are located. (More people will see your hosted game!) The Zone.com software will load and display the games-in-progress page.

5. A new page will appear showing dozens of host/join circles (see Figure 13-10, shown earlier). Scroll down until you see a gold-colored circle with a Host button. Click Host. You can also select the Quickhost button at the top of this page to find the next open circle.

6. The Host window appears. Click Settings at the bottom of the window to access the Settings dialog box, as shown below. Type a description of the type of game you would like to host and set the maximum number of players. Also, determine if you will accept team play (2 on 2, for example). You can also create a private game (password required). Click OK when you're ready.

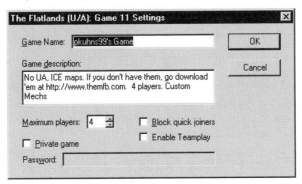

7. Sit back and wait. It may take a few minutes for players to find your game and enter it. When a new player appears, you can chat with the player in the chat window (see Figure 13-11, shown earlier).

8. Wait until the maximum number of players is in your room and everyone agrees it's time to play. Click Launch when you're ready, and your game will begin!

Hosting Other Internet Games

Hosting other types of Internet games is a bit more complicated, involving setting up a game server, which is a PC available through the Internet that can host a large multiplayer game. For

13

example, to host a Quake III Arena game, you set up a Quake III server, and then give players the server's IP address. Everyone enters the IP address of the server into their Quake multiplayer screen and launches the game. Players "spawn" (appear) in real time as they enter the game.

When you host a game, you often need to give other gamers your IP address. They will enter this IP address into their game, and then wait while the game scours the Internet looking for your PC. Afterward, their PC and your PC will initiate a conversation allowing the user to join in on your game. Some huge multiplayer games also require you to specify your PC's current IP address.

If you are accessing the Internet from home over a modem, your IP address most likely changes every time you dial up. If you're running Windows Me, you can easily find your PC's current IP address. Just open the Games menu (click Start, Programs, Games) and select Get IP Address. You'll see the IP Configuration window, as shown below, Copy down your IP address. (Remember, if you are disconnected in the middle of a game, when you reconnect, you will have a new IP address.)

IP Configuration
Ethernet Adapter Information
PPP Adapter.
Adapter Address	44-45-53-54-00-00
IP Address	216.225.80.180
Subnet Mask	255.255.255.0
Default Gateway	216.225.80.180
OK	Release	Renew
Release All	Renew All	More Info >>

*You can also find your IP address the traditional way in Windows 95/98/Me. Open a DOS window (click Start, Run), and then type **command.com** in the Open field. When the DOS window appears, enter **ipconfig** and press ENTER. Or try **ipconfig /all** to see complete Internet connection information.*

Voice Chatting While Playing Games

The ability to voice chat while playing games has been available on special modems since 1997. Voice chat at that time required special software and hardware. Microsoft incorporated this feature into Windows Me and simplified the process. Microsoft's Voice Chat feature enables gamers to call up their friends using NetMeeting, invite them into a game, and then begin playing the game while they continue to chat!

To use the Voice Chat feature, each gamer must be playing a game that uses DirectPlay, a component of DirectX. You can determine if your game uses DirectPlay by reading the game box.

To set up Voice Chat for your PC, open the Control Panel (select Settings, Control Panel from the Start menu), click Gaming Options, and then click the Voice Chat tab. The Voice Chat page appears, as shown here.

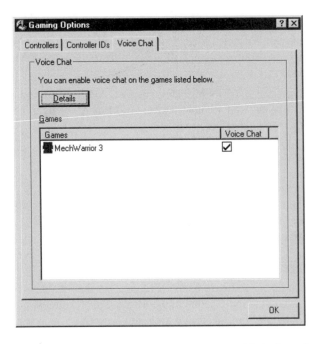

Check the box next to a game listed in the Games box to enable it for voice chat. If no games are listed, either the games installed on your PC do not use DirectPlay or the games already include voice chat capabilities. Only games listed in the Voice Chat page can be played while chatting over the Internet.

If this is the first time you are turning on Voice Chat, the Sound Hardware Test Wizard appears. Follow the wizard's steps to test your sound card (this is required to make sure that your sound card is compatible with your modem).

Inviting Others Into Multiplayer Games

You can invite your friends to play an Internet game. Both Outlook Express and MSN Messenger provide this capability. All games published by Microsoft since 1999 are compatible with MSN Messenger and Outlook Express invite capabilities.

Using Outlook Express to Invite Players

Windows Me's version of Outlook Express allows you to invite friends in your Outlook Express Contacts list to multiplayer games. Before you can use this feature, make sure you and your friend meet the following requirements:

■ Have the same game installed in your CD-ROM drive or on the PC. Most multiplayer games require each player to have a copy of the game you want to play.

13

■ Have the game on Windows Me with Outlook Express version 5. (This is the version included with Windows Me.). If one of the players is using Windows 98 and Outlook Express version 4, you will not be able to view MSN Messenger friends in Outlook Express.

■ Are all players members of MSN Messenger and are online at the same time? (It is possible to invite players who are not members of MSN Messenger, as explained in the "Inviting Others to Games" section.)

■ Have Outlook Express configured correctly. Your Outlook Express settings must be configured to start MSN Messenger automatically.

To invite a friend to play a game through Outlook Express, open Outlook Express 5 and look at the Contacts column in the main window. If your friend is online and has MSN Messenger open, he or she will appear in your Contacts list. Double-click your friend's name, select Send an Invitation, and click To Start *game*. The game will start, and you'll be playing in minutes.

Using MSN Messenger to Invite Players

Microsoft has added an invite capability to its MSN Messenger service that enables gamers to invite their friends they see online into a game immediately. This feature works with games that include the DirectPlayLobby interface (a feature built into DirectX), which is true of most new games that were developed using DirectX 7.

To invite an MSN buddy into a game, when you log into MSN Messenger, click on a gaming buddy, and then open the Tools menu and select Send an Invitation. You'll see the games you can invite your friend to listed in the submenu, as shown here.

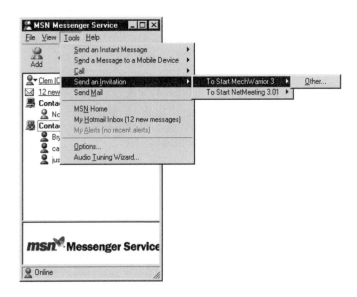

Your friend will receive an instant message with an invitation that says, "*Your name* is inviting you to start using *game*. Do you want to **Accept** (Alt+T) or **Decline** (Alt+D) the invitation?" If your friend accepts the invitation (by pressing ALT+T), the game will start automaticallyt! However, you will still need to initiate the multiplayer gaming option inside each game.

Only games that are compatible will be listed in the Send an Invitation submenu. If you are playing a relatively recent game and it is not listed in this window, check to see if an update for the game is available on the Web. Recent "patches" to the game may include this feature and the capability to host the game from the MSN Gaming Zone Web site.

Inviting Others to Multiplayer Games

Suppose your friend Horseshoe loves Falcon IV but doesn't have an MSN Messenger account. If you know Horseshoe is online (because he appears in your AOL IM buddy list or elsewhere), here's how you can invite him into a multiplayer game:

1. In Outlook Express 5 or MSN Messenger, click Tools, Send an Invitation, To Start Falcon IV, Other.

2. In the Send an Invitation dialog box, enter Horseshoe's e-mail address and click OK.

3. MSN will send Horseshoe an e-mail message that includes a link to join MSN Messenger. Horseshoe then will download the MSN Messenger software and sign up. After that, you can begin playing.

Installing Game Hardware

If your PC's CPU is fast enough for today's 3D games, you rarely need to alter any other part of your hardware. In addition, almost all PC's now have CD-quality audio on the motherboard, so there is rarely a need for a sound card. What almost always is required is a newer, faster video card or a game controller such as a joystick for your favorite game. You may also want to have multiple monitors. The following sections describe how to install game controllers and multiple monitors. See Chapter 13 for instructions on adding a new video card.

13

The only game that currently supports multiple monitors is Falcon 4. This game enables you to have two separate views onscreen at one time. However, games that can be played in a window can, in a sense, be used on multiple monitors. You could display one game on monitor 1 and another game on monitor 2.

Installing Joysticks and Controllers

Windows Me has made hardware installation easier than ever. Joysticks, steering wheels, flight yokes, VR helmets, and foot controllers are as easy to add as plugging in and restarting your PC. The hardest part of adding these game controllers to your PC is figuring out which ones to buy!

If you have Windows 95 or 98, installing a new game controller isn't difficult. These operating systems are Plug-and-Play as well, but only Windows 98 Second Edition has the drivers for the latest game controllers. If you are using Windows 98 Second Edition, just plug in the device and Windows should detect it.

If you are using a new game controller with Windows 95 or 98 version A or B, you will need the driver for your device on your PC or a floppy disk that came with the controller. If you can't find the floppy, you can download the latest driver for your device from the Internet. Visit a search engine such as Yahoo! and enter the name of the company that made your controller and include the word "driver" or "drivers." Once you locate the correct driver, download and save it on your computer; then plug in the device. Windows will ask for the latest driver in the Add Hardware wizard. Specify the location of the driver and Windows will install the device.

Windows Me includes many built-in drivers, but it may not have the driver you need for an older or more obscure controller. If you can find your older driver disk, you can install it for the controller.

To install a new controller, Make sure you have a joystick port on the back of your PC. Sound cards always include these ports, and most PCs now have these controllers built into the back of the PC. Attach the device to the port. Then click Start, Settings, Control Panel and select the Game Controllers icon. Click Add to open the Add Game Controller dialog box, as shown in Figure 13-15. Scroll through the list box to find the device you want to configure. Select it and click OK. Now you'll need the Windows Me CD. Place the Windows Me CD in the CD-ROM drive and click Next.

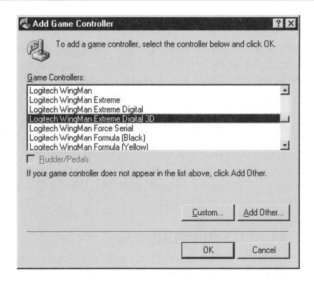

FIGURE 13-15   Adding a game controller

Installing a Generic or Custom Controller

If you don't see the exact name of the device listed in the Add Game Controller dialog box, such as Thrustmaster Flight Control System or Logitech WingMan, you can try selecting a generic device such as three-axis, two-button joystick or whatever most closely describes your controller. This is only a stopgap solution, because the choices available probably do not match your controller feature for feature. A number of features, such as a three-axis joystick or multiple firing buttons, are not available.

An alternative is to create a new, custom configuration for your controller by double-clicking on Custom (at the top of the list in the Add Game Controller dialog box). This brings up the Custom Game Controller dialog box, shown in Figure 13-16.

If your game controller fits any of the Special Characteristics profiles, select the appropriate option (for a joystick, game pad, flight yoke/stick, or race car controller). This does away with any second-guessing about axes and buttons. If your joystick or controller has a "hat"—a small, eight-position thumb controller—check the Has a Point of View Control check box. The Custom Game Controller dialog box also provides three- and four-axis options for more advanced joysticks. (A four-axis joystick represents a three-axis joystick with a throttle.) Although the Custom Game Controller dialog box has a number of options for setting up more advanced joysticks and controllers, installing the driver that came with your controller is still your best bet.

13

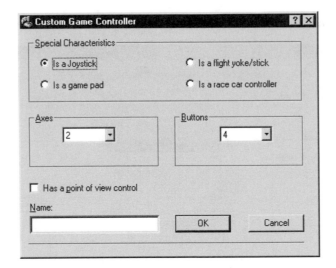

FIGURE 13-16   The Custom Game Controller dialog box allows you to configure more advanced controllers or homemade controllers

The most common problem associated with controllers such as joysticks and gamepads is outdated drivers. If you connect a controller and it doesn't function properly or isn't recognized by Windows, you probably need to obtain a more updated driver. The best solution is to visit to the manufacturer's Web page and see if a newer driver is available. If your controller is an older product, make sure you obtain the latest 32-bit drivers for the device. These drivers, or VxDs, work in DOS games and in Windows, unlike the ones for the older games.

Installing a Controller with a Driver Disk

If your controller came with a driver disk, insert the floppy drive or CD-ROM and click on Add Other in the Add Game Controller dialog box. Find the controller in the list supplied, as shown in Figure 13-17, or click Have Disk and select the appropriate drive (the floppy or the CD-ROM drive).

If this disk doesn't work, you either have a damaged floppy disk or the disk has its own Windows setup program on it. To see if there is a setup program on the disk, open Windows Explorer, click the drive containing the program, and look for a setup.exe or an install.exe program. Double-click this to begin the installation of the driver.

If you don't see any .exe files on the floppy and you can't get the driver to install from the floppy disk supplied with the controller, scroll down the list of manufacturers until you see the company that makes your controller. Don't forget to look in the Microsoft section (select Microsoft in the Manufacturers list) for the correct device. It might be listed there.

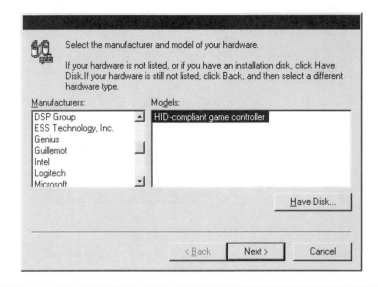

FIGURE 13-17　Installing a controller that came with a driver disk

After you install your controller, you can set up profiles for multiple game controller devices through the Windows Me Controller Profile Manager. This extension to the Gaming Options dialog box provides multiple setups for each controller and how it will be used in a game. You can reach this new dialog box by clicking Start, Settings, Control Panel, Gaming Options. When the Gaming Options dialog box appears, click Controllers to access the Controller Profile Manager area. Here, you can set up profiles for multiple game controller devices. You can also test your controller in its own test suite, as shown in the example in Figure 13.18. This test environment comes with the Logitech Wingman controller. Your controller will most likely have a different test environment, or one that relies strictly on the game controller test environment provided with Windows.

NOTE   *Each device has its own controller ID. When you remove a joystick and attach your newest flight yoke, for example, Windows Me immediately recognizes the device and assigns the correct settings to the device.*

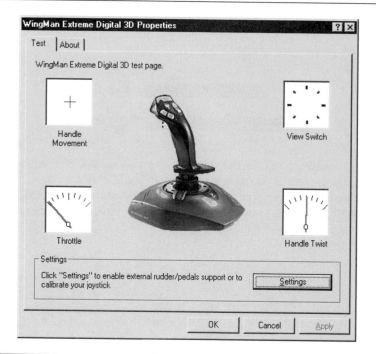

13

FIGURE 13-18   The test area for the Wingman Extreme digital joystick

Running Multiple Monitors

Windows 98 and Windows Me enable gamers to connect up to nine monitors to a PC. Each monitor must have its own dedicated video card. If you would like to play Quake II across three 19-inch monitors, for example, you'll need three video cards.

Because most PCs only have a maximum of six slots (and IRQ addresses), the number of monitors that you can run is limited only by the free slots in your PC. One of these slots is dedicated to a video card—the AGP slot. The AGP slot enables the video card to talk to the CPU at or above the speed of the motherboard. Only one of these slots is available on most PCs. This forces you to decide on a configuration:

- **AGP for monitor one and PCI for monitor two**   Most gamers who want to add a second monitor will choose to install a PCI-based 3D video card or possibly an older video card. This is usually the fastest and least expensive solution. Unfortunately, today's hottest AGP cards contain features and CPU speeds not available on PCI cards. In addition, the PCI bus speed, up to 66MHz on newer machines, doesn't allow video cards to keep pace with AGP's 2x and 4x motherboard bus speeds. Gamers who choose this path will need to configure their games for the less powerful PCI video card. If you're unsure about whether you have AGP or PCI slots, you need to unscrew the case to your machine, and see what kind of slots are inside of your machine. By comparing this graphic with your motherboard, you should be able to tell whether you have an AGP or PCI slot.

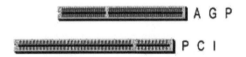

- **PCI for both monitors**   Older PCs that do not include an AGP slot require you to install a PCI video card. If you have a new PC with an AGP slot, however, you can pretend it doesn't exist, swap out the AGP card, and put in two identical PCI cards, such as the older Voodoo III PCI card. This is a bad choice for most gamers, because good hardware and a faster bus slot are going to waste.

- **A "dual-head" video card**   A more expensive but elegant option is to use a new dual-head card that controls two monitors. Currently, only one video card manufacturer has this type of card available. The Matrox G450 is a single AGP video card that can control two monitors. The drawback to this solution is the G450 card is more expensive than most 3D video cards, and it doesn't support the latest T&L (Transform & Lighting) capabilities of new 3D games.

Setting up for Two Monitors

Most users who want to run a second monitor for gaming will opt to keep their AGP video card and install a PCI video card in a free PCI slot. First, you need to make sure that you have a free PCI slot in your PC. Look at the back of your PC and see if any slots are available. See the following illustration for an example of a PC with free PCI slots. You'll also need the video card's driver disk or the Windows CD-ROM and a Philips head screwdriver before you begin this procedure.

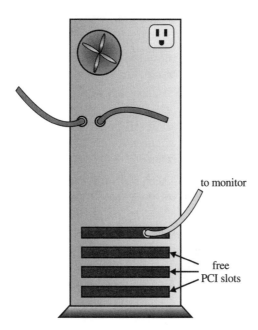

to monitor

free
PCI slots

13

If you have a free PCI slot, follow these steps:

1. Shut down your PC and remove its power cord.

2. Remove the PC's case. If your PC is a tower PC, lay it on it side. Tower cases are always easier to work with when they're on their side.

3. Remove the monitor cable connected to your current video card. It will undoubtedly be in the way if you don't.

4. Ground yourself by touching the metal case with your hands. Do this before touching anything inside the case.

5. Unscrew and remove the PCI slot metal protector on any of the free PCI slots.

 Make sure the power cord is unplugged from the PC before proceeding with the next step. You will fry the motherboard if it isn't!

6. Place your PCI video card in the PCI slot and press it down firmly. Make sure it's seated correctly in the PCI slot.

7. Before you screw down the video card or replace the case, test to make sure that the new video card is detected. Connect your monitor to your existing AGP card, connect the second monitor to the PCI card, connect the power cord, and turn on the PC.

8. Windows should auto-detect the video card and either ask you for a driver disk or install its own. If the card is not detected when you boot your PC, chances are good you didn't insert the PCI card properly. You will need to shut down your PC, unplug its power cord, and then try to reseat the video card.

9. After Windows successfully auto-detects the video card, it will try to install the best video card driver it can find. You will either need to have a driver disk for your video card or the Windows CD-ROM.

10. Now you need to set the primary monitor in Windows. The Display Properties dialog box will appear on the desktop and show you visually which monitor it thinks is the primary monitor, as shown in Figure 13-19. If this window does not appear, right-click the desktop, select Properties, and then click the Display tab.

Troubleshooting Multiple Monitor Problems

You may have some problems when you try to install and set up multiple monitors. You might find that Windows recognizes your second card as the default monitor, and won't recognize your first monitor at all. In this case, you'll need to delete both display adapters and then restart Windows so that it will detect the cards again. Here's how to do it:

1. Make sure you have your Windows CD in the CD-ROM drive. Then open the Control Panel and select System.

2. When the System Properties dialog box appears, click on the Device Manager tab.

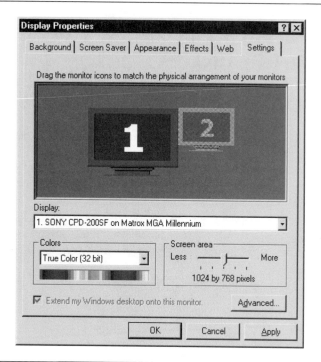

FIGURE 13-19	The Display Properties dialog box allows you to set the primary monitor

3. Expand the Display Adapters list and delete both entries.

4. Restart your PC. Windows should detect both devices and install drivers for both. Whether it chooses your original monitor as the default monitor or as the secondary monitor depends primarily on Plug-and-Play's detection whims.

13

Another problem you could experience is that the graphics in your game look horrible on the second monitor. This is probably because your second video card or monitor can't support the current colors, resolution, or frame rate of your primary video card. Chances are good that the second video card does not have more than 8M of video RAM or does not support 3D features. You will need to lower the screen resolution for both cards and possibly run 3D features in software (instead of using the primary display driver for your video card). Games that support Direct3D can emulate hardware functionality in software. If you want to play the latest 3D games on two monitors, make sure the game can be played in a window and then purchase two 3D cards, such as a 16M or 32M Voodoo III card or an NVIDIA TNT II PCI card.

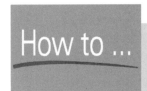 **Install a Video Card Without the Driver Disk**

If you've lost your Windows CD-ROM or can't find the video card driver disk, you can still install a second video card. When Windows boots after inserting the video card, set up the new video card as VGA. Windows has the VGA driver built in and doesn't require the Windows CD. Next, follow these steps:

1. Restart your computer. When the desktop appears, log onto the Web through your ISP or network.

2. Visit a page such as http://www.yahoo.com or http://www.excite.com. Search for the video card manufacturer's Web site, or access your video card manufacturer's Web page directly. The following sites are a few popular 3D manufacturer sites for the latest drivers:

   - www.nvidia.com/Products/Drivers.nsf
   - www.creative.com/support/files/download.asp
   - www.3dfxgamers.com/drivers/latest_drivers.stm
   - support.atitech.ca/drivers/index.html
   - www.matrox.com/mga/drivers/home.htm

3. Download the latest video card drivers for your video card.

4. After you've downloaded the driver into a temporary directory, right-click the desktop and select Properties.

5. When the Display Properties dialog box appears, click the Settings tab.

6. Click Advanced, and then select the Adapter tab. Finally, click Change.

7. The Update Device Drivers Wizard will start, allowing you to update your new video card driver. When the wizard asks whether to search for the new driver, click Specify the Location of the Driver (Advanced), and then click Next.

8. In the next window, make sure that the Search for a Better Driver Than the One Your Device Is Using Now (Recommended) option is selected. Then click Specify a Location, and then Browse. Navigate to the location where you downloaded the driver file and click OK.

9. Click Next. The wizard will display the devices similar to your video card. Select your video card from the list, and then click Next. The wizard will install the driver.

10. When the wizard finishes, reboot your PC. The new driver for your video card should be in use when Windows restarts.

Troubleshooting a New Video Card

Suppose that you've installed a new video card so you could play your new 3D action game, and one of these things happens:

- During startup, the game displays a dialog box that says something like "Your video card does not support 3D."
- You try to start your game and all you see is a black screen.
- The game crashes and returns you to the Windows desktop.
- The game starts but everything is gray.

Any of these events might mean that your video card does not support Microsoft's DirectDraw API or cannot handle 3D textures. Sorry, but you'll need to get a different video card.

If you already have a 3D video card installed, then you may have installed older or incorrect drivers. Windows NT and Windows 2000 drivers differ from Windows Me drivers. You can check the drivers you have currently installed by following these steps:

1. Right-click the desktop and select Properties. The Display Properties dialog box will appear.
2. Click the Settings tab. Click the Advanced button on this page.
3. Click the Adapter tab. Your PC's video card driver settings will appear on this page.

TIP
Going through the Display Properties dialog box, as described here, is an alternative to going through the Device Manager tab of the System Properties dialog box, as explained earlier in the chapter. Both methods display information about your video card (display adapter).

If you don't have the correct driver, go to your video card manufacturer's Web site and download the most up-to-date driver for your system and video card.

13

Chapter 14

Going Mobile

How to...

- Choose a laptop
- Share document and mail files between a laptop and a desktop PC
- Play games on a laptop
- Choose a handheld PC
- Beam data between handhelds
- Read and edit documents on a handheld
- Access the Internet using a handheld
- Play games, read e-books, and paint pictures on a handheld

Your desktop computer has a lot going for it: a stylish case; a thousand times the processing power of the computer that took Neil Armstrong to the moon; and a bunch of cool peripherals like a printer, gaming joystick, and punchy speakers. But it's not perfect. For one thing, it's so, well, static. You can't take it with you when you want to sit on the front porch or drive across town. Your software is of little use when you are away from the desk.

That wasn't so important a few years ago, but we're more mobile than ever now. Many of us need a portable solution that offers computing power, Internet connectivity, and more. Today, there are two main kinds of portable devices: laptops (also called notebooks) and handheld computers (also called PDAs, or Personal Digital Assistants).

Laptops are fully functioning, fully equipped microcomputers that can go on the road. You can use them like a desktop computer to edit Word and Excel documents, play SimCity, scan pictures, print documents, and so on.

Handheld computers are small enough to fit in your pocket. Since handhelds are so much smaller than laptops, they have much less in common with a desktop PC, but they have their own special role to play. They are great for keeping track of your schedule, listening to music, reading your e-mail, paging, and other "handheld" tasks.

In this chapter, we'll look at the tools of the mobile trade. We'll discuss the kinds of portable PCs available, how to share data with a desktop PC, and how to use portable computers for your work and play.

Using a Laptop

In Chapter 1, I addressed the question "Laptop Versus Desktop PC: Which Is Better?," and told you that for me, the laptop choice wins. Since many laptops can perform the same functions as a desktop PC, most of the topics in the other chapters of this book apply to laptops and desktops. Here, we will just look at some laptop-specific subjects, including the types of laptops, sharing data and mail with a desktop computer, and playing games on a laptop.

Choosing a Laptop

What kind of laptop might you want? All portable PCs are not the same. Larger ones are hard to take away on trips, but they have more power and features. Smaller, lighter laptops sacrifice some features in order to make them more portable.

Desktop Replacements

Do you want just one computer—a portable—instead of a laptop and a desktop? Sure, that's possible. There's an entire class of laptop designed to replace your desktop PC. It's called, not surprisingly, the desktop replacement.

Instead of dealing with multi-PC hassles, you can consolidate all of your needs into a single desktop-replacement laptop computer. If your laptop does double duty at home as a desktop PC, you'll need to get a fast one, with a Pentium II or faster processor under the hood. You'll also need a large hard drive. Graphic capabilities are another important issue to consider. A full-featured 3D graphics chipset allows your system to play games, as well as to run new multimedia software and business applications.

There's one other main concern when you're making a laptop your full-time PC—expandability. In a traditional desktop PC, most of your expansion comes through drive bays and PCI slots. In a laptop, there are no PCI slots, so you need to have USB ports and PCMCIA slots for the capability to add peripherals externally.

You might also want a docking station or port replicator. These peripherals make it easy to convert the system into a desktop configuration, without plugging in or removing a lot of cables individually. A pair of docks, one at home and one in the office, makes it convenient to move your PC and all of its data between a pair of well-endowed desks, complete with monitor, printer, mouse, and more. The downside is that a docking station, especially one with PCI slots and other features like built-in Ethernet, can be quite expensive. Also, docking stations are typically not compatible with other laptops, even laptops that are made by the same company. This means that a complete desktop replacement can be an expensive affair. Personally, I feel that a good laptop with a sizable screen (14" or 15") is every bit as usable as an external monitor, even clearer, so I don't bother with docking stations.

A full-featured desktop replacement also exacts a stiff weight penalty. These big laptops typically weigh at least 7 pounds, and often as much as 9 or 10 pounds. That's a lot of laptop to carry around frequently. Larger notebooks are so big, in fact, that they're difficult to open and operate in a typical airline seat, especially if the passenger in front of you reclines his or her seat.

Most "road warriors" (those folks who travel all of the time) opt for lighter systems, even if it means owning a desktop PC and a laptop. Smaller laptops are called slimlines and subnotebooks.

Slimlines

What makes a notebook "slim"? In general, slim PCs weigh in at about 5 pounds or less, a significant relief from laptop PCs that weigh nearly twice that much. But you'll need to give up some things when you opt for this lighter and thinner version.

14

Slim PCs often have somewhat slower processors, because there isn't as much room internally to dissipate heat. However, you can still find reasonably powered lightweight portables in the mid-Pentium II range, even Pentium III if you're willing to pay a bit more. That's generally enough processing power for just about any business-oriented task you might want to perform.

The real sacrifice in slimlines comes in the form of missing drives. Instead of the convenient three-spindle (drive) systems you'll find in the large, desktop-replacement class, lightweight PCs shave pounds and inches by removing the floppy and CD-ROM drives, as you can see in Figure 14-1. If you're traveling and have no need to read or write data, you're in luck—your portable PC is quite light. But if you anticipate the need for floppy and/or CD-ROM drives, you'll need to pack them, too. They generally take the form of external drives that plug into special ports or the PC Card bus of your laptop.

NOTE   Spindles *are a shorthand way of talking about the drives in a laptop, referring to the floppy, hard disk, and CD-ROM drives. A three-spindle computer has all three. A two-spindle laptop leaves the CD-ROM or floppy drive out. You generally need to connect a missing drive via a connection cable, or the laptop might have a bay that lets you remove one device and insert another. One- and two-spindle computers are less convenient than three spindle systems, but they often weigh a lot less.*

FIGURE 14-1   Many portables have modular bays in which you can install different kinds of drives or additional battery

Subnotebooks

If you want the lightest, smallest PC on the market that still retains the complete Windows operating environment, get a subnotebook. The Sharp Actius, shown in Figure 14-2, weighs about 3 pounds and is just a hair over 1-inch thick. The Sony Vaio is even thinner, shaved to .87 inch at one end.

In exchange for the small size, you'll be giving up built-in drives. Virtually all subnotebooks offer the floppy and CD as external peripherals. They also shrink the screen to a measly 13.3 inches (the smallest VAIO is 10.4 inches) or so, and sometimes even chop the ports off the case and transplant them to a port replicator-like peripheral. If all you need is a word processor for the road, you can cart along a 3-pound portable and get by just fine. If you need to plug into a video projector and the CD-ROM drive, you'll be packing external devices that will drive up the weight and overall bulk. Also, battery life is significantly shorter than larger versions, since the battery packs are physically smaller.

Sharing Data with a Desktop PC

You may have both a desktop and laptop computer, or you might need to share your laptop data with desktop PC users. What's the easiest way to get the data you need from a desktop to a laptop and back again?

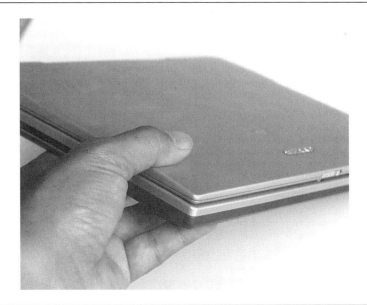

14

FIGURE 14-2   Subnotebooks are so small they're almost invisible in a backpack

One of the easiest methods to share data between two PC is through a handy Windows tool called the Briefcase. The Briefcase stores files that you plan to edit on a different PC. For examples, suppose that you want to take some files that are on your desktop PC at home with you on a trip and work on those files on your laptop. When you get home, you want to have copies of the most up-to-date versions of your files on both your laptop and your desktop PC. Here's how to do that:

1. Create a new Briefcase on the desktop PC by right-clicking on the Windows desktop and choosing New, then Briefcase. A New Briefcase icon will appear on your Windows desktop, as shown here.

2. Add files from your desktop PC to the Briefcase. The easiest way to do that is to drag the document icons from their ordinary folder (such as My Documents) to the Briefcase icon on the Windows desktop.

3. Move the Briefcase to your laptop. You can do that by using a network connection, a LapLink cable, a floppy disk, or a Zip disk.

4. Once the Briefcase is on your laptop, you can open it as if it were an ordinary folder and work on the files.

5. When you return home from your trip, it's time to synchronize the files. To do that, connect the notebook to the desktop PC using a network connection, or just copy the Briefcase to the desktop PC with a floppy disk or a Zip disk. Then right-click the Briefcase and choose Update All.

6. After the Update Briefcase dialog box appears, click the Update button to synchronize the files.

Using this technique, you will never accidentally overwrite an important file with an older version or lose track of file updates when you're traveling.

Sharing Mail Files with a Desktop PC

The Briefcase is a powerful tool for keeping files in sync when you're on the road, but it's hard to use the Briefcase for e-mail. What if you have a powerful information manager like Microsoft Outlook and want access to old mail, contacts, and your calendar while you're on the go with a laptop? The solution is to copy the mail data file to your laptop just before you leave.

The exact procedure varies depending on which e-mail program or information manager you use. To give you the general idea, here are the steps to take if you have Microsoft Outlook 2000:

1. Close Outlook 2000. (If you leave it open, the data file will be locked, and you won't be able to copy it.)

2. Find the data file. For Outlook 2000, open C:\Windows\Local Settings\Application Data\Microsoft\Outlook. (Yes, Microsoft certainly hides it well.) You want the file called Outlook.pst.

3. With your laptop connected to a network or using a removable storage disk of sufficient size, copy the data file to the same location on your laptop. A CD-R drive or a network connection works best, since these files can get large. (My Outlook.pst file is well over 200M.)

4. After copying the file, you can open Outlook on the laptop and access the same data as you had on the desktop computer.

If you make changes to your e-mail or program or information manager data on your laptop, you can copy it back to the desktop PC by using the above steps in reverse.

NOTE *Outlook Express doesn't use a single .pst mail file like Outlook does. Instead, it creates a .dbx file for each email folder you have. This makes it a little messier to copy your mail between computers, but this arrangement does let you copy individual mail folders, rather than taking all your mail with you. To find where Outlook Express stores your mail, choose Tools, Options, Maintenance, and click the Tools Folder button. The folder location will be displayed in the dialog box.*

Playing Games on a Laptop

What good is taking a computer on vacation without some gaming? To play today's crop of high-performance games, you need a laptop that has modern 3D graphics support in its video subsystem. Without this support, you are limited to playing non-3D or non-action oriented games.

If you have the hardware, you can play games on your laptop, at least for a little while. Games chew up your batteries much faster than ordinary business applications. So if you want to play Quake Arena for more than an hour or so, here are some tips that can help you do that:

■ If your laptop has SpeedStep or a similar feature that slows down the processor to conserve power, enable it.

■ Reduce the screen brightness as much as possible.

■ Use headphones so the laptop doesn't need to drive the speakers, which use more power.

■ Carry a second, fully charged battery on long trips.

Also, you'll probably want to bring a real mouse. The touchpad or pointing stick that most laptops use for pointer control isn't a lot of fun to use in games. You can plug a real mouse into the PS/2 port on the back of your laptop, just as you would connect a mouse to a desktop PC.

14

Using a Handheld Computer

Handheld computers offer ultimate portability and very handy functions. In addition to the standard "organizer" type applications (memo pads, phone lists, and so on) and business tools, there are all kinds of things you can do with your handheld computer. Attach a GPS receiver, for instance, and you can navigate by satellite anywhere in the world. If you have a Visor, you can plug in the MiniJam MP3 player and listen to CD-quality music, essentially turning your Palm into a portable music player. (See Chapter 11 for details on using a portable MP3 player.)

Choosing a Handheld Computer

You've seen them everywhere from the athletic club to business meetings. Now you want a little handheld computer of your own. What are your choices? There are basically two main kinds of handheld computers: the Palm organizer and the Pocket PC.

Palm Organizers

The Palm handheld organizer (sometimes called by its old name, the PalmPilot) is far and away the most popular handheld computer on the market. There are a few reasons for that. First of all, the Palm was designed from the ground up to be a simple device that did just a few essential things very well. As a result, it's extremely compact and has an excellent set of key built-in applications, including a date book, address book, to-do tracker, and memo pad.

More important than its built-in features are the thousands of additional programs for the Palm that you can download and install. There are more games, applications, and utilities available for the Palm than for any other handheld computer in the world. Programs range from text editors and spreadsheets, to satellite navigation systems, to e-mail and Web browsers. There is also an incredible array of games, including card and board games, strategy titles, puzzles, and even racing games.

The Palm synchronizes with desktop PCs in a very elegant way. Just slip the Palm into its desktop cradle, press the HotSync button, and all of your important data—like appointments and notes—are updated on both your desktop computer and Palm, so you have identical records on both devices.

Palm Computing sells a family of Palm devices, but they also license the operating system to other companies. That means there are a number of Palm clones available, and some are very cool. Here are the most interesting Palm handhelds currently available:

- **Palm m100**   This model features curvy lines, new software, and a clock display on the front. Priced around $149, it's the least expensive Palm on the market, suitable for casual users and students. (About $150)

- **Palm III**   One of the oldest members of the Palm family, the Palm III has a number of peripherals designed to fit it. There are a few models in the Palm III family, each offering a different amount of memory, but you can get the 8MB version for $249.

- **Palm IIIc**   This is the first color Palm. Its 256-color display is great for pictures, games, and even reading text. It costs about $399.

- **Palm V**   This thin Palm has a classy brushed aluminum finish and integrated rechargeable batteries, so you never need to worry about losing power on the road. It's priced around $399.

- **Palm VII**   With an integrated wireless modem, you can check e-mail and surf the Web as easily as flipping up the antennae on this Palm. It costs $449, and you also need to pay a small monthly fee for your wireless Internet access.

- **Visor**   The Visor, from Handspring, has a unique Springboard slot that lets you slip peripherals—like modems, extra memory, radios, and pagers—into the back as easily as you can add games to a GameBoy. Like the m100, the Visor starts around $149.

- **TRG Pro**   This $329 Palm, made by TRG, looks just like a Palm III, but it includes a compact flash slot that accepts extra memory and applications.

- **Sony CLIE**   Sony's newest Palm device is available in grayscale and will shortly also be available with a 256-color screen. The device is interesting because it includes built in video playback tools, a fancy job wheel for one-handed operation, and a Memory Stick slot. In other words, it's a PDA as only Sony can make it. The grayscale CLIE sells for about $399, though the color version's price had not been set as this book went to press.

> **TIP**   *You can read more about these handheld models at www.palm.com, www.handspring.com, www.trgnet.com, and www.sony.com.*

Memory defines how many databases, electronic books, games, and other programs you can fit in your handheld computer. On average, most Palm models come with about 2M of memory, although 4M units are also available. At the top of the line in the Palm universe, the Palm V*x*, Visor Deluxe, and TRGpro all have 8M. The latter two models also afford high levels of expandability. The Palm III*x* has an internal expansion slot, but the only add-on currently available for it is a memory card (manufactured by TRG, interestingly).

> **TIP**   *While I suggest buying a handheld computer with the most memory you can get your hands on, don't be discouraged if the one you're eyeing has "only" 2M. That's enough to hold thousands of records (a lot more than most people have), plus plenty of third-party software. But if you consider yourself a power user, or think you might evolve into one, buying a model with more memory might make sense.*

14

PocketPCs

While most people seem to like the Palm models, they don't appeal to everyone. Some folks consider the Palm to be too small. Others don't like the small screen. The Palm uses a 160 x 160-pixel display, and you can practically count the pixels if you look at the screen closely enough. But the biggest complaint of all is that Palms have trouble with common Microsoft Office documents. The antidote is the PocketPC family of handheld computers. An example of a PocketPC is shown here.

PocketPCs are based on Microsoft's Windows CE operating system, which bears more than a passing resemblance to the Windows on your desktop computer. Each PocketPC model comes with basic software like a calendar, address book, and memo pad. In addition, Pocket PCs come with special versions of Word, Excel, Outlook, and Money that are optimized to run on the smaller screen and with less memory. These applications synchronize perfectly with their desktop equivalents, so it's a snap to work on a document in Word on the desktop PC, transfer it to the PocketPC, and continue reading or editing it on the road.

Some PocketPC models also support up to 65,000 colors and significantly more memory than the Palm. PocketPCs typically come with 16M to 32M of memory. Of course, the Windows-like environment of those units requires more memory than the Palm does, but the larger memory also allows you to store more applications and files.

Some PocketPC models are priced comparably to the Palm models. The Compaq iPAQ, for instance, lists for $299. Casio's E-115, on the other hand, costs a more considerable $599.

 You can get more information about PocketPC models at www.pocketpc.com.

Interacting with a Handheld

Using a handheld model is a lot different than using a laptop. For starters, most handhelds do not have a keyboard. The vast majority, including both the PocketPC and Palm models, use some form of handwriting recognition to understand what you're trying to say.

No matter what kind of handheld you have, you can enter data in your desktop PC, synchronize the computers, and thus get your information into the handheld. But that's not very practical, is it?

You'll need to learn how to speak your handheld's language if you want to get real work done or have fun with your pocket-sized PC.

On the Palm, there are four ways to enter data:

- Using Graffiti, the Palm's handwriting-recognition system
- Using the small on-screen keyboard
- Entering text into the PC and then performing a HotSync
- Connecting a real keyboard to your Palm and typing the ordinary way.

A clip-on keyboard is particularly handy if you plan to enter a lot of data, such as writing long memos. The Palm Keyboard, shown here, is an ingenious device that folds up to about the size (and comfort) of a deck of cards, but unfurls to the size of a full-size laptop keyboard.

If you're at your desk, you might find it easier to enter data into the Palm directly, and then perform a HotSync, since your desktop computer sports a full-sized keyboard.

Graffiti is a specialized handwriting-recognition system that allows you to enter text into the Palm. Unlike other handwriting-recognition systems, Graffiti does not interpret your ordinary handwriting, nor does it learn or adapt to the way you write. Instead, you need to modify the way you write slightly and make specific kinds of keystrokes that represent the letters, numbers, and punctuation you are trying to write. Don't worry, though, it's not hard to do. You can learn the basics of Graffiti inside of a day; in fact, you can probably master most of the characters in an hour or less.

When entering text into your Palm, you can't write directly on the part of the screen that the Palm uses as a display. Instead, you write inside the small rectangle at the bottom of the display.

 *Be sure to write on the correct side of the rectangle, or you won't get the results that you expect from Graffiti. The right side is for numbers, the left side is for letters, and either side works for punctuation. Small arrows on the top and bottom of the Graffiti area draw an invisible line between the text and numeric portions.*

Your Palm came with a Graffiti cheat sheet, either as a laminated card or a sticker, which you can apply to your Palm. Take a look at the Graffiti guide, and you'll see that most characters are single-stroke shapes (which are called *gestures* in Graffiti-ese). The characters must be drawn in the direction indicated on the Graffiti guide; the heavy dot indicates the starting position. To write a character, mimic the Graffiti guide by drawing the shape starting with the dot and, in most cases, finish the character in a single stroke without lifting the stylus. Most Graffiti gestures bear a strong resemblance to their normal, plain English counterparts.

The easiest way to learn Graffiti is simply to practice writing the alphabet a few times. Use the Graffiti reference card that came with your Palm or Table 14-1 as a guide. Table 14-1 also shows a few alternative gestures that may make certain characters easier to draw consistently.

Beaming with Your Palm

The Palm has a very cool feature that could very well be the reason it has become so popular. A small IR (infrared) port lets you communicate with any other Palm handheld, regardless of its vendor. That means a Palm III can communicate with a Visor, TRG, or Sony. What kinds of things can you communicate? Glad you asked... here's a short list of things you can do with your Palm's IR port:

- Beam any calendar, address, note, or to-do item to another user.
- Beam your contact information as a kind of digital business card.
- Play two-player games like Battleship and Chess.
- Send documents like text files and spreadsheets to other users.
- Print documents with an IR-enabled printer.

Beaming with your Palm is a snap. While the exact procedure for beaming data may vary from program to program, it works more or less the same way in all applications. As an example, suppose that you found a cool, free game on the Internet and installed it on your Palm. A friend wants you to beam it to her. Here's how to do it:

1. Tap the Applications button on your Palm so you can see the program icons on your Palm screen.

Letter	Gestures		Letter	Gestures
A	∧		S	S 5
B	B B 3		T	7 ⟩
C	C <		U	U ∨
D	D D △		V	V V
E	E ξ		W	W W
F	Γ Γ		X	X X
G	G G		Y	y γ
H	h h		Z	Z 2
I				0	O O U
J	J ⌐		1		∧
K	α		2	2 2
L	L ∠		3	3
M	m m		4	L <
N	N X		5	5 5
O	O O		6	6 6
P	P P		7	7 ⟩ ⟩
Q	℧ ℧		8	8 8 8
R	R R		9	9 ξ

TABLE 14-1   A Guide to Graffiti Gestures for Letters and Numbers

14

Graffiti Tips and Tricks

Despite Graffiti's simplicity, there are a few tips and tricks that will make writing on the Palm a lot easier:

■ Draw your characters as large as possible, especially if you're having trouble with the Palm misinterpreting what you're writing. Use all of the Graffiti area if necessary.

■ Make sure that you make your gestures on the correct side of the screen to get the characters you want, and don't cross the line between the letter and number portion of the Graffiti area.

■ Don't write at a slant. Some handwriting-recognition engines can account for characters being drawn at an angle to the baseline, but Graffiti can't. Vertical lines should be perpendicular to the Graffiti area baseline.

■ Don't write too fast. Graffiti doesn't care about your speed, but if you go too fast, you won't have sufficient control over the shape of your gestures. You are much more likely to make mistakes.

■ If you have a hard time making certain gestures consistently, try the character a different way. (See Table 14-1 for a list of primary and secondary gestures for each character.) Use the ones that work best for you.

2. Tap the menu button and choose App, then Beam from the menu, as shown here.

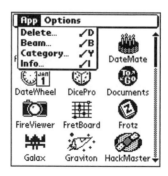

3. After the Beam screen appears, scroll down the list until you find the program that you want to beam to another Palm (DicePro in this example). Tap the program you want to beam, as shown below, and then tap the Beam button.

4. Point your Palm at the other Palm so the IR ports line up and are within about a foot of each other.

5. Wait until the program has finished beaming. The other Palm should ask its owner if he or she wants to accept the new program. The recipient can accept the program, and then run it.

Reading Documents on Your Palm

Like most handheld computers, the Palm and its siblings have several core applications that you can use to track your schedule, look up phone numbers, and take notes in meetings. However, if you want to read documents (or e-books, as you'll read about later) on your Palm, you'll need a special tool.

Reading Desktop PC Files

What if you want to read documents that you created on your desktop computer? In other words, you want to open a Microsoft Word, Microsoft Excel, or perhaps a Corel WordPerfect file right on the Palm. That's not as easy as it sounds, since there is no conduit built into the Palm to grab documents from the desktop computer and display them on the Palm. That's why you need some alternate options.

Perhaps the most effective tool for displaying Office-style documents on your Palm is Documents To Go (available at www.dataviz.com). If all you want to do is read documents on your Palm, this program may be your best bet. Documents To Go has both Palm and desktop computer components for shuffling documents to the Palm. You can use the Windows component to add programs to the Palm, and they'll be copied to your handheld after the next HotSync.

14

Reading Palm Doc Files

When Palm users talk about Doc files—text documents in the Doc format—they're not gabbing about Microsoft Word's .doc format. Instead, they're referring to a text format popularized by a program called AportisDoc and generally considered the de facto standard among Palm text readers today. A *reader* is a program that displays such a Doc file on your Palm device. Some let you edit as well as read.

While any Doc file can be read by almost any Doc reader/editor for the Palm (and vice versa), the Doc format is totally incompatible with the version used by Microsoft Word. On the plus side, you can convert a .doc format file to Doc and back again (as described in the next section).

There are plenty of Doc viewers out there, all of them reasonably priced (and a few of them free). Here's a rundown of some of your choices, all available from www.palmgear.com:

- **CSpotRun**   This reader is free, supports auto-scrolling and rotating text, and has a clever name.
- **Isilo**   This reader supports HTML and text (.txt) files as well as Doc files.
- **QED**   This program doubles as a text editor. It includes a utility for converting Doc files back to Windows format.
- **SmartDoc**   This is a text editor as well as a reader. It supports auto-scrolling and bookmarks, and offers a choice of four font sizes. See the next section for details on using SmartDoc to create and edit documents.
- **TealDoc**   This reader supports images and links between documents. It also includes advanced search options.

Creating, Editing, and Sharing Documents with SmartDoc

Viewing existing documents is all well and good, but what happens if you want to create a new document from scratch or edit a Word document that you decided to bring along on your Palm? In these cases, a simple document viewer won't do the trick. Instead, you need a document editor.

I recommend a great little document editor/viewer called SmartDoc, from Cutting Edge Software, which you can find at www.palmgear.com. The application is easy to use. It looks similar to the Palm's memo pad in that it has two views: a list view and a document view. SmartDoc begins in list view, which is where you choose your document to work with.

To create a new, blank document, tap the New button or just start writing in the Graffiti area. To open an existing document, simply tap on it. Once you're in the document view, note the Editable icon at the top, just to the right of the Doc tab. If the icon has a line through it, you can't edit the document. Tap on it to enter Edit mode. Now you can insert, cut, copy, and delete text as necessary, as shown here.

*Unless you're actively editing a document, leave SmartDoc's Edit mode turned off.
That way you won't accidentally change the contents of a file you're simply reading.*

Once your document is finished, you probably want to get it off your Palm and make it available to others. You actually have two choices:

- Beam the document to other Palm users
- Upload it to your PC, where you can open it in Microsoft Word

Beaming Documents

Before you beam your document, you should first prepare it by choosing Doc, then Prepare for Distribution from the menu. This simply performs a few housecleaning operations that make your document presentable to others. Specifically, it does the following:

- Moves the cursor to the top of the document
- Sets the category to Unfiled
- Turns off Privacy (if it was set)
- Makes the document searchable (sets the Global Find setting to the default)
- Compresses the document to allow it to beam faster
- Sets the document to back up to the PC on the next HotSync

Then you're ready to beam your document to another Palm. Just tap the document's Action Icon and choose Beam. Or, if the document view is open, choose Doc, then Beam from the menu.

*You can beam documents to other users. However, in order for them to read the files,
they'll need some kind of Doc reader on their Palm.*

14

Moving Documents to the PC

Getting your document from SmartDoc to the PC is also pretty easy, but making it usable from that point on is a little trickier.

When you make changes to a document, it is automatically flagged in SmartDoc for automatic backup on the PC. You can also manually set a file for backup to the PC, by using one of these methods:

- In the list view, tap the Backup region of the screen to display the Backup icon.
- From the document view, choose Doc, then Prepare for Distribution. Make sure that the Backup on HotSync option is checked.
- From the document view, tap the Info button and select the Backup on HotSync option.

After your document is ready for its trip back to the PC, your work isn't done yet. Before you commence the HotSync, you need to make sure the conduit is properly configured. On the desktop PC, choose the HotSync Manager icon in the system tray and choose Custom. At the bottom of the list, you should see an entry called System. Set it to Handheld Overwrites Desktop (by default, this is usually set to Do Nothing). Close the HotSync Manager, and then perform the HotSync.

After the HotSync is over, any documents set for backup will be copied to the PC. You can find them in the backup folder for your user name. On most PCs, the file is stored as C:\Palm\ *username*\Backup. Open this folder and look for the file. You should find that it has a .pdb file extension, and Microsoft Word won't open it. Now what?

You need one more piece of the puzzle: a program that can translate the Palm PDB file format into a text file that Word can understand. PalmDocs, available from www.palmgear.com, is such a program. PalmDocs installs a macro in Microsoft Word that acts as an indirect conduit to your Palm. Here's how to use it:

1. Install PalmDocs. The program only affects Microsoft Word by adding a macro to its default template.

2. After installing PalmDocs, close Word (if it was previously open) and reopen it. You should see a new menu called PalmDocs.

3. Choose Open PDB File from the PalmDocs menu, as shown below.

4. The Open dialog box will appear, showing the Add-on folder by default. Navigate to the Backup folder and find your document. Then click on Open.

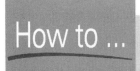 **Work with Word Documents on Your Palm**

In a nutshell, here is what you need to know to work with Microsoft Word documents on the Palm:

- To read Word documents, all you need is a program like Documents To Go.

- To create or edit long documents on your Palm, you need an editor like SmartDoc.

- When you transfer completed SmartDoc documents to the PC, they end up in the Backup folder.

- To get those Palm documents into a usable format on your PC, use PalmDocs to import them into Word.

The document will open in Word. Now you can edit, save, print, or e-mail the file just as if you had created it in Word from the beginning.

Sending E-mail and Browsing the Web with a Handheld

A question I hear often is, "Is it possible to get e-mail on a handheld PC?" The answer is an unequivocal "Yes." While most handheld PCs don't come with modems, there are a lot of ways to get on the Internet anyway. Here's a quick guide to your modem and Internet options with a Palm handheld:

- **Desktop connection**   Most Palm handhelds come with a mail program that you can use to read e-mail and create new messages. The mail is transferred when you use HotSync. This means that you can check e-mail at your desk, and then read and reply to it when you leave the office. When you get home again later, the next HotSync sends the e-mail.

- **Modem**   Modems are available for most Palm models, including the Palm III and Visor families. Just plug your Palm into a nearby phone line to send and receive e-mail or surf the Web with a Palm Web browser. My favorite browser is ProxiWeb, available via a free download from www.palmgear.com. You can also use AvantGo (www.avantgo.com) as a simple Web browser.

- **Wireless**   The Palm VII has a wireless modem built in, allowing you to send and receive e-mail as well as browse the Web in a limited capacity. If you have a Palm III, Palm V, or a Visor, you can use the Minstrel wireless modem (www.novatelwireless.com) to access the Web and get e-mail.

14

■ **Phone**   Perhaps the most clever solution around, the PocketMail Backflip (www.pocketmail.com) is a device that clips onto Palm III models and sends and receives e-mail using any phone—cellular, landline, or PBX—using high-frequency audio tones. The Backflip ensures that you can get e-mail no matter where you are or what kind of phone line you might have to work with.

Playing Games with a Handheld

Some of the most common applications for handheld computers are games. Sure, the display is smaller and the processor isn't as fast, which can limit the kinds of games you play. Nonetheless, your Palm is a great game machine for passing the time in an airport, on the train, in a meeting (while you look like you're taking notes), or any other place that you are bored with doing productive activities.

But where's the joystick? There is none, silly. Most action games on the Palm use the buttons on the Palm case to control the action. While the game is running, the Date Book, Address Book, Memo Pad, and To Do List buttons are diverted to game controls and will not switch you to the usual applications. To find out which buttons do what in a given game, you can experiment or check the game documentation. In most games, you can find basic instructions by checking the game's Help option on the menu. Figure 14-3 shows how the buttons work in HardBall, a game that is included on the Palm CD-ROM.

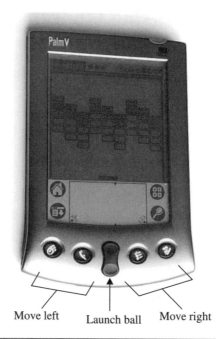

Move left   Launch ball   Move right

FIGURE 14-3   The arcade game HardBall, found on the Palm CD-ROM, uses the four buttons on the case to move the paddle left and right

TIP
Do you want to pause a game? Just turn your Palm off. The game will remain frozen until you turn it back on again. But be aware that, in many cases, switching to another application will end the game, so don't do that unless you want to start from scratch later.

Where can you find the games? They're everywhere, or at least that's what it will seem like once you start looking. The best all-around site for downloading games is www.palmgear.com.

Reading E-Books

Since the dawn of time, one seemingly insurmountable problem has plagued the human race: how to read in bed without disturbing one's spouse. Torches didn't work—they crackled too loudly and tended to set the bed on fire. Battery-operated book lights didn't work—they made books too heavy, leading to carpel reader syndrome. But finally there's an answer: the Palm device. Just load up a novel and turn on the backlight. You'll have no trouble seeing the screen in the dark, and your spouse won't even know it's on.

There are dozens of online sources for e-books, both free and commercial. Commercial titles are not unlike what you can buy in a bookstore; they've simply been converted to an electronic format and authorized for sale online.

However, before you start trying to read e-books, make sure that you have a Doc viewer. Many people make this mistake: They download a bunch of nifty e-books from MemoWare (or wherever), load them onto their Palms, then spend a lot of time trying to figure out why they can't "see" their e-books. (Normally, when you install a piece of software, you see an icon for it.) The reason is that they don't have a Doc viewer installed. Without one, there's no way to view Doc files. See the "Reading Palm Doc Files" section earlier in this chapter for more information about Doc viewers.

Finding the Free Stuff

If there's one site that's synonymous with Palm Doc files, it's MemoWare (www.memoware.com). Here, you'll find thousands of texts divided into categories such as business, history, travel, biography, sci-fi, and Shakespeare. Whether you're looking for a collection of Mexican recipes, a Zane Grey western, a sappy love poem, or a classic work by Dickens, this is the place to start. There's enough reading material here to last you decades, and 99 percent of it is free. (MemoWare is also affiliated with Electron Press, a site that offers contemporary works for a small fee.)

MemoWare offers a convenient search engine, so you can just type in a title or keyword to quickly find what you're looking for. It also has links to other e-book sites, although none are as comprehensive. Finally, MemoWare provides numerous links to software programs that turn computer documents into Doc files.

Finding the Commercial Stuff

The thing about public domain e-books is that most of them are, well, old. Somerset Maugham and Jack London are all well and good for catching up on the classics you promised yourself you would read one day, but sometimes you just want a little Stephen King or Mary Higgins Clark. Fortunately, you can have them all on your Palm, provided you're willing to pay for them.

Peanut Press (www.peanutpress.com) has long led the charge in bringing contemporary, mainstream fiction and nonfiction to Palm devices. The company started in late 1998 with just a couple dozen lesser-known titles, but now offers hundreds of books from some very well-known authors. Most of them are discounted by up to 30 percent, and you don't need to take a special trip to the bookstore to get them. The following are some of the more prominent and popular titles available from Peanut Press:

- *Angela's Ashes*, by Frank McCourt
- *The Girl Who Loved Tom Gordon*, by Stephen King
- *Message in a Bottle*, by Nicholas Sparks
- *Star Trek: First Strike*, by Diane Carey
- *Like Water for Chocolate*, by Laura Esquivel
- *The Dictionary of Concise Writing*, by Robert Hartwell Fiske
- *Monica's Story*, by Andrew Morton
- *Hope of Earth*, by Piers Anthony

Looking Elsewhere

Peanut Press may be the largest source for commercial e-books, but there are other Web sites that offer contemporary works as well. Here are a few to get you started:

- **Books2Read.com**   Touted as an Internet bookstore, this site has a small but growing collection of Palm-formatted titles (reminiscent of early Peanut Press).
- **ElectronPress.com**   This site offers a couple dozen original fiction and nonfiction titles, all priced at $5 or less.
- **Tale.com**   Here, you'll find dozens of original novels and short stories spanning numerous categories. You get to read the first part of any story for free, then pay a small fee if you want to buy the rest (a novel might cost $3; a short story may go for a quarter). These titles are delivered to you in the standard Doc format, so you'll need a viewer like CSpotRun or SmartDoc.

Painting on the Palm

You're probably wondering why you might want to paint on a handheld computer so small it fits in your pocket. Well, in the world of computers, the answer very often is "because you can." Programmers have never let something as silly as a technical limitation get in the way of doing something. When the Palm came out, it seemed like programmers literally scrambled to be the first to create a paint program for their favorite handheld PC.

But aside from that admittedly flippant answer, the ability to sketch things out on your Palm is a handy feature. You can draw a map to sketch the way to lunch, outline a process, or design a flowchart. You can also just doodle—use the Palm as a high-tech Etch-a-Sketch when you're bored.

Painting on your Palm is fun and productive, but you need to keep these limitations in mind:

- Some Palm paint programs allow you to make use of grayscale or color modes (depending upon which Palm you own), but for the most part, you're stuck with black-and-white, two-color screens.

- The Palm has a resolution of 160 x 160 pixels. There isn't a lot of room in which to draw. You'll find that after transferred to a PC, the images will be very small (the smallest resolution in Windows is 640 x 480 pixels, and most people run their displays at 1024 x 768 pixels). So it's generally not possible to draw something on the Palm that you later plan to export to, say, a PowerPoint presentation.

- Not all Palm paint programs support printing, which means that, in some cases, what you draw on the screen pretty much stays on the screen. If you can print your work of art, it will print just as rough and jagged on paper as it looked on your screen.

Perhaps the most full-featured paint program for the Palm, TealPaint seems to do it all. The program has a complete set of painting tools, including lines, shapes, fill tools, an eraser, and a variety of brushes. Even better, it supports 16 levels of gray for fully-utilizing your Palm's grayscale screen. TealPaint also comes with a Windows utility for viewing and saving images within Windows. The main paint interface looks like this:

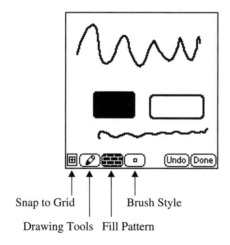

Snap to Grid   Brush Style

Drawing Tools   Fill Pattern

14

Using TealPaint, you can copy and paste selections of your image, not just within the same picture but in any picture in your database. To copy and paste, first select what you want to transfer. Tap the Tool button and choose the Selection tool. Drag a rectangle around some part of your image. Then use the Copy Selected and Paste Selected items on the Edit menu. After you paste a copy of your image, you can drag it around on the screen to suit your taste.

TealPaint is also an animation tool. You can use TealPaint to create animations by playing all the images in a particular database in sequence. Download this program from www.palmgear.com and have fun experimenting!

Chapter 15

Networking Your PC

How to...

- Install a network in your home or office
- Share printers across a network
- Share files and CD-ROM drives among your computers
- Back up your files over a network
- Share a single Internet connection among multiple computers (including Macintosh)
- Protect your network

If you have more than one computer in your house, you've probably run into at least one of the following situations:

- Your Quicken checkbook files are on the computer in the den, but your kids are playing on that one, and you're left with the old computer (without your files or even Internet access).
- You've spent an afternoon toting Zip disks back and forth between the computer with the scanner and the computer with the good printer.
- You're tired of tying up two phone lines when two of you surf the Internet.

If any of this sounds familiar, it might be time to install a network to connect your computers together. You'll be in good company—between the years 2000 and 2003, the number of networked home computers is expected to grow from 2–18 million.

Networking Basics

If you've looked inside your computer, you've seen that there are a bunch of parts connected by electrical cables. These cables carry electrical signals back and forth between the components in your computer: the hard drive, the floppy disk drive, and the computer processor on the motherboard. The computer components are separate devices that communicate with each other, transmitting information back and forth.

A network works on the same principle, connecting separate computers so that they can send information back and forth. After all, if the computer processor can read information from the hard drive by sending signals over the short cables inside the computer case, why shouldn't it be able to read files from a hard drive in another room, over longer wires? That's just what a network does: It lets two or more computers quickly transmit information over special electrical cables running between them. Computers communicate over a network using networking protocols.

Networking Protocols

Computers are nothing if not organized, and this goes for networks as well. The information sent back and forth must be organized by the networking software according to protocols. *Networking protocols* are agreed-upon formats for the messages, requests, answers, and data that the network carries. In fact, when any conversation takes place, whether between computers or people, some sort of protocol is required so that all parties understand how to interpret the conversation and know what is expected of them.

You might be familiar with the human protocol for ordering lunch at the local drive-in. You pull up to the drive-through window's order location, and a voice says "May I take your order?" You say, "I'd like a cheeseburger." The voice says, "Fries with that?" You say, "No, thanks." The voice says, "That'll be $2.50 at the front window." You say, "Thank you," and then move up to pick up your order. If the communication was successful, you'll get your cheeseburger.

Computer networking protocols follow a pattern surprisingly similar to this, although the dialogue necessary to view and read files from a remote hard drive is a bit more complex. In any case, in order to get your burger or data, the conversation needs to follow a pattern that both parties expect, using a common language.

There are many different networking protocols in common use these days. You may have heard of TCP/IP, which is the protocol used for all Internet communication. Other protocols include NetBEUI, which Microsoft developed on its own before anybody guessed that the Internet would ever reach outside of universities and government labs, and IPX/SPX, which was popularized by Novell Corporation for its NetWare networking product. Your Windows computer can be set up to use any of these protocols to share files and printers, as long as each computer on your network is set up with at least one protocol in common with the rest.

What Can You Do on a Network?

Thanks to the networking software built into Windows, a network will let you view files and folders on the hard drive, floppy disk, or CD-ROM of another computer, exactly as if the drive were in your own computer. For example, in the Folders list (in a Windows Explorer window) shown below, you can see into the hard drive of my computer (drive C:) and another networked computer named Java (drive J:). With my network, I can look at, edit, copy, and manipulate files on Java's hard drive just as if it were part of my own.

A network can share printers in the same way, sending document data through the network to a printer attached to another computer. Besides sharing files and printers, a network can also let you share a single Internet connection with all the computers in your home or office simultaneously, and it can let you play interactive games between your computers and with other people on the Internet.

This chapter should give you enough information to get a network working in short order. If you want more information on home networking, you might check these Web sites:

- http://help-data.excite.com/members/homenetwork/index.htm

- http://www.homepclan.com/

- http://www.rockvilleliving.com/cg.html

Choosing the Right Network for You

There are three basic options for types of technology that you can use to connect your computers: Ethernet, Phoneline, and wireless. The simplest and least expensive option is to connect your computers with Ethernet, which is a tried-and-true standard used all over the world. Phoneline networking connections use your existing household phone wiring to carry the network signal. Wireless networking uses radio signals sent over the airwaves, using the same radio-frequency band used by cordless phones.

All three of the networking options operate at at least 10Mbps (million bits per second), which is plenty fast enough for all but the most demanding network applications. In choosing an option, a primary consideration is the convenience in setting up the wiring. Here's what I suggest:

- If you plan on sharing a high-speed DSL or cable modem Internet connection, use Ethernet. Buy a hardware Internet connection-sharing device for the added security. The extra expense is well worth it.

- If your computers are close together, again, go with Ethernet. It's the least expensive, and you won't have much of a problem with the cables.

- If your computers are far apart but near phone jacks carrying the same phone extension, use Phoneline networking.

- If your computers are far apart but the phone extensions aren't already installed, it's up to you. You could run Ethernet cables along baseboards and through walls, but most likely you'll be better of with in-the-wall wiring. If you do that, you'll need to install cables with either Phoneline or Ethernet, so go with whatever you feel most comfortable with. Either way, you can hire a phone wiring contractor to install the necessary wiring in your home or office.

- If you want to be able to surf the Internet with your laptop from any location, and you can afford it, go with a wireless network. The cost of wireless networking ranges from $150 to more than $400 per computer, and at least $500 more if you need to connect the network to a standard DSL or cable modem. What you get for this much money is the complete freedom to move your computers about.

After you decide on which type of network to use, you will need to purchase networking hardware to connect your computers. Don't worry though—the price of networking equipment has fallen drastically in the past few years. Network devices were once costly specialty items, but they're now such a basic commodity that you can find them at your local computer store, and big stores such as Office Depot, Staples, OfficeMax, and CompUSA. You can also find great bargains at online stores like www.buycomp.com, www.egghead.com and www.cmpexpress.com. But don't hesitate to pay a few dollars more at a local shop, where you can get help from a real, live person should you run into trouble.

The following sections describe how each of the networking options work, their advantages and disadvantages, and the equipment you'll need.

NOTE *If you are thinking about sharing an Internet connection, read "Sharing your Internet Connection" later in this chapter before deciding on a network setup. Windows comes with Internet Connection Sharing software built-in, but other solutions offer greater protection from hackers for a small expense.*

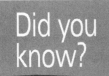

Did you know?

Networking Terminology

Networking has a language all its own, and bunches of acronyms (computer people *love* acronyms). Here are some of the terms you're likely to run across in the course of buying and installing a network:

LAN (local area network)	A group of computers with a high-speed data connection between them. This chapter tells you how to set up your own LAN.
NIC (network interface card)	Also called a *network adapter* or *network card*, a hardware device plugged into a computer to transmit and receive network signals. Not all NICs are "cards"; some are external boxes connected to your computer's USB port.
Ethernet	A fast, efficient networking technology, developed in the 1970s and still popular today.
UTP (unshielded twisted-pair) cable	A type of cable that is similar to phone cabling but specially manufactured to be able to carry high-speed data without distortion. It's widely used for Ethernet networks.
10BaseT	Ethernet networking using a 10Mbps data rate over UTP cable.
100BaseT	Also called *100Base-Tx* or *Fast Ethernet*, Ethernet networking at 100Mbps over UTP cable.
CAT5	UTP cable certified to work properly with networks. (Cable also comes in the CAT3 variety, but CAT5 is the one to use.)

15

Hub	A device into which you plug the cables going to each computer in a 10BaseT or 100BaseT network.
Switch	A hub on steroids that permits faster network transfers when there are many computers transmitting and receiving at the same time.
Router	A device that transfers information between separate networks, such as between a LAN and the Internet.
Firewall	A router or a software package that can selectively block data from a network for security purposes.
10/100	Also called *dual-speed*, denotes a NIC or hub that can operate at either 10Mbps or 100Mbps, depending on the capabilities of the device(s) to which it's connected.
RJ45	A wider version of the familiar modular phone jack, used for network cabling.
Patch cable	A UTP cable used to connect a NIC to a hub.
Crossover cable	A special type of patch cable that can be used to connect one computer directly to another without a hub. It's useful when there are only two computers that need to be connected.

Ethernet Networks

Ethernet network hardware transmits data at either 10Mbps or 100 Mbps. A speed of 100Mbps is fast enough to transmit the entire contents of this book in a few seconds, but 10Mbps is fast enough for home and small office use. Is 10Mps good enough to get you through an intense session of an interactive action game? Yes, it should be plenty fast enough. Games actually transmit very little information between computers. (The image generation department is where speed matters, and that depends on your computer's processor and graphics card, not the network. See Chapter 13 for details on what you'll need to play games on your computer.)

Advantages of Ethernet include its high speed and low cost, which can run as low as $25 per computer. The disadvantage is that you need to run cables between your computers and a central hub.

Ethernet networks send data over special twisted-pair network cables. The cable gets its name from the fact that inside its jacket, the wires running from end to end are twisted together in color-coded pairs. Each computer will need a NIC (network interface card) and some twisted-pair cabling. If you have three or more computers you'll also need a hub to connect the cables coming from each computer, as illustrated in Figure 15-1.

If you want to share a single high-speed DSL or cable Internet connection for all your computers, Ethernet is your best choice. You can buy a hardware device for about $125 to connect your DSL or cable modem directly to your network, and these devices usually include a built-in hub.

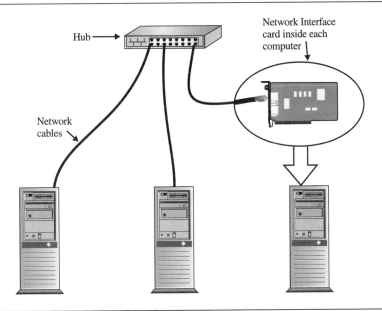

Hub →

Network Interface
card inside each
computer

Network
cables

FIGURE 15-1   An Ethernet network using a hub

You can use inexpensive cables called *patch cables* like extension cords between the computers and the hub when they're less than 100 feet from each other. Alternately, you can install in-the-wall wiring when the computers are in different parts of your home or office, or when running cables along the floor, walls, or ceiling isn't appropriate.

As for speed, for a basic home network, there's not much practical difference between 10Mbps and 100Mbps networking. Unless you plan on transferring really huge files on a daily basis, go with 10Mbps (10BaseT) equipment—it's a bit less expensive, and the network is less finicky about the quality of the cabling you use.

The equipment you'll need includes NICs, cables, and a hub (if you'll be connecting three or more computers). The following sections provide more details about these items for Ethernet networks.

15

NOTE
Some manufacturers sell packaged kits of NICs, cables, and a hub in one box. Be sure to check the prices of the package and the separate items before you invest in a kit. In many cases, you'll end up paying almost double for the kit. However, if you find one at a good price and with adequately long cables, there's no reason not to buy the packaged deal.

Ethernet NICs

For an Ethernet network, you'll need one NIC per computer. You can get internal cards (called PCI cards) for modern, standard desktop computers, PCMCIA or PC Card adapters for laptops, or USB models for either type of system. Common brands are D-Link, Linksys, 3COM, Intel,

Netgear, SMC, SiS, Sohoware, CNet, Hawking, and Farallon. You buy either 10Mbps 10BaseT cards or 10/100 Fast Ethernet cards. (As I said earlier, 10Mbps is fast enough for most small networks.) Try to get identical NICs for each of your computers.

NOTE   *All modern desktop computers accept "PCI" type plug-in adapters. If you're going to network an old desktop computer, though, it might require an "ISA" adapter. The difference is in the size and shape of the connector into which the adapter fits. Read the computer's manual to be sure, or look inside the computer. If there are two connectors lined up end to end behind each empty slot, you need an ISA adapter.*

Ethernet Cables and Hubs

If you're connecting only two computers and no additional equipment, you don't need a hub. Just buy a CAT5 UTP *crossover* cable to connect the two computers directly. These cables come in lengths from 2–100 feet. For longer cables, shop around carefully. You'll find that the price can range from 10 cents to $1 per foot.

If you're connecting three or more computers or other devices, you'll need to buy a hub with enough ports for every computer or network device. Hubs come with 4, 5, 8, or more ports each. If you're using 10Mbps (10BaseT) network adapters, get a standard Ethernet hub. If you're using 100Mbps adapters, or a mix of 10Mbps and 100Mbps, get a 10/100 (or dual-speed) hub. (In fact, dual-speed hubs are a good choice even if you don't yet have mixed-speed equipment; you might add some later.) Prices range from as little as $20 for a generic four-port 10BaseT hub to $80 or more for a five-port 10/100 switching hub.

NOTE   *Hubs can run into the hundreds of dollars, but there's no need to spend that much for a small network. Hubs called switches or switching hubs can make a complex network run faster, but for simple networks, they're not necessary.*

To determine the length of cables to buy, pick a location for the hub somewhere between the computers, and then measure the distance from each computer to the hub. If you're going to install in-the-wall wiring, there are two ways that you can connect to your computers and hub:

■ You can have connectors added directly to the ends of the wiring.

■ You can have the wiring run between special RJ45 network jacks (similar to phone jacks) placed near each computer. Then connect the hub and computers to these jacks with patch cables.

Figure 15-2 illustrates both of these methods. Using RJ45 jacks is a little more expensive, but it's neater than direct connections.

Decide how you're going to run the wires, consult with your wiring installer if you're going to use in-the-wall wiring, and then determine the number and length of patch cables you'll need. For longer runs, you may be able to have a local computer store make custom cables for you at less expense than purchasing manufactured ones.

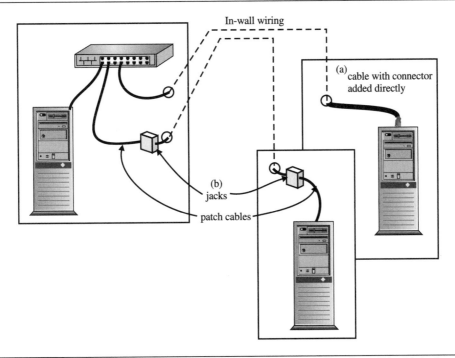

In-wall wiring

(a) cable with connector added directly

(b) jacks

patch cables

FIGURE 15-2   Two ways of connecting in-the-wall wiring: (a) directly or (b) with jacks and patch cables

TIP   *If you're going to use a hardware DSL/cable sharing device to share an Internet connection, research that item before buying your network gear. You may not need to buy a hub at all, because most of the sharing devices include a built-in four-port hub as part of the package.*

Phoneline Networking

Some brands of Phoneline NICs are designed go inside your computer; others connect to your computer's USB port. Then they plug into a phone jack and send the network data over the house's existing wiring using a weak radio signal. This signal doesn't interfere with your phone service or DSL line; in fact, they can all be used simultaneously. The newest Phoneline equipment supports 10Mbps transfers, and the hardware costs about $40–$75 per computer.

Phoneline networking has the advantage of not needing new network cables or a central hub, so it's quick and easy to set up. The disadvantages are that the equipment is a bit more expensive than Ethernet hardware, and you need to have a jack carrying the same phone extension at each computer. Also, if you want to set up a shared high-speed DSL or cable Internet connection,

15

you'll need to use Microsoft's Internet Connection Sharing or an add-on software package to manage the shared connection. This offers much less hacker protection that the Ethernet hardware solution.

Before you decide to purchase a Phoneline network, be sure that you have phone jacks where you want to install your computers, and that the jacks are all wired for the same phone number. To check this, you need two phones and an assistant. Plug a phone into each of two jacks near your computers and see if you can talk to your assistant when you pick up the receivers. Leave one phone in place, and check any other jacks you want to use with the other phone. If you can't hear your assistant, the jacks are on different extensions and won't work for Phoneline networking. You'll need to move a computer or get a new jack installed before you can use the network at that location. If you don't already have the phone jacks installed, Ethernet might be a less expensive solution.

If you're setting up a Phoneline network, you'll need to buy one NIC per computer. Brands include the following:

- Netgear Home Phoneline 10X
- Intel AnyPoint Home Network 10Mb
- Linksys HomeLink Phoneline 10Mb
- Diamond HomeFree Phoneline 10Mb
- D-Link 10Mb Home Phoneline Network
- 3COM HomeConnect Home Network Phoneline

By the time you read this, there probably will be several more Phoneline packages available. Home networking is a growing industry! Whichever brand you buy, be sure to get 10Mbps devices only, and be sure they're listed as complying with the HomePNA 2.0 standard. HomePNA is a standards committee made up of manufacturers, and compliance means that the network adapters you buy will work with models made by other manufacturers.

 Avoid 1Mbps equipment and any adapter that connects through your computer's parallel printer port. These are obsolete devices, and there's simply no need to use such slow equipment these days. If the box doesn't mention 10Mbps or 100Mbps on the outside, don't buy it.

Most Phoneline network adapters can be purchased in kits with two or more cards, and unlike their Ethernet cousins, these kits seem to be a good buy. Many come with additional software to share a single dial-up or DSL/cable Internet connection with all of the computers on the network.

Wireless Networking

If you're going to take the plunge and install a truly wireless network, be prepared for sticker shock! You'll need one wireless NIC per computer, and they cost from $150–$400 each. Brands include 3Com's AirConnect, Diamond's HomeFree, Farallon's SkyLine, Intel's AnyPoint, Proxim's Symphony, Sohoware's CableFree, WebGear's Aviator and Aviator Pro, and Zoom

Telephonics' ZoomAir. Most of these manufacturers make both 1Mbps and 11Mbps models. I recommend purchasing only 11Mbps equipment listed as 801.11b certified. This guarantees that it will operate with equipment from another manufacturer.

If you need a connection to a wired Ethernet network or a DSL or cable modem, you have two choices:

- You can use the manufacturer's *gateway* software in one of your networked PCs.

- You can buy an *access point*, which is a little box sporting a network cable connection on one end, an antenna on the other, and a $400+ price tag in between.

Installing Your Network

Installing and configuring a network used to be incredibly complex. The good news is that wiring and setting up a network has gotten much easier. In fact, you can have a three-computer network up and running in an hour once you've done your shopping.

I suggest that you start with two computers, placed side by side on a table. This way, you can test your equipment and software setup without running back forth between two rooms. Once you have these computers working correctly, move them to their final locations and install the cables between them. Test again, and if all is still working, set up any additional computers you're adding to your network. Using this approach, the following basic steps are involved in the job:

- Install the NICs
- Connect two computers
- Configure the software
- Test the network
- Finish and test the installation

If you carefully work through each step, your network installation should go smoothly.

Installing NICs

If you are using external USB-connected network adapters, just plug the network adapters into a free USB jack or into a USB hub with the included USB data cable. Windows will prompt you to insert the software floppy disk provided by your adapter manufacturer and will restart the computer. When this is done, go onto the next section, "Connecting Two Computers for Testing."

If you are using internal network adapters that plug into the motherboard inside your computer, you'll need to open your computer case. It's not that difficult, really. Refer to Chapter 17 for a full discussion about installing hardware devices. If you're already comfortable doing this, here's the procedure in a nutshell:

1. Unplug the computer's power cable. Open the computer case and set the cover aside.

2. Locate an empty adapter card socket on the motherboard and remove the screw and metal cover plate covering the hole next to the socket.

15

3. Pick up the plastic bag holding the NIC with one hand and touch the computer's metal chassis with the other. Remove the card from its plastic bag and hold it by its metal bracket. With your free hand, touch the computer chassis again. (If it sounds like I'm having you do the Macarena, I apologize. This strange ritual is needed to prevent static electricity from damaging the network adapter.)

4. Carefully fit the adapter card into the motherboard socket, as shown here. Gently press it into the socket with a forward and back rocking motion until the card is fully seated.

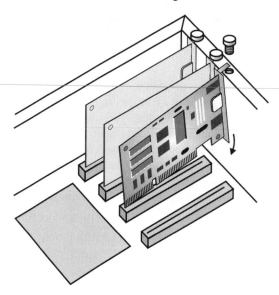

5. Attach the card's metal bracket to the computer frame with the screw you removed from the cover plate.

6. Close the computer case and reconnect the power cable.

Connecting Two Computers for Testing

Once you've installed network adapters in two computers (for initial testing), you'll need to connect the adapters together. How you do this depends on the type of network you're setting up.

Ethernet Network with Crossover Cable

If you bought a crossover cable (you're not using a hub), connect the two network adapters with the crossover cable now.

Ethernet Network with Hub

If you are using an Ethernet hub, use two patch cables to connect the two computers to jacks on the hub. The setup should look like that in Figure 15-1 (shown earlier in the chapter), but with only two computers. Plug in the hub and turn on the computers.

NOTE   *If one of the jacks on your hub is marked Uplink, don't use that jack. If there is a switch labeled Uplink/Normal, make sure that the switch is in the Normal position.*

Phoneline Network

If you're setting up a Phoneline network, connect the network adapters in the two computers with an ordinary phone extension cable, as shown here. These are included with the adapters. Just connect a jack on one card directly to a jack on the other. There are two jacks on each card. It shouldn't matter which you use unless the manufacturer's instructions say otherwise. If so, use the jacks marked Wall or Line, not Phone.

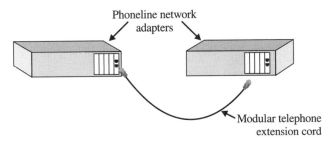

Phoneline network adapters

Modular telephone extension cord

Configuring Software

When you turn on each computer after installing a new network adapter, Windows will automatically detect the new hardware and start up the Add New Hardware Wizard. The wizard will take you through the process of adding the driver software that Windows uses to control the network adapter. Then you'll go through the steps of setting up the networking software and Windows. This might look like a long and complex procedure, but if you're careful and follow all of the steps, it should go quickly and smoothly.

Before you start, gather any diskettes provided with your network adapters and the Windows CD-ROM disks provided with your computers.

Installing Network Adapter Driver Software

If your network adapter came with instructions for installing its driver software under Windows, your best bet is to follow those specific instructions. I'll give you generic instructions that work in most cases:

15

1. When Windows starts up the first time after you've added your network adapter, it will display the message "Windows has detected new hardware and is locating the software for it." If Windows next displays the message "Windows is installing the software for your new hardware," you're lucky: Windows came with your network adapter's software preinstalled. You may need to insert your Windows CD-ROM. After a few moments, you'll be asked "Do you want to restart your computer now?" Click Yes. When Windows restarts, go on to step 3.

2. If Windows can't automatically find the required software, it will ask for help. In the window that appears, select the Automatic Search for a Better Driver option, as shown

here. Then get the floppy disk or CD that came with your network adapter, insert it into your computer's floppy drive, and click OK. Windows will locate and install the necessary software, and then ask if it's okay to restart the computer. Remove the floppy disk and click Yes.

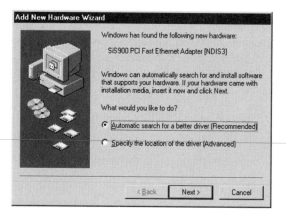

3. When your computer has restarted, right-click on My Computer on your desktop and select Properties. Select the Device Manager tab.

4. Be sure there are no yellow exclamation point icons displayed under Network Adapters. These icons are bad news. They mean that the hardware isn't functioning correctly or isn't installed properly. In the example shown below, there's an exclamation point indicating a problem with a PCI Communication Device, but the network adapter is fine. If you see an exclamation point next to the entry for your network adapter, highlight it and click the Properties button. The "Device status" message will tell you what you need to do to fix the problem.

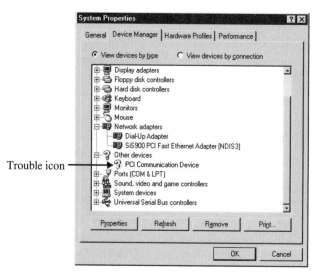

Configuring Network Protocols

After your network adapters and their drivers are installed, you'll need to set up the network protocol software that Windows uses to organize the messages it sends across the network.
Here are the steps:

1. Click Start and select Settings, Control Panel. Double-click the Network icon. (You may need to click View All Control Panel Options, on the left side of the Control Panel window, to see the Network icon). Click the Configuration tab.

2. See if NetBEUI appears in the list of network components installed. If it does, skip ahead to step 5.

3. Click the Add button. Select Protocol and click Add.

4. Select Microsoft in the Manufacturers list and NetBEUI in the Network Protocols list, as shown below. Then click OK. NetBEUI should now appear in the list of installed components.

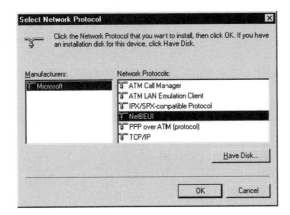

5. Click NetBEUI to highlight it. (If NetBEUI appears more than once, click on the entry that reads NetBEUI -> *xxxx* Adapter, where *xxx* is the brand name of your network adapter.) Click on Properties, click the Advanced tab, and check the Set This Protocol to Be the Default Protocol option. Click OK.

6. See if TCP/IP appears in the list of installed components. If it does, skip ahead to step 9.

7. Click the Add button. Select Protocol and click Add.

8. Select Microsoft in the Manufacturers list, select TCP/IP in the Network Protocols list, and click OK.

9. Click the File and Print Sharing button. Select the I Want to Be Able to Allow Others to Print to My Printer(s) option and click OK.

15

10. Click OK to close the Network applet. Windows may ask you to insert its installation CD-ROM. When the process is finished, Windows may ask to restart your computer. If it does, click No. Don't restart now. Just go ahead to the next section, "Configuring Network Software."

Be sure to follow these steps carefully with *each* of your networked computers.

If you are familiar with networking, you may be wondering why you need to install NetBEUI. It turns out that the browser service doesn't function properly on a TCP/IP-only setup, at least with Windows Me. Also, automatic IP address assignment doesn't work with Windows 95. NetBEUI lets all versions of Windows work together without hassles. Using NetBEUI also lets us disconnect file sharing from TCP/IP to provide security against Internet hackers.

Configuring Network Software

Now that Windows can communicate with your network adapters, the next step is to set up the file sharing software.

First, think of a name to give each of your computers. You'll use these names to identify the computers on the network, so choose names that will make sense to each of the people using your computers. You can use names like Mom, Bob, Laptop, Kitchen, and so on. (I use the names of Indonesian islands, so I don't need to worry about running out—there are more than 14,000 to choose from.) It's best to pick single-word names, with eight or fewer letters and no punctuation characters or spaces.

The next steps depend on the version of Windows you have available. Follow one of these three paths:

- If your computers all use Windows Me, follow the steps under "Configuring Windows Me."

- If you have some computers with Windows Me and some with Windows 95 or 98, set up the Windows Me computers first, using the steps under "Configuring Windows Me." You'll create a networking diskette to use with your Windows 95/98 computers. Then follow the steps under "Configuring Windows 95/98 with the Wizard."

- If you have only Windows 95 or 98, follow the steps under "Configuring Windows Manually." You can use this technique with *any* version of Windows even if the wizard is available to you.

The Home Networking Wizard simplifies network setup, but it does not take steps to protect your network from hackers on the Internet! Be sure to read the "Protecting Your Network" section at the end of this chapter to find out what you need to do to protect your computers.

Configuring Windows Me

Windows Me comes with a Home Networking Wizard program to help you set up your network in a few simple steps. Here's how:

1. Start the wizard by clicking Start, Programs, Accessories, Communications, and then Home Networking Wizard.

2. If you have Windows 95 or Windows 98 computers in your network, select the I Want to Create a Floppy Disk option, and then click Next.

3. In the Internet Connection window, indicate how this particular computer will access the Internet:

   ■ If you won't be using the Internet with this computer, select No, This Computer Does Not Use the Internet, click Next, and go on to step 5.

   ■ If you are setting up Microsoft's Internet Connection Sharing on your LAN, but the connection will be made by another computer, select Yes, This Computer Uses the Following, then choose A Connection to Another Computer, and click Next. Continue with step 5.

   ■ If this computer will use a modem, a direct connection to a high-speed DSL or cable connection, or a connection-sharing hardware device on your LAN, select Yes, This Computer Uses the Following. Then choose A Direct Connection to My ISP Using the Following Device and select the appropriate dial-up connection or LAN adapter name from the drop-down list, as shown in Figure 15-3. Click Next and continue with step 4.

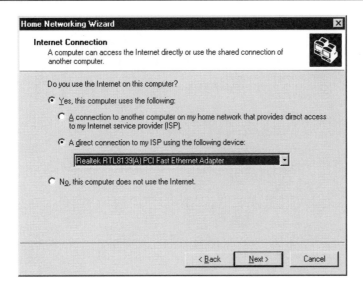

FIGURE 15-3   Choosing a direct Internet connection

15

4. If you indicated that you use a dial-up Internet connection, you will be offered the choice of sharing it with the rest of the computers on the LAN. You can check Yes or No. If you check Yes, be sure to select your LAN adapter as the Device Which Connects this Computer to Your Network. Then click Next.

5. In the Computer and Workgroup Names window, enter the unique name you chose for the computer in the Computer Name box. For the workgroup name, select Use the Default Workgroup Name MSHOME, as shown in Figure 15-4. Click Next.

6. In the Share Files and Printers window, select the My Documents Folder and All Folders in It check box if you want to share your My Documents folder with the rest of the LAN. If you do this, click Password and enter a password to protect these files from unauthorized access. If you have any printers physically connected to this printer, check the box next to each printer's name, as shown in Figure 15-5. Click Next to continue. If you're not creating a setup disk, skip to step 8.

7. If you chose to create a setup disk for Windows 95/98 computers in step 2, you will be asked to insert a blank, formatted floppy disk. Follow the on-screen instructions.

8. The wizard will complete its work. Click Finish. If you're asked to restart your computer, click Yes. Then proceed to configure each of your other computers. Be sure to enter a different computer name for each computer!

Once your computer has restarted, you will find a new icon on your desktop named My Network Places. If necessary, you can open this and double-click Home Networking Wizard to make changes to your file sharing setup. Now, skip down to "Testing Your Network."

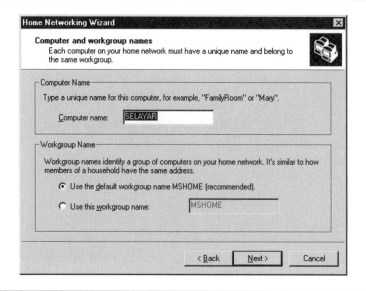

FIGURE 15-4   Specifying computer and workgroup names

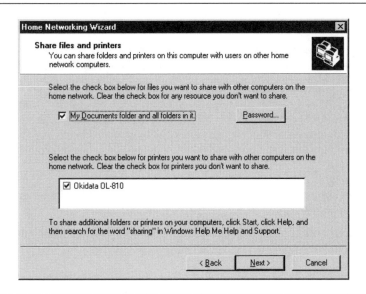

FIGURE 15-5   Choosing to share files and printers

Configuring Windows 95/98 with the Wizard

If you had the Windows Me wizard create a disk for your Windows 95 and/or 98 computers, take the diskette to your Windows 95/98 computers. Insert the diskette and open the My Computer icon on your desktop. Open the floppy disk icon, and double-click on the Setup.exe icon. This will run the Home Networking Wizard. Next, follow the steps outlined in the previous section for configuring Windows Me.

On Windows 95/98 computers, the My Network Places icon doesn't appear on the desktop. You'll need to use the Network Neighborhood icon instead. When I talk about using the Home Networking Wizard, remember that you'll need to run it from the floppy disk. It doesn't appear in Network Neighborhood as it does in My Network Places.

Configuring Windows Manually

If the wizard isn't available on your computer, you can set up the network manually. To be honest, it's not much more work than using the wizard! Here's what to do:

1. Click Start, Settings, Control Panel, and double-click the Network icon (not Dial-up Networking). If Network is not one of the choices displayed, click View all Control Panel Options, on the left side of the Control Panel window. Click the Configuration tab.

2. If the list of installed components already includes Client for Microsoft Networks, go on to step 4. Otherwise, click Add, Client, Add.

15

3. Select Microsoft from the Manufacturers list, and Client for Microsoft Networks from the Clients list. Then click OK.

4. If the installed component list already includes TCP/IP, skip to step 5. Otherwise, click the Add button. Choose Protocol and click Add. Select Microsoft and TCP/IP. Click OK.

5. If you want to share any printer(s) attached to this computer with the rest of the network, click on the File and Printer Sharing button and select I Want to Be Able to Allow Others to Print to My Printer(s). If you want to share file folders or drives on this computer with the rest of the network, select I Want to Be Able to Give Others Access to My Files. Click OK.

6. For the Primary Network Logon option, select Client for Microsoft Networks.

7. Click the Identification tab. For your computer name, enter the unique name you chose for this computer. For the workgroup, enter **MSHOME**. Click OK.

8. Windows might ask to you insert the Windows CD-ROM. When it has finished its installation, it will ask you to restart the computer. Click Yes.

The manual method won't automatically share your My Documents folder or your printers. You can do that following the steps in the "Sharing Your Printer with Others" and "Sharing Your Files with Others" sections later in this chapter.

 *If you use Windows 95 or 98, the My Network Places icon won't be present on your computer. You need to use the Network Neighborhood icon instead. Network Neighborhood does most of the same things as My Network Places.*

Testing Your Network

When you've installed the network adapters in your first two computers, connected them, and set up the networking software, you're ready to test your new network to make sure that it's working correctly. Here are the steps:

1. Double-click the My Network Places icon (Network Neighborhood, if you use Windows 95 or 98) on either computer.

2. Double-click Entire Network. Click on View the Entire Contents of This Folder.

3. You should see an icon labeled MSHOME. Double-click it, and you should see two icons, one for each of your computers, as in the example shown next.

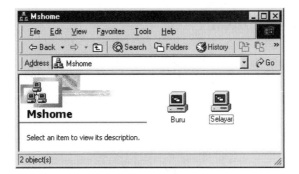

If you don't see the two computers listed, you'll need to do some detective work to find out what's wrong before proceeding any farther. Here are some suggestions:

- Look at the back of the NICs in your computer. Most have a green LED indicator which lights up when there is a proper electrical link between the cards, or for Ethernet networks, between the cards and the hub. Hubs also have indicator lights for each port. If your Link indicators aren't lit up, check your cabling before proceeding any further.

- Restart both computers, wait 10 minutes and look at My Network Places again. Sometimes it just takes a little time for a new network to get going.

- Right-click My Computer, select Properties, and view the Device Manager. Check for yellow exclamation point (!) icons next to the entries under Network Adapters. If you see any, you'll need to resolve the hardware problems first. Highlight the network adapter entry and click Properties to see the diagnosis.

- Open the Control Panel's Network applet on both computers (by right-clicking on My Network Places and selecting Properties). Click the Identification tab. Check that the computer names are different and the workgroup names are the same on both computers. Click on the Configuration tab. Check that at least Client for Microsoft Networks, NetBEUI, and a network adapter are listed on each computer's component list.

- Be sure that *at least* one computer has "I want to give others access to my Files" and/or "I want to give others access to my Printers" checked, and that it's booted up. At least one computer with sharing enabled has to be online in order for the list of networked computers to appear.

15

Finishing the Installation

When your first two computers appear under Entire Network in My Network Places, your network is functioning correctly. Move the computers to their final location, finish their final wiring, and test again. Then, if everything works properly, configure and connect the remaining computers. As you add each one, check the Entire Network contents in My Network Places of the new computer to see if it's working. The new computer might not appear on the other computers for several minutes.

When all of your computers are in place and wired, once again check Entire Network in My Network Places to be sure that each computer is visible. You may need to wait 10 minutes or so for them all to appear. When all your wiring and configuration is working correctly, you can start to use your new network.

After your network is set up, Windows gives you a quick way to get to the Network applet in the Control Panel, in case you need to make changes. Right-click My Network Places on the desktop and select Properties.

The following sections provide some pointers for finishing your Ethernet, Phoneline, or wireless network installation.

Finishing an Ethernet Network

If you're installing an Ethernet network, move your computers to their final locations and connect the network cables. If you have only two computers, use your crossover cable to connect the network adapters directly. Otherwise, connect each computer to your network hub and confirm that an indicator light comes on at the hub and on the back of the network adapter for each computer, when everything is powered up.

For best operation, follow these guidelines when laying out your network cabling:

- Don't pull, stretch, kink, or sharply bend network cables.
- Don't staple cables to walls or furniture with anything but rigid clips or staples designed for the purpose. If you want to tack the cables down, use coaxial cable clips, which are available at hardware stores or electrical supply stores. If you're running wires along your baseboards or around doors, etc., you can get rigid "wiring channels" to cover and protect the cables. (As an alternative, you can run your cables through clear vinyl tubing, for that "high-tech" look!)
- Place network cables where they won't get stepped on, squashed by desk chair wheels, run over by kids on roller skates, and so on.

You can save a bit on installation by putting the hub near one computer and buying one short patch cable for that connection. Then have in-wall wiring run from the hub to the remaining computers.

If you're going to have wiring installed inside your walls, consider hiring the job out to a wiring contractor. It's a bit tricky to install network cabling yourself, and for only a few computers, the tools will end up costing more than hiring a professional. Call a competent phone wiring installer and ask if he or she is familiar with network wiring. Be sure to ask for and check references. Also make sure that the contractor uses certified CAT-5 cabling, jacks, and connectors throughout.

Finishing a Phoneline Network

If you're installing a Phoneline network, plug each of your computers' network adapters into a phone jack. If the jack was already used by a phone, answering machine, or modem, plug the network adapter directly into the wall jack. Then plug the phone, answering machine, or modem into the network adapter, as shown here.

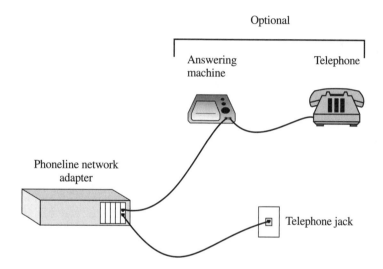

Don't wire anything else, especially a modem, in between the network adapter and the wall jack. Modems like to disconnect other devices when they're making a call, and this will disrupt your network connection.

Test your network by viewing Entire Network in My Network Places. If any computers are missing, check their configuration using the steps outlined earlier in the "Testing your Network" section. Also, be sure that each computer is plugged into the same phone extension line. To check this, follow the procedure described in the "Phoneline Networking" section earlier in this chapter.

Finishing a Wireless Network

If you bought a wireless network, you're about to enjoy the payoff. Just set up any remaining computers, move them to their final location, and that's it!

Check the documentation provided by the manufacturer to see if you need to configure any additional security features of your wireless network cards. Some manufacturers provide an encryption feature that makes it more difficult for others to electronically eavesdrop on your network signals (but don't kid yourself—government agencies and other such folks probably can).

Sharing Printers

After you've installed the network, you can immediately start taking advantage of it. The first use you might want to make of your network is printer sharing. Your network gives you the ability to use any of your printers from any computer on the network, regardless of which computer the printer is physically attached to.

One point to remember is that the computer that is physically attached to the printer must be turned on in order for anyone else to use the printer. Consider installing your favorite printer on the computer most likely to be turned on so that it will be available when you want it.

Sharing Your Printer with Others

If you're just now adding a new printer, refer to Chapter 16 for details on how to get it properly installed and working. Once you have a printer properly working with a given computer, you can use the Home Networking Wizard to let other networked computers use it, as explained in the "Configuring Windows Me" section earlier in this chapter.

If you use Windows 95, follow these steps:

1. Go to the computer that has the printer physically attached to it.

2. Open the Control Panel's Network applet (right-click My Network Places and select Properties). Click the Configuration tab. Click File and Print Sharing and select I Want to Allow Others to Be Able to Print to My Printer(s). Click OK, and then close the Network dialog box and Control Panel.

3. Open the Printers folder by clicking Start, Settings, Printers.

4. Find the icon corresponding to the printer you want to share, right-click on it, and select Sharing, as shown here.

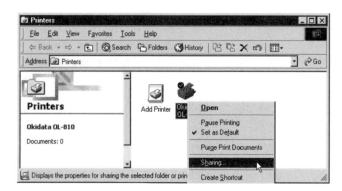

5. Click the Shared As button and enter a name in the Share Name box, as shown in the example here. Choose a short name that will differentiate this printer from others you own. For example, you might enter ColorInk or Laserjet4. Choose a name with eight or fewer characters, without spaces or punctuation. Then click OK.

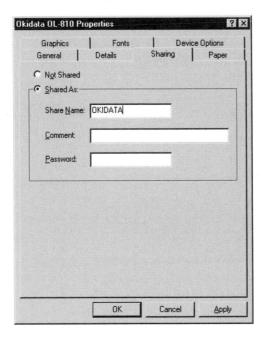

This printer is now available to everyone on the network. To make it a private printer again, just view the Sharing properties and select Not Shared.

Using a Printer Installed Elsewhere on the Network

To use a printer on another networked computer, you first need to install the printer on your computer. You'll just need to do this once. After the networked printer has been installed, you can use it whenever you like.

15

Installing a Networked Printer

Here's how to install a networked printer on your own computer:

1. Make sure that the computer that is physically connected to the printer is turned on.

2. Go to your computer and open the Printers folder by clicking Start, Settings, Printers.

3. Double-click Add Printer, and then click Next. Windows asks how the printer is connected to your computer. Choose Network Printer and click Next.

4. Click the Browse button. Windows displays a list of the computers on your network and the printers that are available for shared use, as shown here. It might take a few seconds for this list to appear.

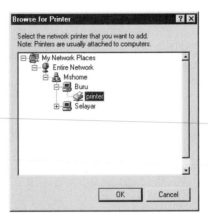

5. Find the printer you want to use. You mighty need to poke into the list view, opening the Entire Network item, then your workgroup, then individual computers to find the printer. Highlight the printer and click OK.

6. If you use this computer with old MS-DOS applications installed on your computer, select Yes. Then click Next.

7. Windows will ask for a name to give this printer on your computer. You can probably use the name it suggests. Click Next.

8. Leave Print a Test Page set to Yes and click Finish.

9. Windows might ask you to insert your Windows CD-ROM and select the appropriate printer manufacturer and model. If so, follow the same procedure you use when installing a printer on your own computer (see Chapter 16). Usually, Windows can get any necessary printer drivers directly from the other computer, through the network. (Is this nifty or what?)

That's all there is to it. Now that this printer is in your Printers folder, you can use it anytime you wish. It will appear in your application's Print dialog box as a printer choice. When you choose the network printer, Windows will send the printer data over the network, and it will be output on the printer you selected. You can add as many networked and local (directly connected) printers as you wish to your Printers folder.

If you want to use this particular networked printer most of the time, you can make it your default printer. Just right-click it in your Printers folder and select Set as Default. This way, each Windows application will assume you want to use this printer unless you specify otherwise.

Saving Print Jobs When a Networked Printer is Offline

Keep in mind that in order for printing to occur, the computer to which the printer is physically attached must be turned on. However, there is a way to store the printer data until a networked printer is available.

If your computer is disconnected from the network or the other computer is not turned on, you can right-click the printer icon in your Printers folder and select Use This Printer Offline. Any printing you attempt will be saved on your own computer. Later on, when the other computer is back online, uncheck Use This Printer Offline. All of the saved printing will be sent out. It's a great feature for laptops when you're working away from the LAN. But be careful if you use this. If you forget to uncheck Use This Printer Offline, your output will never appear, and you'll be wondering why!

Managing Shared Printers

You might already be wondering what happens if two people try to send something to the same printer at the same time. Will your spreadsheet and someone else's tofu recipe print on the same sheet of paper? No! Windows manages the printers using a *queue*, or list of work to be done. This way, the printer takes care of everyone's printing tasks on a first-come, first-served basis.

The Windows Printer Manager works for networked as well as local printers. Just double-click any printer in your Printers folder to see the documents currently printing or waiting to be printed. You can cancel documents by highlighting them and clicking Document, Cancel (you can do this from any computer on the network).

If you try to print a document but nothing comes out of the printer, before you try the Print command again, open your Printers folder, double-click the printer's icon, and see if your document is listed in the window. If it is, the screen will tell you why it's not printing. For example, the printer may be out of paper. If the document does not appear in the window, be sure the printer is turned on.

15

Sharing Files and CD-ROMs

Sharing your computer's drive and file folders is only a bit more complex than sharing a printer. File sharing makes your hard drive's folders visible on other computers on your network. Therefore, you need to be careful what you make available, to avoid the chance the someone else might accidentally delete or damage some of your files.

The best way to avoid problems is to share only particular file folders, and only if necessary. If all you want to do with your LAN is make a small group of files available to several people, there's no need to share your entire C: drive, when you can just share a single folder. So before you get started, think about what you want to make available from each of your computers. One handy folder to share is My Documents.

If you have one scanner to be shared by all of your computers, you might be disappointed to find that Windows doesn't let you share access to a scanner over your network the way it shares access to files and printers. However, you can still make life easier by sharing the folder in which your scanner software saves files. That way, the people in your home or office can come to the computer with the scanner, scan images, and then go back to their own computer to work with the files they saved.

Sharing Your Files with Others

If you use Windows Me, the Home Networking Wizard will let you share your My Documents folder with the network, with a minimum of fuss. You can use Windows Explorer to share *any* folder or drive on your computer.

Sharing My Documents

If you want to share your My Documents and you use Windows Me, the Home Networking Wizard will set this up for you, as described in the "Configuring Windows Me" section earlier in this chapter. When this is done, other computers will be able to see a mydocuments icon representing your My Documents folder in their My Network Places window, as shown here.

If you use Windows 95, you can still share your My Documents folder, it's just a bit more work. Use the procedure described in the next section.

Sharing any Drive or Folder

Before you begin the procedure for sharing a drive or folder, decide whether you want to share the entire contents of a drive (which would make sense for CD-ROM or floppy drives) or just a certain folder and its contents (which would make sense for your hard drive).

Then follow these steps:

1. Open the Control Panel's Network applet and click on the Configuration tab. Click the File and Print Sharing button. Select I Want to Be Able to Give Others Access to My Files. Click OK and close the Network dialog box and the Control Panel.

2. Start Windows Explorer and view the drive or folder. You can use My Computer, Windows Explorer, or any other desktop view.

3. Right-click the drive or folder and select Sharing. Windows will display the Sharing page of the drive or folder's Properties dialog box, as shown in Figure 15-6.

4. Click Shared As. You can either accept the name Windows selects as the share name or enter another one in the Share Name box. If you choose your own share name, it's best to stick to names of eight or fewer letters without spaces or punctuation, such as SCANS, CDROM, or CDRIVE.

5. Decide how much access you want to give other network users to your shared files. Choose Read-Only (the default) if you want people to only view and read your files. They will not be able to create new folders, delete files, or change files. Choose Full if you want others to be able to modify, create, delete, and rename files and folders in your shared folder. Choose Depends on Password if you want to grant different access to different people.

6. You can leave the password box(es) blank if you want *anyone* to be able to view these files. I recommend that you choose passwords for your network. Enter them here, and then click OK.

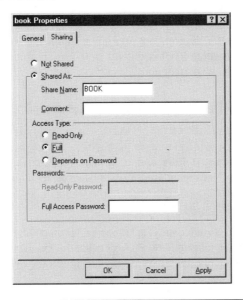

15

FIGURE 15-6   The Sharing page of a folder's Properties dialog box

 *If you leave the password boxes blank, and then connect to the Internet without taking the precautions I outline at the end of this chapter, anyone in the world will be able to read and/or delete your files. Even with the precautions, do not take this risk! Set up passwords!*

You can repeat this procedure with several different folders, if you want.

When a folder is set up for sharing, its folder icon in Windows Explorer changes to show a hand offering the folder to others, as shown here.

book

Setting up Personal Folders

If you move around from computer to computer, you've probably found it frustrating to find that the file you want is *there*, while you're working *here*. You can get around this problem by setting up a folder on one of your computers in which you keep all or most of your files. Share this folder, and give it a name like Bobfiles. In fact, it's handy to set up one such shared folder for each person in your household or office. That way, everyone can get to their files from any computer anytime.

You can even make My Documents on each computer use this shared folder automatically. Just right-click your My Documents folder and select Properties. In the Target box, type *computername**sharename*, where *computername* is the name of the computer sharing your personal folder, and *sharename* is the name you used when sharing the folder (for example, \\Bobfiles). This way, the My Documents folder on each of your computers stores its files on one computer (Bali in this example).

For this to work, the computer sharing your personal folder needs to be on all of the time; otherwise, you won't be able to get to My Documents from any computer! Also, you need to be very careful to back up that computer frequently.

Using Files Stored Elsewhere on the Network

Once a drive or folder has been shared on the network, you can get to it from any other computer on your network. If you've been using Windows for a while, you've probably noticed that there are often several ways to do the same thing, and using shared folders is no exception. Let's take a look at three approaches: My Network Places, Windows Explorer, and My Computer.

Browsing My Network Places

My Network Places is a feature available only on Windows Me and Windows 2000 (not Windows 95 and 98). It lets you collect shortcuts to network folders and Internet file sites for quick access.

If you double-click My Network Places, Windows displays three or more icons:

■ The Add Network Place icon runs a wizard that lets you enter the name of a shared folder, an Internet site with Microsoft's Web Folder feature, or an Internet FTP file repository.

■ The Home Networking Wizard icon lets you change your Home Networking settings using the setup wizard.

■ The Entire Network icon lets you view all of the computers on your network, their shared folders, and the files inside the folders using a standard Explorer view. Just double-click to dig into the folders it displays.

■ Windows automatically displays an icon for each shared folder or drive on each computer on your LAN. This is a handy feature, new to Windows Me, that you can use to get to any shared file without much hunting around.

The easiest way to find files elsewhere on your LAN is to use the Entire Network and shared folder icons in My Network Places.

> **TIP**
>
> *If there is a particular shared folder (or a subfolder inside it) that you will use frequently, you can drag a shortcut to it to your desktop. Just hold down the* ALT *key while dragging the icon from My Network Places or from an opened folder to your desktop. Even though the actual folder is on another computer on your LAN, you can have a shortcut to the folder for quick access.*

Opening Shared Folders with Windows Explorer

You can get to shared folders directly by entering their network path into the Address bar of Windows Explorer. You might already be familiar with paths to files, like C:\My Documents\ Recipe.doc. This path tells Windows that the file is stored on the C: drive in a folder named My Documents, and the file itself is named Recipe.doc.

You can view shared files and folders with a network path name as well. The network path follows the UNC (Universal Naming Convention) format. For example, the path \\Bali\Workfiles\ Project1\Plans.doc tells Windows that the file is on the computer named Bali, in a shared folder with the network name Workfiles, and the desired file named Plans.doc is in a subfolder named Project1. (In this example, Workfiles is that network name given when the folder was shared.)

If you know the name of a computer and the names of its shared folders, you can explore the files or folders directly using this new type of path name.

Adding a Shared Drive to My Computer

If you use a program that expects to find its files using a old style path name with a drive letter, you can actually make a drive letter on your computer pick up its files from another computer on your network. This process is called *mapping*.

Follow these steps to map a network drive:

1. Open Windows Explorer and choose Map Network Drive from the Tools menu.

2. Choose a drive letter that is not used by your own computer's internal drives.

15

3. Enter the path (in the UNC format *computername\sharedfoldername*) to the other computer, as in the example shown here.

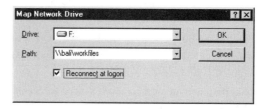

4. Select the Reconnect at Logon check box to make this setting work every time you use your computer. Click OK.

Now, the chosen drive letter will seem like it's part of your computer, but its files actually sit on another computer on your LAN. The new "drive" appears in My Computer along with your floppy drive, C: drive, and CD-ROM, as in the example shown here.

New drive F: →

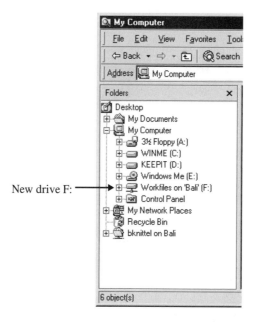

Sharing CD-ROMs

Using file sharing to make a CD-ROM available over the network is handy if you have a computer without a CD-ROM drive. Or, if you find that you use several different CD-ROMs frequently and hate needing to keep switching disks, you can put the CDs in different computers and use them from your own desktop.

To share a CD-ROM drive, open My Computer, right-click the entry for the CD-ROM drive, and select Sharing. Click Shared As and enter a name like CD or CDROM. Leave the access set to Read-Only and the password blank. Click OK. Do this on all your computers, if you want.

To access a remote CD-ROM, you can use the same techniques available for using files stored on the network (described in the previous sections). If you use a software package that needs to know the location of its CD-ROM files, you may need to assign a drive letter to the networked CD-ROM drive, as described in the "Adding a Shared Drive to My Computer" section.

NOTE

CD file sharing works for data disks, but doesn't work with music CDs.

Backing Up Files over the Network

You can use free space on another computer to back up files from your own hard drive. This way, if your own computer is damaged or you accidentally delete the files, you may be lucky enough to have spare copies on another computer.

The easiest way to back up files is to simply copy them from a folder on your computer to a folder on another computer. Create a folder on the remote computer named something like My Backups. Then you can drag files and whole folders from your computer into the shared backup folder.

You can also use a backup utility that lets you save a backup set in a file. Perform a backup configured for maximum compression and save the result on a shared folder on another computer. (Windows doesn't come with a backup program capable of this, but you can purchase one. You might take a look at Ultrabac at www.ultrabac.com. The free version can back up local files to file on another computer. The paid version lets you back up shared folders from other computers at the same time. With the paid version, you could back up *all* the computers on your network at once!

Sharing Your Internet Connection

If you use a modem or high-speed DSL or cable Internet connection, you can make this one connection available to all of the computers on your network. Since most of the time you are just looking at the computer screen and aren't downloading data at full speed, you usually won't even notice that the connection is also in use by others. Sharing one connection is a great way to save on ISP bills and the expense of extra phone lines. Once you have a network, sharing a connection is a snap!

15

NOTE

If you have an Apple iMac or Macintosh computer at home, you'll be happy to know that a shared Internet connection will work with your Mac. Just connect the computer to your network using an Ethernet cable or Apple-compatible phone-line networking adapter, and set up the Mac's network adapter for DCHP automatic configuration.

NOTE

You should know that certain network software such as NetMeeting and CUSeeMe works only partially or does not work at all over a shared connection, because of some unfortunate technical limitations.

Sharing Dial-up Connections

If you currently use a modem to establish an Internet connection, you can tell Windows to use a feature called Internet Connection Sharing to make the dial-up connection available to every computer on your LAN. Windows 98 Second Edition and Windows Me have this feature. You can also download the Connection Sharing update for the original version of Windows 98.

One computer is set up with a modem and configured to establish a dial-up connection to your ISP, in the usual way. This connection is shared with the rest of the LAN, as illustrated below. When any computer on the LAN tries to access the Internet, the one computer automatically dials up and passes Internet data between the LAN and the Internet on behalf of the other computer. When the connection goes unused for a few minutes, it automatically hangs up.

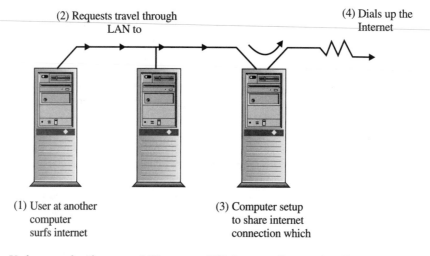

(2) Requests travel through LAN to

(4) Dials up the Internet

(1) User at another computer surfs internet

(3) Computer setup to share internet connection which

> **NOTE**   *Unfortunately, if you use AOL as your ISP, Internet Connection Sharing won't work. If you want to share a connection and still access AOL, you might consider getting a standard ISP account and accessing AOL services over the Internet. Contact AOL's customer support for information about doing this. Free ISP accounts like FreeISP and AltaVista won't work either. Their connection software requires you to view ads while you're connected, and the Internet Connection Sharing software isn't compatible.*

To set up Internet Connection Sharing, start at the computer that actually has the modem you'll use for dialing to your ISP. Set up and test dial-up access to the Internet first.

Next, run the Home Networking Wizard from My Network Places and click Next until you get to the Internet Connection page (refer to Figure 15-3). Specify that you want to use a direct connection to the Internet and select the appropriate dial-up connection, as described in the "Configuring Windows Me" section earlier in this chapter. Click Next to get to the Internet Connection Sharing page. Check Yes and select your LAN adapter as the device that connects this computer to your network. Click Next until the wizard finishes. When you're finished, restart your computer.

Then go to each of the other computers on your LAN and run the Home Networking Wizard from them. Go to the Internet Connection page and specify that you want to use a connection to another computer on your home network. Click Next until the Wizard finishes, and then restart the computer.

Now, whenever any computer tries to access the Internet, the computer that is sharing its connection will dial your ISP automatically.

> **NOTE** *All you're sharing is the connection to your ISP. Each computer can still be set up to retrieve mail from different e-mail accounts. If your ISP doesn't provide multiple mailboxes, your LAN users can always sign up with a free service like Hotmail, Yahoo!, and others. See Chapter 7 for details on using e-mail.*

Sharing DSL and Cable Connections

High-speed DSL and cable modems normally use an Ethernet connection between the special modem and one computer. There are two ways you can set up your network to share a high-speed connection with your LAN: using the Microsoft Internet Connection Sharing software or using a special-purpose hardware device called a connection-sharing router or firewall.

With Microsoft's software approach, you need to install an additional Ethernet NIC in one of your computers, to which you connect the modem. The total cost is about $20 for an adapter card and a patch cable. The computer with the actual connection is called the *gateway* computer, and this computer needs to be turned on for any of the other computers to reach the Internet. There are also commercial software packages like WinRoute and SyGate which work the same way.

Hardware connection-sharing devices or routers have built-in software much like Microsoft's Internet Connection Sharing, but they have a special advantage: Because they sit in between your LAN and the DSL or cable modem, they can filter out hacker activity before it gets to your computer. Microsoft Internet Connection Sharing doesn't prevent the outside world from getting to your LAN. A hardware router does.

I strongly recommend using a hardware device because it has the following advantages:

- Provides faster performance
- Doesn't require that a gateway computer be left on for the other computers to get to the Internet
- Offers excellent protection from Internet hacking

> **NOTE** *If your DSL service requires you to use a "connection" program to sign on with a user name and a password, you will need to use a hardware device to share this type of connection. Microsoft's Internet Connection Sharing can't be set up to transmit the password your ISP requires.*

15

Using a Hardware Connection-Sharing Device

Hardware connection-sharing devices cost about $125, and most include a four-port Ethernet hub in the same box. Brands include Linksys, D-Link, 3COM, Netgear, and others. I've tested the Linksys DSL/Cable Modem Sharing Router myself, and it works well.

> **NOTE** *When you shop for a hardware connection-sharing device, check that its box says it supports PPPoE. This is the network protocol used to perform the sign-on step.*

With the hardware device, you simply connect the device to your network hub with one patch cable and to the DSL or cable modem with another. In fact, most of these devices have a hub built into them, so you can simply plug each of your computers into the device and skip the hub altogether, as illustrated here.

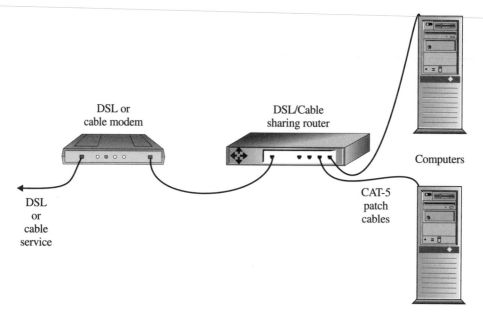

Configure the router as instructed in its owner's manual. You may be provided with special wizard setup software on a floppy disk, or you may be instructed to use Internet Explorer to enter setup information via a Web page built right into the router. You'll enter the information provided by your ISP into a page called WAN Settings.

Once the router is configured with information provided by your DSL or cable ISP, go to each computer on your LAN and follow these steps:

1. Open the Control Panel (select Settings from the Start menu and click Control Panel) and double-click the Internet Options icon.

2. Click the Connections tab, and then click Setup.

3. Choose I Want to Set Up My Internet Connection Manually and click Next.

4. Select I Connect Through a Local Area Network. Click Next and finish the wizard.

5. Restart each of the computers.

When this configuration is complete, the entire LAN will be able to use the high-speed connection.

Using Microsoft Internet Connection Sharing

To share your high-speed connection with Internet Connection Sharing, choose one computer to serve as the gateway computer, which is the one that receives the actual DSL or cable modem connection. Buy an extra 10Mbps (10BaseT) Ethernet adapter, if this computer doesn't already have an extra one. This card is in addition to the one used in your own network. I recommend using a different brand of NIC than you used for your own network. Then, when you open the Control Panel's Network applet, you will be able to differentiate between the adapter that connects to the network and the adapter that connects to the cable or DSL modem.

Install and configure the new adapter as instructed by your DSL or cable ISP. Connect the DSL or cable modem to the computer with two NICs, as illustrated here.

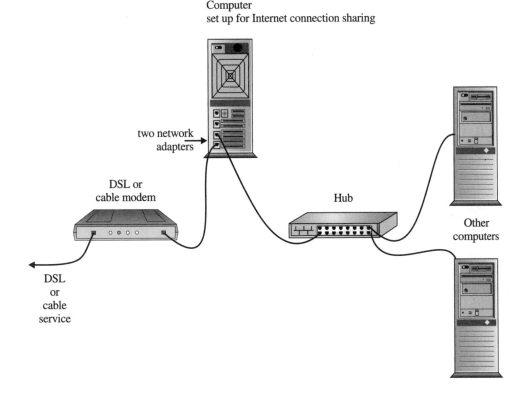

Computer
set up for Internet connection sharing

two network →
adapters

DSL or
cable modem

Hub

Other
computers

DSL
or
cable
service

15

When this network adapter is set up, you should be able to use Internet Explorer to reach the Internet from this computer. Be sure this works before proceeding.

Next, follow the instructions in the "Sharing a Dial-Up Connection" section, except that instead of choosing a dial-up connection to share, choose the network adapter corresponding to the connection to the DSL or cable modem. Be careful to select the adapter that connects to the modem, *not* the one that connects to your LAN. Don't forget the step of configuring all of your other computers to use a LAN Internet connection. Finally, restart all your other computers.

From now on, as long as the gateway computer is turned on, all of your computers should be able to reach the Internet through your high-speed connection. However, there is no firewall in place, and all your shared files are exposed to the Internet. Be sure you take the security steps outlined in the "Protecting Your Network" section at the end of this chapter.

 *If you enable Internet Connection Sharing but don't take adequate precautions, hackers on the Internet can and will probe your computer's files. They may even install viruses or erase your data.*

Playing Games Across Your LAN

As you learned in Chapter 13, which is all about playing games on your computer, many computer games are designed to allow several people to interact. The game software sends information about user actions back and forth over a LAN or over the Internet, so each player can see what the others are doing.

In fact, many people set up a home network just to play interactive computer games. If you don't care about file and printer sharing, just follow the network installation instructions provided earlier in the chapter and skip the parts about sharing and using shared resources.

Playing a game across your own LAN is pretty much the same as playing across the Internet, except that you'll find that interaction across your LAN will be much faster than over a dial-up connection. Game software instructions should tell you how to connect to other users. Here are some tips:

- Most games that permit play across the Internet will let you play with other computers on your LAN as well. The instructions for your game will tell you how. Usually, you will just need to type in the name of another computer on your LAN to make a connection to it. You can find your computer's name by right-clicking My Network Places, selecting Properties, and viewing the Identification page.

- If your game requires you to enter an IP address (the Internet equivalent of a phone number) in order to connect to another user, you can find the addresses of each of your computers by clicking on Start, selecting Run, typing **winipcfg**, and pressing ENTER. Select your LAN adapter to find your IP address on the LAN, as shown here. Use this number to play with other people in your own home. Your IP address may change from time to time, so you should check this number each time you want to play a game.

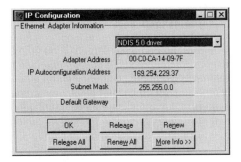

If you use a shared Internet connection, you might not be able to play some games with users on the Internet. If the software says it doesn't work with NAT (Network Address Translation), it won't work on a shared connection.

Protecting Your Network

Your network makes it possible to get at information in any of your computers, but you don't want to make it *too* easy. You'll need to consider ways of protecting your network from the damage that can be done by mistake, as well as maliciously.

Protecting Your Files

When you're sharing your computer's contents across a couple of networked computers, that leaves them vulnerable to all of the things that can go wrong with the chances multiplied by the number of computers and users accessing them. You'll need to carefully consider ways to protect your files. After all, you don't want a family member's accidental keystroke in another room to erase all of your files, by remote control!

Here are some suggestions:

- Before sharing a folder or entire hard drive, be sure you really need to. There's no sense exposing your files unnecessarily.

- When others don't need to modify your files, use the Read-Only option when sharing. That way, others can see the files, but not change or delete them.

- Remember that Windows offers no real user/password security. Anyone can walk up to your computers and read any file there, password or no password. If the contents of some files are sensitive, consider using an add-on file security product to encrypt and protect them.

Risks from within are bad enough, but today, with almost everybody using the Internet, risks from without are far worse. What follows is probably the most important part of this chapter.

15

Protecting Your Network from the Internet

It seems like you can't open a newspaper these days without seeing another story about hackers stealing personal information, credit card numbers, or government secrets. It's no surprise, really. When we're sitting in front of our computers, we're alone and it's quiet. It's very difficult to believe that someone across the world might be perusing our hard drive at the same time. So, few of us worry about the problem enough to take precautions. With tens of millions of computers joining the Internet every year, it's now a hackers' paradise. Take action today to prevent yourself from becoming another hacking statistic tomorrow.

You set up your LAN to make it easy to get at your files from other computers. But you want "other" to mean just *your* computers. The problem is that Windows does nothing to set such boundaries, so when you're connected to the Internet, your shared files can be read, written, and erased from just about any computer in the world. If you use a dial-up connection to your ISP, you are only exposed to hackers during the time that your modem is connected. Still, wily hackers are scanning the Internet constantly, so this is a small consolation.

If you use a hardware connection-sharing device or router to share a high-speed Internet connection with your LAN, that device will provide a great deal of protection against hacking. It acts as a filter to prevent outside people from accessing your shared files—in computer lingo, it's called a *firewall*. This provides excellent protection, and it's the one I recommend.

If you use a modem or a high-speed connection without a hardware firewall device, you'll need to do something to protect your shared files from exposure. There are three things you can do (listed from the least to the most effective):

■ Be absolutely sure that each shared folder on each computer on your LAN requires a password. This provides a *minimum* of protection. It's difficult to enforce this though, because anyone can set up a new shared folder at any time.

■ If you use Microsoft's Internet Connection Sharing, *do not* enable file or printer sharing on the computer that manages the shared connection to your ISP. Open the Control Panel's Network applet, click File and Printer Sharing, and make sure that neither option box is checked. This is a small inconvenience for the additional security you gain.

■ For the most protection, you can prevent Windows from using TCP/IP for its file sharing work. This is like making Windows speak a foreign language on your LAN so that the conversation can't work its way out across the Internet, and more to the point, so Windows can't understand anything sent in by hackers. You can still access the Internet, and you can still share files, but outside computers won't be able to connect to your shared files. This is a good idea whether you use a modem or a high-speed Internet connection.

To get the highest level of security available without a hardware firewall device, set up each of your computers as follows:

1. Open the Network applet in the Control Panel.

2. Select the TCP/IP entry in the list of installed network components and click Properties. (If there is more than one TCP/IP entry, start with the first one.)

3. Select the Bindings tab and uncheck the File and Printer Sharing for Microsoft Networks option and the Client for Microsoft Networks option. Click OK. When Windows complains that you have not selected any drivers, click No.

4. If there are any other TCP/IP entries in the list of components, repeat step 3 with each of them.

5. Close the Control Panel. You might need to insert your Windows CD-ROM, and when the setup process has finished, Windows will ask to restart your computer. Click Yes.

Be sure to follow this procedure exactly, on each of your computers. If you enable or disable file or printer sharing on any computer at a later date, follow this procedure again to be sure that these settings are still correct.

This might seem like a lot of work, but it's essential to protect your data. And remember, with a hardware firewall/connection-sharing device, none of this is necessary.

15

Part IV

Upgrading, Maintaining, and Troubleshooting Your PC

Chapter 16

Adding Peripherals

How to...

- Connect your peripherals to you PC
- Add printers
- Add scanners
- Add storage devices
- Upgrade your monitor
- Use surge suppressors and UPSs

Okay, you have your PC out of its box, plugged in, and powered up. You have even become proficient at a few applications. Unfortunately, without external *peripherals*—such as printers, monitors, scanners, and drives—you will probably find your imagination and newfound knowledge a bit restrained.

This chapter covers some of the more common types of peripherals that you might want to add to your system. But first, it explains the ways that you can connect those peripherals to your system.

Getting Connected

Before you can determine which type of connection is best for your peripherals, you need to understand how data is transferred between your system and a device. In Chapter 1, you learned that computers process information as *bits* (switches that can be on or off, represented by a 1 or 0), which are organized into groups of eight bits, called *bytes*.

The speed at which these bits are transmitted depends on the interface. The *interface* is what connects your device to your system. Think of it as an information manager. Like human managers, some interfaces are faster and more efficient than others when it comes to handling data. A speed of one megabit per second (1Mbps) is equal to one million bits per second. A speed of one megabyte per second (1MBps) is equal to one million bytes per second. Notice the difference of the lowercase *b* versus the uppercase *B* in the acronym. This is good stuff to know when weeding through computer supply catalogs.

Technology advances so quickly, even teenagers have a difficult time keeping up. In the olden days (a few years ago, in computer time), there were two popular ways in which computers communicated with printers and other external devices: through serial and parallel ports. Then PS/2 ports came along. Now we have USB (Universal Serial Bus) and Firewire ports, designed to meet the need for better and faster connections.

Serial, Parallel, and PS/2 Connections

Serial and parallel ports come standard on most computer systems and still have a wide variety of uses. Newer systems take advantage of PS/2 (bus) ports.

A serial port is like a single-lane road, or the lines for rides at your favorite theme park. A parallel port is like a multiple-lane highway. The serial port is commonly used for connecting a serial mouse, printer, digital camera, or joystick. The parallel port, also known as the printer port, is commonly used for connecting a printer, a scanner, or an external drive. PS/2 ports connect the keyboard and mouse (some people call them keyboard and mouse ports). The PS/2 standard sparked the idea of a universal interface that supports multiple devices simultaneously. Figure 16-1 illustrates these three types of ports, as well as the USB port (discussed in the next section).

Obviously, you are limited to the number of devices you can connect to your system through these ports. If you want to attach one of your new computer toys, you must reach behind your system and swap one device connection for another. This often involves shutting down your system first. Serial and parallel connections can also be painfully slow. USB and Firewire connections offer a solution.

USB Connections

The USB standard was developed in 1996 as a better way of connecting peripherals to a system. Most modern PCs provide at least one USB port (something to look for when you are buying a new PC). This technology was designed as an alternative to the PS/2 standard, which supports multiple devices simultaneously.

USB offers the following key features:

- Support for both low- and high-speed devices (1.5 to 12Mbps)
- Simple Plug-and-Play installation, which means that you do not need to set any switches
- Support for hot swapping, which means that you can remove and connect peripherals without shutting down your computer
- Support for up to 127 devices per port, through a hub, which is a port extender of sorts
- Power supply to low-power devices

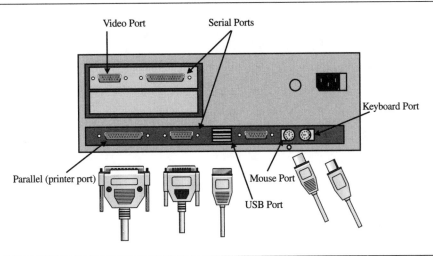

.FIGURE 16-1   Typical computer ports

16

NOTE *The USB interface requires only one IRQ address, irrespective of the number of devices connected to the port. This address is used by your system to acknowledge a request for processor time, kind of like raising your hand in class when you have a question.*

To expand your port's capabilities so that it can support multiple (up to 127) devices, you need to invest in a USB hub. These handy devices are like power strips. They turn one connection into multiple connections. Some hubs are modular, meaning that you can configure them to fit your specific needs. Less-expensive hubs are not modular and simply expand your single USB port to four or more ports, as in the example shown in Figure 16-2.

Most hubs are expandable and flexible enough to connect all of your peripherals to one central station. A hub can also be used to configure a low-cost universal docking station for your laptop computer. Figure 16-3 illustrates how peripherals connect to the USB hub.

Some USB interfaces provide load-sharing capabilities, which distribute the line speed evenly across all connected devices. This means that all of the devices can operate simultaneously without impacting performance.

Firewire Connections

A better and faster communication standard, known as IEEE 1394 or Firewire, was developed by Apple Computer, Inc., as a way to connect high-speed devices such as digital video camcorders, digital cameras, disk drives, printers, and music systems. Firewire is significantly faster than

FIGURE 16-2   A USB hub that supports four ports

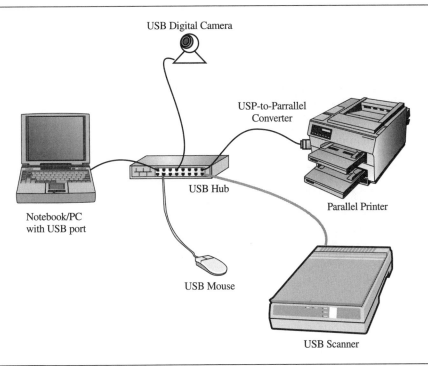

USB Digital Camera

USP-to-Parrallel
Converter

USB Hub

Notebook/PC
with USB port

Parallel Printer

USB Mouse

USB Scanner

FIGURE 16-3   Connecting devices to a USB hub

USB and is, therefore, recommended for high-performance devices. The average data speed for Firewire connections is currently 400Mbps. Like its slower, more economical counterpart, USB, Firewire is fast and hot swappable.

Firewire cables can span up to 15 feet and have either two 6-pin connectors for data and power, or one 6-pin and one 4-pin connector for data only. Figure 16-4 illustrates the Firewire connector systems.

A Firewire network can support up to 63 devices. Unlike USB, Firewire does not require a hub to connect multiple devices. They simply *daisy-chain* together, so one device connects to the next, which connects to the next, and so on.

16

TIP

Although a hub is not required to connect multiple Firewire devices, hubs for Firewire connections are available. You may find this a worthwhile convenience if you frequently hot swap devices and don't want to interrupt the chain between connections.

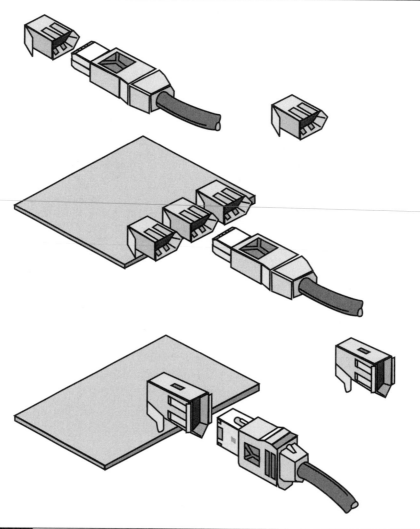

FIGURE 16-4 Firewire connector systems

Connecting USB or Firewire Devices

USB and Firewire devices connect directly to the interface port or hub. There is no need to configure hardware settings, IRQs, or any other address.

The device you are connecting should come with cables and any device drivers that are required by that device. Simply connect your device, load your drivers, and have fun playing. It is important that you follow the installation instructions that come with your device. In most cases, the software is self-starting, meaning that when you load the disk that came with the device, the setup program launches automatically. All you need to do is follow the onscreen instructions, and voilà, your driver loads successfully (hey—magic happens).

NOTE   *Device drivers provide instructions for your system so that it knows how to communicate with the device. For example, when you purchase a printer, it usually comes with a user's guide. This guide gives you the information you need to operate that printer. Since computer systems cannot read manuals, their instructions need to come in the form of device drivers. The software that makes up the device driver runs in the background, meaning you do not see it running.*

Firewire devices are designed for daisy-chaining, so that one port on the device connects to a port on another device or a Firewire interface card. If you are using a Firewire hub, you will use only one port on the device.

Just to get you started, here is a short list of vendors who supply USB and Firewire hubs and interfaces for PCs:

Ariston Technologies	http://www.ariston.com
Belkin Components	http://www.belkin.com
Interex	http://www.interex.com

Converting Serial or Parallel Devices

What about that serial mouse you love so much and that diehard parallel printer that has served you for many years? Can they, too, take advantage of USB and Firewire technology? In a word, yes. There are several manufacturers of serial and parallel converters, or *adapters*, that enable you to connect serial or parallel devices to USB or Firewire interfaces.

NOTE   *Serial and parallel devices cannot be daisy-chained. Since they are not USB or Firewire compliant, they cannot be used as pass-through devices. You can, however, connect them to a hub or to the end of a chain.*

Before buying an adapter, make certain it is designed for the device you are connecting. Adapters do not always work with all serial or parallel devices. Some devices may require additional drivers. Check with the vendor or manufacturer prior to making the investment to be sure that you are buying the right adapter for your device.

16

Installing Devices

Some Windows systems support a technology called Plug-and-Play. This means that if you connect a compatible Plug-and-Play device—such as a printer, scanner, or monitor—to your computer, the next time you start up your computer, it will automatically recognize the device. Plug-and-Play makes it easy to add peripherals to your system. You just make the physical connections with the appropriate cable and connectors, insert the software that came with your new device into the appropriate disk drive (floppy or CD-ROM), and follow the directions that appear on the screen.

If your new peripheral is not a Plug-and-Play device, you will need to use the Windows Add New Hardware Wizard to let your system know about it. From the Windows desktop, click on the Start button, choose Control Panel, and double-click Add New Hardware. Then follow the instructions on the screen.

Adding a Printer

To really express yourself, you need to produce some tangible form of your creative genius. Even though we are moving toward a more paperless society, physical forms of information—printed material—still provide a purpose. The only question is, which printer is best for your specific needs?

There are several types of printers available. Some printers are more costly than others, but provide various features. You need to consider the the quality you want for your printouts, as well as the speed at which your printer produces its output. The following sections will tell you about each type of printer and its advantages and disadvantages.

> TIP
>
> *Most printers support the standard letter-sized print stock. Others are capable of printing on larger stock. If you intend to produce various sizes of output, make certain the printer you are considering will handle the paper and sizes you require.*

Dot-Matrix Printers

Dot-matrix printers are primarily used for printing multipart forms. They are still out there, although they are not as popular as they once were. These printers are very affordable and provide text-quality output in the form of dots.

A print head consisting of seven to nine firing pins strikes a pin against an ink ribbon to make an impression on the page. Some dot-matrix printers are capable of printing between 300 to 600dpi (dots per inch). This type of quality is fine for text, but not for graphics in most cases.

Here's a summary of the benefits and drawbacks of dot-matrix printers:

Benefits	Drawbacks
Low cost	Moderate print quality
Easy to maintain	Difficult-to-find replacement ribbons
	Prone to jamming and misalignment
	Noisy operation
	Slow speed

Ink-Jet Printers

Ink-jet printers are primarily used for printing medium-quality documents. They are available in black-and-white models, as well as in affordable color models. These printers are a good choice for printing color proofs, short documents, and even high-resolution photographs. The print quality can be good to excellent, depending on the dots-per-inch settings. The higher the setting, the more ink you use, and the slower your printer will print.

Ink-jet printers work by directing a very small spurt of ink onto the page. Each color has its own jet head. Unfortunately, on most ink-jet printers, if you run out of one color, the entire color cartridge must be replaced, even if you have ink in the other color compartments. The only color that can be swapped out separately is black.

Some companies offer recycled toner and ink cartridges. This is often a tempting alternative to purchasing expensive cartridges from the local stationary store. Be careful. If the product used to fill these cartridges is not compatible with your printer, you may end up with a very expensive repair bill. Purchase your cartridges from a reputable source.

Ink-jet printers must be maintained periodically to achieve a good print quality. This maintenance is relatively simple, yet a bit time-consuming. The print heads need to be aligned with a software utility included with the print driver. If the print heads becomes clogged, this same software utility is used to clean them or flush them out. Depending on how often you use your printer, this may need to be done each time you start up your printer or after a period of not being used. Some printers perform this task automatically.

Ink-jet printers have the following benefits and drawbacks:

Benefits	Drawbacks
Affordable color output	Slow to moderate speed
Medium print quality	Moderate head maintenance
Affordable to maintain	Moderate noise
Moderate size	Require ink-jet paper for high-quality printouts
Low noise level	Often require expensive add-on software to support PostScript

Photo Printers

Photo printers often use six colors instead of four, though this trend is changing now that nozzle sizes have been refined to the point of producing droplets as small as four picoliters. For best results, these printers require a special design. If you want to ensure that your photos don't fade over time, you'll want to invest in "archival quality" inks, some of which guarantee a photo life of 200 years. You can print photos on normal-quality paper, but the results will pale in comparison to using high-quality glossy photo paper.

Here are the benefits and drawbacks of photo printers:

Benefits	Drawbacks
Affordable color output	Slow speed
Excellent print quality	Moderate head maintenance
Affordable to maintain	Moderate noise
Moderate size	Requires ink-jet paper for high-quality proofs
Low noise level	Often requires expensive add-on software to support PostScript

16

Laser Printers

If you require high-speed and high-quality output, a laser printer is a good choice. Laser printers are primarily used for black-and-white documents. Color laser printers are also available, but at a considerable cost. Laser printers are much faster than ink-jet printers, but they can be rather costly to maintain, depending on the model.

Laser printers work by charging the paper with positive ions where letters or an image should appear. Toner is negatively charged and, therefore, is attracted to the page where it has been charged. A fusing unit bakes the toner onto the page.

There are various laser printer parts that need to be replaced on a regular basis, including charge coronas, belts or drums, and toner cartridges. In most models, the toner cartridge replaces everything all at once; that is why they are so expensive. In other models, you may need to purchase these items separately. It is a good idea to ask about the printer's maintenance requirements when considering a purchase.

Laser printers have the following benefits and drawbacks:

Benefits	Drawbacks
High speed	Typically expensive toner cartridge replacements
High print quality	High cost for color cartridges or color models
Low maintenance	Large size
Quiet operation	Used cartridges are harmful to the environment so you should dispose of them properly
Moderate cost for black-and-white models	
PostScript support	

Connecting Your Printer

Printers can connect to your system in a variety of ways. They can connect directly to a port on your computer or to a network so that multiple computers can print to the same printer.

 Some printers do not come with a printer cable. Make certain you know what type of connection your printer accepts. You may need to purchase the cable separately.

After connecting your printer to your system, you will need to install the driver that came with the printer. Follow the installation instructions for your specific device.

Adding a Printer on the Printers Folder

In Windows, you manage your printers and print jobs through the Printers Folder, as shown in Figure 16-5. To access a printer from various applications, you must add the printer to your Printers Folder. Many printer driver installation programs do this for you automatically.

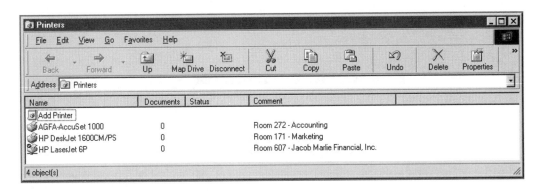

FIGURE 16-5   The Printers Folder

If your new printer does not appear in the Printers Folder, you can add it as follows:

1. From the Windows desktop, click Start and select Settings, Printers.

2. In the Printers Folder, double-click Add Printer.

3. Follow the Add Printer Wizard's instructions to add the printer.

Picking the Printer for a Print Job

You may have more than one printer connected to your system or network. From the Printers Folder, you may select the printer you use most often as your default device. This will be the device on which documents will print when you click the Print icon or button from an application. In the Printers Folder, the default printer is indicated by a check mark in a circle. To specify another printer as the default, right-click it and select Set as Default from the pop-up menu.

If you want to use a printer other than the default for a specific print job, open the File menu from any application and select Print. The application will display the Print dialog box, as shown in Figure 16-6. In this dialog box, you can select any printer that your system knows about (any printer listed in the Printers Folder).

Adding a Scanner

16

Scanners are peripherals that reverse the magic of printers. They take tangible material and convert it into something your computer understands: a complex gathering of shaded dots. Okay, so it is a bit more complicated than that, but to use a scanner, you don't need to know the details of how it operates.

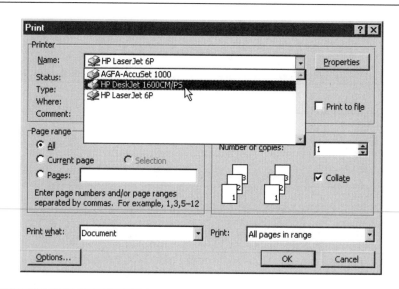

The Print dialog box

All kinds of wonderful things can be scanned. For instance, you can scan your baby's first picture, and then e-mail the photo to the entire family. If you would like to alter a scanned picture, open the image in your favorite image-editing application and use its tools. (Some scanners even come with an image-editing program as a bonus.) Textures and 3D objects can also be scanned to create interesting backgrounds and fills.

Scanners and Resolution

There are several types of scanners on the market today. Some are adequate for scanning in photos to send to family and friends; others are suitable for more serious tasks. A 300dpi scanner will scan in images and produce a 300dpi image that will print on a 300dpi printer just fine. If you take this image and output it to a high-resolution printer that produces 1,440dpi, the image will still look like it did on the 300dpi printer, because you cannot produce more dots than the image has (unless you have an expensive image-enhancing application).

Now, if you take that same image and scan it on a scanner that produces high resolutions, you will end up with an image that can be output to various devices. The trick is to scan the image at the appropriate resolution for the output device. (You can find formulas for determining the most efficient combination in many graphic application books, if you are interested.)

The higher the resolution, the more disk space you need to store the image. For most purposes, a 300dpi scan works just fine. If you intend to enlarge the image, do so while you are scanning it. For instance, if you want the picture to be a half a size larger than the original, scan it in at 150 percent.

> **TIP**
>
> *For Web and other work that will only display on the screen, the rule of thumb is to scan at 72dpi. Anything over 100dpi will be wasted onscreen because of its relatively low display resolution.*

What to Look for in a Scanner

When you are shopping for a scanner, look for one that will do what you need it to do today and in the future. Consider how you intend to connect it to your system. Ask the following questions:

- Does it require a specific interface card? Some scanners require an interface card that may or may not come with the scanner. Make sure the interface card is compatible with your system and that you have a spare slot available.

- Is it parallel, USB, or Firewire compatible? Know how you are going to connect the scanner to your system. You are limited to the number of parallel devices you can connect to your system. You might want to consider a USB or Firewire connection.

- What is the largest size image it can scan? You don't want to buy a scanner and then find out that it can't accommodate the big pictures you want to scan.

- What is the highest resolution it produces? You may want something that can produce more than one resolution. A scanner that can produce an image at 50dpi to 1440dpi is recommended for most applications and can be found at a reasonable price.

- If you want to scan in lots of old photos and/or slides, you need a specialized scanner called a "slide scanner". Check the Web for details. HP and Nikon make particularly good ones. The HP units are among the best bargains.

- Is the stated resolution of the scanner "optical" resolution or "interpolated"? Interpolation is not true resolution, but a software trick to approximate a higher resolution.

Adding Data Storage

Nearly everyone who owns a computer runs out of disk space at one time or another. And there is always that first time when you could just kick yourself for not backing up your work after the only copy you have suddenly becomes inaccessible.

One way to add data storage is to install a new hard drive on your computer, as discussed in Chapter 17. Alternatively, you can use an external drive, or removable-media (diskettes, CDs, and tape) device, to provide extra data storage space.

Drives are funny hardware beasts, so you need to carefully consider the connection you will use:

- If you intend to connect a drive to your USB port, check whether your USB interface supports load balancing. If it does not, you do not want to connect the drive on a bus that supports a printer, scanner, or other load-demanding device, or this will impact your drive's performance. It is like having one bowl of food in front of eight hungry puppies. One is bound to leave hungry.

16

- For the best performance, you may want to consider connecting to a Firewire port.
- Another type of connection you might use is SCSI, the slower alternative to Firewire. A SCSI drive is a bit more complicated to connect. You must configure the drive with a unique SCSI address and ensure the last device on the bus is terminated.

CD-ROM, CD-R, and CD-RW Devices

The CD-ROM (compact disc-read only memory) drive enables your system to read CDs, including audio recordings. As the name implies, you can only read data with this device; you cannot use it for backing up your data.

The CD-R (compact disc-recordable) drive enables you to record up to 650MB of data onto a single disk. This type of device is also known as a WORM (write once read many) device, because you can only record a CD one time; it cannot be erased and rewritten. However, a CD-R can be read many times by any CD device. CD-Rs are cost-effective. If you purchase them in packs of 20 or more, they cost less than a dollar a disk. CD-R disks are recommended if you intend to record music. You can typically record up to 74 minutes of music on one CD-R.

NOTE *See Chapter 11 for details on playing audio CDs and recording music on CD-Rs. For more information about CD-ROM, CD-R, and CD-RW, see Chapter 17.*

If you do not like the idea of being able to record on a CD only once, you may consider purchasing a CD-RW device, which enables you to rewrite over the same CD more than once. Keep in mind, however, that CD-RW disks can only be rewritten a finite number of times. CD-RWs cost considerably more than the CD-Rs.

When you purchase a CD, CD-R, or CD-RW device, make certain it is compatible with your system. It is recommended that you buy one that connects to a USB or Firewire interface. If your system already has SCSI devices installed, you may consider a SCSI solution. In any case, you must install the device driver that comes with your CD drive.

Most CD-R or CD-RW devices come with an application that enables you to easily create a CD. Since the process of creating a CD can be complicated, it is a good idea to have such an application. For example, Hewlett-Packard provides a very intuitive utility that makes creating a CD a pain-free experience.

NOTE *If you want to be able to use the CD-ROM drive while booting from a diskette (in the event your operating system goes berserk), make certain you copy the device drivers and configure your boot diskette—the one your operating system recommends you create.*

For the maximum ease of use of CD-R and CD-RW devices, I suggest that you purchase a program called Adaptec Easy CD Creator Deluxe and DirectCD. DirectCD makes your CD-R or CD-RW as easy to use as a disk drive. You can drag and drop files, rename files, delete files, and create new directories right on your CD-R or CD-RW. The CD-R or CD-RW drive appears just like any other drive in My Computer, Windows Explorer, and file dialog boxes. You can easily save files directly from your word-processing software, spreadsheet, and other applications directly to the CD-R or CD-RW. For tons of more information about choosing CD-R and CD-RW drives, as well as answers to every question you could imagine about recording CD-R, CD-RW, and DVD, see http://www.fadden.com/cdrfaq/.

DVD-ROM Drives

DVD-ROM drives allow your system to read DVDs (digital versatile discs) and CDs. These devices require a high-speed interface to perform optimally. Before considering this type of purchase, make certain your system is equipped with enough RAM (random access memory) and the appropriate interface the DVD device requires. A Firewire interface is highly recommended for DVDs.

Another thing to consider is your video card. A high-performance graphics accelerator card is recommended for watching movies recorded on DVDs. Most of the new PCs sold today are equipped with interfaces that support multimedia devices such as DVDs.

Zip and Jaz Drives

Zip and Jaz devices are wonderful for backing up data. They operate very similarly to a large-capacity floppy disk. The disks they use are compact and easy to transport. The Zip drive, from Iomega Corporation, can store up to 100MB or 250MB of data onto a single disk. These drives are very easy to install and are supported by most print vendors.

The Jaz drive, also from Iomega Corporation, can store up to 1GB or 2GB of information on a single disk.

The driver that comes with these drives makes them simple to install. If you purchase the model that connects to your parallel port, it offers a pass-through port that connects to your parallel printer. This enables you to use your single parallel port for two devices. This type of connection, however, hinders the performance of the drive. If speed is important, you should consider a USB or Firewire connection.

TIP   *For more information regarding Zip and Jaz devices, visit http://www.iomega.com.*

Upgrading Your Monitor

You learned about the essentials of shopping for a new monitor, as part of your PC system, in Chapter 1. As your computer efficiency improves, you may discover that your screen is just not large enough to display all of your stuff, or the image is not as clear as you would like it to be.

When you shop for a better monitor, keep your video card in mind. The video card is the main interface between your system and monitor. If you have a low-end video card, it may inhibit the way a high-performance monitor renders an image or text. A VGA (Video Graphics Accelerator) card with at least 2MB of memory will support most monitors on the market today.

16

The Bigger the Better?

Larger screens allow you to view more data at one time, depending on the resolution you have set. The resolution determines how an image displays on the screen. A higher resolution uses more dots to display the image on your screen, thus making it clearer and sharper.

As explained in Chapter 1, resolution describes the number of dots that are displayed on your screen at any given moment. The higher the resolution, the smaller and clearer your image will be. For example, if you set your display to 640 x 480, your screen will paint the image with 640 *pixels* (dots) across and 480 pixels down. This gives you a total of 307,200 pixels of brilliant color on your screen. If you set your resolution to 1,024 x 768, you will have a total of 768,432 pixels, so you can fit more information on the screen. The image will appear smaller and much clearer than it did at 640 x 480 because it is not as spread out. Unfortunately, the font will also be much smaller. The trick is finding the appropriate balance between resolution and your particular screen size. The larger your screen size, the higher you can set your resolution without going blind.

Document monitors are taller than they are wide. They are designed to display a full document page in readable format. In other words, you can proof an entire page without needing to squint or enlarge the font.

A popular and affordable size for monitors is 17 inches. Anything larger will cost you significantly more money. If you do a lot of work with graphics, you might consider purchasing a 19-inch monitor. Be careful, though—once you use one of these big screens, you may have a difficult time adjusting to something smaller.

Flat Versus Fat

LCD (liquid crystal display) screens, also known as flat screens, were praised in Chapter 1. They display a very sharp picture and do not require a lot of room on your desk. Their downside is that they can be difficult to see under some types of light, such as sunlight. They can also cost you quite a bit more money.

If you decide to get an LCD screen, you can choose between active (active matrix, also called TFT, for thin film transistor) and passive (also called dual scan). The active display has a very fast refresh rate and is more expensive. The passive, dual-scan screen has a slower refresh rate and is somewhat less expensive than the active type. Depending on your personality, one can either fit your work style or drive you completely nuts. If you like a snappy screen that reacts with your every command, then you should consider only active screens. If you don't mind waiting for the cursor to catch up with your lightning-fast mouse action, then the less expensive, slower, passive screen will be sufficient. Some LCD panels can pivot so you can work in either Landscape or Portrait mode. They come with special screen drivers to rotate the image when you swivel the screen. Working in Portrait mode is especially great for Web browsing.

Using a Surge Suppressor

Anything electrical from your computer, modem, printer, scanner, or other electronic device needs to be plugged in, and this leaves them vulnerable to power surges. Most people are familiar with the most spectacular surges—those from lightning. However, other power surges happen constantly, when equipment in your building cycles on and off, causing voltage changes. Although these surges are tiny compared to lightning bolts, they can easily reach 1,000 volts. Gradually, they cause deterioration in circuits and can lead to problems down the road.

To help protect your computer, and those other electronic components connected to it, most computer sellers recommend adding a *surge protector* or *surge suppressor*. If a sudden power surge comes into your home or work space, surge suppressors are designed to grab that extra dose of electricity and displace it safely, avoiding damage to the important and sensitive electronics of your computer's motherboard. However, some surge suppressors simply do not work properly. Those $5 surge suppressors may actually do more harm than good.

Surge suppressors contain small devices called MOVs (metal-oxide varistors), which are designed to absorb surge damage before it reaches your equipment. Basically, MOVs commit suicide to prevent surges from reaching your computer. However, MOVs wear out with use. As an MOV ages, the operating characteristics change making it more sensitive and likely to dissipate more heat (and possibly start a fire!).

Another potential problem is caused by shunting (moving to an alternative course) surges to the ground wire. Your electronic devices are connected to each other through the ground circuit. Conventional surge suppressors using MOVs direct destructive voltage into the network through the "back door" when they divert surges to the ground wire.

In a nutshell, an ineffective surge suppressor can actually cause damage to a computer's motherboard and scramble data sent to interconnected computers, printers, scanners, and modems.

Surge Suppressor Standards

Most suppressors today have the UL (Underwriters Laboratories) 1449 classification (or at least, they should) and are looking to add the UL 1449, Second Edition. However, this is a safety classification, not a performance classification.

NOTE

Underwriters Laboratories, whose "UL" seal is easily recognized on electrical devices in America, has understood the potential fire hazard posed by the failure of certain types of surge suppressors. In the new version of the Standard UL 1449, Transient Voltage Surge Suppressors, surge suppressors must now pass a more stringent fire-safety test to earn the "UL 1449, Second Edition" label. To meet this standard, some manufacturers now use metal enclosures, some have converted to high-temperature plastic, and some use thermal cutout devices.

16

Because there has been no third-party independent testing criteria for surge suppressors, the U.S. government recently developed a set of criteria, using some of the UL's classifications, which in turn use the national standard based on the IEEE's (Institute of Electronic and Electrical Engineers) C62.41-1991 standard.

For interior building use, there are three grades, A, B, and C. Each grade rates the harshness of a surge environment. The IEEE's harshest interior environment, called Category B3, can experience 100 surges of 6,000 volts, 3,000 amps in one year's time. A 6,000-volt surge is the largest voltage transient that should occur in the interior of a building. UL now tests a point-of-use surge suppressor to 1,000 surges of 6,000 volts, 3,000 amps, which is equivalent to 10 years of IEEE's harshest environment! This test, along with UL's lowest suppressed voltage rating category of 330V (UL has established a series of voltages for identifying the voltage-suppression performance of suppressors), is what the government uses in defining a Grade A classification. If a surge suppressor maker meets these specifications and can prove it, you can almost bet the house that you will never have a surge-related failure.

According to one manufacturer, before you buy a suppressor, you should compare the rated service life for various surge levels. Be sure you get one that will do the job for the area you live in. According to the industry guide IEEE 587, a medium-exposure location could have one 6,000-volt surge per year, and a high-exposure location could produce forty 6,000-volt surges per year. So, if you think you are in a high-exposure location, and expect a five-year life from your surge suppressor, it should be designed to withstand at least two hundred 6,000 volt, 3,000 amp surges.

Types of Surge Suppressors

There are two main types of surge suppressors:

- **Shunt mode suppressors**   Many of the low-priced suppressors available today are of the shunt mode variety, which is an older technology. These shunt mode types usually divert power surges to the safety ground wire, using circuits described as "all three modes of protection." Yet, these resulting surges diverted to the ground wire can exceed 1,000 volts, which can harm your computer. Any surge suppressor that diverts surges to the ground wire is called a Mode 2 suppressor. Computers with modems or data lines to other equipment, such as networks and shared printers or scanners, should avoid using Mode 2 surge suppressors.

- **Series mode suppressors**   A new form of surge suppressor uses a series type of suppression. It captures residual energy in a series of capacitors and slowly and harmlessly releases it to the neutral line. There is no surge current diverted to the ground wire, nor are there any MOVs that can wear out. Series mode suppressors are offered by a company called Zero Surge. This company's surge suppressors are rated Grade A endurance, Class 1 performance, and Mode 1 application. These suppressors have a zero response time, unlike the shunt types, which need time to react (letting through spikes).

Using a UPS

Perhaps you have never experienced a power spike, drain, or outage. But if you ever do, you will be happy you have a good surge suppressor. Power drains are often referred to as "brown-outs." These will become important when you are working on the perfect novel and you encounter a power drain before you can save your work. In some cases, a power drain can actually cause your system to reboot.

This is where a UPS (uninterruptible power supply) device saves the day. The basic and sole purpose of a UPS is to provide an uninterruptible source of power for whatever is plugged into it. In your case, it's your computer. If you work on sensitive information or are in a situation where it would be detrimental to have a power loss, consider purchasing a UPS.

Most people have their computer plugged into a power strip or surge suppressor, which in turn, is plugged into your wall outlet. This is the only source of power for the computer. When the lights go out, there is no electricity flowing into the outlet, and the computer goes dead immediately.

A UPS is actually a backup power source that keeps things running for a certain period of time (15–60 minutes), giving you extra time to save your work and shut down the computer properly.

A UPS uses the primary power from your outlet and a secondary backup battery. The primary power is used until the power fluctuates beyond the safety threshold. When this happens, the secondary power kicks in for a short time. Once the primary power is restored, the UPS switches back to the primary power source.

UPS devices work in both AC and DC power arrangements, depending on the type of UPS you purchase. The power from the outlet is always AC. Power from the battery is DC. So, UPS devices contain components (transformers) that switch or convert AC power to DC. A device called an inverter converts the DC battery's reserved power to AC, so you can continue to operate your computer when the outlet source goes dead. When the primary source is used, the battery is recharged.

UPS devices vary in cost as they do in size and power. The bigger the backup battery, the longer it can run your equipment when the power goes off, and usually the more the UPS costs. Some UPS devices provide extra bells and whistles, such as warning sounds or the ability to shut down your computer before the UPS goes dead, too.

A standby UPS, also called an SPS (standby power supply) is one of the least expensive and more popular models. However, in this type, the battery charger is on standby waiting to go into action when the power goes out. Unfortunately, the switch to battery power is not instantaneous, so a small delay occurs. Avoid these types if it is critical that your system does not shut down. Instead, be sure to get a UPS device that is a true online UPS device, where the primary power source is the UPS's battery, and outlet power is the *secondary* power source (the reverse of the standby UPS). Online UPS devices always have current flowing.

Remember that no matter which model you use, the UPS gets plugged into the wall. Your computer and peripherals should be plugged into the UPS device. There are some UPS devices that have an outlet for a surge suppressor, and some UPS devices have built-in surge suppression.

16

Smart UPSs

If you require a bit more functionality from your UPS, many manufacturers offer Smart UPSs that enable you to manage your system remotely, which means you can dial into your system via a modem or connect through a network. Some models can even be set to automatically shut your system down in the event of a power outage.

Another cool feature of some Smart UPSs is a built-in wiring fault indicator, which detects faulty wiring prior to you plugging in your valuable equipment. They also offer two to six outlets so you can plug your system, monitor, printer, and any other device you want protected.

Since battery backups cannot last forever, these Smart UPS devices actually monitor their battery through microprocessor-controlled circuitry. Some models even offer a quick charge feature. In the event that your battery does get low and power restoration is not going to happen soon enough, you can hot swap the batteries without having to shut down your system.

An average Smart UPS for your home or office PC will cost around $300, which is minimal if you compare it to the amount of trouble it will save you in the event of a power outage or brownout. More expensive models are available for servers and network configurations.

TIP

If you have a laptop rather than a desktop computer, you're in luck! You already have a UPS built into your computer. Yup, it's in the form of the laptop's battery. As long as your battery is connected (inserted into the laptop) and charged, you're protected if the AC power blacks out or your dog pulls the plug out of the wall. Your laptop battery will take over automatically, without a hiccup. In my opinion, this is one of the strong advantages of laptops over desktop computers. It has saved me from losing my work more than a few times.

Chapter 17

Upgrading Your PC from the Inside Out

How to...

- Add more RAM to your PC
- Upgrade your hard disk
- Add internal CD, CD-R, and CD-RW drives
- Replace your video card
- Install a new motherboard

In the last chapter, we covered how to expand your computer's abilities by connecting new items to it, sort of like creating a many-headed hydra. But what about adding stuff inside your PC to make it perform better, run quicker, or hold more information?

Some simple upgrades to the innards of your computer can enhance your computing experience significantly. In Chapter 1, I talked quite a bit about choosing a computer system, so you already know that the CPU speed is a prime determinant of the system's speed. But there are other factors that affect your computer's speed and performance, such as the RAM and the hard disk. In this chapter, you'll learn how to upgrade your computer's RAM and hard disk, as well as its video card and motherboard.

NOTE   *Some computers, such as laptop computers and some desktop machines (like the Compaq Ipaq), are intentionally limited in their internal expansion options. These machines can't easily be expanded by putting new cards, drives, and so forth inside of them. You just connect external peripherals to these computers via USB, serial, parallel, PCMCIA, and Firewire ports, as described in Chapter 16. If your computer falls into one of these classes, you can skip this chapter.*

Ramming in More Memory

Windows loves memory, and it intelligently uses the memory it finds in your system. The cheapest and easiest way to improve the speed of your PC is to add RAM. RAM refers to the chips on the motherboard that store your work temporarily while you have a document or program open and running. Think of it like a blackboard in a classroom. When the class is over, the blackboard gets erased. When you're working, RAM is where all your writing and calculating happens. When you turn off your computer, the contents of RAM are erased.

If your computer seems to "hit the hard disk" (sounds sort of like a quiet garbage disposal and cause a little light on your PC to blink on and off a bunch) and run more slowly every time you click on something or move the mouse around, your PC needs more RAM. You should be able to quickly switch between five to ten open programs without a lot of complaining from your PC.

Microsoft states the minimum amount of RAM required for the Windows operating system, but you really need more than that minimum. For example, the published minimum for Windows Me is 32M of RAM, but you'll want at least 64M, and preferably more like 128M.

In general, the more memory you have installed the better. I'm writing this on a 300Mhz Pentium II laptop that has 128M of RAM, and it's plenty zippy. I typically have more than ten programs or windows open doing all manner of things, such as exchanging e-mail and browsing the Web. Another machine of mine has only 64M of RAM and hits the hard disk more, slowing me down.

Shopping for RAM

There are several different types of RAM. RAM is classified based on its speed in storing and retrieving data. Always check with the manufacturer of your computer or motherboard when adding RAM, or you could get something that doesn't work. Here are some of the popular types of RAM, listed in order of speed:

- DRAM (Dynamic RAM)
- EDO (Extended Data Out)
- SDRAM (Synchronous Dynamic RAM)
- RDRAM (Rambus DRAM)
- *n*DRAM

Go shopping for some new memory that matches the kind of board you have (read the motherboard or your PC's manual). If you have a choice of RAM type for your computer, choose the fastest that it can take advantage of. Don't buy faster RAM than the computer can use. It will just be a waste of money!

Be careful where you buy your new RAM. RAM is something you can get really gouged for. It's also a commodity that can be sold in a sub-par quality without your ever knowing it. All you'll know is that your computer suddenly crashes all of the time. You'll want a quality product from a known RAM manufacturer such as Viking or Kingston. If you can buy directly from a good manufacturer, do so. Manufacturers tend to support their products well. They usually offer a lifetime guarantee, and have knowledgeable personnel who can answer specific questions about installation and applications.

Another fairly good source, though the price may be a little higher, is the catalog houses such as CDW or PC Warehouse. Catalog sales are one of the fastest growing marketing tools for the computer industry, just as Web sales are. Make sure to get a good guarantee on the product. In real terms, that means a 30-day return policy, as well as a lifetime warranty. That way, if the memory fails at any point, you can ask for a replacement. If it's well manufactured, memory seldom fails (it has no moving parts except electrons), so this is not a big risk on the memory vendor's part. Besides, the way technology keeps changing, a lifetime warranty really amounts to a 4- to 6-year warranty, even on the most advanced machines. Beyond that amount of time, your system will end up in a museum, if you didn't already donate it to your local charity.

As a last resort, you can buy your RAM from the manufacturer of your computer. But look out! Computer makers typically take you to the cleaners on RAM upgrades, and they usually don't make their own RAM. I have noticed as much as a 300-percent markup in RAM prices advertised by computer makers, relative to competitive "street" prices for direct-from-manufacturer brands.

Installing RAM

Today's computers will automatically detect any memory you install (no switch setting is necessary). Windows will read this setting and use it as necessary. Most RAM comes on DIMM (double-inline memory modules) and is held in place with friction only, as opposed to SIMMs (single-inline memory modules), which use clips.

To avoid damaging your PC, *carefully* install the memory. Here are the basic steps:

1. Unplug the computer.

2. Open the PC case.

3. Find the RAM slots.

4. Touch the metal case with your other hand before inserting the RAM. (RAM chips are very susceptible to damage by static electricity.)

I would suggest buying an air can to blow out the ram slot before inserting. Mine have generally had quite a buildup of dust after a year or so of use.

5. Firmly insert the DIMMs in place, making sure that the module is flush and that all the pins are connecting.

Whenever you insert or remove memory, be careful not to seriously flex the motherboard by pulling or pushing. This could result in a cracked board, which, in effect, wrecks your computer.

6. Replace the cover to the computer and reconnect the cables.

7. Restart your computer. As it boots, check to see that the system reflects the additional RAM you just installed. The system will display the amount of RAM with its other BIOS program reports when it boots Windows. If you miss this line on the screen or want to double-check it, open the Control Panel (click Start, Settings, Control Panel) and select the System icon. The General tab of the System Properties dialog box should show your computer's RAM amount, as in the example in Figure 17-1.

Troubleshooting Added RAM

If the BIOS detects the RAM, you can be assured that it will be detected in Windows, so don't worry about any settings within Windows per se. However, if you've just added RAM to your computer and it doesn't seem to show up in the computer's report of total RAM when it is booting (or from within the BIOS program), there are several things to check:

■ Make sure you purchased the correct type, speed, form factor (physical shape), and capacity of RAM.

■ Make sure you inserted the RAM in the correct slot. Most computers have a few slots for RAM. Many motherboards require that RAM slots be filled in a specific order, or auto-detection of RAM will not work.

■ Double-check that the RAM was inserted correctly and is firmly seated in the computer. With the power off, try removing and reinserting it.

■ If it's still a no-go, remove the RAM (turn off the power first, of course), carefully package the RAM in an antistatic bag, and return it to the dealer to be tested.

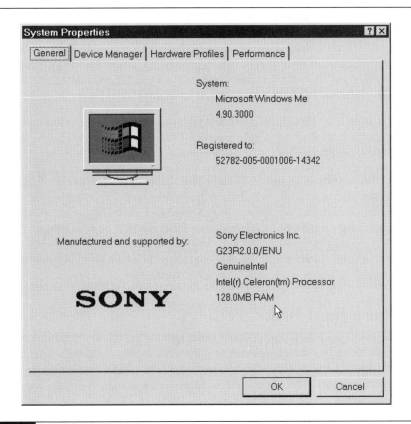

FIGURE 17-1   Checking the amount of RAM in your system

Upgrading Your Hard Disk

If it hasn't happened to you already with some computer, it will one day soon. You'll see an error message from Windows telling you that you are pushing the limits on hard disk space. When a hard disk is near full, it can effectively strangle the operating system, bringing your PC to a crawl. You can free some hard disk space by getting rid of stuff you don't need and by using some hard disk maintenance tools (discussed in Chapter 19), but there are limits to the reclamation possibilities. If you need to store more data than your hard drive will permit, installing a higher-capacity drive may be the best way to go.

17

TIP   *Hard disks are not the only way to get more space, especially if you want the freedom of an infinite amount of storage. See Chapter 16 for information about using removable media, such as CD-ROMs, CD-Rs, Jaz drives, and Zip drives, and later in this chapter for installation of internal CD-R and CD-RW drives.*

If you decide to upgrade your hard drive, you can either replace the existing drive or add another drive. Replacing your old drive has a drawback: You have a lot of good stuff on it that you use and definitely want to keep. There are ways to back it all up, install a new blank drive, and then copy all your old stuff over to it, but that's generally a hassle. Usually, it's easier to just add a second drive and leave the first one in place. Then you'll have a new drive in My Computer (typically labeled D or E) that you can use for storage.

While it can be a hassle to do this, putting your operating system and main programs on a faster drive, such as upgrading from a 5,400–7,200 can result a large speed improvement in your system.

There are two basic types of drives: SCSI and EIDE. Unless you have a pretty fancy PC, you'll have an EIDE drive in it. Today's PCs limit the number of EIDE drives to four. If you need to use more than four drives, you should be running SCSI drives. However, SCSI drives require that you purchase a special SCSI controller card and install it into the computer along with the SCSI drives. Those controllers tend to be expensive, too. Think twice about using SCSI unless you know you need it. People usually only upgrade to SCSI for very specific reasons, such as for high-speed network servers or nonlinear video editing.

Shopping for a Hard Disk

Though SCSI used to be the hands-down winner in the speed wars, the newer Ultra-DMA (sometimes called Ultra-ATA) drives are cheaper and almost as fast. An Ultra2/Wide SCSI and a high-spindle-speed (10,000 RPM) drive will transfer data at 80M bits/second. (Fast-Wide SCSI and Ultra-SCSI are only 20M bits/second, incidentally.) Ultra-DMA drives can transfer data at 66M bits/second.

Your motherboard's BIOS needs to support Ultra-DMA to take advantage of the faster EIDE drives. Some motherboards will support Ultra-DMA 33 only, so an Ultra-DMA 66 drive will only run at 33M bits/second on that machine. Your extra expenditure will be wasted.

Also, look for a drive with a fast access time, with less than 10ms (milliseconds) average access time. (*Average access time,* sometimes called *seek time,* is a specification that will likely be advertised along with the drive's price.)

If you intend to do video editing, you might want to buy a drive that is AV-certified (audio/video certified) and has a 7,200 RPM or faster spindle speed. These drives have faster data transfer and are more consistent in data throughput.

You can check your local computer shop (or discount store that sells it all) or a Web site such as www.buycomp.com for the latest prices on hard disks. As with everything else, they continue to plummet. For less than a couple hundred dollars, you'll be able to get a huge hard disk. I've seen 80G drives for around $300. By the time you read this, that will probably sound old hat.

Installing a Hard Disk

Just as when adding RAM, modern motherboards auto-detect and configure hard disks when you insert them. Using EIDE, you'll have a pretty easy time of getting a drive up and online. They typically come preformatted, but read the instructions with the drive for details. As mentioned earlier, the EIDE specification allows for four drives, one of which is probably your CD-ROM. That typically leaves room for three hard disks (unless you have a CD-RW in your PC, too).

Before you install your new hard drive, read the instructions that came with your new EIDE drive. There usually are drawings and explanation of what to do. If it conflicts with what you read here, follow *their* instructions, not these.

Also, make sure that you have a hard-drive cable that can connect two hard disks in a daisy-chain fashion. It should have three connectors on it: one that goes to the motherboard and two others for connecting to your two hard drives. If you don't have this type of cable, go to a computer store and purchase one.

Here are the steps for installing a hard disk:

1. Unplug the power.

2. Open the PC case.

3. Set the jumper on the new drive to "slave." Make sure the existing (boot) drive is set as the "master" drive. These jumpers are on the back end of the drive and there should be a little plaque or label showing how to change the jumpers. They are typically little, black plugs that you pull off and then push on in a different arrangement. It's a good idea to pull out the primary drive and look at how the jumpers are set on it. If you don't have a little booklet for the drive, it's a good idea to look up the drive maker's Web site and search for the page devoted to your drive. A technical drawing of the jumper settings can likely be found there.

4. Install the new drive in an open bay close enough to the old drive so that the cable will connect easily and properly. Screw in the drive carefully to secure it.

5. Install the data cable so that the two drives and motherboard are all connected. Be sure that everything fits snugly.

6. Locate and connect an extra power-supply wire to power the new drive. There usually are one or two extra ones floating around inside the computer. This wire will come from the power supply and have a plastic molded connector on it with just a few (typically four) wires in it that will plug into a small connector on the back of the drive.

7. Replace the cover to the computer and reconnect the cables.

8. Restart the system. The new drive should be detected.

17

9. Open My Computer to check that you have a new drive listed there. It should show up with about the same capacity available as the box it came in says, but not quite as much (some of the disk's capacity is lost in the formatting process that should have been performed at the factory).

Troubleshooting a New Hard Disk

If your new drive doesn't show up in My Computer (or Windows Explorer), here are several possible reasons:

- There isn't any power to the drive. Check that you wired up the power connector. If there wasn't a spare one, you'll need a power-cable splitter (available at stores like Radio Shack for a buck or two).

- The data cabling is bad. Check that the cables are tight. Try a different cable.

- You didn't set the master and slave jumpers correctly. Look carefully at the back of the drives. If the drives are from two different manufacturers, the arrangement may not look the same. Jumpers could be in different arrangements and locations.

- Although most new computers will do this automatically, you may need to tell the computer's BIOS to auto-detect the drive. Read the manual for the computer to learn how to enter the BIOS settings and adjust this setting.

- Your new drive was not preformatted when you purchased it. Virtually all over-the-counter hard drives these days are preformatted (ready to rock and roll with Windows), but you could have one that is not preformatted. This gets complicated. Refer to a book on hard disks or PC upgrading such as *Troubleshooting, Maintaining, and Repairing PCs, Fourth Edition* (ISBN 0072126868) and read about the FDISK and FORMAT commands, or call the manufacturer of the hard drive for technical support.

Internal Mass Storage

Chapter 16 discusses adding various types of external mass-storage devices, such as CD-RW, Jaz, and Zip drives as peripherals. When you add them internally, there are some additional considerations to keep in mind. Take a look at this list of devices, and their relative storage capacities:

Drive type/name	Storage per disk or cartridge
Zip drive	(100MB/250MB)
Jaz drive	2GB (note: SCSI only)
LS-120 drive	120M
CD-R	650MB
CD-RW	650MB
Tape backup unit (TBU)	Wide variety
Orb drive	2.2 GB

CD-R and CD-RW have fast become the most cost-effective way to do backup, although they are a little tricky to work with. I love CD-RW drives because you, on a single CD, can write about 650MB worth of stuff, and rewrite it virtually as many times as you like. Many experts believe that CD-RW disks will be a popular storage medium until DVD devices become widely available. (DVD can potentially store up to 17GB of data on a CD-sized disk, though we're probably not going to see more than half of that in consumer-grade PCs.) I recently purchased CD-R media for as little as 10 cents per disk! Compare that to a spare 2GB Jaz drive disk, which runs about $100. Admittedly, Jaz drives are much faster, though.

With the exception of the Jaz, they are all available as EIDE devices, which means you'll hook them up much like the hard disk installation described in the section above. Remember that you are only allowed four EIDE devices in a PC, so if you have already have a situation such as this:

- Hard drive   Master on EIDE channel 1
- Hard disk   Slave on EIDE channel 1
- CD-ROM   Master on EIDE channel 2

then you only have room for one new device. It will have to be a slave, on channel two.

Internal expansion drives such as CD-R and CD-RW drives often have jumpers on them just like hard drives do. Make sure to check their settings and read the manual carefully when installing an internal drive to make sure you have the master/slave relationships set properly, or the drive(s) on that channel may fail to work at all.

You should have hard drives on the same cable (also called a *channel*), and slower devices on the other channel. This is because a channel is limited by the slowest device on it. Hard drives are way faster than the devices listed above. So, things like CD-RW and Zip drives should go on the second EIDE channel.

Upgrading Your Video Card

As you learned in Chapter 13, if you have a weak video card, you will not be able to play many of the great 3D games that are available for PCs. If you want to keep up with the video-game industry, you may need to purchase a new video card every 12 months. Another reason you might need to install a video card is to be able to run multiple monitors on your system (which was covered in detail in Chapter 13). Finally, you may want to add a single card that has multiple functions such as video capture and TV tuning.

Shopping for a Video Card

Before you begin shopping for a video card, you should determine whether your PC comes with an AGP video card or a PCI type video card. You'll need to buy the correct type of video card for your PC. If you have a new PC (one built in the year 1999 or 2000), it almost certainly uses an AGP-type video card. AGP (Accelerated Graphics Port) was developed with gaming and live-motion video in mind, so the computer display can keep up with the action. Some older video cards plug into the PCI connectors, which can do a credible job for most work and play.

17

In Chapter 1, we talked about the available slots your computer might have for inserting cards. Most likely, your computer has a few PCI slots, and it probably has an AGP slot as well. Refer to Figure 1-8 in Chapter 1 for a picture of a motherboard with these slots.

Many motherboards have AGP-based video chips built into them. If you pop the top of such a computer, no external card will be plugged in or visible, so you might wonder where the video card is or what kind you have. One way to check your video card (display adapter) type is through the Control Panel (click Start, Settings, Control Panel). Select the System icon and click the Device Manager tab. Then click on the + sign next to Display Adapters to see the type of card installed, as shown in Figure 17-2.

The technology for video cards changes very rapidly, and prices steadily drop. Good cards are available for as little as $100, although you can pay $300 or so for a very fast one. Better video cards typically have a lot of their own RAM on them (called VRAM, for video RAM).

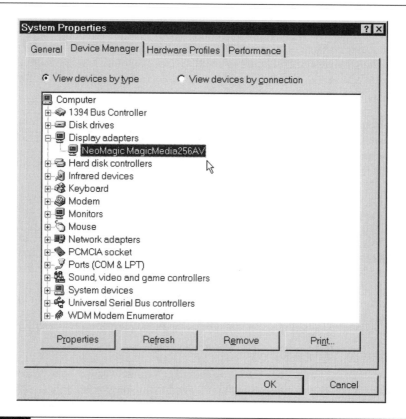

FIGURE 17-2　Checking your video card (display adapter) type

The RAM on these cards actually stores the screen image in it, with each little dot on the screen corresponding to RAM locations in the chips on the video card. (This is called *memory-mapped video*). A *co-processor* chip on any decent video card does most of the work of moving the image around, which frees your system's CPU for other work.

If you're getting a new video card because you want to play games, make sure that it's a 3D card, preferably a powerful 3D card based on the Voodoo or Nvidia chips. Today's 3D action games and strategy games *require* a 3D card. This means the chip on the video card must be capable of drawing in three dimensions (X, Y, and Z). Older, 2D video cards simply cannot do this.

> **NOTE** *Older games were very accommodating to gamers. Even if you had a generic 2M video card, you could still play games such as Duke Nukem, Doom, and Quake. However, if you buy a newer game, released in 1999 or later, 3D hardware acceleration is required to play the game. The reason for this is that the game places enormous demands on the video card during gameplay.*

Competing brands of video card makers make great claims about their co-processors and their proprietary video-card design. I suggest checking out computer magazines or gaming magazines, if you're upgrading primarily to play games. For other applications, you can check with the maker or documentation supplied with the program(s) you want to run. For example, if you're running photographic or video software, a specific card with an accurate color-matching system may be recommended by your software maker to ensure that your printed output matches what you see on the screen.

Installing a Video Card

If your computer has a built-in adapter, you may need to manually disable the onboard one before installing a new video card; otherwise, there will be a conflict. This is often achievable from the computer's BIOS settings. For example, some motherboards make you disable the on-board video via a jumper or other switch on the motherboard; others will detect a new video card and disable the on-board automatically. Check your computer's manual for any special instructions regarding the addition of a new video card.

To install a new video card, follow these instructions:

1. Unplug the computer. Put it up on a table so you can see what's going on.

2. Remove the cover and set it aside. After you've removed the case, lay the PC on its side.

3. Find the video card in your PC. To find it, look at the back of your PC monitor. Follow the cable that connects your monitor to your PC. Your monitor cable is almost certainly connected to your video card.

17

> **NOTE** *As noted earlier, some PCs do not use a video card, but rather have their video chip on the motherboard. If you can't find your PC's video card, chances are the video is on the motherboard; usually "business" PCs have this setup. (People at work shouldn't need to upgrade their video card!) These PCs can be difficult to reconfigure for a new video card.*

4. Detach the monitor cable from the video card. Unscrew the screw holding down the video card. You will need a Philips head screwdriver for this screw.

5. Ground yourself by touching the metal case.

6. Using two hands, pull out the video card from its slot. This is a delicate operation. You will need to grab the video card on its edge and somewhere on the top, and then gently but firmly pull the video card straight out of its slot. This should require a little force because the card will be seated in the slot tightly.

7. Lay the old video card on a table or a chair. Do not put it on a carpet or rug, or it could get fried by an electric shock.

8. Line up the new video card connector with the connector slot on the PC's motherboard.

NOTE *If you've inherited an older PC, it may have a 3D video card and an older 2D video card. This is often the case for older Voodoo 3D cards. These types of two-card systems are now obsolete. Remove both cards and go buy a new 2D/3D video card instead.*

9. Screw in the new card securely.

10. Replace the cover to the computer and reconnect the cables

11. Restart your computer.

12. Windows will probably recognize that you have a new video card. It may prompt you to insert the Windows CD. (Check the manual or quick setup guide that came with the video card to determine how to proceed.) Most likely, you'll need to insert the CD or floppy disk that came with the video card and run its installation program. Follow the instructions.

13. The adapter may have a fine-tuning tool or an addition to the Control Panel's Display tool. Use it for adjusting various aspects of your new video card.

NOTE *For information about installing a second video display card (typically for gaming) and installing a video card when you don't hade the necessary driver, please see Chapter 13.*

Replacing Your Motherboard

As mentioned in Chapter 1, the *motherboard* is the main circuit board in your PC. It holds the CPU, the RAM, and expansion cards, among other things. Some people who get into playing computer jock take to buying a new motherboard on a regular basis as a means of speeding up their computer. With the price of motherboards being what they are (not very expensive unless a CPU chip and RAM chips are installed in them), it's not a bad way to go. Every couple of years, motherboard technology improves radically, and so swapping out the old for the new can actually result in significant speed improvements, even if you don't change anything else (such as the hard disk and CD-ROM).

Unless you know what you're doing and like to tinker with your computer, I recommend buying a complete and tested system from a name-brand manufacturer, rather than replacing your motherboard. If all you want to do is increase your hard disk space or add RAM, you can upgrade either one, as explained earlier in this chapter.

Shopping for a Motherboard

When shopping for a motherboard, ideally you'll want a modern one that will support a high-speed CPU. Look for the following features:

- Compatible with your Windows operating system
- Plug-and-Play (PnP); check that it has an actual Plug-and-Play BIOS
- Support for the ACPI power management scheme (not just APM)
- A reasonably quick processor (in the 500 to 800MHz range), such as a Pentium Celeron, Pentium II, Pentium III, AMD K6 2, or AMD K6 III
- A 100MHz internal bus or faster
- Support for AGP graphics
- A flashable BIOS for later upgrading
- Designed around the speed and type of processor you have in mind for your system.

You can easily check if a type of motherboard is compatible with Windows Me (or the Windows version you're using). Microsoft regularly tests equipment of various types to ensure that it is compatible with its various operating systems, and adds the results to its Hardware Compatibility List. You can view this information at www.microsoft.com/hcl, as shown in Figure 17-3.

There are many sites on the Web that sell motherboards, such as www.motherboards.com. There is also a raft of information about motherboards on the Web, as well as newsgroups about the topic. Figure 17-4 shows the list of newsgroups about motherboards I found in just a few seconds, using Outlook Express. (See Chapter 8 for more information about newsgroups.)

Choosing a motherboard is somewhat complicated, and you'll want to read up on the latest technology before you invest in one. Pay particular attention to the bus speed and the support chipset. The *chipset* is the collection of chips that handle the interaction of the CPU, RAM, and other elements of the motherboard. Some people claim that the chipset is even more important than the CPU itself in determining the overall performance of a computer. The Triton 2 and Triton 3, from Intel, are two of the fastest Pentium chipsets. You can upgrade your computer's CPU, memory, and hard disk, but the motherboard has been designed around the capabilities of the chipset. Until you change the motherboard, your PC will function largely the same way. You cannot upgrade the chipset on a motherboard; you need to replace the whole motherboard.

Also, check that the motherboard you purchase matches the power supply and chassis you already have, or you'll end up needing to buy a new chassis and power supply to go along with your new motherboard. Chassis and power supplies come in two types: ATX and AT. The size

17

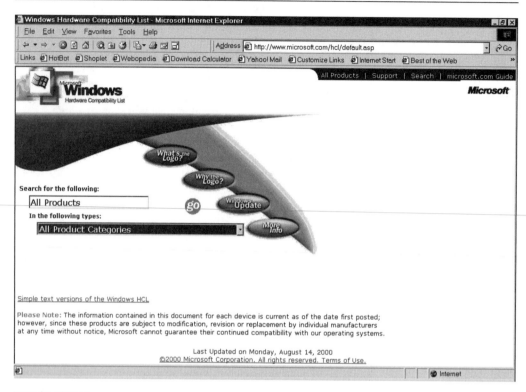

| FIGURE 17-3 | Use the online Microsoft Hardware Compatibility List to check any kind of hardware before you purchase it |

and placement of connectors, as well as the spacing of the expansion slots, differ between AT and ATX types. The primary advantage of an ATX motherboard is that it has more elaborate power management. For example, the power supply can be shut down and activated through software controls.

Installing a Motherboard

Installing a motherboard is tricky business, because there are a lot of screws and wires to connect. Here are a few points to keep in mind when replacing a motherboard:

- Unplug all external AC connections and external cables before you begin.
- Put the computer on a table in a well-lit workspace.
- Remove the cover completely and get it out of the way.

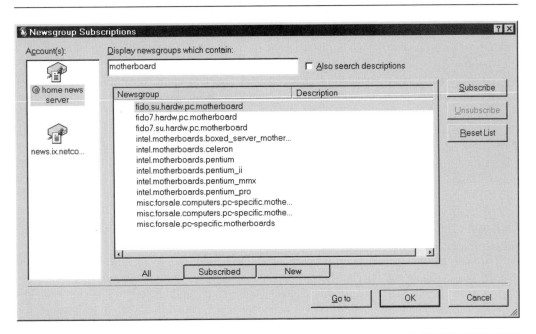

FIGURE 17-4   Newsgroups about motherboards abound

- Make a drawing of where the cables go and how they are connected. You may want to label them. Remember that you'll need to put them back on the new motherboard.

- Make sure the motherboard isn't stressed, bent, warped, or touching the metal chassis except at the support points after you install the new one.

- Don't connect or disconnect any cables while power is applied to the motherboard.

- Handle RAM chips carefully. Make sure you are grounded and have neutralized any static charge before you handle RAM chips. Touch the chassis first, then handle the RAM; otherwise, you may damage the chips' innards.

Troubleshooting a New Motherboard

Once you get into the finer points of installing and testing new motherboards, you'll likely become at least a little obsessed with making your new baby run as quickly and smoothly as possible. It's sort of analogous to souping up a hot-rod car by swapping in a new engine. (I used to do that too, but got really tired of having grease under my fingernails!) Troubleshooting and tweaking your motherboard can be a lot of fun. Be sure to check the manufacturer's Web site for troubleshooting help should you need it. Most motherboard makers have extensive support information on their sites, including flash-BIOS and driver downloads.

17

Chapter 18

Tweaking Windows

How to...

- Customize your desktop's look and feel
- Add and remove fonts
- Adjust mouse settings
- Assign sounds to system events
- Set Internet Explorer options
- Remove programs
- Set e-mail options
- View system properties

Windows is a flexible operating system that you can tweak to suit your own needs and preferences. Most of the tools you will use to customize your system reside in the Control Panel. As its name implies, the Control Panel contains applets (mini-applications) that allow you to control the way that your system looks and adjust some of its behavior.

You have quite a few choices when it comes to customizing the appearance of your screen. If you're the creative type, you'll enjoy playing with your wallpaper, screen saver, colors, and fonts.

Behavior options include modifying your mouse's button and speed settings, selecting distinct sounds that let you know what's going on with your system, defining specific characteristics for your Web browser, and setting your system's date and time. You also have the power to remove applications from your system. (Just don't get too carried away with this tool, or you may end up removing something you need.)

Accessing the Control Panel

Because the Control Panel is your path to many tasks, you've read about some of its applets in previous chapters. To access the Control Panel, click the Start button, select Settings, and then select Control Panel. You'll see the Control Panel window, as shown in Figure 18-1.

 Depending upon the toys and applications you have installed, this Control Panel may have a few more options than are standard with your operating system. For example, some modems have a utility program that enables you to organize mail and faxes. This chapter concentrates on common, standard Control Panel options that enable you to customize your system environment to your satisfaction.

Okay, so now you have the Control Panel open. Just what do all of those icons do? Here are brief descriptions of the most commonly used icons in the Windows Me Control Panel:

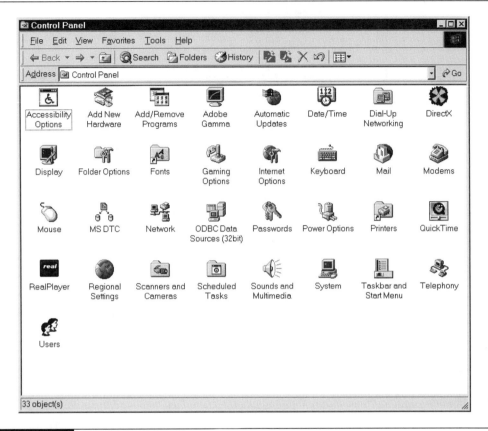

FIGURE 18-1 The Control Panel

Add/Remove
Programs

Walks you through the process of adding or removing applications

Date/Time

Lets you change the date and time settings on your system

Display

Allows you to set the colors and fonts for your application windows

18

Fonts

Lets you add or remove fonts that are available to your applications

Internet
Options

Defines how your Web browser (Internet Explorer) behaves

Mail

Allows you to set up e-mail services on your system

Mouse

Defines the way your mouse behaves, depending on your personal preferences

Sounds and
Multimedia

Lets you tweak your sound card, video, and CD settings, as well as pick the sounds played when the system performs a given task like booting up, starting an application, or displaying an error

Printers

Enables you to add, remove, and manage the printers that are available to your system (this applet is discussed in Chapter 16)

System

Displays information regarding your system's performance and configuration

Customizing Your Desktop's Appearance

By far, the most popular way in which you can customize your system is by altering the look and feel of your desktop—the virtual one that greets you every time you launch Windows. Figure 18-2 shows an example of a plain desktop, ripe for some enhancements.

If you do not fancy the standard Windows color scheme, you can change it, along with the screen fonts and wallpaper. Yes, you read that correctly—*wallpaper* is the background image behind all of those icons. By default, the wallpaper is set to a very stylish shade of green. How boring is that?

FIGURE 18-2   You can make a desktop like this more visually interesting

To change the way your desktop looks, open the Control Panel window and double-click the Display icon. You'll see the Display Properties dialog box, as shown in Figure 18-3. By default, the Background page is active when you open the Display Properties dialog box. To view another page's options, click the tab for that page at the top of the dialog box.

TIP   *As a shortcut to the Display Properties dialog box, you can also place your mouse pointer anywhere on an empty area of the desktop area (not on an icon) and click your right mouse button. From the pop-up menu, select Properties.*

Picking a Pattern

The Background tab offers two background options: Pattern and Wallpaper. Patterns are an economical to way to flash a bit of color onto your desktop without paying the price of memory. Patterns are made up of lines and dots instead of a rendered bitmap image. Therefore, they do not

18

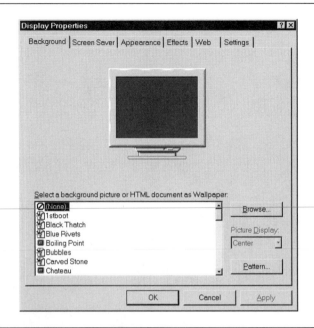

FIGURE 18-3   The Display Properties dialog box allows you to customize the look and feel of your desktop

require as much RAM (random access memory) as wallpaper. With most new computers, you don't need to worry about the amount of RAM consumed by your choice of desktop background, but you just might prefer a soothing pattern.

NOTE   *When an application is launched, it knows how much RAM it requires for frequently accessed files and allocates (reserves) that amount of memory in RAM. So, when your operating system boots up, it knows what it needs to display on your desktop and allocates that amount of memory in RAM. See Chapter 17 for more information about RAM and adding RAM to your system.*

Patterns can be only one color and do not vary much. You can select one of the many standard patterns or edit a pattern to make it more interesting.

To select a pattern, follow these steps:

1. Click the Pattern button in the Background tab of the Display Properties dialog box (refer to Figure 18-3).

2. In the Pattern dialog box that appears, click the name of the pattern you want displayed. You'll see a preview of the pattern in the monitor at the top of the dialog box.

3. If you want to edit that pattern, click the Edit Pattern button. Change a color square to black by clicking the square (pixel). If you want to change it back, click the square again.

4. When you are finished, click the Done button.

5. Click OK to close the Pattern dialog box.

6. Make sure that the Wallpaper selection is set to None, then click the Apply button. (To see the pattern, you must set the Wallpaper selection to None.)

The background color for all patterns is determined by the Desktop color on the Appearance tab. If this color is set to black, you will not see any patterns.

Selecting Wallpaper

Wallpaper is nothing more than a bitmap, which is an image that was rendered from a complex arrangement of pixels (dots). Since bitmaps can consist of several color and pixel combinations, the resulting file requires more memory to display than patterns require.

To select a wallpaper image, click on the name of the wallpaper image you want displayed in the Background tab of the Display Properties dialog box (refer to Figure 18-3). The bitmap images that are used as wallpaper on your desktop are commonly stored in the WINDOWS directory under the C: drive, and these are the choices that you see in the dialog box's list box. If you were to look for this path in Windows Explorer, it would look like C:\WINDOWS. Under this directory, all files that end with the extension .bmp, are available in the Wallpaper list. If you have a bitmap image stored in another location, you can click on the Browse button to select that image from its associated location.

Next, choose how you want to display the image by selecting an option in the Picture Display drop-down list. There are three ways wallpaper can be displayed on your screen:

- **Tiled**   If you have a small bitmap image, it is best to tile it over your screen. This repeats the image over the entire display space, sort of like the tiles on a wall.

- **Centered**   If you have a larger image, it looks best centered on the screen.

- **Stretched**   High-resolution images (greater than 72dpi) can be stretched to fit the display. However, unless the image was designed for this purpose, it does not always look as good as you might imagine.

The monitor at the top of the dialog box will show what your selected wallpaper looks like. When you're satisfied with your choice, click on the Apply button.

TIP   *If you are surfing the Web and happen to come across a fine-looking picture you would like to display on your desktop, right-click over the picture. From the pop-up menu, select Set as Wallpaper. Some photo-editing or graphics applications have a similar menu choice.*

18

Active Desktop

If you want, you can add some interesting Web-like features onto your desktop using a feature called *Active Desktop*. With Active Desktop, you can keep your Internet Explorer home page right at hand even when you don't have a Web browser open, or you can view online information in real-time. For example, you might want to monitor a stock ticker, local ski conditions, or the weather.

To enable Active Desktop, click the Web tab of the Display Properties dialog box. Check the box for the Show Web content on my Active Desktop. Now you have to choose the Web content you want to display on your desktop. If you just want to see your current home page (as set in Internet Explorer), put a check mark next to My Current Home Page. So for example, if you if your home page is currently www.nytimes.com, you'll see the *New York Times* front page as your desktop, with the icons sitting right on top of it.

To check out other options, such as stock tickers, weather, daily comic strips, etc., connect to the Internet and click New, Visit Gallery. The Gallery Web page will list lots of Active Desktop items you can choose from. Follow onscreen instructions to add them to your list of options. Next, put a check mark next to the ones you want to display and click Apply. Once they are displaying, you can position the Active Desktop items on your desktop by moving the pointer over them and then dragging them from their title bars. Figure 18-4 shows my desktop with a weather map, sports updates, and a very weird clock with flying numbers.

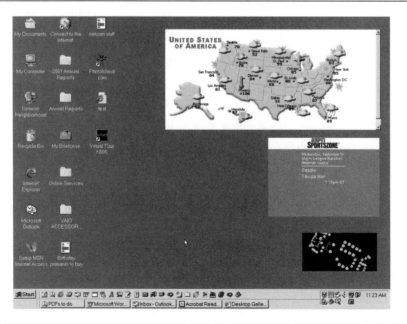

FIGURE 18-4   You can make your desktop come alive with streaming information by turning on Active Desktop

When the Active Desktop concept was first introduced, people were excited about it. It turned out to be a little buggy, though. As a result companies other than Microsoft, have begun to offer similar alternatives to this so-called "push" functionality. For example, AOL Instant Messenger (www.aol.com) and Entry Point (www.entrypoint.com) have news and stock tickers you might also want to check out.

NOTE *The Web option requires a bit more memory to operate than the standard desktop. If you find your performance is hindered, you may not want to use this option.*

Setting Other Display Properties

The other pages of the Display Properties dialog box allow you to further modify the way your desktop and windows look.

The Screen Saver page, shown in Figure 18-5, lets you set a screen saver for your desktop. A screen saver is an image that appears after a certain period of system inactivity. For example, you can set a picture of outer space to appear on your screen after your computer has not been used for 20 minutes. You can also specify a password, so that after the screen saver comes on, you must enter a password to reactivate your system. This is a security measure that prevents just anyone from using your computer when you are away from it.

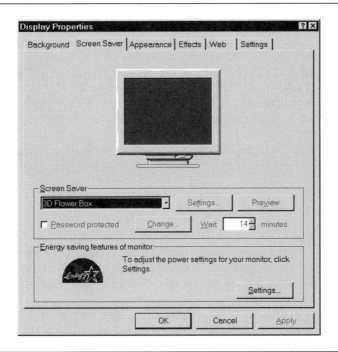

 FIGURE 18-5   The Screen Saver page of the Display Properties dialog box includes a choice of screen savers and screen saver settings

18

Originally, screen savers were designed to save your monitor. If a monitor displayed the same image for a long period of time, the phosphors on the screen began to burn and an image was left on the screen as a ghost-type image. Modern monitors do not have this burn-in problem. Nowadays, screensavers are mostly for fun.

Most of the time, computers sit around twiddling their thumbs waiting for something interesting to happen, such as you typing on the keyboard or clicking your mouse. This is especially true when a screen saver is running. Basically, it's a waste of energy. Since your computer could actually be doing something useful when the screen saver is running, scientists at the University of California in Berkeley got the idea to harness that wasted computing power to create the world's largest supercomputer. Over 1.5 million PC owners have signed up over the Internet to let their PCs be used for a big scientific experiment during those otherwise wasted periods. The experiment, called SETI@home (SETI stands for Search for Extraterrestrial Intelligence, a NASA program that listens for radio noises from space), hopes to detect signs of life from other planets. Install the SETI@home screen saver, and your computer becomes part of the supercomputer, sifting through millions of bits of radio noise from outer space, looking for that special squeak, warble, grunt, or mathematical secret code from ET saying "Hi." Visit http://setiathome.ssl.berkeley.edu/ for more on how it works and how to participate in this exciting program.

The Appearance page, shown in Figure 18-6, enables you to fine-tune the way your windows look. Here, you can change your background color, window colors, and fonts. You can even name your personalized settings by clicking on the Save As button. To change the look of an element on your computer's screen, click on it in the example area of the dialog box, and then choose the color, font size, and so on. For example, to change the color of your desktop, click the desktop area (or choose it from the Item list), and then click the Color selector.

If you are less inclined to customize everything, there is a variety of predefined schemes from which to choose.

The Settings page, shown in Figure 18-7, includes settings for the system colors and the screen's resolution (the number of dots that display on the screen at a given time).

Be careful not to set the refresh rate above what your monitor can support, or you run the risk of damaging the monitor.

By changing the resolution, you can get more stuff on the screen at one time. Of course, there's a price to pay for this: everything will be become smaller to the eye. On a 17-inch monitor, I like running at 1,024 x 768 pixels. But if that is too blurry, try out 800 x 600 pixels. If you have an LCD screen, remember that this type of screen is always optimized for one specific resolution, typically 800 x 600, or 1,024 x 768. Changing it to a resolution other than the optimized one will result in a blocky display, or on some machines will decrease the size of the display area.

FIGURE 18-6   The Appearance page of the Display Properties dialog box controls the look of windows and dialog boxes

Managing Fonts

Fonts provide a variety of text styles that can spiff up your documents and better convey your message to the audience you are hoping to reach. Let's consider some basic font terminology before getting into how to install, view, and remove fonts. Actually the word *font* as used with PCs replaces the word *typeface* that professional typesetters traditionally use. You might have noticed that many of your applications allow you to choose the font you are typing in, as well as the *typesize* of the font.

Serif fonts, such as Times Roman, have extra strokes on the end of each letter. This type of font is easy to read in printed form and is commonly used for paragraph text. The text you are reading here is printed in a serif font, in fact. *Sans serif* fonts, such as Arial, resemble block-style lettering. This type of font is commonly used for headings and online documentation because it is easy to read on a monitor. *Script* fonts have the look and feel of handwriting, only neater and easier to read. This type of font is reserved for special uses such as invitations or announcements. A final category of font is called *display type,* and is used very judiciously, typically for signs, posters, flyers and the like.

18

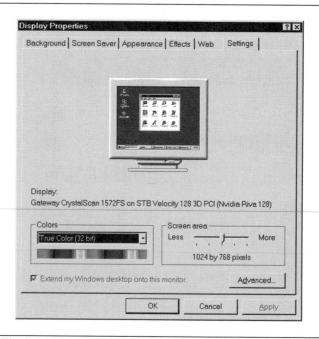

FIGURE 18-7 The Settings page of the Display Properties dialog box lets you set the colors and resolution for your screen

Fonts also break down into two groups called *proportional* and *monospaced*. Most modern fonts are proportionally-spaced, meaning that thin letters such as "l" take up less horizontal space than wider ones such as "W." This makes the text pack together to get more on a line and improves its aesthetic. Times Roman, for example, is a proportionally-spaced font. By contrast, Courier is a monospaced font. Courier is often used when you want all letters and numbers to be given the same amount of horizontal space, forcing vertical columns of letters or numbers to line up properly. (Aligning columns can be achieved with proportionally-spaced fonts too, but you have to use a tab stops, tables, or some other trick to make the spacing work out.) Using monospaced fonts lets you align columns just like using a typewriter—you adjust the alignment by pressing the keyboard's spacebar or backspace key.

TIP *If you intend to share your files with other people, it is highly recommended that you use a standard Windows font, such as Times New Roman, Arial, Veranda, or Courier New. That way, they are more likely to be able to see and read the file as you laid it out. If the recipient of a file doesn't have the intended font installed in their system, Windows will substitute a similar, though not identical, font. To get around this, there are ways to "embed" fonts into your files (even into Web pages). This ensures your readers can see them, but it might require some study to understand the best ways to implement this feature. In MS Word, check the Tools, Options, Save dialog box, and turn on "Embed TrueType Fonts."*

Fonts can be stored anywhere on your system, but they must be added to the Fonts folder before they can be accessed by your applications. The Control Panel's Fonts applet is your entry to the Fonts folder. When you double-click on the Fonts icon in the Control Panel, you see the Fonts folder window, as shown in Figure 18-8.

 If your applications are taking longer than usual to start up, you might have too many fonts installed.

You may notice that some fonts in your Folders window have a printer, a TT, or an O icon preceding the font name. The printer icon means the font is a PostScript font. If your printer does not support PostScript, this type of font may not print the way you expect it to. For example, a bullet may look rather interesting—instead of the expected dot, you might see something like a symbol. The TT icon means the font is a True Type font. True Type fonts appear the same on the screen as they do in your printed output. (If you are sending your files that contain TrueType fonts to a service agency for printing, make sure their printer supports True Type fonts.) The O stands for OpenType, the successor to TrueType.

Fonts are available from many locations, including from professional font "foundaries"— companies that specialize in the design of beautiful and functional typefaces. They are also available quite freely over the Internet. In general, you get what you pay for. Cheap fonts can look just that way—cheap. Professional fonts can include special features such as foreign characters, old-fashioned numerals, small caps, ligatures, symbols, and kerning "hints" that

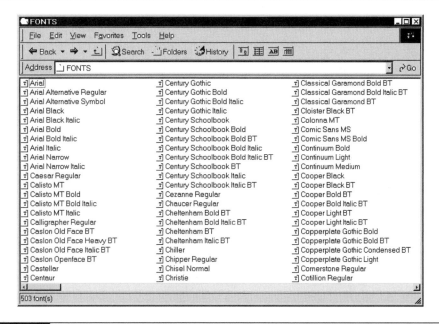

FIGURE 18-8   The Fonts folder shows the fonts that your applications can access

18

make the font print out more attractively. For professional fonts, check out www.monotype.com, www.bitstream.com, www.adobe.com. You can find inexpensive or free fonts at www.buyfonts.com and www.fontcafe.com/showcase/.

When you download a font from an Internet site, save it to a personal font directory on your hard disk. Then install it in your Fonts folder, as follows:

1. Open the Control Panel and double-click the Fonts icon to access the Fonts folder window.

2. Click the File menu and select Install New Font. The Add Fonts dialog box will be displayed.

3. From the Add Fonts dialog box, select the drive and folder containing the fonts you want to install.

4. Turn on Copy Fonts to Fonts Folder if you want the font files stored in the Fonts folder. They don't have to be copied there, though I suggest doing so, just so you have all your fonts in one location.

5. Once the list of fonts is displayed, select the fonts you want to install, and then click OK.

To delete a font, just access your Fonts folder through the Control Panel, select the font to remove, and press the DEL key.

If you want to select more than one font, select the first font, then hold your CTRL *key down to select other fonts.*

Viewing a Font

You can display a font to see what it looks like by double-clicking it in the Fonts folder. This will open a window showing all the letters of the font in different sizes. The copyright information is also displayed in this window.

Tuning Your Mouse

The Control Panel's Mouse applet lets you adjust features associated with your mouse, including some button functions and pointer actions. When you double-click on the Mouse icon in the Control Panel, you'll see the Mouse Properties dialog box, similar to the one shown in Figure 18-9. The specific settings available for your mouse depend on the type of mouse you have installed. Here, we'll look at the common mouse functions that can be tweaked with most mouse drivers.

The actual mouse icon shown in the Control Panel, as well as the properties, may vary. For example, if you have a Logitech mouse and its associated drivers, you will see a little, purple mouse icon, which launches a custom mouse properties dialog box when selected.

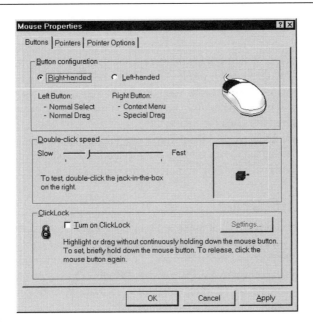

FIGURE 18-9   The Mouse Properties dialog box allows you to control your mouse settings

Configuring Mouse Buttons

Many mice are designed for either right-handed or left-handed people. Some devices are ergonomically designed for one hand or the other. Through the Buttons page of the Mouse Properties dialog box (see Figure 18-9), you can specify how you want your buttons to work. Typically, on a right-handed mouse, clicking or double-clicking with the left command button makes selections or opens items such as folders and files. Clicking with the right command button opens a pop-up menu for the selected item. If you switch your mouse buttons to operate as a left-handed mouse, the button assignments are reversed.

 For lefties, mouse instructions can get confusing, such as when someone tells you to right-click on an item. For left-handed users, it is really a left-click. Of course, "southpaws" are accustomed to such idiosyncrasies. Some may find it fun to switch the buttons just to drive the right-handed folks nuts.

Some mice also include a third button or a mouse wheel. The middle (third) button can be set to perform a variety of actions. For example, you can set it to copy selected text to the Clipboard when clicked. That is a very helpful function if you do a lot of copying. The mouse wheel often

18

doubles as a middle button when pressed. This handy little feature acts like a scroll bar. Instead of needing to click the up and down arrows in your right scroll bar, all you do is turn the wheel. This is a very cool tool when you are surfing the Internet or viewing documents.

Some mouse drivers allow you to change the way that the mouse behaves when selecting or opening files or folders. You might see a single-click option that causes a file to open when the mouse is clicked only once, as opposed to the standard double-click action. If the single-click option is selected, a file will be selected automatically when the cursor is placed over the file name, and then opened when you click the button once.

You can also adjust the double-click speed if you find it difficult to open folders or files. If you have a slow clicker finger, reduce the double-click to a comfortable speed. If, on the other hand, you have a super-speedy clicker finger, increase the double-click speed.

Picking a Pointer Scheme

Mouse pointers are the little graphics that move across your screen when you move the mouse. They let you know where your cursor is currently located.

The Pointers page of the Mouse Properties dialog box, shown in Figure 18-10, allows you to customize the various mouse pointer icons. Just for fun, Windows provides some rather cool pointer schemes to keep you entertained, including animated icons that do special things when you perform given actions such as opening a file or program.

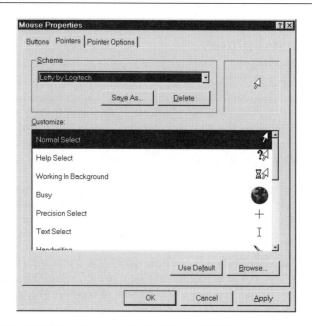

FIGURE 18-10   The Pointers page of the Mouse Properties dialog box lets you customize your mouse pointer scheme

Setting Pointer Options

This Pointer Options page of the Mouse Properties dialog box, shown in Figure 18-11, offers options to adjust your mouse speed, behavior in a dialog box, and appearance.

This page has three sections of options you can set:

■ **Pointer Speed** The slider in this section sets the speed at which the cursor moves across your screen when you move your mouse. Some people like this movement to be slow and steady like a bicycle; others like it to be extra responsive, like a race car. The Accelerate button lets you set the pointer acceleration. The difference between speed and acceleration is similar to that on a car. When you press down on the accelerator, do you want your car to jump off the line or accelerate slowly? The same is true for your mouse. The slower the acceleration speed, the more control you have, but the response is a bit delayed. If you like the mouse to move quickly, adjust the speed and acceleration to match your preference.

TIP *If you are new to using a mouse and find it a bit awkward, you might want to slow the speed and acceleration down a bit until you gain better control.*

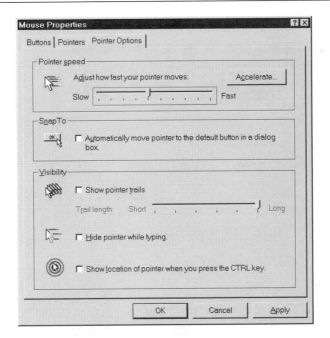

| FIGURE 18-11 | The Pointer Options page of the Mouse Properties dialog box includes speed, snap-to, and visibility settings |

18

- **SnapTo (sometimes called Auto Jumps)**   This section contains a single, very slick option. When you select this option, your cursor will automatically jump to the default button when a dialog box opens. For example, if a dialog box offers OK and Cancel buttons, the cursor will jump directly to the default button, which is usually OK. This means that all you need to do is click your mouse button to accept the default.

- **Visibility**   This section contains three options that you can enable or disable. If you select the Show Pointer Trails option, you can also set the length of the trails, using the slider below the check box. A pointer trail is a ghost-type image of the pointer's path—like the example you see to the left of the check box. If the pointer distracts you when you're entering text, select the Hide Pointer while Typing check box. Then the pointer won't appear on the screen when you're typing. Finally, if you sometimes lose track of the pointer, you can select the last check box on the page. When this option is enabled, you can press the CTRL key to put a "spotlight" on the cursor.

Hearing Bells and Whistles

The Sounds and Multimedia applet in the Control Panel gives you control over your computer's sound and audio settings. The Sounds page, shown in Figure 18-12, lets you select from an interesting variety of sounds for specific Windows events. It also lets you set the sounds for certain programs that have assignable sounds.

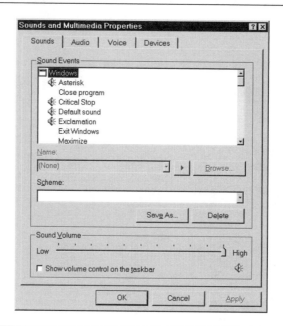

FIGURE 18-12   The Sounds tab of the Sounds and Multimedia Properties dialog box offers a variety of system sounds

For instance, you might want to hear a whistle whenever you launch a program. If you would like to hear a sound, select it from the list, and then click on Play if you want to preview (prehear) it. Your settings do not take effect until you click OK. If you just want to play around, you can always click Cancel to leave this setting unchanged. Listening to the available sounds also provides a good test for any newly installed speakers.

The Audio page lets you choose your preferred devices for playing back and recording sounds. You can also fine-tune your audio device performance and your speakers.

On the Voice page, you'll find settings for recording voices for games and such.

To see a list of the multimedia devices installed on your system, click the Devices tab. This page lists your audio, mixer, video-capture, and other multimedia devices. You can select a device from the list and click the Properties button to see the status of the device and its properties.

Choosing Internet Options

The Control Panel's Internet Options applet, shown in Figure 18-13, allows you to tweak the way that Internet Explorer behaves. It has several pages, including some with more advanced features that you usually will not need to change. Here, we'll discuss the most commonly used controls.

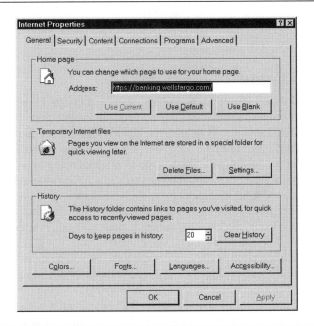

FIGURE 18-13   The Internet Properties dialog box has pages of settings for controlling Internet Explorer

18

Setting Your Home Page and Housekeeping

The General page of the Internet Properties dialog box (see Figure 18-13) includes options to set your home page and manage your temporary Internet files and History folder.

Your home page is the first page displayed when you open your browser window. You can change from the default home page displayed by your browser to another home page. For example, if you do home banking, you might want to go right to the sign-in page when you double-click the Internet Explorer icon on your desktop. The easiest way to set your default home page is to enter the exact address. For example, if you wanted your home page to take you right to Yahoo! mail, you would enter http://www.mail.yahoo.com in the Address box. Click the Use Current button to accept that address as your default home page.

TIP *You can also set this page from your browser window. Just open the page that you want to be your default, then open the Tools menu and select Internet Options. Your current address should already appear in the Address box. Click the Use Current button to set it as your default home page.*

Temporary Internet files store Web pages that you've already viewed. You can quickly view these pages again, even when you're offline. Although they're convenient, temporary Internet files can consume a lot of disk storage space. To delete all the temporary files currently stored and free that space, click the Delete Files button.

The History folder is another convenient way to return to Web sites you've visited in the past. You can set the amount of days that the pages are saved in your History folder, as well as clear the History files to start fresh.

Controlling Web Content

The Content page of the Internet Properties dialog box, shown in Figure 18-14, has settings for enabling Web ratings, using certifications, and storing personal information.

If you have curious children, you may be interested in the Content Advisor feature. Click on the Enable button in the Content Advisor section to see the Content Advisor dialog box, as shown in Figure 18-15. Select the category for the type of material that you would like to restrict, and then move the slider to indicate the level you want to allow. When you are finished setting the content restrictions, click OK.

A certificate is a security mechanism for identifying you or others that you connect to through the Internet. You can use the Certificates and Publishers buttons to identify the certificates Internet Explorer should accept.

The Personal Information section of the Content page allows you to specify whether you want Internet Explorer to use your stored personal information to fill in common fields in forms used on the Internet.

The AutoComplete feature is handy if you find yourself entering the same information in various forms. For example, if you do a lot of home shopping on the Web, you probably don't want to need to enter your e-mail address and home address over and over again. Click the AutoComplete button to open the AutoComplete Settings dialog box, as shown in Figure 18-16.

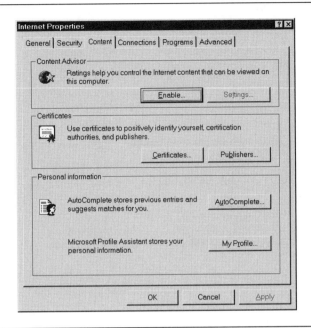

FIGURE 18-14   The Content page of the Internet Properties dialog box allows you to control what content can be viewed, use certificates, and store personal information

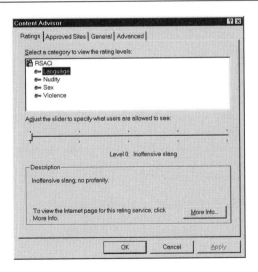

FIGURE 18-15   The Content Advisor dialog box

18

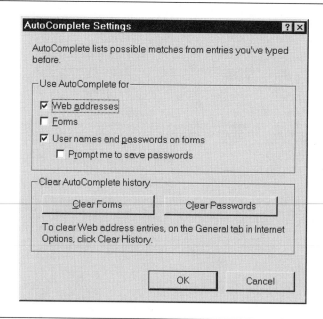

FIGURE 18-16   The AutoComplete Settings dialog box

Here, you can define the type of information you want completed automatically. Then, depending on which options you chose, when you enter a Web address or information in a Web form, all you need to do is enter the first character, and Internet Explorer will open a list of possible entries.

Setting the Date and Time

By default, Windows displays the current time, according to your system's built-in clock, on the right end of the taskbar. Sometimes, your system clock is not perfectly accurate.

If you need to set the time and/or date on your computer, open the Date/Time applet from the Control Panel. You'll see the Date/Time Properties dialog box, as shown in Figure 18-17. Select your region and set the current date and time. Selecting the Automatically Adjust Clock for Daylight Savings Changes check box at the bottom of the dialog box tells Windows to take care of adjusting your clock automatically during daylight savings and standard time changes.

TIP   *You can also open the Date/Time dialog box by double-clicking on the clock on your taskbar.*

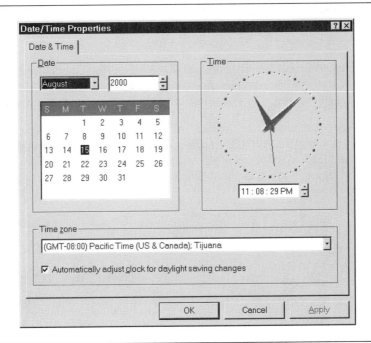

FIGURE 18-17   The Date/Time Properties dialog box has a calendar and clock for setting
your system's date and time

Removing Programs

Even pack rats need to let go of a few of their collections to make room for new toys and
treasures. You may be faced with something that makes computer-literate people quake in their
boots: low disk space. Many years ago, a 10M disk seemed like a waste of free space. No one
ever thought that data would require that much storage capacity. Wow, have times changed!
Nowadays, 10M is not nearly enough to contain your operating system, let alone any applications.

In the event you need to remove an application, there are a few ways in which to do it
successfully:

- Run the uninstall program that is installed by the application's installation program.
- Use the Control Panel's Add/Remove Programs applet.
- Manually remove the program's shortcuts and files from your disk.

18

The first two methods listed above will remove the program and also take care of some of the entries the program added to the Windows Registry (the database of system information). Manual deletion does not remove any Registry entries from your system.

NOTE *Although the icon in the Control Panel says Add/Remove Programs, the only programs that you can easily add through this applet are those that came on your Windows CD. You add other programs using their own installation programs, as explained in Chapter 3.*

The best-case scenario is running the application's uninstall program, usually accessible through the Start menu's Programs list. (Check the documentation that came with the software if possible.) For example, if for some reason you wanted to remove the WinZip program, you would click Start, Programs, WinZip, Uninstall WinZip, as shown here.

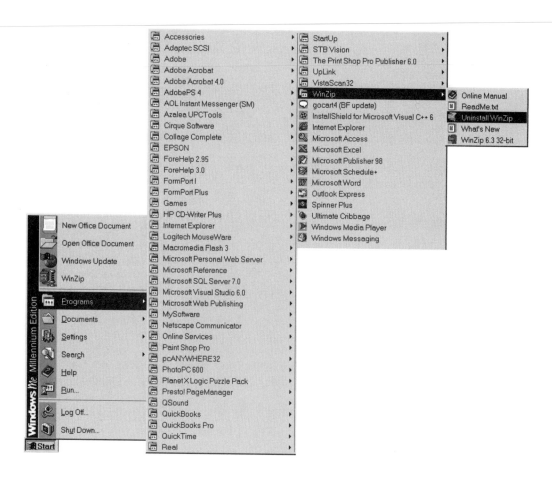

If the application did not supply an uninstall program, it may be compliant with Microsoft's uninstall utility, which is run by the Add/Remove Programs Wizard. To find out if your application is compliant, open the Control Panel and double-click the Add/Remove Programs icon to access the Add/Remove Programs Properties dialog box. Scroll through the list of software applications to find the one you want to remove. If it is listed, select it, and then click the Add/Remove button. If it is not listed, the program does not support this tool.

During an uninstall process, you may be asked whether or not you want shared files to be removed. Make sure that you do not answer yes if another application requires that shared file. If you are uncertain, answer no.

The worst-case scenario is removing your programs manually. It is highly recommended that you read the installation instructions for the application you want to remove. Make certain the software does not provide you with a proper means for removing the software from your system prior to removing it manually. If you absolutely have no choice, you can remove the directory where the software is installed, then remove any shortcuts that are associated with that program. To remove a directory or shortcut, select it, then press the DEL key. Keep in mind that this is not the recommended way of doing things—it is simply a last resort. If the program registered itself in the system registry, its entry in the registry will not be removed using this removal technique, but that's not likely going to cause a problem.

Getting Information About Your System

To get a glimpse at how your system is performing, you can double-click on the System icon in the Control Panel. Some of the settings in this dialog box can affect your computer in ways that you don't want to happen, so they are best left alone unless you know what you're doing.

Two pages of the System Properties dialog box can be helpful if you want to see information about your system and its performance status:

- ■ The General page, shown in Figure 18-18, reports information regarding your operating system, processor, and RAM.

- ■ The Performance tab, shown in Figure 18-19, displays information regarding your resources. If your system resources are less than 50 percent free, your system is a bit overburdened. You might want to consider closing a program or two or increasing your RAM. (See Chapter 17 for details on adding RAM.)

18

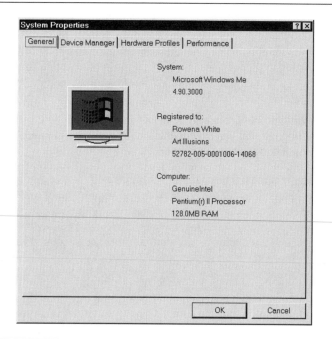

FIGURE 18-18   The General page of the System Properties dialog box shows your operating system, registration information, and computer system information

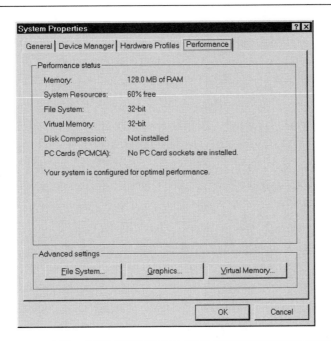

FIGURE 18-19   The Performance page of the System Properties dialog box shows your resource status

Chapter 19

Fixing and Avoiding Computer Problems

How to...

- Recover lost data
- Avoid out-of-memory and out-of-space errors
- Recover from a program or computer crash
- Start up a crashed computer
- Restore a computer to a previous configuration
- Solve printing problems
- Troubleshoot Internet connection problems
- Run hard-disk maintenance programs

Whether you are new to computers or an old hand, you're going to run into some problems now and again. Computers just aren't as smart as we would like them to be. Until they can respond as effortlessly as the ship's computer in the *Star Trek* TV series (Picard says, "Tea, Earl Gray, hot," and what he gets is tea, not a ham sandwich), you should be prepared for a sometimes infuriating relationship with your computer.

What you'll find is this chapter is a kind of "brain dump" of common annoyances and major problems I've dealt with when using my own computers, along with a compilation of the things my friends love to hate about theirs (and about Windows).

You might read this chapter so you'll be prepared for the worst. More likely, you'll be seeking the solution to a problem you're currently experiencing. To help you locate the discussion of your particular problem, the chapter is organized as follows:

- Data loss
- Memory and disk space error messages
- Frozen (crashed) programs and computers
- Computers that won't start up
- Printers and printing
- Internet connections

Once you learn some of these troubleshooting tricks, you might just find you mysteriously have more friends that you thought, and you'll need an answering machine with a larger message capacity. Well, if you're willing to share what you know, at least it's a very effective way to meet new people.

This chapter also covers a topic closely related to solving computer problems: keeping your hard disk healthy. Since your hard disk is the repository of your computer's data, keeping it in good shape will help you to avoid some major computer problems.

Data Loss Problems (or What to Do After Losing Your Ph.D. Thesis)

When comparing computer war stories, "The computer ate my report" story is one of the saddest and possibly the most common. Suddenly losing a precious document you've been slaving over for hours is a major bummer, and it has probably happened to you, or will happen, at least once. (It could be worse—you could be driving down the street and watching your laptop slip off the roof of your car onto the freeway and under the wheels of a semi.) Even the most diligent backup artist still occasionally watches in horror as the computer, like some mythical Greek god punishing the helpless mortals for some unfathomable transgressions, mangles her work.

The saying, "An ounce of prevention is worth a pound of cure," is all too true with computers. Your first line of defense with work in progress is to save it regularly. Beyond that, there are a couple of tricks you can use as a hedge against software snafus and system crashes that work against you even if you're persistent at regularly saving.

If you accidentally deleted a file (by clicking on it in a file folder and then pressing DEL or right-clicking and choosing Delete), there's hope. As discussed in Chapter 3, you can recover files you accidentally deleted from the Recycle Bin, as long as you rescue them before you empty the Recycle Bin. If you accidentally deleted a program file (files with the extension of .dll, or exe.), you can recover those using the System Restore feature in Windows Me, as explained in the "Restoring Your System with Restore" section later in this chapter.

TIP	*You should have an emergency startup disk on hand in case of a serious system problem. See the "Using Your Emergency Startup Disk" section later in this chapter for details on creating and using an emergency startup disk.*

Using a Program's Auto-Backup Features

Realizing that people hate losing their work and can easily become disenchanted with a product that doesn't protect their data for them, more and more programs have options you can set to automatically back up your files for you. To find out if a particular program supports this feature, read its manual or look through its Help file.

As an example, Figure 19-1 shows Microsoft Word's Save options (choose Options from the Word Tools menu and click on the Save tab to open this dialog box).

Of particular importance is the Save AutoRecover Info Every ___ Minutes option. If you set this to 5, as in Figure 19-1, your work will be automatically saved every 5 minutes, even if you forget to do it. If Word or Windows crashes (appears frozen for an extended period of time) or some other problem crops up, such as a power outage, you can just reboot and run Word again. The file should be opened automatically by Word, with *(recovered)* after the file name in the title bar. At that point, you need to make sure to save the file again, just like it's a new document.

Another helpful setting is Always Create Backup Copy. With this option turned on, when you open a existing document, a copy of it is made. Let's say you're working on a file called Chapter 21. The backup copy is called Backup of Chapter 21 and is stored in the same folder

19

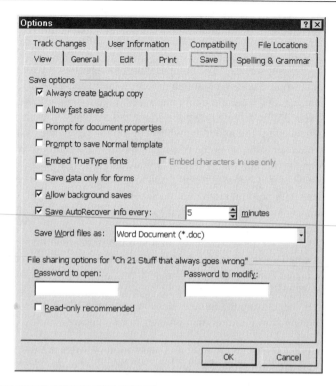

FIGURE 19-1 Auto-backup options in Microsoft Word

as the original. Each new backup copy replaces the previous backup copy. This way, if something happens to the original (say, you accidentally save a document that you've messed up), you can go back to the previous version of it. Just open the folder where it's stored and double-click on the backup version, as shown here.

Each set of auto-backup options applies only to one particular program (and remember that not all programs have options that protect you against catastrophe or your own shenanigans). The settings you make for, say, Word, will not have any effect on Excel or Outlook Express. Make sure to check the manual and Help file for each specific program and set the appropriate options in it. If your program doesn't have automatic backup features, you can make your own backups as you work, as described in the next section.

If you have a Palm handheld organizer and use the Palm Desktop software that came with it, you probably run it and leave it open all of the time your PC is on. You may not know that it doesn't save new entries automatically. To avoid losing your entries, you should get in the habit of manually using the Save command every time you enter new information, such as an appointment or contact.

Saving Your Work in Multiple Places

As you know, you save a file in almost any program (such as your word processor), by opening the File menu and choosing Save or Save As. As discussed in Chapter 2, if it's the first time you've saved the file, you'll name the file and specify where to store it. After that, you prudently save your file on a regular basis as you're working on it. Let's consider where you're saving your files.

Typically, people save their work onto the hard disk, in a folder such as My Documents or a folder within My Documents. No matter which folder you use, the file is going onto your hard disk somewhere. If calamity should cause your hard disk to fail, then you're likely up the creek. You won't be able to recover your document short of sending your hard disk to a service that specializes in data recovery. This could cost you plenty (easily in the hundreds of dollars, possibly thousands).

Even if your program automatically makes backup copies, it is storing those copies on your hard disk, along with the original. As a quick line of defense, you can make an *extra* copy each time you save a file. Here's how:

1. Save the file as usual. Give it a name and save it on the hard disk somewhere.

2. Before doing any more, save the file again to another location, such as on another machine on the local area network, on another hard disk, or on a floppy disk.

3. Continue to do you work. The next time you save the file, save it in the original location again.

4. The next time you save the file, save it in the other location.

5. Continue to alternate between locations when you save the file—every other save is on another drive.

With this method, if you save fairly frequently, you should always have a fairly recent backup of your work to revert to, if necessary.

TIP

Suppose that you're working on a document and you've really messed up. You would like to start over again. If you haven't used the Save command to save the file during the time that you've made the changes you want to erase, you may be in luck. Some programs, such as Word, let you back out of all of the changes you made during an editing session and haven't manually saved. Close the file; when the program asks if you want to save your changes first, say no. Then you can reopen the file, and it will be in the same state it was when you last saved it. But be aware that some programs, such as Quicken, automatically save file updates each time you make a change to a document.

Recovering a Word File—A Last Resort

What if you've lost a Word file due to a system or Word crash, and its automatic recovery feature doesn't seem to work? There may still be a way to recover that file. (From personal experience, I can assure you that this tip alone may be worth the price of this book!)

This approach takes advantage of the fact that Word, like many programs, does not actually save your file completely until you manually quit the program and close the document file. Suppose that you created a file yesterday and you're working on it again today. When you open the file, Word creates a temporary file to store your work in as you edit. It's not until you actually close that document (or Word) that yesterday's file it overwritten to match what is in the temporary file. Then the temporary file is erased from the disk.

Here are the steps to take to recover a Word file after a crash:

1. After the crash, shut down and reboot the computer.

2. Run Word. If Word's AutoRecover feature worked, a "recovered" version of the file will be opened automatically by Word. If so, save the file, and you're back in business. If Word did not automatically open the file, continue with the steps here.

3. Reopen the file you were working on, manually. If it's the old version, the one without your latest work in it, or an empty file with nothing in it (this can happen, too), just close it. Don't save it.

4. You need to find the temporary file that Word created for your lost document. The temporary file is a hidden file with a weird name, but it's there on your hard disk somewhere, usually in the C:/Windows/Temp folder or the same folder as the original file. Word starts temporary file names with the characters ~W. To search for the file, open the Start menu and select Search.

5. Click on Search Options to bring up the advanced options. For the search criteria, enter ~W*.* as the file name and specify files created during the last 1 day. Click Search Now and the search results will show a list of temporary files, as shown in the example in Figure 19-2.

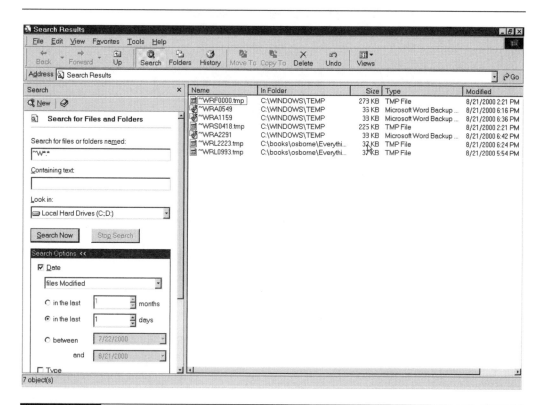

FIGURE 19-2   Searching for an elusive, lost Word file after a crash

6. Notice the time the files were created (you may need to adjust the column heads or scroll horizontally). A number of these files were created by Word in the last 24 hours. If the location and time looks reasonable, it just might be the file you were working on. Try opening suspected files manually in Word. The easiest way do to this is to right-click a file and choose Open With. In the Open With dialog box, choose Microsoft Word and deselect (remove the check from) the Always Use This Program to Open These Files check box at the bottom of the dialog box, as shown next. Click OK. The file will open in Word (or at least Word will try to open it.)

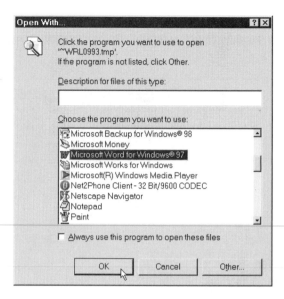

7. If it's the right file, you're in luck. If not, close it, and repeat step 6 with another file from the Search Results window.

8. When you find the correct file, save the file in your work folder, giving it a reasonable name. You're finished—you just recovered your file (and maybe even your job).

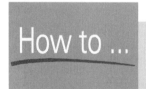 **Avoid Losing Your Work**

Losing a document can be a catastrophe, and it happens all too often. Here's a checklist for saving your work:

- Save your work whenever you've done enough that you would really hate to, or couldn't afford to, redo it. You be the judge of your time's worth.

- If your program has an automatic-save option, turn it on, and set it to a relatively short amount of time, such as every 5 or 10 minutes of work.

- Occasionally make a backup of your work. Either close the file and copy it via My Computer or use the File Save As command in your application. Or, alternatively save a file on one disk drive, then on another.

- Study up to understand how your programs save your work.

Memory and Disk Space Errors

As you've learned in previous chapters, RAM (random access memory) refers to the memory Windows uses for temporary storage of your applications and documents during a computer session. Your system needs enough RAM to keep everything running smoothly. Your computer's hard disk stores all of your computer's contents, whether the computer is on or off. If you don't have enough space on your hard disk, your PC will have trouble operating, and you may lose files because you can't save them to disk.

Dealing with "Low-on-Memory" Error Messages

You may be working away on your PC, switching among several open applications on your desktop. You try to open one more window, and Windows presents you with a message telling you that you're low on memory. Here are some things you can try when you see this type of error message:

- Try closing some programs and/or documents.
- Empty the Recycle Bin.
- Use Windows Explorer or My Computer to delete some unnecessary files. Then empty the Recycle Bin again.
- Make sure you have at least 10M of free space on your hard disk.
- If you have less than 64M of RAM in your computer, upgrade to at least 64M, preferably 128M. (See Chapter 17 for details on upgrading RAM.)

Dealing with "Out of Disk Space" Error Messages

Suppose that you've finally finished some extensive editing of a document and press CTRL-S to save it. Instead of dutifully saving your file to disk, your program responds with a message about being out of disk space. Here are some things that you can do to try to recover some space on your hard disk so you can save your file:

- Empty the Recycle Bin.
- Delete files you don't need. Poke around your folders and desktop and see what detritus you have collected and never use.
- Open My Computer, right-click your hard drive, choose Properties, Disk Cleanup. Windows will run the Disk Cleanup utility, which deletes temporary Internet files, temporary program files, the Recycle Bin files, and offline Web pages (if you give your approval).
- Remove programs that you never use. Use the program's uninstall program or the Add/Remove Programs applet in the Control Panel to remove programs. (See Chapter 18 for details on removing programs.) You might also consider using a third-party program

19

like Norton CleanSweep or McAfee's Uninstaller, which let you safely remove all unwanted software wasting space on your hard drive. They also allow you to make compressed backup copies of removed programs, so you can reverse the process with just a few clicks of the mouse.

- Archive rarely-used files to some other drive or backup medium, such as CD-Rs or CD-RWs. (See Chapters 16 and 17 for details on CD-Rs, CD-RWs, and other removable media.)

- Compress files and folders you don't use often. If you're using Windows 95 or 98, you need to compress files manually by using a Zip utility such as WinZip. (You can download Zip programs from the Internet.) In Windows Me, you can have the system automatically compress files for you through the Compressed Folders tool. To activate Compressed Folders, open the Add/Remove Programs applet in the Control Panel. Choose Windows Setup, select System Tools, and click Details. You'll see a list of System Tools components, as shown in Figure 19-3. Check the box next to Compressed Folders to add it.

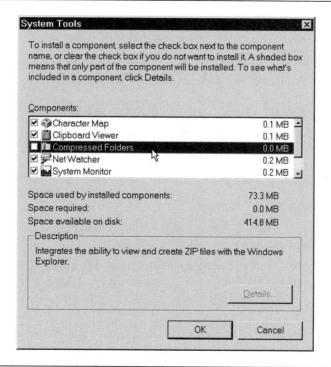

FIGURE 19-3   Windows Me includes the Compressed Folders system tool

With Windows Me Compressed Folders tool, you can store your files in a fraction of the space they normally take up. You can drag and drop files into Zip-formatted folders, and Windows compresses and decompresses them effortlessly and automatically for you. Read more about using Compressed Folders in Windows Help.

■ Purchase a higher-capacity hard disk. (See Chapter 17 for details on upgrading your hard disk.)

See the "Keeping Your Hard Disk Healthy" section later in this chapter for information about avoiding hard disk problems and other ways to recover hard disk space.

Frozen (Crashed) Computer or Program Problems

You'll become familiar with this scenario soon enough, if you haven't already, sorry to say! Windows is improving all the time, but there are still situations that can cause your computer or a program to crash. A *crash* isn't as terrible as it sounds. Your computer or program just gets stuck, and you'll need to reboot the machine to get back to work. You might lose some work as a result, but nothing terrible will happen to your computer, except in rare situations. (See the "Data Loss Problems" section earlier in this chapter for ways of mitigating data loss as a result of crashes.)

Your computer may crash after you've added something new to your computer (such as a new printer, application, or internal modem) or you've changed some system settings on your computer. In this case, you can try using the System Restore feature in Windows Me. See the "Restoring Your System with System Restore" section later in this chapter for details.

When Your Computer or Program Is Stuck

Here are some steps to take when your computer or a program you're using seems to be stuck, frozen, or crashed (all these terms mean the same thing):

■ First, press the ESC key once or even twice. Sometimes, this stops the computer from doing what it's doing or gets it out of a mode in which it doesn't want to respond to the keyboard.

■ If your program is still stuck, try pressing ALT-TAB or using the taskbar to switch to another program to see if Windows is dead or it's just a problem with a single program. (ALT-TAB is the standard keyboard combination for switching from one program to another.)

■ If the taskbar is in auto-hide mode and doesn't appear, press the WINDOWS key on the keyboard to bring up the Start menu. (Or press CTRL-ESC, which is the standard keyboard combination for keyboards that don't have a WINDOWS key.) You may be able to change to another program that way.

19

■ If you can switch to other programs, save any documents you are working on in those programs, and then close those programs if possible.

■ If one program seems to be stuck, press CTRL-ALT-DEL *once*, and then wait. In a few seconds, a list of programs should appear, as shown here. Select the program that is listed as not responding and click the End Task button. If other programs are listed as not responding, select and end those as well.

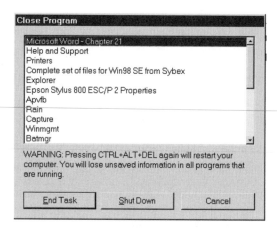

■ If possible, open the Start menu, select Shut Down, Restart to reboot the computer. If your computer won't open the Start menu, press CTRL-ALT-DEL twice. If pressing CTRL-ALT-DEL doesn't reboot your computer, you'll need to press the power switch. You might have to hold the button in for about four seconds to force the machine to power down.

If your PC has been shut down in an ungraceful way (either it totally froze and you had to press CTRL-ALT-DEL or someone tripped over the power cord to your computer), a program called ScanDisk will run the next time you boot up. Even though it's annoying and takes a few minutes, you should let it run. It checks the integrity of the hard disk files to make sure that the file allocation table is not damaged. The file allocation table (FAT) is like the directory that tells Windows where your files are, so ScanDisk helps keep your precious documents (and the operating system itself) from becoming partially or fully scrambled. In fact, you should occasionally run ScanDisk intentionally, as explained in the "Running ScanDisk" section later in this chapter.

About Illegal Operations and the Blue Screen of Death

One day, you'll be typing along, playing a game, viewing your digital photos, cruising the Web, or whatever you do with your computer—then, suddenly, blam! You see some unfriendly message, sporting a big, red X, about how you or some program has just "performed an illegal operation" and will be shut down.

How to ...   **Revive a Dead Mouse**

If your mouse stops responding, try this:

1. Press the WINDOWS key (or CTRL-ESC).

2. Press the up arrow key once so that Shut Down is highlighted.

3. Press Enter. This will bring up the Shut Down dialog box.

4. Use the arrow keys to select Shut Down.

5. Press the TAB key until the OK button has a little box in it.

6. Press the spacebar. This will shut down your computer.

7. Check the mouse connection to the computer. Wiggle it and make sure it's tight, or plug in a different mouse.

8. Restart the computer.

Sounds like a warning from a hospital, doesn't it? Actually, a guy this happened to phoned me once, all shook up, concerned about how the authorities knew he was using a piece of copied software! I explained it was merely a coincidence that his illegally obtained program just happened to have a problem with it (a *bug*). The moral of the story is not to take it personally when this kind of message pops up.

Illegal operations are usually caused by a negative interaction between the operating system and a program you're running. Not all programs are well written, and if a program tries to do something such as interfere with the operating system, Windows will shut it down. It's possible that even though an errant program may be shut down when it acts out of line, it can still leave the operating system somewhat unstable. Everything might look okay after an errant program is shut down, but if you're doing important work and can't afford for the system to crash or act a little weird, I suggest you close your work and reboot the computer. That will probably set things straight again.

If a program really steps on the operating system significantly, you might experience what's affectionately called the Blue Screen of Death (BSOD). The Windows desktop disappears, and your entire screen goes blue with a message in white letters. It will tell you that the operating system has become unstable or that Windows is waiting for something to happen, such as a program to close. You'll be given the option of waiting or pressing CTRL-ALT-DELETE keys simultaneously to restart your computer. You should always try to exit Windows gracefully when possible, so try waiting a bit, get back to the Windows screen by pressing the spacebar, and see if you can close down your open programs, save your work, and restart via the Start menu's Shut Down command.

19

When Your Computer Won't Shut Down

Some computers can have difficulty powering down under software control. Actually they almost power down, they just don't make it all the way. You'll end up staring at a screen that reminds you to wait until you're told it's okay to shut down, or a message that says Windows is shutting down, but that's it. This happens mostly on older computers running Windows 98. Newer computers and Windows Me have addressed this issue.

Suppose that you've gone through the standard procedure to shut down (chosen Start, then Shut Down, then Shut Down), then waited and waited, but the PC doesn't shut down or show the message telling you it's okay to turn off you computer now. In this case, you should just go ahead and turn it off, using the power switch. This might require holding in the power switch for over 4 seconds.

When Your Laptop Won't Reboot

When a laptop computer locks up, pressing CTRL-ALT-DEL sometimes won't restart it. It's even possible that holding in the power switch for four seconds won't power down the laptop. The trick is to remove all sources of power:

1. Unplug the AC power source.

2. Remove any removable batteries.

3. Wait a few seconds and reinsert the battery(ies).

4. Plug in the AC power source if the batteries are depleted.

5. Restart the computer.

Computer Startup Problems

Whether it's because you've just installed a new program or a new device, or because of some damage to operating system files or hard disk, your PC might not be able to start up. You try to start it up and it just hangs. Here are some points to consider:

■ Since normal booting up can take up to a minute or so, don't assume there's really a problem unless there is absolutely no activity on the screen. Sometimes, the only movement you'll see is in the little blue, cloud-like bar at the screen's bottom.

■ Check that the power is connected, the monitor is on, the brightness isn't turned down, that the monitor cable is secure, and that there's no floppy disk inserted in drive A. The computer could actually be booting, but if the monitor is off, you'll never know it.

■ If the problem persists, press the reset switch or turn the computer off, wait a few seconds, and turn it on again. Let it try to boot again. Windows is pretty good at repairing itself. It notes when a bootup has been unsuccessful, and it will try to boot one way or another. It may take some time, grinding away on the hard disk for a few minutes.

What can you do if your computer still won't start up? There's still hope. You can try Safe mode and System Restore. If they don't work, you can use your emergency repair disk to start your computer.

Entering Safe Mode

If your computer won't boot the regular way, you can try booting into Safe mode. *Safe mode* loads just the minimum amount of the system software to get your computer started.

1. Click Start, Shut Down, and then choose Restart and click OK.

2. Press and hold down the Ctrl key until the Windows Start Menu appears. (On some computers, you can press F8 instead of CTRL.)

3. Choose Safe Mode and press Enter.

NOTE

Another means of entering Safe Mode is to press and hold down the left SHIFT key while Windows is booting. This takes you directly to Safe Mode without displaying the Startup menu.

While booted up in Safe mode, you have three options:

■ Sometimes, just shutting down and rebooting again after a successful boot into Safe mode will result in a proper full bootup.

■ If you have some knowledge of how device drivers work, you can investigate your system while in Safe mode in hopes of determining which setting (such as a screen driver) was wrong. Do this using the Control Panel's System icon.

■ The best approach is to use the System Restore feature to return to the computer to a known good state, as described in the next section.

Restoring Your System with System Restore

If your system will only boot in Safe mode, or it starts acting weird after you've installed something, you can run System Restore. System Restore is a feature included in Windows Me (it's not in Windows 98). System Restore is a way to turn back the clock, in effect. It's sort of like having a time machine so you can undo changes made to the computer.

System Restore takes a snapshot of the system files and settings on a regular basis from time to time (you can set the schedule if you want, but the factory setting is fine). When you run System Restore, you choose a time to revert the system to (called a *restore point* or *system checkpoint*), and System Restore does the rest. Then you reboot, and your system should be fixed. You can also undo a restoration, in case it made things worse, or you can choose an earlier checkpoint in case the problem wasn't repaired as you had hoped.

19

System restore can do the following:

- Restore your computer to a more stable situation.
- Retain your work files (personal documents). Items like documents, e-mail messages, and browsing history are saved when you use System Restore.
- Typically store about one to three weeks of system changes.
- Watch to see when you delete program files (.exe and .dll files) and restore those. If one of your applications becomes corrupted, you might be able to fix it.
- Keep track of restore points for you automatically.
- Let you reverse a restoration.
- Let you create a new restore point if you're about to make some system changes.

About Restore Points

The actual number of restore points that System Restore saves depends on how much stuff you've been doing with your computer and the size of your hard disk or the hard disk *partition* that contains your Windows folder (partitions are discussed later in this chapter, in the "Keeping Your Hard Disk Healthy" section). You can manually change this setting to include more restore points if you have enough hard disk space. If you don't use your computer every day, some days may not have any restore points. If you use your computer frequently, you may have restore points almost every day, and some days may have several points.

As a default, System Restore creates restore points even if you don't make any changes to your system. It does this on the following schedule:

- Every 10 hours that your computer is on
- Every 24 hours in real time
- If your computer is off for more than 24 hours, the next time you turn it on

If you wonder why the computer has a lot of hard disk activity going on when you're doing nothing with it, it could be creating a restore point.

System Restore must use some hard disk space to save snapshots of the system from time to time. So, occasionally, it needs to remove all old restore points to make room for recording new changes. This means that the calendar of available points only goes back so far.

> **TIP** *You might want to consider creating your own restore point when you anticipate making changes to your computer that are risky or might make your computer unstable. Start System Restore, as described in the next section, and choose Create a Restore Point.*

Running System Restore

There's a lot of information about System Restore in the Windows Help file, because it's a powerful tool. Just open Help from the Start menu and do a quick search for System Restore. Then click through the links and read all about how it works and the options you have. There's also a link on the first page of Help for running a System Restore.

If you're more interested in just getting your system working again, you can run the program, and the wizard will walk you through it. Here's how:

1. Click Start, Programs, Accessories, System Tools, System Restore. You'll see the first System Restore window, as shown in Figure 19-4.

2. To fix your computer, select Restore My Computer to an Earlier Time and click Next. Now you'll see the window for choosing your restore point.

3. Click on a bold date in the calendar. The exact restore point times appear in a box to the right of the calendar, as shown in the example in Figure 19-5. Choose one to roll the system back to.

> *In this example, there are no restore points between August 15 and 20. It just so happens these are dates that I wasn't working on this computer. But from August 1–14, I was using it heavily, so I can choose restore points in that range.*

NOTE

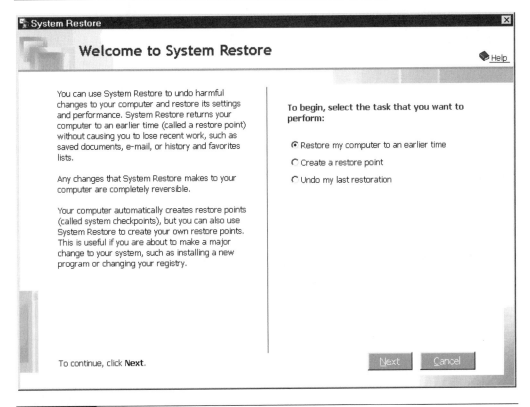

FIGURE 19-4   System Restore's opening window

19

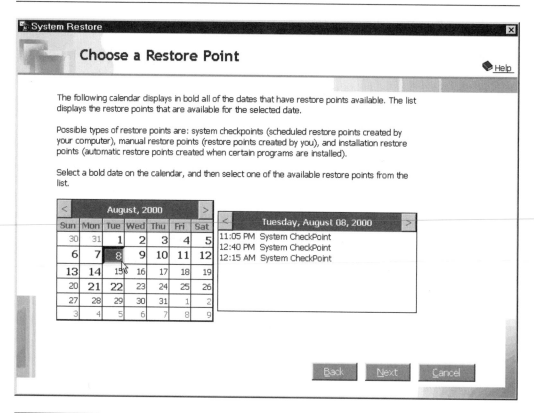

FIGURE 19-5 Choosing a restore point

4. Click Next. System Restore will display the warning shown here.

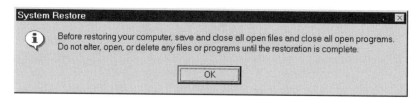

5. Close your files and programs, and then click OK. The system restoration will take place. You'll be told what to do. With any luck, your system will now be more stable!

If you roll back to a point before a program was installed, the program will not work after restoration. If you want to use the program again, you must reinstall it. Also, regarding applications, System Restore does not replace the process of uninstalling a program. To completely remove the files installed by a program, you must remove the program using the Add/Remove Programs applet in the Control Panel or the program's own uninstall program.

Undoing a System Restore

A failed restoration is automatically reversed by System Restore if it detects that the computer didn't boot. But what if you've run System Restore, and your system doesn't work as it should? This is rare, but it's possible. You might have changed some hardware in between the restore point and the restoration, so the system might now be using drivers that are incompatible with your current hardware.

In any case, if you do not like the state of your computer after restoring it, you can undo the restore or select another restore point. All successful restorations are reversible. Simply run System Restore (as described in the previous section) and select Undo My Last Restoration (see Figure 19-4). Then follow the onscreen instructions.

Using Your Emergency Startup Disk

You were prompted to create an emergency startup disk when you upgraded your computer to Windows Me (or whatever version of Windows you're running). You should always have an emergency bootup floppy around. You can create one through the Control Panel's Add/Remove Programs applet. Click the Startup Disk tab, and then click Create Disk. You must create your startup disk when your system is stable. You cannot create one once your system is unable to start Windows.

If you can't even boot from the hard disk into Safe mode, insert your emergency startup disk in your floppy drive and turn the computer off and on again. If your computer won't start and you can't find this disk, you may be in trouble. Try creating one on another computer that has your version of Windows on it and booting your dead computer with it. This might work.

If you see the "Starting Windows" message, but things get stuck after that, restart and hold down the left SHIFT key. Then choose Safe Mode from the resulting menu and work from Safe mode to clear up the problem.

If the last action you performed on your computer before starting with the startup disk was a restoration, then a message appears that recommends that you revert your last restore. Type **1** to select Revert the Restore Changes Made to my System (Recommended). If you select **2**, you will not have the opportunity to revert this restoration from the startup disk again. To repair the condition you were originally trying to fix, use System Restore again to roll back to another restore point.

If you had to use your emergency startup disk after using System Restore, don't make other system changes while booted from the floppy. If you do, you won't be given another chance to revert to the system state before the failed restoration. Your first action should be to choose to undo the restoration.

19

Printing Problems (or Why Won't This @#$ Thing Print?)

Printing is a notorious cause of PC headaches. Truly, the technology of printing is a complex one, both for your computer and for your printer. The actually appearance of a successful printout is something of a miracle.

For a computer document to print, it must to be translated into myriad complex instructions that your particular brand and model printer can understand. Only then can the printer spit out the millions of microscopic dots in just the right colors, positioned correctly on the final page, with correct font sizes and styles—all adjusted so it looks identical to the onscreen document.

Before we go over some typical printing problems and possible solutions, let's look a little closer at how printing happens. Understanding the printing process will give you a better idea of how to clear up printing problems.

Understanding the Printing Process

The software that does much of the printing work is called the printer *driver*. Just like a bus driver, the printer driver's job is to get the document's data from the computer into the printer. Each brand and model of printer has its own specialized printer driver.

When you tell your program to print a document, the program passes basic information about the document to the operating system (Windows) page by page. Windows, along with your printer driver, then turns the image into a huge string of commands and data that are sent out through the correct port, or over the network, to your printer. Your printer then interprets all of the commands, accepts the data, and begins printing. In the case of larger documents, the printer and computer continue to communicate for some time, as the computer passes only the amount of information the printer can accept, while the pages print (this is called *spooling*).

Obviously, the driver is an important part of the printing process. So first, make sure that you have installed the printer driver for your brand of printer. Your printer most certainly came with instructions about how to install the driver so that it can work with Windows. Windows comes with drivers for hundreds of popular printers, so it's quite possible that you can install the printer driver without needing the driver from the manufacturer. However, it's still best to use the software supplied with the printer, because it may include more printing features, color controls, and utility programs.

If you don't have a manufacturer-supplied disk with software on it for your printer, and if your printer is a USB or Plug-and-Play model, Windows may detect it when you simply plug in the printer according to the printer's manual. Just follow the on-screen instructions. If nothing happens when you plug in the printer, and you don't have a CD-ROM or floppy disk with software from the printer's maker, you should manually add the new printer to your computer system through the Printers window. (See Chapter 16 for details on adding printers.)

Handling Printing Problems

As noted earlier, printing problems are common. The following sections address some specific printing problems you may bump into and possible solutions for them.

You can get printing help from the Windows Help file. There is a troubleshooter built into Windows, reachable from the Printers folder. Right-click the printer and choose Properties. Click Print Test Page. If the page doesn't print correctly, click No. The Printing Troubleshooter will appear. Choose the option that describes your problem best, and click Next.

Nothing Happens When You Try to Print

If you use the Print command to print a document and nothing at all happens, try the following:

- Check that the printer is on, online, filled with paper, and wired securely. Look to see that the cables are really connected well. Is the printer actually plugged into the AC power outlet?

- You can have Windows try to print a test page for you to check the printer. Open the Printers folder (click Start, Settings, Printers), right-click the printer, and choose Properties. Then click Print Test Page. If the page prints, the problem is with your document or application program, not the printer or Windows.

- Check that the printer is assigned to the correct port. Right-click on the printer in the Printers folder and choose Properties. Click the Details tab and make sure that the correct port is set for the printer (typically it will be LPT1).

- If all else fails, remove the printer (right-click on the printer's icon in the Printers folder and choose Delete). Then follow the manufacturer's instructions for installing the printer again.

The Printout Doesn't Look Right

The printed version of your document may not look like the one on your computer screen. Here are some areas to check:

- Make sure the paper size you are using matches the document size you are printing. Your program might have a setting in it for paper size that exceeds the size of the actual paper you're using.

- If a partial page printed, check the page orientation. It may be set to Landscape, and your paper is loaded in the Portrait (long way up and down) orientation.

- Check the page-layout command in the program you are printing from *and* in the Properties box for your printer (click the Details tab, and then click Settings). If just the edges of the printout are missing, decrease the margins for your document and try again.

- If you get PostScript error codes or pages of really weird letters and curly braces instead of whatever you're trying to print, either you are trying to use a PostScript printer driver with a non-PostScript printer or the printer needs to be set to PostScript mode. Add the printer to your computer again using the Add Printer Wizard.

Printing Is Slow

When your printer is printing more slowly than usual, you can check the spool settings. Open the Properties box for the printer, and click on the Details tab. Make sure that the Spool Print Jobs option is turned on. If this option is selected, and you're waiting a long time for a printout to appear, click Spool Settings in the Details tab, and then click Restore Defaults. Try printing again. If things don't improve, open the dialog box again and try changing the spool setting from EMF to RAW.

The Colors in Your Printout Look Bad

If you're printing to a color printer and one of the colors, (red, green, or blue) seems to be missing in your printouts, first check your printer's cartridges. As explained in Chapter 16, color ink-jet printers have removable ink cartridges. If you're running low on a color, you will need to replace the color cartridge.

It's possible that just the nozzle for a color (the nozzle spits out the color ink onto the paper) is clogged. Most printers offer a way to clean the nozzles. You can often do this through the Printers folder. Click Start, Settings, Printers. Right-click the printer and choose Properties. Look for a Utilities tab, such as the one for an Epson printer shown here, or some other mention of tools such as nozzle cleaning.

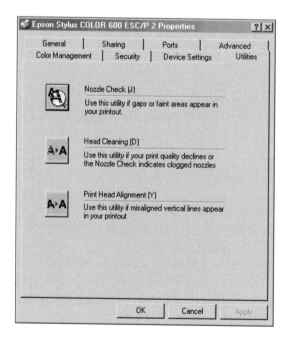

Nozzle cleaning uses up a fair amount of ink. Ink for ink-jet printers isn't cheap, so you might not want to do nozzle cleaning too often. Use nozzle cleaning as a last resort before you go out and buy new cartridges.

Internet Connection Problems

Internet connection problems make themselves known indirectly. For example you might be unable to receive your email, cruise the Web, or interact with newsgroups. Be aware that slow Web browsing can be caused by problems unrelated to your modem or other connection to the Net. There might be heavy network traffic or the server storing the Web site or email you're trying to access is down. So, try a couple of major Web sites before you assume the problem is with your computer's connection. If you continue to see "The page cannot be displayed" (in IE) or "There was no response" (in Netscape) regardless of the Web site you attempt to connect with, it's likely your Internet connection is troubled.

There are two kinds of connection problems when accessing the Internet: one you can fix and one you just get to complain about. The connection from your PC to the ISP may be faulty. That you can fix, even if it involves a support call to the ISP. The other kind of problem is when the Internet itself is totally bogged down, and no amount of magical incantations directed at your PC can fix that.

Here are some things you can check on your own:

- If you're using a dial-up connection, check the phone line. Plug a phone into your modem line and see if you get a dial tone.

- Check the phone cords connecting your modem to the phone jack, and replace them if they look shabby.

- With an external modem, you have a serial cable from the modem to the PC, so make sure it's tight. Double-check the AC adapter while you're back there.

- Whether you're using a dial-up connection, DSL, or cable, the lights on an external modem can tell you a lot about your connection. Some manufacturers of internal modems (notably, 3Com) provide software that mimics these lights. My cable modem has three green lights on the front, all of which have to be on before I can connect to the Internet. Make a point of knowing what a healthy connection looks like on your cable, DSL, or analog modem.

- If you have cable Internet service, verify that your cable modem is getting power and the connections are good. If you have cable TV service, check the TV to see if you are receiving TV signals. Having TV doesn't mean necessarily that you should also have Internet access, but if there is no TV signal, it's likely that the cable ISP service is down, too.

- If you have DSL Internet service, check that your DSL hookup is attached properly.

19

Once you've checked your modem, your connections, and your phone line, that's about all you can do. You'll need to call in the cavalry. Call your ISP's technical support jock while you're seated at your PC. You might want to jot down some notes in case you run into the same problem again.

Other Resources for Solving Problems

You've tried all of the solutions recommended and nothing worked. Now what? It's time to turn to some other resources:

- Use the Windows Help system. On the first page of the Help system, look for the Troubleshooting link. Click on it. You'll have a number of troubleshooting options to choose from. Alternatively, search through Help for information about your specific problem. (See Chapter 2 for more information about using the Windows Help system.)

- On your computer or another, use Microsoft online help via a Web browser. Go to www.microsoft.com and click the Search button.

- Microsoft has a "knowledge base" that contains help on many PC-related subjects. This comprehensive database is updated daily and contains more than 50,000 detailed articles with technical information about Microsoft products, fix lists, documentation errors, and answers to commonly asked technical support questions. Check out the site at http://search.support.microsoft.com/kb/c.asp.

- On your computer or another, read the additional Help text files included on the Windows CD-ROM (network.txt, printers.txt, and so on). You can find them using My Computer. Open the file appropriate to your problem (such as, printers.txt if you're having a printing problem). The file will open in Notepad (or WordPad if it's too large for Notepad).

- Send messages to a newsgroup about Windows. You'll find hundreds of people online who can give you advice. You may find someone who knows about the problem you are having. (See Chapter 8 for details on how to join newsgroups and find communities of people who have interests or needs common to yours.)

- Go the library or bookstore and procure some more advanced books.

- Hire a professional who has a good track record and comes with a recommendation from someone you know. (Find out how much the consultant charges for these services first, or you may be stuck with a huge bill, along with a problem that couldn't be fixed.)

Keeping Your Hard Disk Healthy

Your hard drive is a very special part of the computer. It holds your operating system and all of the applications and data files that you create. Keeping your hard drive healthy and in good working order is paramount to having a safe and reliable computing experience.

A simple precaution is to make sure that the placement of your computer provides for good airflow around the drive. This will help reduce heat buildup and protect the drive. Do not put your computer in an area where the temperature, humidity, or vibration is a problem.

Also, be careful not to bump into your hard drive if you are moving your computer or running a maintenance program or reconfiguring the hard disk. You could damage the drive and lose data.

Along with the physical treatment of your hard disk, there are several steps you can take to ensure that you are getting the best performance from your hard drive. These include partitioning your disk, defragmenting your disk, and scanning your disk for errors.

Partitioning Your Hard Disk

When you purchase a PC, it usually comes preconfigured and ready to go. The hard drive is formatted and loaded with an assortment of software.

In most cases, the hard disk comes configured with one partition—one large volume—that is the whole hard drive. It is one big repository containing the operating system and all of the applications and files available to you. Unfortunately, if you use it this way, you could be wasting a lot of useful disk space—in some cases, more than 40 percent!

The way that your data and applications are stored on your hard drive is in the form of data *clusters*. The larger your hard drive, the larger the cluster size. The larger the cluster size, the greater the waste of space on your hard drive.

If you are using a hard drive that is greater than 2G, you may want to partition it. Dividing a hard drive into several partitions lets you efficiently organize operating systems, programs, and data. However, there is a trade-off between having your files spread over all those partitions because it's annoying to jump around between drive letters (C:, D:, E:, etc.) to find your files. I don't recommend having more than five partitions on your computer. Whether and how you partition your drive(s) depends on what you are doing. If you are capturing video to disk, you are going to need a huge partition—and hopefully, you will keep that huge partition for video data only, using your main partition (a smaller one) for you programs and operating system. I have recently purchased a secondary 40G hard disk that I keep all as one partition, for video editing, but my main drive C: is a 13G, partitioned into two halves.

You can use commercial partitioning programs like PowerQuest's Partition Magic (www.powerquest.com/partitionmagic), which you can launch without leaving Windows. You can launch it from within Windows, but it leaves Windows and enters its own graphical user interface (GUI) that looks much like Windows, and then reboot Windows once finished. It supports partitions of hard drives larger than 20G. You can use it with FAT, FAT32, NTFS, HPFS, and Linux ext2 file systems. Partition Magic will also convert partitions of one type to another, such as FAT to FAT32.

You can also use Symantec's Partition-It (www.symantec.com/region/sg/product/partition-it/main.html) to partition your hard drive. Partition-It is similar to Partition Magic in that it frees valuable hard drive space by creating smaller partitions and hence smaller cluster sizes.

> **CAUTION** *If you reformat a drive larger than 8G with cluster size less the 8K (kilobytes), you might have problems running Scandisk or Defrag. So use a larger cluster size.*

19

If you've upgraded to Windows 98, use the FAT32 conversion utility that's included with Windows 98 to improve your file and memory management capabilities. This rids you of the FAT16 filing system used in previous Windows versions.

Defragmenting Your Hard Drive

There are many ways files can get corrupted on your hard disk. As you constantly use your hard drive, bits and pieces of files end up scattered all over the hard drive. The files are not stored in one continuous block of space; instead, the information is stored in the first available free space. Fortunately, your system knows where all these pieces are stored and can put them together again. Yet all of this storing, moving, and deleting can make things a bit messy on the hard drive. It also increases the chances of things going wrong.

The more files you create, save, and delete, the more cluttered your hard drive becomes. Your hard drive needs to work harder to find all of the pieces to put back together. This process of splitting files all over the hard drive is called *file fragmentation.* Too much fragmentation can slow Windows to a crawl and cause your computer to crash.

You can easily put the pieces back together by using a software program called a defragmenter. By defragmenting the hard drive, you are reorganizing all your files, making them closer or together once again. Your computer will spend less time trying to find all the data, and thus the performance of your hard drive will increase. To keep your PC operating at optimum speed, you should consider defragmenting the hard drive regularly, perhaps once a month (if you have a large hard drive and a lot of file activity).

Do not defragment your hard drive unless you have your computer attached to a reliable power source, like a UPS device. If you are defragmenting and the power goes out, there is a slight risk that you may lose the file that was being relocated at the time of the power outage.

Windows comes with a defragmenting program called Disk Defragmenter. Follow these steps to defragment your hard disk:

1. Back up your important data before you defragment (in case of problems).

2. Clean out unnecessary files from your hard disk so you don't have to bother defragmenting them too. Right-click on the hard disk file in question and choose Properties, Disk Cleanup.

3. Turn off your screen saver, because you don't want it to run while you're defragmenting your disk. Right-click the desktop, select Properties, and click the Screen Saver tab. Change the screen saver time to 0.

4. Click Start, Programs, Accessories, System Tools, and then Disk Defragmenter. Alternatively, you can right-click the partition in Windows Explorer or My Computer, and select Properties. Then you can run the defragmenter from the Tools tab.

5. Select the drive you want to defragment and click OK to start the process. You'll see a progress report, as shown next.

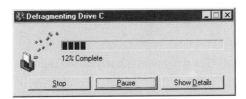

6. To see what the Disk Defragmenter is actually doing, click the Show Details button. The program will display a window representing your hard drive and the data on it. Click the Legend button in the lower-right corner of the window to see what it all means, as shown in Figure 19-6.

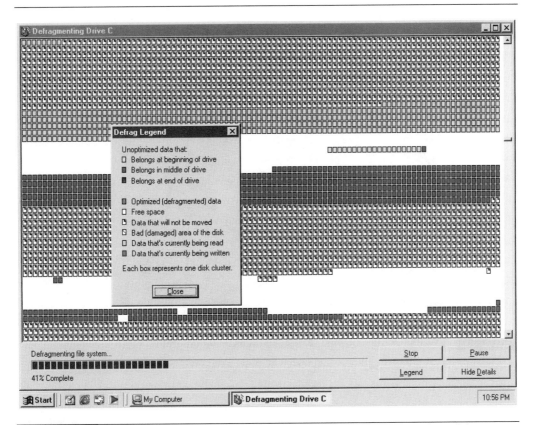

FIGURE 19-6   Click the Show Details button to view a graphical representation of the defragmenter's work behind the scenes

19

If Disk Defragmenter stops and displays a message telling you it cannot defragment the drive, run the ScanDisk program first in Thorough mode, as described in the next section. Then try defragmenting again.

Windows 98 includes a utility that will automatically run ScanDisk and Disk Defragmenter for you, called the Maintenance Wizard. You can run the Maintenance Wizard from the System Tools submenu (the same place you find the Disk Defragmenter), and it will let you set up a routine maintenance schedule.

There are commercial defragmenters that you can use. For example, Symantec's Norton Utilities (www.symantec.com) and McAfee's Office 2000 (www.mcafeemall.com) are excellent programs. An example of the Norton Utilities defragmenting program is shown in Figure 19-7.

Executive Software offers a free 30-day trial of its Diskeeper software at www.diskeeper.com. It comes with an excellent analysis tool, and it will defragment hard drives in the background so that your work is not disrupted. In addition, an event log will record every action taken on each file by the program. Figure 19-8 shows the Diskeeper screen.

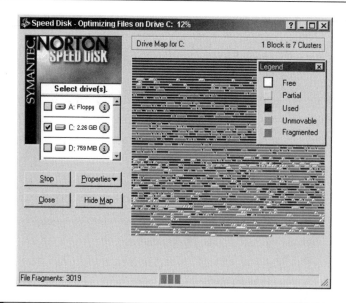

FIGURE 19-7   Norton Utilities includes a disk defragmenting program

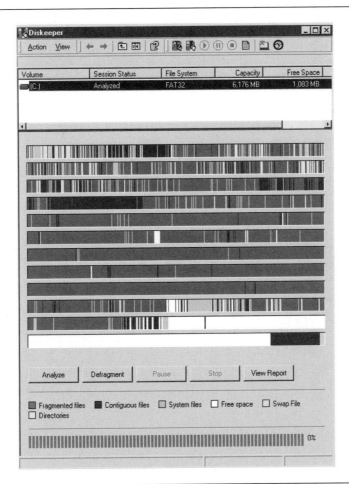

FIGURE 19-8   Diskeeper from Executive Software is a deluxe disk maintenance tool

Running ScanDisk

ScanDisk is a great utility that does just what its name implies: It scans your hard disk looking for problem files and fixes any problems it finds automatically.

19

To run ScanDisk, select Programs from the Start menu and click Accessories, System Tools, ScanDisk. You'll see the ScanDisk window, as shown in Figure 19-9. Select the drive that you want to scan and the type of test. The Standard option takes care of most problems and takes less time than the more intensive Thorough option. Running ScanDisk in Standard mode once a week is a good idea. Running it in Thorough mode once a month is probably a good idea if you use your machine heavily.

There are other commercial and shareware programs that will check your hard drive for problems and fix them. For example, Ontrack Data Advisor (www.ontrack.com/freesoftware) is a freeware program that scans your hard drive. Norton Utilities and McAfee's Office 2000, mentioned in the previous section, have disk-scanning utilities as well as defragmenters.

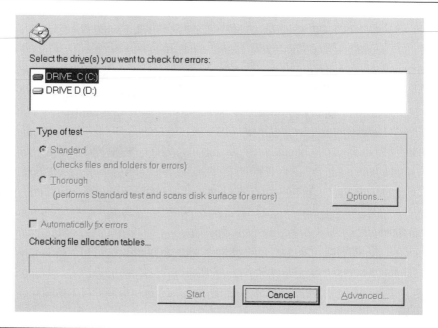

FIGURE 19-9   ScanDisk checks for errors on your disk and tries to fix them automatically

Glossary

applet   A small application, such as a utility program or limited-function spreadsheet or word processor. Java programs are usually called Java applets, because they are relatively small in size.

application   Any data entry, update, query or report program that processes data for the user. It includes the generic productivity software (spreadsheets, word processors, database programs, etc.) as well as custom and packaged programs for payroll, billing, inventory and other accounting purposes.

back up   To make a copy of important data onto a different storage medium for safety.

baud rate   The signaling rate of a line, which is the number of transitions (voltage or frequency changes) that are made per second. The term has been used erroneously to specify bits per second. However, only at very low speeds is baud equal to bps.

binary   Meaning two, it's the principle behind digital computers. All input to the computer is converted into binary numbers made up of the two digits 0 and 1 (bits). For example, when you press the "A" key on your personal computer, the keyboard generates and transmits the number 01000001 to the computer's memory as a series of pulses. The 1 bits are transmitted as high voltage; the 0 bits are transmitted as low. The bits are stored as charged and uncharged memory cells in the computer or as microscopic magnets on disk and tape. Display screens and printers convert the binary numbers into visual characters.

BIOS   (basic input output system)   An essential set of routines in a PC, which is stored on a chip. It provides an interface between the operating system and the hardware. On startup, the BIOS tests the system and prepares the computer for operation by querying the CMOS memory (a small, battery-backed memory bank) for drive and other configuration settings. It then loads the operating system and passes control to it.

bit (*binary digit*)   The smallest element of computer storage. It is a single digit in a binary number (0 or 1). The bit is physically a transistor or capacitor in a memory cell, a magnetic domain on disk or tape, a reflective spot on optical media, or a high or low voltage pulsing through a circuit. Groups of bits make up storage units in the computer, called characters, bytes, or words, which are manipulated as a group. The most common is the byte, made up of eight bits and equivalent to one alphanumeric character. Bits are widely used as a measurement for transmission. Ten megabits per second means that ten million pulses are transmitted per second. A 16-bit bus means that there are 16 wires transmitting the bit at the same time. Measurements for storage devices, such as disks, files and databases, are given in bytes rather than bits.

bitmap   A binary representation in which a bit or set of bits corresponds to some part of an object such as an image or font. For example, in monochrome systems, one bit represents one pixel onscreen. For gray scale or color, several bits in the bitmap represent one pixel or group of pixels. The term may also refer to the memory area that holds the bitmap. A bitmap is usually associated with graphics objects, in which the bits are a direct representation of the picture image. However, bitmaps can be used to represent and keep track of anything, where each bit location is assigned a different value or condition.

board   See *card*.

boot   Causing the computer to start executing instructions. Personal computers contain built-in instructions in a ROM chip that are automatically executed on startup. These instructions search for the operating system, load it and pass control to it. The term comes from the word "bootstrap." Since bootstraps help you get your boots on, booting the computer helps it get its first instructions. The term is used erroneously for application software. You might hear for example, "let's boot WordPerfect," whereas the correct usage is "load WordPerfect."

browser   A program that lets you look through a set of data. Common Web browsers are Internet Explorer and Netscape Navigator.

button   (1) A knob, such as on a printer or a mouse, which is pushed with the finger to activate a function. (2) A simulated button on screen that is "pushed" by clicking it with the mouse.

byte (*binary table*)   The common unit of computer storage. It is made up of eight binary digits (bits). A ninth bit may be used in the memory circuits as a parity bit for error checking. A byte holds the equivalent of a single character, such as the letter A, a dollar sign or decimal point. For numbers, a byte can hold a single decimal digit (0–9), two numeric digits (packed decimal) or a number from 0 to 255 (binary numbers). The primary specifications of hardware are rated in bytes; for example, a 10-gigabyte (10GB) disk holds 10 billion characters of instructions and data. A 64-megabyte (64M or 64MB) memory allows 64 million characters of instructions and data to be stored internally for processing. With database files and word processing documents, the file size is slightly larger than the number of data characters stored in it. Word processing files contain embedded codes for layout settings (margins, tabs, boldface); therefore, a 100,000-byte document implies slightly less than 100,000 characters of text (approximately 30 pages). Database files contain codes that describe the structure of the records; thus, a 100,000-byte database file holds somewhat less than 100,000 characters of data.

card   A flat board that holds chips and other electronic components. The board is made of reinforced fiberglass or plastic and interconnects components via copper pathways. The main printed circuit board in a system is called a system board or motherboard, while smaller ones that plug into the slots in the main board are called boards or cards. The printed circuit board of the 1960s connected discrete components together. The circuit boards of today interconnect chips, each containing hundreds of thousands and millions of elementary components.

CD-R (CD-Recordable)   A recordable CD-ROM technology using a disc that can be written only once. The drive that writes the CD-R disc is often called a one-off machine and can also be used as a regular CD-ROM reader. CD-Rs create the equivalent of pits in the disc by altering the reflectivity of a dye layer. Different dyes can be used, including cyanine (green), pthalo-cyanine (yellow-gold) and metal-azo (blue). CD-R discs are used as a means to distribute large amounts of data to a small number of recipients. CD-Rs are also used for archiving data. Their major advantage over other media is that they can be read in any CD-ROM reader.

CD-ROM (Compact Disc Read Only Memory)   A compact disc format used to hold text, graphics and hi-fi stereo sound. It looks like an audio CD, but uses a different track format for data. The audio CD player cannot play CD-ROMs, but CD-ROM players can play audio discs. CD-ROMs hold 650MB of data, which is equivalent to about 250,000 pages of text or 20,000 medium-resolution images. Sometimes 680MB is used as the capacity, depending on whether the total number of bytes (681,984,000) is divided by 1,000,000 or 1,048,576 (see *binary values*). A CD-ROM drive (player, reader) connects to a controller card, which is plugged into one of the computer's expansion slots. Earlier drives used a proprietary interface and came with their own card, requiring a free expansion slot in the computer. Today, CD-ROMs use SCSI or EIDE and can be installed without taking up an extra slot.

CD-RW (CD-ReWritable)   A rewritable CD-ROM technology. CD-RW drives can also be used to write CD-R discs, and they can read CD-ROMs. CD-RW disks have a lower reflectivity than CD-ROMs and CD-Rs, and MultiRead CD-ROM drives are required to read them. Initially known as CD-E (for CD-Erasable), a CD-RW disk can be rewritten a thousand times.

chip   A set of microminiaturized, electronic circuits that are designed for use as processors and memory in computers and countless consumer and industrial products. Chips are the driving force in this industry. Small chips can hold from a handful to tens of thousands of transistors. They look like tiny chips of aluminum, no more than 1/16-inch square by 1/30-inch thick, which is how the term "chip" originated. Large chips, which can be more than a half inch square, hold millions of transistors. It is actually only the top one thousandth of an inch of a chip's surface that holds the circuits; the rest is just a base. The terms *chip*, *integrated circuit* and *microchip* are synonymous.

compress   To compact data to save space.

CPU (central processing unit)   The computing part of the computer. Also called the processor, it is made up of the control unit and ALU. Today, the CPUs of almost all computers are contained on a single chip. The CPU, clock and main memory make up a computer. A complete computer system requires the addition of control units, input, output and storage devices and an operating system.

data   (1) Technically, raw facts and figures, such as orders and payments, which are processed into information, such as balance due and quantity on hand. However, in common usage, the terms data and information are used synonymously. The amount of data versus information kept in the computer is a tradeoff. Data can be processed into different forms of information, but it takes time to sort and sum transactions. Up-to-date information can provide instant answers. A common misconception is that software is also data. Software is executed, or run, by the computer. Data is "processed." Software is "run." (2) Any form of information whether in paper or electronic form. In electronic form, data refers to files and databases, text documents, images and digitally-encoded voice and video. (3) The plural form of datum.

database   A set of related files that is created and managed by a database management system (DBMS). Today, DBMSs can manage any form of data including text, images, sound and video. Database and file structures are always determined by the software. As far as the hardware is concerned, it's all bits and bytes.

desktop   An on-screen representation of a desktop, where your tools, files, and documents are found.

dialog box   A small, onscreen window displayed in response to some request. It provides the options currently available to the user.

digital camera   A video or still camera that records images in digital form. Unlike traditional analog cameras that convert light intensities into infinitely variable signals, digital cameras convert light intensities into discrete numbers for storage on a medium, such as a hard disk or flash disk. As with all digital devices, there is a fixed, maximum resolution and number of colors that can be represented. Digital cameras record color images as intensities of red, green and blue, which are stored as variable charges in a charge coupled device (CCD) matrix. The size of the matrix determines the resolution, but the analog-to-digital converter (ADC), which converts the charges to digital data, determines the color depth.

display   (1) To show text and graphics on a CRT or flat panel screen. (2) A screen or monitor.

document   A word-processing text file.

DOS (disk operating system)   Pronounced "dahss." A single-user operating system from Microsoft for the PC. It was the first OS for the PC and is still the underlying control program for Windows 3.1. Windows 95/98 and Windows NT build in their own version of DOS to support existing DOS applications. The DOS version that Microsoft developed for IBM is PC-DOS, and the version that all other vendors have used is MS-DOS. Except for DOS 6, which contains different versions of various utilities, PC-DOS and MS-DOS commands and system functions are the same. All releases of PC-DOS and MS-DOS are generally called DOS.

drive   An electromechanical device that spins disks and tapes at a specified speed. Also refers to the entire peripheral unit, such as a disk drive or tape drive.

DSL (digital subscriber line)   A modem technology that increases the digital speed of ordinary telephone lines by a substantial factor over common modems. DSL technologies are either asymmetric or symmetric. Asymmetric provides faster downstream speeds, which is suited for Internet usage and video on demand. Symmetric provides the same rate coming and going. DSL uses packet switching technology that operates independently of the voice telephone system, allowing telephone companies to provide the service without locking up circuits for long calls. For this reason, DSL is not as well suited to video conferencing as is ISDN. Circuit-switched ISDN keeps the line open and connected throughout the session. The transmission rate of DSL technologies is very much tied to the distance between the telephone company and the customer.

DVD-ROM   A read-only DVD disk used for storing data, interactive sequences as well as audio and video. Expected to become the CD-ROM of the 21st century, DVD-ROMs run in DVD-ROM or DVD-RAM drives, but not in DVD-Video players connected to TVs and home theaters. However, most DVD-ROM drives will play DVD-Video movies. DVD originally stood for Digital Video Disc. Since it spanned both the movie video and computer worlds, it was later called Digital Versatile Disc. Today, the acronym has become its name. DVD stands for D-V-D.

e-mail   The transmission of memos and messages over a network. Users can send mail to a single recipient or broadcast it to multiple users. With multitasking workstations, mail can be delivered and announced while the user is working in an application. An e-mail system requires a messaging system, which provides the store and forward capability, and a mail program that provides the user interface with send and receive functions. Most Web browsers have a built-in e-mail function.

ergonomics   The science of people–machine relationships. An ergonomically-designed product implies that the device blends smoothly with a person's body or actions. Although ergonomically-designed seats, keyboards and mice are important to a computer user's well-being, perhaps the most beneficial aspect of ergonomics is teaching people to get up from the computer periodically and stretch.

extension   File types, or file categories, that are added to the end of DOS and Windows file names. The extension is separated from the file name with a dot such as LETTER.DOC. An extension can contain up to three letters or digits. Executable files use .EXE, .COM and .BAT extensions; for example, NOTEPAD.EXE is the text editor that comes with Windows. All programs and most data files use extensions. However, some word processing files do not, in which case you could create your own filing system; for example, CHAP1.NOV and CHAP2.NOV could be chapters in a novel.

file A collection of bytes stored as an individual entity. All data on disk is stored as a file with an assigned file name that is unique within the directory in which it resides. To the computer, a file is nothing more than a string of bytes. The structure of a file is known to the software that manipulates it. For example, database files are made up of a series of records. Word processing files contain a continuous flow of text. Following are the major file types. Except for ASCII text files, most files contain proprietary information contained in a header or interspersed throughout the file.

Type	Contents
data file (table)	data records
document	text
spreadsheet	rows and columns of cells
image	rows and columns of bits
drawing	list of vectors
audio	digitized sound waves
MIDI	MIDI instructions
video	digital video frames
Web page	text
batch file	text
source program	text
executable program	machine language

FireWire A high-speed serial bus developed by Apple and Texas Instruments that allows for the connection of up to 63 devices. Also known as the IEEE 1394 standard, the original spec calls for 100, 200 and 400 Mbits/sec transfer rates. IEEE 1394b provides 800, 1,600 and 3,200 Mbps. FireWire supports hot swapping, multiple speeds on the same bus and isochronous data transfer, which guarantees bandwidth for multimedia operations. It is widely used for attaching video devices to the computer.

floppy disk A reusable magnetic storage medium introduced by IBM in 1971. The floppy was the primary method for distributing personal computer software until the mid-to-late 1990s, when CD-ROMs became the preferred medium. Floppies are still widely used for backup and to transfer data between users that are not attached to a network. Today's common floppy is the 3.5" microfloppy, developed by Sony, that holds 1.44MB. Also called a "diskette," the floppy is a flexible circle of magnetic material similar to magnetic tape, except that both surfaces are used for recording. The drive grabs the floppy's center and spins it inside its housing. The read/write head contacts the surface through an opening in the plastic shell or envelope. Floppies spin at 300 rpm, which is from 10–30 times slower than a hard disk. They are also at rest until a data transfer is requested.

folder   In the Macintosh and Windows 95/98/Me, a simulated file folder that holds data, applications and other folders. A folder is the same as a DOS or Windows 3.1 directory, and a folder within a folder (subfolder) is the same as a DOS or Windows 3.1 subdirectory. Folders were popularized on the Mac and later adapted to UNIX and Windows.

font   A set of type characters of a particular typeface design and size. Usually, each typeface (Times Roman, Helvetica, Arial, etc.) is made available in four variations: normal weight, bold, italic and bold italic. Thus, for bitmapped fonts, which are fully generated ahead of time, four fonts would be required for each point size used in each typeface. For scalable fonts, which are generated in any point size on the fly, only four fonts would be required for each typeface.

gigabyte   One billion bytes. Also GB, Gbyte and G-byte.

graphics   The creation and manipulation of picture images in the computer. Two methods are used for storing and maintaining pictures in a computer. The first method, called vector graphics, maintains the image as a series of points, lines, arcs and other geometric shapes. The second method, called bitmapped graphics and also known as raster graphics, resembles television, where the picture image is made up of dots.

hard disk   The primary computer storage medium, which is made of one or more aluminum or glass platters, coated with a ferromagnetic material. Most hard disks are fixed disks, which are permanently sealed in the drive. Removable cartridge disks are gaining in popularity and are increasingly available in greater variety. Most desktop hard disks are either IDE or SCSI. The advantage of SCSI is that seven or more devices can be attached to the same controller board. Hard disks provide fast retrieval because they rotate constantly at high speed, from 3,000–10,000 rpm. In laptops, they can be turned off when idle to preserve battery life. Older hard disks held as little as five megabytes and used platters up to 12 inches in diameter. Today's hard disks can hold several gigabytes and generally use 3.5-inch platters for desktop computers and 2.5-inch platters for notebooks.

hardware   Machinery and equipment (CPU, disks, tapes, modem, cables, etc.). In operation, a computer is both hardware and software. One is useless without the other. The hardware design specifies the commands it can follow, and the instructions tell it what to do. Hardware is "storage and transmission." The more memory and disk storage a computer has, the more work it can do. The faster the memory and disks transmit data and instructions to the CPU, the faster the work gets done. A hardware requirement is based on the size of the databases that will be created and the number of users or applications that will be served at the same time. How much? How fast? Software is "logic and language." Software deals with the details of an ever-changing business and must process transactions in a logical fashion. Languages are used to program the software. The "logic and language" involved in analysis and programming is generally far more complicated than specifying a storage and transmission requirement.

hertz   The frequency of electrical vibrations (cycles) per second. Abbreviated "Hz," one Hz is equal to one cycle per second. Named for Heinrich Hertz, who detected electromagnetic waves in 1883. A megahertz (MHz) is one million cycles per second.

home page   The first page retrieved when accessing a Web site. It serves as a table of contents to the rest of the pages on the site or to other Web sites. See *World Wide Web* and *URL*.

HTML (Hypertext Markup Language) The document format used on the World Wide Web. Web pages are built with HTML tags, or codes, embedded in the text. HTML defines the page layout, fonts and graphic elements as well as the hypertext links to other documents on the Web. Each link contains the URL, or address, of a Web page residing on the same server or any server worldwide, hence "World Wide" Web.

hypertext A linkage between related text. For example, by selecting a word in a sentence, information about that word is retrieved if it exists, or the next occurrence of the word is found. Hypertext is the foundation of the World Wide Web. Links embedded within Web pages are addresses to other Web pages, either stored locally or in a Web server anywhere in the world. Links can be text only, in which case they are underlined, or they can be represented as an icon of any size or shape. The hypertext concept was originally coined by Ted Nelson, one of the pioneers of the microcomputer revolution, as a method for making the computer respond to the way humans think and require information.

icon In a graphical user interface (GUI), a small, pictorial, on-screen representation of an object, such as a document, program, folder or disk drive.

IDE (Integrated Drive Electronics) A type of hardware interface widely used to connect hard disks, CD-ROMs and tape drives to a PC. IDE is very popular because it is currently the least expensive way to connect peripherals. Starting out with 40MB capacities years ago, multi-gigabyte (GB) IDE disk drives have become entry level, costing less than five cents per megabyte.

Internet An internet is a large network made up of a number of smaller networks. "The" Internet is made up of more than 100,000 interconnected networks in over 100 countries, comprised of commercial, academic and government networks. Originally developed for the military, the Internet became widely used for academic and commercial research. Users had access to unpublished data and journals on a huge variety of subjects. Today, the Internet has become commercialized into a worldwide information highway, providing information on every subject known to humankind. The Internet's surge in growth was twofold. As the major online services (America Online, CompuServe, etc.) connected to the Internet for e-mail exchange, the Internet began to function as a central hub for e-mail outside of the Internet community. A member of one online service could send mail to a member of another, using the Internet as a gateway. The Internet glued the world together via electronic mail. Second, World Wide Web servers on the Internet link documents around the world, providing an information exchange of unprecedented proportion that is growing exponentially. With the advent of graphics-based Web browsers such as Mosaic and Netscape, this wealth of information became easily available to users with PCs and Macs rather than to only scientists and hackers at UNIX workstations. The Web has also become "the" storehouse for drivers, updates and demos that are downloaded via the browser. Daily news and information is also available on the Net. Usenet (User Network) newsgroups have been delivering timely information on myriads of subjects long before the Web was created. The news can be selected and read directly from your Web browser. Chat rooms provide another popular Internet service. Internet Relay Chat (IRC) offers multiuser text conferencing on diverse topics. Dozens of IRC servers provide hundreds of channels that anyone can log onto and participate in via the keyboard. Today, all the major online services provide full Internet access. DELPHI was the first, and the others followed suit. In addition, thousands of Internet service providers (ISPs) have come out of the woodwork to offer individuals and organizations access.

intranet   An in-house Web site that serves the employees of the enterprise. Although intranet pages may link to the Internet, an intranet is not a site accessed by the general public. Intranets use the same communications protocols and hypertext links as the Web and thus provide a standard way of disseminating information internally and extending the application worldwide at the same time. The term as originally defined here has become so popular that it is now often used to refer to any in-house LAN and client/server system.

ISDN (Integrated Services Digital Network)   An international telecommunications standard for transmitting voice, video and data over digital lines running at 64 Kbps. The telephone companies commonly use a 64 Kbps channel for digitized, two-way voice conversations. ISDN service is available in most parts of the U.S.

ISP (Internet service provider)   An organization that provides access to the Internet. Small Internet service providers provide service via modem and ISDN while the larger ones also offer private line hookups. Customers generally are billed a fixed rate per month, but other charges may apply. For a fee, a Web site can be created and maintained on the ISP's server, allowing the smaller organization to have a presence on the Web with its own domain name. The major online services, such as America Online and CompuServe, provide Internet access but are still known as "online services," not ISPs. They generally offer the databases, forums and services that they've created in addition to Internet access. While they may host a customer's home page, they typically do not host Web sites with unique domain names.

joy stick   A pointing device used to move an object onscreen in any direction. It employs a vertical rod mounted on a base with one or two buttons. Joy sticks are used mainly for playing computer games, as well as in some drawing systems.

JPEG (Joint Photographic Experts Group)   Pronounced "jay-peg." An ISO/ITU standard for compressing still images that is becoming very popular due to its high compression capability. Using discrete cosine transform, it provides lossy compression (you lose some data from the original image) with ratios up to 100:1 and higher. It depends on the image, but ratios of 10:1–20:1 may provide little noticeable loss. The more the loss can be tolerated, the more the image can be compressed. Compression is achieved by dividing the picture into tiny pixel blocks, which are halved over and over until the ratio is achieved.

keyboard   A set of input keys. On terminals and personal computers, it includes the standard typewriter keys, several specialized keys and the features outlined below. See *PC keyboards*.

ENTER (RETURN) KEY   In text applications, it ends a paragraph or short line. In data applications, it signals the end of the input for that field or line.

CURSOR KEYS   The four arrow keys move the cursor on screen. They are used in conjunction with shift, alt and control to move the cursor in bigger jumps; for example, CONTROL UP ARROW might scroll the screen. Some earlier keyboards didn't have cursor keys, in which case control or alt was used with some letter key.

CONTROL, ALT, COMMAND & OPTION KEYS   Used like a shift key, these keys are held down while another key is pressed to command the computer in a variety of ways.

ESC KEY   Commonly used to exit or cancel the current mode such as exiting from a menu. Also used to clear an area or repeat a function such as redrawing the screen.

NUM LOCK   Locks a combination number/cursor keypad into numeric mode only.

HOME & END KEY   Commonly used to move the cursor to the extreme left or right side of the current line. Often used in conjunction with shift, control and alt; for example, CONTROL HOME and CONTROL END usually move the cursor to the beginning and end of a file.

PAGE UP/PAGE DOWN KEYS   Used to move the cursor up and down a page, screen or frame. Often used in combination with shift, control and alt.

FUNCTION KEYS   Used to call up a menu or perform a function, they are located in a cluster on the left side or in a row across the top of the keyboard (F1, F2, etc.). They are often used with the shift, control and alt keys to extend the number of options.

BACKSPACE KEY   Used to delete the character to the left of the cursor (erase typos) and may be used with the shift, control and alt keys to erase segments of text. The extra-wide, typewriter-style key is preferred.

DEL KEY   Used to erase the character at the current cursor location. Used in conjunction with the shift, control and alt keys, it is used to erase any segment of text, such as a word, sentence or paragraph.

INSERT KEY   Usually a toggle switch to go back and forth between insert and overwrite mode. Also used to "paste" a segment of text or graphics into the document at the current cursor location.

REPEATING KEYS   Most computer keys repeat when held down, a phenomenon first-time computer users must get used to. If you hold a key down that is used to command the computer, you'll be entering the command several times.

AUDIBLE FEEDBACK   Keyboards may cause a click or beep to be heard from the computer when keys are pressed. This is done to acknowledge that the character has been entered. It should be adjustable for personal preference.

LAN (local area network)   A communications network that serves users within a confined geographical area. It is made up of servers, workstations, a network operating system and a communications link. Servers are high-speed machines that hold programs and data shared by network users. The workstations (clients) are the users' personal computers, which perform stand-alone processing and access the network servers as required. (See *client/server*.) Diskless and floppy-only workstations are sometimes used, which retrieve all software and data from the server. Increasingly, "thin client" network computers (NCs) and Windows terminals are also used. A printer can be attached to a workstation or to a server and be shared by network users. Small LANs can allow certain workstations to function as a server, granting users access to data on another user's machine. These peer-to-peer networks are often simpler to install and manage, but dedicated servers provide better performance and can handle higher transaction volume. Multiple servers are used in large networks. The controlling software in a LAN is the network operating system (NetWare, UNIX, Windows NT, etc.) that resides in the server. A component part of the software resides in each client and allows the application to read and write data from the server as if it were on the local machine. The message transfer is managed by a transport protocol such as TCP/IP and IPX. The physical transmission of data is performed by the access method (Ethernet, Token Ring, etc.) which is implemented in the network adapters that are plugged into the machines. The actual communications path is the cable (twisted pair, coax, optical fiber) that interconnects each network adapter.

laptop computer A portable computer that has a flat screen and usually weighs less than a dozen pounds. It uses AC power and/or batteries. Most have connectors for an external monitor and keyboard transforming them into desktop computers. Most laptop computers today fall in the notebook computer category. (See *notebook computer.*)

link On the World Wide Web, an address (URL) that takes you to another document on the same server or on any remote server.

Linux Pronounced "linn-icks." A free version of the UNIX operating system (OS) that runs on PCs and is seen as a potential alternative to Windows. Although Linux is "freeware;" it is often sold along with proprietary add-ons and technicals by vendors such as Red Hat Software, Caldera, and TurboLinux. The distribution CD-ROMs from such vendors include hundreds of tools, applets and utilities, as well as the full source code. Due to its stability, Linux has gained popularity with Internet service providers (ISPs) as the OS for hosting Web servers. Its use as a server OS for businesses is expected to grow; and as graphical user interfaces such as KDE and GNOME become more user-friendly, Linux may become a viable desktop alternative to Windows. In 1990, Finnish computer science student Linus Torvalds turned Minix, a popular classroom teaching tool, into Linux. Torvalds created the core Linux kernel, while most of the supporting applications and utilities came from the GNU project of the Free Software Foundation. The many programmers who have freely contributed to the Linux/GNU system have become known as the "open source" software movement.

Macintosh A family of personal computers from Apple, introduced in 1984. It was the first computer to popularize the graphical user interface (GUI), which, along with its hardware architecture, has provided a measure of consistency and ease of use that is unmatched. The Macintosh family is the largest non-IBM compatible personal computer series in use in what is essentially a PC versus Mac world.

maximize In a graphical environment, to enlarge a window to full size.

megabyte One million bytes. Also MB, Mbyte and M-byte.

megahertz One million cycles per second. Also written as MHz.

memory The computer's workspace (physically, a collection of RAM chips). It is an important resource, since it determines the size and number of programs that can be run simultaneously, as well as the amount of data that can be processed instantly. All program execution and data processing takes place in memory. The program's instructions are copied into memory from disk or tape and then extracted from memory into the control unit circuit for analysis and execution. The instructions direct the computer to input data into memory from a keyboard, disk, tape or communications channel. As data is entered into memory, the previous contents of that space are lost. Once the data is in memory, it can be processed (calculated, compared and copied). The results are sent to a screen, printer, disk, tape or communications channel. Memory is like an electronic checkerboard, with each square holding one byte of data or instruction. Each square has a separate address like a post office box and can be manipulated independently. As a result, the computer can break apart programs into instructions for execution and data records into fields for processing. Oddly enough, the computer's memory doesn't remember anything when the power is turned off. That's why you have to save your files before you quit a program. Although there are memory chips that do hold their content permanently (ROMs, PROMs, EPROMs, etc.), they're used for internal control purposes and not for the user's data. "Remembering" memory in a computer system is its disks and tapes, and although they are also called memory devices, many prefer to call them storage devices in order to differentiate them from internal memory. Perhaps in time, memory will refer to disks exclusively and RAM will refer to working memory. Until then, its usage for both RAM and disk only adds confusion to the most confusing industry on earth. Memory is such an important resource that it cannot be wasted. It must be allocated by the operating system as well as applications and then released when not needed. Errant programs can grab memory and not let go of it even when they are closed, which results in less and less memory available as you load and use more programs. In addition, if the operating system is not advanced, a malfunctioning application can write into memory used by another program, causing all kinds of unspecified behavior. You discover it when the system freezes or something weird happens. If you were to look into memory and see how much and how fast data and instructions are written into and out of it, you might think it's a miracle that it works at all!

menu　An onscreen list of available functions, or operations, that can be performed currently. Depending on the type of menu, selection is accomplished by (1) highlighting the menu option with a mouse and releasing the mouse; (2) pointing to the option name with the mouse and clicking on it; (3) highlighting the option with the cursor keys and pressing Enter; or (4) pressing the first letter of the option name or some designated letter within the name.

microprocessor　A CPU on a single chip. In order to function as a computer, it requires a power supply, clock and memory. The first-generation microprocessors were Intel's 8080, Zilog's Z80, Motorola's 6800 and MOS Technologies 6502. The first microprocessor was created by Intel, whose family of x86 chips remains the most popular type of microprocessor.

minimize　In a graphical environment, to hide an application that is currently displayed on screen. The window is removed and represented with an icon on the desktop or taskbar.

modem (*modulator-dem*odulator)　A device that adapts a terminal or computer to a telephone line. It converts the computer's digital pulses into audio frequencies (analog) for the telephone system and converts the frequencies back into pulses at the receiving side. The modem also dials the line, answers the call and controls transmission speed.

monitor　A display screen used to present output from a computer, camera, VCR or other video generator. A monitor's clarity is based on video bandwidth, dot pitch, refresh rate and convergence.

mouse　The most popular pointing device. It was called a mouse because it more or less resembled one, with the cord being the mouse's tail. Graphical interfaces are designed to be used with pointing devices, but key commands may be substituted. However, graphics applications, such as CAD and image editing, demand a mouse-like device. Mouse movement is relative. The screen cursor moves from its existing location. The mouse could be moved across your arm, and the screen cursor would move as well. After years of use by millions of users, it is now widely known that mice can be hazardous to your health. Many applications require endless clicking and dragging to accomplish tasks. Continuous use puts enormous stress on the wrist, and constant double-clicking can be the most strenuous function.

MP3 (MPEG Audio Layer 3)   An audio compression technology that is part of the MPEG-1 and MPEG-2 specifications. It compresses CD-quality sound by a factor of 12, while maintaining the same high fidelity. Greater compression ratios are also obtainable that provide reasonable sound quality.

MPEG (Moving Pictures Experts Group)   Pronounced "em-peg." An ISO/ITU standard for compressing video. MPEG is a lossy compression method, which means that some of the original image is lost. MPEG-1, which is used in CD-ROMs and Video CDs, provides a resolution of 352x240 at 30 fps with 24-bit color and CD-quality sound. Most MPEG boards also provide hardware scaling that boosts the image to full screen. MPEG-2 is a broadcast-quality standard that provides better resolution than VHS tapes. MPEG-2 is used in DVD movies. *.mpg* is the extension used on files stored in the MPEG file format.

multitasking   The running of two or more programs in one computer at the same time. The number of programs that can be effectively multitasked depends on the type of multitasking performed (preemptive versus cooperative), CPU speed and memory and disk capacity. Programs can be run simultaneously in the computer because of the differences between I/O and processing speed. While one program is waiting for input, instructions in another can be executed. During the milliseconds one program waits for data to be read from a disk, millions of instructions in another program can be executed. In interactive programs, thousands of instructions can be executed between each keystroke on the keyboard.

network   An arrangement of objects that are interconnected. In communications, a network consists of the transmission channels interconnecting all client and server stations as well as all supporting hardware and software.

notebook computer   A laptop computer that weighs from approximately five to seven pounds. A notebook that weighs under five pounds is usually called a *subnotebook*.

operating system   The master control program that runs the computer. It is the first program loaded when the computer is turned on, and its main part, called the kernel, resides in memory at all times. It may be developed by the vendor of the computer in which it's running or by a third party. It is an important component of the computer system, because it sets the standards for the application programs that run in it. All programs must "talk to" the operating system. PCs primarily use Windows (including Windows 3.x, Windows 95/98/Me, and Windows NT/2000), or they may run the increasingly popular Linux operating system. Macintoshes use the Mac OS (System 9 and OS/X being the most recent versions). Minicomputers and workstations typically use a variety of UNIX operating systems.

parallel port   A socket on a computer used to connect a printer or other parallel device via the computer's parallel interface.

PC (personal computer)   Although the term PC is sometimes used to refer to any kind of personal computer (Mac, Amiga, etc.), in general the term "PC" refers to computers that conform to the PC standard originally developed by IBM. Today, PC hardware is governed by Intel and PC operating systems by Microsoft. The PC is the world's largest computer base. PCs are used as stand-alone personal computers or as workstations and file servers in a LAN (local area network). They predominantly run under Windows, although DOS systems still linger. If an Intel-based PC is used as a network server running UNIX or other operating system, it is typically called an Intel-based server, or x86-based server, not a PC. Although there are literally thousands of PC vendors, from mom and pop shops to large mail order houses (Dell, Gateway, etc.) to the major computer companies (Compaq, HP, etc.), and of course IBM, still one of the world's largest PC makers, all PCs use an Intel x86 or compatible CPU.

peripheral   Any hardware device connected to a computer, such as a monitor, keyboard, printer, disk, tape, graphics tablet, scanner, joy stick, paddle and mouse.

pixel   (*pix* [picture] *el*ement) The smallest addressable unit on a display screen. The higher the pixel resolution (the more rows and columns of pixels), the more information can be displayed. In storage, pixels are made up of one or more bits. The greater this "bit depth," the more shades or colors can be represented. The most economical system is monochrome, which uses one bit per pixel (on/off). Grayscale and color displays typically use from four to 24 bits per pixel, providing more than 16 million colors.

plug in   An auxiliary program that works with a major software package to enhance its capability. For example, plug-ins are widely used in image editing programs such as Photoshop to add a filter for some special effect. Plug-ins are added to Web browsers such as Netscape to enable them to support new types of content (audio, video, etc.). The term is widely used for software, but could also be used to refer to a plug-in module for hardware.

pointer   A symbol used to point to some element on screen.

printer   A device that converts computer output into printed images. Laser printers and LED printers employ the electrophotographic method used in copy machines. Ink jets have become the most popular form of desktop, personal printer. Almost all units can print in color or have a color option. Ink jets propel droplets of ink directly onto the paper.

printed circuit   The "printed" circuit is really an etched circuit. A copper foil is placed over the glass or plastic base and covered with a photoresist. Light is shined through a negative image of the circuit paths onto the photoresist, hardening the areas that will remain after etching. When passed through an acid bath, the unhardened areas are washed away. A similar process creates the microminiaturized circuits on a chip (see *chip*).

RAM (Random Access Memory)   A group of memory chips, typically of the dynamic RAM (DRAM) type, which functions as the computer's primary workspace. The "random" in RAM means that the contents of each byte can be directly accessed without regard to the bytes before or after it. This is also true of other types of memory chips, including ROMs. However, unlike ROMs, RAM chips require power to maintain their content, which is why you must save your data onto disk before you turn the computer off.

ROM (Read-Only Memory)   A memory chip that permanently stores instructions and data. Its contents are created at the time of manufacture and cannot be altered. ROM chips are used to store control routines in personal computers (ROM BIOS), peripheral controllers and other electronic equipment. They are also often the sole contents inside a cartridge that plugs into printers, video games and other systems.

save   To copy the document, record or image being worked on onto a storage medium. Saving updates the file by writing the data that currently resides in memory (RAM) onto disk or tape. Most applications prompt the user to save data upon exiting. All processing is done in memory (RAM). When the processing is completed, the data must be placed onto a permanent storage medium such as disk or tape.

SCSI (Small Computer System Interface)   Pronounced "scuzzy." SCSI is a hardware interface that allows for the connection of up to seven or 15 peripheral devices to a single expansion board that plugs into the computer called a SCSI host adapter or SCSI controller. Single boards are also available with two controllers and support up to 30 peripherals. SCSI is widely used from personal computers to mainframes.

scanner   A device that reads a printed page and converts it into a graphics image for the computer. The scanner does not recognize the content of the printed material it is scanning. Everything on the page (text and graphics objects) is converted into one bitmapped graphics image (bitmap), which is a pattern of dots. Optical character recognition (OCR) systems perform the same scanning operation, but use software to convert the dots into coded ASCII or EBCDIC characters. Digital cameras are similar to desktop scanners, except that they focus into infinity, whereas desktop scanners accept paper, one page at a time or in a continuous feed like a copy machine (see *digital camera*).

screen saver   A utility that prevents a computer display from being etched by an unchanging image. After a specified duration of time without keyboard or mouse input, it blanks the screen or displays moving objects. Pressing a key or moving the mouse restores the screen. It would actually take many hours to burn in an image on today's color monitors. However, the entertainment provided by these utilities (swimming fish, flying toasters, etc.) has made them very popular.

scrollbar   A horizontal or vertical bar that contains a box that looks like an elevator in a shaft. The bar is clicked to scroll the screen in the corresponding direction, or the box (elevator, thumb) is clicked and then dragged to the desired direction.

serial port   A socket on a computer used to connect a modem, mouse, scanner or other serial device via the computer's serial interface. The Macintosh uses the serial port to attach a printer, whereas the PC uses the parallel port. Transferring files between two personal computers can be accomplished by cabling the serial ports of both machines together and using a file transfer program.

shortcuts   Windows allows you to create pointers, or shortcuts, to your program and data files. The shortcut icons can be placed on the desktop or stored in other folders. Double-clicking a shortcut is the same as double-clicking the original file. However, deleting a shortcut does not remove the original. Shortcut icons have a small arrow in their lower-left corner pointing northeast. To create a shortcut to a program file, drag the icon from a folder or Explorer window and drop it on the desktop or into another folder.

slot   (1) A receptacle for additional printed circuit boards. (2) A receptacle for inserting and removing a disk or tape cartridge.

software   Instructions for the computer. A series of instructions that performs a particular task is called a program. The two major categories of software are system software and application software. System software is made up of control programs such as the operating system and database management system (DBMS). Application software is any program that processes data for the user (inventory, payroll, spreadsheet, word processor, etc.). A common misconception is that software is data. It is not. Software tells the hardware how to process the data. Software is "run." Data is "processed."

sound card   Also called "sound board" and "audio adapter," it is a personal computer expansion board that records and plays back sound, providing outputs directly to speakers or an external amplifier. The de facto standard for sound card compatibility in PCs is Creative Labs' Sound Blaster.

spreadsheet   Software that simulates a paper spreadsheet, or worksheet, in which columns of numbers are summed for budgets and plans. It appears onscreen as a matrix of rows and columns, the intersections of which are identified as cells. Spreadsheets can have thousands of cells and can be scrolled horizontally and vertically in order to view them. The cells are filled with:

- ■ Labels—any descriptive text, for example, RENT, PHONE or GROSS SALES

- ■ Numeric values—actual numeric data used in the budget or plan, and the formulas command the spreadsheet to do the calculations; for example, SUM CELLS A5 TO A10

- ■ Formulas—created by saying "this cell PLUS that cell TIMES that cell"

Formulas are easy to create, since spreadsheets allow the user to point to each cell and type in the arithmetic operation that affects it. The formulas are the spreadsheet's magic. After numbers are added or changed, the formulas will recalculate the data either automatically or with the press of a key. Since the contents of any cell can be calculated with or copied to any other cell, a total of one column can be used as a detail item in another column. For example, the total from a column of expense items can be carried over to a summary column showing all expenses. If data in the detail column changes, its column total changes, which is then copied to the summary column, and the summary total changes. Done manually, each change would require recalculating, erasing and changing the totals of each column. The automatic ripple effect allows users to create a plan, plug in different assumptions and immediately see the impact on the bottom line. This "what if?" capability makes the spreadsheet indispensable for budgets, plans and other equation-based tasks.

surge protector   A device that employs some method of surge suppression to protect electronic equipment from excessive voltage (spikes and power surges) in the power line. The most common method uses a metal oxide varistor (MOV) component to shunt the surge to the neutral and ground lines. Another method is series mode, which actually absorbs the energy. Surge protectors may use both methods.

synchronous   Refers to events that are synchronized, or coordinated, in time. For example, the interval between transmitting A and B is the same as between B and C, and completing the current operation before the next one is started are considered synchronous operations.

system   A computer system is made up of the CPU, operating system, and peripheral devices.

taskbar   An on-screen toolbar that displays the active applications (tasks). Clicking a taskbar button restores the application to its previous appearance. Windows 95 popularized this feature.

TIFF (Tagged Image File Format)   A widely-used bitmapped graphics file format developed by Aldus and Microsoft that handles monochrome, gray scale, 8- and 24-bit color. TIFF allows for customization and is compressed using several compression methods .*tif* is the extension used to identify TIFF files.

trackball   A stationary pointing device that contains a movable ball rotated with the fingers or palm. From one to three keys are located in various positions depending on the unit.

UPS (uninterruptible power supply)   Backup power used when the electrical power fails or drops to an unacceptable voltage level. Small UPS systems provide battery power for a few minutes; enough to power down the computer in an orderly manner. Sophisticated systems are tied to electrical generators that can provide power for days. A UPS system can be connected to a file server so that, in the event of a problem, all network users can be alerted to save files and shut down immediately.

URL (uniform resource locator)   The address that defines the route to a file on the Web or any other Internet facility. URLs are typed into the browser to access Web pages, and URLs are embedded within the pages themselves to provide the hypertext links to other pages. The URL contains the protocol prefix, port number, domain name, subdirectory names and file name. Port addresses are generally defaults and are rarely specified. To access a home page on a Web site, only the protocol and domain name are required. For example, http://www.osborne.com retrieves the home page at Osborne/McGraw-Hill's Web site. The *http://* is the Web protocol, and *www.osborne.com* is the domain name. If the page is stored in another directory, or if a page other than the home page is required, slashes are used to separate the names. If a required page is stored in a subdirectory, its name is separated by a slash. Like path names in DOS and Windows, subdirectories can be several levels deep. For example, the components of the following hypothetical URL are described here:

http://www.abc.com/clothes/shirts/formal.html

http://	protocol
www.abc.com/	domain name
clothes/	subdirectory name
shirts/	subdirectory name
formal.html	document name (Web page)

USB (universal serial bus)   A hardware interface for low-speed peripherals such as the keyboard, mouse, joystick, scanner, printer and telephony devices. It also supports MPEG-1 and MPEG-2 digital video. USB has a maximum bandwidth of 1.5 Mbytes/sec, and up to 127 devices can be attached. Peripherals can be plugged in and unplugged without turning the system off. USB ports began to appear on PCs in 1997, and Windows 98/Me fully supports it.

utility program   A program that supports using the computer. Utility programs, or "utilities," provide file-management capabilities, such as sorting, copying, comparing, listing and searching, as well as diagnostic and measurement routines that check the health and performance of the system.

video card   An expansion board that plugs into a desktop computer that converts the images created in the computer to the electronic signals required by the monitor. It determines the maximum resolution, maximum refresh rate and the number of colors that can be sent to the monitor. The monitor must be equally capable of handling its highest resolution and refresh.

virus   Software used to infect a computer. After the virus code is written, it is buried within an existing program. Once that program is executed, the virus code is activated and attaches copies of itself to other programs in the system. Infected programs copy the virus to other programs. The effect of the virus may be a simple prank that pops up a message onscreen out of the blue, or it may destroy programs and data right away or on a certain date. It can lie dormant and do its damage once a year. For example, the Michaelangelo virus contaminates the machine on Michaelangelo's birthday. A common type of virus is a boot virus, which is stored in the boot sectors of a floppy disk. If the floppy is left in the drive when the machine is turned off and then on again, the machine is infected, because it reads the boot sectors of the floppy expecting to find the operating system there. Once the machine is infected, the boot virus may replicate itself onto all the floppies that are read or written in that machine from then on until it is eradicated.

wallpaper   A pattern or picture used to represent the desktop surface (screen background) in a graphical user interface. GUIs come with several wallpaper choices, and third-party wallpaper files are available. You can also scan in your favorite picture and make it wallpaper.

window   A scrollable viewing area onscreen. Windows are generally rectangular, although round and polygonal windows are used in specialized applications. A window may refer to a part of the application, such as the scrollable index window or the text window in a database, or it may refer to the entire application in a window.

Windows   The most widely-used operating system for PCs. Windows provides a graphical user interface and desktop environment similar to the Macintosh, in which applications are displayed in resizable, movable windows onscreen. The greatest advantage to Windows is the huge wealth of application programs that have been written for it. It is the de facto standard for desktop and laptop computers worldwide with more than 200 million users. Microsoft is in complete control of Windows and does its best to introduce advancements to keep up with the times. Windows is, however, a complicated operating environment that has its roots in DOS, which was developed for the first PCs. Each version of Windows has to support applications written for previous versions of Windows as well as DOS applications. Certain combinations of hardware and software running together can cause problems, and troubleshooting can be daunting. Considering that Windows has its roots in a hardware platform that grew as disorderly as the wild west, it is a wonder that it works as well as it does.

World Wide Web   An Internet facility that links documents locally and remotely. The Web document is called a Web page, and links in the page let users jump from page to page (hypertext) whether the pages are stored on the same server or on servers around the world. The pages are accessed and read via a Web browser such as Netscape Navigator or Internet Explorer. The Web became the center of Internet activity, because Web pages, containing both text and graphics, were easily accessible via a Web browser. The Web provides point and click interface to the largest collection of online information in the world, and the amount of information is increasing at a staggering rate. The Web is also turning into a multimedia delivery system as new browser features and browser plug-in extensions, coming at a dizzying pace, allow for audio, video, telephony, 3D animations and videoconferencing over the Net. Newer browsers also support the Java language, which allows applications of all variety to be downloaded from the Net and run locally. The fundamental Web format is a text document embedded with HTML tags that provide the formatting of the page as well as the hypertext links (URLs) to other pages. HTML codes are common alphanumeric characters that can be typed with any text editor or word processor. Numerous Web publishing programs provide a graphical interface for Web page creation and automatically generate the codes. Many word processors and publishing programs also export their existing documents to the HTML format, thus Web pages can be created by users without learning any coding system. The ease of page creation has helped fuel the Web's growth. Web pages are maintained at Web sites, which are computers that support the Web's HTTP protocol. When you access a Web site, you generally first link to its home page, which is an HTML document that serves as an index, or springboard, to the site's contents. Large organizations create and manage their own Web sites. Smaller ones have their sites hosted on servers run by their Internet service providers (ISPs). Countless individuals have developed personal Web home pages as many ISPs include this service with their monthly access charge. Individuals can post their resumes, hobbies and whatever else they want as a way of introducing themselves to the world at large. The Web spawned the intranet, an in-house, private Web site for internal users. It is protected from the Internet via a firewall that lets intranet users out to the Internet, but prevents Internet users from coming in. The World Wide Web was developed at the European Center for Nuclear Research (CERN) in Geneva from a proposal by Tim Berners-Lee in 1989. It was created to share research information on nuclear physics. In 1991, the first command line browser was introduced. By the start of 1993, there were 50 Web servers, and the Voila X Window browser provided the first graphical capability for the Web. In that same year, CERN introduced its Macintosh browser, and the National Center for Supercomputing Applications (NCSA) in Chicago introduced the X Window version of Mosaic. Mosaic was developed by Marc Andreessen who later became world famous as a principal at Netscape. By 1994, there were approximately 500 Web sites, and, by the start of 1995, nearly 10,000. In 1995, more articles were written about the Web than any other subject in the computer field. Today, there are millions of Web sites with new ones coming online non-stop. Many believe the Web signifies the beginning of the real information age and envision it as the business model of the 21st century.

zip   To compress a file with PKZIP or WINZIP.

Index

And Don't Forget These...

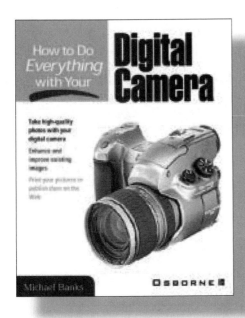

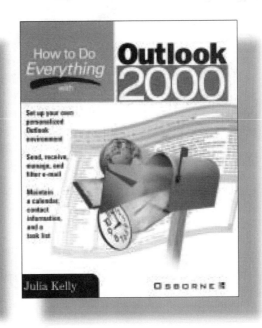

How to Do
Everything with
Your Digital
Camera

Michael Banks
$24.99
ISBN: 0-07-212772-4
Available: December 2000

How to Do
Everything with
Outlook 2000

Julia Kelly
$24.99
ISBN: 0-07-212431-8
Available

How to Do
Everything with
FrontPage 2000

David Plotkin
$24.99
ISBN: 0-07-212575-6
Available

How to Do
Everything with
Your iMac,
Second Edition

Todd Stauffer
$24.99
ISBN: 0-07-212416-4
Available

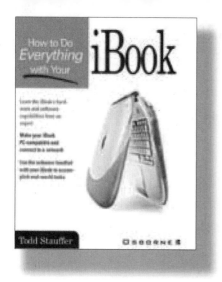

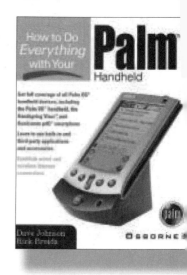
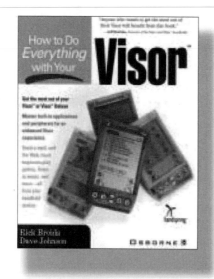